POSTCOLONIAL
THEORY
AND THE
UNITED STATES

POSTCOLONIAL THEORY AND THE UNITED STATES

Race, Ethnicity, and Literature

Edited by
Amritjit Singh
and Peter Schmidt

University Press of Mississippi
Jackson

www.upress.state.ms.us
Copyright © 2000 by University Press of Mississippi
All rights reserved
Manufactured in the United States of America

08 07 06 05 04 03 02 01 00   4 3 2 1
⊗

Library of Congress Cataloging-in-Publication Data

Postcolonial theory and the United States : race, ethnicity, and literature / edited by
Amritjit Singh and Peter Schmidt.
p. cm.
Includes bibliographical references and index.
ISBN 1-57806-251-9 (cloth : alk. paper)—ISBN 1-57806-252-7 (paper : alk. paper)
1. American literature—Minority authors—History and criticism.   2. American
literature—20th century—History and criticism.   3. Ethnic groups—United
States—History—20th century.   4. Postcolonialism—United States.   5. Decolonization
in literature.   6. Ethnic groups in literature.   7. Minorities in literature.   8. Ethnicity in
literature.   9. Race in literature.   I. Singh, Amritjit.   II. Schmidt, Peter, 1951 Dec. 23-
PS153.M56 P67   2000
810.9'920693—dc21   99-087192

British Library Cataloging-in-Publication Data available

CONTENTS

Preface vii
Introduction xi

IDENTITIES, MARGINS, AND BORDERS: I

On the Borders Between U.S. Studies and
Postcolonial Theory 3
Amritjit Singh and Peter Schmidt

IDENTITIES, MARGINS, AND BORDERS: II

Postcolonialism, Ideology, and Native American Literature 73
Arnold Krupat

"Where, By the Way, Is This Train Going?":
A Case for Black (Cultural) Studies 95
Mae G. Henderson

Refiguring Aztlán 103
Rafael Pérez-Torres

Denationalization Reconsidered: Asian American
Cultural Criticism at a Theoretical Crossroads 122
Sau-ling C. Wong

HISTORICAL CONFIGURATIONS

Indian Literacy, U.S. Colonialism,
and Literary Criticism 151
Maureen Konkle

Capitalism, Black (Under)development, and the
Production of the African-American Novel in the 1850s 176
Carla L. Peterson

Postcolonial Anxiety in Classic
U.S. Literature 196
Lawrence Buell

Romancing the Empire: The Embodiment
of American Masculinity in the Popular
Historical Novel of the 1890s 220
Amy Kaplan

Neither Fish, Flesh, Nor Fowl: Race and Region
in the Writings of Charles W. Chesnutt 244
Anne Fleischmann

Postcolonialism after W. E. B. Du Bois 258
Kenneth Mostern

CONTEMPORARY CONTESTATIONS

How (!) Is an Indian? A Contest
of Stories, Round 2 279
Jana Sequoya Magdaleno

Revisioning Our Kumblas: Transforming
Feminist and Nationalist Agendas in Three
Caribbean Women's Texts 300
Rhonda Cobham

Arab-Americans and the Meanings of Race 320
Lisa Suhair Majaj

Broken English Memories: Languages of the Trans-Colony 338
Juan Flores

"Born-Again Filipino": Filipino American
Identity and Asian Panethnicity 349
Leny Mendoza Strobel

South Asian American Literature: "Off the
Turnpike" of Asian America 370
Lavina Dhingra Shankar and Rajini Srikanth

Can You Go Home Again?: Transgression and
Transformation in African-American Women's and
Chicana Literary Practice 388
Inés Salazar

Hybridity in the Americas: Reading Condé,
Mukherjee, and Hawthorne 412
Bruce Simon

Contributors 445
Name Index 451
Subject Index 465

PREFACE

Postcolonial Theory and the U.S.: Race, Ethnicity, and Literature represents a new chapter in the emerging conversations about the importance of borders on a global scale. Borders may be defined not just as the lines dividing one country from another but also the ways in which difference is deployed across societies and cultures to mark distinctions of power. A series of events since the eighteenth century has reshaped not just boundaries on maps but how societies are internally structured: European imperialism, the assumed cultural superiority of Europe that was its close companion, and the continuing power of European thought in our knowledge paradigms; slavery, the Middle Passage, and the Black diaspora; the American Revolution; the Haitian Revolution of 1804; the 1857 Mutiny (which Indian historians call the First War of Independence); Freedom Movements in India, Africa and elsewhere; the 1955 Bandung Conference of African and Asian nations; the Civil Rights and anti-Vietnam War movements in the U.S.; and the dismantling of South African apartheid in the 1990s—to name just a few.

The U.S. has been involved in almost all these world-shaping events, both as the oldest self-conscious democracy and the youngest "superpower" with a sense of its own "manifest destiny." The rise of global capitalism and neocolonialism, plus more than a century of immigrant life in the U.S.—coupled with other migrations around the world throughout the twentieth century—have kept in constant flux our understandings of assimilation and resistance, assent and dissent, descent and consent. The growing recognition in the last two decades of hybrid cultures around the globe calls into question, more sharply than ever before, the validity of old binaries such as West and East, North and South, white and non-white, developed vs. developing nations, First and Third Worlds.

As we enter the twenty-first century, in response to such developments some older ways of reading and teaching U.S. literature and cultural history are being supplemented by newer ones. At the swirling heart of these changes is not just a fundamental shift in how the "national" qualities to a literary tradition are conceived but also how the nation defines itself. For admirers of U.S. literature, it is much more difficult than it was a generation ago to focus on a heroic act of cultural rebellion against England as the defining feature of this tradition. In that familiar narrative of origins, U.S. authors claimed their centrality in the canon by using the resources of the English language to found and continue a new American literary tradition, just as the colonists used English and Scottish legal traditions to declare newfound rights and independence. Similarly, it is rarer now in U.S. literary study to assume a single-file "American procession" (Alfred Kazin's phrase) of great, mostly white male, authors succeeding each other with masterworks that reimagine the founding moment of this shared tradition.

Recently U.S. studies—especially the growing scholarship on race, ethnicity, immigration, and empire—has once again sought an international focus. U.S. literature past and present is increasingly being studied within the context of the global literatures in English, and a search for a single "origin" of the "American self" has become considerably more problematic than it was a generation ago. Simultaneously, the long and sinuous history of the *borders* of English within the U.S.—the many ways in which languages and cultural traditions other than English have crossed into and helped shape U.S. culture and literature—is being rethought and rewritten, though the deep debt to England and English literature is hardly denied. Like many other changes in U.S. society, these changes in academic scholarship and teaching strategies owe a profound inspiration to the U.S. Civil Rights movement of the 1950s and 1960s. Without that movement (as well as the related and parallel events that brought political independence to many Asian and African countries), it would be impossible to think afresh about the "master narratives" that shape the consciousness of most Americans.

We may be said now to be in a "transnational" moment, increasingly aware of the ways in which local and national narratives, in literature and elsewhere, cannot be conceived apart from a radically new sense of our shared human histories and our growing global interdependence. *To think transnationally about literature, history, and culture requires a study of the evolution of hybrid identities within nation-states and diasporic identities across national boundaries.* How best to understand these global matrices is a source of intense debate and urgency.

What is curious about this sense of millennial transition in U.S. studies, however, is how old it is—it is part of a recurring pattern of crisis in U.S. culture in the process of redefining its core values and shared history. Our declarations of independence and new beginnings, cultural and otherwise, are haunted by a sense of both eternal recurrence and perpetual incompleteness. Today's cultural moment eerily mimes that of approximately one hundred years ago, when Frederick Jackson Turner and W. E. B. Du Bois offered their competing theses about which was more significant—the western frontier or the color-line—in forming U.S. identity. Du Bois was hardly alone in formulating a conception of the making of Americans that challenged Turner's. Consider, for example, José Martí's essays from the same period, Charles W. Chesnutt's "The Future American" essays (1900), or Randolph Bourne's critique of the boundaries of "America" in "Trans-National America" (1916). We might even claim that exploring the tensions between national and transnational identities created key insights for Alexis de Tocqueville in his *Democracy in America* (1835–39). (Coincidentally, 1835 is also the year of Thomas Macaulay's "Minute on Indian Education," which initiated the process of transforming the cultural identities of most South Asians by introducing English into British India.)

Postcolonial Theory and the U.S. collects essays that raise new and troubling questions about how the legacies of colonial history might be defined for past and present U.S. literary culture. Studies addressing issues of race, ethnicity, and empire in U.S. culture have provided some of the most innovative—and controversial—contributions to recent scholarship, and much of this research has been enabled by a spirited dialogue with what is now called "postcolonial" theory. We have collected essays written in the 1990s that exemplify some of the best of this new work by both well established and up-and-coming scholars, drawing on both unpublished writings and previously printed essays. We have selected several essays from some of the most respected and diverse journals in U.S. studies—such as *American Literary History*, *American Literature*, *Callaloo*, *Aztlán*, and *Amerasia Journal*—and almost all of these contributors have chosen to revise their essays specifically for this volume. We wanted essays that would be accessible, well-focused resources for college and university students and their teachers. We were especially interested in essays that displayed both historical depth and theoretical finesse as they attempted close and lively readings of specific literary texts and/or cultural events. Further, we tried to shape an anthology that included more than one discussion of each literary tradition associated with major "racial" or ethnic communities. Such a gathering of diverse and often competing or complementary viewpoints, we believed, would provide good introductions to cultural traditions and surrounding issues with which some readers might not be familiar. The volume opens with two essays by the editors: first, a brief survey of the arguments of the individual essays chosen for this volume; and second, a longer essay that places current debates in U.S. ethnicity and race studies within both the history of "American Studies" as a whole and recent developments in postcolonial theory. This latter essay is our contribution to the debates on identities, margins, and borders explored further in Part II.

We would like to acknowledge the following colleagues who gave us advice, suggested sources, and cast a skeptical eye on our words when they most needed it. They have given us a new appreciation for the meaning of *collegial*. A shout out and deepest thanks to:

T. J. Anderson, Wendy Barker, Ellen Bigler, Jay Birje-Patil, John H. Bracey, Stephen N. Brown, Gert Buelens, P. S. and Vijay Chauhan, Joseph Conforti, Patty Chu, Gaurav Desai, Miguel Diaz-Barriga, Robert Elliot Fox, Jacqueline Goldsby, Tomo Hattori, Jon Hauss, Udo Hebel, Michelle Hermann, Robert E. Hogan, Chuck James, Abdul JanMohamed, Kathryn Kalinak, Ketu Katrak, Susan Koshy, Arnold Krupat, Alejandro Lugo, Kenneth Mostern, Seiwoong Oh, Babu Patel, David and Judy Ray, Maureen Reddy, Marjorie Roemer, Frank Ken Saragosa, Lavina Dhingra Shankar, Barbara Schapiro, Ridgway Shinn, Bruce Simon, Werner Sollors, Rajini Srikanth, David Thomas, Sarah Willie, Rafia Zafar. Aware as we are of the collaborative nature of our scholarship, we are sure there are others who should be mentioned here. We also owe thanks to Anupama Arora and Reshma Singh for their assistance at several critical junctures. The work of preparing a comprehensive cross-index for this volume could not have been accomplished without the generous assistance of friend and colleague, Daniel M. Scott III, and several *aficionadoes* of the project—including Aradhana Arora, Patrick Brennan, Sharon Fisher, Anita Hellstrom, and Regina Vinluan.

At Rhode Island College, graduate students Carol Maloney, Brett Palana, and Rahul Gairola have served as research assistants at different stages of this project, which has taken us at least four years to complete. Bruce Johnson of the University of Rhode Island has been immensely helpful through the latter half of this process with suggestions and library research, as well as occasional calls to various contributors on our behalf—sometimes a kind of unofficial assistant editor. Other students who have assisted in various ways include Le-Ann Elgie, Kristen Gagne, Amy Pennington, Timothy Shirley, and Caleb Cabral. Thanks are also due at Rhode Island College to the Faculty Research Committee and Joan Dagle, Chair, Department of English, and Dean Richard Weiner for their strong support of this project; and to Swarthmore College for a leave semester that coincided with a crucial phase of the work.

We would also like to thank Seetha Srinivasan and Anne Stascavage at the University Press of Mississippi for their cheerful faith in the anthology. All our contributors and editors have shown remarkable patience and cooperation and we thank them sincerely.

This anthology is dedicated to Prem Singh and Lisa Aaron for their love and companionship.

INTRODUCTION

Amritjit Singh and Peter Schmidt

Postcolonial Theory and the U.S.: Race, Ethnicity, and Literature opens with essays
that are broadly comparative in scope and raise crucial questions regarding the
interconnections between postcolonial critique and U.S. ethnic studies—especially
Black, Asian American, and Latino/a and Native American studies. These essays all
present different ways of understanding the interchange between poststructuralist and
postcolonial theory on the one hand and U.S. ethnic studies theory and practice on
the other.

Our introductory essay, "On the Borders Between U.S. Studies and Postcolonial
Theory," was written especially for this volume. Our thesis is that recent U.S. race
and ethnicity studies splits into two groups with rather different premises, the "borders" school and the "postethnicity" school, and that this division can only be fully
understood by placing it in two different contexts. First, although these debates in
U.S. studies are one of the symptoms of the "culture wars" of the 1980s and 1990s,
we believe these debates have an older genealogy: they may be traced back not just
to the 1950s but to the early modern period of the 1890s through the 1920s, when
"American Studies" was being first constituted as a field in the academy. The second
context important for understanding arguments over the role of ethnicity and race in
U.S. culture is developments in postcolonial studies. We briefly survey key developments in this field. Then, in the last section of the essay, we focus on three exemplary
areas of interaction between postcolonial and U.S. race/ethnicity studies—
transnationalism, "whiteness" studies, and feminism. We also make the case that our
analysis of current trends in U.S. studies has great relevance for understanding the
contradictions in current theories of "globalization." We conclude the body of the
essay by presenting what we believe are key challenges to the emerging "borders"
paradigm in U.S. studies.

In Arnold Krupat's "Postcoloniality, Ideology, and Native American Literature," he gives both a wry deconstruction of how representations of "authentic" Native American cultures and voices have become fashionable both inside and outside of the academy in the 1990s and a vigorous argument for making what he terms "anti-imperial translation" at the heart of any valid sense of the "postcolonial," especially as it may apply to Native Americans. He also outlines some reasons for his skepticism towards the applicability of this newly fashionable term to Native Americans' life and art, including literature. In his view, contemporary Native American literatures cannot quite be classed among the postcolonial literatures of the world for the simple reason that there is not yet a "post- " to the colonial status of Native Americans while considerable number of Native people exist in conditions of politically sustained subalternity. Yet some Native American fiction clearly looks and sounds like other postcolonial fiction published elsewhere but also performs ideological work that appears quite analogous—especially when it comes to issues of translation and boundary-crossing. Because historically specifiable acts of translative violence marked the European colonization of the Americas from Columbus to the present, it seems to Krupat particularly important to reappropriate the concept of translation for contemporary Native American literature. To do so is not to deny the relationship of this literature to the postcolonial literatures of the world but, rather, to attempt to specify a particular modality for that relationship. Krupat's essay concludes with a reading of Leslie Marmon Silko's *Almanac of the Dead* (1991). It is reprinted from *The Turn to the Native: Studies in Criticism and Culture* (Nebraska UP, 1996).

Mae Henderson's essay, originally published in *Callaloo* in 1996, gives a comparative history of Black Studies in the 1960s and 1970s and the present and argues that the infatuation of many U.S. scholars with British cultural studies and postcolonial theory in general erases the contributions of U.S. Black Studies to the interdisciplinary study of transnational cultures, while greatly overstating the contrasts between the "nationalist" 1960s and the supposedly "transnationalist" present. Her essay then presents several models for "recovering" the historical evolution of Black Studies as a source for models of cultural studies, particularly via interdisciplinary and cross-cultural modes. She argues that any valid narrative we construct of the genealogy of cultural studies in the United States must create a place for Black Studies as a scholarly and political enterprise that transformed the university into a space of contestation and negotiation over the production and construction of knowledge. The advent of Black Studies was an inaugural moment and remains central to the formation of the contemporary cultural studies project. Its introduction into the American academy has paved the way for the articulation of a series of claims and counterclaims which have made the case for feminist studies, ethnic studies, postcolonial studies, gay and lesbian studies, and cultural studies as well.

Rafael Pérez-Torres's "Refiguring Aztlán" addresses the multiple and often complex roles that the image of the Aztec homeland has played within a variety of Chicano/a cultural and political discussions. Noting that various constituencies have invoked Aztlán in order to defend or defy particular articulations of Chicano/a identity, this essay argues that Aztlán serves as an empty signifier. By reclaiming Aztlán in various contexts and for various purposes, Aztlán never ceases taking on numerous forms in the continuing process of Chicana/o self-identification on a cultural, social and political level. The image of Aztlán suggests a homeland, yet it is a place whose contours are ever contested. Any position—whether nationalist, culturalist, feminist, queer—erases certain aspects of what Aztlán may represent in order to foreground others. This essay offers a genealogy for Chicano critical discourse. It traces the lines of descent by which the term *Aztlán* has been passed down since its reclamation for the Chicano Movement in 1969. Rhetorically, the term represents a strategy of indigenous affirmation reminiscent of the development of a Mexican nationalist discourse following the Revolution. Politically, it is used to stake a claim for legitimacy and land in the face of military and social oppression against Mexicans and Chicanos begun in 1848 at the close of the war between Mexico and the United States. Culturally, the term comes to represent a kind of spiritual or ethical component to the development of Chicano and Chicana identities. In each case, the term *Aztlán* contests the continued exploitation of Mexicans and Chicanos by evoking an image that suggests a claim to place before the incursion of European powers. Needless to say, the call to an originary indigenous past can lead to essentialisms and erasures that have persistently bedeviled conceptualizations of Chicano/a identities. It is these erasures that draw Chicano and Chicana critics back to the complex relationship between self and place in order to reclaim, rearticulate, and refigure Aztlán. In the end, Pérez-Torres sees Aztlán functioning most vitally as an "absent unity" that inspires continual reinterpretation and transformation of both Mexico and the U.S. The essay was originally published, appropriately enough, in 1997 in *Aztlán: A Journal of Chicano Studies*.

Sau-ling C. Wong's essay, similarly, shows a sophisticated understanding of the many ways in which critiques of nationalism associated with postcolonial theory have influenced Asian American studies. But she is simultaneously aware of how often Asian American histories have been erased or oversimplified where "theory" is concerned. Given current American political and cultural realities, she argues that multiple strategies are needed in both community-building and scholarship to emphasize both the unities and the differences of Asian American experiences and cultures— some strategies stressing pan-Asian American unities and others opening space for complexity and difference ("denationalization") as needed. Such a balance is the "theoretical crossroads" she promotes. In this Sau-ling Wong shares a position similar to those articulated recently in revisions to their own work made by Gayatri Spivak, Lisa Lowe, and David Palumbo-Lui, among others. Wong's essay has been frequently cited (and argued with) since its original publication in *Amerasia Journal* in 1995, and we are pleased to republish it here along with a new headnote specially written for this anthology by the author, in which she chronicles and reflects upon the interpretations the essay has received and the ways in which Asian American studies has evolved since the mid-1990s.

The second section of this anthology focuses on nineteenth- and early twentieth-century literary and cultural conflicts, yet the essays exhibit a striking set of contrasting assumptions about applying "postcolonial" theory to U.S. social history.

Maureen Konkle's contribution focuses on the early nineteenth-century Native American writer William Apess, which in turn inspires a critique of some of the current assumptions in Native American studies. She argues that William Apess describes U.S. colonial epistemology in his *Eulogy on King Philip*, which situates a critique of the

emerging nationalist historiography of New England and the U.S. as a whole in relation to Native arguments for the sovereign status of Indian nations in the removal
era, particularly those of the Cherokee, which were well known at the time. Apess's
critique shows that the purpose of the production of knowledge about the identity of
Indians is to displace the fact that the Indian treaty, which is necessary to legitimate
the authority of the U.S. government, concedes the political autonomy of Indians.
Apess thus joins the Native political leaders and intellectuals who preceded him and
he serves as a precursor of those who followed, for Native people have pointed to the
treaty as the demonstration of Europeans' recognition of their political autonomy and
heterogeneity virtually since the beginning of the written record, through to the present day. Apess goes a step further than his predecessors, however, in that he explicitly
connects the systematic oppression of Native peoples with the production of knowledge, thus linking politics and epistemology. Apess's critique thus has far-reaching
significance for the criticism of Native American literature, which continues to produce knowledge about the psychological or cultural identity of Indians without addressing the history of that preoccupation. Apess's rejection of European notions of
Indian identity as mere cover for political objectives and his profound knowledge of
what writing had done to Native people and what it could do demonstrate that new
vocabularies of critical discourse are necessary to address the history of Native writing
and the peculiarities of colonialism in North America and the U.S. Konkle's essay,
especially revised for this volume, originally appeared in *American Literature* in 1997.

Carla L. Peterson's essay asks why a comparatively large number of novels written
by African Americans were published in the 1850s—after more than a decade in
which the primary attention of Black writers had focused on other genres, particularly
the ex-slave narrative. Her answer explores how fiction could shape responses to economic and cultural exploitation and underdevelopment in both the North and the
South that were significantly different from how other literary forms challenged those
inequities. Peterson notes that one of the first conventions these new fictive narratives
challenged was that of framing and endorsing the "authenticity" of a Black-authored
text by a white writer. She then gives an extended discussion of the role that revising
inherited genres and generic expectations—particularly tragic mulatta and picaresque
plots—could play in response to colonialism in fiction. The mulatta figure, for instance, could appeal as an exotic and sexualized narrative commodity to be consumed
by readers in both North and South, thus paralleling the "surplus" or luxury value
that lighter-skinned mistresses had within the slave economy. But in the hands of
Black writers the mulatta's story could also bring the inequities of the slave economy
sharply into focus while also embodying acts of resistance. The essay originally appeared in *American Literary History* in 1992.

When Lawrence Buell's essay was first published in *American Literary History* (also
in 1992), it caused controversy for perhaps too easily equating the responses of canonical European American nineteenth-century writers such as Cooper, Bryant, Whitman,
Melville, and Thoreau vis-à-vis the United Kingdom with the dilemmas faced and
strategies employed by contemporary postcolonial writers such as Achebe and Ngugi.
Yet Buell's original essay acknowledged the difficulties and dangers of what he was
trying to do, while urging that U.S. studies of white mainstream/canonical writing

not ignore postcolonial studies because of these complications. In particular, Buell framed the challenge as exploring the border (that is, the *link*) between "American postcolonialism and American imperialism." The version of Buell's essay presented in this anthology is revised and rethought, a beneficiary of skeptical but also supportive criticism he received from U.S. studies scholars. To the extent that U.S. literary culture is thought in terms of postcoloniality, the place criticism understandably tends to begin is with internal colonization of racial and other minority groups and voices, and their resistance to that. But the dominant Yankee culture during the early years of national history also exhibited a number of defining traits analogous to formations associated with the so-called newer English literatures, particularly but by no means exclusively settler culture discourse. Ironically, it is in so-called "classic" American literature, i.e., the work of the subsequently canonized nineteenth-century white male writers, that one especially finds these parallels. Buell's essay attempts to define, account for, and reflect on some of the broader implications of this peculiar situation.

Amy Kaplan's essay argues that traditional definitions of empire as "expansionist" are inadequate, particularly for the U.S. in the late nineteenth century. America's new empire of democracy, according to Brooks Adams and Franklin Giddings, defined itself ideologically against the territorially based colonialism of the old European empires. Kaplan shows that a complex double discourse of American imperialism emerged in the 1890s: politicians, intellectuals, and businessmen on both sides of the debate were redefining national power as *disembodied*—that is, divorced from contiguous territorial expansion. In the same period, and often the same breath, masculine identity was reconceived as *embodied*—that is, cultivated in the muscular robust physique and a "romance" narrative in which this chivalric hero rescued white women and engaged in cultural uplift in "frontier" spaces within past U.S. history, or kingdoms set in the past or future, or countries undergoing colonial crises, particularly in Latin America or the Pacific. Under Kaplan's eyes, these imperial romance narratives conflate and make exotic the threatening poles in contemporary political rhetoric of old-world "tyranny"—empire—and new-world "anarchy"—revolution—against which the U.S. intervenes and defines itself. Kaplan explores links between fictional narratives and U.S. adventures in Cuba, the Philippines, and elsewhere; she also provocatively investigates connections between these fictional soldiers of fortune and the discourse of the "new woman" in this period. She reads a number of once hugely popular novels against this ideological matrix, including Richard Harding Davis' *Soldiers of Fortune* (1897); Mary Johnson's *To Have and To Hold* (1900); George Barr McCutcheon's *Graustark* (1901); and Owen Wister's *The Virginian* (1902). The essay was originally published in *American Literary History* in 1990.

Anne Fleishmann's essay on Charles Chesnutt places his paradoxical conceptions of both racial and regional identity as a response to developments in the late nineteenth and early twentieth century in the U.S. In doing so, she also critiques currently influential readings of Chesnutt's work (especially Eric Sundquist's) while in general agreeing with recent reconceptions of the period that make Chesnutt as important as Mark Twain to an understanding of the Gilded Age's obsession with guilt as well as gilt, the color-line as well as the production line. Fleischmann argues that Chesnutt's "The Wife of His Youth" is about the demise of mixed-race identity following the 1896

Plessy v. Ferguson decision. In the story, two particular characters and their abilities to "pass" or not are allegories for race discourses in the South—Mr. Ryder is a biracial, "freebawn" black man whose skin tone allows him to pass as white, while 'Liza Jane is a darker-skinned former slave. Throughout the narrative, different moves are made to "whiten" 'Liza Jane and mask Mr. Ryder's own biracial identity, raising questions concerning the allegiance of either character to their social history. Recent postcolonial theoretical formulations—those that reject a manichean racial duality and affirm the possibility of hybridity—suggest however that rather than simply resolving his dilemmas by finally privileging of his "black" self, Mr. Ryder's choice illuminates how the *Plessy* decision reinscribed the two-race system of white dominance and black oppression by denying the possibility of creating and cultivating hybrid or syncretic racial and cultural identities. Fleishmann's essay has been accepted for publication in the *African American Review*.

Kenneth Mostern's "Postcolonialism After W. E. B. Du Bois" argues that if the term "postcolonialism" is understood as the name for certain textual moods (ambivalence), styles (hybridity), and tendencies (interdisciplinarity) rather than as the name for a historical period—as famous definitions by both Homi Bhabha and Gayatri Spivak suggest—then Du Bois' *The Souls of Black Folk* is clearly a postcolonial text. Mostern suggests that ambivalence, hybridity, interdisciplinarity and the forging of new aesthetic paradigms are best understood not as unique historical events but as the tendency of a class fraction—that of the elite educated "minority" scholar in the twentieth century. Mostern's reading seeks to define the relationship between particular minoritized subjectivities, which we call "races" and "ethnicities," and what marxism would call their class fractions. Further, it also claims that "postcolonial" subjectivity (including Du Bois') does not adequately represent all minority subjectivities—those minority subjectivities that are not formed in the western academy are not representable within postcolonialism. Mostern's essay is scheduled also to appear in the volume *Rethinking Marxism*, from Guilford Press.

The final section of the anthology, focusing on cultural developments in the U.S. since World War II, is the longest in the anthology because we want readers to confront the paradox that since the Civil Rights movement of the 1950s and 1960s colonial and postcolonial questions of power have become more rather than less prevalent in U.S. literature and cultural studies.

Jana Sequoya Magdaleno's contribution was originally published in 1993; it has been specially revised and expanded for this volume. It meditates on how ongoing attempts to define "Indianness" in literature and culture are emblematic of global struggles to contain and control difference in modern societies. Building upon premises similar to those in Krupat's essay but pushing her argument further, Sequoya Magdaleno directly faces two contentious issues of cultural appropriation: the ethics of publishing Native American oral sources that are part of the tools of survival of endangered communities, and the politics of the appropriation of Native American studies by the academy in the name of the postcolonial. She also considers the paradox that the concept of the mestizo or the métis refers to historically cohesive cultures in the Americas, but within the U.S. —especially for Native Americans—such an emphasis on mixed-blood and mixed-culture tends to produce fragmentation and dispersal of identity and identification rather than cohesiveness. Her arguments on these points should be central to any historical understanding in cultural studies of the virtues and dangers of "hybridity." Sequoya Magdaleno's essay also tests her points with comments on works by N. Scott Momaday and Leslie Marmon Silko, among others. In its earlier incarnation, entitled "Round 1," this essay appeared in 1993 in *New Voices in Native American Literary Criticism*, edited by Arnold Krupat.

Rhonda Cobham's piece focuses on three Caribbean authors writing in English: Merle Hodge, Erna Brodber, and Paule Marshall. Marshall's work is most obviously relevant for the themes of this volume, for she has lived for many years in the U.S. , but by including this essay covering two other Caribbean-based writers we do *not* mean this as a gesture "annexing" them as U.S. writers—and this is certainly not Cobham's intention either. Rather, Cobham's essay, like this anthology, in effect argues that a full understanding of U.S. cultural history is impossible without a comparative and transnational cultural approach. Thus Avey, the U.S.-born heroine of Marshall's *Praisesong for the Widow*, cannot fully understand how her identity has been shaped via exclusions as well as inclusions until she journeys to the Caribbean. Cobham's essay also demonstrates that Marshall should be considered not just in terms of how she revises U.S. cultural history but from within a primarily Caribbean literary and historical context. Further, Cobham argues that Brodber, Hodge, and Marshall—in contrast to some cultural nationalist and radical feminist writers—seem singularly committed to that oldest of female/colonial responsibilities of maintaining and renewing the sociosymbolic order. All the three novelists discussed are members of that Black middle-class strata of women who have benefited from the intersection of class, racial and sexual bias. The cultural spaces (here figured as "kumblas") that have protected them do not exist for the majority of their lower-class sisters. The narrative and metaphorical experiments of the writers discussed, however, deliberately thematize these representational limitations, so that the texts themselves come to function as a critique of the process they embody. Their openness to the possibility of subversion, while constantly working towards the consolidation of a functioning sociosymbolic order, differentiates their work from the deconstructive strategies common to writers and critics within Western discourse, where the unraveling of the dominant discourse is often represented as a liberating breakdown of all social order. An earlier version of Cobham's essay was published in *Callaloo* in 1993.

Counting Konkle, Buell, Kaplan, and Lisa Majaj, among others, this volume's essays present perspectives that investigate the privileges of whiteness in American culture in what may be taken to be postcolonial terms. In "Arab Americans and the Meanings of Race," Lisa Majaj notes that Arab Americans are in the unique position of being largely excluded from both majority and minority status as currently defined in the U.S. —what Majaj calls the "ethno-racial pentagon" (Black, Asian, Hispanic, Native American, and white) established as normative during the Nixon administration (1968–74). Arab Americans' inconsistent and contradictory history of racialization may shed new light on the inconsistencies of the color-line as it functions in U.S. legal traditions. Majaj also traces the contentious history of the use of the word "Arab" in the U.S. , noting that it functions unevenly and contradictorily in all of its uses—as a racial and an ethnic category; as a referent to a language (Arabic) shared by many but not all; as a religious category that often functions as a code-word for Islamic (even though many Middle Eastern Americans are Christian); and as a strange form of shorthand in which a single ethnic group (Arab) designates many, rather as if "Chinese American" were to be the preferred pan-ethnic/racial term over Asian American. (And like "Oriental," of course, the word "Arab" in English is embedded with its own complex colonial history.) Majaj shows that although some prefer the term "Middle Eastern American," the name "Arab American" since the 1970s oil crisis has emerged as the most workable pan-ethnic term than can aid groups' organization as a political and economic and cultural force in U.S. life. In short, it joins a long history of pan-ethnic terms that aid Americanization, but are themselves not necessarily an endorsement of assimilation or postethnic identity as often defined in current U.S. cultural debates. Majaj's article ends with a helpful survey of Arab American autobiographies, fiction, and poetry of the past century. After World War II, she argues, there is a significant shift away from narratives adopting an ethnographic stance "explaining" Islam to the West while the authors (often Middle Eastern Christians) dissociate themselves from Islam. Contemporary authors such as Diana Abu-Jaber and the Lebanese-American Lawrence Joseph attempt to negotiate ethnic identity in the U.S. within a racialized framework by examining its contradictions rather than confirming its authority.

Juan Flores's contribution to this volume argues for the centrality of Arcadio Díaz-Quiñones's essays, particularly *La memoria rota: Ensayos sobre cultura y política* (published in Puerto Rico in 1993), in contemporary U.S. studies. He shows how Díaz-Quiñones's work corrects much earlier cultural commentary coming out of Puerto Rico which treated primarily as an afterthought the cultural issues faced by Portorriqueño communities within the U.S. His essay also includes a cogent discussion of how Díaz-Quiñones's concept of *memoria rota* (broken memories) is deeply rooted in U.S./Puerto Rican history and expresses a sense of new possibilities, not just brokenness, that is comparable to (and influenced by) such concepts from postcolonial theory as Homi Bhabha's articulation of the importance of a "third space" in culture breaking up some of the binary hierarchies of colonial and neocolonial practices. Flores' essay originally appeared in *Modern Language Quarterly* in 1996; the revised essay appears both in this anthology and in Juan Flores' *From Bomba to Hip Hop: Puerto Rican Culture and Latino Identity* (Columbia University Press, 2000).

Leny Mendoza Strobel focuses on contemporary issues in Filipino American cultural identity and their implications for Asian American panethnic consciousness. Behind the "new face" of the Filipino American community in the mid-1990s are significant shifts that need to be articulated in how cultural identity and Asian panethnic consciousness are understood. The Filipino American presence within Asian American Studies needs to be expanded beyond the Bulosan and Philip Vera Cruz generation, the literary contributions of the "flip" generation, and the oral history books by Cordova, Vallangca, and Espiritu. While there is an emerging body of scholarly work, the post-1965 community has yet to be extensively studied. Numerous materials have been generated in the last ten years by the community itself, however, such as the Filipino American Experience Research Project at San Francisco State University, newspapers and magazines, television programs, and cultural productions in California such as the

Filipino American Arts Exposition project of the Philippine Resource Center. Strobel's article gives an overview of some of these materials, along with data from her own interviews with students, writers and artists, and other community members. In particular, she focuses on examples of attempts to develop community institutions that would make access to indigenous knowledge and narratives of decolonization available not just to academics but to all sectors of the community. The essay also discusses the importance of community arts festivals across the U.S. and gives a brief survey of emerging Filipino American writers and artists of the 1990s beyond fairly well-known names such as Hagedorn, Gonzalez, Bacho, and Villanueva—including Ruth Mabanglo, Eileen Tabios, Cecilia Manguerra-Brainard, and Bino Realuyo. Strobel's essay has been revised and updated especially for this anthology; an earlier version was published in *Amerasia Journal* in 1996.

Lavina Dhingra Shankar and Rajini Srikanth's essay, written especially for this volume, asks how the increasing presence of postcolonial diasporics—such as the South Asians—in the United States is changing the definition of Asian America/n, and hence altering ethnic American literature. While some South Asian Americans are comfortable with an Asian American identification, many consciously and actively "dis-identify" themselves from this ethno-racial category. Part of this disidentification stems from the recognition by many South Asian Americans that Asian American social and cultural spaces have historically been dominated by literary artists and scholars of East Asian ancestry even though South Asians were among the earliest immigrants to the United States in the nineteenth century, and South Asian Americans today outnumber the Japanese Americans. Highlighting the ambivalent position of postcolonial South Asians within Asian American literary and cultural studies, this essay locates four South Asian American writers of diverse backgrounds who occupy the interstitial "third space" in Homi Bhabha's phrase—Agha Shahid Ali, Shani Mootoo, Tahira Naqvi, and Abraham Verghese—and analyzes their works within the rubric of the U.S. ethnic canon. Shankar and Srikanth argue that South Asian American literature offers a unique vantage point from which to view and comprehend this critical time of flux within the Asian American and North American demographic landscape. The equivocal position of South Asian American literature within Asian American studies epitomizes many South Asians' desire to be a part of yet remain apart from the rest of Asian America.

Inés Salazar's wide-ranging, comparative essay—also written especially for this anthology—stresses the power of cultural memory and cultural revision in Toni Morrison's *Sula*, Toni Cade Bambara's *The Salt Eaters*, and Helena Maria Viramontes' "The Moths." Much of the literature by African-Americans and Chicanos is marked by an acute awareness of the condition of diaspora and a concomitant longing for "home," that is, a place of belonging. However, the literature by women studied in this essay suggests that they experience the condition of diaspora differently from men. For them, "home" as a site of nostalgia for uncomplicated return is fraught with potential peril. Simplistic invocations of home, both materially, as in "the family," and figuratively, as in "culture," are often aligned with patriarchal values. Just as significantly, the texts discussed also weave a complex critique of mainstream American society for its role in subjugating women of color politically, socially, and economically. Thus, figures in these texts engage in transgressive behavior by actively opposing the expectations both of their own communities and of larger American society. In doing so, they create an alternative to conceptions of community engendered either by a strictly race-based analysis or by white feminist theory. These writers also invoke a long legacy of activism by women of color that does not owe a debt to white feminism and in fact often precedes it. This legacy in turn serves as a foundation for new, more inclusive figurations of community. In this model, women of color lead the way transforming the very meaning of American society.

Bruce Simon's essay "Hybridities in the Americas" concludes our anthology. Simon uses the work of three novelists (Hawthorne, Condé, and Mukherjee) to demonstrate the advantages of comparative readings of cross-cultural migrations and reconfigurations. Simon also presents an exemplary instance of how contemporary literature reshapes our interpretation of canonical texts—Hawthorne's *Scarlet Letter*, in this case—and suggests that our sense of what is at stake in such reimaginings becomes profounder when we see these events in postcolonial terms: Mukherjee's and Condé's revisions of Hawthornian romance seek in divergent ways to emplot the powerful repressions that lie under claims to authority and the ability to "speak" for others. Simon's essay has not been previously published. Its breadth and historical range and its central focus on issues of ethnicity and colonial power bring this volume to an appropriate close.

IDENTITIES, MARGINS, AND BORDERS: I

ON THE BORDERS BETWEEN U.S. STUDIES AND POSTCOLONIAL THEORY

Amritjit Singh and Peter Schmidt

in memory of Toni Cade Bambara and Alfonso Ortiz

"I think the major choice faced by the intellectual is whether to be allied with the stability of the victors and rulers or—the more difficult path—to consider that stability as a state of emergency threatening the less fortunate with the danger of complete extinction, and take into account the experience of subordination itself, as well as the memory of forgotten voices and persons. As Benjamin says, 'to articulate the past historically does not mean to recognize it "the way it was." . . . It means to seize hold of a memory (or a presence) as it flashes up at a moment of danger.' "

—Edward Said, *Representations* 35 [Said's ellipses]

"When I first ran across Dr. Du Bois's passage [about the Negro being born with a veil at the beginning of *Souls of Black Folk*] as a girl, I had a problem straightaway. It conflicted with what I'd learned early on through Eldersay, namely, that the seventh son (or seventh son of the seventh son) who was born with a 'veil' (some said 'caul,' which I heard as 'call' as in having a calling) was enhanced by it, was gifted. . . . Second sight enabled the person to see things others couldn't see. Persons born with the veil were, if not clairvoyants, at least clear-seeing. They could see through guise and guile. They were considered wise, weird, blessed, tetched, or ancient, depending on the bent of the describer. But they were consulted in the neighborhoods, occasionally revered. . . . When I came to the bit about looking at your own self all the time through the eyes of people who either pity you or hate you, that did not sound like the second sight I'd heard of."[1]

—Toni Cade Bambara, 310–11

For those scholars for whom questions of race, ethnicity, and empire are central, U.S. studies in the 1990s has gained immensely from dialogue with the emergent field called "postcolonial studies," which provided comparative historical analyses of these issues from global or transnational perspectives. We believe, however, that much of this new work in U.S. studies exhibits a split or contradiction, bifurcating into two

3

groups with different premises—the "postethnicity" school and the "borders" school. We offer below definitions of these terms and a brief survey of the working premises of these two schools. Then, in the second section of this introduction, we place this split in the context of the culture wars of the 1980s and 1990s. We argue that these debates have a genealogy: they can be traced back not just to the 1950s but to the early modern period of the 1890s through the 1920s, when "American Studies" was being first constituted as a field in the academy in the midst of a surge in immigration, new forms of racial segregation and industrial labor, a more varied mix of students attending universities, and the closing of the western "frontier" coupled with newly global ambitions for U.S. power.

In the third part of this introductory essay, we give an overview of developments in postcolonial studies worldwide, and in the fourth section we reflect on parallel developments between the borders school in U.S. ethnic studies, the "cultural studies" movement in England, and postcolonial studies. We stress three shared emphases—on the "transnational" or diasporic, on "whiteness" studies, and on feminist analysis. We then consider recent developments in both "globalization" and "postcolonial" theory, making two essential points. First, we perceive a set of contradictions in current narratives of globalization that is quite similar to that in U.S. ethnic studies—a split between those who argue for a simple contrast between (world) citizenship and market participation vs. tribalism, and those who argue that contemporary developments are much more complicated than that. These dissenters to dominant globalization theory—many of whom are associated with "postcolonial" scholarship—critique narratives that claim causal connections between "opening" countries to multinational corporations and the rise of human rights and democratic values. In general, postcolonial intellectuals urge that such claims be placed in the context of a critical history of the rise of the *first* multinational enterprises associated with colonialism—including their colonial discourses of markets, "civilized values," and economic and cultural development.

Our final point is that U.S. borders studies and postcolonial scholarship are best engaged together. We believe that this is already happening but predict even richer examples of cross-fertilization in the coming decades. U.S. ethnic studies, in our view, has sometimes been unfairly contrasted with the various fields of postmodern, postcolonial, and British cultural studies—with claims that U.S. studies tends to be more provincial and idealistic, naively stressing narratives of self-determination against cultural stereotyping. We will argue instead that many of the concepts associated with postcolonial studies that have proven so influential—such as double-consciousness; mobility; hybridity and revision; a "third space" that is neither assimilation nor otherness; histories of coalition-building and transnational diasporic connections—have a rich genealogy in U.S. ethnic studies as well, especially with reference to people of color. In general, U.S. ethnic studies need not perceive the new influence of postcolonial studies as a threat but as an opportunity for doing even more ambitious comparative and transnational work. Much of this new U.S. cultural studies scholarship shares enough premises to be called a school—the borders studies school—and so greatly did its influence within U.S. studies grow in the 1990s that we believe a new "borders" paradigm has emerged that may be as influential over the next decades as Frederick

Jackson Turner's "frontier" thesis was over one hundred years ago. We will end our introductory essay, however, on a cautionary note, raising some difficult but necessary questions about the possible limitations and dangers of the emerging borders paradigm in relation to both U.S. and postcolonial studies.

Let our intentions in assembling this anthology not be misunderstood: we are *not* suggesting that U.S. studies must be central or primary in the field of postcolonial studies—only that its present role should be rethought by interested cultural critics in all fields involved. Similarly, we certainly don't want to reify U.S. borders and cut off a study of groups "within" these borders from a transnational context. U.S. studies scholarship has sometimes been woefully under-informed about U.S. studies work produced outside of the U.S.; it would be unfortunate if new theories labeled "postcolonial" received attention at the expense of work produced by U.S. studies scholars living outside the U.S. We hope the arguments of this essay and the quality of the essays in this anthology may inspire a reassessment of the assumptions governing both U.S. and postcolonial studies and the "borders" they share and cross.[2]

I
OVERVIEW: POSTING BORDERS

The U.S. may be understood to be the world's first postcolonial *and* neocolonial country. Anti-colonial resistance at its founding worked to secure an economy that thrived by appropriating the labor of racially-defined "aliens" not allowed the "inalienable" rights of full citizenship. While the U.S. defined itself as the world's first independent and anti-colonial nation-state it simultaneously incorporated many of the defining features of European colonial networks—including the color-line—into its economic and cultural life. Narratives of world power dating from the era of colonialism informed the way the country imagined its military, political, economic, and cultural authority as an expanding nation and, since the Civil War and especially since World War II, as a world power. U.S. foreign policy ventures in the 1990s—since the much celebrated end of the Cold War—project a continuing "self-image" as the world's only superpower.

In the nineteenth century in particular the U.S. also sought to contrast its destiny with that of other colonial empires, arguing that it was not composed of a home and a set of colonies but instead was a nation with an ever-expanding frontier integrating new and mostly contiguous territories into the old. This was to make its fate exceptional: an "empire for liberty" not following the rise and then fall-into-decadence pattern of past empires.[3] Yet the very language with which it imagined this exceptional fate was as oxymoronic as its own internal stratifications were contradictory. For example, the founding fathers' refusal to acknowledge the conflicts between slavery and the nation's democratic ideals is at the heart of many contemporary debates centered on the history of color, race, class, and global capitalism. "Empire" and "home" were not only interdependent, they were almost coterminous, sharing the same territories. This interdependency and proximity intensified the desire to police the borders of class- and color-lines. Yet for some citizens such internal stratifications or boundary-lines were temporary and crossable with a good work ethic, while for others such aspirations to cross social borders were seen not as an inalienable right but as a fundamental threat.[4] Ironically, immigrant success narratives so dominate the mythology of the U.S. as a nation that those who were native-born to the territories the U.S. claimed—most notoriously, Native Americans and Mexicans—were either to die off, become immigrants in their own land, or become a separate, colonized, cultural space within the "American" national body. Similarly, in such master narratives of nationhood, the history of slavery and its aftermath was often rewritten as an exception that proves the rule—the descendants of slaves are either redeemed to serve as a shining example of expanding democratic pluralism or damned as a case study in the pathology of willful separatism.

U.S. studies scholars trying to make sense of these contradictions have since the 1960s split into at least two groups. We advocate calling the first of these groups the "postethnicity" school. Those in this group acknowledge American cultural contradictions but tend to stress a progressivist narrative of the U.S. as a society of increasing inclusion, especially after 1965—a world in which ethnic identities should be understood as a prelude or base through which to join a society "beyond ethnicity" where cultural identities are formed by "consent," voluntary pluralism, and "postethnic" or hybrid cultural multiplicities. Many argue that such a conception of identity (as well as economic expansion) is progressively loosening the pre-modern caste structures such as class and color that previously stratified U.S. society. Prominent intellectuals who have recently articulated such narratives of American culture include Arthur J. Schlesinger, Jr., David Hollinger, Shelby Steele, and Francis Fukuyama. Such a reading of American history and the American future has strong links both with the "ethnicity school" of American studies led by Werner Sollors in the 1980s and earlier American studies scholarship, such as Günnar Myrdal's and Oscar Handlin's in the 1940s and 1950s and Frederick Jackson Turner's in the 1890s—work which argued that American culture was continually self-correcting towards inclusiveness and that placed as paradigmatic the comparative histories of upward mobility of European American immigrants.[5] Indeed, it would not be too much of an overstatement to claim that today's postethnicity school represents a new incarnation of the basic principles of the "consensus" historians of the 1950s and the "progressivists" of the 1890s-1920s. (We will argue the validity of such parallels below.)

The most articulate critiques of such a "progressivist" vision of the American present and future have come from cultural critics often conversant with U.S. ethnic and labor history, community organizing, and (more recently) colonial and postcolonial studies. We think that the "borders school" is an appropriate (though obviously somewhat over-simplifying) name for this group for several reasons. First, theorizations of U.S. "borders" and their history and effects have recently become central in numerous contemporary disciplines participating in both U.S. and postcolonial studies.[6]

Second, these analyses of borders do not focus solely on the vexed history of the U.S./Mexican border. They aim to *link* analyses of both external and internal borders and to place these accounts in a historical context. Studies by the borders school seek to merge an ideological history of an expanding frontier in a colonial context with both a history of internal stratification and with contemporary obsessions about prote geographic and cultural boundaries.

Third, we make the case that one of the term's great advantages is its flexibility. We believe it will facilitate much needed *comparative* discussion of the role played by internal stratification and cultural histories within the U.S. More inter-ethnic investigations of Asian American cultural histories are needed, for example, but also more *intra*-ethnic or multiracial comparisons of, say, Asian Americans, blacks, Latinos, and whites in ways that will not treat their cultural histories as if they developed autonomously. "Borders" analyses must be able to focus on what connects such groups as well as what separates them.

Fourth, we argue that "borders" is the best term available to link the study of cultural differences internal to nation-states like the U.S. to the study of transnational or diasporic connections in the context of globalization. In contrast to postethnicity scholars, the borders school asks whether class and color hierarchies will simply proliferate in new guises within the U.S. and the global economy, taking different configurations in the agricultural, industrial, service, finance, information-processing, and cultural sectors.[7] Just as the postethnicity/borders studies school rift is at the heart of current arguments about American citizenship and culture, so is there a similar tension involved in the cultural politics of difference as they function on a global scale.

Borders. To connect and to divide. Not a frontier, its deadly imagination of a line between the savages and the civilized. Not exodus, with its mirage of a promised-land to end the wandering, and not simply exile or diaspora, with its involuntary sense of never-never-home. But borders. A part yet apart, home and not-home, neither "here" nor "there." A boarder who can suddenly become uninvited. Borders on the edge and on the inside. Not just for those on whom America descended, making them wanderers in their own homeland. Not just for those about whom America had "reservations" regarding whether they could be or should be American—or even human. And not just for those forced to be immigrants against their will and then resident aliens—not pilgrims—in plantations in Hawaii, Mississippi, and elsewhere. But borders also for those strangers from a different shore who chose to be an immigrant, or were forced to choose, and then found their very presence made alien one generation after the next. Even for their descendants, whose border-zones and -towns may not be always so dramatically marked but are there still, in daily events such as the question "but where are you *really* from?" Borders. A new America that isn't bounded by such borders so much as *defined* by them.

Used in the context of cultural history, the term *borders* refers to the construction and mobilization of difference. By "borders" in U.S. ethnic and cultural history we mean both examples of internal stratification within an ethnicity or a nation and the ways in which cultural differences may be used to define transnational connections and tensions. In *Racial Formation in the United States* (1986), Michael Omi and Howard Winant made a distinction between racial dictatorship and racial hegemony that is a working premise of the borders school. Such a distinction is largely unacknowledged by postethnicity progressivists, or treated as less applicable after the 1960s than it once was.[8] Like those in the postethnicity school, scholars in the borders school emphasize hybridity and the paradoxes and contradictions of "American" identity, but in doing so they stress how some groups may be "included" in American culture primarily in coercive ways that keep them marked and subordinated as separate "minorities." This perspective emphasizes how ever-changing national frontiers and internal borders marked in part by class and color create social divisions for capital to exploit. The borders school stresses how the affected groups invented strategies of border crossing, "passing," hidden cultural memories, and alternative public spaces in order to survive. Equally important, borders school studies challenge dominant narratives of ethnic difference and exclusion that intertwine with and support simplistic narratives of pluralistic inclusion. These narratives of difference are narratives of the American nightmare rather than the American dream—ways of marking individuals and peoples with cultural and/or genetic traits that make them threatening aliens. To counter both such myths, the borders school emphasizes multiple strategies of coalition-building and the transgression of definitional boundaries of all kinds. In literary studies, equivalent strategies have been devised to criticize both the politics of inclusion (how new "ethnic" American writings are often evaluated by comparing them with "classic" and "representative" and "already established" American works) and the politics of difference (how a work may be too easily marked with traits defining it as "representative" of a certain class or color or gender).

Border school scholars also try to balance a study of unities within and among U.S. groups with emphases on difference and internal complexity. Rather than conceiving of ethnicity using a "national" model that implies a bounded territory and a unified cultural tradition, their understanding of ethnicity is close to Stuart Hall's, which stresses multiple "points of attachment," not a single one: "[T]he new forms of ethnicity are articulated, politically, in a different direction. By 'ethnicity' we mean the astonishing return to the political agenda of all those points of attachment which give the individual some sense of 'place' and position in the world, whether these be in relation to particular communities, localities, territories, languages, religions, or cultures" (*Critical Dialogues* 236–37).[9]

Both these "schools" of U.S. ethnic and racial studies—but especially the borders school—have recently sought to redefine themselves in a transnational or global context. They have also been influenced by recent postcolonial theory as it has countered earlier intellectual trends—especially European-centered structuralism and poststructuralism—that have proven inadequate to analyze global change in the last thirty years. The postethnicity school has suggested that the American dilemma and its solution—a gradual opening of society to include groups once "marginalized"—is increasingly not exceptional but paradigmatic for other countries (especially those which emerged from former colonized territories) that seek to form a unified democratic culture with a racially and culturally mixed populace. In their view, the U.S. is prophetic: its dilemma of finding an *unum* among the *pluribus* of mixed races and ethnicities is now shared by most of the world's nations, and the U.S.'s uneven evolution toward democratic pluralism represents the only realistic and hopeful model for a future beyond class warfare along the color-line. The borders school agrees, but tends to have a much sharper sense of the U.S.'s imperfect realization of its ideals, and consequently a more ambivalent attitude toward implying the U.S. is a "model" for the rest of the world.

II

U.S. ETHNIC STUDIES AS THE FRONTIER
IN THE CULTURE WARS: A BRIEF HISTORY

"As the recording machine played one of [Ellington's] most recent compositions, a combination of Cuban music and the unmistakable Ellington rhythm, he talked about dissonance.

'That's the Negro's life,' he said. 'Hear that chord!'—he set the needle back to replay the chord. 'That's us.'

'Dissonance is our way of life in America. We are something apart, yet an integral part.' "

—spoken to John Pittman in 1941, as quoted in Mark Tucker, *The Duke Ellington Reader* 150

Counternarratives from the "Center" as Well as the "Right"

To check the rising influence of postcolonial theory and ethnic studies—especially the "borders school"—commentators on the right and those who claim the center have arrayed a set of counternarratives that show strange symmetries despite the apparent difference of origin. An inordinate amount of attention was given to Allan Bloom's *The Closing of the American Mind* (1987) and its thesis that the decline and fall of American civilization is due to its failure to teach classic Humanities texts in the universities. More serious and shrewd attempts to link academic events with cultural trends at large have come from other quarters—including Arthur M. Schlesinger, Jr., and Francis Fukuyama. Both have attempted to update the turn-of-the-century historian Frederick Jackson Turner's "frontier thesis"—and, in Fukuyama's case, to make the clever assertion that what once made the U.S. exceptional has now become the goal of all liberal democracies.

Schlesinger's position in *The Disuniting of America* (1991) was an updated form of 1890s-style progressivism, though his intellectual roots, like Turner's, go back much deeper, to de Tocqueville, Crevecoeur, Franklin, Jefferson, and the Puritans. He conceded that American democracy in the past has imperfectly realized the ideals of life, liberty, and the pursuit of happiness for all citizens, especially when the history of American racism is considered, but he argued that an imperfect history in implementing these ideals does not invalidate them but rather makes them more necessary. He also asserted that these ideals are explicitly the heritage of Western civilization (especially "classical" and Anglo-Saxon) and that it is this heritage alone that can provide the common ground improving our democratic culture rather than fragmenting it: the health of U.S. civilization for him comes from the fact that it will allow people of all races and creeds to consent to be governed by these ideals and traditions. Like Oscar Handlin and Günnar Myrdal before him, but writing after the 1960s Civil Rights accomplishments, Schlesinger suggested that the U.S. had entered the final stage of its democratic development by extending the possibility of full citizenship and upward mobility to all U.S. minorities—imperfectly, perhaps, but also irrevocably.

Fukuyama in *The End of History and the Last Man* (1992) updated not just Progressivists and Puritans but returned to the European Enlightenment itself, in particular the reinterpretation of its ideals embodied in the work of Hegel. He adopted the central premises and paradoxes of Hegel's historiography—that only certain individuals and cultures are progressive, seeking to have their individuality recognized and embodied in a nation-state on the world historical stage—in order to argue that Western liberal democracies, whatever their internal imperfections, are the highest form of political and cultural evolution that human beings can imagine, and are thus the "end of history," with "end" defined not as a point of perfection that we have necessarily yet reached but as a guiding goal or telos, *the* master narrative. Like Schlesinger (and Hegel), Fukuyama argued that such a view of history is fundamentally Western and is the "common ground" making a culture resilient. He did edit Hegel's Eurocentrism and racism to stress the irony that such ideals are often now most endorsed by people coming from cultures and traditions that Hegel would have assumed were incapable of aspiring to Enlightenment freedom realized in the form of the State. Although Fukuyama offered his narrative and his thesis as a description of future world cultural development, its importance for cultural debates within the U.S. is clear when Fukuyama is read in conjunction with Thomas Sowell and Arthur Schlesinger, Jr.: Sowell's and Schlesinger's prescriptions through which new immigrant groups will revalidate classic "American" ideals become in Fukuyama a prophecy for success in any postcolonial situation within an emerging global economy dominated by multinational corporations and institutions like the International Monetary Fund.[10]

Now consider a range of seemingly different master narratives proposed by a variety of academics studying the roles played by race and ethnicity in U.S. history—academics whom we have loosely grouped into the "postethnicity school" of American studies. Werner Sollors, the author of the influential *Beyond Ethnicity: Consent and Descent in American Culture* (1986), may like Schlesinger be seen as an intellectual heir to Turner, Crevecoeur, and de Tocqueville. He stressed the complicated interaction between narratives of descent (inherited family and ethnic and/or national ties) and narratives of consent (chosen identities and imagined communities) in the making of the American self, in which a "new" identity is shaped out of citizens coming from many different ethnic and racial backgrounds. He updated his predecessors (and must be contrasted with Schlesinger) in his stress on the long and complex histories that narratives of both "consent" and of "descent" have within U.S. social history; no simplistic opposition between "unities" and ethnic otherness grounds his work, as it does *The Disuniting of America*. Without modifying his primary narrative, Sollors in *Beyond Ethnicity* even conceded the importance of "antagonistic acculturation" for U.S. ethnic history—the fact that a group may become acculturated in the U.S. by identifying not with its dominant figures but with its models of internal resistance, especially those embodied in black American culture. But many commentators since 1986 have followed Sollors' lead in criticizing the importance of "race" and arguing that to be truly "American" is to choose to be postethnic.[11]

Interestingly, while Sollors' *Beyond Ethnicity* is congruent with a dominant strain in U.S. studies that we have called the "postethnic" school (and is one of its most balanced and complex products), Sollors' later work to some degree has revised his thesis to give greater prominence to the history of U.S. narratives of exclusion and difference. Or perhaps his later work has elaborated more fully some ideas such as the following that were only tentatively sketched in *Beyond Ethnicity*: "one may ask whether the two systems of widely shared consent bias and severe de jure discrimination of totally descent-defined groups were not intimately interrelated" (38). Such a shift in emphasis can be seen most clearly in Sollors' introduction to *The Invention of Ethnicity* (1989); " 'Of Plymouth Rock and Jamestown and Ellis Island'; or, Ethnic Literature and Some Redefinitions of 'America' " (1992); the *Black Columbiad* anthology (1994); *Neither Black Nor White Yet Both: Thematic Explorations of Interracial Literature* (1997); and *Multilingual America: Transnationalism, Ethnicity, and the Languages of American Literature* (1998).[12] Sollors' career is a good example of how our division of U.S. studies broadly into "postethnicity" and "borders" schools is ultimately too schematic to capture the nuances of recent developments, though we believe such a characterization of the debate is helpful for understanding its broad patterns and how much is at stake. Sollors' reconsiderations—plus his continuing emphasis on the importance of the study of multi-lingualism in the U.S.—can also rightly be taken as an indication of the rising influence of the borders school and of the role that Sollors' own work has played in articulating the alternative paradigm.

The Significance of the Border(s) in U.S. Historiography

So rapidly has the influence of the borders school been growing that we believe it is not an overstatement to claim that in the 1990s it became a cultural paradigm for the study of race and ethnicity in U.S. studies as significant (and as fiercely contested) as Frederick Jackson Turner's "frontier" thesis was over one hundred years ago. (We are aware of the irony of such a claim—more on this in a moment.) The relevance of Turner's frontier paradigm to current debates within U.S. studies is worth briefly re-examining here, precisely because his thesis is not usually mentioned by historians of either the postethnicity or the borders schools as they debate colonialism, the nation-state, acculturation, and race and ethnicity.[13] Much can be gained if current arguments in U.S. studies are historicized, and all the topics just mentioned (if not their current nomenclature) are embedded within Turner's argument.

Turner's central point was that an ever-expanding frontier was a "consolidating agent" (15) to the nation-state: "In the crucible of the frontier the immigrants were Americanized, liberated, and fused into a mixed race, English in neither nationality nor characteristics" (23). Note that Turner's thesis anachronistically placed the most marginalized and least Americanized "immigrants" at the frontier, not in the cities. Why, then, was it so influential? Delivered as an address to historians attending the World's Columbian Exposition in Chicago in 1893, Turner's "The Significance of the Frontier in American History" pointedly raised the question of whether a new location in American culture could perform the amalgamating function of the frontier now that the frontier had closed. Yet the site of Taylor's speech—in both the real city of Chicago and the utopian "white city" of the Fair—and its timing—just as a new wave of immigration from Europe was beginning to crest—suggest an answer. That is, Turner implied that cities and factories would have to perform the frontier's role in the new, post-frontier phase of American history, or else the American nation-state would disintegrate. Or perhaps new frontiers would have to be found—in the Caribbean, Latin America, or the Philippines.

The postethnicity school never shows its descent from Turner more clearly than when its exponents in effect substitute for Taylor's vanishing frontier the disappearing boundaries of inherited ethnic or racial identities. Both borders function as the location where an ethnicity defined by descent is, in Turner's words, "liberated and fused" into new hybridities. Similarly, for both Turner and for members of the postethnicity school "American" national unity is jeopardized if this process is interrupted or compromised. Though contemporary narratives of diaspora and consent are usually not as European-centered as Turner's was ("Our early history is the study of European germs developing in an American environment" [3]), the telos of the narrative may be fundamentally the same beneath the different terminology.

Turner's narrative of nation-building downplayed the violence of the frontier in favor of defining it as a space of freedom, "a gate of escape from the bondage of the past" (38). Most historians influenced by Turner focused on the cities as the significant site where "American" identity was produced. In such books as Günnar Myrdal's *An American Dilemma* (1944), Oscar Handlin's *The Uprooted* (1951) and *Race and Nationality* (1957), Turner's progressivism was revised to argue that the internal American racial frontier would vanish as inexorably as the geographical frontier once did— provided that premodern caste or racial distinctions were outgrown. Myrdal and Handlin also recast Turner by seeing this newly defined frontier essentially negatively, as a space of the victimized and socially disorganized who became socially functional again only after they assimilated.

Another historian from the mid-century, Walter Prescott Webb, took a different tack and emphasized the virtue of frontier violence as Turner did not. For Webb, the Southwest was the site where marginal citizens could prove their right to assimilate by marking and subduing others as aliens: the frontier was the violent, advancing edge of the dominant narrative of Anglo-Saxon assimilation and development. We mention Webb here on purpose: a critique of Webb's work and the production of an alternative way of interpreting the history of the Southwest was a central goal of Américo Paredes. Paredes' work from the 1930s through the 1960s played an indispensable role in the emergence of Chicano studies in the 1960s and therefore demonstrates precisely how the borders school is not a 1990s phenomenon but must be seen as a new phase of a long-standing critical tradition of resistance to the paradigms that have dominated American historiography.[14]

Américo Paredes articulated an alternative way of understanding both the manichean Southwestern frontier history of Webb and the consensus narratives of a Günnar Myrdal or Oscar Handlin or Robert Park. But Paredes' critique should also be read in conjunction with the contemporaneous work of Richard Wright, James Baldwin, John Hope Franklin, Carter Woodson, or Melville Herskovits—not to mention other international figures such as C. L. R. James, Frantz Fanon, or Aimé Césaire. Similarly, in the modernist period from the 1890s through the 1920s, alternatives to Turner's thesis about the formation of "American" identity existed in the diverse work of writers such as Lydia Maria Child, Maria Ámparo Ruiz de Burton, José Martí, Frances E. W. Harper, W. E. B. Du Bois, Horace Kallen, and Randolph Bourne—as well as Chief

Simon Pokagon (Potawatomi), who, like Turner, also gave an address in Chicago in 1893, though hardly from the same podium. (It is revealing how rarely Chief Pokagon is even mentioned when Turner's address is discussed. Angered by the exclusion of Native Americans from the World's Columbian Exposition, Pokagon gave a masterful jeremiad called "The Red Man's Rebuke," one version of which he sold as a pamphlet to fair attendees [Walker 209–20]). A history of such competing readings of "Our America" would be of immense value.

Contemporary borders school scholars adopt Turner's frontier thesis but cast it in significantly different light, as a strategy of empire and alien-making fundamentally in contradiction to American claims of democracy based on inalienable rights. And the borders school puts forth a compelling counter-paradigm of its own—a paradigm that seeks to tell the history of a different (and plural) cultural space, the border or *la frontera*, that is neither the site of assimilation nor the marking of an alien Other. It treats such a space as definitive for an ever-growing number of U.S. residents and explores it as a realm of exile, mobility, survival strategies, and the emergence of alternative and multiple identities mixing old and new that cannot be easily or accurately assimilated into earlier dominant narratives of "American" identity.

Perhaps even more powerfully, the borders school suggests that such a third cultural space is not a recent emergence in U.S. history. Rather, it argues that this space has been present within the history of U.S. settlement from the beginning—that it is in fact constitutive of U.S. identity, central rather than marginal. In a way, the borders school is attempting to reconfigure *both* Turner's frontier thesis *and* Martí's and Du Bois' paradigms of double consciousness and the multiple, conflicting identities and languages of "our" America that are continually being contested and creolized. And unlike the postethnicity school it does not posit such a state as the ultimate form of "consent" narrative, when past conflicts are left behind (made "post-") for a radically remade identity transcending the past. Instead, the borders school understands that such divided or border identities descend eternally from the contradictions within modernity itself, from the moment that the "Americas" were "discovered" and the struggle began to define whether these "Americas" were an alternative to or a proof of Europe's claim to be the superior civilization.

The borders school is undertaking new histories of both U.S. immigration and U.S. racial contradictions. Instead of a diasporic model that stresses the progress from descent to consent, uprooting to assimilation, the new ethnic history focuses on networks and associations that are transplanted and yet continually mobile, extending outside the U.S. but also branching in multiple ways within its cities and countryside. As the work of Jorge Duany and Juan Flores demonstrates, while Puerto Ricans value their U.S. citizenship and the freedom of movement it confers, their journeys back and forth between the two nations challenge the traditional territorial definitions of national identity, while transnational identities gain greater weight. In Chicano/a studies, Gloria Anzaldúa's 1987 exploration of contemporary border zones of cultural connections and resistance is deservedly well known and we will not rehearse her arguments here. Instead, we suggest that Anzaldúa's influence on American *historiography* as well as literary study needs to be charted; her influence also needs to be compared and contrasted with Paredes'. For just one example, consider George Sánchez's book *Becoming Mexican American* (1993).

Sánchez's study of Chicano identity formation attempts to synthesize the insights of Paredes, Anzaldúa, Renato Rosaldo and others, and it may prove as influential an example for new U.S. ethnic histories as Oscar Handlin's work was in the 1950s. Sánchez does not use a bipolar model suggesting a choice between fixed models of either "Mexican" or "American" identities; he stresses the changing "Mexican" experience of different generations (due in part to the changing U.S. presence in Mexico and the "southwest," alternatively known as El Norte) and also focuses on the shifting U.S. context, including the ironic effects of nativist agitation that usually strengthened the very Chicano communities it was intended to discourage. Sánchez emphasizes the internal diversity of the Chicano communities in Los Angeles, the many sites (home, community centers, workplace, schools, voting booths, and cultural festivals) in which they shaped their identities; he demonstrates that the barrios Chicanos called home, especially in the 1930s, were not centralized but widely dispersed communities that depended all the more on their ties of interconnection and their alliances with other ethnic groups—a part of the story of the southwest that has largely been untold. Sánchez also stresses the crucial role that mass culture as well as "high" culture played in Chicano community formation, including the profound influence of Cuban and African American popular culture, especially music and fashion. Influenced by such transnational and transethnic styles, Chicano culture could develop in border zones that allowed for creative hybridities and a critical stance toward some dominant forms associated with both Mexican and American culture. Analogous developments have also been occurring rapidly since the 1960s in literature, though this is not Sánchez's primary focus.[15]

In sum, borders school scholars emphasize the continual need for attention to the following topics:

- archives for the cultural history of particular groups; defining gaps in those archives; and confronting the challenges of recovering oral sources of cultural memory
- double- or multiple-consciousness, heterogeneity, strategic anti-essentialism: the emphasis on diverse histories and voices within a "single" group or location
- diaspora and exile and multiple locations both geographically and culturally, with attention to class and gender differences as they affect mobility, work, leisure, neighborhoods, and cultural production
- a recognition of the experience of linguistic borderlands and the cultural politics of negotiating multiple languages and dialects
- pan-ethnicity—the importance of making alliances among Native American tribes, Asian American or Latino/a ethnicities, etc., as well as the strategies for using new understandings of shared cultural history for "bonding in difference," for making ties across cultural boundaries
- strategically emphasized racial and community unity as needed to combat racism and economic oppression and to increase political power

- how to rethink the past and future of "whiteness": for more on this, see part IV below
- transnational perspectives, so that the histories of groups "within" the U.S. are also placed within the context of global forces and diasporas
- a workable balance between activist work within local communities and scholarly and teaching and mentoring responsibilities
- a focus on the ways in which all forms of culture, including literature, may dramatize all of the above issues in particularly complex and memorable ways

The borders school's contribution to U.S. ethnic studies cannot be understood without also considering this work in a transnational or diasporic context. If U.S. ethnic studies once evolved by shifting from Handlin's 1950s "uprooted" analogy to a 1970s stress on immigration as the transplantation of support networks, the 1990s work of the borders school significantly revises both these roots-centered paradigms. It is not just that narratives of assimilation to an "American" identity are being critiqued, as postethnicity scholars frequently complain. It is that the very definition of national identity is being revised, both from within and from without. Borders school analyses such as Gary Okihiro's *Margins and Mainstreams* argue that U.S. definitions of citizens' freedoms within the nation have often been expanded significantly by the civil rights claims of ethnic minorities, not by the majority. Simultaneously, such studies have complicated upward mobility and assimilation narratives by arguing for the relevance of diaspora (or migrant, or exilic) paradigms for the experience of a growing number of people who reside in the U.S. That is, the borders studies school has been central in demonstrating the necessity of studying U.S. ethnicity in a transnational context where the assimilation of immigrant ethnicities is not the primary focus. It is precisely in the analysis of diasporic vs. assimilationist models for the study of ethnicity where the relevance of postcolonial studies is clearest for U.S. ethnic studies. Before considering this last topic at some length in section IV, we should first turn to a brief look at several important developments in postcolonial studies.

III

LOOKING BACKWARD, MOVING FORWARD: POSTCOLONIAL STUDIES IN RETROSPECT

"If history moves forward, the knowledge of it travels backward, so that in writing of our recent past we are continually meeting ourselves coming the other way."

—Terry Eagleton, 190

"And the strength is not in us but above us, in a voice that drills the night and the hearing like the penetrance of an apocalyptic wasp. And the voice proclaims that for centuries Europe has force-fed us with lies and bloated us with pestilence,

> for it is not true that the work of man is done
> that we have no business being on earth

that we parasite the world
that it is enough for us to heel to the world
whereas the work has only begun
and man still must overcome all the interdictions wedged in
    the recesses of her fervor and no race has a monopoly on
    beauty, on intelligence, on strength

and there is room for everyone at the convoction of conquest. . . .

—Aimé Césaire, *Notebook of a Return to the Native Land*, in *Collected Poetry* 77

Edward Said's *Orientalism* and Eurocentric Representations

Most scholars regard Edward W. Said's *Orientalism* (1978) as the foundational text of what has come to be known as "Postcolonial Studies." In this groundbreaking work, Said charts the Western world's construction(s) of "an inferior East" by underscoring how the authorizing/authoritative "Occident" continues to produce an objectified and negatively stereotyped "Orient." Drawing from both Michel Foucault's definition of "discourse" and Antonio Gramsci's conceptualization of "hegemony," Said traces the evolution of European power/knowledge paradigms and their Western epistemologies—which he collectively calls "Orientalism"—and links them with imperialism. These Western paradigms and epistemologies are invested in the various forms and modes of representation—including TV and films, paintings and advertisements. For Said, fiction and journalistic writings are critical forms of representation. In his analysis of textual representations of the "Orient," Said clarifies how these representations can never be fully realistic. According to Said, "In any instance of at least written language, there is no such thing as a delivered presence, but a re-presence, or a representation. The value, efficacy, strength, apparent veracity of a written statement about the Orient therefore relies very little . . . on the Orient itself" (21).

Like "race" and "gender" in the West, what passes as the Orient (or the non-West) in Western forms of knowledge is a construction that calls for an interrogation of its ideological content, including its links to imperialism. Orientalism, for Said, is a major revolution in epistemology that reveals a European development of an image of the East that determines Europe's understanding of its territorial accumulations. For Said, chief among the inherent dangers of such Eurocentric epistemological production of the East are the ways in which "European culture gained in strength and identity by setting itself off against the Orient as a sort of surrogate and even underground self" (3). In his view, the Orient's attempts at self-authentication have become problematic due to the West's hegemonic discursive practices beginning with the eighteenth century and especially since the Industrial Revolution. More insidiously, the imperialistic gaze that has co-existed with the growth of Eurocentric epistemologies has been internalized by the non-Western Others to such a degree that there is a real danger that the East's perception of itself has been permanently altered. Not unlike bell hooks—who, in her preference for the use of the term "white supremacy" over "racism"—gives herself room to critique the complicity of black people in the pervasive institutional structures that maintain their second-class status in the U.S., postcolonial theorists—

from Frantz Fanon to Gayatri Spivak—have commented on the effects of Euro-American constructions of the former colonies (whether called Third World against First World, or South against North) on the self-images of individuals and societies so defined.

Although those material conditions that produced the colonialist discourses of colonizer/colonized between West and East may have become dismantled, the socio-cultural practices which supported these economic and political matrices still exist. Thus, while colonialism may have, in a large measure, ended "officially" in the early 1960s, institutionalized practices such as language acquisition, education, and religion remain operational to the degree that previously colonized peoples essentially remain dominated by Western cultural constructs. Hence, the meaning of "postcolonial" could be as diverse as the nations it hopes to give agency to, and many critics have often noted the risk in using the term to homogenize the diverse historical experiences of colonized peoples around the globe.

Building on Said's methodology in *Orientalism*, postcolonial studies as an approach has come to represent a vital if controversial field of study. The field has been enriched by the continuing work not only of Said himself but also that of scores of scholars and imaginative artists. Postcolonial novelists, poets and scholars have all advanced the unmasking of imperialism's ideological guises initiated by Said, and helped us to recognize forms of marginality across seas and border that are reinforced by various forms of cultural production, including and especially popular culture. For example, the domain of postcolonial studies includes a consideration of diasporic populations from the former colonies and the related issues of mimicry, complicity and hybridity that this global phenomenon has generated. The work of many U.S. studies scholars—such as Henry Louis Gates, bell hooks, Ketu Katrak, Abdul JanMohamed, Barbara Christian, Trinh T. Minh-ha, Sara Suleri, Gauri Viswanathan, Chandra Talpade Mohanty, Satya Mohanty, David Lloyd, Robert Elliot Fox, Carol Boyce Davies, Anthony Appiah, Lisa Lowe, Hazel Carby, José David Saldívar, Inderpal Grewal and Caren Kaplan— who have in recent decades focused their scholarship on race, immigration, ethnicity, or challenges to bourgeois white feminism, also manifests a postcolonial awareness: an alertness to issues of otherness and creolization in global and transnational contexts— pointing to a confluence of ideas and paradigms between postcolonial studies and ethnic U.S. studies that is at the heart of this volume.[16] One may point in this context to the parallel work in Canada by scholars such as Linda Hutcheon and Arun Mukherjee and novelists M.G. Vassanji, Rohinton Mistry, and Michael Ondaatje, as well as the growing influence of perspectives shaped by Stuart Hall and Paul Gilroy and novelists Salman Rushdie and Caryl Phillips out of the United Kingdom.

Since 1989, several overviews and a couple of critical anthologies have helped to consolidate the field and to clarify conflicts over definition and domain, a necessary precursor to the academic legitimacy "postcolonial studies" has now received in classrooms around the world as well as in those anthologies of theory and critical approaches that are the hallmark of most introductory courses for English majors. It is important here to acknowledge the pioneering if controversial contributions of the Australian team comprising Bill Ashcroft, Gareth Griffiths, and Helen Tiffin, whose three edited volumes have been critical to an adequate classroom exploration of postcolonial issues and approaches in literary study: *The Empire Writes Back: Theory and Practice in Post-Colonial Literature* (1989); *The Post-Colonial Studies Reader* (1995); and *Key Concepts in Post-Colonial Studies* (1998). Their reader was preceded by and complements *Colonial Discourses and Post-Colonial Theory: A Reader* (1993) edited by Patrick Williams and Laura Chrisman. Several recent monographs that would, singly or together, serve as useful texts for an undergraduate course in postcolonial literature and theory include Elleke Boehmer, *Colonial and Postcolonial Literature: Migrant Metaphors* (1995); Leela Gandhi, *Postcolonial Theory: A Critical Introduction* (1998); Dennis Walder, *Postcolonial Literatures In English: History, Language, Theory* (1998), and Ania Loomba, *Colonialism/Postcolonialism* (1999).

While Bill Ashcroft, Gareth Griffiths and Helen Tiffin have "use[d] the term 'post-colonial' . . . to cover all the culture affected by the imperial process from the moment of colonization to the present day" (1989: 2), most critics concur that the term "post-colonial" describes the combination of material, economic, social, and cultural practices an indigenous (and/or creolized) population engages with *after* the removal of the physical presence of a colonizing nation. Under this rubric, for example, India is defined as "post-colonial" after August 15, 1947, but not before. Patrick Williams and Laura Chrisman characterize Said's *Orientalism* as colonial discourse theory or analysis because it analyzes "the variety of textual forms in which the West produced and codified knowledge about non-metropolitan areas and cultures, especially those under colonial control" (1994: 5), and for their purposes "post-colonial" theories focus on the effects such colonial discourses continue to have on the colonized after the colonizer as physical agent has been removed. As a result, the promotion of a nation from colonial to post-colonial gives birth to new issues like nationality, partition, "common-wealthizing" and economic regeneration. Through this definition of post-colonial, we must ask ourselves: when a nation ceases to be part of an empire, at the moment of its transformation to post-colonial status, does a nation become "Third World?" If so, what factors "drop" a country from a global status more privileged than "Third World" aside from the departure of the colonized? Is the presence of a European colonizer a prerequisite to joining the "First World" club?

In her lucid and wide-ranging monograph, Boehmer not only distinguishes between "postcolonial" and the hyphenated "post-colonial," but offers succinct definitions of terms such as "imperialism" ("the authority assumed by a state over another territory"), "colonialism" (which "is manifested in the settlement of territory . . . and the attempt to govern the indigenous inhabitants of occupied lands"), "colonialist literature" ("literature written by and for colonizing Europeans about non-European lands dominated by them"), and "postcolonial literature" ("that which critically scrutinizes the colonial relationship") (2–3). Boehmer helpfully draws the distinction between "postcoloniality"/"postcolonial," which she defines as "that condition in which colonized peoples seek to take their place forcibly or otherwise, as historical subjects" and the hyphenated "post-colonial," which she qualifies as "another period term designating the post-Second World War era" (3).[17]

Again, within this framework, India is defined as a "post-colonial" country since it achieved independence after World War II. But, ironically, as other critics have argued, countries like India have experienced a loss of clear and coherent identity even more after the sun finally set on the British Empire in that part of the world. During the freedom movements, maybe it was easy to view much in culture in binary terms. But today, as a result of an explicit cultural barter transposed between the colonizer and colonized, subsequent generations of Indians not only uphold but hallow the hegemonic remnants of Western culture. This translation of culture, language and ideology, described by Simon During as imperial "residue," is smeared upon the landscapes of all post-colonial nations. And yet this "residue" is constantly in a state of flux and both culture and capital remain shifting realities—subject not only to the postcolonial paradigms of complicity and hybridity, but also global capitalism and market economy.[18]

A second vital term that has emerged in the evolution of Said's unmasking crusade is "neo-colonial." Viewed through a Marxist/Jamesonian lens, most theorists agree that "neo-colonial" primarily refers to the combination of the economic conditions of global capitalism that continue to subjugate post-colonial nations as they strive to resist the material (after)effects of the invasive economical tactics of colonizing nations. Paraphrasing Kwame Nkrumah, the celebrated Pan-Africanist and first president of independent Ghana, Ashcroft, Griffiths, and Tiffin report, for example, that "although countries like Ghana had achieved technical independence, the ex-colonial powers and the newly emerging superpowers such as the United States continued to play a decisive role [in neo-colonial strategies] through international monetary bodies, through the fixing of prices on world markets, multinational corporations and cartels and a variety of educational and cultural institutions" (Ashcroft et al *Key Concepts* 162–63). Here, contemporary imperialism is remasked in the guise of international money—ideology funnels itself into the global economy and polices, even pathologizes the "Third World."

Having established a methodology in *Orientalism* for examining both how and why the colonizing West has constructed the colonized East during the last few centuries, Said has since given particular attention to specific historical and material conditions that produce cultural artifacts like literature, music, art and other integral cultural expressions that highlight imperialistic epistemologies. Expanding on his focus in *The World, the Text, the Critic* (1983), in which he underscores how the "necessary interplay" between "a text and its circumstantiality" limits, or restrains "both the interpreter and his interpretation," Said's *Culture and Imperialism* (1993) provides an examination of texts that inevitably foreground the theoretical continuum from pre- to post-colonial temporality. In this landmark work, Said primarily examines nineteenth-century literature as he elaborates two critical concepts that guide his more recent criticism. The first, "a structure of attitude and reference" (62) that can be experienced in novels by Jane Austen and Rudyard Kipling, for example, primarily highlights how the "world beyond [England] is [never] seen except as subordinate and dominated," and how these novelists "refin[ed] and articulat[ed] . . . the 'status quo' " (74–77) of imperial Britain. Even more important than these observations of how the British novel participates in the perpetuation of cultural hegemony through colonial discursive practices, however, is Said's emphasis on the necessity for a "contrapuntal reading" of these texts. In such a reading one "must take account of both [the] processes . . . of imperialism and that of resistance to it, which can be done by extending our reading of the texts to include what was once forcibly left out" (66–67). Thus, for example, the reader of Austen's *Mansfield Park* should take note of how, though it essentially provides the family material wealth, the Bertrams' sugarcane plantation in Antigua is virtually marginalized throughout this text. Avoiding a reductive demonization of Austen for what might be interpreted as her complicit role in this imperialistic enterprise, however, Said prefers to examine "how [a] body of humanistic ideas co-existed so comfortably with imperialism" in works like *Mansfield Park* (82).[19]

The Antecedents of Postcolonial Thought

Since *Orientalism*, a considerable amount of scholarship has focused not only on the historical underpinnings of Orientalist epistemologies, but, perhaps more importantly, on the anti-colonial strategists who had challenged the ideological and material conditions of colonizing nations long before Said's book was published. Although the contributions of individuals like Trinidad's C. L. R. James and Cape Verde's Amilcar Cabral continue to receive acknowledgment, it is Frantz Fanon who has received the most critical attention in the last few decades. A Martiniquan psychiatrist who actively confronted the colonizing French in Algeria, Fanon's most important works include *Black Skin, White Masks* (1952), in which he foregrounds the intersections among racism, sexual desire and colonialism, and *The Wretched of the Earth* (1961), which outlines strategies for decolonization and movement towards native autonomy.

Informed by both Marxism and psychoanalysis, Fanon ultimately developed his concept of the "comprador" class, or "intellectual native bourgeoisie," which was comprised of an elite, privileged class of natives whose 'black skin' became 'masked' by their desire to engage in the economic and socio-cultural practices of white colonizers. While Said is quick to observe that Fanon was not ignorant of pre-colonial class divisions, he also highlights what he refers to as Fanon's "critical nationalism," which stressed how "the future would not hold liberation but an extension of imperialism" (*Culture and Imperialism* 323) if the comprador class did not involve itself in liberation efforts.[20]

As many critics note, Fanon's work had a marked influence on black consciousness movements in Great Britain, France, and the U.S. in the 1960s and the 1970s. By drawing attention to the internalization of negative self-images among colonized natives, Fanon's name and work have become associated with African and Caribbean writers of the "negritude" movement such as Leopold Senghor and Aimé Césaire, as well as with earlier African American activists such as W. E. B. Du Bois and Jamaica-born Marcus Garvey, all of whom have variously posited a distinct "African personality" which was perceived as a unified, pro-active response to the dehumanizing processes of both the external colonization of African nations and the internal quasi-colonial practices that perpetuated hegemonic racial differences in countries like the United States. While these thinkers focused on colonial conditions that forced the diasporic displacement of generations of Africans, they also underscored the intersections between what Boehmer refers to as "the double vision of the colonized" (115), who felt alienated both from their own homeland and from the interloping colonizers, and Du Bois's concept of "double consciousness," which speaks specifically to the fragmented condition suffered by African Americans. Indeed, in this volume, Kenneth Mostern argues that it is Du Bois's 1903 publication of *The Souls of Black Folk* that essentially inaugurated postcolonial theoretical frameworks. This connection between dualities, one in the colonial homeland and the other in the postcolonial promised land, illustrates the inevitability of multiple identities for people of color.

In addition to drawing parallels between the negritude movement, decolonization, and the alienating "double consciousness," some critics have begun to underscore the complementary theoretical and political practices of early twentieth century modernist writers and certain (post)colonial writers whose poly-cultural affiliations include access to metropolitan centers. According to Boehmer, "the preoccupation with the displace-ment and loss of identity shared by the new colonial writers corresponded to the breakdown in universal systems of understanding with which metropolitan modernists were concerned" (124). Thus, writers such as Katherine Mansfield, Claude McKay, Jean Rhys, Raja Rao, and C. L. R. James essentially shared with Ezra Pound, T. S. Eliot, James Joyce and Virginia Woolf feelings of alienation and displacement that they had begun to absorb and sometimes "mimic" in the metropolitan centers of Paris and London. However, as Boehmer asserts, although this "metropolitan modernism" encouraged both "a displacement of conventional perspectives" and "a process of global transculturation" (124, 129–30), it could not transcend the structures of impe-rial authority that were ingrained in the canonical modernist writers, and even found their places in the fictional narratives of their novels. *A la* Said on *Mansfield Park*, Boehmer does not condemn these writers for being implicated in imperialist dis-courses, though she highlights the inherent limitations of being able to "deviat[e] from the norm" (167).

Besides Du Bois, Harlem Renaissance figures—Alain Locke, a Howard University philosophy professor who mentored several young black writers in the 1920s, and Claude McKay, a Jamaica-born poet who spent many nomadic years in Europe and North Africa—deserve special attention in relation to a transnational modernist re-sponse to colonialist conditions. For example, in *The New Negro* (1925) Locke claims that "Harlem has the same role to play for the New Negro as Dublin has had for New Ireland," and compares the New Negro Renaissance to freedom movements in India and elsewhere. African-Americans' struggle toward self-determination in a post-bellum, post-slavery, but still race-ridden, quasi-colonial United States is illustrative of what Elleke Boehmer describes as "the double process of *cleaving*" in the early days of anti-colonial cultural imperialism in both India and Africa: "*cleaving from*, moving away from colonial definitions, transgressing the boundaries of colonialist discourse; and, in order to effect this, *cleaving to*: borrowing, taking over, and appropriating the ideological, linguistic, and textual forms of the colonial power"(105–06). McKay's novel *Banjo* (1929) explores issues concerning diasporic black identities[21] even as the Back-to-Africa movement, led by fellow Jamaican, Marcus Garvey, denounces Euro-centric colonial hegemonies by inverting the West's obsession with racial stereotypes. Ultimately, as Paul Gilroy notes in *Black Atlantic*, most black intellectuals who trav-eled between the United States and Europe literally and figuratively "desire[d] to transcend both the structures of the nation state and the constraints of ethnicity and

national particularity" (19). Gilroy's perspective is arguably an attempt to acknowledge the hybridizing, creolizing power of the African experience in the West, possibly
the nemesis of the Afrocentrist ideas associated with the work of Molefe Asante. As
Sieglinde Lemke remarks in *Primitivist Modernism* (1998), "Gilroy deftly argues that
black cultural expressions are necessarily 'modern because they have been marked by
their hybrid creole origins.' . . . By claiming that hybridity marks modernity, Gilroy
makes an important contribution to conventional definitions of the 'modern' condition" (15).

Nativism, Mimicry, Hybridity, Complicity

As may be surmised from the above, "nativism"[22] is another issue that links postcolonial studies to new understandings of the U.S. Anthony Appiah—a Ghanian educated in the U.K. and a U.S. resident since the 1970s—has critiqued nativist
tendencies in debates of African culture and identity as well as responded to Afrocentrism on the U.S. scene. Nativism ranges from Afrocentric appeals to purity and racial
solidarity on the American scene (ranging from Molefe Asante to the Leonard Jeffries
variety) to negritude and Ngugi's nativist assertions on African Literature in African
languages. In *Islands and Exiles*, Chris Bongie suggests that "regardless of whether the
appeals of a Molefi Keti Asante are more popular than those of a Homi Bhabha to
cultural hybridity, . . . this (ineradicable) opposition is itself at the foundation of
postcolonial theory" (47). Bongie attributes the ambivalences, divisions, and mixtures
that define this opposition to what Paul Gilroy has called "the fragmentation of the
self (doubling and splitting) which modernity seems to promote" (*Black Atlantic* 5).[23]
Observing the essentialist nature of most identity formation projects, Gilroy contends
that furthering an awareness of this modernity has been less fashionable than "appeals
to the notion of purity as the basis of racial solidarity." Gilroy mentions in particular
the wide appeal of Spike Lee's "campaign against difficulty, complexity, and anything
else that does not fit the historical binary codes of the American racial thought" (*Small
Acts* 185–86).

Simon During—taking a more sympathetic view—makes a case for a "post-colonialism" defined as "the need, in nations and groups which have been victims of
imperialism, to achieve an identity uncontaminated by universalist or Eurocentric concepts and images" (33). He distinguishes someone like Salman Rushdie—complicit
with the legacy of colonialism in their unwillingness to "jettison the language and
culture of the imperialist nations"—from, say, Ngugi wa Thiong'o, who identifies
"with the culture destroyed by imperialism and its tongue" and attempts to recreate
an uncontaminated political space and literary language. The cause of cultural nationalism that might foster and shape indigenous structures and institutions (including
theater) led Ngugi around 1980 to write in Gikuyu, eschewing the languages of
Europe. In *Decolonising the Mind: The Politics of Language in Africa* (1981), Ngugi sets
up this distinction in sharper terms as between "imperialist tradition" and "resistance
tradition" and asserts a strong belief in "the coming inevitable revolutionary break
with neo-colonialism"—arguing that a truly African literature will overtake the "hy-

brid tradition," associated with his fellow African writers such as Wole Soyinka, Chinua Achebe, Ousmane Sembene, and others—for Ngugi, "a tradition in transition, a minority tradition that can only be termed as Afro-European literature; that is, the literature written by Africans in European languages" (26–27).

Echoing the implicit or explicit assaults on Senghor's Negritude by Richard Wright, Wole Soyinka,[24] and others, Anthony Appiah notes that "the very category of the Negro is at root a European product; for the 'whites' invented the Negroes in order to dominate them. Simply put, the overdetermined course of cultural nationalism in Africa has been to make real the imaginary identities to which Europe has subjected us" (*Father's House* 62). Appiah has, in fact, provided a most trenchant critique of "nativism"—an ideology enshrined in "that now-classic manifesto of African cultural nationalism," *Towards the Decolonization of African Literature*, whose three Nigerian authors have argued that "African literature is an autonomous entity separate and apart from all other literature . . . [with] its own traditions, models, and norms" (Chinweizu). For Appiah, this campaign for "apartness" is shaped by the dictates of the West's Herderian legacy, its notion of a *Sprachgeist*, and its involvement in what Nietzsche called "the problem of race [Rasse]": namely, that "it is simply not possible that a human being should *not* have the qualities and preferences of his parents and ancestors in his body, whatever appearances may suggest to the contrary" (Nietzsche, *Beyond Good and Evil*, 214 [section 264], cited in Bongie 49). According to Appiah, the "reverse discourse" of these Nigerian writers is derived from the very discourse it would contest and which made possible the invention of "Negroes" in the first place. In *In My Father's House*, Appiah argues passionately for the need to "transcend the banalities of nativism—its images of purgation, its declarations, in the face of international capital, of a specious 'autonomy,' its facile topologies" (71–72). For Appiah, this transcendence will come about only when we leave behind "the language of empire—of center and periphery, identity and difference, the sovereign subject and her colonies" (72), and recognize that "we are all contaminated by each other" (155).

This "contamination" is at the heart of concepts such as hybridity, mimicry and complicity that have come to be associated with postcolonial theory. In colonial discourses of the Other—as in official multiculturalism—each national (or racial/ethnic) group is viewed as pure and homogeneous, representing an authentic and unified culture. In this knowledge paradigm, any deviation from the "norm"—assertions or display of strong individual experience or "multiple identities"—would be seen as impure, even betrayal.

In response to such a denial of the ambiguity of belonging—especially visible in migrant and diasporic communities, Homi Bhabha, for example, has highlighted the concept of "hybridity" to describe a fundamental effect of colonialism and colonialist discourses. In his analysis, Bhabha stresses the interdependence and the mutuality of subjectivities that mark the relations between the colonizer and colonized. For him, all cultural systems and stances are constructed in the ambivalent and contradictory space that he calls the "Third Space of enunciation"(*Location of Culture* 37). Cultural purity is untenable because cultural identity emerges in this "Third Space" which is both ambivalent and contradictory. Although Bhabha views hybridity primarily as an empowering force because "[it] displays the necessary deformation and displacement of all sites of discrimination and domination" (*Location of Culture* 112), he also aligns it with a few other controversial concepts that do not necessarily lead to the synthesis of different cultures that is privileged in Gilroy's analysis of trans-Atlantic black cultural production. For example, in his representation of the colonial subject's "mimicry" of colonial authority, Bhabha argues that mimicry aids the colonizer because it helps create "a recognizable Other." For Bhabha, mimicry is a process by which the colonized subject is reproduced as "almost the same, but not quite . . . so that mimicry is at once resemblance and menace" (*Location of Culture* 86). It becomes a threat or a "menace" to colonial authority, because it highlights the colonial subjects' "difference" from the colonizer. A gap is produced by this difference (what Bhabha refers to as "slippage") that ultimately fixes the colonial subject as an incomplete, or "partial presence." This "partial presence," in turn, threatens or "menaces" the colonial authority because it produces another knowledge of the colonizer's cultural norms that the colonizer is unwilling to accept, i.e., the "partial presence" acts as a disturbing mirror of the dominant culture's self-proclaimed, self-aggrandizing " 'normalized' knowledges and disciplinary powers."

Thus, mimicry remains subversive to the colonizer though the colonized may not be fully conscious of this effect. So, postcolonial writing is not a menace just because of its opposition to colonial discourse, but even more from its disruption of colonial authority, from the real possibility that its mimicry is also mockery. This double-edged aspect of mimicry—homage as well as menace to the colonizer's identity and authority—is present in the idea of brown-skinned Englishmen—"a class of person Indians in blood and colour, but English in tastes, opinions, in morals, and in intellect"—who would serve as "interpreters" in Macaulay's "Minute on Indian Education"(1835) and also fictionalized in V. S. Naipaul's *The Mimic Men* (1967). In contrast to Naipaul, Salman Rushdie appears much more willing to celebrate such mimicry and ambiguity of space in diasporic lives through highlighting the creative possibilities of expatriation and exile in essays such as "Imaginary Homelands" as well as in his fictional practice in *Midnight's Children* and elsewhere. Asserting the significance of the "double perspective" that the Indian diasporic writers in U.K. could bring to bear on their "imaginary homelands, Indias of the mind," Rushdie observes: "Our identity is at once plural and partial. . . . But however ambiguous and shifting this ground may be, it is not an infertile territory for a writer to occupy. If literature is in part the business of finding new angles at which to enter reality, then once again our distance, our long geographical perspective, may provide us with such angles" (15).

Cognizant of the complicated ways in which mimicry shapes hybridity, the British critic Robert J. M. Young is broadly in agreement with Bhabha's conceptualization of hybridity because it signifies both a "challenge and resistance against a dominant colonial power . . . [and] deprives[s] the imperialist culture . . . of its own claims to authenticity" (23). However, while Bhabha tends to view hybridity as a productive "third space of enunciation" from which the colonized initiate the process of self-authentication, Young warns that hybridity can perpetuate a reductive sense of the Other because, at the height of imperialist discursive practices, the derogatory term "hybrid" frequently connotes a native's return to a pre-colonial, "primitive" subject-position, as the term "native" itself sometimes does. Thus, although Young is drawn to hybridity's employment of "a double logic which goes against the convention of rational either/or choices" (26), he is wary of using such a term that has its historical foundations in racist discourses. Young is not the only one who is skeptical about the assumption of advantage in hybridity. Others such as Aijaz Ahmad, Benita Parry, and Chandra Talpade Mohanty have pointed to the neglect of local differences in this idealist aspect of colonial discourse analysis. As Ashcroft et al have noted, "the assertion of a shared post-colonial condition such as hybridity has been seen as part of a tendency of discourse analysts to de-historicize and de-locate cultures from their temporal, spatial, geographical, and linguistic contexts, and to lead to an abstract, globalized concept of the textual that obscures the specificities of particular cultural situations" (*Key Concepts* 118–19).

Another prominent figure who has expanded our understandings of hybridity and complicity is Gayatri Chakravorty Spivak, whose theoretical contributions emanate from a critical nexus of "subaltern studies," deconstruction, feminism and Marxism. Since 1976, when Spivak published her translation of Jacques Derrida's *Of Grammatology*, in which her notoriously dense and self-reflexive "Translator's Preface" introduces readers in many ways to her commitment to deconstruction, Spivak has, as noted by Donna Landry and Gerald MacLean in their valuable introduction to *The Spivak Reader* (1996), "increasingly expanded her interests beyond the European literary and philosophical traditions to the history of imperialism and non-elite or subaltern insurgency" (8). While these expanded interests have gained Spivak new audiences among individuals and groups focused on studying race, gender, and nation, she appears to have been marginalized by the deconstructive establishment. As Landry and MacLean point out, "while [Spivak] remains one of the few intellectuals actually carrying out the suggestions made by the post-Enlightenment ethical movement associated with Derrida and Emmanuel Levinas, scholars who have engaged in high ethical debates in the recent past seem to have ignored her contributions. . . . It is as if Spivak's work had been contaminated by too long an association with Marxism, Third Worldism, and international feminism to possess a theoretical position pure enough to be entertained any longer as high ethical discourse" (*Spivak Reader* 9).[25]

Because of the centrality of the deconstructive idea in Spivak's *oeuvre*—from her "Translator's Preface" to Derrida's *Of Grammatology* (1976) through *In Other Worlds: Essays on Cultural Politics* (1987), *The Post-Colonial Critic* (1990), and *Outside the Teaching Machine* (1993), to *A Critique of Postcolonial Reason: Toward the History of the Vanishing Present* (1999)—Spivak has sometimes been misread as anti-historicist. Her "anti-historicism" (if at all it could be called that) does not exclude the project of deconstructing imperial history, but she is committed even more to destroying the ideology of a "hegemonic historiography" that presents the history of colonialism as a coherent Western narrative. Thus, Spivak, like Said, is invested in debunking orientalist epistemologies which construct the "Third World" through Western imperialist representations. In fact, she would like to promote heterogeneous discursive representations that create the space for a new "worlding of the world" (*In Other Worlds*).

Nowhere is Spivak's view of historicist projects illumined better than in her relationship to the work of the Subaltern Studies Collective, whose introduction to Euro-American audiences she is often credited with. This group, which initially included

Ranajit Guha, Shahid Amin, Partha Chatterjee, Gyan Pandey, David Arnold, and David Hardiman, was organized in 1982 in Calcutta, India, and took its name from Gramsci's conceptualization in *Prison Notebooks* (1971) of the "subaltern" (one who is "of inferior rank") as a subject dominated by oppressive, hegemonic power structures. Since their inception, the Subaltern Studies group has been committed to addressing critically the ways in which academic writing has, until recently, manufactured "elitist interpretations" (Guha *Subaltern Studies I*: vii) of South Asian historiography, i.e., how the history of South Asia had become a chronicle of elites: kings and viceroys, high castes and upper classes, etc. Retrospectively, Guha, in his Introduction to *A Subaltern Studies Reader*, reflects on the disillusionment of the 1970s politics in India—"the years between the Naxalbari uprising and the end of the Emergency"—that gave rise to two kinds of questions for the Collective:

> 1. What was there in our colonial past and our engagement with nationalism to land us in our current predicament—that is, the aggravating and seemingly insoluble difficulties of the nation-state?
> 2. How are the unbearable difficulties of our current condition compatible with and explained by what happened during colonial rule and our predecessors' engagement with the politics and culture of the period?

Reminiscent of Fanon's warning against the ways in which the "native intellectual bourgeoisie" of a colonized country become complicit in the deformation of pre-colonial subjectivities, scholars associated with the Subaltern Studies Collective emphasize the inherent dangers in constructing historiographies that are dependent upon privileged bourgeois epistemologies. According to Spivak, the Collective do offer a theory of change—the agency of change, for them, being located in the insurgent or the "subaltern"—even though "they generally perceive their task as making a theory of consciousness or culture rather than a theory of change" (*Spivak Reader* 205–206). But how does one write the "subaltern" history of India—from the point of view of peasant insurgency, when there are "no subaltern testimonials, memoirs, diaries or official histories" (*Spivak Reader* 203)? Ranajit Guha has continued to assert the need to "focus on this consciousness as our central theme, because it is not possible to make sense of the experience of insurgency merely as a history without a subject" (*Spivak Reader* 220).

In her influential essay, "Can the Subaltern Speak?" Spivak expands on the subject of native autonomy by openly questioning whether subaltern classes can "speak" from a position beyond the Western hegemonic discourses that have produced them. Including Spivak's remarks about how the "gendered subaltern" does not speak for herself and therefore disappears, this essay, in Leela Gandhi's words, interrogates the "contesting representational systems [that] violently displace/silence [this] figure" (Gandhi 89). This essay has caused unending debate and confusion and Spivak has felt compelled to clarify and expand on her original articulations from the mid-1980s for well over a decade. Admitting that the original essay "was so uncontrolled that only someone else could cut it" (*Spivak Reader* 288), Spivak has pointed out how the use of the term "subaltern" has become so slippery in recent Euro-American usage as to be almost meaningless. In both *The Spivak Reader* and *The Critique of Postcolonial Reason* (announced several years ago as *An Unfashionable Grammatology: Colonial Discourses Revisited*, an "archival and theoretical study of gender and colonial discourse"), Spivak has attempted to bring readers back to a consideration of Guha's original definition: "The social groups and elements included in this category represent *the demographic difference between the total Indian population and all those whom we have described as the 'elite'* " (*Spivak Reader 203*; Spivak's italics).[26]

In response to those who criticize Spivak's position on the inevitability of a subaltern subjectivity that is always-already contextualized by confining discursive practices,[27] Spivak has introduced the concept of "strategic essentialism," which utilizes the effectiveness of a strategically positioned essential identity that can be implemented to combat the oppressive tactics of colonial structures. While such an "essentialist" ideology may sound antithetical to theories of deconstruction, Spivak explains her position in an interview with Elizabeth Gross by pointing out that "as a deconstructivist . . . I cannot in fact clean my hands and say I'm specific. In fact I must say I am an essentialist from time to time" ("Criticism, Feminism, and the Institution" 183).

Spivak's work is emblematic of the ways in which, as Leela Gandhi notes, postcolonial studies have become a contested matrix for the playing out of Marxist and poststructuralist theories. Certainly, for example, just as Foucault's concept of "discourse" influenced Said, Derrida's deconstructive theories have informed much of Spivak's poststructuralist formations of identity. Moreover, Spivak's concomitant application of Gramscian "hegemony" to her work necessarily invokes some of the inherent tensions/ paradoxes in postcolonial studies that continue to engage a variety of critics in the discourses surrounding "high theory," postcolonial studies, and transnational feminism. One of these tensions/paradoxes which Spivak's work has always problematized in a range of global contexts and which has received special attention in *A Critique of Postcolonial Reason* is the deconstructive stance of "persistently to critique a structure that one cannot not (wish to) inhabit," or, restated in the words of Landry and Mac-Lean, "[t]he critique of essentialism is predicated upon essentialism. That is why it is important to choose as an object of critique something which we love, or which we cannot not desire, cannot not wish to inhabit, however much we wish also to change it" (*Spivak Reader* 7). Spivak has consistently held that an obsessive opposition to a presumed European "center" is counterproductive and merely reifies the center, confining one to the "margins."[28] This nexus of desire and resistance—as noted in other ways by bell hooks—is at the heart of what Spivak has called the "productive complicity" of "native informants" like herself. In *Critique* (171–173)—after offering her multi-pronged approach for native informants to resist and subvert marginalization in their ability to address the issues of colonialism and neocolonialism, internal colonization and essentialism against the "double bind of Eurocentric arrogance and unexamined nativism"—she reiterates the continuing significance of deconstruction in the following words: "Deconstructive cautions would put a critical frame around them (we can never be fully critical) and in between them, so that we do not compound the problem by imagining the double bind too easily resolved. In fact, and in the most practical way, double binds are less dangerously enabling than the unilaterality of dilemmas resolved" (173). Salutary words for all of us working in the field of cultural studies!

Immigration and Diaspora

Addressing the need to theorize more closely the ways in which ideologies of resistance are operational in postcolonial theories and literatures, Ashcroft, Griffiths, and Tiffin published *The Empire Writes Back* in 1989. These critics outline the growth of modern post-colonial literatures and record the emergence of discourses that have evolved from writings in colonial, imperialistic English to the post-colonial works written in English. According to Ashcroft, et al, there is a "need to distinguish between what is proposed as a standard code, English (the language of the erstwhile imperial center), and the linguistic code, English, which has been transformed and subverted into several distinctive varieties throughout the world" (8). The appellation "English," then, serves as a linguistic marker for those "peripheral" texts that "write back" to an imperialistic center that has both displaced and dislocated pre-colonial native identities. These critics not only analyze the ways in which writers such as Lewis Nkosi, V. S. Naipaul, Michael Anthony, and R. K. Narayan engage in "subversive" discursive strategies such as abrogation, appropriation, and creolization, but they also survey how indigenous literary theories (e.g., Indian, African, Caribbean) intersect with post-colonial theories to "construct . . . a 'unique' voice [that is] distinct from the language of the centre" (117).

The net effect of these discourses is to give color to the understanding and deconstruction of what has come to be known in the U.S. as ethnic studies and, somewhat extravagantly, American Studies. Like the cultural "residue" earlier described by Simon During, the act of immigration is, within itself, symbolic of the "transcendent" postcolonial who is not only able to break away from the colonizer on a national level, but is also able to transfer his or her existence globally to the "promised land," the United States—or for that matter, Canada, or the U.K. Still, such a monumental shift is not without consequences—the postcolonial immigrant is tossed into the great "salad bowl" of the U.S., immediately experiencing the joy of immigration and the sadness of exile. Many transnational women writers—such as Tsitsi Dangarembga and Meena Alexander—have testified that while gender was the primary battle for them in their homelands, "race" and their exoticization through the combined prism of both race and gender shape major identity challenges for them in the West. Alexander expresses her complex of reactions both in her powerful memoir, *Fault Lines* (1993), and in a book of reflections and writerly statements entitled *The Shock of Arrival* (1997), wherein she informs her readers that the Asian experience of arrival to the new world manifests itself in the art of Asian Americans. As Alexander puts it, "Rendered Other in the new world, one is interrogated, asked who one is, made to respond" (153). Like many immigrant, African American and other ethnic American writers, Alexander illustrates how postcolonial women—more than their male counterparts—are exoticized and fetishicized in the U.S., treated as prize possessions or viewed as living proof of desired diversity even as their voices are ignored or silenced.

In their introduction to *Memory and Cultural Politics: New Approaches to American Ethnic Literatures*, editors Amritjit Singh, Joseph Skerrett, Jr., and Robert E. Hogan attempt to link postcolonial studies to the numerous intersections of ethnicity, identity, memory and history in the U.S.: "Postcolonial discourses have extended and complicated our understandings of how changing patterns of racial formulation and immigration are affecting the emergence of a new American identity" (12). On the one hand, Singh, et al, acknowledge the fruitful application of postcolonial studies to readings of the United States as a nation—its long ill-treatment of Native Americans; its conquest of Mexico; its ambiguous relationship to Puerto Rico, Hawaii, and Panama; and its many colonial and neo-colonial ventures in the Philippines and around the world (see in this context the essays in this volume by Arnold Krupat, Lawrence Buell, and Amy Kaplan). On the other hand, Singh, et al, remind us that "*each* diasporic community is shaped by its own specific histories of class, religion, language, race, and region, and that [we need] to remain alert to the dangers of totalizing tendencies inherent in some postcolonial discourses" (12).

As noted by Singh, Skerrett and Hogan, the "dialogue between the ethnic self and the dominant culture is a significant part of the process by which both the individual and the group confront the socio-political challenges of American life" (13). In the context of U.S. nationality, Boehmer's "double vision of the colonized" and Du Bois' concept of "double consciousness" themselves become masked, or, more appropriately, expand themselves to accommodate the vast amalgam that they attempt to empower. In fact, the colonizer/colonized binary in traditional postcolonial studies can no longer suffice in the deconstruction of diasporic identities within the U.S. borders. Identity becomes multi-faceted, and results in what Arjun Appadurai views as a mess of hyphens in which the "sides of the hyphen will have to be reversed and we become a federation of diasporas, American-Italians, American-Haitians, American-Irish, American-Africans" ("Heart" 804). And, even if our shared U.S. citizenship were to take precedence over our other identities fragmented by "race," ethnicity, gender, national origin, etc., we cannot but acknowledge that we are all a part of a most powerful imperialist, capitalist democracy whose global agenda most of us acquiesce in through silence, indifference, arrogance, and/or media influence. It is for this reason that we represent the borders school as an important new paradigm for approaching diasporic histories and constructions of the U.S. within and outside its geographical boundaries.[29]

IV

THE BORDERS SCHOOL AND POSTCOLONIAL THEORY: NEW ETHNICITIES

"In this particular segment, ladies and gentlemen, we have adjusted our perspective to that of the kangaroo and the didjeridoo. This automatically throws us either down under and/or out back. And from that point of view it's most improbable that anyone will ever know exactly who is enjoying the shadow of whom."

—Duke Ellington, describing an excerpt from his suite *The Afro-Eurasian Eclipse* in 1971 (Mark Tucker, *The Duke Ellington Reader* 379–80n)

"Renato Rosaldo has noted the way ethnographers, accustomed to viewing cultures as self-enclosed, have similarly treated immigrants: . . . 'Immigrants and socially mobile individuals appeared culturally invisible because they were no longer what they once were and not yet what they could become.' "

—George Sánchez 11

Postcolonial studies and the borders school in U.S. ethnic studies have interacted in a number of complex ways over the last decades. We would like to focus here briefly on three (of many) instances of such cross-fertilization—transnationalism, feminism, and whiteness studies—and then turn to reflections on the current state of "globalization" theory and some upcoming challenges we see facing the borders school.

Transnationalism, Diaspora, and Immigration Narratives

Recently, U.S. studies has once again sought an international focus—this time, prompted by shifts in ethnic and postcolonial studies as well as by global developments outside the academy. Today's cultural moment eerily mimes that of approximately one hundred years ago, when Frederick Jackson Turner and W. E. B. Du Bois offered their competing theses about which was more significant—the western frontier or the color-line—in forming U.S. identity. Turner's question of what new site in U.S. culture would replace the frontier in creating new Americans parallels much current writing expressing anxieties about the breakdown of traditional sites of assimilation to a "national" culture. Turner's assumptions were not Du Bois'. Arguing that the color-line was even more significant to U.S. identity than the frontier, Du Bois saw a country that engineered violence restricting access to citizenship rights. His life work was devoted to demanding equality of rights in law but pluralist possibilities in cultural history. Similarly, borders studies scholars today ponder the paradoxes of class- and color-lines, and usually with the same transnational as well as internal emphasis that Du Bois brought to his work after 1903.

"No existing conception of Americanness can contain this large variety of transnations," Arjun Appadurai has recently written (*Modernity at Large* 172), but his sentence could easily be at home in one of Martí's essays, Charles W. Chesnutt's "The Future American" essays (1900), or Randolph Bourne's critique of the boundaries of "America" in "Trans-National America" (1916). Appadurai's emphasis is shared by a broad spectrum of U.S. studies scholars. The 1996 American Studies convention topic was "Global Migration, American Cultures, and the State," and in 1998 both *American Literary History* and *American Quarterly* (to pick two influential journals) published essays reflecting critically on the confluences between postcolonial studies and new developments within U.S. studies, especially emphases on "transnationalism," or diasporic forms of identity that cannot be fully bound within narratives of citizenship or exclusion within fixed nation-states.[30]

What is new as we enter a new century is the central role played by scholars of color from both postcolonial studies and the borders studies school in shaping these revisions for the study of ethnicity and race and culture. Not only is a wide variety of disciplines represented—particularly sociology and anthropology and history as well as literary and media studies and older interdisciplinary sites such as Black Studies—but significant transnational exchanges of ideas are involved, especially in the area of how exilic or diasporic consciousness poses a challenge to traditional nation-state narratives of identity and majority/minority dichotomies.

Of all writers associated with the U.S. borders studies school, Gloria Anzaldúa has probably had the widest influence both within the U.S. and internationally—she is indeed a significant instance of how borders studies scholarship has impinged upon postcolonial theory as well as the reverse. (Most influential: Anzaldúa's approaches toward studying external borders, internal borders "within" a single ethnicity, mixed languages, and the reinterpretation of origin narratives. Also vivifying has been Anzaldúa's revisionary approach to form—her writing mixes the analytical and the anecdotal, prose and poetry, and various "levels" of both Spanish and English.) In the words of Gita Rajan and Radhika Mohanram: "Diaspora acts as a mediator, a catch-all term to house the postcolonial condition. But recent critical focus has shifted from exile and diaspora to borders, and the crossing and recrossing of physical, imaginative, linguistic, and cultural borders. Gloria Anzaldúa's groundbreaking work, *Borderlands/ La Frontera* [1987], is largely responsible for this new direction in postcolonial studies" ("Introduction" 5).

Yet just as clearly, postcolonial theorists' innovations have profoundly redirected traditional U.S. ethnic studies analyses since the 1970s so that it is not so centripetally focused on immigration and assimilation narratives. There are significant parallels between the Caribbean-born British cultural studies theorist Stuart Hall's "new ethnicities" paradigm developed in the 1980s and early 1990s and contemporaneous "new ethnicities" history in the U.S. that we have named the borders school. "Denationalization" is a common theme, both in the sense of challenging the hidden racial biases of national narratives and in contesting how minorities within those same nation-states adopted nationalist narratives to define unity in opposition. There remains a shared emphasis on new strategies for defining panethnic "unities" and claims for rights without succumbing to nationalist assumptions. The following sentence from "Culture, Community, Nation" is representative of Hall's complex thought: "We need to be able to insist that rights of citizenship and the incommensurabilities of cultural difference are respected and that *the one is not made the condition of the other*" [Hall's italics].

Without too much distortion this complex double move of Hall's could be said to be central to Lisa Lowe's *Immigrant Acts* or José David Saldívar's *Border Matters*, as well as the essays included in the second section of this anthology. Both Lowe and Saldívar argue that Asian American or Latino/a American studies must focus on transnational perspectives that cannot be simply aligned with one country or another, but with a heterogeneous group in diaspora and in resistance. Both books ambitiously position their transnational cultural studies paradigm as being indispensable for U.S. ethnicity studies as a whole. Both also, like Hall's work, stress the need to find the proper balance between analyzing strategies of racial unity (to resist racism) and strategies highlighting difference (to critique homogeneous unities based on supposedly primary racial or ethnic identities).

In sum, border studies' critique of the dominance of traditional immigration/assimilation narratives within U.S. ethnic studies would be impossible to contemplate without the influence of postcolonial theory, though its sources of inspiration are by no means solely coming from outside the U.S. This scholarship profoundly seeks to change how we understand the meaning of "immigrant" acts, by exploring the tension between diasporic identity and nation-state citizenship and portraying in new ways both the local community contexts in which cultural production takes place and the global matrix within which it must also be understood.

Feminism, Postcolonialism, and U.S. Studies

In *The Empire Writes Back*, Ashcroft, Griffiths, and Tiffin observe several parallels between feminist and postcolonial discourses. Both discourses seek to decenter the hegemonic and recuperate the marginalized; both open possibilities of re-reading canonical texts and/or subverting patriarchal literary forms; and both are practical in orientation, seeking social change (175–77).[31] In a variety of postcolonial and U.S. multicultural contexts, feminism has been a vehicle for transforming the intricate relationships between women and the numerous fragmented identities they assume in their respective former colonies and the contemporary U.S. In the various historical contexts shaped by colonialism and whiteness, the biological signifiers of "female" differ—and are at times unequal—when they come into contact with other theoretical discourses, both European and indigenous.

For example, as part of the European states' need to justify slavery and colonialism, the categories of male and female became racially marked and the difference between the private and public realms they were identified with was subsumed by the new compulsions of the colonial and nationalist projects. As both Partha Chatterjee (1993) and Mrinalini Sinha (1995) have noted, the colonial mind established parallels between the characteristics of English women and Bengali men, and both were deemed incapable of participation in public or political realm. By focusing on practices such as arranged marriage, purdah, and sati, colonization assumed "sympathy with the unfree and oppressed womanhood of India" and also transformed this female figure into "a sign of the inherently oppressive and unfree nature" of the entire Indian culture (118). In response, the nationalists sought a specific site of resistance for their cultural identity while fighting for political independence, making the dichotomy between "world/ home" and "spiritual/material" the center of their nationalist project. So, Hindu Bengali women were educated in classical Hindu scriptures and learned the virtues of "orderliness, thrift, cleanliness, and a personal sense of responsibility, . . . accounting, hygiene, [etc.]. . . . Once the essential femininity of women was fixed in terms of certain culturally visible qualities, they could go to schools, travel in public conveyances, watch public entertainment programs, and in time even take up public employment outside the home" (130). The woman in the colonies was, thus, re-configured into a carefully defined space and role by both the colonial mind and the nationalist project (Chatterjee 33–157; Sinha 33–68).

In the U.S. context too, the woman of color, unlike her white counterpart, is marked "doubly other" by both her race and sex. Echoes of this dilemma resound in Sara Suleri's urgent observation that there is no available dichotomy that can redefine postcoloniality as necessarily sharing "feminism's most vocal articulation of marginality, or the obsessive attention it has recently paid to the racial body" (757). Consequently, the traditional tenets of postcolonialism need to be re-contextualized to create spaces for the representation of all marginalized women. The void of such a hermeneutic strategy becomes filled by a counter-discourse that, whether it intends to or not, polices female identities simply by existing—in other words, that denial of agency conversely results in the application of another agency which the figure being represented does not necessarily consent to. In this context, the relationship between ethnic studies and postcolonialism engages in an ideological tug-of-war in which the colored woman is constantly (de)centered. Both these discourses face a nearly impossible task: to seek and reinforce consensual spaces that address women outside of their pervasive stereotypes. Though one might assume that this doubling up of powerful discourses is the key that unlocks the souls of women, both respective discourses can also doubly "other" the woman.

This is the critical juncture at which we must deconstruct and historicize those very critical tools that are essential to interpretation. Yet within this juncture exist more bifurcations that problematize feminist studies, especially the issue of authority and who has the right to speak for and against minority women. In her paradigmatic essay, "Under Western Eyes: Feminist Scholarship and Colonial Discourses," Chandra Talpade Mohanty critiques those Western feminist writings that "discursively colonize the material and historical heterogeneities of the lives of women in the third world, thereby producing/re-presenting a composite, singular "Third World Woman"—an image which appears arbitrarily constructed, but nevertheless carries with it the authorizing signature of Western humanist discourse."[32]

One can find plenty of examples of this arbitrary construction of the Third World woman in film and other forms of Western popular culture—from director David Selznick's black mammy in *Gone With the Wind* to Madonna's recent dual fetishization of the popular Western images of the exotic Indian *gopi* and the oriental Japanese geisha—the latter an image she flaunted at the 1998 Grammy Awards after capturing four of them. This exploitation of third world women, however, takes on a different effect beyond the hallowed halls of Tinsel Town. Trinh T. Minh-ha notes, "Authenticity in such contexts turn out to be a product that one can buy, arrange to one's liking, and/or preserve. Similarly, the Third World representative the modern sophisticated public ideally seeks is the unspoiled African, Asian, or Native American, who remains more preoccupied with his/her image of the *real* native—the *truly different*—than with the issues of hegemony, racism, feminism, and social change (which s/he lightly touches on in conformance to the reigning fashion of liberal discourse)" (Ashcroft et al, *Post Colonial Reader* 267). Hence, to capture agency in some Western discourses, the colored woman must necessarily "revert" to her ancestral culture to get back to "her roots," like Trinh T. Minh-ha's unspoiled objectified subject, or delve into American culture to assimilate into a modern woman, the spoiled subjectified object.

What, then, is the specific pivotal point of ethnic self-reflection in an American context? For many women, this occurs with the physical, ideological and emotional act of bodily re-placement—the act of immigration. Like their biological sex and gender markers, immigration and personal history becomes an integral force in both personal and societal perceptions of the foreign self. In *Immigrant Acts*, Lisa Lowe argues, "To consider testimony and testimonial as constituting a 'genre' of cultural production is significant for Asian immigrant women, for it extends the scope of what constitutes legitimate knowledges to include other forms and practices that have been traditionally excluded from both empirical and aesthetic modes of evaluation" (156).

How does the "Third World" woman's geographical "testimony" of immigration get played out? How does one's gendered identity get transformed through migration? What is the relationship between the homeland and the promised land in terms of third-world women's identities? For example, in her film, *A Tale of Love*, Trinh T. Minh-ha associates her protagonist, Kieu, with a Western-feminist need for physical and psychological space. Kieu incorporates elements of U.S. individuality into her new conception of family and community. But Kieu's Vietnamese-American aunt views this new understanding as a betrayal of homeland traditions. In a similar articulation of a diasporic woman's experience of passing and immigration, writer Meena Alexander describes in *The Shock of Arrival* the ethnic questions and looks she is constantly subjected to. She writes, "The questions that are asked in the street, of my identity, mold me. Appearing in the flesh, I am cast afresh, a female of color—skin color, hair texture, clothing, speech, all marking me in ways that I could scarcely have conceived of" (66). In this sense, the act of immigration magnifies the *consciousness of identity*—in other words, whereas marked identity and its accompanying questions and looks may not be anomalous for women in their homeland, it becomes an elusive entity after immigration necessarily questioned by white Americans. As further illustrated by Alexander, her choice to wear a sari in contrast to jeans becomes a "flag for 'Indianness . . .' India, that strange land, far away. Land of maharajahs and snake charmers and poverty so desperate it ends in the plague" (64).

Unlike the marginalized African American woman, the Asian woman occupies a tenuous space between the color lines. Whereas the Asian woman is usually perceived as a reticent, mail-order bride type, the black woman is often marked as a survivor of generational slavery and/or sexual promiscuity—a powerful individual, in many senses, but one without a strong enough morality to remain docile. bell hooks addresses this all-American, essentialized version of the African American woman, noting "I became fascinated by how a lot of the stereotypes for Asian women ("passive," "nonassertive," "quiet") are just the opposite of the stereotypes that plague black women ("aggressive," "loud," "mean"). It's like we exist in two radically different poles in the economy of racism. And it's those positionings that make it hard for Asian women and black women to come together . . . but I think we have to be more public in *naming* the ways that we dare to cross those boundaries and come together" (*Outlaw Culture* 218).

With such a varied amalgam of issues brewing in U.S. studies, it is no wonder a single discourse cannot comprehensively synthesize intersections of feminism and postcolonialism in the American context. Scholars of U.S. studies are likely to observe and experience these ever shifting boundaries and masks, and how they relate to sex and gender markers—alerting us to the risks of fostering positions based on current power relationships in the world and breezily accepting labels such as First World and Third World. In the words of Harveen Sachdeva Mann, "As feminist studies become increasingly globalized, it is imperative that we—students and scholars from both the first and third worlds, now studying/theorizing/practicing in the west—examine postcolonial women's experiences within their specific historical and material contexts rather than as extensions of or variants upon western ontologies, as minor illustrations

of western feminist theories, or as components of an other, homogenous category"
(70).[33]

Postcolonialism and Whiteness Studies

For both postcolonial and U.S. ethnicity studies, defining the cultural history of
"whiteness" is central to their projects. This work has arguably had precedents in the
work of Albion Tourgée, Frances E. W. Harper, W. E. B. Du Bois, and Richard
Wright in the U.S., Prem Chand and Mulk Raj Anand in India, and J. M. Coetzee
and Nadine Gordimer in South Africa (to choose just a few examples).[34] At one level,
these figures and others gave expression to what ordinary folk experienced under Jim
Crow in the U.S. or under English colonialism in India, which maintained close ties
with older feudalist and casteist elements in India. Surely, "low-down folks" (Langston
Hughes's phrase) might be credited with the experiential knowledge that forms the
basis of what has emerged recently as "whiteness studies." Both "house negroes" and
"field negroes" under slavery preserved a sense of their human dignity even under the
unending, brutal assault of assumed white superiority in their lives, and created in
their folklore and "sorrow songs" patterns of resistance and transcendence. For example, in the popular antebellum black folktales that were collected and published in the
early to mid twentieth century by Zora Neale Hurston and others, the subversive acts
of black trickster figures emphasized how slaves attempted to resist the hegemonic
socio-economic order constructed and perpetuated by the white slave owners. Ultimately, folktales such as the ones that recorded how the unyielding and clever slave
"John" negotiated the inequities of power between himself and his unwitting "Old
Marster" led writers like Charles W. Chesnutt—in the Uncle Julius stories, for example—to explore how the blacks attempted and often succeeded in manipulating the
system of their oppression to their advantage. Not unlike the discursive genealogy of
how the term "bad" became resignified in the Middle Passage (what was "bad" for
the slave traders was quite often "good" for the Africans being forced into slavery),
the genesis of whiteness studies may best be contextualized against the literary output
of Chesnutt and other more recent African Americans who have effectively reconstituted "blackness" by subverting and challenging the power hierarchies underlying
most contemporary conceptualizations of "whiteness." Informed by what bell hooks
calls the " 'special' knowledge of whiteness gleaned from close scrutiny of white people" (Frankenberg, *Displacing Whiteness* 165), many African American writers and intellectuals have historically attempted to undermine white hegemony in the U.S. by
exposing how the dominant white culture can only enjoy certain privileges at the
socio-economic expense of a black underclass maintained by instruments and institutions of power.

For our purposes, a very early document in whiteness studies is the delightful 1929
essay, "Our Greatest Gift to America" by novelist and journalist, George S. Schuyler.
Schuyler suggests wryly that the greatest contribution of black Americans to the U.S.
is not bridges and buildings, King Cotton or Duke Ellington, but the sense of superiority the presence of blacks allowed new European immigrants to feel and nourish as

they adjusted to the painful realities of their American experience. Schuyler observes how this false superiority inspired the "hope and pride" of European immigrants, and spurred them on to "great heights of achievement." Indeed, in his 1995 monograph, *How the Irish Became White*, Noel Ignatiev traces the genealogy of how the Irish gained both cultural and economic capital by distancing themselves socio-politically from blacks. Paraphrasing Theodore W. Allen (*The Invention of the White Race*, 1994), Ignatiev accounts for "the change that Catholic Irish underwent on emigration to the United States, from being victims and opponents of racial oppression to upholders of slavery and white supremacy"(187). Further, as Valerie Babb as argued in *Whiteness Visible* (1998), whiteness has since the eighteenth century been strategically used as a glue to bind together European immigrants of diverse religious, class, and language backgrounds as defined against Native Americans and Africans. Like Ignatiev, Babb too declares that, although the non-propertied and indentured European labor class had much in common with blacks and American Indians, middle- and upper-class Europeans males pre-empted any possibilities of solidarity by defining themselves through skin color and "race." Once whiteness had been established as a prerequisite for American citizenship, Babb posits, the consolidation of white power was rapid.

Babb's conclusions are both enriched and complicated by Ian F. Haney Lopez's *White by Law: The Legal Construction of Race* (1996), which attempts to "unearth and elaborate some of the perduring, seemingly fundamental characteristics of Whiteness, particularly as these have been fashioned by law" (xiv). Haney Lopez is concerned specifically with how whiteness became increasingly entrenched in the U.S. legal system at the turn of the century, especially in relation to immigration, marriage, naturalization, and citizenship. In examining a series of cases from the first half of twentieth century in which state and federal courts decided who was "White enough" to naturalize as a citizen, Haney Lopez reveals the difficulties and contradictions judges faced and created in trying to define whiteness, resorting, as they saw fit, to "scientific" classifications or to the "common man's understanding of 'race.'" Broadening the focus on law and racial identity that was first broached by Virginia Dominguez in *White by Definition* (1986) with regard to the Creole populations of Louisiana, Haney Lopez suggests that being white "depends in part upon other elements of identity—for example, on whether one is wealthy or poor, Protestant or Muslim, male or female—just as these elements of identity are given shape and significance by whether or not one is white" (xiii). So, "being White is not a monolithic or homogenous experience, either in terms of race, other social identities, space or time. Instead, Whiteness is contingent, changeable, partial, inconstant, and ultimately social. . . . [H]owever powerful and however deeply a part of our society race may be, races are ultimately a human invention" (xiv).

In the African American literary tradition, there has always been a sharp awareness of "race" as a social construction.[35] Half a century after Schuyler's ironic analysis of how "blackness" has shaped and sustained the "whiteness" of European immigrants, Ralph Ellison in his 1981 introduction to *Invisible Man* (1952) noted how the American Negro's "darkness . . . glowed . . . within the American conscience with such intensity that most whites feigned moral blindness toward his predicament." A decade after Ellison's pronouncement, Toni Morrison has continued to interrogate this "moral blindness" not only in her powerful fiction but also in *Playing in the Dark* (1992)—an important work of literary analysis that articulates how "blackness" has been a necessary condition for the articulation of "whiteness" in canonical texts by mostly male white writers. As Morrison puts it, "through significant and underscored omissions, startling contradictions, heavily nuanced conflicts, through the way writers peopled their work with the signs and bodies of this presence—one can see that a real or fabricated Africanist presence was crucial to their sense of Americanness" (6). Morrison's commentary includes brief suggestive re-examinations of works by authors such as Poe, Melville, Twain, Cather, and Hemingway to engage with the hitherto black presence underpinning the exploration of such American themes as freedom and adventure, autonomy and authority, "newness and difference."

In a phrase prescient of Homi Bhabha's point that white colonizers intend colonized people (of color) to feel the sting of being "almost but not quite white," Morrison declares that in the "construction of blackness *and* enslavement could be found not only the not-free but also, with the dramatic polarity created by skin color, the projection of the not-me" (38). However, while Bhabha argues that this "almost white" status of the colonized ultimately poses a threat to European colonial cultures because they are forced to view disturbing mirrors of their own subjugating practices, Morrison conversely implies how the color line's imbrication in U.S. system of slavery actually compels colonizing white mentalities to more completely distance themselves from the plight of non-whites and affirm for them the "not-me" status of people of color. In this sense, Morrison helps to bring into focus Ellison's earlier statement about the ways in which wave after wave of new immigrants—such as Mr. Yacobowski in Morrison's *The Bluest Eye*—"refuse to recognize the vast extent to which they too benefited from [the American Negroes'] second class status." Given the stigma of slavery and its consequences for race and power relations, immigrants—whether from Europe or Asia—have generally kept away from African American communities and their culture.

In his own way, of course, Ellison throughout his career helped to destabilize notions of racial essentialist identity—as, in 1973, when he told a Harvard University audience that "all of us are part white, and all of y'all are part colored." Further deconstructing the socially constructed binary of black/white in the U.S., he would later assert that he did not recognize "any white culture . . . [and that there is] no American culture which is not a partial creation of black people" (Graham and Singh xiii). In blurring the borders between black and white, Ellison anticipates the chief value of whiteness studies today—namely to show that whiteness, however constructed, is not a "natural" category and that its articulation as a locus of identity is intimately connected to issues of power and material wealth. Indeed, as Ellison suggested, the racial matrix in the U.S.—symbolized by the ghettoization of African Americans—is undergirded by "economic, not cultural" conditions. In this context, whiteness studies is linked to postcolonial studies and ethnic studies both in its examination of the socio-cultural benefits that accrue from whiteness and its unpacking of the economic and political power that propels it.

Many critics have also observed the connections between "whiteness" and the many levels of hierarchies it generates among post-colonials and other peoples of color in the U.S.—this is reflected, for example, in the layers of misperception between, on the one hand, African Americans, and on the other, Latinos and new immigrants from Asia, Africa, and the Caribbean (A. Singh, "Possibilities of Radical Consciousness"). These hierarchies, often dovetailing into skin color codes, can fetishize postcolonials in their new environments in Europe and North America. Not unlike Tsitsi Dangaremb-ga's novel *Nervous Conditions*, several of bell hooks' essays—especially "Eating the Other: Desire and Resistance" in *Black Looks*—offers a gendered update of Fanon's earlier recognition of the economy of desire, colonialism and resistance. In "Eating the Other," hooks argues—with examples from real life observations and her readings of films such as Sandra Bernhard's *Without You I am Nothing*—that an encounter with the Other does not require relinquishing forever one's "mainstream positionality." As she explains it, "when race and ethnicity become commodified as resources for plea-sure, the culture of specific groups as well as bodies of individuals"—for instance, the desire of certain young white males at Yale to sleep with as many women from other racial/ethnic groups as possible before graduation—constitute an arena wherein "members of dominating races, genders, sexual practices" affirm their powers-over in intimate relations over the Other"(*Black Looks* 23). By extension, as a result of such a desire to exoticize and feminize the Other, the post-colonial immigrant—now a new ethnic—becomes an integral part of the *re*-essentialization of the former colonial sub-ject even in the diaspora. hooks places her faith in vigilance and critique as a way out of working through the problematic of desire and resistance in a colonial situation. As she puts it, "Within a context where a desire for contact with those who are different is not considered bad, politically incorrect, or wrong-minded, we can begin to concep-tualize and identify ways that desire informs our political choices and affiliations. Ac-knowledging ways the desire for pleasure, and that includes erotic longings, informs our politics, our understanding of difference, we may know better how desire disrupts, subverts, and makes resistance possible. We cannot, however, accept these new images uncritically" (39).[36]

Despite its emphasis on transnationalism, feminism, and whiteness studies—or perhaps precisely because of it—borders studies scholarship remains quite controver-sial within U.S. studies as a whole, both within the academy (especially for such groups as the American Historical Association, in contrast to the American Studies Associa-tion) and within larger cultural fields. Rather than analyzing the controversies further, we shift the focus now to two final topics: first, whether an equivalent to the postethnic/borders studies split in U.S. studies is also discernible within competing contemporary analyses of *globalization*; and second, difficult questions that we believe borders studies scholarship must now face if it is to enter a new phase of influence.

The Borders of Globalization Theory

A critical history of contemporary theories of globalization is sorely needed. We think current theories of globalization exhibit a split that almost exactly parallels the divide we discerned within U.S. ethnic studies. That is, a large set of analysts argue that the way to understand current trends is really very simple: peoples and nations face a basic moral choice between globalization and tribalism, true modernity and democracy vs. economic dysfunction and religious and ethnic isolationism. Arguments by globalization theorists such as Theodore Levitt, Samuel Huntington, or Thomas L. Friedman, for instance, make the dangers of tribalism and isolationism really very similar to those noted by postethnicity scholars. Such scholarship sees itself as the only proper way to study the globalization of markets and cultures in an allegedly postnational world; indeed, like Frances Fukuyama, this scholarship claims or implies that its definition of the global is the proper "end" for all nations and civilizations in the universal narrative of historical progress. A revised form of Hegelianism provides the essential philosophical underpinnings for this school, for it assumes that freedom and progress must be realized not solely in the form of a State but rather in a State's approved participation in global markets. This group's confident attempt to exert hegemony over the proper meanings of the word "global"—which as they use it is really synonymous with Hegel's term "world-historical"—makes us willing to cede the term to them, naming them (not without some irony, for this school may be decidedly myopic and classist) as the "globalization" school.[37]

Most theorists who call their work "postcolonial" question the major assumptions behind this discourse linking globalization and progress. Like U.S. borders school scholars, they place at the center of their analyses the study of inequities of power rather than the progress of allegedly "universal" truths of development. They compare and contrast late twentieth-century global flows of people, goods, and cultural signs dominated by multinational corporations with earlier world-wide transformations during the "colonial" period. From a postcolonial perspective, to be part of a global population flow is not analogous to transferring money across national borders, even if those who hire workers and those workers who transfer money elsewhere both use electronic financial connections. Multinational capital may not destabilize local or premodern inequities of power in societies in favor of more democratic structures, as much globalization theory contends. Instead, there are usually great economic advantages to be gained when multinational capital aligns itself with local elites to reinforce inequities in a society and a market: contemporary capitalism both undermines *and* reinforces national hegemonies and the structural divisions within nation-states.

Postcolonial theorists also see diaspora or exile as the generic form of modernism for many of the world's people, not identification with a nation-state as it enters the world stage. Such peoples' citizenship in the world, when it can be imagined at all, is defined as a doubleness or contradiction: a way of using transnational capital and cultural flows to sustain connections with more than one place while practicing hybrid understandings of citizenship. In the words of Azmi Bishara, an Israeli Arab, "Our citizenship is Israeli, but our national identity is Palestinian"; or, in the words of a character in a Harif Kureishi movie-script, "We are not British, we are Londoners."[38]

To recognize oneself in diaspora means not only to question the meaning of national identity, as Clifford, Said, Kaplan and Grewal, Radhakrishnan, and many others have suggested. Diaspora as a powerful concept for cultural critique should also destablize dominant narratives of *globalization*. Stuart Hall has reminded us that neither the term *postcolonial* nor words such as *diaspora, migrant*, or *transnational* can be truly oppositional—that is, useful—if they are used in such a broad way as to erase the many constituencies and communities of people as they struggle to reweave connections in the stresses and tears of global movements. Global diaspora theorists pointedly try to refuse the *telos* that governs globalization theory—the belief that a single, universal calculus of measurement may be used to determine a nation's "progress" in the realms of a market economy, democracy, human rights, etc. In James Clifford's words, "Transnational travels and contacts—of people, things, and media—do not point in a single historical direction" (*Routes* 9). Yet as Anne McClintock has said, postcolonial theory remains "haunted by the very figure of linear 'development' that it sets out to dismantle" ("Angel of Progress" 292).

Arjun Appadurai, among many, is exemplary of the revisionary energy of postcolonial cultural theory as it presents counternarratives to the messianistic clichés of globalization theory. In *Modernity at Large: Cultural Dimensions of Globalization* (1996), Appadurai draws on a host of theorists from anthropology and postcolonial studies to argue that globalization at the turn of the millennium is producing heterogeneity, not homogeneity, on both local and global scales. His focus is on how to understand the role of disjunction and difference in the global cultural economy—in particular, in the varied and contradictory movements of people, technology, money, cultural forms, and ideas across ethnic, racial, class, and national borders. In the process, he exposes much current globalization theory to be the dreaming of the elites. Appadurai also focuses on the links between the global and its apparent contradictions, the national and the local, critiquing the way these terms are often juxtaposed as antithetical in globalization theory. For Appadurai, the construction of primordialist "ethnic" or "tribal" identities has in the past and the present proved central, not marginal, to nation-state modernization. He also ponders the paradox that modern primordial sentiments are primarily transnational and deterritorialized; these new forms of ethnicity attempt to appropriate older modes of nationalism in compensation. None of these phenomena, furthermore, can be studied apart from the history of colonial empires— whether Western or Ottoman—and their aftermath. Finally, like many other postcolonial theorists, he seeks to explore ways in which the "diasporic public spheres" constructed by ordinary people in diaspora rather than the elites counter all narratives of globalization that make the nation-state or the market the primary loci for global citizenship. Unlike Edward Said in "Intellectual Exile: Expatriates and Marginals," Appadurai does not see national identity as primarily collective and exilic identity as primarily individualistic; he stresses how new technologies in particular allow for a diasporic public sphere to some extent to create diasporic unities and counter nation-centered narratives of identity.[39]

In short, we need to place debates about the politics of difference "inside" the U.S. within the context of the new cultural politics of difference operating in globalization theory, including the ways it governs discourses defining "human rights" and "the global economy." In doing so, we must critique the ways in which U.S. elites in particular are seeking to dominate not just narratives of the proper forms of ethnicity in "American" but also the proper forms of world citizenship for both individuals and nations. Whatever the counternarratives to dominant current globalization theories are called—Spivak's "transnational cultural studies," Appadurai's "diasporic public spheres" and "disjunctive cultural flows," San Juan's "new dialogic alliances," Jan-Mohamed's "specular border intellectuals," Lowe's "immigrant acts," etc.—the contributions of both the U.S. borders studies and the postcolonial studies fields should prove central. But to be truly *counter*narratives rather than a recycling of dominant assumptions, such theories will have to keep Spivak's warning in "Diasporas Old and New" in mind: she sees global diasporas as an index of "the increasing failure of a civil society in developing nations"; for her, transnationality is not necessarily a utopian site of resistance but a symptom of how severely damaged the possibilities are for the social redistribution of wealth within developing nation-states and the global economy.

Difficult Questions for the Borders School

The renewed emphasis on difference, borders, and the transnational in U.S. ethnic studies is productive—so long as it remains genuinely critical and comparative. We need many more studies focusing on transnational cultural exchanges within and among specific ethnic groups. We also need a good comparative history of ideas of "nationalism" within particular racial/ethnic groups.

Dangerous questions must also be asked. To what extent, for instance, do "transnational," "diasporic," and "borders" paradigms theorize cultural difference and cultural mobility in incompatible ways—or are these terms basically synonymous? How must the new transnational studies improve upon older diaspora/migration models and all-too-simple contrasts between "home" and "exile"? In what ways have the limitations of old nationalist narratives been reincorporated into the "transnational" or the "borders" paradigms? And how may an emphasis on new cultural hybridities privilege cosmopolitan culture created by elites, especially men, as Kirin Narayan and Gloria Anzaldúa have warned (see Wald, "Minefields and Meeting Grounds" 207–08)?

The borders school also needs to examine more critically than it has so far done the limitations of its own paradigm, asking questions such as:

- Can borders analysis be a new form of American exceptionalism, rather than its critique, reinforcing a "melting pot" version of multiculturalism?
- How can borders school cultural studies avoid simplistic classifications of literary or other artwork as either "assimilationist" or "diasporic"? (This has already occurred.)
- How should "internal" vs. external borders be theorized for groups or nations (compare Etienne Balibar and Immanuel Wallerstein)?
- Must not border zones be seen as functioning differently even within a "single" ethnicity, when different Chicano/a communities in the southwest or the northeast are compared, for example? To what degree will a focus on race and ethnicity obscure the functioning of other axes of affiliation within and across ethnic boundaries—such as class, economic niche, religion, gender, or sexuality? Border analyses that privilege ethnicity over religion, for instance, cannot well examine the roles that Islam or Catholicism might play in sustaining mixed diasporic/ immigrant communities.
- How should transnational contacts best be interwoven in U.S. studies—the influence of U.S. Latino communities and literatures on the Caribbean and Latin

America, and vice versa; or the interchanges between varied Asian American communities and Asian countries? (And what of the study of cross-ethnic, -national, and -racial influences?)

- What about class and other economic issues in cultural production? How well will border studies analyses be able to handle these?
- Comparative ethnic studies histories of many cultural forms are needed—music, movies and videos, performances that center in community centers, from street festivals to pow-wows—perhaps along the lines of work by George Lipsitz. This anthology, for instance, has just a few comparative essays, and its focus is primarily on "high" literary prose forms.

Perhaps the most important question is: can a trope developed in context with Anglo U.S./Mexican border history really be applied to other interactions, even if the broad outlines of discrimination and resistance (for instance) may be similar? Other Latino/a U.S. groups have histories of occupation and diaspora that both parallel and diverge significantly from those of Mexican Americans—will these nuances be erased if analogies of cultural "border zones" are stressed?

Or consider the idea of borders as applied to Native Americans in their interactions with others and with themselves. There are over 500 recognized Native American nations within the U.S. alone, with many registered members who do not reside exclusively on a particular "reservation"; in what ways must our current understanding of all of the above terms be revised or discarded when Native American cultural production is viewed as central? Or to what degree may the necessity of borders and transnational emphases be truly confirmed—especially when debates about "authenticity" and identity and who may claim to speak on behalf of tribal communities have such huge consequences?

How well served by borders analogies is the study of African American history? At first glance the answer might seem to be not so well at all, since from the beginning Africans were forcibly enclosed within the borders of U.S. society to define its "bottom," not its edges. But rather than seeing borders analogies as being imported, Black Studies has historically been central in exploring just the kinds of analyses of alternative cultural "spaces" that we have said define the borders school: spatial and cultural matrices that recognize power and difference but destroy simplistic notions of cultural centers, tops, bottoms, and margins. Indeed, the synthetic qualities of "black" culture that have repeatedly crossed social barriers and influenced people of other racial and ethnic groups would appear to provide a classic test case for the borders school's cultural paradigms stressing the migration of cultural forms, not their separateness or homogeneity.[40]

In addition, recent debates within Asian American studies about the role of South Asians also provide reason for cautionary optimism. The borders school's emphasis on building coalitions while decentering artificial unities imposed from without could not be more timely here. Without a concept of shared universals, arguably, coalition-building of any kind would be impossible. Each "group" would begin to self-divide infinitely if only difference is stressed without a balancing emphasis on hybridities and shared experiences in diaspora. For instance, South Asians are hardly a unified cultural group "in" the Indian subcontinent, much less "in" Asia, except perhaps under the colonial or provincial American gaze. And South Asians have come to the United States in multiple stages, including those who are "immigrants" from Africa or the Caribbean, with different waves of migration dominated by different professions and education levels. As Sucheta Mazumdar has noted, it would be thoroughly ironic— though hardly unprecedented in U.S. cultural history—if Asian American studies "should become the vehicle for a process of homogenization of immigrants which strips away multiple layers of ethnic identity in favor of a single census category" (67). Lavina Shankar and Rajini Srikanth have argued that the ways in which South Asian experience often contradicts the narratives of Asian American immigration or the Asian American literary canon should be seen not as a problem for Asian American studies but as an opportunity to make its own cultural analyses more complex.

Such a revisionary swerve is indeed occurring in many fields in U.S. ethnic studies, and for similar reasons. Adopting a "borders" paradigm to study such changes will hardly inoculate scholarship against overgeneralization or the erasure of questions of power, however. Our own essay's claim that a borders paradigm is emerging in U.S. ethnic studies may of course be just as dangerous a form of overgeneralization as Fredric Jameson's 1986 assertion that "national allegories" and anti-colonial resistance were shared strategies defining "Third World" cultural production. Yet we believe there is indeed a central dialectic driving current U.S. ethnic studies scholarship, and we have tried to name it. More to the point: we believe that the borders school's ideas have spread rapidly because they begin to bring into focus what is unique about this cultural moment and the ways in which it is reconfiguring our past and future. We believe that the borders school's emphasis on complexity, contradiction, and power in its historical contexts will prove better for building bridges among diverse groups in the U.S. than the older emphases on being either uprooted, transplanted, or assimi-lated—precisely because borders school analogies emphasize the in-betweenness, the migrant rather than *im*migrant displacements and crossings that many populations are currently living through.[41]

V
IN CONCLUSION

The U.S. Civil Rights movement, global decolonization efforts, the often forced mobility of populations, and the rise of multinational corporations have influenced a number of intellectual movements in the academy that strikingly challenge the para-digms of the previous generation in cultural studies—postcolonial and cultural studies abroad and the "borders school" within the U.S. Many of the influential scholars associated with the borders school have been grounded in ethnic studies and/or labor history programs, both of which emphasize the resilience of racial and class divisions in U.S. history and the multiple strategies that have been created to resist and cross these divisions. The best of these models do not deny the importance of narratives of descent or consent in the making of identities in the U.S., nor do they downplay the importance of cultural interchange across race or class or national boundaries. We predict that the borders school's paradigms for engaging in the study of U.S. racial and ethnic history (and the ways in which these histories intersect with other strains in U.S. culture) will become one of the most productive fields in U.S. studies over the next decades, and that one of its best sources of inspiration will come from the contemporary field of postcolonial or diasporic studies. Indeed, both trends are already established.

Admittedly, the postethnic school in U.S. studies is attractive for its stress on the dangers of racial and ethnic separatism and the illusions of homogeneity. But its neo-progressivist insights are also its greatest blind spot; most critical responses to its visions of the future begin with the gut response, *"who* has the kind of freedoms to invent new identities that you're so celebrating?" The borders school is attractive for its pragmatic skepticism and its knowledge that social stratifications do not go away by acts of individual choice. It also stresses that a truly democratic community is built best out of complexity and contradiction: it continually reinvents the meaning of *dissent* as well as descent. The dangers faced by the borders school lie in so emphasizing difference or other aspects of the "postmodern" that any sense of interconnectedness or historical context is lost. It would also be dangerous to so italicize its sources of inspiration in postcolonial studies that the borders school's own diasporic connections to earlier U.S. studies debates in the 1940s–1960s and the 1890s–1930s become forgotten.

When postethnic progressives imply that the borders school is primarily divisive and negative and essentialist, they should be reminded that it is the scholarship of the borders school past and present that has made many of the most important breakthroughs in studying intercultural connections, community-building, and democratization in U.S. history. It is also those groups most oppressed by the status quo that historically have made the most decisive alliances across racial, ethnic, class, and other boundaries in order to survive—and then commemorated those acts in powerful and innovative cultural inventions, such as the Sorrow Songs as reinterpreted by the Fisk Jubilee Singers that Du Bois celebrated in the last chapter of *The Souls of Black Folk.*[42] Such cultural works understand that new forms of community may arise when people from many different backgrounds come together to resist undemocratic power. But as Edward Said has reminded us (in the quotation used as a epigraph for this essay), such advances are often created in an emergency, a moment of danger, and they come at great cost. Studying the history of the new cultural alliances and artistic forms that rise up out of such moments of crisis and remembrance may be the single most important research topic in all of U.S. studies as we try to meet the challenges of a new century.

In short, paraphrasing Du Bois, we may say that in U.S. cultural studies the main problem of the twenty-first century will be the problem of the *border-lines*. We hope that the essays collected here will do more than interest readers in their specific subjects and readings of U.S. cultural history. Our goal in selecting these writings and providing this introduction was to prove by example our maxim that both U.S. studies and postcolonial studies have much to teach each other. We believe workers in these fields can best contribute to current cultural debates and enliven the minds of students in the next generation only if they cross and question the borders constantly being erected to keep them separate.

Notes

1. The Du Bois passage to which Bambara is referring is of course the famous definitions of "double-consciousness" and seeing from "behind the veil" that open *The Souls of Black Folk* (1903). Bambara's revisionary response to Du Bois is a singular instance of the sense of U.S. cultural traditions that this introduction will argue is much needed in "postcolonial" theory. Bambara does not just name the role of elders in the community in which she grew up; she capitalizes this presence as if it were an empowering ancestor who authorizes her to revise a predecessor such as Du Bois, doubling his double consciousness so that it is no longer so fixated on the color-line as a frontier of either exclusion or inclusion on another's terms. For other considerations of double consciousness and its relevance for American culture, see Bernard Bell; Bruce; Early; Adell; A. Singh, "Possibilities of a Radical Consciousness"; and Gilroy, *Black Atlantic*.

2. We have preferred "U.S. studies" over "American studies" to indicate the range of academic discourses in relation to the United States. But to the extent our volume engages the long shadow of U.S. cultural politics and foreign policy adventures in the "other Americas" as well as Africa and Asia, our volume represents a form of "American Studies" in the broadest sense. Recent articles that more thoroughly make the point about U.S. studies' sometime provincialism include Jane Desmond and Virginia Dominguez's "Resituating American Studies in a Critical Internationalism"; Carolyn Porter's "What We Know That We Don't Know: Remapping American Literary Studies"; and Patricia Wald's "Minefields and Meeting Grounds: Transnational Analyses and American Studies." One possibly hopeful sign is that MELUS, the U.S.-based Society for the Study of Multi-Ethnic Literatures of the U.S., is helping to foster a number of adjunct MELUS organizations in Europe, Latin America, and Asia to encourage transnational scholarly exchange. Yet it remains to be seen whether such organizations help create a culture of genuinely critical transnationalism and exchange rather than sites of export for U.S. ideas of how properly to study the U.S. Regarding the issue of borders between U.S. and postcolonial studies, there are a number of recent signs that the boundaries of these "fields" are being questioned and rethought: anthologies such as Lavie and Swedenburg's *Displacement, Diaspora, and Geographies of Identity* and Wilson and Dissanayake's *Global/Local: Cultural Production and the Transnational Imaginary* (both 1996), for instance, and McClintock, Mufti, and Shohat's *Dangerous Liaisons: Gender, Nation, and Postcolonial Perspectives* (1997) include a number of essays focusing on the U.S. from transnational and postcolonial perspectives.

3. For a trenchant analysis of Jefferson's ideological oxymoron in historical context, see Dimock. For succinct arguments that certain minority groups in the U.S. are "internal colonies," see Blauner; Bracey's introduction to *Black Nationalism in America* (lvi-lix); Acuña; and Spivak's comments in an interview with Alfred Arteaga (*Spivak Reader* 22–25). It appears that "internal colony" is now being used in much more limited ways than when it was adopted in the 1960s: for one discussion comparing the efficacy of the "internal colonization theory" with that of competing theories of oppression, such as the "power-differential" and "split-labor-market" theories, see Parrillo 117–121. More recently, Pease, "New Perspectives"; Kaplan, "Left Alone with America"; Lawrence Buell; Schueller; Sumida; Ashcroft, Griffin, and Tifflin; Omi and Winant; San Juan; and Sharpe have all in different ways suggested that the U.S. is simultaneously neo- and postcolonial in its racial formations. On the subject of diasporas, James Clifford's essay is a lucid introduction to the complexities of the topic very applicable for U.S.

studies, but see also Hall's "Cultural Identity and Diaspora"; Grewal, "The Postcolonial, Ethnic Studies, and the Diaspora"; and Spivak, "Diasporas Old and New." We do not propose to worry a definitional distinction in this essay between "race" and "ethnicity," other than to note that distinctions of culture and language often pass for distinctions of blood and race and vice versa, so that if these terms are studied as they function as time-bound historical constructs (as they should be), they had better be investigated together, not apart. For a good introductory summary of the meanings of "ethnicity" as used in anthropology and in relation to "race" and "nationalism," see Banks.

4. Consider Alan Marcus' discussion of how municipal services in Cincinnati grew out of a desire to regulate the "non-American" behavior of groups such as blacks and poor new immigrants (Singh, Skidmore, Sequeira, eds., *American Studies Today*). For another view of the symbiotic relationship of blacks to new immigrants, see George S. Schuyler, "Our Greatest Gift to America."

5. For one contemporary use of the terms "caste society" and "opportunity society," see DeMott; see also Myrdal (1944). For representative examples of disputes over immigration and Americanization in the first two decades of this century in American Studies, see Edward Ross (1914); Randolph Bourne (1916); Horace Kallen (1924); and H.P. Fairchild (1926). Two excellent interpretations of the disciplinary and generational "crises" that have marked American Studies are Gene Wise's and Guenter Lenz's; see also Kaplan's and Pease's much briefer surveys, focusing on the "denial of empire" as a recurrent strain in American studies. Wise's essay is well-known and indispensable. Lenz's piece is particularly interesting in his claim that the "myth-symbol school" in American Studies in the 1950s were indebted to cultural concepts developed in the 1930s, particularly those associated with radical historians of the period and synthesized by Caroline F. Ware in *The Cultural Approach to History* (1940)—a collection whose essays stress contention and struggle, not harmony, in U.S. history (see pp. 89–90 in Lenz in particular). Lenz's and others' tracing of various strains of counter-Progressivist and counter-consensus movements within American Studies is no doubt an analogue for our own consideration of the clashing paradigms of the postethnicity and border schools at the century's end. (We should also note the regrettable absence of any reference to historians of color, even Du Bois, in Lenz's 1982 survey.) As Philip Gleason has noted, the origins of "American Studies" as an approach and "disciplinary holding company" are closely linked to the emergence of the U.S. as a superpower after World War II and the desire to promote "democratic ideology" and the "American way of life" around the world. But until challenged in the early 1970s by the Radical Caucus and the National American Studies Faculty (NASF), the American Studies Association (ASA) and its projects were characterized by white male domination, resisting the integration of emerging perspectives from women, African Americans, and other minorities: see Allen F. Davis' "The Politics of American Studies," which was the 1989 ASA Presidential address. In literary U.S. studies, issues of reading the particularities of African American experience pioneered the focus on race and ethnicity in recent decades. One comprehensive view of these developments may be found in A. Singh et al, *Memory, Narrative, and Identity* (3–25).

6. Aside from Gloria Anzaldúa's influential *Borderlands/La Frontera* (1987), which we discuss further below, recent examples of cultural histories theorizing the concept of borders include Abdul JanMohamed's "Worldiness-Without-World"; D. Emily Hicks' *Border Writing*; José David Saldívar's *Border Matters: Remapping American Cultural Studies* and Guillermo Gómez-Peña's *The New World Border*; Michaelsen and Johnson's anthology *Border Theory* (especially recommended: the editors's introduction, plus essays by Lugo, Johnson, Sáenz, and Chang); Giroux's *Between Borders*; and Myrsiadis and McGuire's *Order and Partialities: Theory, Pedagogy, and the "Postcolonial,"* published as part of a "Border Testimonies and Critical Discourses" series. Lugo's essay is instructive for its argument that border theory must be situated in the context of changing late twentieth-century discourse on cultures and the nation-state, especially his use

of Gramsci and Foucault on power to illuminate the work of Benedict Anderson and Renato Rosaldo. Those interested in an archeology of the term *border*'s circulation in critical discourse should discover Jacques Derrida's 1979 essay "Living On/Border Lines." But they should begin by investigating how sociologists in the 1950s such as Robert Park and E. Franklin Frazier revised Frederick Jackson Turner to theorize "racial frontiers" and "contact zones" as sites of cultural and racial hybridity as well as conflict. Note: Park's and Franzier's work should be read together with Américo Paredes' writings from the 1950s (cf. footnote 14 below). For background on Parks' influence in sociology, see Wacker's essay in Fine's *A Second Chicago School? The Development of a Postwar American Sociology*; and Gregory Stephens (1–11, plus notes). One contemporary permutation of "contact zone" theory is Mary Louise Pratt's.

7. Using the term *borders* to name so many phenomena in U.S. studies has obvious dangers. As an analytical concept for the study of ethnicity, it was first developed within Chicano cultural studies, where it is applied both to the politics of a specific and continuous national border and as a term to investigate the complex dynamics of Chicano critiques of both Mexican and U.S. narratives of cultural and national history. Applying this term even to other Latino/a cultural groups with different histories is problematic, much less using it in even more disparate cultural contexts. For more on these dangers, contrasted with the advantages the term brings as a paradigm for cultural difference, see Michaelsen and Johnson, who argue that contemporary "border studies" applies not just to the U.S./Mexican borderlands but to multiple borders defining the U.S. and its relations to the Americas and the world, including U.S./Canadian, Mason-Dixon, Indian reservation, and urban diasporic boundary lines and cultural histories. We strongly agree, and for these reasons prefer using "borders" in its plural form when its relevance for U.S. studies is being discussed. See also the last section of Part IV in this essay.

8. Omi and Winant argue that climactic events spurred by the Civil Rights movement (particularly the 1965 passage of voting rights bills and new immigration legislation loosening quotas from non-European countries) moved the U.S. into a new era of "racial hegemony," in which a still-dominant white majority focused not on mostly excluding people of color from immigration rolls and internal political and economic power but on setting the terms for inclusion. Omi and Winant stress politics and economics somewhat to the exclusion of other realms of culture, such as the role that the arts play in maintaining or challenging racial formations, yet it seems possible to argue that rules for racial hegemony and transformation were first experimented with in the realm of popular culture before such moves were made in other spheres (cf. George Lipsitz's work, for instance). The role of the arts in racial formation and transformation has consequently been a primary focus of the cultural historians of the borders school.

9. Influential recent examples of work in the borders school in U.S. studies include Annette Kolodny's essay "Letting Go Our Grand Obsessions: Notes toward a New Literary History of the American Frontiers"; *Criticism in the Borderlands: Studies in Chicano Literature, Culture, and Ideology*, edited by Hector Calderón and José David Saldívar (1991); Hortense Spillers's introductory essay, " 'Who Cuts the Border': Some Readings on 'America,' " in the anthology of pan-American essays she edited entitled *Comparative American Identities: Race, Sex, and Nationality in the Modern Text* (1991); Ronald Takaki's *A Different Mirror: A History of Multicultural America* (1993); *An Other Tongue: Nation and Ethnicity in the Linguistic Borderlands*, edited by Alfred Arteaga (1994); Lisa Lowe's *Immigrant Acts: On Asian American Cultural Politics* (1996); King-Kok Cheung's *An Interethnic Companion to Asian American Literature* (1997); José David Saldívar, *Border Matters: Remapping American Cultural Studies* (1997); Rafia Zafar's *We Wear the Mask: African Americans Write American Literature, 1760–1870* (1997); Michaelsen and Johnson's anthology *Border Theory* (1997); Werner Sollors' *Multilingual America* (1998); Lavina Shankar and Rajini Srikanth's *A Part, Yet Apart: South Asians in Asian America* (1998); William V. Spanos'

America's Shadow: An Anatomy of Empire (2000); Ellen Bigler's *American Conversations: Puerto Ricans, White Ethnics, and Multicultural Education* (1999); and John Carlos Rowe, *Literary Culture and U.S. Imperialism*. But many other works could be cited, and influential publications in all the primary fields in U.S. ethnic studies—Native American, Latino/a, Black, Asian American, and European American history, as well as new works on U.S. narratives of nationhood such as Priscilla Wald's *Constituting Americans* (1995) and Cheryl Walker's *Indian Nation: Native American Literature and Nineteenth-Century Nationalisms* (1997)—increasingly test premises we argue are constitutive of the borders school, reminding us of the new challenges to ethnic U.S. studies from global and transnational perspectives.

10. For another reading of Fukuyama's work stressing parallels with Frederick Jackson Turner, see Fredric Jameson's *The Cultural Turn*. In addition to Hegel, nostalgia for the arguments of Daniel Bell's *The End of Ideology* (1960) in Fukuyama and his supporters needs to be investigated. Regarding Thomas Sowell, his definition of the broad patterns of recent postcolonial as well as American history meshes with Schlesinger's in many ways. Where Sowell supplements Schlesinger is in his updating of arguments making the Protestant work ethic central to democracy. In works like *Ethnic America* (1981) and *Migrations and Cultures: A World View* (1996), Sowell expanded the Puritan paradigm to argue that many different religious and cultural traditions—Confucianism, for example—may give particular groups the work ethic and the strong family ties that will allow them to succeed as immigrants in a new culture. These values are an individual's and a group's "cultural capital" and when strong allow immigrants to overcome whatever cultural and structural barriers—including racial prejudice and rapid economic changes in a global economy—are encountered. The hidden argument within Sowell's master narrative, of course, is that a person's and a group's character is its fate: this character, and not the culture at large, determines success or may be blamed for failure. In studying American history (or the history of any recently postcolonial country), the primary emphasis for Sowell should not be on structural inequities or cultural contradictions but on individual opportunities and what is made of them. Other influential thinkers associated with the center or the left, many of them white, offer positions similar to Schlesinger's in crucial ways, most explicitly in their lament for the loss of "common ideals" and in their blaming the decline of "common culture" and civic responsibility on "identity politics" (especially racial and ethnic separatism) and the supposed heritage of self-indulgence fostered by the 1960s. A number of names could be cited, including E. J. Dionne, Jr., Todd Gitlin, Christopher Lasch, and Michael Tomasky.

11. Sollors' validation of chosen or constructed identities in "A Critique of Pure Pluralism" and *Beyond Ethnicity*, as many critics have pointed out, tends to make illusory or secondary the difference that class or gender or historical period can make. Even more seriously, it can't really allow analysis of America's historical obsession with racial identity; race tends to be systematically translated into yet another variety of ethnic difference in *Beyond Ethnicity*. Tellingly, two of the sections of *Beyond Ethnicity* that attempt to face the issue of race most directly are quite short: "Race and Ethnicity" (37–39) and "The Problem of Cultural Dominance" (191–95). In them, there is an unresolved tension between Sollors' decision to see race as "merely one aspect of ethnicity" (36) and his claim that "(t)his choice does not represent an attempt to gloss over the special legacy of slavery and racism in America" (37). Sollors's narratives of descent and consent, though powerful, have trouble investigating whether or not "ethnicity" as defined in U.S. culture is *primarily* a product of the country's obsession with whiteness—the form by which an increasing range of European (and occasionally non-European) migrants were deracialized and granted supposedly race-free privileges as valuable citizen-ethnics, while others remained racially marked as aliens. Being marked as a racial alien is "beyond" (or beneath) ethnicity in a way different from Sollors' use of the term.

Numerous other recent commentators from diverse backgrounds might be aligned with the working premises of Sollors' *Beyond Ethnicity*: Herbert Gans, "Symbolic Ethnicity" (1979); Mary C. Waters, *Ethnic Options* (1990); Shelby Steele's *The Content of Our Character: A New Vision of Race in America* (1990); Lawrence W. Fuchs's *American Kaleidoscope: Race, Ethnicity, and the Civic Culture* (1990); the editor Philip Fisher's introductory essay in *The New American Studies: Essays from Representations* (1991); Stanley Crouch's *The All-American Skin Game, or the Decoy of Race* (1995); David A. Hollinger's *Postethnic America: Beyond Multiculturalism* (1995); Dinesh D'Souza's *The End of Racism: Principles for a Multiracial Society* (1995); and Eric Liu's *The Accidental Asian: Notes of a Native Speaker* (1998), among others. Not coincidentally, many of these works are published by major commercial houses, not university presses.

12. For another example of Sollors' possible shift in emphasis, compare this key sentence from Sollors' "A Critique of Pure Pluralism," "[a] growing number of literary scholars are pursuing postpluralist, postethnic approaches in studying American literature" (277), with the following from " 'Of Plymouth Rock' ": "The 'old-stock'/'new immigrant' distinction on which much of the thinking about 'America' and 'ethnicity' rested did not, of course, apply to all ethnic groups" (226–27). The section on pp. 226–35 of " 'Of Plymouth Rock' " (the conclusion) contains Sollors' primary revisions and qualifications and is meant to be signified by his title's reference to "Jamestown" (the site of the first importation of slaves to the North American colonies). For commentaries on Sollors' *Beyond Ethnicity*, see the editors's introduction to *Memory, Narrative, and Identity* by A. Singh, Skerrett, and Hogan; and—more critical of Sollors—Alan Wald; Steinberg; and Wong. Books such as George Hutchinson's *The Harlem Renaissance in Black and White* (1997) and Gregory Stephens' *On Racial Frontiers* (1999) are clearly indebted to Sollors' approaches. For yet a different take on Sollors' legacy, see Walter Benn Michaels' *Our America: Nativism, Modernism, and Pluralism* (1995). Michaels' distinction between Progressivist and Modernist racisms, where Progressivist racism emphasizes the importance of assimilation to Anglo-Saxon ideals and Modernist pluralism in fact emphasizes separate and unequal, is a direct challenge to Sollors' *Beyond Ethnicity* but is somewhat indebted to Sollors' article "A Critique of Pure Pluralism." Michaels argues that the narratives of descent, of "blood" ties, that he studies in the Progressivist and Modernist periods contain contradictions so serious that they must be seen, ironically, as fictive "descent" narratives whose audience may "consent" to believe are true. For a critique of Michaels' book, however, see Glass.

13. Exceptions to this generalization about Turner include Amy Kaplan, "Left Alone with America"; Jameson, *The Cultural Turn*; and José David Saldívar, *Border Matters* 172–73. A useful general introduction to the issue of Turner's influence on American Studies is Warren I. Susman's. On Turner's historical context and his interpreters in the next generation, see in particular "A Centennial Symposium on the Significance of Frederick Jackson Turner" [under 'C' in our Works Cited]; Nash; and Thomas.

14. Contemporaries of Webb's at mid-century offering very different and more revisionary interpretations of the frontier include Robert Park, E. Franklin Frazier, and Henry Nash Smith. The work of Smith and his successors Richard Slotkin, Richard Drinnon, and Roy Harvey Pearce needs now to be read *alongside* Paredes' work, but Paredes is still too often studied separately, if studied at all. For recent studies of Paredes' importance and a summary of earlier discussions of his work, see Bruce-Novoa and José David Saldívar, "Américo Paredes and Decolonization." Also placing Paredes' work in a larger cultural context are José Limón's *Dancing with the Devil: Society and Cultural Poetics in Mexican American South Texas* and two essays by Ramón Saldívar: "The Borders of Modernity: Américo Paredes's *Between Two Worlds* and the Chicano National Subject" and "Border Subjects and Transnational Sites: Américo Paredes's *The Hammon and the Beans and Other Stories.*"

15. For a review stressing the importance of Sanchez's study for U.S. ethnic studies, see Ethington. See also Sanchez's placement of his own study in the context of critiques of Oscar

Handlin: 277–78, notes 7–11. Ethington's use of the phrase "borderlands school" has to some degree emboldened our own broader argument for a "borders school", as has Donald E. Pease's contrast between the "multiculturalists" and the American "new historicists"; Pease argues that the tension between these two "strategies" for interpreting the U.S. "may well determine the future of the field" (25). Perhaps mercifully, our "borders school" trope seems so far uncommon in U.S. studies, despite the great increase in the 1990s of studies with "border" in the title (see note six above).

16. In their introduction to the *Scattered Hegemonies* anthology, Inderpal Grewal and Caren Kaplan offer definitions of the global and transnational feminisms that might serve well as pointers in all work on issues of identity, diaspora, nation. In this view, the domestic and the global are both viewed transnationally. For Grewal and Kaplan, "transnational feminism is not an ahistorical theory of worldwide gender oppression," which they call "global feminism." In contrast, transnational feminism examines the "relationship of gender to scattered hegemonies" throughout the globe based on various structures of power. Transnational feminism (an idea also more visible in the recent pronouncements of Gayatri Spivak) privileges modes and methods of analysis that focus on geopolitical forces in specific historical contexts to expose linkages and complicities in a global frame instead of a comparativist approach that looks for similarities among differences in search of homogenizing paradigms. For our purposes, the "transnational" is a warning against presumptions that the U.S. alone might provide models and examples of "border crossings" in gender, ethnicity, region, and language in a world of several multi-racial democracies from which the U.S. too should be willing to learn significant lessons.

17. While recognizing the distinction between "postcolonial" and "post-colonial" made by Boehmer—a distinction Ashcroft et al have not maintained in their three synthesizing volumes—we have in this volume used "postcolonial" more consistently to suggest our interest in the historical roots of postcolonial thought—hence our interest in figures such as Du Bois, Alain Locke, Fanon. See Gandhi, 3–4, for slightly variant definitions.

18. It is appropriate here to record the reaction of novelist Amitav Ghosh as symptomatic of one kind of reaction among contemporary India's writers and intellectuals to the label "post-colonial": " I must say I have no truck with the word at all. . . . I don't know a single Indian writer of my acquaintance who does not detest it. . . . It completely misrepresents the focus of the work I do. . . . What is post-colonial? When I look at the works of critics such as Homi Bhabha, I think they have somehow invented this world which is a set of representations of representations. They have retreated into a world of magic mirrors and I don't think anyone can write from that sort of position." This quotation, cited with glee and approbation by critic Meenakshi Mukherjee in the August 1998 *Newsletter* of IACLALS (Indian Association for Commonwealth Literature and Language Studies), appeared originally in an interview with Amitav Ghosh published in the Special Number (India and Pakistan, 1947–1997: A Celebration) of *Kunapipi: A Journal of Post-colonial Writing*, edited by Shirley Chew. Ghosh's point is well-taken because not *all* South Asian (or, for that matter African) writers are self-consciously postcolonial, but that does not rule out postcolonial readings of a novel such as Ghosh's own *The Shadow Lines* (1989). Ghosh's response is in synch with other attacks on postcolonial theory from critics such as Aijaz Ahmad (see note 19) and Arif Dirlik, who, like Ahmad, views postcolonialism as an exercise among mostly First World-privileged diasporic South Asians ("Postcolonial Aura").

19. Admirers of *Orientalism* include Gayatri Spivak and Partha Chatterjee, but the book has had its detractors too, chief among them the Marxist critic, Aijaz Ahmad. Ahmad attacks Said for his close ties to the culturally myopic poststructuralist thought and views *Orientalism* as symptomatic of the late 1970s, when many intellectuals covered their anti-Marxism by guiltily taking shelter in Third-Worldism. He faults *Orientalism* in regard to both the text and the socio-cultural conditions that led to its production. Citing what he perceives to be the implicit link

between upper class immigrants to the West and the "metropolitan intelligentsia," Ahmad attributes much of the success of *Orientalism* to a specific temporal location in which non-Western intellectuals "needed . . . narratives of oppression that would get them preferential treatment" (*In Theory* 196) in Western academies. Accordingly, for Ahmad, Said's text fit the bill because it helped to produce the subject-positions of oppressed non-Western Others who were constructed by the hegemonic epistemologies of Western imperialists. Conversely, perhaps ironically, Said has accused Marxist theory of being an example of a "self-policing, self-purifying community" that is marked primarily by "the official sequential or ideological [stories] produced by institutional power." Said, as Leela Gandhi has noted, views Marxist theory as a failed project because it does not "accommodate the specific needs and experiences of the colonized world" (71). This is a somewhat curious critique, parallel to Ahmad's own proclamation—especially in the latter's denunciation of Jameson—that not enough attention is given to the heterogeneity of "Third World" literatures. Indeed, as Leela Gandhi later points out, Said "fails to engage with the enormous contribution of Marxism" (73) to his own postcolonial theorizing. Ahmad's attacks on poststructuralist influence in postcolonial theory invite a comparison with Steven Watts, "The Idiocy of American Studies: Poststructuralism, Language, and Politics in an Age of Self-Fulfillment" (1991).

Ahmad, of course, has focused his invective not only against postcolonial theorists, but has also aimed it squarely at fellow Marxist, Fredric Jameson, in an important example of how postcolonial studies can serve as little more than a battleground between other competing disciplinary or ideological formations (Marxism, feminism, poststructuralism). In his now-(in)-famous essay, "Third World Literature in the Era of Multinational Capitalism," Jameson states: "all third-world texts are necessarily . . . allegorical, and in a very specific way: they are to be read as what I will call 'national allegories' " (67). Responding to what he perceives as Jameson's facile homogenization of "Third World" texts, Ahmad decries Jameson's lack of critical analysis in which "the enormous cultural heterogeneity of social formations within the so-called Third World is submerged within a singular identity of 'experience.' " For Ahmad, Jameson's interpretative strategy not only epitomizes the Western academy's propensity for presenting universal and totalizing discourses by focusing solely on nationalist issues, but also ignores the connections between private, personal experience and what Ahmad refers to as a public "collectivity"—"class, gender, caste, religious community, trade union, political party, village, prison" ("Jameson" 5, 21). Beyond his quarrels with fellow Marxist Jameson and his assaults on Said and other postcolonial critics, Ahmad has a larger problem with poststructuralism and its universalizing and homogenizing tendencies: "Politically we are Calibans all. Formally, we are fated to be in the poststructuralist world of Repetition with Difference; the same allegory, the nationalist one rewritten, over and over again" (*In Theory* 102). More to the point, poststructuralist theory, for Ahmad, is reactionary and implicated in the demise of Marxism, resulting in the fashionable and flabby references among the late 1970s intellectuals to "Third World, Cuba, national liberation, and so on" (192).

20. See Henry Louis Gates' "Critical Fanonism" for a consideration of "successive appropriations" of Fanon in postcolonial theory.

21. For further comment, see Amritjit Singh, *The Novels of the Harlem Renaissance*, esp. 47–53; and P.S. Chauhan's "Re-reading Claude McKay."

22. "Nativism" in this context has somewhat different resonances from its use to suggest the "anti-immigrant" tendencies discussed in works such as John Higham's *Strangers in the Land;* Arnold Shankman's *Ambivalent Friends: Afro-Americans View the Immigrant*; and David Hellwig's "Strangers in Their Own Land: Patterns of Black Nativism."

23. Gilroy's work represents a shift from Said's emphasis on inter-national demarcations toward—in the words of Julie Rivkin and Michael Ryan—"an understanding of "para-national

and trans-regional flows of culture. From the Caribbean to New York to London, black cultural influences and migrations tend not to heed traditional literary boundary lines, and these new realities demand new modes of non-national critical thinking" (853).

24. One recalls Soyinka's oft-quoted remark—"the tiger doesn't proclaim his tigeritude"—on issues of African particularism in Negritude movement. But in *Myth, Literature, and the African World*, Soyinka states: "negritude, having laid its cornerstone on a European intellectual tradition, . . . was a foundling deserving to be drawn into, nay, even considered a case for benign adoption by European ideological interests" (134). As late as 1978, in an interview with Jacqueline Leiner, Aimé Césaire maintained that for him (and possibly for Léopold Sédar Senghor), "black culture had never had anything to do with biology and everything to do with a combination of geography and history" (*Collected Poetry* 6).

25. In *The Spivak Reader*, the editors Landry and MacLean refer to two 1993 issues of *Diacritics* with essays by Rey Chow (# 1), Judith Butler (# 4), and Robert Baker (# 4) to make their point about the neglect of Spivak in "high theory" debates on the Other. While Rey Chow's essay, "Ethics after Idealism," discusses Spivak as an energetic post-Marxist writing today, the essays by Butler and Baker do not even mention Spivak. Caren Kaplan and Inderpal Grewal have noticed a similar neglect of Spivak's contributions in the discourses of "masculinist marxism" (for example, Aijaz Ahmad's *In Theory* does not even mention Spivak once) and Anglo-American feminism ("in feminist film and literary studies, where psychoanalytic paradigms are dominant, Homi Bhabha's work may be more assimilable"). See Kaplan and Grewal, "Transnational Feminist Cultural Studies: Beyond the Marxism/Poststructuralism/Feminism Divides."

26. Spivak's "Can the Subaltern Speak" was based on a 1983 lecture but first published in its entirety in 1988 and reprinted since and now carefully reconfigured into the chapter called "History" in *A Critique of Postcolonial Reason* (1999). In a 1993 interview with Landry and MacLean, included in *The Spivak Reader*, Spivak further clarifies her position: "In the essay, I made it clear that I was talking about the space as defined by Ranajit Guha, the space that is cut off from the lines of mobility in a colonized country. You have the foreign elite and the indigenous elite. Below that you have the vectors of upward, downward, sideward, backward, mobility. But then there is a space which is for all practical purposes outside those lines. Now if I understand the work of the Subalternites right, every moment of insurgency that they have fastened onto has been a moment when subalternity has been brought to a point of crisis: the cultural constructions that are allowed to exist within subalternity removed as it is from other lines of mobility are changed into militancy. In other words, every moment that is noticed as a case of subalternity is undermined. We are never looking at the pure subaltern. There is then something of a not-speakingness in the very moment of subalternity" (*Spivak Reader* 288–89).

27. In an oft-cited attack on Spivak's essay, for example, Benita Parry accuses Spivak of denying the possibility of agency to subaltern classes. Parry argues that Spivak has a "deliberated deafness to the native voice where it is to be heard" which is ostensibly present in her own writings—thus the subaltern *can* speak, only their voices fall on closed ears. Hence, Parry argues, Spivak denies the postcolonial "the space in which the colonized can be written back into history, even when 'interventionist possibilities' are exploited through the deconstructive strategies devised by the post-colonial intellectual" (Ashcroft et al, *Post Colonial Reader* 40). Parry's attacks on Spivak and Homi Bhabha in the mid-1980s relate to her defense of anti-colonialist nationalism. But as Chris Bongie (1998) has observed, in more recent essays such as "Resistance Theory" (1994), Parry has "come around to a more nuanced position in which, while continuing to argue predictably for 'resistant' nativisms . . . she nonetheless seems more willing and able to acknowledge the constructed (discursive) nature of any and all 'resistant' selves and to re-read 'liberation theories' accordingly. For Bongie, "Parry and Appiah are thus inextricably linked to one another in a mutually contaminatory dialogue—the former offering

. . . 'two cheers for nativism,' the latter countering, as it were, with 'two cheers for hybridity' " (50, 52).

28. In a 1988 interview, Spivak said: "I would like to take away the current notion of marginality, which implicitly valorizes the center. . . . That is the way I think of the margin—as not simply opposed to the center but as an accomplice of the center—because I find it very troubling that I should be defined as a marginal" (*Post-Colonial Critic* 156). She claims, thus, to occupy "the classic deconstructive position, in the middle, but not on either side"—a "third world" woman in a position of power in the U.S. academy, who turns hegemonic narratives inside out through "specific uses" of deconstruction, bringing the outside in.

29. As already indicated, "postcolonialism" as a theory and discourse has had its share of critics (see notes 18, 19, and 27 above). Terry Eagleton observes how the Third World revolutionary nationalism in the 1970s has given way now to "a 'post-revolutionary' condition in which the power of the transnational corporations seems unbreakable" and wherein mistrust of organized mass politics has led to what he views as an overemphasis on culture. As he puts it, "It is not in the end questions of language, skin colour or identity, but of commodity prices, raw materials, labour markets, military alliances, and political forces, which shape the relations between rich and poor nations" (205). Eagleton joins this to an observation on studies of "race" and "ethnicity" in the U.S. that is very relevant to our volume. He says, "In the West, especially in the United States, questions of ethnicity have at once enriched a radical politics narrowly focused on social class, and, in their own narrow fixation of difference, helped to obscure the vital material conditions which different groups have in common" (205). So, for Terry Eagleton, the "cultural relativism" of postcolonial theory, like that of ethnic studies in the U.S., "is for the most part simply imperial dominion stood on its head" (205). While the points Eagleton deserve our attention, his critique is rather harsh and does not anticipate the many ways—as, we hope, this volume demonstrates—in which postcolonial theory and ethnic U.S. studies have transformed our existing understandings of the United States and the rest of the world. No wonder, Dennis Walder has accused Eagleton of aligning himself with Aijaz Ahmad's "bluntly Marxist" *In Theory: Classes, Nations, Literatures* (1992), wherein postcolonial theory "is viewed as the creation of a class fraction of guilt-ridden Western intellectuals and their 'Third World' incorporated colleagues . . . who recycle 'primary' cultural products from abroad for their own consumption, while neglecting more 'independent' local literature in Urdu or Zulu" (4–5). Interestingly, in a footnote, Eagleton himself describes Ahmad's critique of postcolonial theory as "abrasive" (216). For other critiques of postcolonial theory, we recommend beginning with the work of McClintock and Dirlik (especially his "The Postcolonial Aura"); for further reading: Mishra and Hodge; Shohat; Loomba ("Overworlding the Third World"); San Juan; Sumida; Chow; and Grewal, "The Postcolonial, Ethnic Studies, and the Diaspora." Incidentally, while the most influential postcolonial theorists display a salutary and sometimes even devastating skepticism toward their approach to knowledge, the same cannot be said for many of the most quoted "globalization" theorists, as we discuss further in Part IV of this essay.

Other texts and anthologies on postcolonial theory whose value we would like to note as we draw this discussion to a close include Mongia's *Contemporary Postcolonial Theory*; McClintock, Mufti, and Shohat's *Dangerous Liaisons: Gender, Nation, and Postcolonial Perspectives*; Rajan and Mohanram's *Postcolonial Discourse and Changing Cultural Contexts*; and Rosemary Marangoly George's *The Politics of Home: Postcolonial Relocations and Twentieth-Century Fiction*. Stuart Hall's essay collection, *Critical Dialogues in Cultural Studies,* allows one to follow developments in this field as they evolved in the work of one of its prime movers.

30. In a 1998 *American Quarterly* issue, for instance, Nikhil Pal Singh argued that current debates about race, empire, and the transnational must be seen in light of the conflicting analyses of racism offered at the dawn of the postwar postcolonial era by Myrdal, Du Bois, and

C.L.R. James, among others. Singh contrasted Myrdal's view that racism was an outdated caste distinction vanishing with the spread of modernity with Du Bois and James's position that racism was constitutive of modernity, particularly capitalist labor practices and modern discourses of cultural difference. Singh also demonstrated that no responsible history of the transnational can be written without placing primary emphasis on a comparative history of the roles international connections have played for minority vs. majority racial groups—with the implication that U.S. racial and ethnic politics must always be studied within a transnational, not simply national, context. In the same *American Quarterly* issue, Paul Giles undertook a much-needed examination of parallels and contrasts between new ethnic studies in the U.S. and in British cultural studies theory, particularly Stuart Hall's investigation of how older narratives of ethnic identity are inadequate for the "new ethnicities" that he finds in the postcolonial United Kingdom. Giles claims that studies of the mobility of U.S. populations and cultural forms, especially those of minority groups, were a crucial source of inspiration for the postmodern turn in British cultural studies: both C.L.R. James and Stuart Hall began their scholarly careers studying mobility in U.S. culture. By way of more recent comparisons, consider the long shadow of Stuart Hall's influence—extending now through his student Paul Gilroy's work—on Sieglinde Lemke's *Primitivist Modernism* (1998) or Gregory Stephens' *On Racial Frontiers: The New Culture of Frederick Douglass, Ralph Ellison, and Bob Marley* (1999).

For selected recent examples of nation-state theory that have influenced U.S. studies scholars, see Benedict Anderson, *Imagined Communities: Reflections on the Origin and Spread of Nationalism*; Etienne Balibar and Immanuel Wallerstein, *Race, Nation, Class: Ambiguous Identities*; Greenfeld; Bhabha; Gilroy; Cornel West; Frederick Buell; Ketu Katrak, "Colonialism, Imperialism, and Imagined Homes"; and Patricia Wald's review-essay "Minefields and Meeting Grounds: Transnational Analyses and American Studies," on four mid-1990s anthologies on postcolonial and transnational issues. For theorizations and critiques of diasporic and national identities, see Clifford; Said; Grewal; Chow; Spivak, "Diasporas Old and New"; Kaplan; Hall, "Cultural Identity and Diaspora"; Grewel and Kaplan and Radhakrishnan. Also of interest: the special issue of the *Socialist Review* edited by Amarpal K. Dhaliwal dedicated to "The Traveling Nation: India and Its Diaspora" (1994); James Clifford's *Routes: Travel and Translation* (1997); and Jameson and Miyoshi's anthology *The Cultures of Globalization* (1998).

31. The Australian triad has been criticized by Harveen Sachdeva Mann (70–71), Vijay Mishra, and others, however, for breezily implying that an international feminism has now emerged beyond the "exclusivist," "essentialist" Eurocentric locus of the middle-class, white Western feminists in the 1960s. In a review of Arun Mukherjee's *Postcolonialism: My Living* (1998), Mishra states: "the trouble with the Ashcroft, Griffiths and Tifflin conspectus [in *The Empire Writes Back*] is that it has a tendency to homogenize experience, to reduce particularities to a centre-periphery binary and then to locate opposition, from the periphery, in a poorly theorized concept of language as counter discourse. So that there were elisions, some so unnerving and jarring that the book very quickly lost its usefulness" (92). *Key Concepts* (1998) by Ashcroft et al, we may add, is a much more useful book without the "elisions" Mishra complains about.

32. For one response to Mohanty, see Suleri 757–58. Suleri cautions us against the essentialist "claim to authenticity" that Suleri reads in Mohanty's argument.

33. This cannot be the place for anything but the briefest survey of other feminist work in postcolonial and U.S. studies. Particularly recommended for introductory reading: Ania Loomba's "Feminism, Nationalism, and Postcolonialism" in her *Colonialism/Postcolonialism* (215–30); and Frantz Fanon's classic, conflicted meditation on Algerian women and nationalist discourse ("Algeria Unveiled" in *A Dying Colonialism*). *Dangerous Liaisons: Gender, Nationhood, and Postcolonial Perspectives*, edited by McClintock, Mufti, and Shohat (1997), collects essays rethinking the

intersection between gender and narratives of nationhood, as does Grewal and Kaplan's anthology *Scattered Hegemonies*. The topic is also fruitfully explored in essays by Mohanty, Sharpe, Franco, and Kandiyoti in Williams and Chrisman's *Colonial Discourse and Postcolonial Theory: A Reader* (1994), plus Chang's essay in Michaelson's and Johnson's *Border Theory* (1997). Also highly recommended: Ketu Katrak's two essays, "Decolonizing Culture: Toward a Theory for Post-colonial Women" and "Post-colonial Women Writers and Feminisms"; and Kaplan, Alarcón, and Moallem's anthology *Between Woman and Nation* (1999).

34. Prem Chand is the pseudonym of Dhanpat Rai [Shrivastava] (1880–1936), a writer in both Urdu and Hindi, who explored social and political themes in his novels—such as *Karmabhumi* (1925) and *Godan* (1936)—and short fiction against the background of British colonial rule. See his short stories in *The World of Prem Chand*; and Narain. Satyajit Ray's only Urdu film, *The Chess Players (Shatranj ke Khilari)*, was based on a Prem Chand short story. Mulk Raj Anand (1905–), educated in Lahore, London, and Cambridge, is the author of several novels, including *Coolie* (1935) and *Untouchable* (1936), that deal, as their titles suggest, with subaltern characters oppressed by caste and class.

35. African American literary works that explore "race" as a construction are too numerous to list, but our attention has been drawn to Audre Lorde's exploration of this issue through the eyes of a young girl in a short story, "That Summer I Left Childhood." Black writers who have been especially astute in acknowledging their multiple identities without abandoning their commitment to the distinctiveness of African American experience include Audre Lorde and Ishmael Reed in their essays, interviews, and literary works. Reed was the co-founder in 1976 of the Before Columbus Foundation, which advocates a "post-provincial America" and an awareness of "disparate cultures." And yet, as Henry Louis Gates, Jr., has noted, Reed is one of those experimental African American writers who has "consistently managed to consolidate disparate, seemingly unrelated characteristics of black written and unwritten expression, and thereby to define the very possibilities of the novel as a literary form" (cited in Dick and Singh, *Conversations with Ishmael Reed*, xi).

36. Beyond the texts already mentioned in "whiteness studies," we must cite Thomas Y. Gossett's classic *Race: The History of an Idea in America* (1963); Fishkin's indispensable mid-1990s survey of scholarship in the field, "Interrogating 'Whiteness,' Complicating 'Blackness': Remapping American Culture"; also crucial for foundational reading are Omi and Winant's concepts of racial formation and racial hegemony and Peggy McIntosh's discussion of white privilege. Since the mid-1990s, there has been an exponential growth in the number of relevant publications. Frankenberg's book and anthology make the crucial argument that "whiteness" studies will be meaningless if it merely recasts whites as multi-ethnics rather than examines power-relations in their historical context. For other studies on how "whiteness" may be defined and reconstructed, see the journal *Transition*, issue 73 (special issue on whiteness); Henry Giroux; Richard Dyer; Robert Elliot Fox; David Theo Goldberg; Ignatiev and Garvey's *Race Traitor;* Mike Hill's *Whiteness: A Critical Reader;* Susan Gubar's *Racechanges: White Skin, Black Face in American Culture;* and the anthology *White Reign: Deploying Whiteness in America* by Kincheloe et al. Regarding historical perspectives on the U.S., Karen Brodkin's *How Jews Became Whitefolks and What That Says About Race in America* supplements David Roediger's emphasis on Irish Americans in *The Wages of Whiteness* (and Ignatiev's); while Kevin Phillips provides a provocative new synthesis linking the English and American Civil Wars to racial and ethnic politics. Vron Ware focused valuably in her first book on whiteness in Anglo-American women's history. Ruth Frankenberg's anthology *Displacing Whiteness*; Michelle Fine's collection *Off White*; and Samina Najmi and Rajini Srikanth's forthcoming volume, *White Women in Racialized Spaces*, crucially widen the field further; Najmi and Srikanth's anthology covers the United States, Egypt, Cameroon, South Africa, India, and Thailand. To complement Ian Haney Lopez's *White by Law*, see

also the essays in Delgado and Stefancic's *Critical Race Theory* and the work of Patricia Williams. Roediger's *Black on White: Black Writers on What It Means to be White* (which includes such essays as Cheryl Harris' "Whiteness as Property") is also required reading; more anthologies along these and other color-lines should surely be forthcoming. Three books, among many, that examine whiteness from the perspective of individuals in interracial families are: Maureen Reddy, *Crossing the Color Line* (1994), Jane Lazarre, *Beyond the Whiteness of Whiteness* (1996), and James McBride, *The Color of Water* (1996). Unregenerate and other "whiteness" in the U.S. also has its histories: see Thomas Gossett's *Race* and, for perspectives from the 1990s, Giroux; Jessie Daniels' *White Lies: Race, Class, Gender and Sexuality in White Supremacist Discourse*; James Ridgeway's video and book *Blood in the Face: The Ku-Klux Klan, Aryan Nations, Nazi Skinheads, and the Rise of a New White Culture*; and Newitz and Wray's *White Trash*. We take the opportunity here to thank Rajini Srikanth and Samina Najmi for sound advice on this section of this essay.

37. For one critique of such globalist universalisms within the context of colonial and neocolonial history, see Koshy. Regarding Theodore Levitt's work mentioned above, see also Gayatri Spivak's critique in *In Other Worlds* 168–69. Interestingly, Spivak does not note that Levitt appropriates but thoroughly misreads an anecdote from Clifford Geertz's *The Interpretation of Cultures* to support his thesis about the superficiality of national and regional differences when global markets are concerned. Geertz, rather, uses his anecdote to stress the "danger that cultural analyses, in search of all-too-deep-lying turtles, will lose touch with the hard surfaces of life—with the political, economic, stratificatory realities within which men are everywhere contained" (see Levitt 102).

38. Bishara is quoted by Nomi Morris, "Many Arab Citizens Are Seeking to Redefine Their Role in Israel"; for the Kureishi quip, see the movie *Sammie and Rose Get Laid* and also Spivak, *Outside In the Teaching Machine* 252.

39. For one commentary on Appadurai, see Chatterjee. For a Nobel prize-winning economist's critique of dominant globalization theory's assumptions about "development" and "freedom," see Amartya Sen, *Development as Freedom* (1999). Two more narrowly focused studies of global restructuring and ethnic diasporas are: Paul Ong et al, *The New Asian Immigration in Los Angeles and Global Restructuring*; and Dirlik, "Asians on the Rim: Transnational Capital and Local Community in the Making of Contemporary Asian America."

40. For one reflection on the complicated histories of both Black Studies and American Studies scholarship and teaching, see Mary Helen Washington's Presidential Address to the 1997 American Studies Association Convention: " 'Disturbing the Peace': What Happens to American Studies If You Put African American Studies at the Center?"

41. Gayatri Spivak's "Bonding in Difference" is particularly wise and resourceful on these issues.

42. Of a number of authors who have made similar arguments linking U.S. ethnicity and democratic change, we will mention just a few: June Jordan, Gary Okihiro, Ronald Takaki, Taylor Branch, and George Lipsitz. See also the two *Who Built America?* volumes, edited by Levine et al and Freeman et al, respectively; and bell hooks' *Killing Rage: Ending Racism* (1995), which brings to bear new perspectives from the 1990s on Martin Luther King's ideal of a nation as a "beloved community," as does Charles Johnson's 1998 novel *Dreamer*.

Works Cited

Acuña, Rodolfo. *Occupied America*. New York: Harper, 1981.

Adell, Sandra. *Double Consciousness/Double Bind: Theoretical Issues in Twentieth-Century Black Literature*. Urbana: U of Illinois P, 1994.

Ahmad, Aijaz. "Jameson's Rhetoric of Otherness and the 'National Allegory.'" *Social Text* 17 (Fall 1987): 3–25.

———. *In Theory: Classes, Nations, Literatures*. London: Verso, 1992.

Alexander, Meena. *Fault Lines*. New York: Feminist P, 1993.

———. *The Shock of Arrival*. Boston: South End P, 1997.

Allen, Theodore W. *The Invention of the White Race*. New York: Verso, 1994.

Anderson, Benedict. *Imagined Communities: Reflections on the Origin and Spread of Nationalism*. 1983; rpt. London: Verso, 1991.

Anzaldúa, Gloria. *Borderlands: The New Mestiza = La Frontera*. San Francisco: Spinsters/Aunt Lute, 1987.

Appadurai, Arjun. *Modernity at Large: Cultural Dimensions of Globalization*. Minneapolis: U of Minnesota P, 1996.

———. "Disjuncture and Difference in the Global Economy." *Public Culture* 2.2 (1990): 1–24.

———. "The Heart of Whiteness." *Callaloo* 16.4 (1993): 796–807.

Appiah, K. Anthony. *In My Father's House: Africa in the Philosophy of Culture*. New York: Oxford UP, 1992.

———. "Is the Post in Postmodernism the Post in Postcolonialism?" *Contemporary Postcolonial Theory: A Reader*. Ed. Padmini Mongia. New York: Arnold, 1996.

Arteaga, Alfred, ed. *An Other Tongue: Nation and Ethnicity in the Linguistic Borderlands*. Durham: Duke UP, 1994.

Ashcroft, Bill, Gareth Griffiths, and Helen Tifflin, eds. *The Empire Writes Back: Theory and Practice in Post-Colonial Literatures*. New York: Routledge, 1989.

———, eds. *The Post-Colonial Studies Reader*. New York: Routledge, 1995.

———. *Key Concepts in Post-Colonial Studies*. New York: Routledge, 1998.

Babb, Valerie. *Whiteness Visible: The Meaning of Whiteness in American Literature and Culture*. New York: NYU P, 1998.

Baker, Houston. *Modernism and the Harlem Renaissance*. Chicago: U of Chicago P, 1987.

Balibar, Etienne, and Immanuel Wallerstein, eds. *Race, Nation, Class: Ambiguous Identities*. London: Verso, 1991.

Bambara, Toni Cade. "Deep Sight and Rescue Missions." *Lure and Loathing: Essays on Race, Identity, and the Ambivalence of Assimilation*. Ed. Gerald Early. New York: Penguin, 1993.

Banks, Marcus. *Ethnicity: Anthropological Constructions*. New York: Routledge P, 1996.

Bell, Bernard. *The Afro-American Novel and its Tradition*. Amherst: U of Massachusetts P, 1987.

Bell, Daniel. *The End of Ideology; On the Exhaustion of Political Ideas in the 1950s*. Glencoe, IL: Free P, 1960.

Bhabha, Homi, ed. *Nation and Narration*. New York: Routledge, 1990.

———. "Freedom's Basis in the Indeterminate." *October* 61 (Summer 1992): 46–57.

———. "The World and the Home." *Social Text* 1992 10.2–3 (32–31): 141–57.

———. "Postcolonial Criticism." *Redrawing the Boundaries: The Transformation of English and American Literary Studies*. Ed. Stephen Greenblatt and Giles Gunn. New York: Modern Language Association, 1992. 437–65.

———. *The Location of Culture*. New York: Routledge, 1994.

Bigler, Ellen. *American Conversations: Puerto Ricans, White Ethnics, and Multicultural Education*. Philadelphia: Temple UP, 1999.

Blauner, Robert. "Internal Colonialism and Ghetto Revolt." *Social Problems* 16 (Spring 1969): 393–406.

———. *Racial Oppression in America*. New York: Harper, 1972.

Bloom, Allan. *The Closing of the American Mind: How Education has Failed Democracy and Impoverished the Souls of Today's Students*. New York: Simon and Schuster, 1987.

Boehmer, Elleke. *Colonial and Postcolonial Literature: Migrant Metaphors*. Oxford UP, 1995.

Bongie, Chris. *Islands and Exiles: The Creole Identities of Post/colonial Literature*. Stanford: Stanford UP, 1998.

Bourne, Randolph. *War and the Intellectuals: Collected Essays*. Ed. Carl Resek. New York: Harper, 1964.

Bracey, John H, August Meier, and Elliot Rudwick, eds. *Black Nationalism in America*. New York: Bobbs-Merrill, 1970.

Branch, Taylor. *Parting the Waters: America in the King Years, 1954–63*. New York: Simon and Schuster, 1988.

———. *Pillar of Fire: America in the King Years, 1963–65*. New York: Simon and Schuster, 1998.

Brodkin, Karen. *How Jews Became White Folks and What That Says About Race in America*. New Brunswick: Rutgers UP, 1998.

Bruce, Dickson. "W. E. B. Du Bois and the Idea of Double-Consciousness." *American Literature* 64.2 (June 1992): 299–309.

Bruce-Novoa, Juan. "Dialogical Strategies, Monological Goals: Chicano Literature." *An Other Tongue: Nation and Ethnicity in the Linguistic Borderlands*. Ed. Alfred Arteaga. Durham: Duke UP, 1994. 234–7.

Buell, Frederick. "Nationalist Postnationalism: Globalist Discourse in Contemporary American Culture." *American Quarterly* 50.3 (September 1998): 548–91.

———. *National Culture and the New Global System*. Baltimore: Johns Hopkins UP, 1994.

Calderón, Hector, and José David Saldívar, eds. *Criticism in the Borderlands: Studies in Chicano Literature, Culture, and Ideology*. Durham: Duke UP, 1991.

"Centennial Symposium on the Significance of Frederick Jackson Turner, A." *Journal of the Early Republic* 13 (Summer 1993): 133–249.

Césaire, Aimé. *The Collected Poetry of Aimé Césaire*. Trans. Clayton Eshleman and Annette Smith. Berkeley: U of California P, 1983.

Chand, Prem. *The World of Prem Chand*. Trans. David Rubin. Bloomington: Indiana UP, l969.

Chang, Elaine K. "Run Through the Borders: Feminism, Postmodernism, and Runaway Subjectivity." *Border Theory: The Limits of Cultural Politics*. Ed. Scott Michaelsen and David E. Johnson. Minneapolis: U of Minnesota P, 1997. 169–94.

Chatterjee, Partha. *The Nation and Its Fragments: Colonial and Postcolonial Histories*. Princeton: Princeton UP, 1993.

———. "Beyond the Nation? Or Within?" *Social Text* 56 [16.3] (1998): 57–69.

Chauhan, P. S. "Re-reading Claude McKay." *CLA Journal* 34 (1990): 68–80,

Chesnutt, Charles W. "The Future American: A Stream of Dark Blood in the Veins of Southern Whites." *Boston Evening Transcript*, 18 August 1900: 20.

———. "The Future American: A Stream of Dark Blood in the Veins of Southern Whites." *Boston Evening Transcript*, 25 August 1900: 24.

———. "The Future American: A Complete Race Amalgamation Likely to Occur." *Boston Evening Transcript*, 1 September 1900: 24.

Cheung, King-Kok, ed. *An Interethnic Companion to Asian American Literature*. New York: Cambridge UP, 1997.

Chinweizu, Onwichekwa Jemie, and Ihechukwu Madubuike, eds. *Toward the Decolonization of African Literature*. Washington: Howard UP, 1983.

Chow, Rey. *Writing Diaspora: Tactics of Intervention in Contemporary Cultural Studies*. Bloomington: Indiana UP, 1993.

Chuh, Kandice. "Transnationalism and its Pasts." *Public Culture* 9.1 (1996): 93–112.

Clifford, James. "Diasporas." *Cultural Anthropology* 9 (August 1994): 302–38.

————. *Routes: Travel and Translation in the Late Twentieth Century*. Cambridge: Harvard UP, 1997.

Coetzee, J. M. *Waiting for the Barbarians*. 1980; rpt. New York: Penguin, 1982.

Crouch, Stanley. *The All-American Skin Game, or, The Decoy of Race: The Long and the Short of It, 1990–1994*. New York: Pantheon, 1995.

Daniels, Jessie. *White Lies: Race, Class, Gender and Sexuality in White Supremacist Discourse*. New York: Routledge P, 1997.

Davis, Allen F. "The Politics of American Studies." *American Quarterly* 42.3 (September 1990). Rpt. *American Studies Today*. Ed. Amritjit Singh, Max Skidmore, Isaac Sequeira. New Delhi: Creative Books, 1995. 33–51.

Delgado, Richard, and Jean Stefanicic, eds. *The Latino/a Condition: A Critical Reader*. New York: NYU P, 1998.

————, eds. *Critical Race Theory: The Cutting Edge*. Philadelphia: Temple UP, 1999.

DeMott, Benjamin. *The Trouble with Friendship: Why Americans Can't Think Straight About Race*. New York: Atlantic Monthly Press, 1996.

Derrida, Jacques. "Living On/Border Lines." Harold Bloom et al, eds. *Deconstruction and Criticism*. New York: Seabury P, 1979. 75–176.

Desmond, Jane C., and Virginia R. Domínguez. "Resituating American Studies in a Critical Internationalism." *American Quarterly* 48 (Fall 1996): 475–90.

Dhaliwal, Amarpal K., ed. *Socialist Review* 24.4 (1994). Special issue: *The Traveling Nation: India and Its Diaspora*.

————. "Reading Diaspora: Self-Representational Practices and the Politics of Reception." *Socialist Review* 24.4 (1994). Special issue: *The Traveling Nation: India and Its Diaspora*. 13–43.

Dick, Bruce, and Amritjit Singh, eds. *Conversations with Ishmael Reed*. Jackson: UP of Mississippi, 1995.

Dimock, Wai-chee. *Empire for Liberty: Melville and the Poetics of Individualism*. Princeton: Princeton UP, 1989.

Dionne, E. J., Jr. *They Only Look Dead: Why Progressives Will Dominate the Next Political Era*. New York: Simon and Schuster, 1996.

Dirlik, Arif. "The Postcolonial Aura: Third World Criticism in the Age of Global Capitalism." *Critical Inquiry* 20.2 (Winter 1994): 328–56. Rpt. *Dangerous Liaisons: Gender, Nation, and Postcolonial Perspectives*. Ed. Anne McLintock, Aamir Mufti, and Ella Shohat. Minneapolis: U of Minnesota P, 1997. 501–28.

————. *After the Revolution: Waking to Global Capitalism*. Hanover, NH: Wesleyan UP, 1994.

————. "The Global in the Local." *Global/Local: Cultural Production and the Transnational Imaginary*. Ed. Rob Wilson and Wimal Dissanayake. Durham: Duke UP, 1996. 21–45.

————. "Asians on the Rim: Transnational Capital and Local Community in the Making of Contemporary Asian America." *Amerasia Journal* 22.3 (1996): 1–24.

Dominguez, Virginia R. *White by Definition: Social Classification in Creole Louisiana*. New Brunswick: Rutgers UP, 1986.

Drinnon, Richard. *Facing West: The Metaphysics of Indian-Hating and Empire-Building*. Minneapolis: U of Minnesota P, 1980.

D'Souza, Dinesh. *The End of Racism: Principles for a Multiracial Society*. New York: Free Press, 1995.

Du Bois, W. E. B. *The Souls of Black Folk*. 1903; rpt. New York: Penguin, 1989.

During, Simon. "Postmodernism and Postcolonialism Today." *Textual Practice* 1.1 (1987): 32–47.

Dyer, Richard. *White*. New York: Routledge P, 1997.

Eagleton, Terry. *Literary Theory*. Second edition. Minneapolis: Minnesota UP, 1996.

Early, Gerald. *Lure and Loathing: Essays on Race, Identity, and the Ambivalence of Assimilation*. New York: Penguin, 1993.

Ethington, Philip J. "Toward a 'Borderlands School' for American Urban Ethnic Studies?" [Review of George Sánchez's *Becoming Mexican American*.] *American Quarterly* 48.2 (June 1996): 344–53.

Fairchild, Henry Pratt. *The Melting-Pot Mistake*. 1926; rpt. New York: Arno, 1977.

Fanon, Frantz. *Black Skin, White Masks*. Trans. Charles Lee Markmann. 1967; rpt. New York: Grove, 1986.

———. *The Wretched of the Earth*. Trans. Constance Farrington. New York: Grove, 1968.

———. *A Dying Colonialism*. Trans. H. Chevalier. New York: Grove, 1965.

Fine, Gary Alan, ed. *A Second Chicago School? The Development of a Postwar American Sociology*. Chicago: U of Chicago P, 1995.

Fine, Michelle, et al, eds. *Off White: Readings on Race, Power, and Society*. New York: Routledge, 1997.

Fisher, Philip, ed. *The New American Studies: Essays from "Representations."* Berkeley: U of California P, 1991.

Fishkin, Shelley Fisher. "Interrogating 'Whiteness,' Complicating 'Blackness': Remapping American Culture." *American Quarterly* 47.3 (September 1995): 428–66. Rpt. *Criticism and the Color Line: Desegregating American Literary Studies*. Ed. Henry B. Wonham. New Brunswick: Rutgers UP, 1996. 251–90.

Foucault, Michel. "Of Other Spaces." *Diacritics* 16.1 (Spring 1986): 22–27.

Fox, Robert Elliot. "Becoming Post-White." *MultiAmerica: Essays on Cultural Wars and Cultural Peace*. Ed. Ishmael Reed. New York: Viking/Penguin, 1997. 6–17.

Franco, Jean. "Beyond Ethnocentrism: Gender, Power, and the Third-World Intelligentsia." Ed. Patrick Williams and Laura Chrisman. *Colonial Discourse and Post-Colonial Theory: A Reader*. New York: Columbia UP, 1994. 359–69.

Frankenberg, Ruth. *White Women, Race Matters: The Social Construction of Whiteness*. Minneapolis: U of Minnesota P, 1993.

———. *Displacing Whiteness: Essays in Social and Cultural Criticism*. Durham: Duke UP, 1997.

Frazier, E. Franklin. *Race and Culture Contacts in the Modern World*. New York: Knopf, 1957.

Freeman, Joshua, et al, eds. *Who Built America? Working People and the Nation's Economy, Politics, Culture, and Society. Volume Two: From the Gilded Age to the Present*. New York: Pantheon, 1992.

Friedman, Thomas L. *The Lexus and the Olive Tree: Understanding Globalization*. New York: Farrar, Straus, and Giroux, 1999.

Fuchs, Lawrence H. *An American Kaleidoscope: Race, Ethnicity, and the Civic Culture*. Middletown: Wesleyan UP, 1990.

Fukuyama, Francis. *The End of History and the Last Man*. New York: Free P, 1992.

Gates, Henry Louis. "Critical Fanonism." *Critical Inquiry* 17 (1991): 457–70.

Gans, Herbert. "Symbolic Ethnicity: The Future of Ethnic Groups and Cultures in America." *Ethnic and Racial Studies* 2 (January 1979): 1–20.

Gandhi, Leela. *Postcolonial Theory: A Critical Introduction*. New York: Columbia UP, 1998.

Geertz, Clifford. *The Interpretation of Cultures: Selected Essays*. New York: Basic Books, 1973.

George, Rosemary Marangoly. *The Politics of Home: Postcolonial Relocations and Twentieth-Century Fiction*. New York: Cambridge UP, 1997.

Giles, Paul. "Virtual Americas: The Internationalization of American Studies and the Ideology of Exchange." *American Quarterly* 50.3 (September 1998): 523–47.

Gilroy, Paul. *The Black Atlantic: Modernity and Double-Consciousness.* Cambridge: Harvard UP, 1993.

———. *Small Acts: Thoughts on the Politics of Black Cultures.* London: Serpent's Tale P, 1993.

Giroux, Henry A, and Peter McLaren, eds. *Between Borders: Pedagogy and the Politics of Cultural Studies.* New York: Routledge, 1994.

———. "White Noise: Toward a Pedagogy of Whiteness." *Race-ing Representation: Voice, History, and Sexuality.* Ed. Kostas Myrsiades and Linda Myrsiades. London, England, and Lanham, MD: Rowan and Littlefield, 1998.

———. *Channel Surfing: Racism, the Media, and the Destruction of Today's Youth.* New York: St. Martin's, 1998.

Gitlin, Todd. *The Twilight of Common Dreams: Why America Is Wracked by Culture Wars.* New York: Metropolitan, 1995.

Glass, Loren. Review of Walter Benn Michaels' *Our America. Modern Language Studies* 26 (1997): 1–17.

Gleason, Philip. "World War II and the Development of American Studies." *American Quarterly* 36.3 (1984): 343–58.

Goldberg, David Theo. *Racial Subjects: Writing on Race in America.* New York: Routledge P, 1997.

Gómez-Peña, Guillermo. *The New World Border.* San Francisco: City Lights, 1996.

Gossett, Thomas Y. *Race: The History of an Idea in America.* 1963, 1965; rpt. New York: Oxford UP, 1997.

Graham, Maryemma, and Amritjit Singh, eds. *Conversations with Ralph Ellison.* Jackson: UP of Mississippi, 1995.

Gramsci, Antonio. *The Prison Notebooks.* 1971; rpt. New York: Columbia UP, 1992.

Greenfeld, Liah. *Nationalism: Five Roads to Modernity.* Cambridge: Harvard UP, 1995.

Grewal, Inderpal. "The Postcolonial, Ethnic Studies, and the Diaspora: The Contexts of Ethnic Immigrant/Migrant Cultural Studies." *Socialist Review* 24.4 (1994): 45–74.

Grewal, Inderpal, and Caren Kaplan, eds. *Scattered Hegemonies: Postmodernity and Transnational Feminist Practices.* Minneapolis: U of Minnesota P, 1994.

Gubar, Susan. *Racechanges: White Skin, Black Face in American Culture.* New York: Oxford UP, 1997.

Guha, Ranajit, ed. *Subaltern Studies I: Writings on South Asian History and Society.* Delhi: Oxford UP, 1982.

———, ed. Introduction. *A Subaltern Studies Reader, 1986–1995.* Minneapolis: U of Minnesota P, 1997.

Hall, Stuart. "Culture, Community, Nation." *Cultural Studies* 7 (October 1993): 360–61.

———. "Cultural Identity and Diaspora." *Colonial Discourse and Post-Colonial Theory: A Reader.* Ed. Patrick Williams and Laura Chrisman. New York: Columbia UP, 1994. 392–403.

———. *Critical Dialogues in Cultural Studies.* Ed. David Morley and Kuan-Hsing Chen. New York: Routledge, 1996.

Handlin, Oscar. *Race and Nationality in American Life.* Boston: Little, Brown, 1957.

———. *The Uprooted: The Epic Story of the Great Migrations That Made the American People.* Boston: Little, Brown, 1951.

Haney Lopez, Ian. *White by Law: The Legal Construction of Race.* New York: NYU P, 1996.

Hellwig, David. "Strangers in Their Own Land: Patterns of Black Nativism." *American Studies Today.* Ed. Amritjit Singh, Max Skidmore, Isaac Sequeira. New Delhi: Creative Books, 1995.

Hill, Mike. *Whiteness: A Critical Reader.* New York: NYU P, 1997.

Higham, John. *Strangers in the Land: Patterns of American Nativism, 1860–1925.* 1955; rev. ed. New York, ———, 1969.

Hollinger, David. *Postethnic America: Beyond Multiculturalism*. New York: Basic Books, 1995.

hooks, bell. *Black Looks: Race and Representation*. Boston: South End, 1992.

———. *Outlaw Culture*. New York: Routledge, 1994.

———. *Killing Rage: Ending Racism*. New York: Henry Holt, 1995.

Huntington, Samuel P. *The Clash of Civilizations and the Remaking of World Order*. New York: Simon and Schuster, 1996.

Hutchinson, George. *The Harlem Renaissance in Black and White*. Cambridge: Harvard UP, 1995.

Ignatiev, Noel. *How the Irish Became White*. New York: Routledge, 1995.

Ignatiev, Noel, and John Garvey, eds. *Race Traitor*. New York: Routledge P, 1996.

Jameson, Fredric. "Third-World Literature in the Era of Multinational Capitalism." *Social Text* 15 (1986): 65–88.

———. *The Cultural Turn: Selected Writings on The Postmodern*. New York: Verso, 1998.

Jameson, Fredric, and Masao Miyoshi, eds. *The Cultures of Globalization*. Durham: Duke UP, 1998.

JanMohamed, Abdul. "Worldliness-Without-World, Homelessness-As-Home: Towards a Definition of the Specular Border Intellectual." *Edward Said: A Critical Reader*. Ed. Michael Sprinker. Cambridge, MA and London: Blackwell, 1992. 96–120.

Johnson, David E. "The Time of Translation: The Border of American Literature." *Border Theory: The Limits of Cultural Politics*. Ed. Scott Michaelsen and David E. Johnson. Minneapolis: U of Minnesota P, 1997. 129–65.

Jordan, June. *Civil Wars*. Boston: Beacon P, 1981.

———. *Technical Difficulties: African American Notes on the State of the Union*. New York: Pantheon, 1992.

———. *Affirmative Acts: Political Essays*. New York: Archer/Doubleday, 1998.

Kallen, Horace M. *Culture and Democracy in the United States: Studies in the Group Psychology of the American Peoples*. New York: Boni and Liveright, 1924.

Kandiyoti, Deniz. "Identity and its Discontents: Women and the Nation." *Colonial Discourse and Post-Colonial Theory: A Reader*. Ed. Patrick Williams and Laura Chrisman. New York: Columbia UP, 1994. 376–91.

Kaplan, Amy. "Left Alone with America." *Cultures of United States Imperialism*. Ed. Donald Pease and Amy Kaplan. Durham: Duke UP, 1993. 3–21.

———, and Donald Pease, eds. *Cultures of United States Imperialism*. Durham: Duke UP, 1993.

Kaplan, Caren. "Transnational Feminist Cultural Studies: Beyond the Marxism/Poststructuralism/Feminism Divides." *Between Woman and Nation: Nationalisms, Transnational Feminisms, and the State*. Eds. Caren Kaplan, Norma Alarcón, and Minoo Moallem. Durham: Duke UP, 1999. 349–63.

Kaplan, Caren, Norma Alarcón, and Minoo Moallem, eds. *Between Woman and Nation: Nationalisms, Transnational Feminisms, and the State*. Durham: Duke UP, 1999.

Katrak, Ketu. "Colonialism, Imperialism, and Imagined Homes." *The Columbia History of the American Novel*. Ed. Emory Elliot. New York: Columbia UP, 1991. 649–78.

———. "Decolonizing Culture: Toward a Theory for Post-Colonial Women." *The Post-Colonial Studies Reader*. Ed. Bill Ashcroft, Gareth Griffiths, and Helen Tifflin. New York: Routledge, 1995.

———. "Post-colonial Women Writers and Feminisms." *New Nationalist and Post-Colonial Literatures: An Introduction*. Ed. Bruce King. New York: Oxford UP, 1996.

Kazin, Alfred. *An American Procession*. New York: Knopf, 1984.

Kincheloe, Joe L., Shirley R. Steinberg, Nelson M. Rodriguez, and Ronald E. Chennault, eds. *White Reign: Deploying Whiteness in America*. New York: St. Martin's, 1998.

Kolodny, Annette. "Letting Go Our Grand Obsessions: Notes Toward a New Literary History of the American Frontiers." *Subjects and Citizens: Nation, Race, and Gender from Oroonoko to Anita Hill*. Ed. Michael Moon and Cathy N. Davidson. Durham: Duke UP, 1995. 9–26.

Koshy, Susan. "From Cold War to Trade War: Neocolonialism and Human Rights." *Social Text* 58 [17.1] (Spring 1999): 1–32.

Lasch, Christopher. *The Culture of Narcissism: American Life in an Age of Diminishing Expectations*. New York: Norton, 1979.

Lavie, Smardar, and Ted Swedenburg, eds. *Displacement, Diaspora, and Geographies of Identity*. Durham: Duke UP, 1996.

Lazarre, Jane. *Beyond the Whiteness of Whiteness: Memoir of a White Mother of Black Sons*. Durham: Duke UP, 1996.

Lemke, Sieglinde. *Primitivist Modernism: Black Culture and the Origins of Transnational Modernism*. New York: Oxford UP, 1998.

Lenz, Guenter H. "American Studies—Beyond the Crisis?: Recent Redefinitions and the Meaning of Theory, History, and Practical Criticism." *Prospects 7*. Ed. Jack Salzman. New York: Burt and Franklin, 1982. 53–113.

Levine, Bruce, et al, eds. *Who Built America? Working People and the Nation's Economy, Politics, Culture, and Society*. Volume One: *From Conquest and Colonization Through Reconstruction and the Great Uprising of 1877*. New York: Pantheon, 1989.

Levitt, Theodore. "The Globalization of Markets." *Harvard Business Review* 61.3 (May–June 1983): 92–102.

Lim, Shirley Geok-Lin. "Immigration and Diaspora." *An Interethnic Companion to Asian American Literature*. Ed. King-Kok Cheung. New York: Cambridge UP, 1997. 289–311.

Limón, José. *Dancing with the Devil: Society and Cultural Poetics in Mexican American South Texas*. Madision: U of Wisconsin P, 1994.

Lipsitz, George. *Dangerous Crossroads: Popular Music, Postmodernism, and the Poetics of Space*. New York: Verso, 1994.

———. *Time Passages: Collective Memory and American Popular Culture*. Minneapolis: U of Minnesota P, 1990.

Liu, Eric. *The Accidental Asian: Notes of a Native Speaker*. New York: Random, 1998.

Locke, Alain, ed. *The New Negro*. 1925; rpt. New York: Atheneum, 1969.

Loomba, Ania. "Overworlding the Third World." *Colonial Discourse and Post-Colonial Theory: A Reader*. Ed. Patrick Williams and Laura Chrisman. New York: Columbia UP, 1994. 305–23.

———. *Colonialism/Postcolonialism*. New York: Routledge, 1998.

Lowe, Lisa. *Immigrant Acts: On Asian American Cultural Politics*. Durham: Duke UP, 1996.

Lubiano, Wahneema, ed. *The House That Race Built: Black Americans, U.S. Terrain*. New York: Pantheon, 1997.

Lugo, Alejandro. "Reflections on Border Theory, Culture, and the Nation." *Border Theory: The Limits of Cultural Politics*. Ed. Scott Michaelsen and David E. Johnson. Minneapolis: U of Minnesota P, 1997. 43–67.

McBride, James. *The Color of Water: A Black Man's Tribute to His White Mother*. New York: Riverhead, 1996.

McIntosh, Peggy. "White Privilege and Male Privilege: A Personal Account of Coming to See Correspondences Through Work in Women's Studies." 1988; rev. and rpt. *Race, Class and Gender: An Anthology*. Ed. Margaret L. Anderson and Patricia Hill Collins. Belmont, CA: Wadsworth P, 1992. 76–87.

McLintock, Anne, Aamir Mufti, and Ella Shohat, eds. *Dangerous Liaisons: Gender, Nation, and Postcolonial Perspectives*. Minneapolis: U of Minnesota P, 1997.

McLintock, Anne. "The Angel of Progress: Pitfalls of the Term 'Post-colonialism.'" 1992; rpt.

Colonial Discourse and Post-Colonial Theory: A Reader. Ed. Patrick Williams and Laura Chrisman. New York: Columbia UP, 1994. 291–304.

Mann, Harveen Sachdeva. "Women's Rights versus Feminism? Postcolonial Perspectives." *Postcolonial Discourse and Changing Cultural Contexts: Theory and Criticism*. Ed. Gita Rajan and Radhika Mohanram. Westport, CT: Greenwood, 1995.

Marcus, Alan I. "Social Evils and the Origin of Municipal Services in Cincinnati." *American Studies Today*. Ed. Amritjit Singh, Max J. Skidmore, and Isaac Sequiera. New Delhi: Creative Books, 1995.

Martí, José. *Inside the Monster: Writings on the United States and American Imperialism*. Ed. Philip S. Foner. New York: Monthly Review P, 1975.

———. *Our America: Writings on Latin America and the Struggle for Cuban Independence*. Ed. Philip S. Foner. New York: Monthly Review P, 1977.

Mazumdar, Sucheta. "What to Do with All These New Immigrants or Refiguring Asian American History." *Building Blocks for Asian American Studies: East of California Conference*. Ed. Robert G. Lee and Lihbin Shiao. Brown University, Providence RI, September 25–27, 1992.

Michaelsen, Scott, and David E. Johnson, eds. *Border Theory: The Limits of Cultural Politics*. Minneapolis: U of Minnesota P, 1997.

Michaels, Walter Benn. *Our America: Nativism, Modernism, and Pluralism*. Durham: Duke UP, 1995.

Minh-ha, Trinh T. "Writing Postcoloniality and Feminism." *Woman, Native, Other*. Bloomington: Indiana UP, 1989.

Mishra, Vijay. "Dismantling Postcolonialism." [A review of Arun Mukherjee's *Postcolonialism: My Living*.] *Toronto Review of Contemporary Literature Abroad* 17.3 (Summer 1999): 91–95.

Mishra, Vijay, and Bob Hodge. "What is Post(-)Colonialism?" *Colonial Discourse and Post-Colonial Theory: A Reader*. Ed. Patrick Williams and Laura Chrisman. New York: Columbia UP, 1994. 276–90.

Miyoshi, Masao. "A Borderless World? From Colonialism to Transnationalism and the Decline of the Nation-State." *Global/Local: Cultural Production and the Transnational Imaginary*. Ed. Rob Wilson and Wimal Dissanayake. Durham: Duke UP, 1996. 78–106.

Mohanty, Chandra Talpade, Ann Russo, and Lourdes Torres, eds. *Third World Feminism and the Politics of Feminism*. Bloomington: Indian UP, 1991.

Mohanty, Chandra Talpade. "Under Western Eyes: Feminist Scholarship and Colonial Discourse." *Colonial Discourse and Post-Colonial Theory: A Reader*. Ed. Patrick Williams and Laura Chrisman. New York: Columbia UP, 1994. 196–220.

Moon, Michael, and Cathy N. Davidson, eds. *Subjects and Citizens: Nation, Race, and Gender from Oroonoko to Anita Hill*. Durham: Duke UP, 1995.

Morris, Nomi. "Many Arab Citizens Are Seeking to Redefine Their Role in Israel." *Philadelphia Inquirer*. May 6, 1999. A10.

Morrison, Toni. *Playing in the Dark: Whiteness and the Literary Imagination*. Cambridge: Harvard UP, 1992.

Mukherjee, Arun. *Postcolonialism: My Living*. Toronto: TSAR, 1998.

Myrdal, Günnar. *An American Dilemma: the Negro Problem and Modern Democracy*. New York: Harper, 1944.

Narain, Govind. *Munshi Prem Chand*. Boston: Twayne, 1978.

Nash, Gerald D. "The Frontier Thesis: A Historical Perspective." *Journal of the West* 34 (October 1995): 7–15.

Newitz, Annalee, and Matt Wray, eds. *White Trash: Race and Class in America*. New York: Routledge P, 1997.

Ngugi, wa Thiongo. *Decolonising the Mind: The Politics of Language in African Literature*. London: J. Currie, 1986.

Okihiro, Gary. *Margins and Mainstreams: Asians in American History and Culture*. Seattle: U of Washington P, 1994.

Omi, Michael, and Howard Winant. *Racial Formation in the United States: From the 1960s to the 1980s*. New York: Routledge and Kegan Paul, 1986.

———. *Racial Formation in the United States: From the 1960s to the 1990s*. Second Edition. New York: Routledge P, 1994.

Ong, Paul, Edna Bonacich, and Lucie Cheng, eds. *The New Asian Immigration in Los Angeles and Global Restructuring*. Philadelphia: Temple UP, 1994.

Palumbo-Liu, David, ed. *The Ethnic Canon: Histories, Institutions, and Interventions*. Minneapolis: U Minnesota P, 1995.

Paredes, Américo. *"With His Pistol in His Hand": A Border Ballad and Its Hero*. 1958; rpt. Austin: U of Texas P, 1971.

Park, Robert. *Race and Culture*. Glencoe, IL: Free Press, 1950.

Parrillo, Vincent N. *Strangers to These Shores: Race and Ethnic Relations in the United States*. Fifth Edition. Boston: Allyn and Bacon, 1997.

Parry, Benita. "Problems in Current Theories of Colonial Discourse." *Oxford Literary Review* 9.1–2 (1987): 27–58.

———. "Resistance Theory/Theorising Resistance, or Two Cheers for Nativism." *Colonial Discourse/Postcolonial Theory*. Ed. F. Barker, P. Hulme and M. Iversen. Manchester: Manchester UP, 1994. 172–96. Rpt. *Contemporary Postcolonial Theory: A Reader*. Ed. Padmini Mongia. New York: Arnold, 1996.

Pearce, Roy Harvey. *Savagism and Civilization: A Study of the Indian and the American Mind*. Berkeley: U of California P, 1988.

Pease, Donald E. "New Perspectives on U.S. Culture and Imperialism." *Cultures of United States Imperialism*. Ed. Donald Pease and Amy Kaplan. Durham: Duke UP, 1993. 22–37.

Phillips, Kevin P. *The Cousins' Wars: Religion, Politics, and the Triumph of Anglo-America*. New York: Basic Books, 1999.

Porter, Carolyn. "What We Know That We Don't Know: Remapping American Literary Studies." *American Literary History* 6.3 (Fall 1994): 467–526).

Pratt, Mary Louise. *Imperial Eyes: Studies in Travel Writing and Transculturation*. New York: Routledge, 1992.

Radhakrishnan, R. "Ethnicity in the Age of Diaspora." *Transition* 54 (1991): 104–115.

———. *Diasporic Mediations: Between Home and Location*. Minneapolis: U of Minnesota P, 1996.

Rajan, Gita, and Radhika Mohanram, eds. "Introduction: Locating Postcoloniality." *Postcolonial Discourse and Changing Cultural Contexts: Theory and Criticism*. Westport, CT, and London: Greenwood P, 1995. 1–16.

Reddy, Maureen T. *Crossing the Color Line: Race, Parenting, and Culture*. New Brunswick: Rutgers UP, 1994.

Reed, Ishmael, ed. *MultiAmerica: Essays in Cultural Wars and Cultural Peace*. New York: Viking, 1997.

Ridgeway, James. *Blood in the Face: The Ku-Klux Klan, Aryan Nations, Nazi Skinheads, and the Rise of a New White Culture*. New York: Thunder's Mouth, 1990.

Rivkin, Julie, and Michael Ryan, eds. *Literary Theory: An Anthology*. Malden, MA: Blackwell, 1998.

Roediger, David. *The Wages of Whiteness: Race and the Makings of the American Working Class*. London: Verso, 1991.

————, ed. *Black on White: Black Writers on What It Means To Be White*. New York: Schocken, 1998.

Rosaldo, Renato. *Culture and Truth: The Remaking of Social Analysis*. Boston: Beacon, 1989.

Ross, Edward A. *The Old World in the New; The Significance of the Past and Present Immigration to the American People*. New York: Century P, 1914.

Rowe, John Carlos. *Literary Culture and U.S. Imperialism*. New York: Oxford UP, 2000.

Rushdie, Salman. *Imaginary Homelands: Essays and Criticism, 1981–1991*. London: Granta, 1991.

Sáenz, Benjamin Alire. "In the Borderlands of Chicano Identity, There Are Only Fragments." *Border Theory: The Limits of Cultural Politics*. Ed. Scott Michaelsen and David E. Johnson. Minneapolis: U of Minnesota P, 1997. 68–96.

Said, Edward W. *Orientalism*. New York: Pantheon, 1978.

————. *The World, the Text, and the Critic*. Cambridge: Harvard UP, 1983.

————. *After the Last Sky: Palestinian Lives*. New York: Pantheon, 1986.

————. *Culture and Imperialism*. New York: Knopf, 1993.

————. "Intellectual Exile: Expatriates and Marginals." *Grand Street* 12 (Fall 1993): 113–24.

————. *Representations of the Intellectual*. New York: Pantheon, 1994.

Saldívar, José David. *Border Matters: Remapping American Cultural Studies*. Berkeley: U of California P, 1997.

————. *Dialectics of Our America: Genealogy, Cultural Critique, and Literary History*. Durham: Duke UP, 1991.

————. " "Américo Paredes and Decolonization." *Cultures of United States Imperialism*. Ed. Kaplan, Amy, and Donald Pease. Durham: Duke UP, 1993. 292–311.

Saldívar, Ramón. "Border Subjects and Transnational Sites: Américo Paredes's *The Hammon and the Beans and Other Stories*." *Subjects and Citizens: Nation, Race, and Gender from Oroonoko to Anita Hill*. Ed. Michael Moon and Cathy Davidson. Durhan, N.C.: Duke UP, 1995. 373–94.

————. "The Borders of Modernity: Américo Paredes's Between Two Worlds and the Chicano National Subject." *The Ethnic Canon: Histories, Institutions, and Interventions*. Ed. David Palumbo-Liu. Minneapolis: U Minnesota P, 1995. 71–88.

Sánchez, George. *Becoming Mexican American: Ethnicity, Culture, and Identity in Chicano Los Angeles, 1900–1945*. New York: Oxford UP, 1993.

San Juan, E., Jr. *Beyond Postcolonial Theory*. New York: St. Martin's, 1998.

————. *From Exile to Diaspora: Versions of Filipino Experience in the US*. Boulder, CO: Westview P, 1998.

————. *Racial Formations/Critical Transformations: Articulations of Power in Ethnic and Racial Studies in the US*. Atlantic Highlands, NJ: Humanities P, 1992.

Schlesinger, Arthur J., Jr. *The Disuniting of America: Reflections on a Multicultural Society*. Knoxville: Whittle, 1991.

Schueller, Malini Johar. *U.S. Orientalisms: Race, Nation, and Gender in Literature, 1790–1890*. Ann Arbor: U of Michigan P, 1998.

Schuyler, George S. "Our Greatest Gift to America." *Anthology of American Negro Literature*. Ed. V. F. Calverton. New York: Random House, 1929. 405–12.

Sen, Armartya. *Development as Freedom*. New York: Knopf, 1999.

Shankar, Lavina, and Rajini Srikanth, eds. *A Part, Yet Apart: South Asians in Asian America*. Philadelphia: Temple UP, 1998.

Shankman, Arnold. *Ambivalent Friends: Afro-Americans View the Immigrant*. Westport, CT: Greenwood Press, 1982.

Sharpe, Jenny. "Is the United States Postcolonial? Transnationalism, Immigration, and Race." *Diaspora* 4.2 (Fall 1995): 181–199.

————. "The Unspeakable Limits of Rape: Colonial Violence and Counter-Insurgency." *Colonial Discourse and Post-Colonial Theory: A Reader*. Ed. Patrick Williams and Laura Chrisman. New York: Columbia UP, 1994. 221–43.

Shohat, Ella. "Notes on the 'Post-Colonial,' " *Social Text* 31/32 (1992): 99–113.

Singh, Amritjit. *The Novels of the Harlem Renaissance*. University Park: Penn State UP, 1976.

————. "The Possibilities of a Radical Consciousness: African Americans and New Immigrants." *MultiAmerica: Essays on Cultural Wars and Cultural Peace*. Ed. Ishmael Reed. New York: Viking Penguin, 1997. 218–37.

Singh, Amritjit, Joseph T. Skerrett, Jr., and Robert E. Hogan, eds. *Memory, Narrative, and Identity: New Essays in Ethnic American Literatures*. Boston: Northeastern UP, 1994.

————, eds. *Memory and Cultural Politics: New Approaches to American Ethnic Literatures*. Boston: Northeastern UP, 1996.

Singh, Amritjit, Max J. Skidmore, and Isaac Sequiera, eds. *American Studies Today*. New Delhi: Creative Books, 1995.

Singh, Nikhil Pal. "Culture/Wars: Recoding Empire in an Age of Democracy." *American Quarterly* 50.3 (September 1998): 471–522.

Sinha, Mrinalini. *Colonial Masculinity: The 'Manly Englishman' and the 'Effeminate Bengali' in the Late Nineteenth Century*. Manchester: Manchester UP, 1995.

Slotkin, Richard. *Regeneration Through Violence: The Mythology of the American Frontier, 1600–1860*. Middletown, CT: Wesleyan UP, 1973.

Smith, Henry Nash. *Virgin Land: The American West as Symbol and Myth*. Cambridge: Harvard UP, 1950.

Sollors, Werner. "A Critique of Pure Pluralism." *Reconstructing American Literary History*. Ed. Sacvan Bercovitch. Cambridge: Harvard UP, 1986. 250–79.

————. *Beyond Ethnicity: Consent and Descent in American Culture*. New York: Oxford UP, 1986.

————, ed. Introduction. *The Invention of Ethnicity*. New York: Oxford UP, 1989. i–xx.

————. " 'Of Plymouth Rock and Jamestown and Ellis Island;' or, Ethnic Literature and Some Redefinitions of 'America.' " *Immigrants in Two Democracies: French and American Experience*. Ed. Donald L. Horowitz and Gérard Noiriel. New York: NYU Press, 1992. 205–44.

————. *Neither Black Nor White Yet Both: Thematic Explorations of Interracial Literature*. New York: Oxford UP, 1997.

————. *Multilingual America: Transnationalism, Ethnicity, and the Languages of American Literature*. New York: NYU P, 1998.

————, and Maria Diedrich, eds. *The Black Columbiad: Defining Moments in African American Literature and Culture*. Cambridge: Harvard UP, 1994.

Sowell, Thomas. *Ethnic America: A History*. New York: Basic Books, 1981.

————. *Race and Culture: A World View*. New York: Basic Books, 1994.

————. *Migrations and Culture: A World View*. New York: Basic Books, 1996.

Soyinka, Wole. *Myth, Literature, and the African World*. New York: Cambridge UP, 1976.

Spanos, William V. *America's Shadow: An Anatomy of Empire*. Minneapolis: Minnesota UP, 2000.

Spillers, Hortense, ed. *Comparative American Identities: Race, Sex, and Nationality in the Modern Text*. New York: Routledge, 1991.

Spivak, Gayatri Chakravorty. "Criticism, Feminism, and the Institution." Interview with Elizabeth Gross. *Thesis Eleven* 10–11 (Nov. 1984–May 1985).

————. *In Other Worlds: Essays in Cultural Politics*. New York: Metheun, 1987.

————. *The Post-Colonial Critic: Interviews, Strategies, Dialogues*. Ed. Sarah Harasym. New York: Routledge, 1990.

————. "Race Before Racism and the Disappearance of the American: Jack D. Forbers' *Black*

Africans and Americans: Color, Race and Caste in the Evolution of Red-Black Peoples." Plantation Society in the Americas 3.2 (1993): 73–91.

——. *Outside In the Teaching Machine.* Durham: Duke UP, 1993.

——. "Bonding in Difference." *An Other Tongue: Nation and Ethnicity in the Linguistic Borderlands.* Ed. Alfred Arteaga. Durham: Duke UP, 1994. 273–85.

——. *The Spivak Reader: Selected Works of Gayatri Chakravorty Spivak.* Ed. Donna Landry and Gerald MacLean. New York: Routledge, 1996.

——. "Diasporas Old and New: Women in the Transnational World." *Class Issues: Pedagogy, Cultural Studies, and the Public Sphere.* Ed. Amitava Kumar. New York: NYU P, 1997. 87–116.

——. *A Critique of Postcolonial Reason: Toward a History of the Vanishing Present.* Cambridge: Harvard UP, 1999.

Steele, Shelby. *The Content of Our Character: A New Vision of Race in America.* New York: St. Martin's, 1990.

Steinberg, Stephen. *The Ethnic Myth: Race, Ethnicity, and Class in America.* Updated and expanded edition. Boston: Beacon, 1989.

Stephens, Gregory. *On Racial Frontiers: The New Culture of Frederick Douglass, Ralph Ellison, and Bob Marley.* Cambridge: Cambridge UP, 1999.

Suleri, Sara. "Women Skin Deep: Feminism and the Postcolonial Condition." *Critical Inquiry* 18.4 (Summer 1992). 756–69.

Sumida, Stephen H. "Postcolonialism, Nationalism, and The Emergence of Asian/Pacific American Literatures." *An Interethnic Companion to Asian American Literature.* Ed. King-Kok Cheung. New York: Cambridge UP, 1997. 274–88.

Susman, Warren I. "The Useless Past: American Intellectuals and the Frontier Thesis, 1910–1930." *Bucknell Review* 11 (1963): 1–20.

Takaki, Ronald. *A Different Mirror: A History of Multicultural America.* Boston: Little, Brown, 1993.

Thomas, Brook. "Turner's 'Frontier Thesis' as a Narrative of Reconstruction." *Centuries' Ends, Narrative Means.* Ed. Robert Newman. Stanford: Stanford UP, 1996. 117–37.

Tomasky, Michael. *Left for Dead.* New York: Free Press, 1996.

Tucker, Mark, ed. *The Duke Ellington Reader.* New York: Oxford UP, 1993.

Turner, Frederick Jackson. *The Significance of the Frontier in American History.* 1893; rpt. Ithaca: Cornell UP, 1956.

Wacker, R. Fred. "The Sociology of Race and Ethnicity in the Second Chicago School." *A Second Chicago School? The Development of Postwar American Sociology.* Ed. Gary Alan Fine. Chicago: U of Chicago P, 1995. 136–63.

Wald, Alan. "Theorizing Cultural Differences: A Critique of the Ethnicity School." *MELUS* 14.2 (1987): 21–33;.

Wald, Priscilla. "Minefields and Meeting Grounds: Transnational Analyses and American Studies." *American Literary History* 10.1 (Spring 1998): 199–218.

——. *Constituting Americans: Cultural Anxiety and Narrative Form.* Durham: Duke UP, 1995.

Walder, Dennis. *Postcolonial Literatures in English: History, Language, Theory.* London: Blackwell, 1998.

Walker, Cheryl. *Indian Nation: Native American Literature and Nineteenth-Century Nationalisms.* Durham: Duke UP, 1997.

Ware, Caroline F., ed. *The Cultural Approach to History.* New York: Columbia UP, 1940.

Ware, Vron. *Beyond the Pale: White Women, Racism, and History.* New York: Verso, 1992.

Washington, Mary Helen. " 'Disturbing the Peace: What Happens to American Studies If You Put African American Studies at the Center?' " *American Quarterly* 50.1 (March 1998): 1–23.

Waters, Mary C. *Ethnic Options: Choosing Identities in America*. Berkeley: U of California P, 1990.

Watts, Steven. "The Idiocy of American Studies: Poststructuralism, Language, and Politics in an Age of Self-Fulfillment." *American Quarterly* 43.4 (December 1991): 625–60.

Webb, Walter Prescott. *The Great Frontier*. Boston: Houghton Mifflin, 1952.

———. *The Texas Rangers: A Century of Frontier Defense*. Boston: Houghton Mifflin, 1935.

West, Cornel. "The New Cultural Politics of Difference." *Out There: Marginalization and Contemporary Cultures*. Ed. Russell Ferguson, Martha Gever, Trinkh T. Minh-ha, and Cornel West. Cambridge: MIT P, 1990. 19–36.

Williams, Patricia. *The Alchemy of Race and Rights*. Cambridge: Harvard UP, 1991.

———. "The Ethnic Scarring of American Whiteness." *The House That Race Built: Black Americans, U.S. Terrain*. Ed. Wahneema Lubiano. New York: Pantheon, 1997.

Williams, Patrick, and Laura Chrisman. *Colonial Discourse and Post-Colonial Theory: A Reader*. New York: Columbia UP, 1994.

Wilson, Rob, and Wimal Dissanayake, eds. *Global/Local: Cultural Production and the Transnational Imaginary*. Durham: Duke UP, 1996.

Wise, Gene. " 'Paradigm Dramas' in American Studies: A Cultural and Institutional History of the Movement." *American Quarterly* 31 (1979): 293–337.

Wong, Sau-ling C. *Reading Asian American Literature: From Necessity to Extravagance*. Princeton: Princeton UP, 1993.

Wonham, Henry B., ed. *Criticism and the Color Line: Desegregating American Literary Studies*. New Brunswick: Rutgers UP, 1996.

Young, Robert J. M. *Colonial Desire: Hybridity in Theory, Culture, and Race*. New York: Routledge, 1995.

Zafar, Rafia. *We Wear the Mask: African Americans Write American Literature, 1760–1870*. New York, Columbia UP, 1997.

IDENTITIES, MARGINS, AND BORDERS: II

POSTCOLONIALISM, IDEOLOGY, AND NATIVE AMERICAN LITERATURE

Arnold Krupat

In the current climate of literary studies, it is tempting to think of contemporary Native American literatures as among the postcolonial literatures of the world. Certainly they share with other postcolonial texts the fact of having, in the words of the authors of *The Empire Writes Back*, "emerged in their present form out of the experience of colonization and asserted themselves by foregrounding the tension with the imperial power, and by emphasizing their differences from the assumptions of the imperial Centre" (Ashcroft, Griffiths, and Tiffin 2). Yet contemporary Native American literatures cannot quite be classed among the postcolonial literatures of the world for the simple reason that there is not yet a "post-" to the colonial status of Native Americans. Call it domestic imperialism or internal colonialism; in either case, a considerable number of Native people exist in conditions of politically sustained subalternity. I have remarked on the academic effects of this condition in the first chapter;* here I note the more worldly effects of this condition: Indians experience twelve times the U.S. national rate of malnutrition, nine times the rate of alcoholism, and seven times the rate of infant mortality; as of the early 1990s, the life expectancy of reservation-based men was just over forty-four years, with reservation-based women enjoying, on average, a life-expectancy of just under forty-seven years. "Sovereignty," whatever its ultimate meaning in the complex sociopolitical situation of Native nations in the United States, remains to be both adequately theorized and practically achieved, and "independence," the great desideratum of colonized nations, is not, here, a particularly useful concept.[1]

Arif Dirlik lists three current meanings of the term *postcolonial*. Postcolonial may intend "a literal description of conditions in formerly colonial societies," it may claim to offer "a description of a global condition after the period of colonialism"—what Dirlik refers to as "global capitalism," marked by the "transnationalization of production" (348)—and it may, most commonly in the academy, claim to provide "a description of a discourse on the above-named conditions that is informed by the epistemological and psychic orientations that are products of those conditions" (332). Is any one of these meanings useful to describe contemporary Native American literature?[22] Dirlik's first sense of the postcolonial will not work because, as already noted, the material condition of contemporary Native "societies" is not a postcolonial one. His second sense might perhaps come a bit nearer, inasmuch as Native societies, although still in a colonial situation, nonetheless participate in the global economy of a world "after the period of colonialism." To give a fairly undramatic anecdote, in Santa Fe Native Americans sell traditional ceramic work and jewelry (including "traditional" golf tees) across the street from where non-Native people offer the "same" wares made in Hong Kong. In something of a parallel fashion, Lakota people travel to Germany and Switzerland to promote tourism at Pine Ridge. As for the last of Dirlik's definitions, little discourse surrounding Native American literature, to the best of my knowledge, has been self-consciously aware of having been formed "by the epistemological and psychic orientations that are products" of the postcolonial. (And the "nationalist" Native critic seeks to reject any formation whatever according to these "orientations.") Perhaps, then, it may not be particularly useful to conceptualize contemporary Native American literature as postcolonial.

But even though contemporary Native American fiction is produced in a condition of ongoing colonialism, some of that fiction not only has the look of postcolonial fiction but also, as I will try to show in the second part of this chapter, performs ideological work that parallels that of postcolonial fiction elsewhere. Here, however, I want to suggest a category—the category of anti-imperial translation—for conceptualizing the tensions and differences between contemporary Native American fiction and "the imperial center." Because historically specifiable acts of translative violence marked the European colonization of the Americas from Columbus to the present, it seems to me particularly important to reappropriate the concept of translation for contemporary Native American literature. To do so is not to deny the relationship of this literature to the postcolonial literatures of the world but, rather, to attempt to specify a particular modality for that relationship.

To say that the people indigenous to the Americas entered European consciousness only by means of a variety of complex acts of translation is to think of such things as Columbus's giving the name of San Salvador to an island he *knows* is called Guanahani by the natives—and then giving to each further island he encounters, as he wrote in his journals, "a new name" (Greenblatt 52). Columbus also materially "translated" (*trans-latio*, "to carry across") some of the Natives he encountered, taking "six of them from here," as he remarked in another well-known passage, "in order that they may learn to speak" (Greenblatt 90). Columbus gave the one who was best at learning his own surname and the first name of his firstborn son, translating this otherwise anonymous person into Don Diego Colon.

Now, any people who are perceived as somehow unable to speak when they speak their own languages, are not very likely to be perceived as having a literature—especially when they do not write, a point to which we shall return. Thus, initially, the very "idea of a [Native American] literature was inherently ludicrous," as Brian Swann has noted, because Indian "languages themselves were primitive" (xiii). If Indians spoke at all, they spoke very badly (and, again, they did not write). In 1851, John De Forest, in his *History of the Indians of Connecticut,* observed, "It is evident from the enormous length of many of the words, sometimes occupying a whole line, that there was something about the structure of these languages which made them cumbersome and difficult to manage" (Swann xiii).

Difficult for whom, one might ask, especially in view of the fact that De Forest himself had not achieved even minimal competence in any Native language. Further, inasmuch as these were spoken languages, not alphabetically written languages, any estimate that single words occupied the length of "a whole line" could only depend on De Forest's decision to write them that way. De Forest's sense of the "cumbersome and difficult" nature of Indian languages, as I have noted, implies that any literature the Natives might produce in these languages would also be "cumbersome and difficult." Perhaps the Natives would do better to translate themselves or be translated, to "learn to speak"—in this case, to speak English—in order to have a literature. De Forest was wrong, of course, although what most people know as Native American literature today consists of texts originally written in English.

Almost half a century after DeForest, as late as 1894, Daniel Brinton—a man who actually did a great deal to make what he called the "production" of "aboriginal authors" visible to the dominant culture—nonetheless declared, "Those peoples who are born to the modes of thought and expression enforced by some languages can never forge to the front in the struggle for supremacy; they are fatally handicapped in the race for the highest life" (Murray 8). The winners in the "race for the highest life," therefore, would be the race with the "highest" language; and it was not the Indians but rather, as Brinton wrote, "our Aryan forefathers" who were the ones fortunate enough to be endowed "with a richly inflected speech." As Kwame Anthony Appiah explained in reference to Johann Gottfried von Herder, the *Sprachgeist,* "the 'spirit' of the language, is not merely the medium through which speakers communicate but the sacred essence of a nationality. [And] Herder himself identified the highest point of the nation's language in its poetry" ("Race" 284), in its literature. "Whoever writes about the literature of a country," as Appiah elsewhere cited Herder, "must not neglect its language" (50). For those like the Indians with "primitive" languages, there would seem to be little hope, short of translation, for the prospects of literary achievement. Thus, by the end of the nineteenth century, the linguistic determinism expressed by Brinton—and, of course, by many others—worked against the possibility of seeing Native Americans as having an estimable literature at exactly the moment when the texts for that literature were, for the first time, being more or less accurately translated and published.

But here one must return to the other dimension of the translation issue as it affects Native American literatures. For the problem in recognizing the existence of Native literatures was not only that Natives could not speak or, when they did speak, that their languages were judged deficient or "primitive" but also that they did not write.

Here I will only quickly review what I and others have discussed elsewhere.[3] Because *littera-ture* in its earliest uses meant the cultivation of letters (from Latin *littera,* "letter"), just as *agriculture* meant the cultivation of fields, peoples who did not inscribe alphabetic characters on the page could not, by definition, produce a literature. (They were also thought to be only minimally capable of agriculture in spite of overwhelming evidence to the contrary, but that is another story.) It was the alteration in European consciousness generally referred to as "romanticism" that changed the emphasis in constituting the category of literature from the medium of expression, writing— literature as culture preserved in letters—to the *kind* of expression preserved, literature as imaginative and affective utterance, spoken or written. It is only at this point that an oral literature can be conceived as other than a contradiction in terms and the unlettered Indians recognized as people capable of producing a "literature."

For all of this, it remains the case that an oral literature, in order to become the subject of analysis, must indeed first become an object. It must, that is, be textualized; and here we encounter a translation dilemma of another kind, one in which the "source language" itself has to be carried across—*trans-latio*—from one medium to another, involving something more than just a change of names. This translative project requires that temporal speech acts addressed to the ear be turned into visual objects in space, black marks on the page, addressed to the eye. Words that had once existed only for the tongue to pronounce now were to be entrusted to the apprehension of the eye. Mythography, in a term of Anthony Mattina's, or ethnopoetics has been devoted for many years to the problems and possibilities involved in this particular form of media translation.[4]

Translation as a change of names—as a more or less exclusively linguistic shift from "source" to "target" language—may, historically, be traced in relation to the poles of identity and difference, as these are articulated within the disciplinary boundaries of what the West distinguishes as the domains of art and social science. Translators with attachments to the arts or humanities have rendered Native verbal expression in such a way as to make it appear attractively literary by Western standards of literariness, thereby obscuring the very different standards pertaining in various Native American cultures. Conversely, translators with attachments to the social sciences have rendered Native verbal expression in as literal a manner as possible, illuminating the differences between that expression and our own but thereby obscuring its claims to literary status. I have elaborated on these matters elsewhere,[5] and so I will here turn from considerations of the formal implications of translation practices to their ideological implications. I want to explain what I mean by anti-imperial translation and why it seems to me that a great many texts by Native American writers, though written in English, may nonetheless be taken as types of anti-imperial translation.

I base my sense of anti-imperial translation on a well-known, indeed classic text, one that I have myself quoted on a prior occasion.[6] The text is from Rudolph Pann-witz, who is cited in Walter Benjamin's important essay "The Task of the Translator." Pannwitz wrote, "Our translations, even the best ones, proceed from a wrong premise. They want to turn Hindi, Greek, English into German instead of turning German into Hindi, Greek, English. Our translators have far greater reverence for the usage of their own language than for the spirit of the foreign works. . . . The basic error of the translator is that he preserves the state in which his own language happens to be instead of allowing his language to be powerfully affected by the foreign tongue" (Benjamin 180–81). My use of Pannwitz was influenced by Talal Asad's paper, "The Concept of Cultural Translation in British Social Anthropology," originally presented at the School for American Research in 1984 and published in James Clifford and George Marcus's important collection *Writing Culture* in 1986.[7] As will be apparent, I am much indebted to Asad's work.

Asad's subject, like mine, is not translation in the narrow sense but rather translation as cultural translation. The "good translator," Asad wrote, "does not immediately assume that unusual difficulty in conveying the sense of an alien discourse denotes a fault in the latter, but instead critically examines the normal state of his or her own language" (157). Asad notes the fact that languages, if expressively equal, are nonetheless politically "unequal," those of the third world that are typically studied by anthropologists being "weaker" in relation to Western languages (and today especially in relation to English).[8] Asad remarks that the weaker, or colonized, languages "are more likely to submit to forcible transformation in the translation process than the other way around" (157–58). Asad cites with approval Godfrey Lienhardt's essay "Modes of Thought" and quotes Lienhardt's exemplary explanation of anthropological translation: "We mediate between their habits of thought, which we have acquired with them, and those of our own society; in doing so, it is not finally some mysterious 'primitive philosophy' that we are exploring, but the further potentialities of our thought and language" (Asad 158–59). This sort of translation, Asad affirms, should alter the usual relationship between the anthropological audience and the anthropological text, in that it seeks to disrupt the habitual desire of that audience to use the text as an occasion to know *about* the Other, a matter of "different *writings and readings* (meanings)" in order to instantiate the possibility that translation, as a matter "of different uses (practices)" (160), can be a force moving us toward *"learning to live another form of life"* (149).

My claim is that Native American writers today are engaged in some version of the translation project along the broad lines sketched by Asad. Even though contemporary Native writers write in English and configure their texts in apparent consonance with Western or Euramerican literary forms—that is, they give us texts that look like novels, short stories, poems, and autobiographies—they do so in ways that present an "English" nonetheless "powerfully affected by the foreign tongue," not by Hindi, Greek, or German, of course, and not actually by a "foreign" language, inasmuch as the "tongue" and "tongues" in question are indigenous to America. The language they offer, in Asad's terms, derives at least in part from other forms of practice, and to comprehend it might just require, however briefly, that we attempt to imagine living other forms of life.

This is true of contemporary Native American writers in both literal and figurative ways. In the case of those for whom English is a second language (Luci Tapahonso, Ray Young Bear, Michael Kabotie, Ofelia Zepeda, and Simon Ortiz are some of the writers who come immediately to mind), it is altogether likely that their English will show traces of the structure and idioms of their "native" language, as well as a variety of linguistic habits and narrative and performative practices of traditional expressive forms in Navajo, Mesquakie, Hopi, Tohono O'odham, and Acoma.[9] Their English, then, is indeed an English, in Pannwitz's words, "powerfully affected by the foreign tongue," a tongue (to repeat) not "foreign" at all to the Americas. Here the Native author quite literally tests "the tolerance of [English] for assuming unaccustomed forms" (Asad 157), and an adequate commentary on the work of these writers will require of the critic if not bilingualism then at least what Dell Hymes has called some "control" of the Native language.

Most Native writers today are not, however, fluent speakers of one or another of the indigenous languages of the Americas, although their experiences with these languages are so different that it would be impossible to generalize. (E.g., Leslie Marmon Silko certainly heard a good deal of Laguna as she was growing up, just as N. Scott Momaday heard a good deal of Jemez, whereas many of the Native American writers raised in the cities did not hear indigenous languages on a very regular basis.) Yet all of them have indicated their strong sense of indebtedness or allegiance to the oral tradition. Even the mixed-blood Anishinaabe—Chippewa—writer Gerald Vizenor, someone who uses quotations from a whole range of contemporary European theorists and whose own texts are full of ironic effects possible only to a text-based literature, has insisted on the centrality of "tribal stories" and storytelling to his writing.[10] This is the position of every other contemporary Native American writer I can think of—all of them insist on the storytelling of the oral tradition as providing a context, as bearing on and influencing the writing of their novels, poems, stories, or autobiographies.

In view of this fact, it needs to be said that "the oral tradition," *as it is invoked by these writers,* is an "invented tradition." It can be seen, as John Tomlinson has remarked, "as a phenomenon of modernity. There is a sense in which simply recognizing a practice as 'traditional' marks it off from the routine practices of proper [*sic*] traditional societies" (91). This is not, of course, to deny that there were and continue to be a number of oral traditions that "really" existed and continue to exist among the indigenous cultures of the Americas. Nor is it to deny that some contemporary Native American writers have considerable experience of "real" forms of oral performance. I am simply noting that "the oral tradition" as usually invoked in these contexts is a kind of catchall phrase whose function is broadly to name the source of the difference between the English of Native writers and that of Euramerican writers. This "tradition" is not based on historically and culturally specific instances.

A quick glance at some of the blurbs on the covers or book jackets of work by contemporary Indian writers makes this readily apparent. When these blurbs are written by non-Indians (and most are, for obvious reasons, written by non-Indians), reference to "the oral tradition" usually represents a loose and vague way of expressing nostalgia for some aboriginal authenticity or wisdom, a golden age of wholeness and harmony. When these blurbs are written by Native Americans—this generalization I venture more tentatively—they are (to recall the discussion I offered in the first chapter of this book) a rhetorical device, a strategic invocation of what David Murray has called the discourse of Indianness, a discourse that has currency in both the economic and the political sense in the United States. Once more, to say this is in no way to deny that the narrative modalities and practices of a range of Native oral literatures, as well as the worldviews of various Native cultures, *are* important to many of the texts constituting a contemporary Native American literature, and not merely honorifically, sentimentally, or rhetorically.

Anyone who would make the claim that a particular Native text in English should be read as an instance of cultural translation must offer a specific demonstration of how that text incorporates alternate strategies, indigenous perspectives, or language usages that, literally or figuratively, make its "English" on the page a translation in which traces of the "foreign tongue," the "Indian," can be discerned. If one then wants to claim that this translation is indeed an anti-imperial translation, it becomes necessary to show how those traces operate in tension with or in a manner resistant to an English in the interest of colonialism.[11]

In the rest of this essay, I will try to show how Leslie Marmon Silko's novel *Almanac of the Dead* (1991) is a powerful work of anti-imperial translation. Consistent with the methodology I have outlined, I must first point to a dimension of the novel that derives more nearly from an "Indian" than a Euramerican "language." I must then show that the ideological work this "Indian language" figuratively performs is one of resistance to imperialism.

Before doing so, as a context in which to place *Almanac,* I want to open up the question of the ideological work performed by contemporary Native American fiction in general over the past twenty-five years or so, a period that overlaps at least the more recent "postcolonial" period in the rest of the world.

I will be going rather far afield for a theoretical framework to analyze the ideological work of some contemporary Native American novels to Africa and to Kwame Anthony Appiah's account of the postcolonial African novel. I find Appiah's account highly suggestive for the topic of my concern.

Appiah describes the postcolonial African novel as falling into two fairly distinct stages; however, I will place contemporary Native American novels along a continuum—an adjustment I think Appiah would accept. In its first stage, according to Appiah, postcolonial fiction in Africa conceives of itself as specifically "anticolonial and nationalist." These novels of the late 1950s and early 1960s are "theorized as the imaginative re-creation of a common cultural past that is crafted into a shared tradition by the writer. . . . The novels of this first stage are thus realist legitimations of nationalism: they authorize a 'return to traditions' " (149–50). The authors of these novels, trained in Europe and America for the most part, are dependent on the African university, "an institution whose intellectual life is overwhelmingly constituted as Western, and also upon the Euro-American publisher and reader" (149). "In the West," Appiah notes, these authors are known "through the Africa they offer," whereas "their compatriots know them both through the West they present to Africa and through an Africa they have invented for the world, for each other, and for Africa" (149). In Africa, Appiah contends, "from the later sixties on, these celebratory novels of the first stage become rarer" (150), and a much more critical, "postrealist" or apparently postmodernist novel, the sort of novel exemplified by Yambo Ouologuem's *Le Devoir de violence* (1968)—in English, *Bound to Violence* (1968)—began to be produced.

Le Devoir de violence begins with what Appiah calls "a sick joke at the unwary reader's expense against nativism," and Ouologuem's "postnativist" novel continues on to provide "a murderous antidote to a nostalgia for Roots" (151). Novels of this second stage, "far from being a celebration of the nation, are novels of delegitimation:

rejecting the Western *imperium* it is true, but also rejecting the nationalist project of the postcolonial national bourgeoisie" (152). I am not competent to judge the accuracy of this very general account of the postcolonial African novel of the past thirty years or so, or of the particular reading it offers of Ouologuem. But let us see what happens when we bring only this much to the Native American novel of roughly the same period.

The so-called Native American Renaissance, as we noted at the outset of this book, is supposed to have begun with N. Scott Momaday's 1969 Pulitzer Prize for his novel *House Made of Dawn* (1968). It is surely the case that this novel establishes if not a specifically postcolonial stage, at least a self-consciously *new* stage of Native American fiction.[12] Momaday's novel and Silko's *Ceremony* (published in 1977 and in many ways indebted to Momaday's book) seem to work in much the same way as did the first stage of postcolonial African fiction as described by Appiah.

House Made of Dawn opens with its protagonist, Abel, a troubled mixed-blood veteran of World War II, running at dawn, "alone and . . . hard at first, heavily, but then easily and well," in a gray and rainy valley, where "snow lay out upon the dunes" (7). So too does Abel run, once more at dawn, at the novel's conclusion, only now he runs "on the rise of the song, House made of pollen, house made of dawn. Qtsedaba" (191). The final word is from the oral storytelling tradition at Jemez Pueblo, or Wala-towa, where Momaday spent much of his early life, and it echoes "Dypaloh," the first word of the novel and the traditional marker of the onset of Jemez oral storytelling. The phrase "House made of pollen, house made of dawn" is from the Navajo "night chant" and it precedes the final words of the chant proper—"In beauty it is fin-ished"—in which is indicated the completion of the healing or cure that is the primary purpose of the ceremony. Abel has learned these words from an urban Navajo named Benally who has "sung" over him. Short of a further discussion of this rich and com-plex text,[13] let it suffice to say that *House Made of Dawn* appears to "authorize" at least the attempt to "return to tradition," legitimating a tribalism, nationalism (the two are largely synonymous in the Native American context although in opposition to one another in the African context), or conception of "Indianness" that it invents or con-structs in more or less realist fashion "for the world" and also for Native Americans. Like the producers of Appiah's first-stage postcolonial African novel, Momaday has also been dependent on the American university (his much-noted Stanford doctorate with Yvor Winters, for example) and the metropolitan publisher (his book appeared under the imprint of Harper and Row)—and to remark this, I hope it will be clear, in no way denigrates Momaday's very substantial achievement.

Silko's *Ceremony* also appeared through a major eastern trade house, Viking, and Silko's early work was also supported academically.[14] Silko's protagonist, Tayo, is also a mixed-blood World War II veteran severely in need of healing. The novel chronicles Tayo's adventures in which he successfully lives out the vision "seen" for him by a somewhat odd but decidedly powerful Navajo shaman named Betonie. (Betonie's similarities to and differences from Momaday's Benally have been much discussed.)[15] Tayo successfully concludes his "quest" with a return to his people.[16] He is "cured, and the novel ends with a quasi-ceremonial invocation: "Sunrise, / accept this offering, /

Sunrise" (275). The commitment to a "common cultural past," a "shared tradition," and a "return to traditions" is thus worked out in a structure that is circular and reintegrative, a comic structure, relative to a "real" world. Indeed, it is the ideologically functional point of the novel to insist that certain persons (e.g., Ts'eh Montano and her husband, The Hunter) and events (e.g., the appearance of the mountain lion) that might seem to be "mythic" are not mythic but "real." You can go home again, Silko's novel insists, for the traditional world of the Pueblos is available still.

If *House Made of Dawn* and *Ceremony* may thus be said to demonstrate a very distinct "nostalgia for Roots," in Appiah's phrase, it seems to me that this nostalgia is fully expressed in Momaday's long-awaited second novel, *The Ancient Child* (1989), in which a middle-aged painter named Locke Setman, or Set, with the help of a rather embarrassingly fantasized nineteen-year-old woman called Grey, not only leaves his life in the American metropolis but finds that his "true" or "authentic" identity was always-already given in his name, Set, which means "Bear" in Kiowa. Set increasingly "becomes" or discovers the bear in himself, learning that he is a type of "the ancient child," the central figure in a Kiowa story about a boy who became a bear. The novel reaches its climactic moment in the light of a full moon as Set, "an awful quiet . . . in his heart," sees "the image of a great bear, rearing. . . . It was the vision he had sought" (312). Here too, an ideology of legitimation is expressed in an esthetic "eternal return" consistent with the epigraph Momaday has chosen from Jorge Luis Borges (it might also, of course, have come from Northrop Frye): "myth is at the beginning of literature, and also at its end."

For all of this, it is still the case that even *The Ancient Child*'s commitment to the identities of myth cannot entirely ignore the differences of history. If in little else, at least in Grey's (rather trying) fascination with the legend of Billy the Kid and her citations of Shakespeare, James Joyce, Lewis Carroll, and Wallace Stevens, Momaday makes clear his awareness that even a young woman who is finding her identity as a traditional medicine person can do so only in relation to the present-day world and its most notable authors. Momaday had, of course, earlier indicated such an awareness in his portrayal of Benally, deeply attached to Navajo traditionalism yet very much subject to the influences, usually deleterious, of the Euramerican world. And in *Ceremony,* Silko presents Betonie too as someone fully cognizant of the fact that changes were necessary to "keep . . . the ceremonies strong" (133), as someone quite clear that the only way for tradition to sustain itself is for it constantly to change. For all of that, in the three novels I have so inadequately discussed, it does seem to be the case that, like the postcolonial African novels of Appiah's first stage, what is offered "is the imaginative re-creation of a common cultural past that is crafted into a shared tradition by the writer" (Appiah 149–50), an ideological image of Indianness for Native Americans and for the rest of the world. These novels present themselves in an essentially realist mode of representation (as I have said, to insist on the "reality" of the "mythic" is part of the ideological function of these novels) and in more or less comic, reintegrative structures.

Here the complicating instance of James Welch's work must be taken into account. In what follows, I do not claim to offer full readings of the texts I discuss but only to speculate on their ideological work in relation to the issues raised by Appiah. Welch's first novel, *Winter in the Blood,* appeared in 1974, after *House Made of Dawn,* therefore, and before *Ceremony,* and was published by Harper and Row (his subsequent novels have all been with New York trade presses: Harper, Viking, and Norton). His second novel, *The Death of Jim Loney* (1979), followed close on the publication of *Ceremony.* Although Louis Owens has titled his fine chapter on Welch "James Welch's Acts of Recovery" and has written of *Winter in the Blood* as achieving for its unnamed protagonist "a renewed sense of identity as Indian, as specifically Blackfoot" (*Other Destinies* 131), I read that novel as a bit more tentative in its conclusion—and indeed Owens himself later admitted, "The ending isn't exactly happy" (*Other Destinies* 146). And about *The Death of Jim Loney,* Owens quotes Welch himself—"The guy is going to kill himself. No, that's not funny" (*Other Destinies* 145).

Set, Tayo, and somewhat more tentatively, Abel resolve their problems by accepting an "Indian" identity of one sort or another. But this resolution is impossible for Jim Loney. Early in the novel, in response to his lover's rather silly exclamation—"You're so lucky to have two sets of ancestors . . . you can be Indian one day and white the next"—Loney thinks: "It would be nice to think that, but it would be nicer to be one or the other all the time . . . Indian or white. Whichever, it would be nicer than being a half-breed" (14). Later, the narrator, noting that Loney "never felt Indian," has him recall his lover's remark—"She had said he was lucky to have two sets of ancestors"—only to conclude, "In truth he had none" (102). Loney dies violently and alone.

Thus, ideologically, Welch's early fiction seems to fall somewhere between Appiah's first and second stages (hence my preference, at the outset, for conceptualizing these matters along a continuum). It is largely "postnativist"—postnationalist or posttribalist—yet mostly realist (even though *Winter in the Blood* certainly contains scenes that have, not inaccurately, been considered surreal). Nor does it have the sort of corrosive quality that marks Ouologuem's novel or, as we shall see, Leslie Silko's *Almanac of the Dead.* Welch's third novel, *Fools Crow* (1986), explores the Blackfoot past, which it treats as past. To say this puts me once more at a slight tangent to Louis Owens, who wrote of *Fools Crow,* "By imagining, or remembering, the traditional Blackfoot world, Welch attempts to recover the center—to revitalize the 'myths of identity and authenticity'—and thus reclaim the possibility of a coherent identity for himself and all contemporary Blackfoot people, that which was denied Jim Loney" (*Other Destinies* 157). If this is indeed the case, then Welch, by 1986, would have come to a position not far distant from that of Momaday or the Silko of *Ceremony,* authorizing at least a reclamation of, if not a return to, tradition. As I see it, however, Welch, in *Fools Crow,* presents the Blackfoot past as indeed past; the question, then, is whether (and *how*) this past might be a "usable past." Should this be the case, then Welch in some measure has departed from Momaday and the early Silko, coming nearer to those recent novels by Native American authors to which I will presently attend.

My argument thus far is that for all Momaday's and Silko's recognition of the need for tradition to change, in *House Made of Dawn, Ceremony,* and *The Ancient Child* these writers nonetheless insist on the possibility of a recuperation of the traditional—where, to be sure, the exact nature of the "traditional" remains to be specified. Nonetheless, to live in a "traditional" manner, within an organic "Indian" community, is presented as a tentative possibility for Abel and as an imminent reality for Tayo and Set. This is not the case, as I have said, for the protagonists in the first two novels of James Welch.

Neither able to "return to tradition" like Tayo and Set nor wholly cut off from it like Jim Loney—perhaps, then, somewhere between the Native American equivalent of Appiah's first- and second-stage postcolonial novel—are the protagonists in some recent fiction by Louis Owens, W. S. Penn, Diane Glancy, and Betty Louise Bell. Before proceeding, however, perhaps I should again say, as clearly as possible, what I am and am not attempting to do. I am *not* attempting to offer even a partial "survey" of contemporary Native American fiction; to do that would require attention to work by Sherman Alexie, A. L. Carr, Gordon Henry, Adrian Louis, Susan Power, and of course, Michael Dorris and Louise Erdrich, among many others. And I am *not* attempting to establish a canon of contemporary Native American writers, implying that the writers I choose to discuss are somehow the "best." Obviously I think these are very good writers, but their particular interest to me here concerns their relation to varieties of postcolonial ideological work. Demonstrating that relation is what I *am* attempting to do.

In Louis Owens's *The Sharpest Sight* (1992) we have the portrayal of two traditional Choctaw elders, Luther Cole and Onatima, or Old Lady Blue Wood. These two, although they have powers that can shift the compass and change the weather, are nonetheless sophisticated citizens of the modem world; they are college graduates given to meditating on the stories of *Moby-Dick* and *Huckleberry Finn* and to critiquing published histories of their Choctaw people. They offer a sense of "home" to Cole McCurtain, Luther's nephew, and to Cole's father, Hoey. Indeed, the last words of the novel state, "In four days they were at the river, where an old man and old woman were waiting to take them home" (263). But the "home" these elders can offer does not seem to include the promise of reintegration into the sort of traditional community that Silko imagined for Tayo. Owens's meditation on tradition, moreover, is very much a meditation on traditions, inasmuch as the novel concerns not only the relation between Cole and his powerful uncle but also the relation between Mundo Morales, a Mexican American, and his grandfather—who, having died sometime before the story takes place, appears only as a ghost. Near the end of the novel; the grandfather says: "My grandson has become more comfortable with the dead. . . . He knows at last who he is" (262). This suggests that Mundo has also, in some manner, come "home," but I think we will have to look to Owens's further work for a fuller sense of just where and what "home" is.

In Owens's novel, *Bone Game* (1994), Cole McCurtain once more appears, and he is a professor at Santa Cruz, a social location and an identity quite unimaginable, I think, for Tayo or Abel and just exactly the sort of worldly placement that Set abandoned. To help Professor McCurtain through a very difficult time, Luther, Onatima, and Hoey all show up in Santa Cruz, where Cole's daughter, Abby, also has come. At the novel's end, Onatima and Luther return home to Mississippi, where they will talk to the bones of their Choctaw people and "tell them of their granddaughter in these strange, lightning-struck mountains" (242). Hoey by this time "has also found his world there," in Mississippi, and as Onatima says, "When the time comes he will surpass all of us" (242). (And he will surely be the subject of another further novel!)

But for Cole, "home" just now is New Mexico and the house where he and his ex-wife were once happy, where they raised their daughter and where Cole wrote his books. He will take back to New Mexico a reinforced sense of the power of the Choctaw part of his background, but there is no question of a return to traditional community.

W. S. Penn's novel *The Absence of Angels* (1994) offers another portrait of a traditional yet entirely modern person, the narrator's grandfather, whose significant appearances at the beginning and end of the narrative provide a circular frame for the novel. Grandfather appears on the first page of the book, having just made the trip from Chosposi Mesa to Los Angeles—a fifteen-hour drive that "concentration" permitted him to make in eleven hours (in a 1947 Plymouth!). He has come to the hospital where Death hovers at the bedside of his newborn grandson, the sickly Albert Hummingbird, or Alley, the narrator and protagonist of the novel. Grandfather takes Death by the wrist, puts him in the passenger seat of the Plymouth, and drives him away—and Alley lives.

Grandfather not only drives a car but also pedals a bicycle—this too with great concentration—from which he falls, breaking a hip. Death, which had formerly and again recently stalked Alley, now appears at Grandfather's bedside, and the novel, like so many Native American novels, comes full circle in its last scene. Now it is Alley who visits his dying grandfather in the hospital. But Alley knows he cannot, indeed should not, try to drive death away, and Grandfather dies at exactly 10:21 PM on Christmas Eve, an hour and thirty-nine minutes short of the time he had predicted for his passing. Alley, with his lover, Sara Baites, scatters Grandfather's ashes across the desert, thinking about death and life and love and, finally, the life-sustaining value of laughter. Here too, although the power of a traditional person is celebrated, there still can be no return to tradition or to the consolations of "myth."

In Diane Glancy's 1993 collection of stories, *Firesticks,* six of the nineteen stories, each of which is called "Firesticks," form a linked series. *Firesticks* explores the relationship between a forty-two-year-old, part-Cherokee diner waitress named Turle Heppner and a drifter, a "dude" slightly younger than she (but also one-eighth Cherokee, "about a toe's worth" [28], maybe) known only as Navorn. When we meet them, Turle's father, William Bear Hall, is ill and dying, and Navorn agrees to drive Turle to see him in Frederick, Oklahoma, about three hours southwest of Guthrie, where Turle lives and works. Turle's father survives until the penultimate section of the series, when a call comes in to the diner telling Turle of his death.

In the meantime, Turle and Navorn have become lovers and then separated, although Turle now persuades Navorn one more time to drive her to Frederick to make funeral arrangements. Turle's father had asked to be buried on Mount Scott, in the Wichita Mountain range, "state property [and] solid granite" (55), as Turle notes in an explanation of why she has told her father that she could not accede to his wish. Turle says that when she looks at her father, she sees her grandmother's face. "He reminds me of the way she used to look. The few times I saw her" (38). Turle and her grandmother never spoke; "she didn't say anything" (40). Nonetheless, Turle explains: "She still speaks to me in a voice I can hear. It's as though what she had to say to me passed between us without speaking" (40). This silent communication is troubling to Turle, who has been "struggling for a language that would separate us. If I could have heard her, we would have parted like the people after Babel. I might not have liked, nor understood what she said. I would have had a chance to reject it. But we are together in our one language of silence. If she could speak, we could have separated" (40). Even though her mother raised her, Turle, as noted above, sees her grandmother in her father's face, and "it's his family [she] feels on windy days when the dust is up." She adds, "In the red sumac groves I see the circle of their council fires" (41).

These "fires" are not literally those of her father's family, or not recently at any rate; the pronoun "their" seems to extend to people much further back, in a time when Cherokee council fires were struck by "firesticks." Among several visions and "memories" of things she cannot account for as part of her own historical experience, there is Turle's "dream," opening the final section of *Firesticks*, of "the burning firesticks the men used to carry from the holy Keetowah fire to light the smaller fires in the cabins." Turle notes: "It had been a yearly celebration. Light out of darkness. New life from the ashes. I dreamed of the firesticks passed from generation to generation. But now we had lost our ceremonies" (125). Yet Turle comes to understand that words are not only for separation and ending but also for joining and continuation. "Maybe," she says, "words are not always separators. If I speak fight I have light. My words are firesticks" (126).

Navorn drives her to Mount Scott, "Holy ground" (129), as her father had called it, where Turle will bury his pipe and belt buckle. After doing so

> she felt all people again. Those who lived long lives on the prairie, and those who knew extinction of their way of life. . . .
>
> The boulders on Mount Scott kept those faces before [her], frozen in fear and hopelessness. A band of Indians, massacred, their blood mingled with the red Oklahoma soil (130).

Turle discovers that even if the ceremonies have been lost, there was a place to go after all. "The Spirit World kept all things that left. In my vision, the prairie moved again with herds of buffalo and antelope and Indian tribes. My father rode with them, their land restored" (131). *Firesticks* works to an ending in which Turle prays: "Comfort us, Great Spirit. And William Bear Hall, my other father, I'm sorry I did not bury you on Mount Scott like you asked" (131–32). In response, she hears, " 'Forgive me.' The answer was his this time" (132). The story concludes: "I see our words are firesticks finding a way through the dark. Strange warriors. In dreams I hear your talk" (132). The placement of "Strange warriors" as a free-standing fragment is curious. Had there been a comma rather than a period after "dark," "warriors" would have referred to words-as-firesticks. But that is not what the text gives us. Who, then, are these warriors? No doubt they are the Cherokees of old—word-warriors (to use a phrase that has been associated with Gerald Vizenor), carriers of the firesticks of the old council fires. In some measure memories, most particularly dreams and visions, bring them back.[17] But to "have" them, to make them "real" and make them stay, requires words: "our words are firesticks" (132).

Those last words are Turle's words, and words for her are spoken (or unspoken), heard, remembered, and dreamed. But they are not written; Glancy is the writer of words, and *Firesticks* may certainly be taken in part as an affirmation of the author's sense of her vocation. As Silko does in *Storyteller,* Glancy in *Firesticks* presents herself, by implication, as one who writes words "for the people." Turle Heppner can be heard because Glancy gives her the words—words like those of Turle's earlier vision in which she saw "antelope running and . . . saw buffalo, herds and herds of buffalo, as they once had been on the prairie . . . . just as someone someday might get a vision of what our lives had been. They came back not to haunt nor accuse but to remind that they once had been, *and still moved with the swirling winds on the plains and the clouds across the sky*" (93, my emphasis). Turle will go back to work in the diner in Guthrie; she and Navorn will or will not stay together. Outwardly at least, her life will probably not look so very different from the lives of the non-Native inhabitants of her hometown. But the story has made clear that for her, what "once had been" "still moved." The ceremonies are gone, and one cannot reconstitute and live the traditional past. But that past has a presence as well, one that may have powerful consequences.

Like Owens's fiction, Betty Louise Bell's 1994 novel, *Faces in the Moon*, offers a traditionalist couple, and like Glancy's fiction, it shows a move to memory and language as important in the maintenance of tradition. Here, Great-aunt Lizzie and Uncle Jerry are people who provide a center and give a sense of "home" to Lucie, the child the narrator once was. But there is no nostalgia here for "roots." Lucie will not return to the old ways or go "home" again with any prospect of permanence. So far as the novel offers, in Appiah's words again, "a common cultural past . . . a shared tradition," it is a tradition that cannot be discovered in a "return" of any kind but rather remains to be (re-)produced—as with Glancy—in language. But Lucie is not Turle Heppner; she not only will speak but also will become, as she announces on the penultimate page of the novel, the arrogant whiteman's "worst nightmare: . . . an Indian with a pen" (192), more specifically, an Indian *woman* with a pen.

Bell's novel begins powerfully with the following words: "I was raised on the voices of women. Indian women." These voices are sited at "the kitchen table . . . a place of remembering, a place where women came and drew their lives from each other" (4). The novel ends with "the advice" the narrator says was "passed on to [her] by the old people" (193). And what is this "traditional" wisdom passed on by the old ones? It is: "Don't mess with Indian women. . . . That's all. You don't need to know more than that." These words, spoken by the narrator, are echoed by the ghostly voices of other women: " 'Don't mess with Indian women,' the voices whoop" (193). There is imagined here not so much a return to tradition and community as, instead, the necessity of writing, of producing tradition and community, specifically the community of Indian women who today may draw their lives from each other not only at the kitchen table but in a wider world beyond.

Bell's novel—like the work of Owens, of Penn, of Welch, and of Glancy and even like the Native American novels paralleling Appiah's first-stage postcolonial African novel—is written in a sophisticated mode of realism (i.e., a realism *after* modernism). Its form—in this it is like some but unlike others of the novels I have mentioned— contrapuntally plays a circular structure of return (back to the old ones, to kitchen-table talk) against a linear structure of "progress" (forward to self-discovery and writing). The book is a female *kunstlerroman*—a portrait of the artist as a young woman— charting the narrator's progress as an outward (in William Bevis's terms, a centrifugal)[18] movement into the world. But this movement outward depends on a centripetal structure of return, one that, as I have said, takes place in memory or imagination.

Let's return to the final scene of *Faces in the Moon*, which I have only partly described above. It is set in the Oklahoma Historical Society, where Lucie has come to "look at the Cherokee rolls" (190) and fill in the lacunae of her past. Here is an image of the Foucauldian archive, constitutive of what may be known, thought, or spoken or of Virginia Woolf's library of the British Museum, where women exist only insofar as men have pronounced on them. It is in response to "the librarian's" contemptuous grin and his question "Who do you think you are?" (191) that Lucie allows her anger to erupt and then to voice the tough-minded wisdom of the old ones. But her cry, "Don't mess with Indian women," even as it is echoed by ghostly voices, does not conclude the novel. Rather, the book ends with a sentence that on first reading I thought anticlimactic but that I now see as necessary. After the "whoop" of the voices repeating the refrain "Don't mess with Indian women," the narrator says, "And I hear Auney say, slow and pleased, 'Naw, I sure wouldn't wanna do that' " (193).

Lucie's Aunt Auney, her "mother's chorus since birth" (10) and the survivor of four marriages with difficult men, appeared on the first pages of the novel as an image of a strong woman; yet "the closest she came to fighting back was to refuse to forget" (11). Nor will Lucie forget, but she will also most definitely fight back, with her voice and her pen. So again there is a movement out, of "progress" or advance, but as well a movement back, a return in memory to the kitchen table as home. But this return will not ideologically authorize anything like the presumed satisfaction, unity, or plenitude of a precolonial past.

Here I will return at last to Leslie Marmon Silko's *Almanac of the Dead* (1991), a book that is very different from *Ceremony* and that has distinct affinities with Appiah's second-stage postcolonial African novel. In *Almanac* there is no pueblo to which one may return, no kiva in which one may feel related to the gods, the ancestors, and the earth. It is almost as if Silko had taken the celebrated advice given to Marlow in Joseph Conrad's *Lord Jim:* "In the destructive element immerse." For this novel, unlike *Ceremony,* is not set in the mid-1940s but in the horrific present, where drug deals, the pornography of torture, traffic in weapons and body parts, and elaborate and cynical real estate scams define the Western "culture of death" in the Americas.[19] I will try to describe a single strategy of this novel that seems to me to come, figuratively speaking, from a "language" other than "English," a strategy that is deployed in decidedly anticolonial fashion, so that *Almanac,* in the ways I have indicated above, may be read as an example of anti-imperial "translation."

Almanac devotes 763 pages to illustrating the statements Silko has placed in two boxes in the lower left-hand and lower right-hand corners of an annotated "Five Hundred Year Map" of northern Mexico and the southwestern United States; the map is printed just after the table of contents (of the paperback edition). The left-hand box, labeled the "Prophecy" reads: "When Europeans arrived [in the Americas], the Maya, Azteca, and Inca cultures had already built great cities and vast networks of roads. Ancient prophecies foretold the arrival of Europeans in the Americas. The ancient prophecies also foretell the disappearance of all things European." The right-hand box, called "The Indian Connection," states: "Sixty million Native Americans died between

1500 and 1600. The defiance and resistance to things European continue unabated. The Indian Wars have never ended in the Americas. Native Americans acknowledge no borders; they seek nothing less than the return of all tribal lands."

Almanac imagines a contemporary continuation of "The Indian Wars," telling of the movement of apocalyptic armies from north to south and from south to north to rid the Americas of "all"—or at least a great many—"things European." Not all of Silko's Indian warriors are of Native American ancestry, and her cultural politics is not racialized. Thus, from the north, New Age pop spiritualists, guerrilla eco-warriors, homeless Vietnam War veterans, Lakota militants, a barefoot Hopi, and a Korean-American computer genius, among others based in the United States, begin a march southward, while a "People's Army" of Indians from Central America, led by nonviolent twin brothers and a Mayan woman who believes in handheld missile launchers and rockets, marches northward through Mexico. Both groups will eventually converge on Tucson, the eccentric center of the story, and the meeting of these two forces, still to come at the novel's end, will signal the beginning of the end of the dominance in the Americas of the settler culture.

The specific strategy of resistance I want to describe in *Almanac of the Dead* is its insistence on a north-south/south-north directionality as central to the narrative of "our America" (in the phrase of Fernández Rétamar).[20] This shift in the directionality of history in itself works as an ideological subversion of the hegemonic Euramerican narrative, whose geographical imperative presumes an irresistible ("destined") movement from east to West.

As Roy Harvey Pearce claimed more than forty years ago, "The history of American civilization would . . . be conceived of as three-dimensional, progressing from past to present, from east to west, from lower to higher" (49). The image of east-west movement, like other "images of centrality" in Edward Said's phrase, gives "rise to semi-official narratives with the capacity to authorize and embody certain sequences of cause and effect, while at the same time preventing the emergence of counternarratives" (58). East-west images found a "semi-official" narrative of American progress, of the fulfillment of a "manifest destiny," that will take this nation "from sea to shining sea." But "facing west," as Richard Drinnon's powerful study of that name shows, also founds "The Metaphysics of Indian-Hating and Empire-Building." Perhaps I can best convey the depth and persistence of east-west images in the construction of American imperial dominance by citing the words of that great empire builder (and Nobel Peace Prize winner!) Henry Kissinger, who, sometime in the 1980s, said: "You come here speaking of Latin America, but this is not important. Nothing important can come from the South. . . . The axis of history starts in Moscow, goes to Bonn, crosses over to Washington, and then goes to Tokyo. What happens in the South is of no importance" (in Clausen 634). In the hegemonic narrative of the dominant culture, the movement of history is always from east to west, and that movement can neither be reversed (to go from west to east would be the same as going from higher to lower, from civilized to savage, something unthinkable) nor be adjusted to accommodate the south, where, as Kissinger insists, "what happens . . . is of no importance."[21]

It may not be fortuitous that the North-South distinction has gradually taken over from the earlier division of the globe into three worlds, unless we remember that the references of North and South are not merely to concrete geographic locations but are also metaphorical. North connotes the pathways of transnational capital, and South, the marginalized populations of the world, regardless of their location (351).

But it is exactly this inexorable east-west narrative that Silko contests. Insisting that history happens north to south, south to north, she shifts the axis of *where is* important, thus shifting the axis of what is important. The novel concludes with the return to Laguna Pueblo (where Silko grew up) of a "giant stone snake" that had disappeared. The novel's last sentence reads, "The snake was looking south, in the direction from which the twin brothers and the people would come" (763). This "looking south" rather than "facing west" is not only a change of geographical perspective but also a metaphor for a change of cultural and political value. In terms elaborated by Gerald Vizenor, Euramerican "dominance" is, here, challenged by Native American "survivance," the former committed to progress, the latter to "continuance."[22]

Silko's "armies," as I have said, are composed of a ragtag collection of people—African American, Asian American, Euramerican, Native American. Will these poor inherit the earth? If the novel has gone well, we should hope so, whoever we are, and identify with *them.* To say this permits me a return to Yambo Ouologuem's novel *Le Devoir de violence,* in regard to which Appiah wrote, "If we are to identify with anyone, *in fine,* it is with 'la négraille'—the niggertrash, who have no nationality" (152). As Appiah reads Ouologuem, however, this potential identification with "la négraille" is not a happy one. For them, for those "who have no nationality," "one republic," Appiah states, "is as good—which is to say as bad—as any other." In this stage of the African novel, postcoloniality has become . . . a condition of pessimism," "a kind of *post*optimism" (155). Yet Ouologuem's postrealist" "delegitimation" of "nationality" and of "the postcolonial national bourgeoisie" is not strictly consistent with the "postmodernist" project according to Appiah, because it is "grounded in an appeal to an ethical universal . . . a certain simple respect for human suffering" (155). This "ethical universal" Appiah unashamedly names "humanism," noting the way in which this makes the apparently postmodernist, postcolonial African novel "not an ally for Western postmodernism but an agonist from which . . . [Western] postmodernism may have something to learn" (155). I would say much the same for the apparently postmodernist Native American novel.[23] For it too, as Appiah wrote, what "role postmodernism might play . . . is . . . too early to tell" (157).

The choice to respect human suffering and to reject nationalism is, as Appiah reads Ouologuem, a choice of "Africa—the continent and its people" (152), and we may take this observation back to Silko's text. *Almanac,* like the postcolonialist African fiction of Appiah's second stage, is certainly an instance of "postrealist writing," offering a "postnativist politics . . . [and] a transnational rather than a national solidarity" (155), but it is not, for all the grimness of its detail, pessimistic.

Let me take these two matters one at a time. First, my sense of *Almanac'*s commitment to "a transnational rather than a national solidarity" once more puts me at odds with Elizabeth Cook-Lynn, who claims that the book "insists upon the nationalist's approach to historical events" in its creation of "a Panindian journey toward retribution." But Cook-Lynn's very next sentence admits: "[*Almanac*] fails in this nationalistic trend since it does not take into account the specific kind of tribal/nation status of the original inhabitants of this continent. There is no apparatus for the tribally specific treaty-status paradigm to be realized either in the Silko fiction or in the Pan-Indian approach to history" ("Cosmopolitanism, Nationalism" 34). But surely this is to recognize that *Almanac* is not so much failing in its nationalist approach as simply not taking such an approach at all. *Almanac* not only is committed to Pan-Indianism rather than tribal specificity—as Cook-Lynn herself realizes—but also is committed to a kind of Pan-Americanism, in which all those who adhere to tribal values of life and healing may join, regardless of blood quanta or enrollment cards.

As for *Almanac*'s "optimism," perhaps this may derive from the fact that Silko, like other contemporary Native American writers, lives in a postcolonial world but writes, as I have said, from within a colonial context. Materially, that is, sociopolitically, things are not good, but there is everything yet to be done to rid the Americas of bad European things and values. Of course the world of drug deals, body parts sales, and violent pornography that Silko describes is horrible to contemplate, but it is premature for "postoptimism." What Cook-Lynn called "retribution" Annette Jaimes refers to as the dispensation of "a long overdue measure of justice to the haughty current minions of [the] malignant Euroamerican order."[24] This, Jaimes notes, "is what ultimately makes the novel . . . a work of life and liberation rather than death and despair" (57). *Almanac* insists that the prophecies are not to be mocked; the Americas will return to the values of life. These are, to be sure, the old values of indigenous tribal peoples, but they are, today, to be represented by a "transnational" "négraille"; whatever it might mean to speak of a choice of "Africa—the continent and its people," Silko's "armies" are an image of "America—the continent(s) and its people" today: a transnational "tribe" committed to healing, to continuance and survivance.

Notes

*This essay was first published as chapter two in *The Turn to the Native: Studies in Criticism and Culture* (Nebraska UP, 1996). We thank University of Nebraska Press for permission to reprint.

1. Alan Velie has pointed out to me that these statistics should not lead to the general conclusion that all Native Americans are "victims enmeshed in the culture of poverty." In Oklahoma, for example, there are a great many oil-rich Natives; in Connecticut, the Mashantucket Pequots number among the super-rich. For a discussion of the concept of "sovereignty," see chapter one of my *The Turn to the Native*.

2. I again refer the reader to Cook-Lynn, "Cosmopolitanism, Nationalism," for a discussion of these matters from a 'nationalist' perspective.

3. Cf. my "Native American Literature and the Canon" in *The Voice in the Margin* 96–131; and my essay 'On the Translation of Native American Literature—A Theorized History," in Swann. See also Cheyfitz, *Poetics,* in these regards and Murray, *Forked Tongues,* in particular chapter 1, "Translation," and chapter 2, "Languages."

4. For a recent overview, with particular attention to Iroquois and Navajo examples, see Zolbrod's *Reading the Voice.* My own essay "On the Translation of Native American Literature" offers bibliographical references to most of the efforts at mythography or ethnopoetics.

5. See Krupat, "On the Translation of Native American Literatures," in Swann.

6. See Krupat, *Ethnocriticism,* 196–99, 237.

7. A somewhat different version of this paper was presented by Asad and John Dixon in July 1994 at the University of Essex's "Sociology of Literature" conference. This version appears as "Translating Europe's Others," in volume I of the proceedings of the conference, *Europe and Its Others.*

8. In this regard, see John Tomlinson's discussion (in *Cultural Imperialism*) of the linguistic imperialism resulting from the fact that even anti-imperial discourse takes place only in a very few languages, English *primes inter pares.*

9. Recall, however, that although an indigenous language was the first spoken language of these artists, English was their first written language.

10. Vizenor tends to claim ironies for the oral tradition as well, but this is a projection backward of present concerns. Primary orality must minimize irony for the simple reason that it is inimical to direct comprehension and ready recall.

11. It needs to be said that the very fact of difference, whether in form or in content, need not always and automatically work in the interest of resistance. See, in this regard, Fredric Jameson's 1988 account of "the social functionality of culture" (195–96), in which he notes that in spite of the fact that modernist and postmodernist art were both equivalently perceived as obnoxious, the former does in fact function in a manner that is oppositional to the cultural dominant, whereas the second has itself become the cultural dominant.

12. The interesting fiction of earlier Native American writers—writers like John Joseph Matthews, Pauline Johnson, John Milton Oskison, and D'Arcy McNickle, for example—has only recently begun to receive careful critical attention, and it remains to be seen whether a case can be made for considering *them* as the first generation of "postcolonial" or, indeed, anticolonial Native writers. For the present, however, there are good reasons to begin with Momaday.

13. Momaday's work has probably received more critical attention than that of any other Native American writer. Matthias Schubnell's book-length overview of Momaday's work is more hagiography than critical study, and a book-length study of *House Made of Dawn* has been published by Susan Scarberry-Garcia. Louis Owens's chapter on Momaday in *Other Destinies* offers what I believe is the best overall account available. A. Lavonne Brown Ruoff's volume for the MLA gives most of the important references through 1990.

14. Silko was a student of Tony Hillerman's at the University of New Mexico and for eighteen months was a correspondent of the poet and teacher James Wright, whom she met at a writers' conference. For this latter association, see Silko and Wright, The *Delicacy and Strength of Lace.*

15. Ruoff is once more useful for references to the major criticism of Silko. See also the recent volume edited by Melody Graulich, "Yellow Woman."

16. My reference here is to Shamoon Zamir's extraordinary essay "Literature in a 'National Sacrifice Area': Leslie Silko's *Ceremony.*"

17. The role of memory in all of the novels I have discussed so far, and in Betty Louise Bell's *Faces in the Moon,* which I discuss below, is important. Rather than attempt to examine memory as some sort of unique and autonomous expression of Native American culture and value "in its own right," we might find a more fruitful exercise in comparing it with its role, say, in Proust, Woolf, Faulkner, and even Eliot, among other of the canonical modernists. As Franz Boas showed long ago, to assert a "comparative method" as a measurement of *value* (e.g., higher or more "civilized" compared with lower and more "primitive") is to produce inaccuracies, absurdities, or indeed abominations—just what those Native critics committed to cultural or intellectual "sovereignty" and "autonomy" have tried to circumvent. But there are other sorts of comparison available, and to ignore them is unnecessarily to foreclose possibilities for under-

standing. Because I have been misunderstood on this point before, I need to add explicitly that I am *not* suggesting that one should bring the assumptions one brings to Proust to these novels, but rather that one should see whether one can find a critical language that might mediate between Proust and Native American fiction—yet again, as this chapter takes it up, an issue of cross-cultural translation or ethnocriticism.

18. See Bevis, "Native American Novels."

19. The phrase "the culture of death" comes up frequently in Silko's work, as it does as well in the work of Gerald Vizenor, to which I will turn shortly. In his encyclical letter of March 30. 1995, titled *Evangelium Vitae*, or *Gospel of Life*, Pope John Paul II used the term "culture of death" to name a secular humanism that is, in the pope's view, indifferent to "the original inalienable right to life" (*New York Times*, March 31, 1995). Although the pope and certain Native American writers are in agreement in their condemnation of what they variously consider the Western "culture of death," I do not think they would necessarily agree as to what constitutes a life-giving culture.

20. Silko's map does have a single horizontal line indicating the movement of several of the characters eastward, from San Diego to Tucson, and others westward, from El Paso to Tucson. The north-south/south-north directionality seems, however, of central importance.

21. Cf. Dirlik, "The Postcolonial Aura": "It may not be fortuitous that the North-South distinction has gradually taken over from the earlier division of the globe into three worlds, unless we remember that the references of North and South are not merely to concrete geographic locations but are also metaphorical. North connotes the pathways of transnational capital, and South, the marginalized populations of the world, regardless of their location" (351). As we shall see, in similar yet also different ways, Silko's North and South are also both "concrete" and "metaphorical."

22. I'm not sure just where Vizenor first began to develop his concept of "survivance," although most recently it appears fictionally in his *Heirs of Columbus* (1991) and essayistically in his *Manifest Manners* (1994). What is necessary for survivance is healing, something important to Silko.

23. I make the same case in regard to Gerald Vizenor's *Heirs of Columbus* in *The Turn to the Native*, chapter three. I here only repeat that the contemporary Native American novel, although it may perform ideological work that parallels the postcolonial novel in Africa or elsewhere, remains, as a consequence of its sociopolitical situation, a colonial production in a postcolonial world.

24. Justice, for Jaimes, will be dispensed by "the dispossessed/disenfranchised indigenous vanguard swarming northward" ("Review" 57). But there is, as I have noted, a movement southward toward justice and life-giving values as well.

Works Cited

Appiah, K. Anthony. "Race." *Critical Terms for Literary Study*. Ed. Frank Lentricchia and Thomas McGlaughlin. Chicago: U of Chicago P, 1990. 274–87.

————. "Is the Post- In Postmodernism the Post- in Postcolonial?" *Critical Inquiry* 17 (1991): 336–57.

————. *In My Father's House: Africa in the Philosophy of Culture*. New York: Oxford UP, 1992.

Asad, Talal. "The Concept of Cultural Translation in British Social Anthropology." *Writing Culture: The Poetics and Politics of Ethnography*. Ed. James Clifford and George Marcus. Berkeley: U of California P, 1986. 141–64.

Ashcroft, Bill, Gareth Griffiths, Helen Tiffin. *The Empire Writes Back: Theory and Practice in Post-Colonial Literatures*. London: Routledge, 1989.

Bell, Betty Louise. *Faces in the Moon*. U of Oklahoma P, 1994.

Benjamin, Walter. "The Task of the Translator." Ed. Hannah Arendt. *Illuminations*. New York: Schocken Books, 1969.

Bevis, William. "Native American Novels: Homing In." Ed. Brian Swann and Arnold Krupat. *Recovering the World: Essays on Native American Literature*. Berkeley: U of California P, 1987. 580–620.

Cheyfitz, Eric. *The Poetics of Imperialism: Translation and Colonization from "The Tempest" to "Tarzan."* New York: Oxford UP, 1991.

Clausen, Jan. "The Axis of Herstory: Review." *Nation* 258 (May 18, 1994): 634–36.

Cook-Lynn, Elizabeth. "Who Gets to Tell the Stories?" *Wicazo Sa Review* 9 (1993): 60–63.

———. "Cosmopolitanism, Nationalism, the Third World, and Tribal Sovereignty." *Wicazo Sa Review* 9 (1993): 26–36.

Dirlik, Arif. " 'The Postcolonial Aura': Third World Criticism in the Age of Global Capitalism." *Critical Inquiry* 20 (Winter 1994): 328–56.

Drinnon, Richard. *Facing West: The Metaphysics of Indian-Hating and Empire Building*. Minneapolis: U of Minnesota P, 1980.

Glancy, Diane. *Firesticks*. U of Oklahoma P, 1993.

Greenblatt, Stephen. *Marvelous Possessions: The Wonder of the New World*. Chicago: U of Chicago P, 1991.

Graulich, Melody, ed. *"Yellow Woman": Leslie Marmon Silko*. New Brunswick: Rutgers UP, 1993.

Jaimes, M. Annette. "The Disharmonic Convergence: Leslie Silko's *Almanac of the Dead*: Review." *Wicaza Sa Review* 8 (1992): 56–67.

———. *The State of Native America: Genocide, Colonization, and Resistance*. Boston: South End P, 1992.

Jameson, Fredric. *The Ideologies of Theory: Essays, 1971–1986*. Volume Two, *Syntax and History*. Minneapolis: U of Minnesota P, 1988.

Krupat, Arnold. *The Turn to the Native: Studies in Criticism and Culture*. U of Nebraska P, 1996.

———, ed. *New Voices in Native American Literary Criticism*. Washington, DC: Smithsonian Institution P, 1993.

———. *Ethnocriticism: Ethnography, History, Literature*. Berkeley: U of California P, 1992.

———. "On the Translation of Native American Song and Story: A Theorized History." Ed. Brian Swann. *On the Translation of Native American Literatures*. Washington, D.C.: The Smithsonian Institution P, 1992. 3–32.

———. *The Voice in the Margin*. Berkeley: U of California P, 1989.

———. "Poststructuralism and Oral Literature." Ed. Brian Swann and Arnold Krupat. *Recovering the Word: Essays on Native American Literature*. Berkeley: U of California P, 1987. 113–28.

Momaday, N. Scott. *House Made of Dawn*. New York: Harper and Row, 1968.

———. *The Names*. New York: Harper, 1976.

——— *The Ancient Child*. New York: Doubleday, 1989.

Murray, David. *Forked Tongues: Speech, Writing and Representation in North American Indian Texts*. Bloomington: U of Indiana P, 1991.

Ouologuem, Yambo. *Le Devoir de violence*. Paris: Editions du Seuil, 1968. *Bound to Violence*. Trans. Ralph Manheim. New York: Harcourt Brace Jovanovich, 1968.

Owens, Louis. *Other Destinies: Understanding the American Indian Novel*. Norman: U of Oklahoma P, 1992.

———. *The Sharpest Sight*. Norman: U of Oklahoma P, 1992.

———. *Bone Game*. Norman: U of Oklahoma P, 1994.

Pearce, Roy Harvey. *Savagism and Civilization: A Study of the Indian and the American Mind*. 1953; rpt. Berkeley: U of California P, 1988.

Penn, W S. *The Absence of Angels*. Sag Harbor, NY: Permanent P, 1994.

Rétamar, Fernández. "Caliban: Notes toward a Discussion of Culture in Our America," *Massachusetts Review* 15 (1974): 9.

Ruoff, A. LaVonne Brown. *American Indian Literatures: An Introduction, Bibliographic Review, and Selected Bibliography*. New York: Modern Language Association, 1990.

Said, Edward. "Identity, Negation, and Violence." *New Left Review* 171 (1988): 46–60.

Scarberry-Garcia, Susan. *Landmarks of Healing: A Study of "A House Made of Dawn."* Albuquerque: U of New Mexico P, 1990.

Schubnell, Matthias. *N. Scott Momaday: The Cultural and Literary Background*. Norman: U of Oklahoma P, 1985.

Silko, Leslie Marmon. *Storyteller*. New York: Arcade/Little Brown, 1981.

————. *Ceremony*. New York: Viking, 1977.

————. *The Delicacy and Strength of Lace: Letters Between Leslie Marmon Silko and James Wright*. Ed. Anne Wright. St. Paul, MN: Graywolf P, 1986.

————. *Almanac of the Dead*. New York: Simon and Schuster, 1991.

Swann, Brian. "Introduction." *On the Translation of Native American Literatures*. Washington, DC: The Smithsonian Institution Press, 1992.

Tomlinson, John. *Cultural Imperialism: A Critical Introduction*. Baltimore: Johns Hopkins UP, 1991.

Vizenor, Gerald. *Heirs of Columbus*. Hanover, NH: U P of New England/Wesleyan UP, 1991.

————. *Manifest Manners*. Hanover, NH: U P of New England, 1994.

Welch, James. *Winter in the Blood*. New York: Harper and Row, 1974.

————. *The Death of Jim Loney*. 1979; rpt. New York: Penguin, 1987.

————. *Fools Crow*. New York: Viking, 1986.

Zamir, Shamoon. "Literature in a 'National Sacrifice Area': Leslie Silko's *Ceremony*." In Krupat, *New Voices*. 396–418.

Zolbrod, Paul G. *Reading the Voice: Native American Oral Poetry on the Page*. Salt Lake: U of Utah P, 1995.

"WHERE, BY THE WAY, IS THIS TRAIN GOING?"
A Case for Black (Cultural) Studies

Mae G. Henderson

The aim of the contemporary cultural studies investigator is not to generate another good theory, but to give a better theorized account of concrete historical reality.

—Stuart Hall

Black History cannot help but to be politically oriented, for it tends toward the total redefinition of an experience which was highly political. . . . And it recognizes that all histories of peoples participate in politics and are shaped by political and ideological views.

—Vincent Harding

The advent of Black Studies into the academy during the late 1960s and early 1970s represented an irruption of subjugated knowledge that, in a real sense, revolutionized how we look at society, culture, politics, and values. Although the origins of this movement can be traced back at least to the 19th century, the work of scholars, theorists, and artists in the Black Studies and Black Arts movements exposed through practice and precept the racism underlying the mainstream academic project, as well as the ideological assumptions structuring the dominant cultural aesthetic.

The emergence of black cultural studies during the late 1980s and early 1990s continues the Black Studies project in that it takes as its object of investigation the consequences of uneven economic, social, and cultural development. Like Black Studies, cultural studies challenges received and conventional disciplinary paradigms in the construction of knowledge through its multi-disciplinary and cross-cultural focus. And like Black Studies, itself community-based and rooted in community culture, cultural studies has privileged the study of vernacular and mass culture. What I am suggesting here is that many, if not most, of the central concerns of black cultural studies have been anticipated by the Black Studies project and the challenge it brought to the academy two decades ago.

As a recently emergent academic field of study, cultural studies redefines the boundaries delineating traditional disciplinarities. It has shifted, redrawn, and sometimes even dissolved the lines demarcating conventional disciplinary borders by engaging in institutional and ideological analyses. The mode of inquiry in cultural studies entails an examination of material and concrete cultural practices in the context of the conditions of their production and reception. Beyond this rather broad definition of cultural studies are presumptions that attach to its general modes of inquiry, including the interrogation of identity politics and its emphases on the construction of gender, class, race, ethnicity, and nationality as well as the dissolution of boundaries between so-called "high" and "low" cultures as valorized objects of study.

What I wish to address here is the cultural studies project as it relates to the study of African American politics and culture. More specifically, I am concerned with what is currently designated as black cultural studies, and its problematic relation to Black Studies—an area currently subject to critique and assimilation into our contemporary constructions of black cultural studies. Reinforcing the connection between African American Studies and cultural studies, Cornel West poses the crucial place of "race" in this genealogy: "How can the reception of cultural studies in the United States not . . . give [race] a tremendous weight and gravity if we're going to understand the internal dynamics of U.S. culture? . . . It's a different history than the formation of the British Empire. . . . How do we understand the moment of the intervention of Afro-American studies in the academy? Let's read that history next to the intervention of cultural studies in Britain" ("Postmodern Crisis of the Black Intellectuals" 694). In other words, what cultural studies is to British studies, West implies, African American Studies is to the American academy.

As postmodern scholars of African American history and culture, however, we must be cautious in our assessment of the founding days of Black Studies—an intellectual pursuit that was ongoing at the time of its institutionalization in the American academy. Although scholars such as W.E.B. Du Bois and Carter G. Woodson were not working in historically white colleges and universities, their scholarship constitutes a dialogue and critique of hegemonic theoretical and methodological practices, and provides the foundation that has shaped the productions of scholars such as J. Saunders Redding, Darwin T. Turner, Richard Barksdale, John Hope Franklin, and others who worked in the mainstream academy. But in contrast to earlier scholarship, the 1960s' formulations of Black Studies emphasized an interdisciplinarity that relied on historical and cultural contextualization in reconstructing African American experience.

In his historiographical essay, "Beyond Chaos: Black Studies and the New Land," historian and theologian Vincent Harding inadvertently dramatizes the promises and pitfalls of what was then a new field of inquiry: Black Studies. In the context of his evaluation, Harding constructs the origins of Black Studies in a narrative which inscribes an Oedipal tale of black sons (especially with Westernized training) who "seek to devour their fathers." In Harding's narrative, it is Du Bois who serves as founder of African American discursivity, posing the question to which all claimants to scholarly authority must provide an answer: "Where, by the way, is this train going?" A familiar vernacular trope of liberation in both the African American sermonic and folk tradition, the train in this account is bound in the right direction because the new "Black" historians challenged the ideological directions of the previous generation of "Negro" historians who, in making their case for first-class citizenship, emphasized African American patriotism and collaboration in the making of America. The integrationist aims of the "Negro" historians, however, were superseded by black nationalist and Pan-Africanist ideologies that narrativized a struggle against internal and external colonialism. The new direction of the train, indeed, led to a "new land"—the larger American academy as a place where new narratives would have to be fashioned, narratives that would subject the theories, methods, and findings of the traditional disciplines to the scrutiny of investigators figuring as both agents and objects of inquiry.

If the "generational shift" from an integrationist to a nationalist analytic also represented a "paradigm shift," there can be no doubt that a parallel shift from Black Studies to black cultural studies has called into question many of the assumptions of the prior paradigm as well.[1] If, in Harding's nationalist and masculinist narrative, there are no women historians or historical actors, contemporary black cultural studies interrogates not only the categories of race, class, and nationality, but also that of gender in the construction of socio-cultural experience. Clearly, the examination of these categories (and the exclusions they imply) represents a fruitful and necessary methodological direction for the Black Studies project.

In his essay on "The Postmodern Crisis of Black Intellectuals," West writes that "the traveling of cultural studies to the United States must be met with a critical reception—and by critical what I mean is an appropriation of the best: acknowledging where the blindnesses [are], while discussing to what degree British cultural studies can be related to the U.S. context (693). West, then, makes the case for a redeployment of cultural studies that does not entail an uncritical appropriation of European theory into the American academy. Further, his remarks implicitly suggest an application of theory grounded in local contexts that have specific and practical relevance.

Similarly, Manthia Diawara, in his article, "Black Studies/Cultural Studies," cites a genealogy of cultural studies, while at the same time warning of the dangers of reifying the methods and assumptions of British cultural studies in an African American context. Appropriating Antonio Gramsci's notion of *elabore* as a means of setting up a mutual interrogation between the Birmingham school and the Black British school of cultural studies, Diawara proposes to *elaborate* "the one in order to show the limitations of the other." His approach would establish a critique between and within these schools in order to clear a space for African American cultural investigation. The tools of British cultural studies, argues Diawara, need to be elaborated in order to ground black cultural studies in the material conditions of the United States. "Now it is the turn of Black Americans to take the British cultural studies," argues Diawara, "and turn it into a cultural work that is capable of addressing . . . issues [that challenge the black American community]." Rather than expecting the British cultural analysts to show the way, Diawara implicitly invokes the Shklovskian concept of defamiliarization, urging that we read British cultural analysts "in such a way that they do not recognize themselves" ("Cultural Studies/Black Studies" 206). British "diasporic" texts, in other words, must be rearticulated in the context of black American culture.

Diawara also insists on the "anti-essentialist critique" of black cultural studies and the limitations presented by identity politics in revolutionary struggle. Calling attention to the particularizing and homogenizing assumptions that he perceives to be prevalent in Black Studies, Diawara proposes that we abandon this area of study as traditionally conceived in favor of an approach that emphasizes the performative aspects of black culture in the public sphere.

While not in substantial disagreement with this position (one which is underscored by West), I confess that it does raise some troublesome questions regarding the Black Studies project. The problem, as I see it, is that the emergence of black cultural studies threatens to re-marginalize a field of study that became central during the Black Studies movement. The voices and experiences of the objects of investigation—namely, African Americans—are subjected to interpretation by scholars and theorists who draw on paradigms not grounded in African American history and culture. Clearly, such a theoretical move risks appropriating the geographically and historically specific experiences of African Americans to the theoretical exigencies of a non-African American constituency.

Like West and Diawara, I am concerned about the uncritical appropriation of British cultural studies as a model for understanding African American culture and experience. From my perspective, the goal, however, is not simply to "translate" the principles and methodologies of either the Birmingham or the Black British school (with their respective emphases on class and race) in order to define an approach to African American cultural studies; rather it must be to discover in African American culture—its formal and vernacular traditions—indigenous principles and methodologies that reflect the geographical and historical specificities of blacks in the United States. One might ask, for instance, how has black popular culture influenced American culture—both contemporary and historical culture? What kinds of models for cultural study can we find in the forms, structures, and techniques of blues and jazz? How can the paradigm of "internal colonialism" postulated by the black theoreticians of the 1960s serve as a model for studying dominant structures of power? What can the study of African American literature as a "minority literature" tell us about the processes of subversion and complicity at the level of literary expression?

Here I am less concerned about the displacement of African American hegemony in black diasporic studies than I am by the erasure of a historical genealogy for black cultural studies that extends back for at least a century to the African American critique of politics and culture formally inaugurated by W.E.B. Du Bois in his landmark *Souls of Black Folk* (1903), and later elaborated in his many studies, monographs, and autobiographies.

My concern, however, also extends to the intellectual space claimed by the attribution of a British genealogy, as well as to the institutional space claimed for cultural studies, when it threatens to colonize or imperialize the Black Studies project. At issue is the institutional site of production for the discourse of black cultural studies: What space will it occupy in its institutionalization? When we use the term *cultural studies*, are we referring to a method to be practiced by critics of African American culture (and thus a methodology that is compatible with and can be incorporated into existing Black Studies programs)—or are we referring to a new area of study that will seek an institutional space of its own in the academy? In other words, are cultural studies scholars supplementing what is perceived to be a "lack," or displacing what is perceived to be an "absence"?

My own position must be to insist that the emergent project of black cultural studies be situated in the context of Black Studies. As one of the primary oppositional discourses in American political and social history, Black Studies draws upon a tradition that derives in large part from black American writers and scholars. The work begun by W.E.B. Du Bois, Anna Julia Cooper, Carter G. Woodson, Charles Wesley, Dorothy Porter, Alain Locke, Zora Neale Hurston, Richard Wright, E. Franklin Frazier, St. Clair Drake, Horace Cayton, and others has continued in the cultural criticism of Ralph Ellison, James Baldwin, Albert Murray, Angela Davis, Shirley Anne Williams, Henry Louis Gates, Jr., Houston Baker, Jr., Hortense Spillers, bell hooks, Michele Wallace, Gayl Jones, and other contemporary artists and intellectuals.

Distancing his project of cultural studies from the traditional conception of Black Studies, Diawara relegates it (along with feminist and other ethnic studies) to the category of "victim" or "oppression" studies. Surely his intent here is not to valorize a conservative agenda; rather, his tactical appropriation of a conservative vocabulary for progressive ends is meant to affirm the performative dimension of the diasporic aesthetics and culture that are central to his project. Even so, such labels are likely to be controversial in that conservatives have habitually employed precisely this rhetorical code to critique diversity, difference, multiculturalism, and even cultural studies itself.

To examine Black Studies in its ethno-historical dimension is necessary and proper; yet to describe it as simply nationalist is both reductive and ahistorical. The elaboration of Black Studies within the American cultural milieu evolved not only in the context of an intercultural exchange, but also in the context of a rich intracultural dialogue. Moreover, as an intervention into the academy, Black Studies—in its formative stages—had to be insistent upon its integrity and distinctiveness. To criticize it, then, for promoting a naive and essentialist nationalism is to deny the historical and political contingencies of its very inception.

Not only did the institutionalization of African American Studies in the academy in the 1970s help deconstruct what George Lipsitz and others have described as "the consensus myth" of the 1950s and 1960s, but in some respects the argument that Lipsitz makes regarding the relationship between American Studies and European cultural theory obtains equally for that between African American Studies and cultural studies. African American Studies, I would claim, anticipated not only the "cross-disciplinary epistemological and hermeneutic concerns at the heart of contemporary European cultural theory," but also its concerns with comparative and cross-cultural work and, more specifically, its redefinitions of culture in the context of political contestation ("Listening to Learn and Learning to Listen: Popular Culture, Cultural Theory and American Studies" 622–23).

Recovering Black Studies as a model for cultural studies, then, means reclaiming it as a multi-disciplinary, cross-cultural, and comparative model of study which places into juxtaposition the history, culture, and politics of blacks in the U.S., Caribbean, and Africa. Such a program was meant to challenge the conventional disciplinary boundaries of humanistic study as well as to enlarge our conceptions of culture and its relation to history and politics. By introducing a comparative and historical dimension into its methodologies—and this in spite of its avowed nationalist agenda—Black Studies set into motion a revolution in the academy through its challenge to the ethnocentric Euro-American scholarship which had provided the basis for knowledge claims.

What I mean to suggest is that an examination of the Black Studies movement and its political and aesthetic sisters—the Black Power and the Black Arts Movements—may serve to locally and historically ground an African American (and indeed, American) cultural studies movement. Moreover, rather than viewing cultural studies as a means for revitalizing or overcoming the limitations of a moribund Black Studies, the latter can provide the means for rethinking the trajectory of cultural studies outside of a British context—a move which itself interrogates the notion advanced by Paul Gilroy "that much American enthusiasm for cultural studies is generated by its association with England and Englishness" ("Cultural Studies and Ethnic Absolutism" 694). If such an appropriation indeed represents what some have described as a kind of "displaced anglophilia," I would suggest moreover that it represents a residual anxiety in legitimizing African American Studies as an area of inquiry.

Further, I would suggest that, in addition to the oft-cited British works, we ought to reexamine, as founding texts, some of the works published in the 1960s and 1970s documenting the institutionalization of Black Studies. As a colleague of mine puts it, we must not only look to Birmingham, *England,* but to Birmingham, *Alabama,* as a site of historical struggle and contestation—a site whose academic counterpart we still find in Black Studies programs across the country.[2]

Certainly, we must recognize that the Civil Rights and Black Power movements transformed our notions of politics as much as the Black Studies movement transformed our notions of political and cultural critique. Together, they addressed the fundamental role of culture and its relation to the structures and processes of domination. When black students—from the U.S., Africa, and the Caribbean—entered the colleges and universities, their presence as well as their demands challenged many of the received notions underlying our ideas of culture and aesthetic value. For many of these students and scholars, the province of culture was not contained within Eurocentric notions of "high" or "elite" cultures; moreover, these students and scholars subjected such notions to ideological analysis—demonstrating the relationship between politics, culture, and values.

Important to this project which reevaluated Eurocentric knowledge claims was the "vernacularization" of black culture in the scholarship of black critics and theorists like Houston Baker, Jr., Stephen Henderson, Shirley Anne Williams, Henry Louis Gates, Jr., and Gayl Jones,[3] as well as that of white scholars of black culture like Lawrence Levine and John Callahan. Certainly, the contemporary projects of Baker and Gates (and, indeed, my own work) represent a vernacularization of theory which needs to be accounted for in the contemporary black cultural studies project. It is also significant that many of those scholars who used to be associated with Black Studies are now intellectually associated with cultural studies. And some of them, namely Gates and Baker (among others), are still institutionally identified with Black Studies programs. Such relationships are important in that they represent a collapsing or remapping of boundaries within the Black Studies project.

Again, what I am arguing is that the narrative we construct of the genealogy of cultural studies in the United States must create a place for Black Studies as a scholarly and political enterprise that transformed the university into a space of contestation and negotiation over the production and construction of knowledge. The advent of Black Studies was an inaugural moment and remains central to the formation of the contemporary cultural studies project. Its introduction into the American academy has paved the way for the articulation of a series of claims and counterclaims which have made the case for feminist studies, ethnic studies, postcolonial studies, gay and lesbian studies, and cultural studies as well. By challenging the authority and dominance of Eurocentric institutions and paradigms from the perspective of the dominated and oppressed, Black Studies has established the conditions of possibility for the emergence of these areas of study in the American academy. The consequence has been that not only our topics of inquiry, but, in some instances, even the modes of inquiry in scholarly and academic investigations, have been altered and expanded—with the effect of changing the look of our curricula, our classrooms, and our texts.

In conclusion, I would cite scholar Nahum Chandler who says we must "turn up new soil on old ground" and begin to theorize works such as Armstead Robinson's *Black Studies in the University,* John Blassingame's *New Perspectives on Black Studies,* Jack Bass's *Widening the Mainstream of American Culture: A Ford Foundation Report on Ethnic Studies,* and Nathan Huggins's *Afro-American Studies: A Report to the Ford Foundation.* These books contain the rich dialogues and debates that map the trajectory for the Black Studies project, and as such they represent a terrain that we need to revisit—and re-envision—in constructing an appropriate genealogy and institutional space for black cultural studies. Along with those of black British cultural theorists like Stuart Hall, Kobena Mercer, Isaac Julien, and Paul Gilroy, these works need to be examined in light of the contemporary debates on Black Studies, American Studies, cultural studies, and black cultural studies.

What has sustained Black Studies in the past can sustain black cultural studies in the future, and that is the challenge to exclusionary and hierarchic practices—whether social or intellectual. Many will continue to find variations of Pan-Africanism—or what is now more commonly called black diasporic or "black Atlantic world" studies—a productive means of revising a European philosophical and political discourse as it relates to the racial and ethnic Other.

Certainly, these global theories of transnational culture can elucidate our understanding of black cultural practices within the contexts of various and specific localities. Yet we would do well to be reminded of the risks of demarcating new and different boundaries of inclusion and exclusion. In other words, we need not only ask "where, by the way, is this train going?" We need also to ask "where has this train been?"

Acknowledgments

I wish to express my thanks to George Cunningham and Peter Thornton for their critical reading of an earlier version of this essay.

Notes

This essay originally appeared in *Callaloo* 19.1 (1996): 60–67. We are grateful to the editor, Charles Rowell, and to Johns Hopkins University Press for permission to reprint.

1. I am here employing Houston Baker, Jr.'s, terms of analysis in his description of black generational and paradigm shifts in African American criticism. Baker himself draws on the work of Lewis Feuer and Thomas Kuhn for these useful concepts. See his chapter, "Discovering America: Generational Shifts, Afro-American Literary Criticism, and the Study of Expressive Culture," in *Blues, Ideology, and Afro-American Literature* (1984).

2. I am indebted to my colleague Cheryl Wall for this pithy synoptic trope.

3. I refer here to Gayl Jones's critical work, *Liberating Voices: Oral Tradition in African American Literature* (1991).

Works Cited

Baker, Houston, Jr. *Blues, Ideology, and Afro-American Literature.* Chicago: University of Chicago Press, 1984.

Diawara, Manthia. "Black Studies/ Cultural Studies." *Borders, Boundaries, and Frames.* Ed. Mae G. Henderson. New York: Routledge, 1994.

Gilroy, Paul. "Cultural Studies and Ethnic Absolutism." Ed. Lawrence Grossberg, Cary Nelson, and Paula A. Treichler. *Cultural Studies.* New York: Routledge, 1992. 187–98.

Harding, Vincent. "Beyond Chaos: Black History and the Search for New Land." Ed. John A. Williams and Charles F. Harris. *Amistad I: Writings on Black History and Culture.* New York: Vintage, 1970.

Jones, Gayl. *Liberating Voices: Oral Tradition in African American Literature.* Cambridge: Harvard UP, 1991.

Lipsitz, George. "Listening to Learn and Learning to Listen: Popular Culture, Cultural Theory and American Studies." *American Quarterly* 42.4 (December 1990). 622–23.

West, Cornel. "The Postmodern Crisis of the Black Intellectuals." Ed. Lawrence Grossberg, Cary Nelson, and Paula A. Treichler. *Cultural Studies.* New York: Routledge, 1992. 689–705.

REFIGURING AZTLÁN

Rafael Pérez-Torres

One image central to Chicano/Chicana intellectual and social thought has been the figure of Aztlán. Too often, the name of this mythic homeland is either dismissed as part of an exclusionary nationalist agenda or uncritically affirmed as an element essential to Chicanismo. In refiguring Aztlán we move toward a conceptual framework by which to explore the connections between land, identity and experience in relation to Chicana/o populations. Significantly, these connections become centrally relevant in our postmodern times as the political, social and economic relationships between people and place grows ever more complicated and fluid. The problems posed by Aztlán as a site of home and dispossession represent the types of discursive engagements many different constituencies have in their own idiom undertaken. Beyond the dynamic issues posed by the questions of national origin—one in four people living in California today, for example, was born outside the U.S. national border—issues of shifting genders and sexualities, interrogation of national identification, investigation of indigenous ancestry all are areas interrogating the relation between locality and identity.

Within a Chicana/o context, Aztlán as the mythic Aztec homeland has served as a metaphor for connection and unity. It has also served to contest notions of national identity and place defined by hegemonic discourses at the social and—most particularly—cultural levels. Examining the idea of Aztlán helps us focus notions of the "border" and its multiple theorizations referenced in the introduction to this collection. It is true that the idea of borders has become central in various contemporary critical discourses. It is equally true that the U.S.–Mexico border remains a highly contested and dangerous area where naked power is employed in the ideological and economic service of these nation states. This awareness informs the ways in which Chicano/a critical discourse has deployed the idea of Aztlán as an icon of utopian consciousness.

While suggestive of a utopian homeland, the evocation of Aztlán also reveals how power circumscribes notions of home. During the nearly thirty years of its modern incarnation, Aztlán has often been used to represent a nationalist ideal meant to name that place that will at some future point be the national home of a people reclaiming their territorial rights. The current controversy over border control in the Southwest is the latest battle in the retaking of Aztlán, a retaking represented by the migration and immigration of Latinos to the U.S. through both legal and extra-legal means.

Beyond these territorial issues, Aztlán within Chicana/o cultural production more generally stands as the ground on which numerous representations are contested: a site of resistances and affirmations. These multiple meanings of Aztlán indicate how durable the image has been in the Chicano imaginary. Locating the source of its durability, naming what energizes it, forms one of the central tropes in discussions of Aztlán. This essay is no exception. It seeks to trace some of the historical, literary, and intellectual discourses on the meanings of Aztlán. The object is not to conclude that one of these discourses serves to better describe or locate Aztlán. Rather, this discussion is concerned less with the worth of Aztlán as cultural/critical signifier than with its role in shifting the horizon of signification as regards Chicano/a resistance, unity and liberation. In short, Aztlán remains relevant to Chicano discourses because of its status as an empty signifier.

This is not to say that the term Aztlán is meaningless. On the contrary, if anything the term is overdetermined. Three historical moments are suggested by the invocation of Aztlán: the Spanish invasion of the Aztec Empire, the appropriation of Mexican lands by the United States in the nineteenth and early-twentieth centuries, and the immigration to (or reconquest of) the U.S. Southwest by Mexicans and Central Americans in the contemporary era. To be fair, for many in the Chicano "community," Aztlán signifies little if anything at all; it is only the political, social and cultural Chicano/a elite of a particular stripe for whom Aztlán resonates as an icon imbued with some historical meaning. Five hundred years of European presence in the Americas is contested by an assertion of the indigenous, by an affirmation of native civilizations, by the recollection of Aztlán.

Even though it does not quite add up as a political or cultural metaphor, the call of Aztlán seems irresistible to the Chicano intelligentsia. The term inevitably raises difficulties in relation to its self, difficulties that lead the reclamation of Aztlán to take on numerous forms. In part, these forms vary depending on the purposes underlying the evocation of Aztlán. From a literary and cultural critical position, Daniel Alarcón argues that Aztlán can best be understood as a palimpsest, as "a trope that allows a more complex understanding of cultural identity and history" (35). Alarcón notes that "Aztlán has been used to obscure and elide important issues surrounding Chicano identity, in particular the significance of intracultural differences" (36). Cherríe Moraga has rearticulated the nationalist concerns associated with Aztlán, expanding its metaphorical qualities to reconnect it to all different forms of social struggle. Thus Aztlán as a metaphor for land stands as an overdetermined signifier: "For immigrant and native alike, land is [. . .] the factories where we work, the water our children drink, and the housing project where we live. For women, lesbians, and gay men, land is that physical mass called our bodies. Throughout las Américas, all these 'lands' remain under occupation by an Anglo-centric, patriarchal, imperialist United States" (173). From a sociological position, Aztlán becomes for Mario Barrera a locus of difficulty. Aztlán names that site of struggle for Chicano equality and community. This struggle becomes the catalyst driving Chicano political activism and, consequently, the engine leading to an accelerated assimilation "seen most dramatically in the overwhelming loss of fluency in Spanish by the third generation [of Mexican immigrants, but also seen] in the trend toward residential dispersion and the rising rate of intermarriage" (5). I too elsewhere have argued that Aztlán has shifted from signifying a homeland to signaling a complexity of multiple subjectivities called the borderlands.[1]

Each of these positions regarding Aztlán is limited in its scope and can be contested at numerous turns. Viewing Aztlán as a place of mestizaje, a site of multiple and simultaneous subjectivities, elides the way in which notions of the borderlands change depending on its contextualization: whether from a historiographic, sociological, cultural, or ethnographic position. Arguing that assimilation is the problematic result of political engagement avoids the de-indigenization undergone historically by mestizos and erases the complex relations between long-established Chicano communities and recent immigrants. To recast Chicano nationalist concerns within a larger framework of indigenous rights does not fully address the historical and cultural specificities enacted within different localities of political struggle. Understanding Aztlán primarily as a trope does disservice to the geo-political charge the term enacts.

AZTLÁN AND THE PLAN

In large part, the elusive and powerful quality of Aztlán as a signifier has to do with the history of its production. Aztlán was introduced to Chicana/o discourse through "El Plan Espiritual de Aztlán," drafted in March 1969 for the Chicano Youth Conference held in Denver, Colorado. The question in regard to "El Plan Espiritual de Aztlán" is how it enacted Chicano/a self-affirmation and determination. Aztlán marks a matrix where at least two seemingly contradictory strands of Chicano thought meet. On the one hand, the term "Chicano/a" signifies an identification with struggles for change within or the transformation of socioeconomic and political systems that have historically exploited Mexicans and people of Mexican ancestry. The emphasis along this trajectory is on the transformation of material conditions, on gains in a real economic and political sense.[2] On the other hand, the term "Chicano/a" identifies a subjectivity marked by a heritage and culture distinct from and devalued by Euro-American society. The interplay between these two meanings of the term Chicano/a is complex and not at all resolved. Although the claims for Chicano cultural agency have been to a greater or lesser degree effective, their translation into social empowerment has been largely unsuccessful. This tension between the social and cultural polarities within Chicana/o activism is made evident in the various articulations of the term Aztlán.

Aztlán as a signifier marking the completion or return of the Chicano to a homeland suggests both cultural and social signification.[3] As the representation of place,

Aztlán makes claims to a political and economic self-determination not dissimilar to claims asserted by indigenous populations throughout the world. As a symbol of unity, Aztlán suggests a type of cultural nationalism that is distinct from—though meant to work hand-in-hand with—social activism. The sense of a double signification resounds in "El Plan de Aztlán": "Brotherhood unites us and love for our brothers makes us a people whose time has come and who struggle against the foreigner 'Gabacho,' who exploits our riches and destroys our culture. With our heart in our hands and our hands in the soil, We Declare the Independence of our Mestizo Nation. We are a Bronze People with a Bronze Culture. Before the world, before all of North America, before all our brothers in the Bronze Continent, We are a Nation, We are a Union of free pueblos, We are Aztlán" (403). Against the Euro-American, the "Gabacho," the Plan condemns he who "exploits our riches" and simultaneously "destroys our culture." These two spheres in which violence occurs are—within the logic of the Plan—equitable but not identical. One represents the riches of land and labor, commodities within sociopolitical and economic systems of exchange. The other manifests self-identity and cultural independence. The tension between cultural and political autonomy makes itself felt in the image of the Chicano community at once affirming culture ("With our heart in our hands") and nation ("and our hands in the soil"), both coming together in the formation of a "Mestizo Nation." What this Nation consists of—beyond the essentializing and vague vision of a "Bronze People" with a "Bronze Culture" forming a "Union of free pueblos"—remains unspoken.

There are those who want to claim Aztlán as the embodiment of a successful unity between the cultural and political. As a student of both religious studies and legal discourse, Michael Pina argues that Aztlán represents the successful union of the spiritual and social: "On one level Chicano nationalism calls for the re-creation of an Aztec spiritual homeland, Aztlán; on another, it expresses the desire to politically reconquer the northern territories wrested from Mexico in an imperialist war inspired by American 'Manifest Destiny.' These two mythic narratives merged to form the living myth of Chicano nationalism. This myth spanned the diachronic chasm that separates the archaic contents of cultural memory from the contemporary struggle for cultural survival" (36). In effect, Pina argues that the evocation of Aztlán bridges "the diachronic chasm" between past indigenous identity and contemporary social activism as well as spanning the gap between cultural and political agency. Rather than evoke a bridge beyond history, I would argue that Aztlán reveals the discontinuities and ruptures that characterize the presence of Chicanos in history. Although it evokes a Chicano homeland, Aztlán also foregrounds the construction of history within a Chicano context. The difficult articulation of Chicano/a history—a history that speaks of dispossession and migration, immigration and diplomacy, resistance and negotiation, compromise and irony—remains ever unresolved.

AZTLÁN AND DIASPORA

Aztlán can at times be articulated as a rather quaint dream, something of a fantasy: "through Aztlán we come to better understand psychological time (identity), regional makeup (place), and evolution (historical time). Without any one of these ingredients, we would be contemporary displaced nomads, suffering the diaspora in our own land, and at the mercy of other social forces. Aztlán allows us to come full circle with our communal background as well as to maintain ourselves as fully integrated individuals" (Anaya and Lomelí iv). Despite such assertions, Aztlán marks less a sense of wholeness than heterogeneity in terms of identity and geography. It is impossible to ignore the nomadic role Chicanos and Mexican migrant workers have played within a diasporic history in the U.S.

While invoking the diasporic in relation to the Chicano/Mexicano, one might want to tread lightly. From a political scientific perspective, William Safran argues that the concept of diaspora should be expanded to include more than that segment of a people living outside their homeland. His focus is primarily on the contemporary diaspora of "third world" people into Europe. He suggests that the term be applied to expatriate minority communities whose members share a memory of, concern with, and desire for a return to their homelands. As such, Safran notes—in a move that resonates with the conclusions drawn by Mario Barrera—the "Hispanic (or Latino) community in the United States has not generally been considered a diaspora. The Mexican Americans, the largest component of that community, [. . . .] are assimilating at a steady pace" (90). More importantly for the purposes of his argument, Safran argues that "Mexican Americans do not cultivate a homeland myth [. . .] perhaps because the homeland cannot be easily idealized. The poverty and political corruption of Mexico (which is easy enough to observe, given the proximity of that country) stand in too sharp a contrast with conditions in the United States" (90). This is quite a reversal of that favorite Mexican saying: "Poor Mexico. So far from God and so close to the United States." Given the means of mass communication and relative ease of international travel, it is not clear how the proximity of Mexico to the United States significantly affects the comparative de-idealization of it as a homeland in the minds of its diasporic population. More centrally, Mexico—as a national or cultural icon—does at many levels remain significant for most individuals self-identified as Chicano or Mexicano or Mexican-American.

More to the point, the evocation of the diasporic or nomadic indicates that there is no one ideal Subject that encapsulates the multiplicity of Chicano/a subjectivities. One cannot assert the wholeness of a Chicano subject when the very discourses that go into its identity formation—be they discourses surrounding the mutability of gender identity, sexuality, class and cultural identification, linguistic and ethnic association— are incommensurably contradictory. It is illusory to deny the nomadic quality of the Chicano/Mexicano community, a community in flux that yet survives and—through survival—affirms its own self.

This is not to dismiss either the significance of Aztlán or the relevance of "El Plan Espiritual." The Plan does—owing much to Frantz Fanon—articulate an ambitious (if ambiguous) nationalism suggesting that the spiritual longing and physical needs of the subaltern "native" are inexorably bound together. Although Fanon argues in *The Wretched of the Earth* that the immediate effects of a cultural nationalism are difficult to gauge—"I am ready to concede that on the plane of factual being the past existence of an Aztec civilization does not change anything very much in the diet of the Mexican peasant today" (209)—he goes on to argue that "this passionate search for a national culture which existed before the colonial era finds its legitimate reason in the anxiety shared by native intellectuals to shrink away from that Western culture in which they all risk being swamped" (209). By Fanon's argument, the search for an "other" space proves not to be simply an escape from the present. On the contrary, since colonial processes wish to impose rule upon the past as well as the present and future of a colonized people, the quest for a past proves to be a great act of resistance and self-affirmation: "the native intellectuals, since they could not stand wonderstruck before the history of today's barbarity, decided to go back further and to delve deeper down; and, let us make no mistake, it was with the greatest delight that they discovered that there was nothing to be ashamed of in the past, but rather dignity, glory, and solemnity" (210). The affirmation of a glorious past becomes the condemnation of a repressive present.

Evoking a similar sentiment, "El Plan Espiritual de Aztlán" declares: "In the spirit of a new people that is conscious not only of its proud historical heritage, but also of the brutal 'Gringo' invasion of our territories: We, the Chicano inhabitants and civilizers of the northern land of Aztlán, from whence came our forefathers, reclaiming the land of their birth and consecrating the determination of our people of the sun, declare that the call of our blood is our power, our responsibility, and our inevitable destiny" (402–3). The Plan hearkens back to the "forefathers" as a basis for reclamation, a tenuous position at best given the diverse indigenous past of actual Chicanos. The Plan, though influenced by Fanon's thought, strikes wide of the mark in relation to Fanon's final point about national culture: "A national culture is not a folklore, nor an abstract populism that believes it can discover the people's true nature. It is not made up of the inert dregs of gratuitous actions, that is to say actions which are less and less attached to the ever-present reality of the people. A national culture is the whole body of efforts made by a people in the sphere of thought to describe, justify, and praise the action through which that people has created itself and keeps itself in existence" (233). In evoking the quaintly and faintly recalled past, the Plan fails to articulate clearly that which has best served Chicanos and Chicanas in the preservation of self. The Plan does, however, help highlight a sense of historical consciousness— "the brutal 'Gringo' invasion of our territories"—which forms a central trope in Chicano/a cultural criticism. After all, history teaches that U.S. society often has no patience or respect (when it has time to take notice at all) for people of Mexican ancestry, U.S. citizens or not. Employing Aztlán as signifier, Chicano activists, artists and critics constantly write and rewrite history.

The invocation of ancestry by the Plan reclaims a position and a heritage that asserts integrity and agency. This assertion suggests, through the "call of our blood," an essentialized and biologically determined nationalism that proves finally untenable. So problematic is this essentialization that the poet Alurista felt compelled a decade after its writing to defend the Plan in his explanation of cultural nationalism. Alurista was—along with Rodolfo "Corky" Gonzales—one of the drafters of the Plan, as Luis Leal notes in "In Search of Aztlán": "before March, 1969, the date of the Denver Conference, no one talked about Aztlán. In fact, the first time that it was mentioned in a Chicano document was in 'El Plan Espiritual de Aztlán,' which was presented in

Denver at that time. Apparently, it owes its creation to the poet Alurista who already, during the Autumn of 1968, had spoken about Aztlán in a class for Chicanos held at San Diego State University" (20). As a principle player in the articulation of Aztlán, Alurista in 1981 argues that the Plan "clearly stated that 'Aztlán belonged to those who worked it' (not only Xicano workers) and that no capricious frontiers would be recognized—an important point which, in the fervor of an exclusivist narrow national- ism, was quickly overlooked" (25). Alurista disavows what could be interpreted as the most exclusivist elements of nationalism evident in the Plan. At the same time, he insists upon a type of transnational "nationalism," a cultural nationalism distinct from the "exclusivist narrow nationalism" of strict political delineation.

This distinction helps explain the tension between two (ultimately contradictory) veins of Chicano "nationalism" strongly influential in subsequent movements of cul- tural and political identification. Aztlán variously seems to signal a rationally planned nationalist movement and a mythopoetic cultural essence. Although the drafters of the Plan, after Fanon, seem to view a cultural nationalism as simultaneous with a political nationalism, Aztlán came to be the hotly disputed terrain on which either one or another type of nationalism was ostensibly founded. Elyette Labarthe, discuss- ing the development of Aztlán, notes the importance of these disputes in the early development of Chicano self-identity: "On one side an oracular voice crackled over that of reason, on the other side a dispassionate voice piped up above that of the inspired poet, but could not quite blot it out" (79). Militant factions in the Chicano Movement, Labarthe points out, viewed Alurista's nationalism as a hollow and roman- ticized vision that subverted real claims to Aztlán, real political–nationalist interests. The tensions between the locally political and the universally cultural form one of the faultlines that runs through the terrain of Chicano cultural articulations.

AZTLÁN AND NATION

Jorge Klor de Alva implies that this rupture between cultural and political nation- alisms influenced the breakdown of leadership among Chicano communities. With the eye of an anthropologist, he notes:

> On one side are leaders with a humanist bent, often schooled in literature or fine arts, who tend to focus on cultural concerns while emphasizing the cultural autonomy of the individual. Their naive cultural nationalism is ultimately too chauvinistic to promote the unification efforts needed to overcome the divisive forces of monopoly capitalism and the seductiveness of modern fragmenting individualism. On the other side are those primar- ily trained in the social sciences, whose research is delimited by a preoccupation with economic and political issues, and whose eyes are fixed on social structures and the work force. The radicals among them disparage the importance of culture and nationalism while focusing primarily on the significance of class. (137)

Although Klor de Alva goes on to note that this schema is "deceiving in its simplicity," it nevertheless reflects a distancing between "two valuable and necessary camps" (138). The schisms between "the political" and "the cultural" within Chicano discourses run deeply. They spread out over a larger historical and geographic terrain not divided neatly into camps like "political" versus "cultural" or "historical" as opposed to "mythical." The fissures involved in Chicano nationalist claims derive from a number of different historical sources: the nationalist movements—American Indian and Black—current in the political climate of the late 1960s; the Third World struggles for national sovereignty in the 1950s; the "nationless" status of Chicanos who, after fighting in World War II, returned to a country where they were still considered foreigners in the 1940s; the institutionalization, following the Mexican Revolution, of Mexican national culture in the 1920s and 1930s; the usurpation of Mexican territorial rights in 1848; the continuous migrations of Mexicanos before, during, and after the U.S.-Mexican War; the struggle for Mexican independence from Spain begun in 1810. All these form influential trajectories that cross at the matrix of Chicano nationalism.

The influence of the Mexican Revolution on Chicano thinking in particular cannot be minimized. As Leal and Barrón note, "Immigration from Mexico to the United States from 1848 to 1910 was negligible. After 1910, however, and especially during the critical years of the Mexican Revolution (1913–1915), which coincided with the outbreak of World War I and the consequent expansion of American industry and agriculture, large numbers of immigrants crossed the border" (20). The influences on the economic and social conditions of Chicano life in the United States certainly changed as a result of the Revolution. Not the least of these changes was the backlash against Mexicans that came—among other times—in the 1920s.[4]

The nativism so valued by Chicano cultural discourses clearly draws its influence from the construction of postrevolutionary Mexican nationalism. Thus events following the Mexican Revolution—especially the institutionalization of a "revolutionary" ideology—have significantly influenced the articulation of Chicano/a identification. The affirmation of native roots in the cultural identification of the Mexican begins with José Vasconcelos's service as Minister of Education under President Alvaro Obregón (1920–4). Other movements toward Chicano empowerment are prefigured in the Mexican postrevolutionary world as well. In the politico-cultural realm, one finds a strong conflict between Mexican intelligentsia who wish to ally themselves with an international Marxism and those seeking to discover the true character of Mexico. Samuel Ramos undertook *Profile of Man and Culture in Mexico* (1934) as a personality study of Mexico, and Jorge Cuesta's anthology of modern Mexican poetry (1928) serves as an investigation into the meaning of Mexican cultural tradition. Octavio Paz notes: "They both reflect our profound desire for self-knowledge. The former represents our search for the intimate particulars of our nature, a search that was the very essence of our Revolution, while the latter represents our anxiety to incorporate these particulars in a universal tradition" (162). Of course the work of Paz himself has been extraordinarily influential, both as an affirmative point of reference and a sore point of rejection. Of Mexico, Paz argues: "Ever since World War II we have been aware that the self-creation demanded of us by our national realities is no different from that which similar realities are demanding of others. The past has left us orphans, as it has the rest of the planet, and we must join together in inventing our common future. World history has become everyone's task and our own labyrinth is the labyrinth of all mankind" (173). The type of universalism that so interests Paz in this passage (and throughout his writing) forms a common trope in discussions of Chicano culture.

These strong intellectual and cultural associations with Mexico, according to Genaro Padilla, arise from a profound sense of disconnection experienced by Chicana/o writers and thinkers. They have, Padilla argues:

> a nostalgia for the Mexican homeland, especially as it has been imagined in that mythical realm of Aztlán. This impulse has manifested itself intensely in the last two decades, a period during which the Chicano, feeling deeply alienated from the foster parent United States, wished to maintain a vital spiritual link with Mexico, the model of language, culture and social behavior. This explains, in part, why Chicano cultural nationalists not only appropriated the pre-Columbian mythology of Mexico, but also its Revolutionary heroes—Benito Juárez, Emiliano Zapata, Pancho Villa—and affected a kinship with Mexico's common people and their history. (126)

This imagined kinship explains the allegiance found in Chicano nationalist discourses to progressive economic, social, and political agendas. What specific courses those agendas should take—and the role that the culture should play in relation to those agendas—forms part of the discontinuity apparent in the realm of Aztlán.

Aztlán stands as that region where the diverse political, geographic, and cultural concerns gripping the Chicano imagination meet. Alurista, as we have seen, views Aztlán as a sign whose referent is unproblematically present. From Alurista's view, the conflation of a nation and a culture seems to provide no tension. Thus he can assert that Chicano literature "is a national literature, and will have to reflect all the levels that our nation implies, all that IS our people" (Bruce-Novoa 284). From this perspective, Aztlán as a Chicano nation stands as an ontological certainty. The literature that will emerge from it will reflect the same nationalist concerns as any other national literatures. There is a curious elision of nation, literature, people in Alurista's configuration of Aztlán. The term comes to represent not just the fact of sovereignty, but the fact of existence, the very being that is the Chicano—a reflection of the essentializing moves manifested by this strain of Chicano cultural articulation, an essentialization that Alurista seems to speak against elsewhere.

In "In Search of Aztlán," Luís Leal attempts to look upon the idea of Aztlán, and the Plan Espiritual specifically, from a more historical perspective. He traces the effects and traditions of Aztlán by documenting "the rebirth of the myth in Chicano thought" (20). "El Plan Espiritual de Aztlán" forms an important document and turning point in the articulation of Chicano consciousness. In it, Leal argues that the Chicano "recognizes his Aztec origins" as well as "establishes that Aztlán is the Mexican territory ceded to the United States in 1848" (20). The Plan articulates the affirmation of origins, both indigenous (though reified in the form of the "Aztecs") and nationalist. He goes on to note that "following one of the basic ideas of the Mexican Revolution, it recognizes that the land belongs to those who work it," making explicit the connection between Aztlán and the cultural history that enables its articulation. Leal's comments thus point toward the historical loci and salient components that make up the discursive practices associated with Aztlán. This historical perspective quickly dissolves, however, into something else.

Leal concludes with the admonition "whosoever wants to find Aztlán, let him look for it, not on the maps, but in the most intimate part of his being" (22). His discussion, which begins as a historical project, turns into a rhetorical one. Aztlán ceases to exist except as a vague search for spiritual centering. Six years before Leal, Sylvia Gonzales had made a similar discursive move, dissolving the historical ground of Aztlán in favor of an essential and ultimately romantic notion of universal "culture." In her essay "National Character vs. Universality in Chicano Poetry," Gonzales begins by articulating a sociohistorically bound notion of Aztlán: "In recognition of our oppression, the Chicano people searched for identity and awareness as a group, as a nation within a nation. This became the cultural, psychological, philosophical and political nation of Aztlán" (15). Aztlán thus represents a contested, resistant site. Not specifically bound to a geographic reclamation, Aztlán in Gonzales's view is a discursive construction arising out of political necessity. However, her argument moves from focusing on the political to dreaming of the eschatological. Her vision of Aztlán leaves us with a messianic vision of cultural universality: "The world awaits the appearance of a disciple capable of propounding the message, interpreting the underlying language of their work, which has already been proscribed. That disciple will have to be a priest, a magician or a poet" (19). This articulation of Aztlán moves from an assertion of self-determination to a dream of cultural salvation.

LINES OF FLIGHT

What these critics do make clear is that the terrain termed Aztlán represents less a specific geographic locale—though various discourses view it as such—than a means of counterdiscursive engagement. Its efficacy from a strictly political perspective remains questionable. When compared with the other Plans marking El Movimiento, "El Plan Espiritual de Aztlán" does not leave as distinct a political legacy. Elyette Labarthe argues that the power of Aztlán lies in its imaginative conceptualization of Chicano unity: "The socio-economic debate was to be awarded a spiritual dimension and a dynamism that were sadly lacking. The symbol of Aztlán had the power to legitimize the struggles to cement the claims. It was a compensatory symbolic mechanism, fusing poetico-symbolic unity to socio-cultural concerns. The Chicanos who were divided by history, found in it an ancestral territory and a common destiny" (80). Its compensatory function served to make it a lasting image. But as a compensatory strategy, its political effects proved less than prepossessing.

Finally, as the arguments by Gonzales and Leal indicate, the function of Aztlán was to pronounce a minority position that staked claims for legitimacy through a cultural and ancestral primacy. In immediate terms, however, as Juan Gómez-Quiñones argues, the Plan "was stripped of what radical element it possessed by stressing its alleged romantic idealism, reducing the concept of Aztlán to a psychological ploy, and limiting advocacy for self-determination to local community control—all of which became possible because of the plan's incomplete analysis which, in turn, allowed its language concerning issues to degenerate into reformism" (124). The political vagueness of the Plan dissipated its energies along the small faultlines of numerous cultural discourses. And this dispersal, although causing tremors in the cultural terrain of Euro-American society, did little to shake the walls and bring down the structures of power as its rhetoric so firmly proclaimed.

Aztlán as a supposed "common denominator with the claims to the vatos locos, pochos, pachucos, cholos and other mestizos" (Labarthe 80) fails. Purportedly invoked as a politically unifying metaphor, Aztlán becomes something quite different. Although politically and ideologically vague, "El Plan Espiritual de Aztlán" does help establish the discursive habits by which Chicano culture asserts its autonomy. Aztlán thus forms not a national but a critical region for El Movimiento. At its most efficacious moments, it comes to represent a cultural site expressing pride in origins and heritages. The investigation of the past, the reclamation of history, the pride of place embodied in Aztlán manifests itself in the idea of Chicanismo.

The poet José Montoya explains: "*Chicanismo* is a basic concept which embodies both the Indio and the Spanish aspects of our heritage. As Chicano people we now accept the Indio side of our heritage. We somehow never had too much of a problem with our Hispanitude one way or the other. But to be considered an Indio!" (25). The mestizaje of Montoya's exclamations forms a nexus of cultural and personal identity that first gained currency in the nationalist movements of postrevolutionary Mexico. Although the impetus for the celebration of indigenismo emerges from the nationalist discourses of Mexico, hegemonic views on race and culture die long and agonized deaths. Despite the ideological valorization of mestizaje, the racism present in both U.S. and Mexican societies certainly circulate in the "Mexican-American" communities. In a North American context, this means that the members of these communities are under pressure to assimilate particular standards—of beauty, of identity, of aspiration. In a Mexican context, the pressure is to urbanize and Europeanize. Which is to say that in order to belong to larger imagined communities of the nation—particularly in the United States—its citizen-subjects are expected to accept anti-indigenous discourses as their own.

In this respect, Aztlán has allowed for a subjectivity that reclaims the connection to indigenous peoples and cultures. Although it does not offer a platform that would allow for a reclamation of a nation, it has in varied ways provided an alternate national consciousness. It has in problematic ways allowed for another way of aligning one's interests and concerns with community and with history. This may prove to be the most lasting legacy of Aztlán. In crystallizing a sense of rightful place and identity, it has sought to enable a newfound agency. Though hazy as to the precise means by which this agency will emerge, Aztlán has valorized a Chicanismo that reweaves into the present previously devalued lines of descent.

These lines of descent do not come to us without problematic implications. Reimaginings of the past—Mexican, indigenous, Aztec, pure—are understood as true. Their revivification can however only be enacted through their manifestation in a conflicted present. Aztlán thus becomes a terrain of discontinuity, of disjuncture. An infatuation with tradition and the native represents the type of fetishization of Aztec and Mayan themes and icons critiqued by Jorge Klor de Alva: Chicanos "have consistently emphasized the form over the content of native ideology and symbolism by oversimplifying both to the point of caricaturing the intricate and enigmatic codes that veil the meanings of the original texts" (24). While an infatuation with historical "accuracy" is of course suspect, so to an easy manipulation of cultural iconography must be critiqued. In this regard, Daniel Alarcón's redeployment of Aztlán as a palimpsest is very instructive. Aztlán as a cultural/national symbol represents a paradox: it seeks to stand as a common denominator among Chicano populations, yet it divides rather than unifies; it maintains cultural traditions while promoting assimilation into Anglo-American culture; it affirms indigenous ancestry while simultaneously erasing the very historical, cultural and geographic specificity of that ancestry. Consequently, Alarcón astutely maintains: "unless Aztlán is understood in all of its layers, all its complexity, it will never be an attractive model to the diverse culture its leaders seek to encompass within its borders, borders that have been and will continue to be fluid" (62). Aztlán represents not a singular homeland, but rather a borderland between sites of alliance.

In this respect we might think of Chela Sandoval's discussion of U.S. Feminists of color in the 1970s. She notes that feminists of color began to identify common grounds upon which they formed coalitions across boundaries of cultural, racial, class, and gender differences. Their position in the borderlands of feminism enabled a crossing across difference, a recognition of sameness amid difference, a recognition of other countrywomen and countrymen living in a similar and sympathetic psychic terrain. The differences between these men and women—differences signifying struggle, conflict, asymmetry, differences implying dislocation, dispersal, disruption—were never erased. Rather, a fuller process of recognition took place (11). In this context, the borderlands mark a site of profound discontinuity between regions delimiting racial, sexual, gender and economic identities.

To think of Aztlán as a signifier of the borderlands does not negate its historical significance. It still reaches out to the geography of the American Southwest and attempts to represent its distinct material qualities. Yet it is also true that conceptions of the borderlands refutes Aztlán as a fixed entity. Partly, a refutation of the nationalist dreams of the Chicano Movement results from its conflicted message in which revolutionary rhetoric articulated what quite quickly became reformist demands. These reformist positions ultimately offered neither genuine self-determination nor universal liberation. Partly, the refutation of nationalist demands is due to the fact that Latinos, as the fastest growing minority in the United States, have in a sense already reclaimed the Southwest. Partly, there remains the unshakeable belief that the Southwest was never lost. Thus Aztlán as a borderlands marks a site that both belongs and has never belonged to either the United States or Mexico.

The tumultuous histories informing constructions of the U.S. Southwest mark the impossible interstices between imagination and history. In its negative recollection of repressive social forms, Aztlán as signifier marks how historically grounded Chicano consciousness can be. This historical perspective serves to acknowledge the fluid mending and blending, repression and destruction of disparate cultures making up Chicanismo. A tempestuous sense of motion therefore marks that region termed the "borderlands." Not a homeland, not a perpetuation of origin, the borderlands allude to an illimitable terrain marked by dreams and rupture, marked by history and the various hopes that history can exemplify. The borderlands represent the multiplicity and dynamism of Chicana/o experiences and cultures. It is a terrain in which Mexicans, Chicanos, and mestizos live among the various worlds comprising their cultural and political landscapes.

Sergio Elizondo, among others, seeks to give voice to the idea of the borderlands. He discusses a relationship to land that Chicano/a culture has often sought to express:

> We understand now the Border between the United States of America and the Estados Unidos Mexicanos; now we would do well to consider that Borderlands might be a more appropriate term to designate the entire area over which the Chicano people are spread in this country. In so doing, we would come also to understand that the mere physical extension between the U.S.–Mexico border and, let us say, Chicago, is a fact of human dispersion, and not a diaspora of the Chicano people. It is not static for us, but rather it has always been a dynamic and natural motion motivated by laws and processes common to all cultures. Our migrations north of the old historical border have extended the geography and social fabric of Aztlán northward in all directions; we have been able to expand our communal life and fantasies. (13)

Elizondo speaks to a number of repeated issues found in the Chicano cultural imaginary. The problematization of heritage and tradition, the relation between Chicano cultural and social experiences, the significance of land and nation, the expansion of "homeland" and "fantasies" all inform the various movements of contemporary Chicano culture. It is interesting that Elizondo suggests the movement of Chicanos through the United States is not a diaspora but a process "motivated by laws and processes common to all cultures." The desire to make Chicana/o identity "universal" still finds a voice. Nevertheless, Elizondo's statement indicates that the notion of Aztlán has given way to a broader and more diverse vision of Chicano cultural terrain. This cultural terrain expands the realm of desire for Chicanas/os, moving it as it does across the entire face of the United States and beyond; but it also closes a chapter on Chicano cultural identity. No longer grounded exclusively in the Southwest or border region, the borderlands expand the territorial claims of Chicanos. Elizondo portrays this expansion as simply the extension of "the geography and social fabric of Aztlán." His conceptualization does not address at all what that sign "Aztlán" signifies.

As I have sought to suggest, Chicano nationalism failed to perceive the multiplicity and discontinuity evident in the histories and geographies encompassed by the signifier "Aztlán." As a place, or even as a unifying symbol or image, Aztlán erases the vast differences that help form the richness and variety of the terms "Chicana" and "Chicano." The histories of Mexicans in this country are marked by a series of tensions and ruptures—cultural, linguistic, political, economic, racial—that cut across various social and national terrains in which one can and cannot call one's location "home." The interstitial becomes the liminal where the living between becomes a way of moving through such definitions as Other, native, foreign, gringo, pocho, etc.. The performance artist Guillermo Gómez-Peña addresses the multiplicity that makes up identity in the borderlands: "My 'identity' now possesses multiple repertoires: I am Mexican but I am also Chicano and Latin American. At the border they call me *chilango* or *mexiquillo*; in Mexico City its *pocho* or *norteño*; and in Europe it's *sudaca*. The Anglos call me 'Hispanic' or 'Latino,' and the Germans have, on more than one occasion, confused me with Turks or Italians. My wife Emily is Anglo-Italian, but speaks Spanish with an Argentine accent, and together we walk amid the rubble of the Tower of Babel of our American postmodernity" (127–8). The identities Gómez-Peña exposes lead to a decentering of subjectivity accompanied by loss—of country, of native language, of certainty. But this leads as well to gain: a multifocal and tolerant culture, cultural alliances, "a true political conscience (declassicization and consequent politicization) as well as new options in social, sexual, spiritual, and aesthetic behavior" (129–30). The desire to rediscover a homeland within the current climate of Chicano culture fades; the reclamation at hand is much more complex and extensive. It calls for a reclamation of all that is cast between, all devalued by other nationalist identities. Chicano culture traces "lines of flight," movements toward deterritorialization.[5] Chicana/o writers and critics most powerfully enable this type of cultural configuration as they have sought to articulate the difficiencies of a nationalism that presumes the centrality of heterosexual male subjectivity. Their experiences suggest a textured and multifaceted sense of self.

HYBRID WORLDS

In this context, no Chicana author is associated with the borderland more than Gloria Anzaldúa. Caught between the worlds of lesbian and straight, Mexican and American, First World and Third World, Anzaldúa's writing seems to exemplify and reflect the condition of the interstitial and liminal—of being simultaneously between and on the threshold. In the poem "To live in the Borderlands means you," the speaker visits the various characteristics of the borderland. The title reads as the first line of the poem, a device immediately signaling a transgression of borders and marking the thematics of the poem. The title also allows for a shifting in syntactical meaning. Taken alone the title signals a conflation between the "you" the title addresses and the Borderlands of which it speaks. Melding into the poem, the title also signals the mestizaje inherent to the borderlands:

> To live in the Borderlands means you
> are neither *hispana india negra española*
> *ni gabacha, eres mestiza, mulata,* half-breed
> caught in the crossfire between camps
> while carrying all five races on your back
> not knowing which side to turn to, run from. (194)

The borderlands in the poem become a zone of transition and not-belonging. You are not hispanic, Indian, black, Spanish, or white, but mestiza. Identity emerges from the racial, cultural, sexual mixture. It is a land of betrayal where "*mexicanas* call you *rajetas*" and "denying the Anglo inside you / is as bad as having denied the Indian or Black." A mestizaje of linguistic and sexual identity emerges in the borderland as well: "*Cuando vives en la frontera* / people walk through you, the wind steals your voice, / you're a *burra* [donkey], *buey* [steer], scapegoat / . . . / both woman and man, neither— / a new gender." The poem's interlingual expression and evocation of interstitial spaces represents the power of transgression. The borderlands do not represent merely a cultural or national transgression. As the imagery evoked by the poem suggests, sexual and gender identities give way before the transformative forces of a true mestizaje. To live in the borderlands means transgressing the rigid definitions of sexual, racial, and gender definitions.

The battle finally of the borderlands is fought on a ground in which enemies are not without. In the borderlands "you are the battleground / where enemies are kin to each other; / you are at home, a stranger, / the border disputes have been settled / the volley of shots have shattered the truce." There is a discontinuity inherent to the borderland. From this perspective, Elizondo is right in conflating Aztlán with the borderland; they meld one into the other as regions of rupture where self and other perpetually dance around and through one another.

Although one enemy remains the homogenizing elements of society that seek to erase any trace of "race"—the mill that wants to "pound you pinch you roll you out / smelling like white bread but dead"—these enemies do not stand wholly without. These are the lessons internalized through the racism and violence that marks the borderlands. The borderlands represent a home that is not home, the place where all the contradictions of living among and between worlds manifests itself. Anzaldúa articluates the difficulties and problems inherent to this realm of discontinuity. Not offering a vision of another land as the utopian hope for peace or justice, all the poem can offer is advice on how to negotiate through the ruptured terrain of the borderlands: "To survive the Borderlands / you must live *sin fronteras* / be a crossroads." To live without borders means that the subjectivity to which Anzaldúa's poetry points constantly stands at the intersection of various discursive and historical trajectories. The crossroads that subjectivity becomes allow as well for the self to venture down various roads, follow trails that lead across numerous—often discontinuous, often contradictory, often antithetical—regions: European, Indian, Mexican, American, male, female, homosexual, heterosexual. The quest suggested by Anzaldúa's sense of the borderlands is not toward a fixed or rigid identity. The Chicana/o becomes a fluid condition, a migratory self who reclaims not merely the geographic realm of Aztlán. Instead, Chicanos/as come to be seen as transfiguring themselves—moving between the worlds of indigenous and European, of American and Mexican, of self and other.

FILLING THE VOID

The transformation of "Aztlán" from homeland to borderlands signifies another turn within Chicano/a cultural discourse. It demarcates a shift from origin toward an engagement with the ever-elusive construction of cultural identity. As the U.S.-Mexican border represents a construction tied to histories of power and dispossession, the construction of personal and cultural identity entailed in any multicultural project comes to the fore in Chicana/o cultural production. The move represents at this point a liberating one that allows for the assumption of various subject positions. The refusal to be delimited, while simultaneously claiming numerous heritages and influences, allows for a rearticulation of the relationship between self and society, self and history, self and land. Aztlán as a realm of historical convergence and discontinuity becomes another source of significance embraced and employed in the borderlands that is Chicana/o culture.

The tendency in these figurations and refigurations of Aztlán recast it variously as an ontological reality or an epistemological construction. Aztlán thus is repositioned and refigured as a shifting, and thus ambiguous, signifier. Rather than think of it as ambiguous, we might consider it "empty," a signifier which points, as Ernesto Laclau argues, "from within the process of signification, to the discursive presence of its own limits" (36).[6] The shift does not help us fix the significance of the term Aztlán. It does, I hope, sketch out some ideas that may help unravel the bind to which the continued discussions of Aztlán attest. There can be two explanations why we have not arrived, so to speak, at Aztlán. Either the plan to get to Aztlán—representing nation, unity, liberation—has not yet been adequately articulated. (This implies that the proper configuration of Aztlán is still to be enacted at some future utopian date.) Or all the different articulations of Aztlán are equally valid and so we each live our own little atomized Aztlán. The first position is obfuscatory, the second hopeless. Both run counter to that which Aztlán seeks to name.

As an empty signifier, Aztlán names not that which is to be or that has been, but that which is ever absent: nation, unity, liberation. The various articulations of Aztlán have sought to make these absences present in the face of oppressive power based on: racial grounds and the Chicano emergence from the indigenous; historico-political grounds and the struggles over land most clearly indexed by the Mexican-American War of 1846–1848; economic grounds represented by the exploitation of laborers and most specifically farm workers; sexual and gender grounds represented by the colonization of female and queer bodies; and cultural grounds invoked by references to indigenous, folk and popular arts. Whatever its premise, the term "Aztlán" consistently has named that which refers to an absence, an unfulfilled reality in response to various forms of oppression.

This does not help us understand why the signifier Aztlán has so haunted Chicano/a critical thought. Its position of privilege derives, I would argue, from the ways in which ideas about Aztlán crystallize contestations of power. As the editors of this collection note in the introduction, one realization that has emerged in American Studies is the awareness that "empire" and "home" are not only interdependent, they are actually coterminous. Nowhere is this point made more clearly than in the numerous uses to which Aztlán has been put. Aztlán is at once the evocation of a painful and violent history and the invocation of a utopian ideal.

The discourses surrounding Aztlán present themselves as the incarnation of the term: the articulation of unity, of nation, of resistance to oppressive power. Each articulation offers its particular understanding of Aztlán as its fulfillment. This is precisely the reason why Aztlán never adds up. As a sign of liberation it is ever being emptied of meaning just as its meaning is asserted, its borders being blurred by those constituencies engaged in liberating struggles ostensibly named by Aztlán. This simultaneous process of arrival and evacuation does not mark a point of despair, nor is it meant to desparage Aztlán. On the contrary. We cannot abandon Aztlán precisely because it serves to name that we so fondly yearn. As such it stands as a starting point for the struggle to articulate and enact an absent unity and empowerment.

Notes

Reprinted with permission of The Regents of the University of California from *Aztlán: A Journal of Chicano Studies* 22.2 (Fall 1997): 15–41, published by the UCLA Chicano Studies Research Center. Not for further reproduction.

1. See especially Chapter Three of my book *Movements in Chicano Poetry*, "From the Homeland to the Borderlands, the Reformation of Aztlán." There is an unstated teleological position in that discussion I find myself rejecting. Consequently, the present essay attempts to draw upon, elaborate, and clarify that previous analysis. The incisive comments offered by Deena González and David Roman have helped me a great deal in this venture and I thank them. All errors, misrepresentations, slips of logic remain stubbornly mine.

2. Here one finds a dichotomy. As Juan Gómez-Quiñones notes, Chicano leaders of the sixties were impeded by the contradictions between their assertive, often separatist, rhetoric and their conventional reformist demands and programs involving educational reform and voter-registration drives (141–6).

3. Thus Douglass Massey and his associates draw upon the signifier to name their study of transnational Mexican migration: *Return to Aztlán.*

4. See Acuña, *Occupied America* (130–43) as well Ralph Guzmán, "The Function of Anglo-American Racism in the Political Development of Chicanos" (21–4), for examples of Euro-American reactions and ensuent legislation to "stem the tide" of Mexican immigration.

5. The term "line of flight" from Deleuze and Guattari is meant to suggest escape from binary choices. The line of flight is formed by ruptures within particular systems or orders. It allows for third possibilities—neither capitulation to regimes nor unconditional freedom from them. The line of flight is a way out, a means of changing the situation to something other. See *Kafka* (1975) and *Anti-Oedipus* (1972).

6. Laclau's discussion of empty signifiers has helped me think through some of the thorny dilemmas set in motion by the various articulations of Aztlán. While I sympathize with his political project, I do not fully ascribe to his view that modern democracy will begin as "different projects or wills will try to hegemonize the empty signifiers of the absent community" (1996:46). His analysis of the empty signifier itself, however, I find insightful.

Works Cited

Acuña, Rodolfo. *Occupied America: A History of Chicanos*. New York: Harper & Row, 1972.

Alarcón, Daniel Cooper. "The Aztec Palimpsest: Toward a New Understanding of Aztlán, Cultural Identity and History." *Aztlán* 19.2 (1992): 33–68.

Alurista. "Cultural Nationalism and Xicano Literature During the Decade 1965–1975." *MELUS* 8 (Summer 1981): 22–34.

Anaya, Rudolfo A., and Francisco Lomelí, eds. *Aztlán: Essays on the Chicano Homeland*. Albuquerque: Academia/El Norte Publications, 1989.

Anzaldúa, Gloria. "To live in the Borderlands means you." In *Borderlands/La Frontera: The New Mestiza*. San Francisco: Spinsters/Aunt Lute, 1987, pp. 194–5.

Barrera, Mario. *Beyond Aztlán: Ethnic Autonomy in Comparative Perspective.* Notre Dame, IN: University of Notre Dame Press, 1988.

Bruce-Novoa, Juan. *Chicano Authors: Inquiry by Interview.* Austin: University of Texas Press, 1980.

Cuesta, Jorge. *Antología de la poesía mexicana moderna.* Mexico: Contemporaneos, 1928.

Deleuze, Gilles, and Félix Guattari. *Anti-Oedipus: Capitalism and Schizophrenia.* Robert Hurley, Mark See, and Helen R. Lane, trans. Preface by Michel Foucault. Minneapolis: University of Minnesota Press, 1983 [1972].

Deleuze, Gilles, and Félix Guattari. *Kafka: For a Minor Literature.* Dana Polan, trans. Foreword by Réda Bensmaïa. Minneapolis: University of Minnesota Press, 1986 [1975].

Elizondo, Sergio D. "ABC: Aztlán, the Borderlands, and Chicago." In *Missions in Conflict: Essays on U.S.-Mexican Relations and Chicano Culture.* Renate von Bardeleben, ed. Tübingen: Gunter Narr Verlag, 1986, pp. 13–23.

Fanon, Frantz. *The Wretched of the Earth.* Constance Farrington, trans. Preface by Jean–Paul Sartre. New York: Grove Press, 1968 [1961].

Gómez-Peña, Guillermo. "Documented/Undocumented," Rubén Martínez, trans. In *The Graywolf Annual Five: Multi-Cultural Literacy.* Rick Simonson and Scott Walker, Saint Paul: Graywolf Press, 1988, eds. pp. 127–34.

Gómez-Quiñones, Juan. *Chicano Politics: Reality and Promise, 1940–1990.* Albuquerque: University of New Mexico Press, 1990.

Gonzales, Sylvia. "National Character vs. Universality in Chicano Poetry." *De Colores* 1 (1975): 10–21.

Guzmán, Ralph. "The Function of Anglo-American Racism in the Political Development of Chicanos." In *La Causa Política: A Chicano Politics Reader.* Chris F. García, ed. Notre Dame, IN: University of Notre Dame Press, 1974, pp. 19–35.

Klor de Alva, J. Jorge. "California Chicano Literature and Pre-Columbian Motifs: Foil and Fetish." *Confluencia* 1 (Spring 1986): 18–26.

Klor de Alva, J. Jorge. "Aztlán, Borinquen and Hispanic Nationalism in the United States." *In Aztlán: Essays on the Chicano Homeland.* Rudolfo Anaya and Francisco Lomelí, eds. Albuquerque: Academia/El Norte Publications, 1989, pp. 135–71.

Labarthe, Elyette Andouard. "The Vicissitudes of Aztlán." *Confluencia* 5 (Spring 1990): 79–84.

Laclau, Ernesto. "Why do Empty Signifiers Matter to Politics?" *Emancipations(s).* London/New York: Verso, 1996, pp. 36–46.

Leal, Luis. "In Search of Aztlán." Gladys Leal, trans. *Denver Quarterly* 16 (Fall 1981): 16–22.

Leal, Luis, and Pepe Barrón. "Chicano Literature: An Overview." In *Three American Literatures.* Houston A. Baker, Jr., ed. Introduction by Walter J. Ong. New York: Modern Language Association, 1982, pp. 9–32.

Massey, Douglas S., Rafael Alarcón, Jorge Durand, Humberto González. *Return to Aztlán: The Social Process of International Migration from Western Mexico.* Berkeley: University of California Press, 1987.

Montoya, José. "Chicano Art: Resistance in Isolation 'Aquí Estamos y no Nos Vamos.' " In *Missions in Conflict: Essays on U.S.-Mexican Relations and Chicano Culture.* Renate von Bardeleben, ed. Tübingen: Gunter Narr Verlag, 1986, pp. 25–30.

Moraga, Cherríe. "Queer Aztlán: The Re-formation of Chicano Tribe." *The Last Generation.* Boston: South End Press, 1993, pp. 145–74.

Padilla, Genaro. "Myth and Comparative Cultural Nationalism: The Ideological Uses of Aztlán." In *Aztlán: Essays on the Chicano Homeland.* Rudolfo Anaya and Francisco Lomelí, eds. Albuquerque: Academia/El Norte Publications, 1989, pp. 111–34.

Paz, Octavio. *Labyrinth of Solitude.* Lysander Kemp, Yara Milos, and Rachel Phillips Belash, trans. New York: Grove Press, 1985 [1950/1959].

Pérez-Torres, Rafael. *Movements in Chicano Poetry: Against Myths, Against Margins.* New York: Cambridge University Press, 1995.

Pina, Michael. "The Archaic, Historical and Mythicized Dimensions of Aztlán." In Aztlán: Essays on the Chicano Homeland. Rudolfo Anaya and Francisco Lomelí, eds. Albuquerque: Academia/El Norte Publications, 1989, pp. 14–48.

"Plan Espiritual de Aztlán." *Aztlan: An Anthology of Mexican American Literature.* Luís Valdez and Stan Steiner, eds. New York: Knopf, 1973 [1969], pp. 402–6.

Ramos, Samuel. *Profile of Man and Culture in Mexico.* Autin: University of Texas Press, 1962 [1934].

Safran, William. "Diasporas in Modern Societies: Myths of Homeland and Return." *Diaspora* 1.1 (1991): 83–99.

Sandoval, Chela. "U.S. Third World Feminism: The Theory and Method of Oppositional Consciousness in the Postmodern World." *Genders* 10 (1991): 1–24.

DENATIONALIZATION RECONSIDERED
Asian American Cultural Criticism at a Theoretical Crossroads
Sau-ling C. Wong

INTRODUCTION

"Denationalization Reconsidered" first appeared in 1995, in a special issue of *Amerasia Journal* entitled "Thinking Theory in Asian American Studies," edited by Michael Omi and Dana Takagi. I wrote it as part of a field-specific dialog within Asian American studies concerning future scholarly and institutional emphases, without intending it to be a general theoretical pronouncement on ethnicity, postcoloniality, or any number of components of contemporary Asian American experiences. The essay addresses Asian Americanists in the American academy, whose institutional positioning, in my view, calls for priority-setting and choices in one's work. Nevertheless, the essay apparently touched a nerve in a wider circle than I had anticipated. When the editors of this volume kindly afforded me an opportunity to revise the essay, I decided, after some thought, to forgo the chance to further clarify my views, defend them against possible misunderstandings, amend my blind spots, or adjust my biases. Instead, I opted for a reprinting of the original essay together with a brief headnote updating the reader on relevant recent developments in Asian American studies, presented in hybrid chronological/thematic order. I feel that this combination better respects the historical moment at which it was first published and the "life of its own" that it has taken on since then.

The year after the "Thinking Theory" volume appeared, *Amerasia Journal* published a special issue, "Transnationalism, Media and Asian Americans," which, in the words of editor Russell Leong, "gathers together essays that utilize historical analysis, ethnographic approaches, and literary strategies to look at interrelated global and domestic conditions that shape the lives of Asian Americans in the late 20th century" (Leong 1996: iv). In this issue, Arif Dirlik's lead article, "Asians on the Rim: Transnational

Capital and Local Community in the Making of Contemporary Asian America" (1996), reviews the new Pacific formation and raises the question: "The original vision of Asian America may no longer be able to contain the forces shaping Asian America. But is it, therefore, irrelevant?" (15) He calls for a "deeply political answer" (15), part of which is a recognition that many of the problems giving rise to the Asian American movement in the 1960s have persisted in reconfigured form. Citing "Denationalization Reconsidered," he affirms the possibility of a significant role for Asian America in "the reassertion of local welfare against the globalizing forces of transnational capitalism" (18).[1]

A direct refutation of the "denationalization" notion can be found in Susan Koshy's essay, "The Fiction of Asian American Literature" (1996). Koshy argues that the concept is "fundamentally flawed" (340), since it falsely opposes the national and the transnational, the domestic and the diasporic. Even the term itself, with connotations from neoimperialist theory, introduces disturbing potential for right-wing political interventions. Furthermore, she sees a "confusion at the descriptive and conceptual level of key terms like 'transnational,' 'international,' and 'borderless economy' " (341). Koshy takes issue most strongly with my idea of the need for "commitment to the place where one resides," hearing in it painful and ominous echoes of Cold War demands on "loyalty" from Asian Americans (341–2). Thus she judges "Denationalization Reconsidered" "conservative in its conclusions" (342), and suggests that it may hinder new developments in Asian American studies. Calling the term "Asian American" catachrestic—with no literal referent and always exceeded by its postulated meaning—Koshy predicts that "the politics of Asian Americans will be more and more defined by issue-based strategic alliances with other groups as a way of responding to the political complexities of the nineties" (341).[2]

Lisa Lowe's *Immigrant Acts: On Asian American Cultural Politics* (1996) is a theoretical analysis of Asian American racial formation and cultural politics based on the premise that from the start, Asian immigration to the United States has been the locus of contradiction between the nation-state and the global economy: that while U.S. capital's needs for labor have placed Asians within the U.S. nation-state, Asian Americans have been marked as "foreign." In this formulation, a global perspective is integral, rather than additional, to any definition of the Asian American formation. "Thus, 'becoming a national citizen' cannot be the exclusive narrative of emancipation for the Asian American subject. Rather, the current social formation entails a subject less narrated by the modern discourse of citizenship and more narrated by the histories of war in Asia, immigration, and the dynamics of the current global economy" (33). Lowe's thesis also stresses the structural nature of the othering of Asians in the U.S.: "American national culture takes up the role of resolving the history of inequalities left unresolved in the economic and political domains" (29). She therefore posits an inherently oppositional aesthetic for Asian American culture, "an aesthetic of infidelity and disidentification" (32).

In 1997, Elaine Kim and Lisa Lowe edited a special issue of *positions: east asia cultures critique* to "facilitate new critical discussions between progressive scholars of East Asia and those in Asian American studies" (viii). "As the formation of Asian Americans within the United States is placed in dialectical relation to international histories and locations, the objects and methods of neither Asian American studies nor Asian studies can remain the same" (xiii). The essays selected all "conceptualize Asian Americans as simultaneously formed within both U.S. national and global frameworks" (x). In diverse ways, the contributors address significant shifts in the last three decades impacting Asian Americans: post-Fordist global restructuring, post-1965 immigration and resulting changes in demographics, the colonial and neocolonial role of the United States in the Asian states from which the new "Asian American" communities emigrate, and the failure of citizenship and civil rights toward racialized groups of color in the United States.

Another anthology exploring connections between Asian studies and Asian American studies is edited by Kandice Chuh and Karen Shimakawa. Entitled *Orientations: Mapping Studies in the Asian Diaspora* and forthcoming from Duke University Press, this volume explores such topics as the disciplines and subjects of Asian and Asian American studies; differentiations between "Asianness" and "Asian Americanness"; rethinking the discursive fields in terms of the consequences, benefits, and dangers of looking beyond nationally-defined disciplinary boundaries; and print cultures, specifically journal publications, reflecting some of the aforementioned shifts.

R. Radhakrishnan, one of the contributors to the Chuh and Shimakawa anthology, has collected his many previously published essays on ethnicity and diaspora in one volume, *Diasporic Mediations: Between Home and Location* (1996). Some of these explicitly address Asian American (specifically, Indian American) identity (e.g., "Is the Ethnic 'Authentic' in the Diaspora?"; 203–214); others offer theoretical considerations of terms such as nation, hybridity, subalternity, and postcoloniality relevant to the Asian American condition. All the "meditations" proceed from an understanding of the "diasporic location" as "the space of the hyphen that tries to coordinate, within an evolving relationship, the identity politics of one's place of origin with that of one's present home" (xiii). In "Postcoloniality and the Boundaries of Identity," Radhakrishnan recommends that "the diasporic be named as the 'ethnic' " (176) and defines the "ethnic mandate" as "to live 'within the hyphen' and yet be able to speak" (175–6). He suggests that "diasporic communities need to make a difference within their places/nations/cultures of residence" and ally with each other "relationally" (176).

A different theorizing of the hyphen than Radhakrishnan's is made by David L. Eng in "Out Here and Over There: Queerness and Diaspora in Asian American Studies" (1997), where he argues for "risking the hyphen," or a "hyperbolization" of the hyphen (37), in order to disrupt too comfortable and uncritical an alignment of home and nation-state, and to keep in view the Asian or diasporic element in Asian American studies. Examining contradictions highlighted by the "double meaning of *domestic* as both the "public space of the masculine (nation-state) and the private realm of the feminine (home)," as well as Asian American cultural nationalists' earlier attempts to purchase a public Asian American male identity through devaluation of a "[feminine and homosexual] private realm" (35), Eng proposes a broadened definition of queerness as "a critical methodology for evaluating Asian American racial formation across multiple axes of difference and in numerous local and global manifestations" (39), in a context of continued movements of transnational capital, immigration, and labor. Other scholars who have investigated the intersection between "Asian Americanness" and "queerness"—both of which have been defined as deviance by the U.S. nation-state at various points in its history—including Gopinath (1997) and Puar (1998).

The slash or solidus, rather than the hyphen, is used in David Palumbo-Liu's inter-disiplinary study, *Asian/American: Historical Crossings of a Racial Frontier* (1999), to signal a complex undecidability in Asian American identity. The term Asian/American implies both exclusion and inclusion, both distinction and movement between the two terms. Beginning with the 1920s, Palumbo-Liu analyzes various materializations of Asian American identity in both a nation-state context and a diasporic context.

Another recent book-length study, David Li's *Imaging the Nation: Asian American Literature and Cultural Consent* (1998), while primarily a work of literary criticism, provides a critical theory of Asian American identity in the chapter on "Difference and Diaspora." Among other things, Li argues that the Asian American formation itself is not automatically a solution to, but rather a problem in and of, the contradic-tions of the nation; and that the regional Asia-Pacific idea is not necessarily ameliora-tive.

Though a group-specific anthology, Aihwa Ong and Donald Nonini's *Ungrounded Empires: The Cultural Politics of Modern Chinese Transnationalism* (1997) expounds, in its introduction (Nonini and Ong 1997), a conceptualization of transnationality that would be of interest to Asian Americanist students of diasporic conditions in general. Nonini and Ong take "an affirmative view of diaspora" ' (18) and suggest that the "mobility" of diaspora Chinese, taking the form of a "guerrilla transnationalism," "challenges and undermines modern imperial regimes of truth and power" (19). Each of such regimes to which diaspora Chinese are subject—the Chinese family, the capi-talist workplace, and the nation-state—requires "the localization of disciplinable sub-jects," which the mobile Chinese seek to elude (23) by working the interstices between national spaces and identities. "What is invoked, or when, depends on particular cir-cumstances and the configuration of social relations that constitute our everyday world" (25).

A direction for future investigations of "Asian Americanness," alluded to only tan-gentially in my essay, concerns information technology. Cyberspace has been theorized as a leveler of physical and social differences, a home to all affiliative "imagined com-munities," and the ultimate deterritorializer—"denationalizer," if you will. The im-pact of cyberspace on Asian American subjectivity and community formation merits exploration in light of several facts: the "imagined community" of Asian Americans has been forged on an awareness of, and commitment to resisting, inequalities imposed on their racialized, gendered, sexualized, classed, and otherwise marked bodies; links between Asians in diaspora are facilitated by the internet; Asian Americans have been heavily involved in high tech in a wide range of roles from assemblers and engineers to entrepreneurs and consumers. Complexities in this situation have been analyzed by, for example, Rai (1995), who studies the "crosshatched" dynamics in the construction of a diasporic Hindu identity on electronic bulletin boards; Nakamura (1995), Chun (1999), and Ow (forthcoming), who identify the reinstatement of Euro-American nor-mativity and reinscription of dominant stereotypes of Asians in cyberspace; and Shu (1998), who, using the case of Asian transnational professionals, argues for models of identity formation and mobilization based on participation in information technologies. "Can [the] permeability between Asian and Asian American identities, which has been facilitated and mediated by information technologies, be considered as a new way to reconstruct the conventionally defined 'Other' within the U.S. cultural context?" (Shu 1998: 152). Palumbo-Liu (1999) examines the projection of "Asia Pacific" into liquid capital and a "borderless" cyberspace.

Last but not least, two recent events focus some of the debates touched on in "Denationalization Reconsidered." The 1996 campaign finance scandal, like the 1982 murder of Vincent Chin, emblematizes for many the dangers of conflating Asian and Asian American, foreigner and citizen, and of the revival of the specter of the "Yellow Peril." To the extent that John Huang and his associates can be seen as bearers of and spokesmen for transnational capital, the scandal also raises questions about the meaning of the "Asian American community" and who should represent it. L. Ling-Chi Wang's "Race, Class, Citizenship, and Extraterritoriality: Asian Americans and the 1996 Finance Campaign Scandal" (1996) presents several ways of analyzing the racialization of political corruption and argues for a focus on the restoration of democracy. (See also Palumbo-Liu [1999] for a cultural studies analysis of mainstream media coverage of the scandal.)

Secondly, several Asian economies crashed catastrophically in 1997–98.[3] The events happened too recently to be significantly reflected in scholarship in Asian American studies. Nevertheless, given the role played by the fact—now cast in serious doubt—of Asian ascendancy in certain varieties of theorizing about new concepts of Asian American identity, a newly diminished picture of Asia's promise might provoke yet more rethinking. The chapter "Fear of a Yellow Planet" in Eric Liu's volume of personal essays, *The Accidental Asian* (1998: 115–44), touches on the allures of the idea of a "borderless Chinese tribe" (123) and his misgivings as a Chinese American about them.

In this essay, I would like to address what I consider to be a theoretical crossroads at which Asian American cultural criticism has found itself. For some time now, Asian American cultural criticism—by which I simply refer to implicit or explicit analysis of Asian American subject formation and cultural production—has been undergoing dramatic changes from whose influences no one in the field of Asian American studies can be exempt. Not only have these changes been shaping the practice of individual scholars, but they have been exerting mounting pressure on the field to reflect on its own operating assumptions and, if necessary, modify them. I will use the term *denationalization* to try to capture the complexity of these cultural phenomena, of which I will single out three for scrutiny.

The first is the easing of cultural nationalist concerns as a result of changing demographics in the Asian American population as well as theoretical critiques from various quarters ranging from the poststructuralist to the queer. This has made possible a complication of identity politics as articulated in the 1960s and 1970s, as well as opened up other axes of organization and mobilization including class, gender and sexuality. Concomitantly, permeability has been increasing in the boundaries between Asian Americans and "Asian Asians," once a rallying point for the Asian American movement; as well as between Asian American studies and Asian studies, two disciplines with very distinct histories and institutional locations, and vexed, at times openly antagonistic, relations. The expanding intercourse between the two fields is, among other things, a response to new patterns of economic and political power affecting the relative positioning of Asia and America. In turn, this repositioning arises from a larger global movement of transnational capital, whose cultural consequences include a normalization of multiple subjectivities, migrations, border-crossings.[4] The sweep of the postmodern condition has made it more and more acceptable to situate Asian Americans in a diasporic context—the third component of the denationalizing trend I wish to investigate. A *diasporic perspective* emphasizes Asian Americans as one element in the global scattering of peoples of Asian origin, in contrast to what I call a *domestic perspective* that stresses the status of Asian Americans as an ethnic/racial minority within the national boundaries of the United States. Together, these three changes have taken on the force of something of a paradigm shift in Asian American studies.

The 1995 special "theory" issue of *Amerasia Journal*, whose primary audience appears to be the community of Asian Americanists, provides a perfect occasion for me to air my concerns about denationalization. I believe a political question of constituency and mission underlies questions of application encountered daily by academic practitioners of cultural criticism. This question must be addressed collectively in the face of a trend that, to some, appears to promise novelty, intellectual excitement, delivery from the institutional ghetto of ethnic studies, or even, perhaps, better funding.

THE EASING OF CULTURAL NATIONALIST CONCERNS

I will begin with a clarification. The switching between "Asian American cultural criticism" and "Asian American studies" in the preceding paragraphs is not done randomly. My remarks will concentrate on the former domain, although I believe their implications concern the field as a whole.

On the issue of denationalization, within the Asian Americanist community there has actually been a kind of disjuncture between the history/social science contingent and the literature/cultural studies contingent. The national boundaries of the United States have never been as intense a point of contention for the former as for the latter. From the start, Asian American historians and social scientists have been interested in immigration; of course, in immigration studies border-crossing is more a given than a cultural proposition to be debated.

Furthermore—and I will elaborate on this later—in a sense it is misleading to cast the current debates on "theory" in Asian American studies (of which denationalization is one manifestation) solely in terms of an unprecedented contemporary occurrence due to external influences. The "pre-post" period—the period before concepts from poststructuralism and postmodernist theories found a hearing in Asian American studies—was already witness to much critical interest beyond the domestic American scene. The activists who founded Asian American studies in the late 1960s and early 1970s were influenced as much by the Cultural Revolution in China as by "domestic"

American events like the civil rights movement or the black power movement (Chan 74–75). The anti-Vietnam War movement, which jolted many Asian Americans into recognizing their commonality with the "gooks" as well as among themselves, is inherently transnational in outlook. So too is the internal colonialism model, which, by drawing analogies between colonies in the traditional mode in the Third World and race relations within U.S. boundaries, allowed Asian Americans to talk about their history beyond terms set by narratives of Americanization dominant in the 1940s and 1950s. As Sucheta Mazumdar puts it, "the very genesis of Asian American Studies was international" ("Asian American Studies and Asian Studies" 40). (In this sense, my term "denationalization" is something of a misnomer, as it suggests deconstruction of an establishment where seeds of that deconstruction have been present from the start. For lack of a comparably complex organizing term, however, I will continue to use "denationalization.")

Nevertheless, it remains true that in the early days, transnational concerns had a way of looping back to the domestic once political lessons had been extracted. The linkage between the two was more in the nature of inspiration and analogy, with "foreign" spheres of struggle lending strength and legitimacy to the American minority political enterprise. The Asian American cultural nationalist project as articulated by the *Aiiieeeee!* group[5] was characterized by a cluster of domestic emphases, and the subsequent development of this project did involve a certain ossification of identity politics. Early Asian American cultural criticism was spearheaded by American-born and -raised, Anglophone, mostly male, Asians (Espiritu 50); it features certain premises—anti-Orientalism, valorization of working-class ethnic enclaves, "claiming America"[6]—that explicitly or implicitly discourage, if not preclude, critical attention on things Asian. (Gender enters the equation in that, with things Asian implicitly theorized as feminine, cultural nationalism is committed to an aggressively masculinist agenda.) In fact, it seems anything that threatens to undermine the demonstration of the "indigenization" (the "becoming American") of Asian Americans must be scrupulously avoided.[7] Thus subscription to an indigenization model of Asian American experiences, whereby a person of Asian ancestry has to earn the designation of "Asian American" by acquiring "American" credentials on "American" soil (e.g., railroad-building, writing in English), informs the cultural nationalist project even as it seeks to critique and resist the model's assimilationist teleology. Fear of exoticization so prevailed (compounded by other obstacles such as English monolingualism among many American-born cultural critics) that literature produced by immigrants in the Asian languages has, for a long time, been neglected, and only recently has the disavowal of Asian influences abated noticeably within Asian American cultural criticism (e.g., Cheung, "Woman Warrior"). For the cultural nationalists, then, the U.S. borders turn out to take on as much significance as for white nativists. *Asian America,* a quasi-geographical term that became current in the 1970s and continues to be important,[8] with no territorial sovereignty/ integrity to underwrite it, appears to me to suggest a yearning for the kind of containing boundaries and contained site enjoyed by the dominant society, a nation-state.

While the above account of cultural nationalism has left out much—nuances, contradictions, as well as later developments—there is some truth to the view that since the mid 1970s, some weakening of the aforementioned domestic emphases has been taking place, resulting in a broader cultural space for more Asian Americans. I need not rehearse the details of the feminist critique of cultural nationalism, which has been well presented by Elaine Kim and King-Kok Cheung, among others, and is familiar to most readers of *Amerasia* (e.g., Cheung, "Woman Warrior"; Kim, "Such Opposite Creations"). What may need highlighting is the fact that theoretical challenges have come from other quarters as well. For example, Shelley Wong mounts a class-based critique of the heroic invocation of railroad building in Asian American nation-building, which becomes implicated in American capitalist discourse and the disciplining of the industrial subject. From a gay studies perspective, David Eng notes how Asian American cultural nationalism has been pursuing its agenda of reclaiming masculinity by reinforcing compulsory heterosexuality and suppressing the presence of the Asian American homosexual. Oscar Campomanes has suggested that the presence of Filipino American literature "problematizes some of the claims of Asian American literature as a constitutive paradigm." By calling for a reconceptualization of Filipino writing in the U.S. as a "literature of exile and emergence," rather than a "literature of immigration and settlement whereby life in the U.S. serves as the space for displacement, suspension, and perspective" (49, 51), Campomanes is not only expressing a Filipino American concern. Rather, he is also giving voice to a complaint shared by several other groups. The new Asian American demographics, in which East Asians no longer predominate, have made for a complication of the alignments created in the 1960s and 1970s. For the recently arrived (such as Vietnamese Americans) or long-established but recently vocal groups (such as South Asian Americans), their cultural specificities and historical relationships with U.S. imperialism may be much more complex than has been recognized in an identity politics derived largely from East Asian American experiences.

Shelley Wong, Eng, and Campomanes are just a few of a new generation of critics who have been disrupting the apparently consensual theoretical basis of the Asian American movement. Their moves may or may not lead to a retraining of critical focus beyond U.S. national boundaries, but they all contribute to denationalization in the first sense that I have outlined.

GROWING PERMEABILITY BETWEEN "ASIAN" AND "ASIAN AMERICAN"

Denationalization in the second sense entails a relaxation of the distinction between what is Asian American and what is "Asian," and between Asian American studies and Asian studies. To quote Elaine Kim's succinct formulation in a key document in the denationalization debate, her foreword to Shirley Lim and Amy Ling's 1992 critical anthology, *Reading the Literatures of Asian America* (framed as a revision of the 1982 Introduction to her *Asian American Literature),* "The lines between Asian and Asian American, so important to identity formation in earlier times, are increasingly being blurred" (xiii). As a corollary of this blurring, something of a rapprochement between Asian studies and Asian American studies has been taking place.

There are obvious material bases for this second component of denationalizaton, chief among them the ascendancy of Asia as an economic power of global impact, the coalescence of the Pacific Rim as a geoeconomic entity, and the circulation of Asian transnational capital.[9] Thus instead of being mere suppliants at the "golden door," desperate to trade their sense of ethnic identity for a share of America's plenty, many of today's Asian immigrants regard the U.S. as simply one of many possible places to exercise their portable capital and portable skills. In other words, whereas political instability and economic depression used to occur hand in hand, the Asia of "little dragons" has disentangled the two, creating a situation in which phenomenal economic growth coexists with political uncertainty or repression.[10] While the U.S. is still wildly romanticized in many parts of Asia, the concept of the Pacific Rim as an interconnected economic unit underscores the unevenness of this vast region in which migration is but a rational means of trade-off between security and profit. (In fact, the direction of movement can no longer be assumed to be from Asia to America; many Asian Americans in science and technology are relocating to Asia: see Dunn.) Segments of the Asian professional class have developed their own patterns of trans-Pacific commuting, which obviously affect identity formation in unprecedented ways.

Christopher L. Connery has deftly traced the gradual rise of what he terms Pacific Rim Discourse in the mid-1970s, which has diffused into American culture as an Asia-facing orientation (as opposed to an earlier preoccupation with Europe) and a general awareness of the interconnectedness of Asian and U.S. fortunes. Among the contributing factors he lists are the thaw in U.S.-China relations, the end of the Vietnam War, the recognition of Japan's economic power, and the worldwide economic downturn that forced the U.S. to acknowledge its loss of hegemony. Although Connery notes a decline in Pacific Rim Discourse and an American retreat from internationalism in the late 1980s, the discourse's hold on the American population imagination is still to be reckoned with.

When cultural projects involve trans-Pacific collaboration in material terms, delimiting and designating them as either Asian American or "Asian" become much more difficult, maybe ultimately irrelevant. One good example is the work of film director Ang Lee (*Pushing Hands, The Wedding Banquet,* and *Eat, Drink, Man, Woman*), who grew up in Taiwan, received an American education, draws from both sides of the Pacific for funding, actors and film crew, and deals with characters of varying degrees of biculturality. How exactly should one classify him and his *oeuvre,* not just at credit-claiming time but in a conscientious attempt at valid conceptualization?

Apart from the issue of classification, cultural dissemination, maintenance, and transformation for Asian Americans—a group with a sizable aggregate disposable income—are very different matters today than they were before the advent of cheap jet travel, fax and e-mail, pocket translators, long-distance phone services competing for clients with multilingual support, satellite-typeset Asian-language newspapers, and video and laserdisc rental outlets featuring Asian films. While "trans-Pacific families" (H. Liu) have been a long-standing reality among Asian Americans, today's voluntary immigrants and their descendants, especially middle-class ones, lead a kind of life that tends to blunt the acute binarism between Asian and American with which earlier generations have had to contend strenuously. They need no longer conform to a paradigm of identity formation developed in the steamboat era, when entry into the U.S. more often than not meant a one-way experiment in adaptation. Instead, the voice of family across the ocean could be just a push-button phone call away, and Asian-language media could be brought into one's living room.[11] To paraphrase the title of a book on Southeast Asian Americans, the Far East has come near (Nguyen-Hong-Nhiem and Halpern).

Indeed, the strict demarcation between Asian and Asian American would break down irreparably if we examined the families of so-called "parachute kids" (in Chinese they are often called *xiao liuxuesheng,* or "little foreign students" [Nina Chen]). In view of Asia's vastly superior economic prospects but continued political uncertainty, many middle-class Asian families are splitting their members, sending the children (some-times accompanied by a parent, sometimes not) to study in U.S. schools and/or gain permanent residency while the breadwinner stays in Asia. Family ties are maintained by frequent visits in either direction. (Hence the Chinese nicknames for such families: *kongzhong feiren,* "trapeze artist," or *taikongren,* "astronauts.") Quite apart from citizenship status, the "parachute kids'" lived experience of functioning in this country neither as immigrants nor as foreign (F-1 visa-holding) students, but sharing the situations of both, compels us to reexamine the meaning of "Asian American." As I understand it, the dropping of the hyphen from *Asian-American* in the cultural national-ist period was meant to affirm the indivisible integrity of the Asian American experi-ence, that is, to minimize any negative connotation associated with bilaterality. Now as never before, however, bilaterality is a tangible, physical reality for many at both the family and the individual level.

Not to be overlooked as part of post-1965 demographic changes in the Asian American community is the influx of Asian-born academics (among whom I count myself), whose outlook and research activities further make for closer interactions between Asian and Asian American studies. On the one hand already Westernized before immigration to the U.S.—as Rey Chow points out, this complicates, for good reason, the stereotypical belief in a pristine "native" origin (xi–xii)—these academics, unlike many of their American-born counterparts, are bilingual and biliterate, often retaining a keen interest in the transformations in the Asian cultures in a postcolonial context. To them, the continuities between Asian and Asian American are more abun-dant, the disjunctures less absolute, than to the early cultural nationalists. Especially apparent to the immigrant scholars is the need to denaturalize the U.S. borders as a sort of invisible fence around Asian American cultural criticism.

Their access to and interest in the "Asian" aspects of the Asian American experi-ence are congruent with the attention shift and self-critique among Asian studies scholars: the latter, likewise influenced by the global forces that impinge on the for-mer, have had to rethink their field's area studies roots, Cold War complicities, residual Orientalist assumptions, and racialized stratification of labor in academia. Mazumdar notes: "Drawing boundaries and arbitrarily isolating the immigrants' history and cul-ture of the homeland under the rubric of Asian Studies, and focusing only on [their] existence after arrival in the United States as shaped by the American context, assumes 'America' could be understood independently of 'Asia' or vice versa" (40–41). Neither assumption is conceptually adequate.

Finally, in higher education and academic research settings, Asian and Asian American studies sometimes have to share an institutional location or form a coalition to combat an unsympathetic administration for resources. Whatever the problems with the rhetoric and practice of "multiculturalism" in today's liberal education, it has made Asian-ancestry scholars, regardless of where they are housed, more aware of their common imposed (not always voluntarily adopted) role in the academy and in the racial politics of the larger society. The result is a noticeable rise in collaborative professional activities between Asian Americanists and Asianists, in the form of sessions at each other's conferences, articles in each other's journals, etc.;[12] another form is filling joint appointments, so that the two fields are embodied in one scholar. Certainly it would be a mistake to exaggerate the cordiality between the two fields: Asian American studies is often treated with contempt by sinologist types even now. But considering how long-standing their mutual suspicion, and how much of a *bête noir* the conflation of Asian and Asian American has been to Asian American studies, the current rapprochment is striking.

SHIFTING FROM A DOMESTIC TO A DIASPORIC PERSPECTIVE

The third aspect of denationalization—the shift from a domestic American to a diasporic perspective—follows from the first two but has its own additional set of contributing causes. The increased porosity between Asian and Asian American is but one constituent in a global trend; to paraphrase a character in Salman Rushdie's *Satanic Verses,* the universe is shrinking (cited in Hagedorn, "Exile" 25). In light of the aforementioned combination of multinational capital, cultural homogenization through commodification, and advanced communications technology, not only the Pacific Rim regions, but all regions of the world can be said to be interpenetrating.[13] Furthermore, as Edward Said remarks, in our century forced uprootings of entire populations have attained proportions that are humanistically and aesthetically incomprehensible. "Our age—with its modem warfare, imperialism and the quasi-theological ambitions of totalitarian rulers—is indeed the age of the refugee, the displaced persons, mass immigration" ("Reflections" 357). Though Said's observation is not made in reference to denationalization, the mass movements he describes do point to a world in which identity and culture are increasingly decoupled from geopolitics.

Paul Gilroy argues that one of the principal reasons for going beyond a "national and nationalistic perspective" is that "neither political nor economic structures of domination are still co-extensive with the borders of nation-states": postmodernity has eclipsed the importance of the modern nation-state as a political, economic, and cultural unit ("Cultural Studies" 188). While I question Gilroy's verdict on "ethnic absolutism," the need for a transnational analysis of political, economic, and cultural relationships is undeniable. This appears particularly important when one is studying women, whose relationship with the nation-state has always been conflicted.[14] As Chandra Mohanty points out, "contemporary post-industrial societies . . . invite cross-national and cross-cultural analyses for explanation of their own internal features and socioeconomic constitution" (2; see also Grewal and Kaplan). Beginning with Asian immigrant women garment workers in the U.S. (traditionally the province of Asian American studies), Lisa Lowe has made a compelling case for understanding them in more than a domestic context, linking them to other women of color in the U.S. as well as to transnational capitalism and labor politics worldwide.

(In this connection, let me add that Asian American denationalization is paralleled by changes and debates in other ethnic studies fields. Not only has African-American studies increased its attention to the "Black Atlantic" and scatterings further afield, but Chicano studies has been confronted with the question of including non-Mexican-origin Latino Americans and revising the notion of American culture altogether (e.g., José David Saldívar), and Native American studies must consider professional and political alliances with indigenous peoples elsewhere in the world from a Fourth World perspective.)[15]

As it applies to Asian Americans, a recognition of transnational realities means acknowledging that certain groups classified as Asian Americans by post-1960s prac-tice—Americans of Asian ancestry residing permanently in the United States, regard-less of nativity—have concerns not addressed by that categorization. For example, the cultural productions of, say, Marcos-era Filipino-Americans, Vietnamese- or other South East Asian Americans, or post-Tiananmen Chinese-Americans, necessarily take on a nondomestic cast: the finality of their dislocation co-exists with a perpetual turn-ing of one's gaze toward the lost homeland. This may—or it just as well may not—make for a readier inhabitation of the subject positions assigned by the dominant society. The situation is particularly vexed when displacement is a direct consequence of U.S. imperialism.[16]

Thus a notion of Asian American literature and culture based on putting down roots on American soil—*luodi shenggen,* to cite the title of the first international confer-ence on "overseas Chinese" held in San Francisco in 1992—becomes deeply problema-tized. For some Asian Americans, the impulse to uproot oneself from America at the earliest opportunity may be at least as strong as, if not stronger than, the rooting impulse. (The homeward gaze could last a lifetime.) In such cases, only a diasporic perspective can provide the conceptual room needed to accommodate non-conforming cultural orientations, as well as expose the role of American foreign policy in shaping global patterns of population movement.[17] A diasporic perspective also provides the only way to capture the complexities of multiple migrations and dispersed Asian-origin families, which are not at all uncommon in the population designated as Asian Americans. A Vietnamese American may have gone through Thailand, Hong Kong or France before reaching the US; an Indian American may have lived in Kenya or Britain; a Chinese American family may have branches in Brazil, Singapore, or Ger-many. In light of such migratory patterns, to take the perimeters of the American nation as the limits of one's cultural interests seems arbitrary and myopic. It is pre-cisely on these grounds that a speaker at the session, "Re-examining Diasporas," at the 1994 Association for Asian American Studies Conference in Ann Arbor, Michigan, protested the narrowness of the term *Asian American.*[18] A presenter at the same session, Evelyn Hu DeHart, argued in her paper "What Is a Diaspora?" that the concept of immigration is too linear and limiting, and that an ethnic studies approach is overbur-dened by the baggage of the immigration model such as voluntarism or American triumphalism. (In the same vein, a colleague of mine once told me in a conversation that she resented being pigeonholed as Asian American; instead, she preferred to call herself a world citizen, a term that to her more accurately reflects her past experiences and current mobility.)

Not only scholars but creative writers as well are participating in denationalization in the third sense. Russell Leong's volume of poetry, *The Country of Dreams and Dust,* maps the full sweep of the Chinese diaspora with glances at the Vietnamese diaspora.[19] Jessica Hagedorn describes her own works as being filled with "edgy characters who superficially seem to belong nowhere, but actually belong everywhere"—a phrase that she endows with paradigmatic force and exemplifies in the character Joey Sands in the novel *Dogeaters,* a mixed race homosexual prostitute with the adaptability of a chameleon. Hagedorn stresses the inspiration she gets from the "elegant chaos" of the Philippines' hybrid culture, as well as from the worldwide pop culture perceived as "American." She asserts that "as Asian Americans, as writers and people of color in a world still dominated by Western thinking," we should affirm "a literature that attempts to encompass the world" (Hagedorn, "Exile" 28). For her, Asian American identity formation is not correlated with a sense of belonging to any geographical or political entity. Hagedorn's recent anthology, *Charlie Chan Is Dead,* applies a principle of selection consonant with this belief.

A similar valorization of fluid subjectivity and cultural world citizenship has been voiced by David Mura. In his 1991 memoir *Turning Japanese,* Mura links his "sense of homelessness and defiance of limits" to a ludic aesthetic, citing Yeats, "One day, the poet will wear all masks." Mura's view suggests that denationalizing moves are not peculiar to the foreign-born or those from a heritage as hybrid as the Philippines'. Mura is a Sansei from Minnesota who grew up in a Jewish neighborhood; in his personal life, he has had to grapple with some of the issues with which the Asian American movement contended in the 1960s, and 1970s, as shown by his earlier essay, "Strangers in the Village." Yet Mura, too, appears to have come to regard an Asian American identity as limiting. Poststructuralism is obviously a mediating influence in the case of Barthes-quoting Mura, a product of graduate studies in literature, but one hardly needs it to respond to the alluring possibility of an ever-evolving, never-resolved subjectivity, characterized by instability, endless movement, boundary transgressions, and multiple reference points.

RESERVATIONS

The above, then, are some material circumstances and discursive practices that have contributed to the emergence of a larger, more diverse, more cosmopolitan, one might say more intractable (from a theoretical standpoint) Asian American population. This population calls for vocabularies and concepts about subject formation and cultural production adequate to its perceived realities.

While I have been an early proponent of broadening Asian American literary studies to include immigrant works, which presupposes noteworthy continuities between Asian and Asian American historical experiences and cultural expressions, I have found

myself raising questions about the consequences of an uncritical participation in denationalization, as if it represented a more advanced and theoretically more sophisticated
(in short, superior, though proponents rarely say so directly) stage in Asian American
studies. A developmental or maturational narrative about reconfigurations in Asian
American cultural criticism, whether implicitly or explicitly presented, to me poses
some serious risks. For convenience in discussion, these risks can be grouped into two
categories that are, in fact, inseparable: unwitting subsumption into master narratives
(despite a mandate to subvert master narratives built into the ethnic studies approach),
and depoliticization occluded by theoretical self-critique.[20] While conceding the intellectual and emotional excitement generated by the sense of identity expansion, the
benefits of interdisciplinary commerce, indeed the irreversibility of the material forces
fueling Asian diasporas, I contend that at this juncture in the evolution of our field,
we need to historicize the push to globalize Asian American cultural criticism. Without such historicizing, one of the most important aspirations of denationalization—to
dialogize and trouble American myths of nation—may end up being more subverted
than realized.

I will begin by alluding to a point made earlier in this essay, that the contrast
between the narrow-minded, essentialist 1960s and 1970s and the more enlightened,
deconstructivist and internationalist 1980s is, in many ways, an overdrawn and dehistoricized dichotomy, one based on a "forgetting" of the inherently coalitional spirit of
the pan-Asian American movement. I place "forgetting" in quotation marks to indicate that, of course, the forgetting is itself historically determined and not just a
mistake or a lapse in attention; certainly I do not mean to imply that a "back to
basics" approach would resolve the contestations within the field. However, to me it
is not entirely coincidental that this self-critique echoes the trajectory of "growth"
prescribed for people of color in this country: that minorities need to liberate themselves from their outmoded, inward-looking preoccupations and participate in the
more generous-spirited intellectual inquiries that "everybody else" is engaged in.

Likewise, there are problems with too celebratory a stance toward the loosening of
selected societal constraints on Asian Americans, who have come to be valued in some
Pacific Rim discourse concerning American competitiveness in the Asian and global
marketplace. Again, an underlying developmentalist narrative, tracing a line from
American isolationism to transnational cooperation, elides domestic race relations as
well as the United States's history of exploitation of Asian labor, whether it be manual
or high-tech, at home or abroad. As Aihwa Ong observes, Asian Americans have often
been regarded as the shock troops in America's trade war with Asia.[21] This is the
material basis for certain phenomena that appear, to a casual glance, to be simply an
unalloyed enhancement or enlargement of the cultural life of Asian Americans. Popular rhetoric about the advantages of bicultural literacy, for example, does not merely
represent the triumph and vindication of previous Asian American cultural struggles,
or a confirmation of the need to denationalize. It is all these, but it is also a justification
for using Asian American workers, especially immigrant workers, at various levels
to serve the economic interests of multinational corporations. From this perspective,
language and cultural maintenance is chiefly a business asset, not a matter of community-building. Sometimes I wonder if the current discourse affirming the Asian

American professional's cultural mobility—which encodes usefulness in controlling immigrant laborers on American assembly lines, or negotiating with Asian businesses overseas—would have been as enthusiastically embraced if he/she had not previously encountered frustrations in a purportedly meritocratic, color-blind economy.

It is in this context that I wish to examine a much cited model of identity formation proposed in Lisa Lowe's influential theoretical essay, "Heterogeneity, Hybridity, Multiplicity: Marking Asian American Differences."[22] Among other things, Lowe calls for a redefinition of Asian American subjectivity by holding up, as a "possible model for the ongoing construction of ethnic identity," the transnationally mobile Chinese American family in Peter Wang's film *A Great Wall*. She valorizes "the migratory process suggested by [Peter] Wang's filmic technique and emplotment": namely, a "shuttling between . . . various cultural spaces," so that "we are left, by the end of the film, with a sense of culture as dynamic and open, the result of a continual process of visiting and revisiting a plurality of cultural sites." "We might conceive of the making and practice of Asian American culture as nomadic, unsettled, taking place in the travel between cultural sites and in the multivocality of heterogeneous and conflicting positions" (39). I do not quote this passage here as a summation of the complex arguments in the essay, which, in deconstructing Asian American identity and revealing its internal contradictions, scrupulously affirms the continued need for a Spivakian "strategic essentialism." Lowe's main point is to interrogate the definition of "Asian American" in the 1990s and open up the possibility of "crucial alliances with other groups—ethnicity-based, class-based, gender-based, and sexuality-based—in the ongoing work of transforming hegemony" (39, 40). In that sense, the *Great Wall* example supports but one argument in that essay.

Nevertheless, in view of how central a theoretical document Lowe's essay is in contemporary Asian American studies, and how frequently the passage on *A Great Wall* has been cited by students, Asian Americanists, and other scholars,[23] I would like to raise several issues suggested by it. One is the danger of decontextualization. When the Chinese American father in *A Great Wall* is extracted from his environment to serve as a model of cultural dynamism, what gets left out of the picture are the character's socioeconomic positioning as well as the historical juncture at which the film was made. In the film, the computer scientist's trip to China is precipitated precisely by the kind of career frustration in a racist corporate structure that I touched on above. (He is passed over for a deserved promotion.) In the pre-Tiananmen honeymoon in U.S.-China relations, this frustration could be made into a comic mechanism to trigger a journey of cultural reconsideration and discovery for the entire family; conflicts, where they surface, could be an occasion for light-hearted cross-cultural comparisons. But the hopeful cast to the journeying is less a function of cultural mobility per se than a function of less somber times.

What is more, I wonder to what extent a class bias is coded into the privileging of travel and transnational mobility in Lowe's model—and this is a questioning I extend to some other articulations of denationalization. I understand fully that Lowe's "cultural sites" need not be geographic; however, it is also not entirely accidental, I believe, that *A Great Wall* is about an affluent Chinese American family of the professional class that can take vacationing for granted and have a comfortable home to return to, even when the father has quit his job. After all, as Elaine Kim observes, it is middle-class Asian American youth who can "spend the summer in Seoul or Taipei almost the way middle-class American youth of yore went to summer camp" ("Foreword" xiv). In other words, Lowe's model of identity and cultural formation is, at least in part, extrapolated from the wide range of options available to a particular socioeconomic class, yet the class element is typically rendered invisible. It is from a similar premise, if in much harsher terms, that E. San Juan has faulted Jessica Hagedorn's celebration of her global family and her freedom to put together a fluid, transnational, and cosmopolitan identity. The celebration betrays traces of her own upper-class background: consuming of imported goods is now extended to consuming of cultural products and practices ("From Identity Politics" 129–31).

Class can also be erased when an exilic sensibility is promoted as less narrow than an immigrant one.[24] A preference for exile status is sometimes expressed by middle or upper-middle class immigrant intellectuals who do not want to confront their complicity in emigration and settlement. That is, the severity of the circumstances propelling their exit and preventing their return could have been exaggerated in the interest of ennobling one's self-image. I began pondering this issue when, some years ago, I interviewed two well-known Chinese immigrant writers whose works I taught in a course on Chinese immigrant writing. Even though both left Taiwan under less than life-threatening circumstances and had been living as permanent residents in the U.S. for years, both repudiated the category of "immigrant" (to them probably too materialistic in connotation), preferring to be known as exiles, victims of the cataclysms in recent Chinese history who were displaced from their troubled homeland against their will. Without claiming to know how widespread this phenomenon is,[25] I submit that an elastic definition of "forcible removal" encouraged by the favoring of an exilic identity does have a tendency to depoliticize. Of course, a prolonged exilic sensibility could have been accounted for as well by the less than enthusiastic reception that the U.S. has historically offered Asians. This point has been frequently made in defense of Asian American "sojourning"; further, in his recent typology of Chinese American identity ("Roots"), Ling-Chi Wang has demonstrated the complexities of identification even within a single individual's lifetime. Nevertheless, the potential to glamorize a noncommittal political stance in one's land of principal residence is, to me, a real danger, one that Asian American cultural critics need to recognize.

Even risking culpability of too legalistic a definition of "immigrant," or else too stern a denial of the immigrant's psychic pain, I would like to insist on "claiming America," which was the focus of Asian American cultural politics for fifteen or twenty years after the Third World Student Strikes but is now being contested by denationalization. By "claiming America," I refer to establishing the Asian American presence in the context of the United States' national cultural legacy and contemporary cultural production. Now a diasporic paradigm could conceivably be seen as affording a more flexible and effective purchase on the project of challenging hegemony, whose transnational dimensions are to take precedence over its domestic manifestations. Yet if claiming America becomes a minor task for Asian American cultural criticism and espousal of denationalization becomes wholesale, certain segments of the Asian American population may be left without a viable discursive space. Theresa Tensuan notes that when

Campomanes makes the exile model normative for "Filipino American" writing, the "Flip" writers—American-born descendants of working-class Filipino immigrants—get short shrift.[26] Her observation is worth considering seriously. After all, as John Liu pointed out in a remark at the AAAS conference session referred to above, the term "diasporic" is often deployed as a proxy for "first generation"; in that case, what would be the meaning of preferring a diasporic outlook for the American-born generations? The sentiments and issues ventilated in the cultural nationalist period have not simply become obsolete from shifts in global political, economic, and cultural power. Rather, individual Asian Americans—even first-generation ones, and especially youngsters who have to go through the American educational system—often recapitulate the "old" struggles.[27] These are "old" in the sense of being familiar to Asian Americanists or having been superseded by concerns more amenable to the lexicon of poststructuralism and postmodernity. But they are far from "old" for the subject contending with diverse interpellations, of which the injunction to "Americanize" (often delivered with threats of physical violence) may at times be the most clamorous. Again, what I am challenging is developmentalism, which facilitates reabsorption into master narratives. It would be far more useful to conceive of *modes* rather than *phases* of Asian American subjectivity: an indigenizing mode can coexist and alternate with a diasporic or a transnational mode, but the latter is not to be lauded as a culmination of the former, a stage more advanced or more capacious. In short, there should be no teleology informing our account of the transformations in the world and in the field of Asian American studies.

In an intellectual climate in which "traveling theory" automatically sounds more chic than any "located" theory with a single appellation, we should remember that the concept of *Asian Americans* is one that doesn't travel well, and for good reason: explicitly coalitional, more anti-essentialist than it has been given credit for, it grew out of a specific history of resistance and advocacy within the United States. Conversely, the term *diaspora* attains a global sweep precisely because it has an essentialist core, Stuart Hall's scrupulous redefinition of diaspora as hybridity notwithstanding ("Cultural Identity and Diaspora" 104). In saying this, I am far from suggesting that any group has to be studied in only one theoretical framework; neither am I a purist for whom cultural transformation is measured in terms of deviance from a sacred origin. Finally, even with its essentialist conceptual core, diaspora studies need not abandon sensitivity to oppression or participate in ethnocentrism and cultural chauvinism. Inderpal Grewal has argued persuasively that with a "more inclusive move toward the study of Asian diasporas," Asian American studies could continue the "critique of the state or of the U.S. as empire" that has marked the inception of the field." What I am arguing is that the loosely held and fluctuating collectivity called "Asian Americans" will dissolve back into its descent defined constituents as soon as one leaves American national borders behind.[28] Thus one might study the Chinese diaspora, or the Indian diaspora, and so on. A shared origin, even if it has to be traced a long way back, is constitutive in each case: there is an implicit appeal to common interests which motivates the grouping in the first place. (Indeed, the appeal is often to patriotism for the "motherland" or "fatherland.")[29] But the idea of an "Asian diaspora" would be so inclusive as to be politically ungrounded (in fact ungroundable, given the vastly different interests and conflicted histories of Asian peoples), while the idea of an "Asian American diaspora" is simply quite meaningless. With this reductio ad absurdum, I hope to demonstrate that there is a fundamental tension between Asian American studies with its history of resistance and advocacy, and diaspora studies of specific groups by origin.

But what of the opportunity to build political coalitions across national boundaries? Doesn't diaspora studies provide that?[30] Admittedly formed without as much deep study as I would have liked, my tentative view on this question is that, while I have seen political alliances formed between Asian Americans of different ethnicities to support struggles elsewhere—for example, in aid of pro-democracy dissidents in China or Korean students fighting for reunification—the more typical transnational political alliances seem to be those based on "blood," as a matter of "helping one's own." And given the history of Asian American studies, in which political coalitions formed with other racial/ethnic *domestic* minorities made the very existence of the field possible, I would argue for a continued primacy for this type of association. Elliott Butler-Evans made the point that Rodney King was beaten as a member of an American minority, not as a member of the black diaspora.[31] I think what he meant was that although the violence against African-Americans could be cast in a diasporic context, it is the more immediate context—the status of African-Americans as a domestic American minority—that provides the more compelling explanation and makes for more effective political intervention (at least in the short run). This understanding should thus take precedence over one framed by the African diaspora; that the latter might provide a more theoretically comprehensive account, or be more intellectually gratifying, is a matter of lesser urgency. In the same spirit, I submit that coalitions of Asian American and other racial/ethnic minorities within the U.S. should take precedence over those formed with Asian peoples in the diaspora.

Furthermore, denationalization seems to me to have different valences in the Asian American and African-American contexts. A shift from an African-American domestic to an African diaspora perspective might be more politicizing for African-Americans, while a corresponding move might be depoliticizing for Asian Americans. For African-Americans, the study of diverse other African-origin groups might help counter the group's sense of beleaguerment and constriction imposed by the United States variant of slavery and racism. Connecting to African origins is a powerful means of undoing the cultural amnesia white society attempted to impose. In contrast, a denationalized Asian American cultural criticism may exacerbate liberal pluralism's already oppressive tendency to "disembody," leaving America's racialized power structure intact.

In tracing her own evolving reaction to Theresa Hak Kyung Cha's *Dictee* from the 1980s to the 1990s, Elaine Kim states that this radically destabilizing text demonstrates how "we can 'have it all' by claiming an infinity of layers of self and community" ("Foreword" xvi). While Kim is careful to enumerate the possibilities so claimed, the very fact that a critic like her, known for political commitment and a deep appreciation of historical particularities, should employ a vocabulary of limitlessness testifies to the rhetoric's allure. I believe we can "have it all" only in our consciousness; the infinity of layers of self and community inevitably shrinks when one attempts to translate the claim into material reality. Not only are one's time and energy for action finite, but whatever claiming one does must be enacted from a political location—one referenced to a political structure, a nation. Theoretically I could ascribe a great deal of power to interstitiality and subjectivity-shuttling, which may be wonderful prompters of denaturalizing insights; in practical political terms, however, I can't see how an interstitial, shuttling exercise of power is done.[32] Nations dispense or withhold citizenship, identity cards, passports and visas, voting rights, educational and economic opportunities. For every vision of a borderless world extrapolated from the European Union or NAFTA, there are countless actual instances of political struggles defined in terms of national borders and within national borders. By definition, a world where most travel requires passports and visas is not ready for "world citizenship," a phrase that to me means as much as, or as little as, "just a human being." As ideals both are unimpeachable in their generosity of spirit, their expressed desire to abolish all divisions, all oppositions; as points of purchase for political action both are severely limited in utility, oftentimes disappointingly irrelevant.

In the same sentence where she affirms an "infinity of layers of self and community" Elaine Kim takes care to highlight a word that has an almost old-fashioned ring in today's world—roots: "our rootedness enables us to take flight" ("Foreword" xvi). To Asian Americans the term "roots" could evoke contradictory meanings: either "origin," where one or one's family hails from in Asia; or else commitment to the place where one resides (L. Ling-Chi Wang, "Roots" 187). The second meaning, on which Asian American studies was founded, is what today's Asian Americanists must not lose sight of amidst the enthusiastic call for denationalization.

A Personal Postscript

On the door of the Asian American Studies Program office at UC Berkeley is a sign: THIS IS NOT ASIAN STUDIES, SOUTH AND SOUTHEAST ASIAN STUDIES, OR EAST ASIAN LANGUAGES. Though born out of a practical concern—the frustrated secretary's attempt to minimize misdirected inquiries and interruptions—this sign to me epitomizes the institutional reality within which Asian American studies still operates today. It is a reminder of the precariousness of Asian American studies' discursive space: despite the increasing porosity of boundaries, Asian studies and Asian American studies are still distinct, and collapsing the two will work to the detriment more of Asian Americans as a minority within U.S. borders than of "Asian Asians." For the dropping of the "American" in "Asian American studies" is not only a widespread error—I have yet to hear of someone mistaking Asian American studies for American studies—it is one with potentially serious political consequences. As one of the immigrant academics whose presence has contributed to denationalization, I am mindful of contradictions in my position,[33] and I know that many of the research and teaching interests that come readily to me are not always the ones most needed in the field. Given that, I can no more wish myself out of priority-setting by citing the postmodern condition as my alibi, than I can conjure up an unproblematic multiple subjectivity through an assemblage of poststructuralist terms.

Times are bad, no question about it. Ling-Chi Wang has identified four founding principles of ethnic studies: self-determination, solidarity among American racial minorities, educational relevance, and an interdisciplinary approach (ridiculed as "undisciplined" in the 1960s and 1970s but, like marginality, now fashionable in academia ["Asian American Studies/Ethnic Studies"]). Though these principles might not yield an exhaustive account of Asian American studies, I don't think any of them has been invalidated by changing times. The political imperatives informing Asian American cultural criticism in the early days have not been so firmly achieved that they can be comfortably retired now. In fact, in the age of Newt Gingrich, Rush Limbaugh, Proposition 187, and increasingly vicious attacks on affirmative action and other policies safeguarding the rights of peoples of color, there seems to me to be an even greater need for Asian Americanists to situate themselves historically, to ask where denationalization comes from and where it is headed. To what extent do we want to denationalize our field? To what extent do we want a diasporic perspective to supersede a domestic one? Without subscribing to a narrow, either/or alarmism, I submit these questions for the consideration of my fellow Asian Americanists.

Acknowledgments

Many colleagues and students have helped me keep abreast of developments in the issues I discussed in "Denationalization Reconsidered" and thus helped with my new introduction to this article. I want to thank the following people in particular for telling me about and/or supplying me with relevant sources (some of which are pre-publication copies), and for impressing upon me the importance of some of the topics reviewed in the headnote: Wendy Chun, David Eng, Tomo Hattori, David Li, Kim-An Lieberman, Rachel Lee, Jeff Ow, David Palumbo-Liu, Rob Wilson. I thank the editors of this volume for the opportunity to add this introduction and bring this essay to the attention of a wider readership.

1995: I am indebted to many colleagues for reading earlier drafts of this paper, being exceptionally generous with their critiques and insights, suggesting readings, sharing their work in progress, offering encouragement and support, and providing opportunities for my ideas to be publicized; for lack of space their contributions cannot always be specified: Kum-Kum Bhavnani, Chen Kuan-Hsing, King-Kok Cheung, Inderpal Grewal, Abdul JanMohamed, Caren Kaplan, Elaine Kim, Russell Leong, Lisa Lowe, Colleen Lye, Michael Omi, David Palumbo-Liu, David Parker, Steve Rumpel, Dana Takagi, Dick Walker, Ling-Chi Wang. King-Kok Cheung and I exchanged work in progress; on some issues we independently arrived at shared views, while on others we differ; see her Introduction to *An Interethnic Guide to Asian American Literature*. I am also grateful for feedback from the students in my graduate seminar on Asian American literature, Spring 1993, as well as from the audiences at the following gatherings when earlier versions of the paper were presented: the "Decentering Identity, Recentering Politics" conference at UC Santa Barbara, April 1993, organized by Kum-Kum Bhavnani; the Asian American Literature Discussion Group session at the MLA Convention, Toronto, December 1993; the Townsend Center Humanities Fellowship' meetings, 1993–94; the Ethnic Studies Colloquium. Series, UC Berkeley, Spring 1994; the American Cultures Summer Seminar for Community College Teachers, June 1994. I thank Dorothy Wang and John Zou for their skillful and prompt research assistance, often at short notice.

Notes

1. This essay originally appeared in *Amerasia Journal* 21.1–2 (1995): 1–27. The accompanying introduction was written in 1999 especially for this anthology. We thank Russell Leong, editor of *Amerasia Journal*, for permission to reprint.

Regarding the term "the new Pacific" or "Asia/Pacific," some scholars appear to be moving the "Pacific" increasingly away from consideration of "Asian Americanness" (e.g., Hereniko and Wilson). See also Gima (1998) and Gracewood (1998), which are, however, published under an Asian American rubric.

2. See Hattori (1998) for a related argument on the fictionality of Asian American literature, and by implication Asian American identity.

3. While Japan's economy has been suffering for a number of years, it was the recent collapse of the Thai, Korean, and Indonesian economies, and the weakening of other Asian economies such as Hong Kong's, that most dramatically brought to the attention of Americans the fragility of the Asian economic "miracle."

4. Paradoxically, another cultural consequence may be just the opposite: the rise of various forms of fundamentalism worldwide, with their insistence on purity, absoluteness, and inviolable borders. I am indebted to Abdul JanMohamed for pointing out this phenomenon, which, however, lies beyond the scope of this paper.

5. Frank Chin, Jeffery Paul Chan, Lawson Fusao Inada, and Shawn Wong, eds., *Aiiieeeee! An Anthology of Asian-American Writers* (1974; 1983). The *Aiiieeeee!* editors can hardly be said to have invented cultural nationalist views, which were shared (as well as challenged) by many Asian Americans; other documents from the 1960s and 1970s reflect similar concerns, e.g., Bruce Iwasaki. However, I do take the *Aiiieeeee!* group's statements as a point of departure for discussing cultural nationalism, based on my assessment of their extensive subsequent influence (even if, for some, it only takes the form of continued provocation).

6. The term is Maxine Hong Kingston's, applied to *China Men,* which did not appear until 1980. However, as further elucidated below, "claiming America" is such an important issue in Asian American studies from the start that I find it useful to apply it retroactively to the early cultural nationalist project.

7. I avoid the term *Americanization* here since it calls up too many unwanted associations of coercion and jingoism.

8. Cf. Gee. Some current examples are: *Asian America: Journal of Culture and the Arts,* published at the University of California, Santa Barbara; Bill Ong Hing, *Making and Remaking Asian America through Immigration* Policy; and Karin Aguilar-San Juan, ed., *The State of Asian America: Activism and Resistance in the 1990s.*

9. This phenomenon has generated a great deal of scholarship; see, for example, Deyo; Harris; Shinohara and Lo; and Onis. Parenthetically, the prospect of sharing in Asian prosperity is so attractive that the former British colonies of Australia and New Zealand, previously Europe-oriented and white-identified, are now attempting to redefine themselves as Asian. See, for example, Shi, Zhongxin; Colin James; Bruce Grant. See also Rob Wilson and Arif Dirlik, "Introduction," for a broader contextualization of this redefinition.

10. A recent *Wall Street Journal* article notes that Taiwan, Hong Kong, Singapore, and South Korea are now considered part of the First World: see Biers.

11. A few images from my own experience illustrate the magnitude of this cultural phenomenon: an encyclopedic Chinese video store in Lion City, a giant suburban Asian shopping mall in San Jose, California; AT&T and MCI vying for Asian customers through language and culture-specific ads designed to tug at the heartstrings of trans-Pacific families; second-generation college students at UC Berkeley telling me that they have managed to keep up with their Cantonese through watching Hong Kong movies at home.

12. For example, the new Asian studies journal, *positions: east asia cultures critique,* is also hospitable to submissions on Asian American topics.

13. Frederick Buell, *National Culture and the New Global System*, provides one account of this interpenetration that minimizes the effects of cultural imperialism.

14. Virginia Woolf's famous dictum, "As a woman I have no country," though subject to varying interpretations and put to varying uses in feminist movements, aptly sums up the peculiar relationship of women to the nation-state.

15. See Brotherston, especially 1–4 and 349, for a background history of the concept of the Fourth World.

16. Campomanes in fact argues that the concept of "Filipino American" itself is "inadequate, if oxymoronic," and that Filipino American writers and their works relate to it only ambivalently, the connection "shored up only by its roots in 1960s identity politics" (50, 51).

17. David Palumbo-Liu raises a further question: diaspora is predicated on a relation to home, but the notion of home itself may be unstable and elusive. Personal communication.

18. April 9, 1994, at the University of Michigan. Based on my notes, the speaker in question is of Chinese origin and has lived in Latin America before coming to the U.S.

19. Leong's *The Country of Dreams and Dust* is particularly intriguing given the fact that Leong, the editor of *Amerasia Journal,* has been a significant presence in Asian American studies since the cultural nationalist period.

20. For a particularly incisive critique of the tendency among some Asian American cultural critics to align Asian American literature with a postmodernist aesthetic while bypassing contemporary political history, see David Palumbo-Liu, "The Ethnic as 'Post- .' " Palumbo-Liu's essay "Theory and the Subject of Asian American Studies" raises this pointed question: "does the postmodern present the moment for the ethnic to be conjoined with the universal, as everything is now in a correlate condition of fragmentation and revision, or does this condition erase at that moment the very specificity of ethnicity?"

21. Remark made at the *Luodi shenggen* conference, San Francisco, November 1992, referred to above.

22. Which, interestingly, appeared in the inaugural issue of a journal named *Diaspora*. "Heterogeneity, Hybridity, Multiplicity: Marking Asian American Differences" has since been reprinted as Chapter Three in Lowe's *Immigrant Acts: Asian American Cultural Poltics.* I cite the *Diaspora* page numbers here.

23. Frederick Buell, 194–196, represents a recent example of a non-Asian Americanist using Lowe's essay.

24. I consider "exilic" and "diasporic" to be overlapping, both being referenced to a point of origin and both entailing dispersal. In this essay I use "exilic" when the forcibleness of the removal and the sense of involuntary expulsion are foregrounded by the subject.

25. Nerissa Balce-Cortes observes that some Filipino Americans have been criticized for adopting an "exile" label while enjoying a relatively privileged and terror-free life abroad during the Marcos era. Remark made at a 1993 meeting of the Filipino Studies Working Group, University of California, Berkeley.

26. Comment made in my graduate seminar on Asian American literature at UC Berkeley, Spring 1993.

27. See, for instance, Peter Kiang, Nguyen Ngoc Lan, and Richard Lee Sheehan, "Don't Ignore It: Documenting Racial Harassment in a Fourth-Grade Vietnamese Bilingual Classroom."

28. I am indebted for this insight to Steve Rumpel, who commented on an earlier version of this essay at a 1993–94 Townsend Center Humanities Fellowship meeting.

29. Richard Walker suggests it is no accident that the diasporic notion of "cultural China"

gathered momentum around the time that China's vast market began to open up for investment by the more affluent Chinese in industrialized East Asia. Remark made at a California Studies Group meeting, University of California, Berkeley, March 30, 1995.

30. I am indebted to Angela Davis for raising the question of political alliances at the "Decentering Identity, Recentering Politics" conference, and to Barbara Christian for comparing notes with me on the political of the diasporic perspective in African-American and Asian studies at the 1994 American Cultures seminar at UC Berkeley.

31. Comment made at the "Decentering Identity, Recentering Politics" conference.

32. Except maybe in a state of revolutionary anarchy?

33. For a relevant analysis of the intellectual's location, see Aijaz Ahmad, *In Theory: Classes, Nations, Literatures*, 73–94 and 159. I am indebted to Colleen Lye for this source.

Works Cited

Aguilar-San Juan, ed. *The State of Asian America: Activism and Resistance in the 1990s*. Boston: South End Press, 1990.

Ahmad, Aijaz. *Theory: Classes, Nations, Literatures*. London: Verso, 1992.

Asian America: Journal of Culture and the Arts. Santa Barbara: the University of California.

Biers, Dan. "Now in First World, Asian Tigers Act Like It." *Wall Street Journal*. February 28, 1995. A-15.

Brotherston, Gordon. *Book of the Fourth World: Reading the Native Americas through Their Literature*. New York: Columbia UP, 1992.

Buell, Frederick. *National Culture and the New Global System*. Baltimore: Johns Hopkins UP, 1994.

Campomanes, Oscar V. "Filipinos in the United States and Their Literature of Exile." Ed. Shirley Geok-lin Lim and Amy Ling. *Reading the Literatures of Asian America*. Philadelphia: Temple UP, 1992.

Chan, Sucheng. *Asian Americans: An Interpretive History*. Boston: Twayne Publishers, 1991.

Chen, Nina. "Virtual Asian American Orphans: The 'Parachute Kid' Phenomenon." *AsianWeek* 16:22 (Jan. 27,1995). 1,4.

Cheung, King-Kok. *Articulate Silences: Hisaye Yamamoto, Maxine Hong Kingston, Joy Kogawa*. Ithaca, New York: Cornell UP, 1993.

———. "The Woman Warrior versus the Chinaman Pacific: Must a Chinese American Critic Choose between Feminism and Heroism?" Marianne Hirsch and Evelyn Fox-Keller, eds. *Conflicts in Feminism*. New York: Routledge, 1990. 234–251.

Chin, Frank, Jeffery Paul Chan, Lawson Fusao Inada, and Shawn Wong, eds. *Aiiieeeee! An Anthology of Asian-American Writers*. 1974; rpt. Washington: Howard UP, 1983.

Chow, Rey. *Woman and Chinese Modernity: The Politics of Reading between West and East*. Minneapolis: U of Minnesota P, 1991.

Chuh, Kandice, and Karen Shimakawa, eds. Forthcoming. *Orientations: Mapping Studies in the Asian Diaspora*. Durham, N.C.: Duke UP.

Chun, Wendy Hui Kyong. "Sexuality in the Age of Fiber Optics." Ph.D. diss. Princeton U. 1999.

Connery, Christopher L. "Pacific Rim Discourse: The U.S. Global Imaginary in the Late Cold War Years." In Wilson and Dirlik, *boundary 2* 21:1 (Spring 1994): 30–56.

Deyo, Frederic C., ed. *The Political Economy of the New Asian Industrialism* (Ithaca, NY: Cornell UP, 1987).

Dirlik, Arif. "Asians on the Rim: Transnational Capital and Local Community in the Making of Contemporary Asian America." Special issue: Transnationalism, Media and Asian Americans. *Amerasia Journal* 22.3 (1996): 1–24.

Dunn, Ashley. "Skilled Asians Leaving U.S. for High Tech Jobs at Home." *New York Times* 144:1 (February 28,1995). 1, col. 1.

Eng, David L "In the Shadows of a Diva: Committing Homosexuality in David Henry Hwang's *M. Butterfly.*" Dimensions of Desire: Other Asian & Pacific American Sexualities: gay, lesbian and bisexual identities and orientations. Amerasia journal 20:1 (1994): 93–116.

Eng, David L. "Out Here and Over There: Queerness and Diaspora in Asian American Studies." *Social Text* 52–53 (Fall/Winter 1997): 31–52.

Espiritu, Yen Le. *Asian American Panethnicity: Bridging Institutions and Identities.* Philadelphia: Temple UP, 1992.

Frederic C. Deyo, ed. *The Political Economy of the New Asian Industrialism.* Ithaca, New York: Cornell UP, 1987.

Gee, Emma, ed. *Counterpoint: Perspectives on Asian America.* Los Angeles: Asian American Studies Center, 1976.

Gilroy, Paul. "Cultural Studies and Ethnic Absolutism." Ed. Lawrence Grossberg et al. *Cultural Studies.* New York: Routledge, 1992. 187–198.

———. *The Black Atlantic: Modernity and Double Consciousness.* Cambridge: Harvard UP, 1993.

Gima, Charlene S. " 'Developing' the Critical Pacific: Epeli Hau'ofa's 'The Glorious Pacific Way.' " Special issue: Asian American Spaces. Ed. Gary Y. Okihiro et al. *Hitting Critical Mass: A Journal of Asian American Cultural Criticism* 5.1 (Spring 1998): 29–46.

Gopinath, Gayatri. "Nostalgia, Desire, Diaspora: South Asian Sexualities in Motion." Special issue: New Formations, New Questions: Asian American Studies. Ed. Elaine H. Kim and Lisa Lowe. *positions: east asia cultures critique* 5.2 (Fall 1997): 467–89.

Gracewood, Jolisa. "Sometimes a Great Ocean: Thinking the Pacific from Nowhere to Now and Here." Special issue: Asian American Spaces. Ed. Gary Y. Okihiro et al. *Hitting Critical Mass: A Journal of Asian American Cultural Criticism* 5.1 (Spring 1998): 1–28.

Grant, Bruce. "Australia Confronts an Identity Crisis." *New York Times* . 143, sec. 4 (March 20, 1994). E5, col. 1.

Grewal, Inderpal and Caren Kaplan. "Introduction: Transnational Feminist Practices and Questions of Postmodernity." In Grewal and Kaplan, eds. *Scattered Hegemonies: Postmodernity and Transnational Feminist Practices.* Minneapolis: U of Minnesota P, 1994. 1–33.

Grewal, Inderpal. "The Postcolonial, Ethnic Studies, and the Diaspora: The Contexts of Ethnic Immigrant/Migrant Cultural Studies in the U.S." *Socialist Review* 4 (Winter 1994): 45–74.

Hagedorn, Jessica, ed. *Charlie Chan Is Dead. An Anthology of Contemporary Asian American Fiction.* New York: Penguin, 1994.

Hagedorn, Jessica. "The Exile Within/The Question of Identity." Ed. Lee C. Lee. *Asian Americans: Collages of Identities. Proceedings of Cornell Symposium on Asian America: Issues of Identity.* Ithaca, New York: Asian American Studies Program, Cornell University, 1992. 173–182.

———, ed. *Charlie Chan Is Dead: An Anthology of Contemporary Asian American Fiction.* New York: Penguin, 1994.

Hall, Stuart. "Cultural Identity and Diaspora." Ed. Patrick Williams and Laura Chrisman. *Colonial Discourse and Post-Colonial Theory: A Reader.* New York: Columbia UP, 1994. 392–403.

Harris, Nigel. "The Pacific Rim" [review article]. *Journal of Development Studies* 25:3 (April 1989): 408–416.

Hattori, Tomo. "China Man Autoeroticism and the Remains of Asian America." *NOVEL: A Forum on Fiction.* 31 (1998): 215–36.

Hereniko, Vilsoni, and Rob Wilson, eds. *Inside Out: Literature, Cultural Politics and Identity in the New Pacific*. Boulder: Rowman & Littlefield. Forthcoming.

Hing, Bill Ong. *Making and Remaking Asian America through Immigration Policy: 1850–1990*. Stanford: Stanford UP, 1993.

Iwasaki, Bruce. "Introduction." In Emma Gee, ed. *Counterpoint: Perspectives on Asian America*. Los Angeles: Asian American Studies Center, 1976. 452–463.

James, Colin. "Bye-bye Britannia: Asia Looms into the National Consciousness." *Far Eastern Economic Review* 157: 17 (Oct. 20 1994): 26–27.

Karin Aguilar-San Juan, ed. *The State of Asian America: Activism and Resistance in the 1990s*. Boston: South End Press, 1994.

Kiang, Peter, Nguyen Ngoc Lan, and Richard Lee Sheehan. "Don't Ignore It: Documenting Racial Harassment in a Fourth-Grade Vietnamese Bilingual Classroom." *Equity and Excellence in Education* 28:1 (1995): 31–35.

Kim, Elaine H., and Lisa Lowe, eds. Special Issue: New Formations, New Questions: Asian American Studies. *positions: east asia cultures critique* 5.2 (Fall 1997).

Kim, Elaine. "Foreword." Ed. Shirley Geok-Lin Lim and Amy Ling. *Reading the Literatures of Asian America* . Philadelphia: Temple UP, 1992. xi–xvii.

———. "Such Opposite Creatures: Men and Women in Asian American Literature." *Michigan Quarterly Review* 29:1 (Winter 1990): 68–93.

Koshy, Susan. "The Fiction of Asian American Literature." *The Yale Journal of Criticism* 9.2 (1996): 315–46.

Lee, Lee C., ed. *Asian Americans: Collages of Identities. Proceedings of Cornell Symposium on Asian America: Issues of Identity*. Ithaca, New York: Asian American Studies Program, Cornell University, 1992.

Leong, Russell. "To Our Readers: Transnationalism, Media and Migration." Special issue: Transnationalism, Media and Asian Americans. *Amerasia Journal* 22.3 (1996): iii–vi.

Leong, Russell. *The Country of Dreams and Dust*. Albuquerque, New Mexico: West End Press, 1993.

Li, David Leiwei. *Imaging the Nation: Asian American Literature and Cultural Consent*. Stanford: Stanford UP, 1998.

Liu, Eric. *The Accidental Asian: Notes of a Native Speaker*. New York: Random House, 1998.

Liu, Haiming. "The Trans-Pacific Family: A Case Study of Sam Chang's Family History." *Amerasia Journal* 18:2 (1991): 1–34.

Lowe, Lisa. *Immigrant Acts: On Asian American Cultural Politics*. Durham, N.C.: Duke UP, 1996.

———. "Work, Immigration, Gender: Asian 'American' Women and U.S. Women of Color." *Asian Women United: Making MoreWaves*. 269–277.

Mazumdar, Sucheta. "Asian American Studies and Asian Studies: Rethinking Roots." *Asian Americans: Comparative and Global Perspectives*. Ed. Shirley Hune et al. Pullman: Washington State University Press, 1991. 29–44.

Mohanty, Chandra Talpade. "Introduction: Cartographies of Struggle: Third World Women and the Politics of Feminism." *Third World Women and the Politics of Feminism*. Bloomington: Indiana UP, 1991. 1–47.

Mura, David. "Preparations" [excerpts from Chapter 1 of *Turning Japanese: A Sansei Memoir*, Boston: Atlantic Monthly, 1991]. Ed. Lee C. Lee. *Asian Americans: Collages of Identities. Proceedings of Cornell Symposium on Asian America: Issues of Identity*. Ithaca, New York: Asian American Studies Program, Cornell University, 1992. 9–24.

———. "Strangers in the Village." Ed. Rick Simonson and Scott Walker. *The Graywolf Annual Five: Multi-Cultural Literacy*. Saint Paul, Minnesota: Graywolf P, 1988. 135–153.

Nakamura, Lisa. "Race in/for Cyberspace: Identity Tourism and Racial Passing on the Internet." *Work and Days* 131.1–2 (1995): 181–93.

Nguyen-Hong-Nhiem, Lucy and Joel Martin Halpern, eds. *The Far East Comes Near: Autobiographical Accounts of Southeast Asian Students in America.* Amherst: U of Massachusetts P, 1989.

Nonini, Donald M., and Aihwa Ong. "Chinese Transnationalism as an Alternative Modernity." Ed. Ong, Aihwa, and Donald Nonini. *Ungrounded Empires: The Cultural Politics of Modern Chinese Transnationalism.* New York: Routledge, 1997. 3–33.

Ong, Aihwa, and Donald Nonini, eds. *Ungrounded Empires: The Cultural Politics of Modern Chinese Transnationalism.* New York: Routledge, 1997.

Onis, Ziya. "The Logic of the Developmental State." *Comparative Politics* 24:1 (October 1991): 109–126.

Ow, Jeffrey. "The Revenge of the Yellowfaced Cyborg Terminator: The Rape of Digital Geishas and the Colonization of Cyber-Coolies in 3D Realm's Shadow Warrior." In *Race in Space: Politics, Identity, and Cyberspace.* Ed. Beth Kolko, Lisa Nakamura, and Gil Rodman. New York: Routledge, forthcoming.

Palumbo-Liu, David. *Asian/American: Historical Crossings of a Racial Frontier.* Stanford: Stanford UP, 1999.

———. "The Ethnic as 'Post-': Reading the Literatures of Asian America." *American Literary History* 7:1 (1995): 161–68.

———. "Theory and the Subject of Asian American Studies." *Amerasia Journal* 21:1–2 (1995): 55–65.

Puar, Jasbir K. "Transnational Sexualities: South Asian (Trans)nation(alism)s and Queer Diasporas." In *Q & A: Queer in Asian America.* Ed. David L. Eng and Alice Y. Hom. Philadelphia: Temple UP, 1998. 404–22.

Radhakrishnan, R. *Diasporic Mediations: Between Home and Location.* Minneapolis: U of Minnesota P, 1996.

Rai, Amit S. "India On-line: Electronic Bulletin Boards and the Construction of a Diasporic Hindu Identity." *Diaspora* 4.1 (Spring 1995): 31–57.

Said, Edward. "Reflections on Exile." Ed. Russell Ferguson et al. *Out There: Marginalization and Contemporary Cultures.* New York: The New Museum of Contemporary Art and Cambridge, Massachusetts: The MIT Press, 1990. 357–366.

Saldivar, José David. *The Dialectics of Our America: Genealogy, Cultural Critique, and Literary History.* Durham: Duke UP, 1991.

San Juan, E., Jr. "From Identity Politics to Strategies of Disruption: USA Self and/or Asian Alter?" In Lee, Lee C., ed. *Asian Americans: Collages of Identities Proceedings of Cornell Symposium on Asian America: Issues of Identity.* Ithaca, New York: Asian American Studies Program, Cornell University, 1992. 129–131.

Shi, Zhongxin. "Australia 'Merging into Asia.'" *Beijing Review* 36:3–4 (Jan. 18, 1993): 13.

Shinohara, Miyohei and Fu-chen Lo, eds. *Global Adjustment and the Future of Asian-Pacific Economy: Papers and Proceedings of the Conference on Global Adjustment and the Future of Asian-Pacific Economy.* Tokyo: Institute of Developing Economies, and Kuala Lumpur: Asian and Pacific Development Centre, 1989.

Shu, Yuan. "Information Technologies, the U.S. Nation-State, and Asian American Subjectivities." *Cultural Critique* 40 (Fall 1998): 145–66.

Wang, L. Ling-Chi. "Race, Class, Citizenship, and Extraterritoriality: Asian Americans and the 1996 Finance Campaign Scandal." *Amerasia Journal* 24.1 (1998): 1–21.

———. "Asian American Studies/Ethnic Studies: Politics of Reception and Acceptance." Unpublished paper presented to Columbia University. Graduate School of Education. November 5, 1993.

————. "Roots and the Changing Identity of the Chinese in the United States." Ed. Tu Weiming. *The Living Tree: The Changing Meaning of Being Chinese Today*. Stanford: Stanford UP, 1994. 185–212.

Wilson, Rob, and Arif Dirlik. "Introduction: Asia/Pacific as Space of Cultural Production." Special issue of *boundary 2* 21:1 (Spring 1994): 1–14.

Wong, Sunn Shelley. "Notes from Damaged Life: Asian American Literature and the Discourse of Wholeness." Ph.D. Dissertation. University of California, Berkeley, 1993.

HISTORICAL CONFIGURATIONS

INDIAN LITERACY, U.S. COLONIALISM, AND LITERARY CRITICISM

Maureen Konkle

"If he writes, it is in the character of a white man."

—William Joseph Snelling on William Apess and other Indian writers, *North American Review*, January 1835

"[Apess's *Indian Nullification of the Unconstitutional Laws of Massachusetts*] is written far better than could have been expected from an Indian, and is well worth reading. The only fault we find is, that the author has suffered himself to be exasperated by the persecution he has endured."

—*New England Magazine*, July 1835

"Apes? What has he done? What is he doing now? & with what success?"

—Rev. James Walker, Harvard College's investigator at Mashpee, Fall 1835

The criticism of Native American literature takes for its principal object that literature's expression of Indian identity, a ubiquitous term that generally assumes an inborn Indian consciousness. Most critics hold that Native American literature originates in the oral tradition of the tribes, which is available as literature when scholars translate and write down the various songs, narratives, and ceremonies that they understand to constitute this tradition. These translations strive to be accurate, and it is the scholar who determines what counts as literary, since, most critics agree, traditional Indian cultures do not have a concept equivalent to "literature."[1] Although Indians' oral practices may change over time, the Indian consciousness made available through oral tradition provides an atavistic link to their preliterate past; once Indians move from oral to written practices, their consciousness changes irrevocably. Native writers in English are then most successful in expressing their Indian identity when they provide evidence of what is understood as their culture through themes, forms, narratives, and figures correlated with the oral tradition written down by scholars.[2] The assumption underlying the belief that true Indian identity—the most complete expression of that inborn consciousness—is always associated with the scholar's traces of a preliterate past is that when Indians engage in the practice of writing, they undermine their own identity.[3]

Since William Apess does not provide evidence of his Pequot oral tradition, most critics have agreed that his Christianity and his use of "republican rhetoric" (rights, liberty, citizen) in his *Eulogy on King Philip* (1836) and other writings proves that he had at best a fractured Indian identity, despite whatever admirable qualities he possesses as a writer who may be characterized as antiracist.[4] The current criticism of Native American literature—with its emphasis on the disinterestedness of its knowledge, its ahistorical pursuit of Indian identity, and its insistence on its own apolitical nature—is the legacy of the same U.S. colonialism that William Apess analyzes in the *Eulogy on King Philip*. In the *Eulogy* Apess rejects the notion of an innate Indian consciousness because he understands that the positing of inherent difference between Indians and Europeans is a crucial step in denying Indians' political status. Furthermore, Apess recognizes that the legitimacy of the state itself depends upon that denial. Most criticism of Native American literature perpetuates that denial through its assumption that writing obstructs Indian identity and its assertion that Native American literature is simply the literature of an American minority, representing just one more culture in the multicultural canon of a pluralistic but coherent nation-state.[5]

Contemporary Native intellectuals have argued for some time now that colonialism did occur in the U.S. and that it still determines relations between Native and non-Native people. Native critics of the academy have often pointed out that what determines who is or is not an Indian is a political matter for Indians to decide, not the prerogative of academics. These critics, who include Vine Deloria Jr., Simon J. Ortiz, Gerald Vizenor, Elizabeth Cook-Lynn, Ward Churchill, and Robert Allen Warrior, base their critique on the historical and continued existence of Indian polities that are engaged in an ongoing struggle to establish, or re-establish sovereignty.[6] Although many admit that this term is difficult to define precisely, it is nevertheless validated by the record of treaties and other legal agreements between Native peoples and Europeans from the seventeenth century forward, in which settlers of all nationalities recognized the authority of polities they called "Indian nations."[7] When the poet and fiction writer Simon Ortiz describes oral tradition, he emphasizes its record of the Indian nations' struggles with colonization; literary works continue that tradition of resistance in a different form (9–10). The point of departure for an understanding of Native oral or written traditions is, then, not the existence of an innate Indian consciousness but the existence of a historical and political entity, the Indian nation.

Colonial epistemology begins with Europeans' production of knowledge about native peoples as ahistorical and depoliticized members of a group who share inborn characteristics that mark them as inferior to Europeans and deserving of subjection.[8] It is not possible, however, simply to transfer the insights of postcolonial theory to the United States; indeed, even the most important practitioners of postcolonial theory, when they do occasionally refer to the colonization of North America, figure Native peoples as having been capable of only "prepolitical maneuvers" before their subjection to "wholesale colonization and destruction" (Spivak, "Making of Americans" 783; Said, *Culture* 63). What is required is an analysis of the unique features of U.S. colonialism, and it is this that Apess provides. I will read Apess's *Eulogy on King Philip* in light of several texts that Apess would have known of, that he probably had read, and that certainly bear on his arguments in the *Eulogy*: Supreme Court decisions respecting Indians in the 1820s and 1830s and Edward Everett's *Address at Bloody-Brook* (1835), a speech commemorating King Philip's War published in Boston only a month before Apess gave the *Eulogy* in January 1836. Everett and the justices of the Supreme Court demonstrate that legitimate control of land in North America requires both the recognition and denial of Native political autonomy. They demonstrate as well that the most effective means of denying that dangerous autonomy is the production of knowledge that reduces resistant Indian political entities to an assemblage of inferior, soon-to-be-extinct individuals who, because of their inherent characteristics, cannot claim to form real governments. In the *Eulogy* Apess denies the validity of the concept of inherent Indian difference in order to reassert the primacy of Indian polities, negating the self/other dynamic of colonial discourse by introducing a third term, the Indian nation, the existence of which the U.S. concedes in the treaties. Apess puts forward a fundamental critique of colonial epistemology at the moment of its institutionalization in the U.S.

Modern colonialism is a struggle for territory that takes place in part through the production of knowledge; written records and a reading public are as necessary as technologically sophisticated weaponry or encroaching settlers. William Apess understood that state authority depended on the knowledge produced about Indians as a class of people whose difference precluded their historical and political existence. In calling upon the treaty record to assert that existence, he enters into a history in which Native leaders and intellectuals have returned, again and again, to the treaty as the key point of contention in their struggle against colonialism because in the treaty Europeans must concede Native autonomy. Apess goes a step further than his predecessors however, when he demonstrates that the struggle against colonialism is as much epistemological as it is violent, and that the field of that struggle is not only land, but was and continues to be written English. The determinations of colonial epistemology continue to occlude the political claims and struggles of Native peoples, so much so that the current criticism of Native writing does not have an adequate vocabulary for discussing what is one of Native writing's most important themes, the continuity of Indian nations.[9] Because Apess unequivocally rejects the notion of innate Indian consciousness and articulates the political significance of that rejection, the analysis of his works points toward new critical vocabularies and approaches that can begin to recover the history of colonialism and to discuss the significance of Native writing in English.

While it is commonplace to say that the treaties between Europeans and Native peoples were all broken, such a statement—usually intended to convey the violence of colonization—elides a complex history of political relations between the Europeans who attempted to establish governmental authority in North America and the resisting Native polities (Deloria, "Revision" 87). When the new and unprecedented repub-

lican state was founded in the late eighteenth century, the two-hundred-year-old
tradition of making treaties with Indian nations provided one of the few means of
establishing that state's legitimacy both among the former colonies and internationally
(Deloria and Lytle 2–4). The purchase of land through a treaty from Indian polities
that had authority to sell it guaranteed that the new state controlled territory legitimately. At the same time, since the treaty, duplicitous or not, required the presump-
tion of Indian autonomy in order to be construed as legitimate, it also allowed for
Indians' resistance to U.S. governmental authority: Indians could choose not to sell.
The problem of Indians' conceded autonomy could only be resolved by their disappearance, which was effected in the production of knowledge about their inferiority
and imminent extinction. William Apess seizes on the issues that John Marshall and
Edward Everett inadvertently raise in their attempts to fashion state legitimacy out of
colonial relations: the exact nature of North American "conquest"; the discrepancy
between professed philosophical tradition and actual practice; and the displacement of
recognized Native political entities by a set of notions about the nature and character
of Indians in general.

Marshall argues in *Johnson v. M'Intosh* (1823) that, unlike other conquered peoples
who may be "safely governed as a distinct people," Native people in North America
could not be governed "because they were as brave and as high spirited as they were
fierce, and were ready to repel by arms every attempt on their independence" (590).
Therefore, "[t]he Europeans were under the necessity of either abandoning the country, and relinquishing their pompous claims to it, or of enforcing those claims by the
sword, and by the adoption of principles adapted to the condition of a people with
whom it was impossible to mix" (590). In supporting his argument that European
nations universally recognized the doctrine of discovery—that the European nation
claiming discovery of land held exclusive right to buy that land from Indians—
Marshall reiterates a history of contention among France, England, Spain, and Holland
for control of North American territory (574ff). Marshall's history evades the fact that
each of these European nations made diplomatic alliances with Native peoples as a
means of advancing their own positions, alliances that established nation-to-nation
relations in treaties made by Indian and European governments. Diplomatic history is
not altogether absent from the ruling, however. Even as Marshall argues that Europeans subjected Indians to "conquest," in which land must be "acquired and maintained
by force," this conquest is not solely by force, as he at first implies: "the peculiar
situation of the Indians, necessarily considered, in some respects, as a dependent, and
in some respects as a distinct people, occupying a country claimed by Great Britain,
and yet too powerful and brave not to be dreaded as formidable enemies, required,
that means should be adopted for the preservation of peace; and that their friendship
should be secured by quieting their alarms for their property" (589, 596–97). Marshall
concedes that inter-European contention for control of territory and the vulnerability
of European settlements required the recognition in treaties (the means of preserving
the peace) with Indian nations whose "property" would be defended and whose
"friendship" was necessary.

The supposed conquest of North America presents an unavoidable conflict between what Marshall calls "the actual state of things" and the founding principles of the new state:

> However extravagant the pretension of converting the discovery of an inhabited country into conquest may appear; if the principle has been asserted in the first instance, and afterwards sustained; if a country has been acquired and held under it; if the property of the great mass of the community originates in it, it becomes the law of the land, and cannot be questioned. . . . However [the doctrine of discovery] may be opposed to natural right, and to the usages of civilized nations, yet, if it be indispensable to that system under which the country has been settled, and be adapted to the actual condition of the two people, it may, perhaps, be supported by reason, and certainly cannot be rejected by Courts of justice (591–92).

At the same time that he asserts the principles of the doctrine of discovery, Marshall also allows that the European assertion of authority is an extravagant pretense because settlers clearly understood that North America was inhabited by politically autonomous groups of Indians who defended their territory and their governmental authority. Marshall recognizes that he denies Indian natural rights—rights that precede positive, European law—and that he violates the law of nations in order to support a system of government ostensibly founded on those same republican principles.[10]

The precise nature of the "conquest" that originated European rule in North America and the disposition of the peoples who have experienced that conquest remains contested. In the two *Cherokee Nation* cases, *Cherokee Nation v. Georgia* (1831) and *Worcester v. Georgia* (1832), Marshall transforms the notion of military conquest that he cannot fully support in *Johnson* into a narrative of Indians' consent to be governed. In *Cherokee Nation v. Georgia*, Marshall partially accepted and partially rejected the Cherokee Nation's argument, ruling that although the Cherokee Nation did constitute a state, "a distinct political society, separated from others, capable of managing its own affairs and governing itself," the Cherokee Nation did not "constitute a foreign state in the sense of the constitution" (16).[11] While treaties "recognize [the Cherokee] as a people capable of maintaining the relations of peace and war, of being responsible in their political character for any violation of their engagements . . . the relation of the Indians to the United States is marked by peculiar and cardinal distinctions which exist no where else" (16). Marshall writes that Indians have the right to occupy the land until "that right shall be extinguished by a *voluntary* cession to our government" (17, my emphasis). Until such time as they surrender the land voluntarily, Native tribes "may be denominated domestic dependent nations"; Indians occupy land but remain "in a state of pupilage. Their relation to the United States resembles that of a ward to his guardian" (17). Native tribes are simultaneously politically autonomous with respect to internal government and in the familiar colonial position of inferiority and permanent "pupilage."

In *Worcester v. Georgia*, Marshall details the history of Indians' voluntary cession of land in order to establish the legitimacy of land transfer, a revised history in which his earlier depiction of conquest and implied Indian resistance becomes a series of republican contracts made between the U.S. and Indian nations. This history of scrupulous legality presents a problem, however. If autonomous, self-governing Indian nations exist, the possibility presents itself that rather than willingly giving up their land to the federal government Indians will refuse to sell. Conceding that Indian nations have political authority thus provides an opening for Native historical continuity and political organization that must be closed off. Associate Justice Joseph Johnson recognizes the problem in his concurring opinion in *Cherokee Nation*, when he insists that the Cherokee were a "race of hunters" and notes that any "advancement" of their "society" would put them into direct conflict with U.S. authority (23). In *Worcester*, Associate Justice John McLean elaborates on Johnson's position. For McLean, as for Marshall and Johnson, Indians' inherent difference and inferiority may be taken for granted; the acculturated Cherokee are a "savage people" (573). The inscription of inherent Indian difference must preclude the possibility of future Native political organizations. McLean observes that "the exercise of the power of self-government by the Indians, within a state, is undoubtedly contemplated to be temporary" (593). Autonomous Indian nations within the jurisdiction of a state, McLean writes, "may seriously embarrass or obstruct the operation of state laws," a situation "inconsistent with the political welfare of the states, and the social advance of their citizens" (594). An Indian nation must submit itself to the federal government or "seek its exercise beyond the sphere of state authority" (594). The potential "embarrassment" of which McLean writes is an admission of a possible Native refusal to submit to colonial authority and a return to the violence of European settlement that Marshall sought to avoid.

The history of incomplete "conquest" to which the treaty bears witness must be buried in assertions that Indians willingly gave up their land and conveniently died off. The same political difficulties informing the Supreme Court's decisions underlie Edward Everett's narrative of King Philip's War in his *Address at Bloody-Brook*.[12] From the perspective of historiography rather than jurisprudence, Everett attempts, as did Marshall, to reconcile colonialism with the establishment of the new republican state, and following Marshall, demonstrates that the legitimacy of U.S. state authority depends upon assertions about the inherent difference of Indians.

Although Everett recasts the political conflict between Native peoples and settlers into a moral conflict between opposed races, as is typical of colonial discourses, he must still overcome the problem of Native possession of land. This he accomplishes when, in contrasting the Spanish settlement with the British settlement of the New World (and drawing upon the "black legend" of the Spanish conquest), he introduces the treaty as a signifier of Anglo-American moral superiority. Unlike the violent conquest of Spanish America, "in the Anglo-American settlements, treaties will be entered into, mutual rights acknowledged; the artificial relations of independent and allied states will be established; and as the civilized race rapidly multiplies, the native tribes will recede, sink into the wilderness, and disappear" (590). This disappearance can be measured by the fact that among the New England Indians, "not an individual, of unmixed blood, and speaking the language of his fathers, remains" (590). Settlers make treaties with Indians to acquire land legally; Indians become extinct, and the proof is that there are no more authentic ("unmixed," speaking their native languages) Indians left in New England. As in Marshall's *Cherokee Nation* rulings, the notion of violent conquest conflicts with republican principles, and so the legitimacy of the treaties must guarantee Indian extinction. The treaty's legal significance—its recognition of Native "independent . . . states"—disappears along with the vanishing savage. Everett's position rests on both the recognition of the validity of treaties and the assertion that the inherent difference of Indians will result in their inevitable extinction. It is "deplorable" but "an unavoidable consequence" that Indians are too different to live in the civilized world: "belonging to a different variety of the species, speaking a different tongue, suffering all the disadvantages of social and intellectual inferiority," they cannot survive the onslaught of civilization (590). Treaties may be vacated only when one of the parties or its successors no longer exists; impending Indian extinction dissolves the ties of treaties and clears the land for legal settlement and legitimate government.

Everett recounts the events of King Philip's War in a familiar manner; a violent though noble savage, Philip dies "upon his face in the mud and water, with his gun beneath him" (610). After the state has been secured by the death of its principal threat, Everett can indulge himself in the sentimental portrait of doomed victims and "drop a compassionate tear . . . for these the benighted children of the forest,—the orphans of Providence" (610). Sympathy for Indians teaches settlers and their descendants how to respond to colonial political relations, in effect, how to behave; in his narrative of the state's origins, Everett shows that one ought, as a citizen of the republic, to feel sorry for Indians, but only once they are securely on the road to extinction.[13] Marshall himself, in prefatory remarks to his *Cherokee Nation* ruling, felt the need to mourn the tragic passing of the Indian that the ruling itself required (15).

Sympathy expressed for Indian princesses and noble savages can go only so far, however. "I hope I compassionate the suffering of the Indian," Everett writes; "heaven forbid I should be indifferent to the sufferings of the fathers" (615). The possibility of violence resulting from Indians' unwillingness to cede territory and be governed cannot be set aside easily; historiography must account for the settler violence that was widely acknowledged in Boston at the time.[14] Everett must justify the settlers' conduct even as he establishes them as the state's originators, returning again and again to their possible involvement in "wars of extermination" to refute the notion of settler violence. "No general and indiscriminate slaughter took place," Everett contends, and he must "dwell the more on this point, because it is one of vague reproach to the memory of our fathers; and yet I am not sure, that, unless we deny altogether the rightfulness of settling the continent, . . . I am not sure, that any different result could have taken place" (594).

At stake in Everett's denial of indiscriminate settler violence is the legitimacy of settlement and the government that emerged from that settlement. As a Congressman he recognized the necessity of establishing "the rightfulness of settling the continent" when he supported the Cherokee in their fight against the state of Georgia. In a note to the *Address*, he directs the reader's attention to his published opinions supporting the Cherokee on the basis of treaties being "sacred compacts" between political entities (594 n). Everett adds, however, that the situation of New England Indians has "no applicability" to the situation of the Cherokee in Georgia (594 n). As in Everett's contrast between Spanish military conquest and New England settlement by legal agreement, the Cherokee treaties established settlers' legitimate acquisition of land. Having gained the land by recognizing the ability of the Native tribe to cede it—that is, the Native tribe's status as an "independent state"—the state then cannot tolerate the threat of autonomous Native polities. New England Indians are merely further down the road to vanishing than the Cherokee, a vanishing that makes the treaties obsolete while leaving a residue of legality.

The point at issue in Apess's version of the pilgrim foundation of the republic, as it is in Everett's, is the legitimacy of the state's origins. Apess broaches this point in the second paragraph of the *Eulogy* when, in a reference to the *Cherokee Nation* cases, he observes that settlers are "in possession of [King Philip's] soil . . . only by right of conquest" (277). Apess here invokes the republican narrative of legal land acquisition through treaties and agrees instead with one part of Georgia's argument, that the land had been gained by conquest. The conquest Apess describes is not military, however; rather, it is achieved through duplicitous legal agreements and continuing knowledge production about Indians, in combination with the social and political disruptions caused by settler encroachment. Nevertheless, those legal agreements required settlers to concede Native political autonomy. The keys to Apess's rereading of both the *Cherokee Nation* rulings and New England historiography are his rejection of the notion that Indians are too different from Europeans to live with them and his return to the legal agreements that show that settlers have always recognized autonomous Native political entities with which they needed to coexist. In the figure of King Philip, Apess presents a narrative embodiment of the Cherokees' argument that "from time immemorial the Cherokee nation have composed a sovereign and independent state, and in this character have been repeatedly recognized, and still stand recognized . . . in the various treaties subsisting between this nation and the United States" (*Cherokee Nation* 3). The invocation of time immemorial is an important point made by the Cherokee and by Apess, indicating that since Indian nations have existed in the past they will continue to do so in the future.

In *The Marshall Court and Cultural Change*, G. Edward White states that the elite Cherokee who brought suit again the state of Georgia claimed the "natural rights of ownership" when they argued that the Cherokee Nation constituted a sovereign foreign state (717). Their arguments—ultimately rejected, as were the similar arguments of enslaved Africans before the Marshall Court—stemmed from natural law principles, which theoretically preceded the establishment of positive law and, in these cases, the establishment of the U.S.[15] In repeatedly referring to "nature" and the "natural" in the *Eulogy*, Apess draws upon the contemporary legal sense of the word to depict King Philip's sovereignty. Apess claims that his purpose is to "bring before you beings made by the God of Nature, and in whose hearts and heads he has planted sympathies which shall live forever in the memory of the world, whose brilliant talents shone in the display of natural things" (277). Apess here recalls the Cherokee, who argued that they "[derived] their title [to the land] from the Great Spirit, who is the common father of the human family, and to whom the whole earth belongs" and also the opening lines of the Declaration of Independence, which justify the formation of the new state with an appeal to "the laws of nature and of nature's God" (*Cherokee Nation* 3; Jefferson 919). The "natural sons of an Almighty Being" and Philip with his "natural abilities" are not sentimentalized noble savages, a representation Apess explicitly rejects, but people whose formation of autonomous political entities precedes their relationship with British colonial authority and its successor, the U.S. government (279, 308). Even to be "uncivilized" marks Indians as belonging to a state of nature that is not inferior but socially and politically autonomous. In reference to settler violence and accusations of Indian savagery, Apess observes that "if we have common sense and ability to allow the difference between the civilized and the uncivilized, we cannot but see that one mode of warfare is as just as the other; for while one is sanctioned by authority of the enlightened and cultivated men, the other is an agreement according to the pure laws of nature, growing out of natural consequences" (278). Apess thus attaches to the temporal sense of "nature"—that it precedes European civilization or society in North America—a political sense in order to assert that Indian government precedes European settlement. This is no minor point in the nineteenth century, when the common conception was that as savages in a state of nature Indians were incapable of forming stable political associations.[16]

Indeed, Marshall's concept of "domestic dependent nations" does not recognize that Indians establish stable governments, an act that implies their future existence. The concept defines only the Indian nation's "peculiar" relationship with the U.S. government, not Indian nations' internal political structure (Harring 30). Despite the Justices' effective denial of Indian natural rights, their unwavering belief in Indian inferiority, and their silence on Indian governments, however, they could not evade the substance of the treaties and had to recognize Indians as "citizens" of Indian nations, a historical point that clarifies the apparent ambiguity in Apess's use of the word (White 722). The *Cherokee Nation* rulings explicitly held that Native peoples are not citizens of the republican state. The notion of Indian rights informing the removal struggle refers not to the individual rights of republican citizens but to the collective rights of Native peoples who form Indian nations. In his majority ruling in *Worcester*, Marshall cites several examples of the use of the word "citizen" in reference to Indians, ranging from the first treaty made by the Revolutionary government to the Hopewell treaty of 1802, which was at issue in Georgia's assertion of sovereignty over the Cherokee. The articles of that treaty, Marshall writes, "stipulate for the punishment of citizens of either country, who may commit offences [*sic*] on or against the citizens of the other. The only inference to be drawn from them is, that the United States considered the Cherokees as a nation" (553). In the *Eulogy* Apess extends Marshall's recognition of the Cherokee Nation and its citizens to all Indian nations and their citizens who are engaged in a struggle to protect their autonomy:

> Look at the disgraceful laws, disfranchising us as citizens. Look at the treaties made by Congress, all broken. Look at the deep-rooted plans laid, when a territory becomes a state, that after so many years the laws shall be extended over the Indians that live within their boundaries. Yea, every charter that has been given was given with a view of driving the Indians out of the states, or dooming them to become chained under desperate laws, that would make them drag out a miserable life as one chained to the galley; and this is the course that has been pursued for nearly two hundred years (306).

Apess's use of "treaties" and "citizens" here refers to the Indian nation: the federal government and the states pass laws that disfranchise Indian people as citizens of their own autonomous nations by refusing to recognize either the authority or the boundaries of those nations. Apess had personal experience of such violations when he defended the Mashpee Indians of Cape Cod in their effort to secure self-government from the Commonwealth of Massachusetts. Massachusetts's appointed authorities regulated everything from labor to the use of natural resources on Indian land at Mashpee, preventing Indian people from exercising control over their own lives; the state of Georgia sought to do the same to the Cherokee. It is here worth noting the sign posted on trees around the Mashpee plantation in June of 1833: "Having been . . . degraded and despised, and a much abused people, we have determined to make our own laws and govern ourselves. . . . This is to give notice that we have resolved that if any person is seen on our plantation after the first of July carting or cutting wood, without our leave, or in any way trespassing upon our lands, they shall be bound hand and foot, and thrown off."[17]

Apess writes that "one general law" should apply to both Americans and Native peoples and then adds, directly addressing his audience, "while you ask yourselves, 'What do they, the Indians, want?' you have only to look at the unjust laws made for them, and say, 'They want what I want,' in order to make men of them, good and wholesome citizens" (310). The word "citizens" is used here in the context of an argument for the *coexistence* of the U.S. and Indian nations, a goal that would be achieved when Indian citizens could reside unmolested in Indian nations.

King Philip served an Indian nation violated by settlers, fighting for the recognition of Native government, and prefiguring the political struggle of both the Cherokee and the Mashpee. Although Apess cannot point to specific treaties entered into by King Philip, the *Book of the Indians* by the prolific Boston antiquarian Samuel Gardner Drake does provide him with records of Philip's land sales that establish self-government and territorial boundaries. There is a distinct difference in emphasis between Drake's and Apess's accounts of land transactions, however.[18] Drake writes that the record of land sales shows that the Indians voluntarily sold off their lands in order to "obtain such things as their neighbors possessed" (Drake, *Book of the Indians* III:13). In Apess's version, the land sale record provides evidence of Philip's political authority and its violation by settlers. Philip has a "throne," he "comes into office," he has "counselors and interpreters"; "it appears that he knew there was great responsibility resting upon himself and country, that it was likely to be ruined by those rude intruders around him, though he appears friendly and is willing to sell them lands for almost nothing" (290). Where Drake merely lists, among other legal transactions, a suit against Philip for land and monetary compensation for a promise made by Philip's dead older brother Alexander, Apess stops to consider it. He notes that the court decided in favor of "Talmon, the young Pilgrim," who received "a large tract of land" from Philip to settle the matter (291). "Now let us review this a little," Apess continues: "The man who bought this land made the contract, as he says, with Alexander, ten or twelve years before; then why did he not bring forward his contract before the court? It is easy to understand why he did not. Their object was to cheat, or get the whole back again this way. Only look at the sum demanded, and it is enough to satisfy the critical observer" (291).

In this analysis Apess participates in what may be called a tradition of colonial

discourse in the U.S., in which Indians recite detailed accounts of land swindles perpetrated on them; such accounts appear throughout the historical record, and indeed
continue to appear to the present day. The object of settler duplicity is always the
acquisition of land in a way that may be construed as legitimate; as Everett demonstrates, having acquired Indian land "legitimately," settlers must then deny Indians'
continuous existence in an autonomous Indian nation. Therefore "the records of courts
and legislatures throughout New England" reveal the ongoing, systematic violation
of Indian "natural rights of ownership," as well as of the national "right of sovereignty" that the Cherokee brought before the Supreme Court (291). Apess's analysis
recalls Justice McLean's observations on the potential "embarrassment" presented by
Indian polities. Indian nations may exist only where they are in decline; if these nations
persist, they must be removed beyond the state's boundary or destroyed altogether.
Apess recognizes that that decline was produced and continues to be produced by the
legal system itself, which conceals political motives in a narrative of legitimacy and
fairness. Throughout the *Eulogy* Apess's tactic is to strip away the various forms of
justification for, in Everett's words, "the rightfulness of settling the continent" to
reveal the political motivations beneath.

In Everett's version King Philip can only exemplify Indian vengeance, savagery,
and doom; when Apess separates the figure of King Philip from Everett's notion of
Indian identity, he does not provide an oppositional, "positive" identity for Indians
but asserts instead Indians' political status. Apess's opening paragraphs set out different nations with different heroes—King Philip and George Washington—but Apess's
King Philip contrasts oddly with the usual exemplary figures of the period. Brave,
resourceful, intelligent, and generous, King Philip is also ordinary, understandably
exasperated by settler duplicity, and driven even to cruel acts. Although the eulogy
form invites the audience to identify with King Philip against their own ancestors,
Philip has no specifically "Indian" characteristics they may idealize. Philip has "more
manly nobility in him than . . . all the head Pilgrims put together"; he is more
courageous than Washington crossing the Delaware when he and his men escape the
pilgrims by canoe; he treats settler captives with "a great deal more Christian-like
spirit" than the settlers treat Natives, accepting even his prisoner Mary Rowlandson
as an equal (296, 297, 300). While King Philip may be more humane than his Anglo-
American contemporaries, he is not inherently different from them. When Philip kills
Mohawks and blames the settlers in order to gain the Mohawks' alliance against them,
a story Apess takes from Drake, even this act is evidence of Philip's lack of difference.
Apess writes that Philip "was so exasperated that nothing but revenge could satisfy
him . . . [T]his act was no worse than our political men do in our day, of their strife
to wrong each other, who profess to be enlightened" (299). Indeed, "If [the pious
settlers] were like my people, professing no purity at all, then their crimes would not
appears to have such magnitude. But while they appear to be by profession more
virtuous, their crimes till blacken" (300).

Having established that Indians are not essentially different from settlers, that they
do form sovereign governments, and that settlers have violated those governments,
Apess considers the effects of contemporary "history of New England writers" who
justify settler dominance with their narratives of pilgrim virtue and Indian inferiority

(285). Reading the widely available seventeenth-century record against the grain, Apess concludes that the pious settlers are "lewd" "assassins"; Miles Standish, who by the 1830s had already been mythologized in historiography and fiction, as "vile and malicious" (284).[19] Everett's originators of the republic engage in petty harassment of Indians in order to effect the Indians' decline. When a town passes a law preventing an Indian chief's entrance into its houses without paying a fee of ten beaver skins, Apess asks caustically, "Who could have supposed that the meek and lowly followers of virtue would have taken such methods to rob honest men of the woods?" (285). Historians of pilgrim virtue celebrate duplicity, violence, and death, according to Apess, and use Christianity to authorize the theft of land: "Although in words they deny it, yet in their works they approve of the iniquities of their fathers. And as the seed of iniquity and prejudice was sown in that day, so it still remains; there is a deep-rooted popular opinion in the hearts of many that Indians were made, etc., on purpose for destruction . . . and that God had decreed it from all eternity" (287). Everett's pilgrim "germ of civilization" is not republicanism but colonial dominance, dominance justified and maintained by the production of knowledge about Indians as "made . . . on purpose for destruction" (Everett 615; Apess 287).[20] The missionary who writes that " 'the savage has left the ground for civilized man' " in the West, and that with the Indians gone " 'the rich prairie . . . is now receiving numerous enclosures . . . is now God's vineyard' " is the "son of the pilgrims" who conceals the destruction of Native political organization with a narrative of Christian virtue and Indians' inevitable disappearance (287). Apess makes the political effects of assertions about the difference of Indians quite plain: "must I say, and shall I say it, that missionaries have injured us more than they have done us good, by degrading us as a people, in breaking up our governments and leaving us without any suffrages whatever, or a legal right among men?" (287). If Indians are uncivilized savages and have no real governments, their land may be taken justifiably; it is not the missionary's pursuit of souls that makes him dangerous but his willful destruction of Native political organization for the purpose of gaining Native land.

Apess bears down on the proliferation of settler-produced knowledge about Indians, reminding his audience of the possibility of reading differently. He tells the story of an Indian at Kennebunk who lived on land granted him by the state in a white township. Although "he himself did all that lay in his power to comfort his white neighbors, in case of sickness and death," his neighbors still subjected him to "the common prejudices against Indians" that "[prevented] any sympathy with him" (289). Discouraged by his isolation from his neighbors and by their prejudice, he dug up his dead child's body, and like so many Indians in fiction of the era, went west "to join the Canadian Indians" (289). Apess's interpretation of this story, however, is not the usual one of the noble savage inevitably going west to his fate: the "haughty divines and orators of the day" have perpetuated the knowledge about Indians that provides the foundation for the prejudice that drives away the Indian and justifies taking Native land. "The people were to blame," Apess argues, "for they might have read for themselves; and they doubtless would have found that we were not made to be vessels of wrath, as they say we were. And had the whites found it out, perhaps they would not have rejoiced at a poor Indian's death or . . . would not have called it the Lord killing the Indians to make room for them upon their lands" (289). Although Apess ostensibly writes about a seventeenth-century Indian and his pilgrim neighbors, the reference is undoubtedly contemporary. If Apess's contemporaries had only *read* enough, they would have known that the depiction of Indian savages by "haughty divines and orators" was untrue. Most of the seventeenth-century historians on whom the early nineteenth-century "history of New England writers" relied were "divines": William Hubbard, Nathaniel Morton, John Eliot, and Increase and Cotton Mather. Their writing provided Drake, among others, more than enough cause for condemnation. Orators, though not usually associated with the seventeenth-century settlers of New England, were a common feature of New England life in the antebellum years. Edward Everett and Daniel Webster, both of whom made more than one speech touching on the republic's origins in pilgrim virtue, were often described as New England's most accomplished orators.[21] Apess observes, then, that historians and politicians produce knowledge about Indians' inherent difference and inferiority for the purpose of taking Indian land. They then insist that the material and political effects of such knowledge are actually the signs of Native peoples' inevitable and unassisted extinction.

It is not only the "history of New England writers" who require and perpetuate these disappearing savages; the political use of such conceptions extends to the highest levels of government. Andrew Jackson's professed "parental regard" for the Cherokee must be understood in relation to commemorations of settler violence at Plymouth Rock as well as the pressing concerns of the federal government. Apess asks his audience whether they can "bury the hatchet and those unjust laws and Plymouth Rock together and become friends": "If so, we hope we shall not hear it said from ministers and church members that we are so good so other people can live with us . . . no, even the president of the United States tells the Indians they cannot live among civilized people, and we want your lands and must have them and will have them. As if he had said to them, 'We want your land for our use to speculate upon; it aids us in paying off our national debt and supporting us in Congress to drive you off' " (306–07). In this broad leap from Plymouth Rock to the national debt Apess explicates Everett's unstable narrative of "manifest destiny." Throughout the nineteenth century the federal government's main authority derived from its power to control land. Charles C. Bright notes that "the entire process of acquiring, surveying, parceling, and disposing of Western territories was taken over by the federal government and tied to the [national] debt settlement" (126). Both among the states and internationally, the legitimacy of the U.S. government rested upon its ability to acquire and maintain control of Native land. Native claims on that land had to be vacated, which was accomplished when, as Apess points out, Jackson and the rest of the politicians and historians asserted that Indians were unable to live among whites, unable to govern themselves, and destined to become extinct, conveniently leaving the land for settlers and their government. Celebration of the pilgrim landing at Plymouth Rock becomes an occasion for that reiterated narrative of colonial superiority. Apess thus returns the narrative of the state's origins, which must be represented as providential and beyond dispute, to a history of the complex and necessarily occluded political relations between Native peoples and European settlers.

After considering Apess's analysis of U.S. colonialism, it is revealing to compare critical assessments of him and his writing today and during his lifetime; these accounts are interestingly congruent in their demonstration of the epistemology Apess exposes. Barry O'Connell, the editor of Apess's collected writing, observes in his introduction that for Apess "to write as a Native American could only be an unspeakable contradiction" (xl–xli). The influential critic Arnold Krupat refines his earlier dismissal of Apess as one whose "sense of self, if we may call it that, [derives] entirely from Christian culture," to assert that in the *Eulogy* Apess "attempts with increasing self-consciousness to reconstitute and redefine his 'tribe' and its 'heritage' in Christian terms as a means of constituting and defining himself—this latter process, in typical Native American fashion, hardly self-conscious at all" (*Voice* 145; "Native American Autobiography" 185). Both O'Connell and Krupat make assertions about Native American consciousness, Indians' "typical" or "traditional" characteristics, based on the knowledge produced by the discipline of anthropology, augmented by the researches of literary critics. Because scholars know that Indians are inherently different from non-Indians, any acquisition of "Western" practices or beliefs—writing, Christianity—will cause the "unspeakable contradiction" to which O'Connell refers or, according to Krupat, a disappearance of Indian psychological identity altogether. The "inner" lives of Indians are thus always available to be judged in relation to the critics' imagined better Indian, a more complete Indian than the particular Indian at hand.

A similar assessment was made of Apess in his own day. William Joseph Snelling, who was shortly to become editor of *Indian Nullification of the Unconstitutional Laws of Massachusetts*, Apess's account of the Mashpee struggle for self government (Boston, 1835), began a review of the *Life of Black Hawk* (Boston, 1834) thus:

> [*The Life of Black Hawk*] is a curiosity; an anomaly in literature. It is the only autobiography of an Indian extant, for we do not consider Mr. Apess and a few other persons of unmixed Indian blood, who have written books, to be Indians. They were indeed born of aboriginal parents, but their tastes, feelings and train of ideas, were derived from the whites, and they were and are, in all particulars, civilized men. Human nature is substantially the same every where [*sic*]. Take an Indian child from his parents, in the hope of making him useful as a missionary or instructer [*sic*], give him insight into the truths of religion, and a competent knowledge of the benefits of art, science, and literature, and his expected usefulness is destroyed by the very means used to increase it. He returns to his connections in every respect but color a white man, and is to them what any other white man would be. If he writes, it is in the character of a white man. But here is the autobiography of a wild, unadulterated savage, gall yet fermenting in his veins, his heart still burning with the sense of wrong, the words of wrath and scorn yet scarce cold upon his lips, ('If you wish to fight us, come on') and his hands still reeking with recent slaughter (68–69).[22]

That both Indian writing and Indian Christianity had disruptive political effects can be seen when Snelling's denial of those practices is considered in light of Apess's activities in Boston, which were well known at the time. In addition to organizing a school and a temperance society, in 1833 and 1834 Apess, with the support of the newspaper Snelling edited, led the Mashpee resistance to the Commonwealth of Massachusetts. He drafted and delivered petitions to the governor and president of Harvard College, which supported an almost universally disliked Congregational missionary at Mashpee; denied whites access to natural resources on Mashpee land; wrote articles for the *Boston Daily Advocate* detailing the Mashpee position; represented the Mashpee, along with two other Indian leaders, at the legislature in the winter of 1834; and continued to deliver sermons in which discussion of Native political struggles predominated. The activities of Apess and other Mashpee leaders resulted in a modification of the state's governance of the Mashpee and much public sympathy for their plight. Apess himself, as the accused ringleader of an Indian revolt, earned the wrath of the governor, the administrators of Harvard College, members of the state legislature, and assorted residents of Cape Cod, among others.[23] Apess's notoriety may be gauged by his not needing an introduction to the elite readers of the *North American Review*.

The universal human nature Snelling invokes still allows for an Indian nature that the critic can identify and that European practices destroy, a formulation whose logic both O'Connell and Krupat follow. Snelling's notion of Indian nature is merely less sophisticated—less disciplined—than O'Connell's or Krupat's understanding of Indian identity, and the contemporary notion of inherent Indian consciousness is positive rather than negative. Apess resisted state authority using his ability read, write, and speak English.[24] His preaching and his writing forced Massachusetts legislators—given their vocal support for the Cherokee, their professed republican ideals and Christian beliefs, and their sympathy for Indians—to allow the Mashpee a measure of self-rule. When the governor subverted the agreement, Apess noted the deception and agitated against it in the *Boston Daily Advocate* and in *Indian Nullification*.[25] If Indians do not generally have sufficient military means to resist colonization, when they are literate in English they do have the intellectual means to resist in a state whose legitimacy balances precariously on the production of knowledge about the inherent difference of Indians. It is therefore in the settlers' best interest that Indians be kept as far away as possible from the practice of writing, that the claim be made that Indians who write are no longer really Indians, a claim that obliterates Indians historically and politically, if not physically. The treaty, it bears repeating, is of course a written document. Although it is beyond the scope of this essay to track the exact trajectory from Snelling through ethnology and anthropology to contemporary criticism, it must be pointed out as a first step that the effects of both the historical and contemporary production of knowledge about Indians are the same: the denial to Indians of the practice of writing, which is the denial of their political existence, of their resistance to colonialism, and of their ability to produce works of literature in English comparable to any other literary works.

While academics are seemingly far removed from the political imperatives of the 1830s, the parameters of our thinking about Native peoples and settlers are determined by the relations of 150 years ago and more. Academics continue to engage in an endless production of knowledge about the qualities and characteristics of "Indian identity," but no one, it seems, has ever stopped to ask why we need to know such things or what such knowledge might have to do with larger social relations. No matter how good any particular critic's intentions are, if the categories of knowledge with which we think are not questioned and analyzed, we will continue to participate in that denial of Native political, historical, and material existence so necessary to the legitimacy of the state in which many of us live and work. We might begin to investigate the paradoxes of colonialism in the U.S. and its effects in literary works by doing what Apess exhorts his audience to do and what he himself did: we might read the record carefully and critically. More than that, as Apess's writing demonstrates, we must look to Native intellectual traditions for the means of understanding colonization and its enduring effects on non-Native as well as Native people. Such an approach must begin with the fact that Native people have formed political entities and that they still form political entities. This is only what Indians have always insisted since European settlers first appeared.

Notes

Maureen Konkle would like to thank Edward M. Griffin, Paula Rabinowitz, Carol Miller, Carol Mason, Michelle Lekas, June Reich, Mandy Harris, and the anonymous readers for *American Literature* for their comments on the many versions of this essay. Especially revised for this anthology, this essay originally appeared in *American Literature* 69 (Sept. 1997): 457–86, and the editors would like to thank Duke University Press for permission to reprint it. Copyright 1997, Duke University Press. All rights reserved.

1. See, for example, Krupat, "On the Translation," in addition to the other essays in Swann, *On the Translation of Native American Literature* as well as those in Swann, *Smoothing the Ground*. See also Kroeber and Ramsey. In *Critical Essays on Native American Literature*, Wiget traces the origins of the criticism of Native American literature to nineteenth-century ethnologists such as Henry Rowe Schoolcraft and follows that criticism through twentieth-century anthropology to literary criticism proper. In *Ethnocriticism*, Krupat develops a critical approach to Native American literature derived from ethnography. Scholarly enthusiasm for both creating and interpreting a Native American "oral literature" must be contrasted with the criticism of such practices by many Native scholars. For example, in his anthology *Native American Literature*, Gerald Vizenor observes that such translations "serve dominance rather than the independence of native imagination"; he includes only Native writing in English in his collection (8). What Native writers identify as oral tradition they are often reluctant to put into print directly; see for example, Deloria, *Red Earth* 9–11.

2. For example, Larson charts a developing sense of "Indianness" among Native writers; in *Native American Renaissance*, Lincoln uses anthropological texts to interpret works by Leslie Marmon Silko (chapter 9); see also Lincoln, *Indi'n Humor*, and Velie. Mikhail Bakhtin's concept of dialogism has gained popularity in the criticism of Native American literature in recent years, I would argue, at least in part because of the ease with which the notion of "voices" in "dialogue" can be grafted onto a less theoretical "two cultures" approach. Arnold Krupat, who remains the most influential critic in the field, introduced Bakhtin in his book *The Voice in the Margin*. See Owens for the most extensive application of Bakhtin's writing to Native American literature.

3. In *The Voice in the Margin* Arnold Krupat bases his proposed categorization of Native American literature on the assumption that writing obstructs Indian identity. He writes that "the category of an Indian literature" must be defined "pretty exclusively by reference to the ongoing performances of Native people"; although contemporary oral performances will be influenced by the dominant culture, the orality of that "literature" ensures that the expression

will be "controlled by traditional forms 'internal to the culture' " (209). Later in the same book Krupat defines contemporary Native writing in English as "indigenous literature," which he also refers to as "mixed breed literature" for its combination of "Western" and "Indian modes of literary expression" (214). See Warrior, "A Marginal Voice" for a critique of this approach to Native literature.

4. A. Lavonne Brown Ruoff introduced William Apess and many other early Native writers to literary criticism in her article, "Three Nineteenth-Century American Indian Autobiographers" (1982) and her study, *American Indian Literatures: An Introduction, Bibliographic Review, and Selected Bibliography* (1990). Barry O'Connell must be accorded recognition as the scholar whose work in editing William Apess's writing initiated the minor explosion of interest in Apess; O'Connell's interpretation of Apess's writing in his introduction remains the one from which almost all subsequent readings derive at least in part. O'Connell argues that Apess's republican rhetoric demonstrates his desire to become a citizen of the U.S. (lxxiii–lxxvi), an argument followed by Ashwill, L. Murray, Sundquist, and Walker; that Apess's Methodism helped him to achieve a Pequot psychological and cultural identity (lv), which is the topic of essays by Haynes and Tiro; and that Apess is properly seen as an "antiracist" writer, whose works can be connected to those of African-Americans and abolitionists (xv, lxviii), an argument developed especially by Dannenberg, Sayre, and Peyer. In *Forked Tongues*, David Murray argues that Apess rejects a discourse of "Indianness" and instead exhibits several psychological "identities" in his writing (61, 64). Stevens departs from the trends in the criticism in arguing that Apess achieves a sense of racial identity "through contact with other New England Indians and his own critical reading of American history" (72).

5. Krupat develops the arguments for the inclusion of Native American literature in the canon of American literature most fully in *The Voice in the Margin*. See also Wiget, "Reading Against the Grain." John Guillory analyzes the current academic practice of treating literary works as socially representative in chapter 1 of his book *Cultural Capital*.

6. See Deloria, *Custer Died for Your Sins*; Ortiz; Vizenor, "Native American Indian Literature," "Ruins of Representation," and *Manifest Manners*; Cook-Lynn, "American Indian Fiction Writer" and "Literary and Political Questions of Transformation"; Churchill; and Warrior, *Tribal Secrets*. For an overview of the criticism of the academy by Native scholars and writers, see Littlefield.

7. See Deloria, *Behind the Trail of Broken Treaties* and Deloria and Lytle for analysis of the relations between the U.S. government and Indian nations. Deloria presents an overview and critique of Indian law in "Laws Founded in Justice and Humanity." Harring writes that the term "Indian nation" was first used in colonial treaties, a usage that was taken up by Britain's U.S. successors (57n3). While Harring does not address colonialism in the U.S. per se, his book is indispensable for any consideration of the issue. Colonial treaties with Indian nations varied widely in content and form, but were often written as narratives; for examples, see the series edited by Vaughan.

8. See, for example, Said, *Orientalism*, especially the introduction; JanMohamed; and Spivak, "Rani of Sirmur" and "Can the Subaltern Speak?" My arguments in this essay are influenced by Asha Varadharajan's reappraisal of the role of the object in the work of Edward Said and Gayatri Spivak in her book *Exotic Parodies*.

9. In "Scholarship and Native American Studies" (1993), a response to Littlefield's article "American Indians, American Scholars, and the American Literary Canon," Arnold Krupat attacks Native criticism of the knowledge produced about Native peoples, arguing that such criticism represents the "resentment and anger" of "oppressed people," which often leads them to abandon "logical arguments" to make "statements that may be offered primarily for their rhetorical or political effect" (82). In that same essay, Krupat construes Native sovereignty as a

"right" guaranteed by the U.S. government and asserts that "it remains to be shown" whether or not Native literature in English is a literature of resistance to colonization (87–8; 90). As one of the purposes of his criticism is to "include" Native American literature in the "canon" of American literature, Krupat assumes that Native peoples are merely citizens of the U.S. republic, that citizenship in the republic is a good thing for all of us, and that to insist that there is some other way for Native people to be organized politically makes no sense. Native critics such as Elizabeth Cook-Lynn and Robert Warrior, who have begun to discuss how the political continuity of Indian nations can be understood in relation to the work of Native intellectuals, Krupat labels as "nationalist," apparently without understanding that the discourse of "Indian nations" is not the same—politically or historically—as the discourse of European or postcolonial nationalism. Under the guise of insisting on "democratic inclusion," Krupat merely reiterates the denial of Native political status and struggles that is the main purpose of U.S. colonial discourse. Without an understanding of the political context of Native writing, Krupat's critical approach tends to recirculate ideas about the cultural difference of Indians. Most recently, Krupat's notion of "anti-imperial translation" (which he offers in *The Turn to the Native: Studies in Criticism and Culture*) broadens the concept "translation" to convey what he calls (following Talal Asad) "cultural translation." He argues that Native writers will employ "alternate strategies, indigenous perspectives, or language usages that, literally or figuratively, make its 'English,' on the page a translation in which traces of the 'foreign tongue,' the 'Indian,' can be discerned. If one then wants to claim that this translation is indeed an anti-imperial translation, it becomes necessary to show how those traces operate in tension with or in a manner resistant to an English in the interest of colonialism" (38; see also Krupat's essay in this volume). What Krupat describes does not require a special name; what it does require is a knowledge of the specific history of colonial discourse in the U.S. and a truly *historical* approach to Native writing—neither of which Krupat achieves. Without that specific history, one must rely upon either generalized notions of Indianness or Native American culture/cultures (what else are contemporary writers supposed to employ or depart from?) or, as Krupat demonstrates in this book, equally generalized notions about postcolonial writing (he uses Kwame Anthony Appiah's commentary on the postcolonial African novel as a framework for his comments on contemporary Native novels). My argument in this essay is that our reading of Native literature is determined by the unexamined effects of colonial epistemology: Krupat's criticism largely demonstrates this problem, which cannot be rectified until we examine the peculiar history of colonialism in the U.S., including its epistemological and institutional effects. A large part of that history has been told and continues to be told by Native writers. To attempt to discuss Native literature without knowing that history—and indeed disavowing it—is at the very least mistaken.

10. See White, chapter 10, for his discussion of the Marshall Court's republican philosophy and its effects on African and Native peoples in the U.S., as well as for his discussion of the *Cherokee Nation* cases. See Williams 309–17, for a discussion of what he calls Marshall's "discourse of conquest" in *Johnson*.

11. Several works of literary criticism have addressed the cultural impact of the Supreme Court's rulings on Indians in the 1820s and 1830s. Wald discusses the *Cherokee Nation* cases and Cheyfitz discusses *Johnson* in recent articles. Both of these important and insightful essays rely, however, upon notions of culture and identity that are divorced from the realm of political relations, so that their arguments ultimately concern an American subjectivity. Scheckel discusses the *Cherokee Nation* cases in terms of "questions of national morality and the meaning of American national identity" (103).

12. Everett gave his *Address at Bloody Brook* in September 1835 during his campaign for the governorship of Massachusetts (which he won); it was then published in Boston in December

of that year "by request." See the review of this address in *New England Magazine* (Dec. 1835). There is a strong possibility that William Apess met Edward Everett as early as 1832. Louisa Park, daughter of a prominent Worcester physician and educator and a writer of romances in verse, wrote a letter in April 1832 describing a night of oratory on behalf of the Cherokee that she attended at the Federal-street church in Boston. The speakers were Edward Everett, Elias Boudinot, and an unnamed Indian orator that evidence suggests was William Apess. Park writes about the sympathy Everett evoked in his audience—after his speech, she writes, "[t]he house was still as a tomb and no doubt many eyes were as mine filled with tears"—and about the disbelief, at least on the part of two girls she escorted, that Elias Boudinot, who was "drest like *other people*," was actually an Indian. Of the third orator, Park writes:

> his "palaver" seemed to hit the taste of the audience more decidedly [than Boudinot's]. He was dressed like his companion . . . We now had a few tropes and metaphors, which never failed of applause; some of them were manifestly claptraps; but on the whole I was both surprised and pleased. This man was evidently not quite so well educated, and had not the same familiarity with choice language, and was not so *civilized* as his companion, but there was more native eloquence in his address; his earnestness was evidently sincere, and I felt the difference between hearing an actor on the stage, or even a lawyer defending a client—and listening to a patriot engaged bona fide, with all his heart and soul, in stating the wrongs and pleading the cause of his oppressed country. He was sometimes vehement—and Gen. Jackson had one or two side-knocks, to my great satisfaction.

William Apess was reported to have been a very effective orator in newspaper accounts; he certainly had a habit of mocking Andrew Jackson; and in the *Boston Evening Transcript* for that same week in April 1832 there is a notice that the "Rev. Wm. Apess [sic], of the Pequot tribe of Indians, will give a Lecture . . . at Boylston Hall."

13. Todd points out that "[s]entimental literature is exemplary of emotion, teaching its consumers to produce a response equivalent to the one presented in its episodes" (4). One of the unexamined effects of U.S. colonialism is that many critics still understand sympathy for Indians as a kind of terminal response to American history; it is often noted that one person or another felt compassion for Indians, which is evidently all the needs to be said on the matter. Sympathy for Indians is seldom if ever examined carefully to understand who exactly it benefits, under what circumstances, and for what reasons.

14. The Boston antiquarian Samuel Gardner Drake's variously titled *Book of the Indians*, which he initially published as *Biography and History of the Indians of North America* in 1832, was probably the best known and most widely available work critical of New England's early set-tlers. Many seventeenth-century works were reprinted in the early nineteenth century (and Drake himself edited and reprinted many of these works); their editors often noted the violence and duplicity of their forebears. See, for example, Hubbard viii; Mather 3; Morton 195–96, and Winthrop 134 n. 1. Nathaniel Hawthorne's portraits of morally bankrupt Puritans also date from this period; "Young Goodman Brown" appeared in the April 1835 number of *New England Magazine*.

15. See White, 675–82, for his discussion of what he calls the "reconstituted natural law argument" in nineteenth-century U.S. jurisprudence, which he argues conflates the principles of natural law and the law of nations (676).

16. For example, William Robertson, an eighteenth-century historian of America still popu-lar in the nineteenth century, observed that since Indians "retain a high sense of equality and independence" but lack an "idea of property, . . . no visible form of government is established" (162). Apess refers to Robertson in his appendix to *A Son of the Forest* (55–6).

17. "Nullification. Indian War in Barnstable County" n.p. Apess's account of the Mashpee

struggle in *Indian Nullification* is still the most comprehensive. For a history of the Mashpee Indians' struggles with Massachusetts authorities in the eighteenth and nineteenth centuries, see Campisi, chapters 4 and 5; see also McQuaid and Nielsen.

18. Apess uses Book III, chapters I and II of Drake's 1833 edition of the *Book of the Indians* for the account of King Philip's War at the center of the *Eulogy*, especially chapter II, rearranging, compressing, expanding, editing, and copying Drake's account of the war's events, Philip's character, and settler violence. Callcott writes that such use of another source without citation was a common practice in the era (136). In his edition of the *Eulogy on King Philip*, Lincoln Dexter notes that Drake's third edition of the his Indian book was "no doubt used as a source by Apess" (65). An 1834 edition was not available to me, but because Drake generally only added material to his book through the 1851 edition, I assume that he did not make extensive revisions to the King Philip narrative. Drake took note of Apess in his entry on King Philip in the 1832 edition of *Indian Biography* (268). He complains that Apess misidentifies King Philip as Pequot rather than Wampanoag, a complaint also made in an anonymous review of the second edition of *A Son of the Forest*, which points to Drake as its author (150).

19. For example, Cheney includes Miles Standish as a figure of the noble republican pilgrim. See Gould for an analysis of the puritans-as-republicans theme in antebellum New England writing.

20. See Levin, chapter 4, for an account of the "germ" theory's influence on New England historians in the nineteenth century.

21. Apess acknowledged both Everett's and Webster's support for the Cherokee, as well as that of William Wirt, the Cherokees' lawyer before the Supreme Court, in "An Indian's Looking-glass for the White Man" (160). O'Connell notes the influence of Webster's oratory about pilgrims and the republic (286 n. 15); Reid discusses Everett's contributions to "oratorical culture."

22. After publishing a little-noticed book about his experiences in Minnesota called *Tales of the Northwest* (Boston 1830), Snelling became editor of the anti-Masonic weekly *New England Galaxy*, published several books, and edited others. In *Indian Nullification*, Apess relates that in 1832, when he brought a libel suit against three former Methodist circuit riders, his chief accuser enlisted Snelling to establish Apess's bad character, but Snelling could—or would—not do so (244). O'Connell notes that while Drake listed Snelling as the author of *Indian Nullification* in his own copy of the book, Snelling probably wrote only some prefatory and connecting material (xliii n. 38).

23. In *Indian Nullification* Apess provides the best record of the trouble he caused during the Mashpee revolt, in both his own account and that of the newspaper and other material he reprints. See also *Documents Relative to the Marshpee Indians*, a collection of documents from the Massachusetts government, the overseers of Mashpee, and the Mashpee Indians themselves, that was printed in connection with the Mashpee efforts to gain self-government at the legislature in the winter of 1834. Both the Harvard University Archives (in the collection Mashpee Indians 1811–1841) and the Massachusetts Archives (in the collection Guardians of Indian Plantations) contain records on the Mashpee Indians that shed light on how Apess was perceived. While Apess was active as a preacher when he led the Mashpee revolt, he apparently left the Methodist Church at about that time. Benjamin F. Hallett, editor of the anti-Masonic *Boston Daily Advocate* and lawyer for the Mashpee, reports in his memorial to the Massachusetts legislature [*Rights of the Marshpee Indians* (Boston: J. Howe, 1834)] that Apess left the Methodist church sometime before the winter of 1834 to form his own "Free and United Church" (rpt. *Indian Nullification* 233–34). Despite the availability of this information in O'Connell's edition of Apess's writing, Apess's critics always refer to him as a Methodist. McLoughlin writes that, despite the successes that the Methodists had had in converting many Cherokee people in the 1820s, by the 1830s

they lost much influence when the church hierarchy refused to support their missionaries' endorsement of the Cherokee resistance to removal. Elias Boudinot called the Methodists "abettors of iniquity" in the *Cherokee Phoenix* in January 1831 (qtd. in McLoughlin 57). McLoughlin observes that "[a]fter 1830, to be a Methodist was to be a traitor to the Cherokee Nation" (63). Apess's abandonment of the Methodist church may well have been an act of political solidarity with the Cherokee.

24. By all accounts, Apess was a particularly effective speaker (see note 12 above). Early in the conflict at Mashpee, the *Boston Daily Advocate* reported on 3 Jul. 1833 that Apess was "well educated and a bold speaker" (" 'Flat Nullification' "). During the legislative session attended by Apess, Isaac Coombs, and Daniel Amos as Mashpee representatives, the *Liberator* reported that while Coombs and Amos were varyingly effective in their public speaking, Apess's speech was "fearless, comprehensive and eloquent" (qtd. in *Indian Nullification* 221). After a summary of Apess's speech, the writer observes that the audience—many of whom were members of the Massachusetts House of Representatives—applauded the speakers' "dextrous and pointed thrusts at the whites, for their treatment of the sons of the forest since the time of the pilgrims" (221).

25. The *Boston Daily Advocate* reported in 1835 that Governor John Davis had appointed Charles Marston, a former Mashpee administrator and an ally of the Congregational missionary Phineas Fish, sole commissioner for Mashpee under the new system of government, despite Marston's being "the person whom . . . [the Indians] least wished to have" (rpt. *Indian Nullification* 240–41). The *Daily Advocate* understood the purpose of the governor's choice: "though the Indians are still struggling to advance in improvement, every obstacle is thrown in their way that men can devise, whose intent it is to get them back into a state of vassalage, that they may get hold of their property," an observation that bespeaks Apess's authorship (240–41).

Works Cited

Apess, William. *Eulogy on King Philip, as Pronounced at the Odeon in Federal Street, Boston, by the Rev. William Apess, an Indian.* 1836. *On Our Own Ground: The Writings of William Apess, a Pequot.* Ed. and introd. Barry O'Connell. Amherst: U of Massachusetts P, 1992. 275- 310.

———. *Indian Nullification of the Unconstitutional Laws of Massachusetts; or, the Pretended Riot Explained.* 1835. *On Our Own Ground: The Writings of William Apess, a Pequot.* Ed. and introd. Barry O'Connell. Amherst: U of Massachusetts P, 1992. 163–274.

———. "An Indian's Looking-Glass for the White Man." 1833. *On Our Own Ground: The Writings of William Apess, a Pequot.* Ed. and introd. Barry O'Connell. Amherst: U of Massachusetts P, 1992. 155–161.

———. *A Son of the Forest.* 1829; rev. 1831. *On Our Own Ground: The Writings of William Apess, a Pequot.* Ed. and introd. Barry O'Connell. Amherst: U of Massachusetts P, 1992. 1–97.

Ashwill, Gary. "Savagism and its Discontents: James Fenimoore Cooper and his Native American Contemporaries." *American Transcendental Quarterly* 8.1 (1994): 211–27.

Bright, Charles C. "The State in the United States during the Nineteenth Century." *Statemaking and Social Movements: Essays in History and Theory.* Ed. Charles Bright and Susan Harding. Ann Arbor: U of Michigan P, 1984. 121–58.

Callcott, George H. *History in the United States, 1800–1860: Its Practice and Purpose.* Baltimore: Johns Hopkins UP, 1970.

Campisi, Jack. *The Mashpee Indians: Tribe on Trial.* Syracuse: Syracuse UP, 1991.

Cheney, Harriet Vaughn Foster. *A Peep at the Pilgrims.* Boston, 1826.

The Cherokee Nation v. the State of Georgia. S. Ct. Jan. Term 1831. 10 U.S. Reports (5 Peters) 1.

Cheyfitz, Eric. "Savage Law: The Plot Against American Indians in *Johnson and Graham's Lessee v. M'Intosh* and *The Pioneers.*" *Cultures of United States Imperialism.* Ed. Amy Kaplan and Donald E. Pease. Durham: Duke UP, 1993. 109–28.

Churchill, Ward. *Fantasies of the Master Race: Literature, Cinema and the Colonization of the American Indians.* Ed. M. Annette Jaimes. Monroe, Maine: Common Courage P, 1992.

Cook-Lynn, Elizabeth. "The American Indian Fiction Writer: Cosmopolitanism, Nationalism, the Third World, and First Nation Sovereignty." *Wicazo Sa Review* 9.2 (1993): 26–36.

———. "Literary and Political Questions of Transformation: American Indian Fiction Writers." *Wicazo Sa Review* 11.1 (1995): 46–51.

Dannenberg, Anne Marie. " 'Where Then, Shall We Place the Hero of the Wilderness?': William Apess's *Eulogy on King Philip* and the Doctrines of Racial Destiny." *Early Native American Writing: New Critical Essays.* Ed. Helen Jaskoski. Cambridge: Cambridge UP, 1996. 66–82.

Deloria, Vine, Jr. *Behind the Trail of Broken Treaties: An Indian Declaration of Independence.* 1974. Austin: U of Texas P, 1985.

———. *Custer Died for Your Sins: An Indian Manifesto.* New York: Macmillan, 1969.

———. "Laws Founded in Justice and Humanity: Reflections on the Content and Character of Federal Indian Law." *Arizona Law Review* 31 (1989): 203–23.

———. *Red Earth, White Lies: Native Americans and the Myth of Scientific Fact.* New York: Scribner, 1995.

———. "Revision and Reversion." *The American Indian and the Problem of History.* Ed. Calvin Martin. New York: Oxford University Press, 1987. 84–90.

———. and Clifford M. Lytle. *The Nations Within: The Past and Future of American Indian Sovereignty.* New York: Pantheon, 1984.

Dexter, Lincoln, ed. *The Eulogy on King Philip*, by William Apes. Brookfield, MA: Lincoln A. Dexter, 1985.

Drake, Samuel Gardner. *Biography and History of the Indians of North America.* 3rd ed. Boston: O.L. Perkins, 1834.

———. *The Book of the Indians of North America.* 2nd ed. Boston: Josiah Drake, 1833.

———. *Indian Biography, Containing the Lives of More than Two Hundred Indian Chiefs.* Boston: Josiah Drake, 1832.

Everett, Edward. "Address Delivered at Bloody-Brook, in South Deerfield, September 30, 1835, in Commemoration of the Fall of the 'Flower of Essex,' at that Spot, in King Philip's War, September 18 (o.s.), 1675." *Orations and Speeches on Various Occasions.* Boston: American Stationers, 1836. 587–626.

" 'Flat Nullification' in the Marshpee Indians." *Boston Daily Advocate.* 3 Jul. 1833.

Franklin, Benjamin. *Indian Treaties Printed by Benjamin Franklin.* Philadelphia: Pennsylvania Historical Society, 1938.

Gould, Philip. *Covenant and Republic: Historical Romance and the Politics of Puritanism.* Cambridge, England and New York: Cambridge UP, 1996.

Guillory, John. *Cultural Capital: The Problem of Literay Canon Formation.* Chicago: U of Chicago P, 1993.

Harring, Sidney L. *Crow Dog's Case: American Indian Sovereignty, Tribal Law, and United States Law in the Nineteenth Century.* New York: Cambridge UP, 1994.

Haynes, Carolyn. "'A Mark for Them All to . . . Hiss At': The Formation of Methodist and Pequot Identity in the Conversion Narrative of William Apess." *Early American Literature* 31 (1996): 25–44.

Hubbard, William. *A Narrative of the Indian Wars in New England.* 1677. Worcester, Massachusetts: Daniel Greeleaf, 1801.

JanMohamed, Abdul R. "The Economy of the Manichean Allegory: The Function of Racial Difference in Colonialist Literature." *"Race," Writing and Difference.* Ed. Henry Louis Gates, Jr. Chicago: U of Chicago P, 1987. 78–105.

Jefferson, Thomas. "Autobiography of Thomas Jefferson." *Heath Anthology of American Literature.* Vol. 1. 3rd ed. Ed. Paul Lauter, et al. Boston: Houghton Mifflin, 1998. 919–23.

Johnson and Graham's Lessee v. William M'Intosh. 21 U.S. Reports (8 Wheaton), 543 [1823].

Kroeber, Karl, ed. *Traditional Literatures of the American Indian: Texts and Interpretations.* Lincoln: U of Nebraska P, 1981.

Krupat, Arnold. *The Turn to the Native: Studies in Criticism and Culture.* Lincoln, NE: U of Nebraska P, 1996.

———. *Ethnocriticism: Ethnography, History, Literature.* Berkeley and Los Angeles: U of California P, 1992.

———. "Native American Autobiography and the Synecdochic Self." *American Autobiography: Retrospect and Prospect.* Ed. Paul John Eakin. Madison: U of Wisconsin P, 1991. 171–94.

———. "On the Translation of Native American Song and Story: A Theorized History." Swann, *On the Translation* 3–32.

———. "Scholarship and Native American Studies: A Response to Daniel Littlefield, Jr." *American Studies* 34.2 (1993): 81–100.

———. *The Voice in the Margin: Native American Literature and the Canon.* Berkeley and Los Angeles: U of California P, 1989.

Larson, Charles. *American Indian Fiction.* Albuquerque: U of New Mexico P, 1978.

Levin, David. *History as Romantic Art: Bancroft, Prescott, Motley, and Parkman.* Stanford: Stanford UP, 1957).

Lincoln, Kenneth. *Indi'n Humor: Bicultural Play in Native America.* New York: Oxford UP, 1993.

———. *Native American Renaissance.* Berkeley and Los Angeles: U of California P, 1985.

Littlefield, Daniel F., Jr. "American Indians, American Scholars, and the American Literary Canon." *American Studies* 33 (1992): 95–111.

Massachusetts, Commonwealth of. *Documents Relative to the Marshpee Indians.* Printed by Order of the Senate of the Commonwealth of Massachusetts During the Session of the General Court, A.D. 1834. Vol. 14. Boston: Dutton and Wentworth, 1834.

Mather, Cotton. *Magnalia Christi Americana.* 1702. Hartford, Connecticut: Silus Andrus, 1820.

McQuaid, Kim. "William Apes, Pequot: An Indian Reformer in the Jackson Era." *New England Quarterly* 50 (1977): 605–25.

McLoughlin, William. "Cherokees and Methodists 1824–1834." *Church History* 50 (1981): 56–63.

Morton, Nathaniel. *New England's Memorial.* 1669. Boston: Crocker and Brewster, 1826.

Murray, David. *Forked Tongues: Speech, Writing, and Representation in North American Indian Texts.* Bloomington: U of Indiana P, 1991.

Murray, Laura J. "The Aesthetic of Dispossession: Washington Irving and the Ideologies of (De)Colonization in the Early Republic." *American Literary History* 8 (1996): 205–31.

Nielsen, Donald M. "The Mashpee Indian Revolt of 1833. *New England Quarterly* 58 (1985): 400–20.

"Nullification. Indian War in Barnstable County." *New England Galaxy.* (Boston, Mass.). 6 Jul. 1833.

O'Connell, Barry. Introduction. *On Our Own Ground: The Writings of William Apess, a Pequot.* Amherst: U of Massachusetts P, 1992. xiii–lxxvii.

Ortiz, Simon J. "Towards a National Indian Literature: Cultural Authenticity in Nationalism." *MELUS* 8 (1981): 7–12.

Owens, Louis. *Other Destinies: Understanding the American Indian Novel.* Norman: U of Oklahoma P, 1992.

Park, Louisa Jane to Agnes Major Park. 29 Apr. 1832. Ms. Park Family Papers 1800–1890. American Antiquarian Society, Worcester, MA.

Peyer, Bernd C. *The Tutor'd Mind: Indian Missionary-Writers in Antebellum America.* Amherst: U of Massachusetts P, 1997.

Ramsey, Jarold. *Reading the Fire: Essays in Traditional Indian Literatures of the Far West.* Lincoln: U of Nebraska P, 1983.

Reid, Ronald F. "Edward Everett and Neoclassical Oratory in Genteel America." *Oratorical Culture in Nineteenth-Century America.* Ed. Gregory Clark and S. Michael Halloran. Carbondale: Southern Illinois UP, 1993. 29–56.

Rev. of *Address at Boody-Brook*, by Edward Everett. *New England Magazine.* Dec. 1835: 462–68.

Rev. of *Indian Nullification of the Unconstitutional Laws of Massachusetts; or, The Pretended Riot Explained*, by William Apes. *New England Magazine.* Jul. 1835: 79.

Rev. of *A Son of the Forest*, by William Apes. *American Monthly Review.* Aug. 1832: 150.

"Rev. William Apess, of the Pequot tribe of Indians." *Boston Evening Transcript.* 24 and 25 Apr. 1832.

Robertson, William. *History of the Discovery and Settlement of America.* 1777. New York: J. & J. Harper, 1828.

Ruoff, A. LaVonne Brown. *American Indian Literatures: An Introduction, Bibliographic Review, and Selected Bibliography.* New York: Modern Language Association, 1990.

———. "Three Nineteenth-Century American Indian Autobiographers." *Three American Literatures: Essays in Chicano, Native American, and Asian American Literatures for Teachers of American Literature.* Ed. Houston A. Baker, Jr. New York: Modern Language Association, 1982. 251–69.

Said, Edward W. *Culture and Imperialism.* New York: Knopf, 1993.

———. *Orientalism.* New York: Vintage, 1978.

Sayre, Gordon. "Defying Assimilation, Confounding Authenticity: The Case of William Apess." *A/B: Auto/Biography Studies* 11.1 (1996): 1–18.

Scheckel, Susan. *The Insistence of the Indian: Race and Nationalism in Nineteenth Century American Culture.* Princeton: Princeton UP, 1998.

Snelling, William Joseph. Rev. of *The Life of Ma-ka-tai-me-she-kia-kiak or Black Hawk, Dicated by Himself. North American Review.* Jul. 1835: 68–87.

———. *Tales of the Northwest.* Boston, 1830.

Spivak, Gayatri Chakravorty. "Can the Subaltern Speak?" *Marxism and the Interpretation of Culture.* Ed. Cary Nelson and Lawrence Grossberg. Urbana: U of Illinois P, 1988. 271–313.

———. "The Making of Americans, the Teaching of English, and the Future of Culture Studies." *New Literary History* 21 (1990): 781–98.

———. "The Rani of Sirmur: An Essay in Reading the Archives." *Europe and Its Others.* Vol. 2. Ed. Francis Barker, et al. Cochester, England: U of Essex P, 1985. 128–59.

Stevens, Scott Manning. "William Apess's Historical Self." *Northwest Review* 35.3 (1997): 67–84.

Sundquist, Eric J. "The Frontier and American Indians." *Cambridge History of American Literature, Volume 2: 1820–1865.* Ed. Sacvan Bercovitch. New York: Cambridge UP, 1995.

Swann, Brian, ed. *On the Translation of Native American Literature.* Washington, D.C.: Smithsonian Institution P, 1992.

————, ed. *Smoothing the Ground: Essays on Native American Oral Literature.* Berkeley and Los Angeles: U of California P, 1982.

Tiro, Karim M. " 'Denominated SAVAGE': Methodism, Writing, and Identity in the Works of William Apess, a Pequot." *American Quarterly* 48.4 (1996): 653–79.

Todd, Janet. *Sensibility: An Introduction.* London: Methuen, 1986.

Varadharajan, Asha. *Exotic Parodies: Subjectivity in Adorno, Said, and Spivak.* Minneapolis: U of Minnesota P, 1995.

Vaughan, Alden T. *Early American Indian Documents: Treaties and Laws, 1607–1789.* Washington, D.C.: U Publications of America, 1979-.

Velie, Alan. *Four American Indian Literary Masters: N. Scott Momaday, James Welch, Leslie Marmon Silko, and Gerald Vizenor.* Norman: U of Oklahoma P, 1982.

Vizenor, Gerald. *Manifest Manners: Postindian Warriors of Survivance.* Middletown, Connecticut: Wesleyan UP, 1994.

————. "Native American Indian Literature: Critical Metaphors of the Ghost Dance." *World Literature Today* 66 (1992): 223–27.

————. "The Ruins of Representation: Shadow Survivance and the Literature of Dominance." *American Indian Quarterly* 17 (1993): 7–30.

————, ed. *Native American Literature.* New York: HarperCollins, 1995.

Wald, Priscilla. "Terms of Assimilation: Legislating Subjectivity in the Emerging Nation." *Boundary 2* 19 (1992): 77–104.

Walker, Cheryl. *Indian Nation: Native American Literature and Nineteenth-Century Nationalisms.* Durham and London: Duke UP, 1997.

Walker, James. "Dr. Walker's Queries as to the State of the Indians." Fall 1835. Ms. Mashpee Indians 1811–1841. Courtesy Harvard University Archives, Cambridge MA.

Warrior, Robert Allen. "A Marginal Voice." Rev. of *A Voice in the Margin: Native American Literature and the Canon,* by Arnold Krupat. *Native Nations* 1.3 (1991): 29–30.

————. *Tribal Secrets: Recovering American Indian Intellectual Traditions.* Minneapolis: University of Minnesota Press, 1995.

White, G. Edward. *The Marshall Court and Cultural Change 1815–1835.* Abridged ed. New York: Oxford UP, 1991.

Wiget, Andrew. *Critical Essays on Native American Literature.* Boston: G.K. Hall, 1985.

————. "Reading Against the Grain: Origin Stories and American Literary History." *American Literary History* 3 (1991): 209–31.

Williams, Robert A., Jr. *The American Indian in Western Legal Thought.* New York: Oxford UP, 1991.

Winthrop, John. *The History of New England from 1630 to 1649.* Ed. James Savage. Boston: Phelps and Farnham, 1826.

Samuel A. Worcester, Plaintiff in Error v. The State of Georgia. S. Ct. Jan. Term 1832. 31 U.S. Reports (6 Peters) 515.

CAPITALISM, BLACK (UNDER)DEVELOPMENT, AND THE PRODUCTION OF THE AFRICAN-AMERICAN NOVEL IN THE 1850s

Carla L. Peterson

"Oh, George, never mind the white people," here interposed Mrs. Garie. "Never mind them; tell us about the coloured folks; they are the ones I take the most interest in."

—Frank J. Webb, *The Garies and Their Friends*

In order to protect my children, it was necessary that I should own myself. I called myself free, and sometimes felt so; but I knew I was insecure . . ., till, by dint of labor and economy, I could make a home for my children.

—Harriet Jacobs, *Incidents in the Life of a Slave Girl*

I have signed and sealed the contract with Thayer & Eldridge, in my name, and told them to take out the copyright in my name. Under the circumstances *your* name could not be used, you know. . . . I want you to sign the following paper, and send it back to me. It will make Thayer & Eldridge safe about the contract in *my* name, and in case of my death, will prove the book is your *property,* not *mine.*

—Lydia Maria Child to Harriet Jacobs, 27 Sept. 1860

1
"OF WHAT USE IS FICTION?"

Harriet Jacobs's assertion of the need to own herself, her recognition of "freedom" as a prerequisite to "home" ownership, and her identification of "labor and economy" as the means by which to achieve such ownership are statements that held true for African Americans generally—Northern and Southern, free and slave—in the antebellum period. Indeed, in the decades leading up to the Civil War, black Ameri-

176

cans repeatedly pondered such questions as: How can I escape being a commodity? How can I own myself? How can I possess property? and, more abstractly, How can I achieve and maintain self-possession?

Jacobs's correspondence with Child illustrates the difficulties African Americans faced in their efforts to enter the market of commodity exchange, secure clear title to that which they had produced, and preserve the distinction between *"your* property" and *"mine."* Solutions to these problems were elusive then, as they are now. For, even in its early postcolonial period, the United States was also a neocolonial nation intent on building its economy by appropriating the labor of racially alien populations. As Manning Marable has pointed out, its economic development has been predicated on the systematic exploitation and underdevelopment of black America: *"The constant expropriation of surplus value created by Black labor,"* writes Marable, *"is the heart and soul of underdevelopment"* (7). In the antebellum U.S. the market revolution depended heavily on such black underdevelopment. The economic system of the South relied on slaves whose value lay in their commodity function as capital and in their production function of both a "final good," cotton, and an "intermediate good," slave labor by means of breeding (Conrad and Meyer 97). In the "free" North, industrialization excluded blacks not only from entrepreneurship and capitalist profit but from the ranks of manufacturing labor as well. Policymakers of the period legitimated this exclusion through a recasting of romantic racialism: the moral underdevelopment of blacks, which imprisoned them in a permanent childlike state, deprived them of the competitive drive necessary to become partners in the capitalist enterprise and thereby overcome economic underdevelopment (Takaki 124–27).

To resist underdevelopment, African Americans turned to narrative writing—first to autobiographical and historical discourse and then in the 1850s to fiction—as one of the means of redefining the lives of those "coloured folks" who alone could retain Mrs. Garie's interest (Webb 7). Pauline Hopkins's question in 1900, "Of what use is fiction to the colored race at the present crisis in its history?" was just as pertinent to African-American writers in the 1850s. For fiction, and specifically the novel, makes its appearance at those moments of crisis when, in Mikhail Bakhtin's words, a national culture is decentralized and loses "its sealed-off and self-sufficient character" (370). The 1850s was just such a critical moment for African Americans: it bore witness to the dramatic deterioration of race relations, marked by the passage of the Fugitive Slave Law, the Kansas-Nebraska Act, and the Dred Scott decision, as well as to the consolidation of black underdevelopment signaled by the exclusion of blacks from Northern industrialization and increased demand for slave labor in the South. The African-American novel gave particular expression to such social transformations, becoming, to quote Bakhtin again, "inseparable from social and ideological struggle, from processes of evolution and of the renewal of society and the folk" (67–68). Indeed, between 1853 and 1862, black writers published five texts—two novelized autobiographies, Harriet E. Wilson's *Our Nig* (1859) and Harriet Jacobs's *Incidents in the Life of a Slave Girl* (1861), and three novels, William Wells Brown's *Clotel or, The President's Daughter* (1853), Frank J. Webb's *The Garies and Their Friends* (1857), and Martin R. Delany's *Blake or the Huts of America* (1859–62)—that mark the "beginnings" of African-American novel writing.[1]

In these narratives, the authors consistently sought to disrupt hegemonic notions of history that assumed the permanent fact of black underdevelopment in order to retell African-American history from their own perspective.[2] These writers remained united in their efforts both to represent individual black subjectivity and agency and to affirm the importance of collective identity and experience. And although their narratives reflect varying attitudes toward commodity capitalism and suggest different solutions to black underdevelopment, they all endorse resistance to the expropriation of surplus value created by black labor in order to return it to the community. Yet at the same time, these writers were aware that the black community could never be construed as a pure space. Their narratives depict a community of people characterized by heterogeneity of social class, civil status, and place of origin, whose fluid geographic borders are repeatedly transgressed from within and without; the most visible sign of this transgression is the presence of mixed blood figures, in particular the tragic mulatta. Finally, the writers themselves crossed borders through the very act of composition—in their transition from autobiography to fiction, and in their publication for a white as well as black readership that held the danger of entrapping them in a system of literary commodification over which they had little control.

2
SELF-REPRESENTATION: FROM AUTOBIOGRAPHY TO FICTION

In writing slave autobiographies under the aegis of white abolitionism, black writers all too often found themselves producing conventionalized narratives that offered increasingly stereotyped images of the slave both as narrated and as narrating *I*. Traditional studies of autobiography have theorized the presence of two such *I*s in autobiographical narrative and insisted on the need to view them as distinct entities for whom the use of the same graphic sign is an act of confusion, creating a false unity. In the slave narrative, these two *I*s correspond respectively to the slave still enmeshed in the slave system and the escaped slave whose acquisition of literacy marks him or her as unique. Paul Smith has further argued that a third *I* often emerges in autobiography as the moral "guaranteeing subject" whose function is to vouch for the ideological doxology of the text. This *I* is conceptualized as a fixed and coherent subject, whose effect is to close the enunciatory gap (105). The slave narratives sponsored by white abolitionists underwrite just such a project. Teleological in structure, they conform to an antislavery doxology that mandates the autobiographical *I*'s progression from slavery to a "freedom" whose implications are never fully analyzed. This singular *I* is represented as a coherent guaranteeing subject whose essentialized identity is suggested by the signature "written by himself/herself."

Slave narrators thus discovered that the autobiographical act, far from freeing them from commodification, tended to reinforce their status as commodities. In writing their lives, they often found that they had created alienated images of themselves. And, in agreeing to sell their life experiences on the marketplace, they further exposed themselves to the gaze of an alien audience, whether well-intentioned abolitionists, prurient readers seeking titillation in the accounts of slave nudity or whippings, or simply those eager to consume private lives.[3]

As the 1850s witnessed the appearance of more fictional best-sellers than any previous decade (Mott 122), African-American writers began experimenting with fiction in the hope of reaching a broader audience. These writers produced fiction as a commodity to be sold for profit on the literary marketplace. But they hoped that novelization would enable them to avoid the self-commodification of the slave narrative by disguising those traces of the self they desired to keep hidden. Moreover, as William L. Andrews has noted, these early African-American novels intermingled fact and fiction so that they came to occupy an indeterminate, and potentially empowering, "marginal position between authenticatable history on the one hand and unverifiable fiction on the other" ("Novelization" 26). If such fictional writing could make the consideration of serious political issues more palatable to a readership seeking entertainment rather than edification, its strength also lay in the fact that fiction often is, in Gerald Graff's terms, "hyper-assertive rather than non-assertive," capable of "making stronger, more universalizable" statements than the "factual" discourse of history or autobiography (146). Indeed, the writers' larger goal was to resist underdevelopment through the imaginative reconstruction of African-American history and "local place."[4] Hence, in their fictions they created alternative worlds that, unlike history or autobiography, permitted projections into the future and the invention of new narrative endings. Unlike the slave narrative, finally, these fictions resisted teleology, offering a discursive space for a larger meditation on the "economics of freedom."

Third-person fictional narration in particular provided greater narrational possibilities than did traditional autobiography. By explicitly inscribing the third person within the text, such narration effectively opened up the enunciatory gap closed by slave autobiography, acknowledging the split between narrating and narrated personae. African-American writers took advantage of this split, embodying themselves in the text as character(s) and narrator. As characters, they could turn the alienation of slave autobiography to their advantage by distancing themselves from painful past events; they could further foster personal expansion by reinventing themselves as singular or multiple selves. As narrators, they could adopt authoritative omniscient perspectives denied them by history; they could also provide different perspectives on characters and events, including the reinvented self. Finally, fictional characterization encouraged these writers to dismantle essentialized notions of black subjectivity, conceptualize identity as socially constructed, and explore the multiple facets of African-American experience.

African-American writers' gradual shift from autobiography to novel, from first- to third-person narration, may be traced in the prefatory narrative of *Clotel*, in *Our Nig* and in *Incidents in the Life of a Slave Girl*, suggesting how autobiographical narrative already contains within it subversive fictional techniques, and underscoring the extent to which the grammatical use of person is not a purely formal but a profoundly political act.[5] First, all three texts effectively displace the primary position of the authenticating white abolitionist preface. Brown introduced *Clotel* with an account of his life that proclaimed that the "facts" of a black man's life could authorize his "fiction." Wilson placed the abolitionist documents at the end of her narrative, beginning instead with her own preface, which delivered a stinging attack on "our good anti-slavery friends" and appealed to her "colored brethren" to become her readers. And while the introduction by Child upon which Thayer and Eldridge had insisted is still present, it is preceded by Jacobs's own authenticating preface.

Second, these texts bear traces of the authors' struggle to free themselves from the autobiographical *I* and move toward third-person narration. Brown's prefatory narrative celebrates a form of self-possession as it traces his escape from slavery to a "freedom" that permits him to achieve literacy, enter into the competitive arena of wage-earning labor, and become a successful antislavery lecturer. Anonymously compiled, the first half is written in the third person, separating narrating and narrated personae and underscoring the spuriousness of the guaranteeing ideological *I*. Furthermore, in alternating between third- and first-person pronouns in its second half (by quoting from Brown's autobiographical writings), the narrative unmasks the conventionality of both signs—simultaneously asserting and denying unity of self. Hence, Brown is presented to us not so much as an essentialized self but as the embodiment of the complexity of African-American identity and experience over time.

As female-authored novelized autobiographies, *Our Nig* and *Incidents* bear burdens of narration not evident in similar male-authored narratives. Both Wilson and Jacobs seem to have required a "permission to narrate" necessitated by their vulnerability as black women to the violence of race prejudice and slavery and signaled by their use of fictitious signatures and names. Thus, the common "written by herself" that signs Jacobs's slave narrative is preceded in the title by the pseudonym "Linda," suggested initially by Child as a means of protecting Jacobs's Northern employer, and agreed to by Jacobs who then used it throughout her text. Wilson signed her narrative with the self-consciously objectified signature "Our Nig" and then referred to herself as Frado in her text. In resorting to fictional names to recast their life stories, Jacobs and Wilson were attempting not only to "veil" themselves but also to negotiate feelings of anger and vulnerability, whose expression is often so problematic for women writers, by containing these within a "fictional" world. Hence the presence of the pseudonym here acknowledges the underlying "violence of the letter" that often accompanies the revelation of proper names within an oppressed group in quest of freedom. But it also problematizes essentialist notions of identity and selfhood, and works to resist commodification.

On the level of narration, Wilson established a third-person narrator whose function would be to maintain control over the plot and achieve a perspective of omniscience unattainable in traditional autobiography, while permitting multiple outside viewpoints on the fictional self. At the same time, Wilson sought to conceal her "actual" self and thereby escape commodification by obscuring the distinction between fact and fiction. Thus, while she affirms that her entire narrative is autobiographical, the appended letters confirm as "factual" only the earliest and latest events in her life; the bulk of the narrative, Frado's years in service with the Bellmonts, receives no other textual confirmation. Wilson's difficulties in maintaining narrative distance become evident in the remaining traces of the first person at the beginning and end of the text, the confirmed autobiographical sections.[6] The fact that the first person coheres only around the terms "mother," "father," "home," and "narrative" suggests the degree to which Wilson's autobiography strives, despite the dominance of third-person narration and her attempts to split apart the autobiographical *I*, to unify narrating and narrated *I* into a coherent self.

While maintaining first-person narration throughout *Incidents*, Jacobs also adapted novelizing techniques to the autobiographical mode. She developed forms of double discourse that enabled her to negotiate feelings of anger: chapter titles whose vagueness or banality belie the harshness of the incidents depicted; direct appeals to the reader whose conventionality masks real aggression; maxims whose broad generalizations veil forceful personal judgments. Finally, much like Wilson, Jacobs sought to endow her narrator with much of the authority of omniscience associated with the third person. Thus, Brent relates events and conversations that she herself did not directly witness. And, by relying extensively on dialogue, she seems to turn the narrated *I* into a third-person character, remaining careful, however, not to allow other characters to develop a sustained perspective on her that would lead to commodification. If *Our Nig* is a third-person narration that strains toward the first, *Incidents* is a first-person narration that strains toward the third.

In fact, *Our Nig* and *Incidents* differ radically in their negotiation of necessary compromises with white sponsorship. Having established close relationships with Amy Post and Child, and having openly expressed her distress over Harriet Beecher Stowe's attempts to appropriate her story, Jacobs was able to accept collaboration as historically inevitable and turn it to her advantage. The presence of the conventional discourse of sentimental/seduction fiction in her narrative need not be seen as a sign of Child's editorial encroachment but rather as the shaping of a "floating writing" that suggests the disappearance of the author and emergence of an authorial anonymity through which Jacobs strove to escape commodification and achieve self-possession.[7] In contrast, Wilson's text is marked by an angry acknowledgment of Northern race prejudice and a refusal to compromise with white abolitionism that, given the realities of the 1850s, was highly unrealistic. As a consequence, the third person of the narrative collapses into the ideological *I* of doxological autobiography in Frado's letter reprinted in an appended document, the humility of which belies both the preface's appeal to an exclusively black readership and the narrative's self-assertiveness.

3
THE NOVEL AS COMMODITY

These mid-century African-American writers produced their narratives under pressure from compelling social and economic agendas, and sought to sell their books for profit on the literary marketplace. Wilson hoped to make enough money to care for her sick son, Brown to finance his stay in Britain without having to "beg" his living from white abolitionists. Both Jacobs and Delany were eager to use the proceeds to further their espoused social causes—Jacobs, the antislavery movement; Delany, African-American emigration to the Niger Valley. Their correspondence reveals the extent of their difficulties in achieving these goals. Having completed a draft of her narrative in 1857, Jacobs wrote to Post on June 21 that "I would so like to go away and sell my Book—I could then secure a copywright—to sell it both here and in England" (243). Subsequent events, as we have seen, forced Jacobs to allow Child to take out the copyright in her name. Similarly, Delany orchestrated the publication of *Blake* with great care, securing the copyright to the novel and initially allowing the *Anglo-African Magazine* to publish only three middle chapters in its first issue (Jan. 1859). But, much like Jacobs, he was eventually obliged to appeal to a white abolitionist, William Lloyd Garrison, to intercede on his behalf with "a good publishing house" so that he could "make a penny by it [*Blake*]" (qtd. in *Blake* xi). Apparently receiving no answer from Garrison, Delany finally allowed the successor to the *Anglo-African Magazine*, the *Weekly Anglo-African*, to publish the novel in weekly installments from November 1861 to May 1862.

To interest a good publishing house and remain faithful to their ideological agendas was a complex task for African-American writers. They needed to produce narratives that would construct individual and collective black subjectivity while pleasing both a white audience, unfamiliar with African-American culture, and a black readership seeking to resist underdevelopment. To do so, these writers turned to two fictional types, the tragic mulatta and the picaro, themselves derivations of protagonists of early American seduction fiction and picaresque novels and already legitimated by the dominant cultural discourse as representative aspects of male and female experience in America.[8] Yet they also insisted on revising these conventions from an African-American perspective. In their hands, the tragic mulatta plot increasingly resists conventional "tragic" endings and argues against theories of black underdevelopment; the open-ended form of the picaresque embraces the possibility of black economic development. Finally, both plots force the reexamination of an ideological vision that privileges individual effort and choice. Indeed, African-American fictional narratives of the 1850s explore from different perspectives and to different ends the complex relationship between ideologies of individualism and those of collectivity, in the process thematizing issues of commodity capitalism raised by the authors' literary careers.

Such adaptive strategies suggest how African-American novelistic discourse of the 1850s is marked by hybridity which, as Homi K. Bhabha has suggested in another context, effectively undermines the stark opposition between "the noisy command of colonialist authority [and] the silent repression of native traditions" (154). If the "minority" text comes to voice as a repetition, it is repetition with a difference; it challenges the boundaries of the dominant discourse by questioning the basis of the latter's authority and introducing " 'denied' knowledges" from the native culture (156). In this instance, the denied knowledges are those of African-American community-making—the reconstruction of history and local place in the New World through which African, slave, and Northern black cultural traditions may be heard to echo. As such, hybridity serves here to resist the commodification of the African-American literary text.

4

THE TRAGIC MULATTA AS SURPLUS VALUE

America's first novelistic genre was the seduction novel, whose plot lay bare the economic contract of middle-class marriage in which white women figured as objects of exchange subordinated within the home as regulators of a domestic economy that owed its existence to the labor and capital of their husbands. The plot's ending invariably punished the heroine who resorted to the free expression of her sexuality in an attempt to disrupt this capitalist system of exchange. Although novels of this genre ceased to be written after the 1820s, they continued to be read: cultural anxieties about women's sexuality did not disappear, but were invested in the tragic mulatta plot, in whose heroine sexuality and blackness became conflated. While the convention of the tragic mulatta ostensibly functioned as a socially acceptable literary device that would allow white abolitionist women to speak openly about the plight of the female slave and perhaps even identify with her, it also had its more insidious side. If the tragic mulatta figure erases the physical blackness of the slave woman, as Hortense Spillers and Karen Sánchez-Eppler have noted, it nonetheless reveals the culture's apprehension over what constitutes blackness indicated, for example, in the proliferation of such terms as *mulatto, quadroon,* and *octoroon*. This anxiety over issues of race and sexuality could be allayed only by the sacrifice of the black woman. Thus, beneath its idealized surface, the tragic mulatta plot suggests just how insidiously "romance" privatizes and manipulates the heroine: the object of the white male gaze and desire, the mulatta renders female sexuality available; she legitimates the act of seduction, perhaps even of rape.[9]

As in the seduction novel, however, the sexual plot of the tragic mulatta story is undergirded by an economic one. In the economy of slavery, the mulatta was a commodity sold at high profit as a "fancy girl" or exploited to produce more slaves. Yet, given that the economic system of slavery was underwritten by an aristocratic social code emphasizing luxury consumption rather than accumulation and profit (see Genovese 16–31), the mulatta also constituted a surplus value produced for the personal consumption of the slaveholder. As such, she functions as a fetish, a material object onto which the social properties of aristocratic consumption have been transposed.

From the perspective of black underdevelopment, then, the libidinal surplus of the mulatta is doubled by an economic surplus, and her story becomes the convergence of two plots. In the first, the mulatta is a luxury commodity to be enjoyed (consumed) by the slaveholder. In the second, she is converted into capital and reinvested (through sale or reproduction) in order to accumulate additional capital for the slaveholding class. The convergence of these two plots produces the narrative crisis.

5
RECONFIGURING THE TRAGIC MULATTA PLOT

In their narratives all five writers worked to counter theories of black underdevelopment and to reconfigure individual and collective African-American identity. Brown, Jacobs, and Wilson adopted the tragic mulatta story as a central feature of their narratives, but separated the economic plot from the libidinal, foregrounding the former. Webb and Delany sought to marginalize the tragic mulatta figure; not only does she symbolically feminize the race but her plot prohibits her return as surplus value to the black community. They insisted instead that broader economic issues must predominate.

To tell his tragic mulatta story, Brown shifted from auto/biography to fiction, writing a novel in which the main events of the prefatory narrative function merely as digressions; what is perhaps its most interesting episode, Brown's brief capitalist career as a banker, issuing shinplasters (small promissory notes that are circulated, redeemed, then recirculated), never finds its way into the novel. What becomes the main plot is the story of the mulatta Currer, introduced as Thomas Jefferson's concubine, her two daughters, and three granddaughters. The novel opens with an attack on Southern slave laws, which refuse to acknowledge the marriage relation for slaves, and closes with the happily-ever-after marriage of Clotel's daughter Mary. In between, Brown traces the sad fate of Currer's other progeny, in particular her daughter Clotel.

Borrowing his tragic mulatta plot almost entirely from Child's short story, "The Quadroons," Brown seems to yield to its romantic ideology: the creation of highly socialized and refined mulatta women worthy of the admiration of white men; the blossoming of true love; the tragic ending of the romance due to the laws of slavery. Yet in the novel's opening pages Brown's narrator launches a sharp critique of the tragic mulatta story, exposing its romantic conventions and emphasizing the economic necessity that motivates its heroines: "Reader, when you take into consideration the fact, that amongst the slave population no safeguard is thrown around virtue, and no inducement held out to slave women to be chaste, you will not be surprised when we tell you that immorality and vice pervade the cities of the Southern States. . . . Indeed most of the slave women have no higher aspiration than that of becoming the finely-dressed mistress of some white man" (63).

What is particularly interesting about Brown's adaptation of the tragic mulatta plot is that the lengthy episode of the preface—Brown's production and circulation of shinplasters—reappears as the structural framework of the novel, whose point of departure is the production and inflationary proliferation of a series of tragic mulattas (Currer and her progeny). Its development consists of their circulation, initially as undifferentiated characters, through the libidinal economy of Southern slaveholding society, ostensibly as objects of romantic desire but in fact as luxury commodities designed for the private consumption of the slaveholders. And its conclusion consists of their reconversion into capital for further reinvestment, resistance of course running the risk of death. Yet at least two of the protagonists—Clotel and her daughter Mary—exhibit unconventional forms of agency absent in Child's story; they both attempt escape or resistance by disguising themselves as men. If Clotel must die as a result, Mary escapes to France and marries the heroic mulatto George. While it is impossible to underestimate the significance of marriage as an institution legitimating the sexual relations of African Americans, it is important to note that Mary and George's marriage isolates them from the slave community to which they once belonged and privatizes her within a capitalist economy. Concluding that "a woman's whole life is a history of the affections" (243), Brown, unlike Jacobs, seems unable to conceptualize a role for free black women outside the private sphere.

Brown's tragic mulatta plot differs from Child's in other ways as well, in particular in its emphasis on collectivity. First of all, Brown's incorporation of Child's story in his novel points to his use of oral culture's technique of voice merging that rejects the concept of individual ownership of discourse to insist instead on its collective and shared nature. Second, Brown contextualized his tragic mulatta plot by broadening his focus from individual heroic characters to a larger slave community composed of secondary comic characters. Like the novel's heroines, these characters never achieve real agency; they are freed only through the intervention of the white (and singular) protagonist, Georgiana Peck, referred to as the "liberator" in an echo of both *Uncle Tom's Cabin*'s George Harris and Garrison's abolitionist paper. But below this community's surface lies a resistant and productive slave culture that counteracts underdevelopment by means of an economy of laughter. Through this economy, Brown and his slave characters simultaneously express and disguise black aggression and hostility. Although appearing to conform to a Sambo model, they in fact mock and manipulate the white characters by means of humor. This economy of laughter produces a surplus of pleasure—and psychic relief—for black author, characters, and readers alike (L. Levine 320–21).

In *Incidents in the Life of a Slave Girl*, Jacobs explicitly calls attention to the dominant culture's construction of Linda as a mulatta. But, even more than *Clotel*, Jacobs's narrative radically revises the tragic mulatta story. Dr. Flint's sexual advances do not become the basis for a romantic plot but constitute an attempt at rape. To escape him, Brent realizes that the best strategy of resistance lies in publicity, and that privatization, so common in tragic mulatta stories, can only work to the advantage of the slaveholder. Well aware of this fact, Flint, in a parody of the tragic mulatta plot, seeks to privatize Brent: "In the blandest tones, he told me that he was going to build a small house for me, in a secluded place. . . . I shuddered; but I was constrained to listen, while he talked of his intention to give me a home of my own, and to make a lady of me" (53). It is this attempt that goads Brent to the public action of taking another white man, Mr. Sands, as a lover and bearing his children.

Brent's final escape from slavery begins with a seven-year confinement in her grandmother's attic. Such confinement can be read as a grotesque parody of the dominant culture's efforts to privatize the female, shut her up within the family, and hystericize her body. As one of Brent's friends exclaims: " 'Lor, chile,' she said, putting her arms around me, 'you's got de highsterics' " (108). And indeed, Brent's bodily history ironically prefigures that of later nineteenth-century hysterical women who were to play such an important part in the psychoanalytic discourse of the dominant culture: attempted seduction by an older father figure; the display of such symptoms as numbness, paralysis, loss of speech (*aphonia*), persistent coughing (*tussa nervosa*), unsociability; seclusion within the family; the obsessive concern of the medical profession; and finally, the disruption of the social structure of the patriarchal family. Unlike Freud's later hysterics, however, Jacobs enters the symbolic order to write an autobiography that is based not in hysterical discourse but in a careful manipulation of the conventions of the dominant literary culture.

Brent refuses to accept the traditional fate of the tragic mulatta: commodification, privatization, hysteria, consumption, reinvestment, and ultimately death. Instead, her actions insistently unmask the economic basis of the incidents in her life and her use of "femininity" as a site of resistance to the patriarchal system of slavery. As Houston Baker has noted, Brent deliberately commodifies herself as a sexual object and gives herself to Sands in order to disrupt the slaveholders' control of the slave exchange market. She insists on negotiating her own labor power and later that of her children, first by turning her womb into a site of (re)production, then by means of her mothering and nurturing capacities, and finally by commodifying her children in order to free them (51–54).

To an even greater extent than *Clotel*, *Incidents* underscores the importance of community action in the slaves' efforts to resist commodification and reconstruct local place. Thus, Brent's account of individual destinies is interspersed with descriptions of empowering slave institutions and folkways: the church, the burying ground, John-kannaus celebrations, funeral rituals. Her narrative also suggests the ways in which her life and the lives of other women nurtured by slave culture counter Brown's assertion that "a woman's whole life is a history of the affections"; it elucidates the means by which these women worked to forge homes on the margins of the slaveholders' economy. In particular, it illustrates how Brent's grandmother's home generates an in-house economy, neither private nor public, where children are sheltered, goods produced, and the community provided for, and how her own garret is transformed from a prison into an productive domestic space through the activities of reading, letter-writing, and sewing.

In contrast, the unusually lengthy account of Brent's life after her escape underscores the complexities of black survival in an increasingly urbanized and capitalized North and constitutes a bleak meditation on the economics of freedom. The juxtaposition of the last two chapter titles, "The Fugitive Slave Law" and "Free at Last," questions the meaning of freedom when slave laws can so easily penetrate to the North. Acknowledging her dependent status as a domestic worker, the dispersal of her children, and her lack of a "hearthstone of my own" (201), Brent admits to the difficulties of sustaining home and community. Yet Jacobs never abandons this project. Narration itself becomes a means of forging community as she shifts in the last portion of her narrative from addressing the "women of the North" invoked in her preface to an appeal to members of the black community: "Let every colored man and woman [stand up for their rights], and eventually we shall cease to be trampled under foot by our oppressors" (177). Finally, her nostalgic reference to her grandmother in the very last lines suggests her valuation of "retrospection"—and the narration of retrospection—as a vital means of resisting economic underdevelopment and creating community.

Similar issues of economic survival are explored in Harriet Wilson's *Our Nig*. Wilson's autobiographical Frado is a mulatta who participates in a double seduction plot—her mother's and her own—that strips bare all romance surrounding the tragic mulatta story and exposes both the economic and sexual politics through which capitalism has systematically kept underdeveloped certain classes of people.[10] Frado's mother, Mag Smith, is a poor white woman who is seduced and abandoned; unlike her middle-class fictional counterpart, however, she cannot die but must struggle to survive in undignified poverty. When she does marry, it is out of economic necessity and to a black man, Jim: " 'I can do but two things,' said she, 'beg my living, or get it from you' " (13). This marriage is a union of white and black in which the white partner represents pure economic motivation, interested only "to subserve her own comfort," while the "kind-hearted" and "industrious" black bespeaks "a finer principle," yet covets the white woman as his "treasure" (15, 9, 10, 14); their union reflects that of the nation at large. Jim soon dies of consumption, victim of both disease and hard work; the union between black and white is dissolved and its product, Frado, discarded as waste.

Frado is made to carry the burden of black self-representation alone. From the first, the narrator describes her as a mulatta, but the distance between her and the conventional figure is immense; her function is to expose its romanticization and point to its economic basis. Inverting the convention, Frado follows the condition, not of her mother, but of her "free" father, and becomes Our Nig, an appellation that calls attention to her blackness and erases her mother's whiteness. This inversion underscores the hypocrisy of those laws that define civil status according to the mother and affirms the inescapability of race as the primary social condition in the free North.

Eschewing the conventions of traditional autobiography whereby the perspective of the *I* largely governs the narrative, Wilson allows multiple outside perspectives on her fictionalized self, Frado, seeking in the process to accommodate a double audience of both black and white readers. According to these perceptions, Frado is not socialized into the feminine graces of traditional tragic mulattas. Instead, she is repeatedly represented as a figure of minstrelsy through which the dominant culture constructed and exploited black stereotypes. Like Stowe's Topsy, she is depicted as "a wild, frolicky thing" (18) whom white readers might well have viewed with condescending mockery rather than identification, but in whom black readers might well have recognized a figure of resistance.

Beneath this comic surface, however, Frado is doubly constructed by the Bellmonts as sexual and economic object—represented by the appellation Our Nig—thus bringing to the surface the latent contradictions in the conventional tragic mulatta figure. It is significant that minstrelsy itself both sexualized the black woman in the role of "Negro wench" and undercut her sexuality by masculinizing her, unmasking the male impersonator beneath the female costume at the show's end. Frado is first sexualized by her stepfather in his deliberations about giving her away: " 'There's Frado's six years old, and pretty. . . . She'd be a prize somewhere' " (17). Later, as Our Nig, Frado again functions as a sexual object. The term is invented by Jack, the younger Bellmont son, and is used consistently up to the point where both he and his older brother, James, disappear from the plot. It is clearly sexualized: " 'She's real handsome and bright, and not very black, either' " (25); and Frado participates in this sexualization by becoming attached to both men: "How different this appellative sounded from him [Jack]" (70). If Frado as Our Nig represents black female sexuality to these two men, however, she is seen by others, particularly Mrs. Bellmont, as a desexualized worker to be exploited, a "man, boy, housekeeper, domestic, etc." (116). It is this interpretation of Frado, rather than the sexualized one, that survives to the end of the narrative and even beyond in the appended documents.

Equally importantly, however, the narrative also allows the black narrator's perspective on the white Bellmonts, and hers is a perspective that explodes the dominant ideology of separate spheres. Far from spreading moral beneficence throughout the household, Mrs. Bellmont is depicted as fully preoccupied with the acquisition and accumulation of property. It is she who seeks Aunt Abby's right in the homestead, hopes to marry Jane to a wealthy landowning neighbor, and attempts to preserve her husband's estate by maintaining Frado in indentured servitude and owning her labor power (45, 56). Yet, as a *feme covert*, Mrs. Bellmont owns nothing, and it is this dispossession that is the source of her anger and fear. She fears that Frado's development— her acquisition of education and religion—will end the expropriation of the surplus value created by black labor, encourage an abhorrent socioeconomic equality, and erase racial difference: " 'We should very soon have her in the parlor, as smart as our own girls' " (89). Indeed, the threat of losing Frado's labor fills Mrs. Belmont and her daughter Mary with the fear that they themselves might be forced to engage in domestic work that would reduce them to the status of (black) servant.

In a highly ironic contrast, Wilson portrays the Bellmont men as sentimental. If Frado appears to be Stowe's Topsy transplanted to the North, James embodies the traits of a conventional nineteenth-century heroine. He is a revised Eva, gentle, religious, forgiving, and doomed to an eminently sentimental death. As Hazel Carby has suggested, James represents the well-intentioned but ineffectual Northern abolitionist whose economic interests are ultimately allied with capitalism (44–45). Contradicting the tragic mulatta plot, however, the narrative disallows any romance between Frado and James; indeed, underneath its sentimental surface their relationship is one of labor exploitation as Frado nurses James on his deathbed, thus ruining her health.

The conclusion of *Our Nig* suggests some effort by Frado to control her own labor power; she successfully threatens to withhold her labor in a verbal altercation with Mrs. Bellmont: " 'Stop!' shouted Frado, 'strike me, and I'll never work a mite more for you' " (105). Yet, even after the termination of her indenture Frado finds that she cannot escape economic exploitation. Following her marriage to a black man, who seduces and abandons her, Frado is forced out into the marketplace. The labor that she engages in—the making of straw hats as a form of "rural outwork"—again explodes both the myth of free labor in the North and that of any similarity between black and white women. This industry was fully enmeshed in colonial and slave systems as its raw material, straw, was imported from the Caribbean, and the finished product, hats, were sold South to slaveholders for use by their slaves. And, unlike white women's participation in it, Frado's is not a transition to more remunerative factory work. Hence, by the narrative's end Frado is homeless, deprived of a community of "people of color," and thrown back on public assistance.

Wilson's novelized autobiography is a powerful indictment of the conditions of black underdevelopment in "a two-story White House, North." And, as Gates has contended, Wilson's gesture of signing her text as "Our Nig" is equally powerful since Frado moves from being the object of the dominant discourse to being the subject of her own and reverses the power relation involved in the issue of who names. Yet the fact remains that at the narrative's conclusion as well as in the appended documents the reader is left with a vision of Frado imprisoned in underdevelopment, unable to forge a self-identity independent of the Bellmonts, and yielding to abjection. The ultimate irony is that Wilson was obliged to commodify the one object she owned— herself—to sell on the literary marketplace, but that not even this act of commodification could ensure her son's survival. Such an ending underscores the difficulty of constructing black subjectivity in isolation from community, and suggests the degree to which identity is never individual but part of a larger collective consciousness. As such, the emergence of the ideological *I* around the terms "mother," "father," "home," and "narrative" become fully comprehensible—a desperate gesture to claim self-possession, ownership, relationship.

6
BLACK CAPITALISM AND THE PICARESQUE

Delany's novel *Blake* stands in striking contrast to *Our Nig* as a text that extols the black male hero who self-consciously positions himself above his community in order to forge pan-African nationhood and redirect the course of history. In the process, the tragic mulatta plot recedes to the background to allow the foregrounding of a masculine capitalist plot that challenges black underdevelopment. Delany serialized his novel in 1859 in the *Anglo-African Magazine*, and from 1861 to 1862 in the *Weekly Anglo-African* (the last chapters are missing). Designed for an elite black readership, these organs aimed "to uphold and encourage the now depressed hopes of thinking black men" ("Apology" 3). Thus they were receptive to *Blake*'s radical political message that preached slave insurrection in the South, a black takeover of Caribbean plantation economies, and the development of black commodity and mercantile capitalism on an international scale. The novel fictionalizes a political agenda that Delany had been working out in journalistic form throughout the 1840s and '50s: his call, in the event of a U.S. attempt to annex Cuba, for African Americans to intervene and for enslaved Cubans to revolt; his promotion of African-American emigration to Central America; and his plan for settling the Niger Valley with African-American men who would develop cotton production and encourage the emergence of the black man as capitalist. In constructing a fictional narrative grounded in history, Delany sought new ways to represent both self and community to a broader audience. In *Blake*, he imaginatively explored the mechanisms by which political and economic revolution might be achieved and transformed himself, disguised as the picaresque hero Henry Blake, into an agent of revolutionary change.[11]

The narrative crisis in which Blake is caught up is precipitated in the first chapter by twin occurrences whose relationship only becomes clear in part 2: the refitting of an old ship, the *Merchantman*, by a group of American and Cuban men, among whom figures Colonel Franks, and the sale of Mrs. Franks's favorite slave, the mulatta Maggie, by the colonel. Though the narrator describes these men as "little concerned about the affairs of the general government" and "entirely absorbed in an adventure of self-interest" (3), the plot elucidates the relationship of general government to economic self-interest: the collusion between government and private parties in maintaining the slave system, reviving the slave trade, and opening Cuban sugar plantations to U.S. interests in order to develop external colonization and expand global capitalism. Blake is moved to action not because of these "public" developments, however, but because of the "private" sale of his wife Maggie; he runs away and travels through the Southern states organizing a slave revolt.

At first glance, Blake's planning of rebellion appears motivated by a common interest with his fellow slaves. Blake is a composite of past African-American leaders—Toussaint L'Ouverture, Denmark Vesey, Nat Turner, Madison Washington—and thus represents collective African-American history. Emblematic of those revolutionary acts through which slaves resisted the exploitation of their labor power, Blake, however, remains a single hero—a picaro—who sets himself above the rest of the community. While he seeks to create community by linking the "huts of America" to one another by means of a revolutionary organization, he increasingly positions himself as an elite figure, a freeborn, well-educated, "pure African," untainted by miscegenation, given to "head-work," and detached from the mass of slaves for whom he speaks. Revealing distinctly capitalist tendencies typical of the picaro, Blake denigrates slave culture as primitive superstition, mocking the Maroon survivors of Vesey's and Turner's rebellions. Rejecting both slave conjuration and traditional Christianity as avenues of black empowerment, he relies instead on an organizational strategy that links the huts of America by means of secret rituals, disguises, symbols, and the cult of silence reminiscent of Delany's own organization of the 1858 convention in Chatham, Canada, in which John Brown had participated.[12]

Delany may well have borrowed such forms from the freemason movement of which he was a member and about which he had written a pamphlet claiming freemasonry to be Egyptian—and thus black—in origin. Mark Carnes has recently suggested that freemasonry flourished in the antebellum period as a largely middle-class urban institution that arose in response to male anxieties created by the market revolution. This new capitalist order forced the restructuring of male gender roles, guiding men into competitive capitalism and allowing them sanctuary, not in a feminized church, but in masculine freemasonry. This movement simultaneously adopted the values of the emerging middle class by preaching hard work, sobriety, and self-restraint, *and* subverted these values by creating mysterious rituals that undermined capitalist discipline (32). In the novel, Blake's use of such rituals to create an organization of slaves under his control within an African-American male space reflects Delany's own aspirations as an educated and secularized black man to create a strong black male network that might eventually intervene in the new capitalist order.

Part 1 of *Blake* concludes with the hero's escape to Canada after having thrown slave society into crisis by means of surreptitious killings and monetary bribes, capital figuring here as the "certain passport through the white gap" (43). The narrative action of part 2 shifts to Cuba, where Blake has gone to search for Maggie and further foment slave rebellion. But insurrection is repeatedly deferred, suggesting Delany's great difficulty in conceptualizing the mechanisms of revolution, even in fictional form, and achieving narrative closure. Instead, other problematic social issues come to the fore, pointing to irreconcilable contradictions within Delany's black nationalist capitalist ideology.

Part 2 begins with the reappearance of both the *Merchantman* and Maggie. The sexual and economic plots reconverge here in a twin colonization—that of Cuba by American slaveholding interests, and that of Maggie by the male slave. Indeed, in Delany's plot the tragic mulatta is liberated from the grip of the white slaveholder only to be privatized by black capitalism and disappear from the novel. The rest of part 2 focuses on the attempts by Americans, Spanish, Creoles, and blacks (American and Caribbean) to recolonize Cuba; Delany's depiction of African Americans here is a fictionalization of his own emigration projects. In the novel, the group of blacks in Cuba becomes progressively more inclusive as Delany attempts to negotiate differences of class, gender, religion, and color, and to pay special homage to African culture. In particular, Blake is doubled on the one hand by Gofer Gondolier, a representative of the black folk, and on the other by the aristocratic mulatto poet, Placido. Such an alliance between different social groups remains tenuous, however. Blake himself is revealed to be the son of a wealthy Cuban manufacturer. He becomes increasingly removed from the huts of America as he circulates in the grand domiciles of the Cuban mulatto elite; yet, like Delany, he remains alienated from this mulatto class. His Grand Council meetings end up reduplicating the hierarchies of white patriarchal capitalism. And, though slave culture is represented in part 2 in the form of the Congo dance, it is purely spectacle, not lived and empowering culture. Unable to create a community within a capitalist context that would be nonpatriarchal and nonhierarchical, Delany's narrative defers to the very last (missing) chapters the question of who will win Cuba.

7
THE NOVEL OF COMMUNITY/THE ECONOMICS OF MARGINALITY

Published in London in 1857, Webb's *The Garies and Their Friends* undermines any critical tendency to construct a strict dichotomy between masculine and feminine African-American sensibility whereby women yearn for community and men celebrate heroic individualism. Indeed, the novel seeks a middle ground between ideologies of capitalist individualism and those of collectivity, depicting strong individual characters who work within, and for, the black community of Philadelphia. In his novel Webb imaginatively reconstructs black Philadelphia as an African-American local place grounded in an ethics of collective action. Thus, the very title announces community in its reference to a group of people rather than a single protagonist, whether tragic mulatta or capitalist entrepreneur. Yet it also suggests the separation of the Garies—a Southern slaveholder and his mulatta slave Emily—from their friends; and, in fact, the couple remain isolated throughout the novel. Ostracized by the slaveholding class in the South and hoping to escape the fate of the tragic mulatta, Emily convinces Mr. Garie to resettle in the "free" North; but even as a married couple in Philadelphia, they remain on the margins of both white and black society. Unlike Brown, Webb refuses to offer legal wedlock as a solution to the dilemma of the mulatta heroine; mid-way through the novel, a race riot occurs and the Garies are murdered.

Indeed, the tragic mulatta figure functions more as a pretext for narrative action than as its center. Webb's chief interest is to probe the social and economic conditions of African Americans in the urban North in which black Philadelphia constitutes a hybrid space characterized by a heterogeneity of neighborhoods, social classes, and inhabitants, whom city life brings together in unpredictable ways. If such hybridity appears socially disruptive, it operates in fact as a necessary strategy for African-American survival. The community practices an "economics of marginality" designed to counter black underdevelopment and to translate marginality into social and economic autonomy based on community interdependence.[13]

Webb's novel explores the fictional possibilities of such an economics of marginality in ways that Jacobs's autobiographical narrative could not. On the one hand, it acknowledges black dependence on white social and economic structures—Mrs. Ellis and her daughters sew for white families, while Charlie is put out at service and is later rejected for employment by white businesses. On the other, it illustrates the potential of black entrepreneurship in the figure of Mr. Walters, a wealthy investor in real estate, black craftsmanship in the carpenter, Mr. Ellis, and black small business ownership in the second-hand clothes store of the De Younges. Though the novel openly endorses capitalism as an economic model for black empowerment, it celebrates not so much individual achievement as the way the characters attend to the collectivity, returning surplus value to the community rather than serving their own particular interests. It has in fact little use for those "surplus" individuals, all mulattos, who cannot transcend self-interest: Mrs. Garie, who is doomed by her interracial romance; her cousin, Mr. Winston, who cannot bring himself either to pass or to "bear the isolation and contumely to which [blacks] were subjected" (14) and so leaves the U.S.; and Clarence, the Garies' son, whose life as a tragic mulatto in the North configures an economic plot in which he remains underdeveloped and unproductive, and is ultimately consumed by white society.

Community values emerge most strongly during the race riot and its aftermath, which form the novel's central episodes. Based on a combination of incidents that occurred during the Philadelphia riots of 1834 and 1849, the riot in *The Garies* illustrates once again the conflation of the sexual and economic issues that surround the tragic mulatta. The instigator of the riot, George Stevens, is motivated chiefly by economic self-interest; he plots the Garies' deaths in order to inherit the family fortune. His motives remain hidden, however, as he gives two distinct rationales for the riot to the members of the mob: a sexual motive, which plays on the distaste of whites for interracial marriage, and an economic one, which proposes the destruction of black property resulting in the flight of homeowners, a fall in the value of property, and a consequent cheap buy-out by whites.

The defense of Mr. Walters's house—the bastion of black capitalism—during the riot emblematizes black community interdependence as men and women of all social classes come together to protect it. The Ellis daughters redirect their domestic talents to revolutionary ends as their skilled hands load guns and boil water to pour on the mob below. In contrast, in a futile attempt to warn the Garies, Mr. Ellis is caught by the mob and his hands are mutilated. Deprived of economic resources, the Ellises, an ordinarily self-reliant family, are taken care of by Mr. Walters. Their resilience and ultimate triumph demonstrate the effectiveness of an economics of marginality that resists black underdevelopment, relies on community interdependence, and works to forge collective identity.

In the 1850s, African-American writers turned to fiction writing as a means of resisting conditions of underdevelopment forced upon them by the neocolonial nation-state.

They sought to open up the enunciatory gap between the narrating and narrated *I*s of autobiography and to experiment freely with the construction of narrators and characters. They adapted conventional figures from the dominant literary culture— the tragic mulatta and the picaro—to represent black subjectivity and agency. And although these writers could not always escape the commodification of their literary productions, nonetheless fiction writing enabled them to meditate upon the notion of an economics of freedom, explore the heterogeneity of their communities, and probe the tensions between ideologies of individualism and those of collectivity, both of which work to overcome black underdevelopment.

Notes

An earlier version of this essay first appeared in *ALH* 4.4 (1992): 559–83. We thank Oxford University Press for permission to reprint.

1. Regarding this shift from autobiography to fiction in the 1850s, see Andrews, "Novelization" (23–34), and Yarborough (111–15). The term "novelized autobiography" is from Andrews. For a fuller discussion of many of the points developed in this essay, see chapter 6 of my book, *Doers of the Word.*

2. For a discussion of the formation of individual and collective black identity, see hooks.

3. For book-length studies of these points, see Foster and Andrews, *To Tell a Free Story.* Even doxological slave narratives contained, of course, seeds of "freedom" and techniques of resistance; for example, the many silences—refusals to speak—in Douglass's 1845 *Narrative.*

4. The phrase "local place" is from Said's "Yeats and Decolonization" but applies as well to African Americans under conditions of internal colonization.

5. My discussion of these texts is not meant to be exhaustive. For more extensive analyses see especially Andrews, *To Tell* and "Novelization"; Gates's introduction to Wilson (xi–lv); Yellin's introduction to Jacobs (xiii–xxxiii); Carby (40–61); V. Smith (28–43); Baker (50–56); and Wald (157–71).

6. See also Gates's suggestion that the narrative shifts in *Our Nig* "point to the complexities and tensions of basing fictional events upon the lived experiences of the author" (xxxvii).

7. I adapt the phrase from Lejeune's discussion of collaboration in the autobiographical writings of "those who do not write" (189). The use of the pseudonym may well constitute an example of such collaboration.

8. See especially Davidson's discussion of the seduction and picaresque novels as the earliest American novelistic genres (chs. 5–7).

9. For extremely insightful discussions of the tragic mulatta figure, see Sánchez-Eppler, who places the tragic mulatta plot within the context of nineteenth-century sentimental fiction, and Spillers, who analyzes the mulatto as "a strategy for naming and celebrating the phallus" (168) in twentieth-century fiction.

10. See White for a detailed reconstruction of Wilson's life; see Gardner for a discussion of the actual readership of *Our Nig.*

11. Davidson notes that the picaresque was an early American novelistic genre celebrating difference and acknowledging the aspirations of the economically underdeveloped; it is linked to the rise of commodity and merchant capitalism, and reflects its economic and social instability. Standing as an emblem of this society in flux, the picaro is an isolated individual, both insider and outsider, contemptuous of the dominant culture's devotion to capitalism yet eager

to share its spoils. His story unfolds in a narrative that remains untotalized, filled with ambiguities and irreconcilable contradictions, often ending on a note of irresolution (151–74).

12. Such episodes in *Blake* are direct responses to Stowe's novels and reflect Delany's ambivalence about them. Blake's huts stand in sharp contrast to the more feminized cabins of *Uncle Tom's Cabin*, of which Delany was openly critical. The Maroon chapters are reminscient of *Dred*, a novel that Delany purportedly admired; yet his depiction of the Maroon survivors is highly satirical.

13. See Nash for an extensive discussion of black community activism in antebellum Philadelphia.

Works Cited

Andrews, William L. "The Novelization of Voice in Early African American Narrative." *PMLA* 105 (1990): 23–34.

Andrews, William L. *To Tell a Free Story: The First Century of Afro-American Autobiography, 1760–1865.* Urbana: U of Illinois P, 1986.

"Apology." *Anglo-African Magazine* Jan. 1859: 1–4.

Baker, Houston A., Jr. *Blues, Ideology, and Afro-American Literature: A Vernacular Theory.* Chicago: U of Chicago P, 1984.

Bakhtin, M. M. *The Dialogic Imagination: Four Essays.* Ed. Michael Holquist. Trans. Caryl Emerson and Michael Holquist. University of Texas Press Slavic Series 1. Austin: U of Texas P, 1981.

Bhabha, Homi K. "Signs Taken for Wonders: Questions of Ambivalence and Authority under a Tree Outside Delhi, May 1817." *Critical Inquiry* 12 (1985): 144–65.

Brown, William Wells. *Clotel or, the President's Daughter: A Narrative of Slave Life in the United States.* Ed. William Edward Farrison. New York: Carol, 1969.

Carby, Hazel V. *Reconstructing Womanhood: The Emergence of the Afro-American Woman Novelist.* New York: Oxford UP, 1987.

Carnes, Mark C. *Secret Ritual and Manhood in Victorian America.* New Haven: Yale UP, 1989.

Conrad, Alfred H., and John R. Meyer. *The Economics of Slavery, and Other Studies in Econometric History.* Chicago: Aldine, 1964.

Davidson, Cathy N. *Revolution and the Word: The Rise of the Novel in America.* New York: Oxford UP, 1986.

Delany, Martin R. *Blake; or, the Huts of America: A Novel.* Ed. Floyd J. Miller. Boston: Beacon, 1970.

Douglass, Frederick. *Narrative of the Life of Frederick Douglass, An American Slave.* 1845. Garden City, NY: Anchor/Doubleday, 1973.

Foster, Frances Smith. *Witnessing Slavery: The Development of Antebellum Slave Narratives.* Contributions in Afro-American and African Studies 46. Westport, CT: Greenwood, 1979.

Gardner, Eric. " 'This Attempt of Their Sister': Harriet Wilson's *Our Nig* from Printer to Readers." *New England Quarterly* 66 (1993): 226–46.

Genovese, Eugene D. *The Political Economy of Slavery: Studies in the Economy and Society of the Slave South.* 2nd ed. Middletown, CT: Wesleyan UP, 1989.

Graff, Gerald. "Literature as Assertions." *American Criticism in the Poststructuralist Age.* Ed. Ira Konigsberg. U of Michigan P, 1981. 135–61.

hooks, bell. *Yearning: Race, Gender, and Cultural Politics.* Boston: South End, 1990.

Hopkins, Pauline. "Prospectus." *Colored American Magazine* Sept. 1900: n.p.

Jacobs, Harriet A. *Incidents in the Life of a Slave Girl: Written by Herself.* Ed. and introd. Jean Fagan Yellin. Cambridge: Harvard UP, 1987.

Lejeune, Philippe. *On Autobiography.* Ed. Paul John Eakin. Trans. Katherine M. Leary. Theory and History of Literature 52. Minneapolis: U of Minnesota P, 1989.

Levine, Lawrence W. *Black Culture and Black Consciousness: Afro-American Folk Thought from Slavery to Freedom.* New York: Oxford UP, 1977.

Levine, Robert S. *Martin Delany, Frederick Douglass, and the Politics of Representative Identity.* Chapel Hill: U of North Carolina P, 1997.

Marable, Manning. *How Capitalism Underdeveloped Black America: Problems in Race, Political Economy and Society.* Boston: South End, 1983.

Mott, Frank L. *Golden Multitudes: The Story of Best Sellers in the United States.* New York: Macmillan, 1947.

Nash, Gary B. *Forging Freedom: The Formation of Philadelphia's Black Community. 1720–1840.* Cambridge: Harvard UP, 1988.

Peterson, Carla L. *Doers of the Word: African-American Women Speakers and Writers in the North (1830–1880).* New Brunswick: Rutgers UP, 1998.

Said, Edward W. "Yeats and Decolonization." *Remaking History.* Ed. Barbara Kruger and Phil Mariani. Discussions in Contemporary Culture 4. Seattle: Bay, 1989. 3–29.

Sánchez-Eppler, Karen. "Bodily Bonds: The Intersecting Rhetorics of Feminism and Abolitionism." *American Reconstructed, 1840–1940.* Spec. issue of *Representations* 24 (1988): 28–59.

Smith, Paul. *Discerning of Subject.* Theory and History of Literature 55. Minneapolis: U of Minnesota P, 1987.

Smith, Valerie. *Self-Discovery and Authority in Afro-American Narrative.* Cambridge: Harvard UP, 1987.

Spillers, Hortense J. "Notes on an Alternative Model—Neither/Nor." *The Difference Within: Feminism and Critical Theory.* Ed. Elizabeth Meese and Alice Parker. Critical Theory 8. Philadelphia: Benjamins, 1989. 165–87.

Sundquist, Eric J. *To Wake the Nations: Race in the Making of American Literature.* Cambridge: Harvard UP, 1993.

Takaki, Ronald T. *Iron Cages: Race and Culture in Nineteenth-Century America.* 1979. New York: Oxford UP, 1990.

Wald, Priscilla. *Constituting Americans: Cultural Anxiety and Narrative Form.* Durham: Duke UP, 1995.

Webb, Frank J. *The Garies and Their Friends.* New York: Arno, 1969.

White, Barbara A. " 'Our Nig' and the She-Devil: New Information about Harriet Wilson and the 'Bellmont' Family." *American Literature* 65 (March 1993): 19–52.

Wilson, Harriet E. *Our Nig.* Ed. Henry Louis Gates, Jr. New York: Random, 1983.

Yarborough, Richard. "The First-Person in Afro-American Fiction." *Afro-American Literary Study in the 1990s.* Ed. Houston A. Baker, Jr., and Patricia Redmond. Chicago: U of Chicago P, 1989. 105–21.

POSTCOLONIAL ANXIETY IN CLASSIC U.S. LITERATURE

Lawrence Buell

A s the first of Europe's colonies to win independence, the United States of America has a history that its intellectuals have frequently offered as a prototype for other new nations, yet that they too might find instructive to reexamine in light of later cases. In the field of U.S. literary history, however, such comparisons are still uncommon, and they are confined largely to discussions of margin-center dynamics arising from "neocolonial" domination of racial/ethnic others by Euroamericans, especially its traditional albeit now-threatened white Anglo-Protestant hegemony.[1] By no coincidence is this essay the one discussion in the present collection that approaches "mainstream" writing of the early national phases of U.S. literary discourse as a postcolonial formation.

Indeed, my approach may seem not merely "anomalous" but perverse, judging from some reactions to the original 1992 version.[2] Postcolonial theory has after all based itself in the first instance on the model of reaction by non-European writers to the discourses of European domination. Recently there seems to have been more pluralistic receptivity to alternative models and paradigms,[3] and the argument has been pressed, by Canadian and Australian scholars particularly, for a kind of postcolonial dynamic operating in the vexed relation of settler or white creole cultures ("second world" cultures, as they are sometimes called) to the cultures of their respective imperia, although such arguments still often have an air of self-conscious pleading, for disciplinary if not for substantively historical reasons.[4] And certainly the case of Euroamerica would seem to require the most such, given the present world influence of the U.S. and given that today the preferred narrative of the unfolding dominant ideology of U.S. literary/cultural history is, accordingly, the story of the consolidation of American might from early nineteenth century expansionism to twentieth-century neo-imperialism.[5] To the extent that that revisionist narrative in fact makes sense of history—as to a considerable extent I agree it does, although it is hardly seamless, and hardly the only narrative worth telling—then *prima facie* it may seem a problematic if not positively culpable evasion of the fact of the present imperium to search for marks of a postcolonial past, as if U.S. cultural history should share very much in common with that of Ireland, much less Pakistan or Zimbabwe. Yet without in any sense wanting to argue that all cases are identical, I believe that this sort of reenvisionment can highlight dimensions of U.S. literary and cultural history of much more than merely antiquarian significance.

Promiscuous conflation of different national archives is not the only lumping problem one potentially incurs when broaching the issue of postcoloniality in this or any context. On the one hand, postcolonality talk is also "haunted by the very figure of linear 'development' that it sets out to dismantle" (McClintock 79), tending to carrying the misleading "implication that colonialism is now a matter of the past" (Shohat 105). On the other hand, oppositely, it implies a reduction of the cultures in question to an aftereffect of or response to Eurocentrism.[6] Given these and other possible confusions, I should emphasize that my specific domain of interest is specifically the issue of U.S. settler culture writers' anxiety about literary/cultural liberation from dominance by Eurocentric formations.

1

This experiment began for me with two semi-coincidental perceptions in the mid-1980s: an increasing sense that all branches of "English" literary history must some day radically be rewritten in light of the last half century of global Anglophone literature and postcolonial theory, and an increasing sense of the limitations of the national focus of traditional literary-Americanist thinking, as during the first half-century of its attempted quest for self-legitimation within and against English studies it had come, or so it seemed to me, to overcompensate egregiously in the direction of focusing on the internal teleology of U.S. literary history. In my own special field of antebellum studies, the foundational work, F. O. Matthiessen's *American Renaissance*, was ironically also the last major precontemporary critical *magnum opus* to be informed by a profound appreciation of transatlantic intertextuality: how the five central figures (Emerson, Thoreau, Hawthorne, Melville, Whitman) saturated themselves in the rhetorics of Shakespeare, Milton, metaphysical poetry and prose, neoclassicism, and Romanticism. For almost a half-century thereafter, study of U.S. literary emergence tended to follow the centripetal rather than the centrifugal thrust of Matthiessen's thinking, congealing around such putative nodes of cultural distinctiveness as Puritan inheritance, Adamic innocence, and frontier vigor; around generic patterns like the jeremiad or the captivity or the romance considered as national artifacts; and around lineal succession stories like From Edwards to Emerson, Emerson to Whitman, Hawthorne to James and so forth. Through these devices the unity, the density, and the weight of the field was established.

Perhaps the *ne plus ultra* of this kind of move, all the more telling because not fomented by a card-carrying Americanist and therefore all the more notable as a barometer of how pervasive assumptions of "American difference" had become, was

Harold Bloom's once-influential theory of American poetic succession, an extreme manifestation of the "antinomian" theory of American poesis first codified by Roy Harvey Pearce, though its provenance goes back more than a century to what I am calling the postcolonial period itself.[7] Although Bloom is a reader of impressively cosmopolitan reach, into his Americanist symposium no foreign power is allowed to enter once Emerson begins it; British and U.S. literary histories are kept rigorously distinct, notwithstanding Bloom's presumed awareness that until well into the twentieth century the "strong" American poets read Anglo-European masters more attentively than they read each other. But I do not mean to pick on Bloom especially, when much of the work of most of my own scholarly generation, which perpetrated the revisionary antebellum studies of the 1980s ("the American-Renaissance Renaissance," Michael Colacurcio wittily calls it) generally shows the same cisatlantic foreshortening.[8] Even those during the last quarter century who have developed the narrative of American imperialist consciousness have often sustained a *de facto* exceptionalism of focus in respect to their concentration on the particularity and historical portentiousness of the American national imaginary. The pedagogy and criticism if not the private conviction of literary Americanists still too often fail to break from "the dogmatic focus on discrete *national* dynamics," as Paul Gilroy characterizes it in another context, "which has characterized so much modern Euroamerican cultural thought" (Gilroy 6)—systemically if not intentionally reinforcing the supposition, as William Spengemann writes with pardonable hyperbole, that "an appreciation of American writing depends upon our keeping it separate from the rest of the world" (Spengemann 141).

This kind of conditioning starts with joblist taxonomy and syllabus selectivity in U.S. literature courses, such that one becomes socialized into forgetting that except for Thoreau's debt to Emerson no American Renaissance writer can confidently be said to have formed his or her style chiefly from native influences, nor with the exception of Melville's encomium on Hawthorne is there a clear case on record of one writer of the period now thought major insisting that another ranks with the great world authors. We form the habit of picturing Hawthorne as leading to Melville rather than to, say, George Eliot, even though nothing in the Melville canon follows a Hawthornian pretext more faithfully than *Adam Bede* follows *The Scarlet Letter*.

Today we are in principle better able to combat such parochialisms than a quarter century ago. Feminist and ethnic revisionist critiques of the American canon as it crystallized between the 1920s and the 1960s have suffused a pervasive reflexivity about all our instruments of classification, including literary genealogies, and in African American, Asian American, and Latino/a studies has led to much more fertile reconception of figures and movements in diasporic and/or cross-border terms. Yet scholars continue to think much more about how Whitman's prosodic experimentalism might have been encouraged by Emerson or Poe than by Keats or Tennyson; we know much more about how American writers of domestic fiction related to each other (and how their works construct or critique national ideology) than we do about how they related to Dickens or other popular British sentimentalists of either sex; and even when we place Harriet Jacobs or Frederick Douglass in "context," *pace* Gilroy and other Atlantic world theorists, it is more often a U.S. context than an international one. Obviously there are a number of ways to resist this habituated centripetalism, perhaps the most prevalent of which among Americanists at this particular historical moment are the reimagination of immigration as diaspora; studies of the international circulation of cultural forms like trickster tales, *corridos*, jazz, and carnival; and reconception of "America" hemispherically.[9] My own project is rather to strike at the historical root of U.S. distinctiveness-preoccupations by emphasizing what I take to be the typical aspects of its early canonical expressions to define themselves over against the prior cultural hegemony of the former ruling power, this moment of assertion being also the pivotal moment for subsequent mid-twentieth-century Americanist accounts of U.S. literary/cultural distinctiveness *and* subsequent "new Americanist" interrogations of the ideological character of those critiques. From my standpoint, *both* the traditional and revisionist Americanist accounts tend to understate the postcolonial anxiety of the "classic" writers of United States literary history, and this ironically on account of the fact that each account is in its own way legatee of the more rarefied anxiety of the modern academic Americanist quest for self-legitimation: the traditional account self-consciously so by reason of having to argue the case for cultural distinctiveness and literary value, the revisionist account by its orthogenetic vision of the emerging nation-state and its attendant cultural forms as an eventual world power. Through the particular lens I use here, the icons of the traditional account may look more interestingly and persuasively vulnerable for being less exceptional, and the "dominant" cultural forms they express more persuasively unstable and transculturally imbricated.

I certainly do not mean to *deny* all distinctiveness to antebellum U.S. literary culture, neither to claim that the archive of American Anglophone writing can be conflated with the British, nor that U.S. cultural nationalism equals Australian or Nigerian. My aim is simply to take more fully into account than is customarily done the degree to which the practices and innovations of the iconic figures of U.S. literary history arose out of "a culture in which the ruled were constantly tempted to fight their rulers within the psychological limits set by the latter," to quote Ashis Nandy's characterization of the intellectual climate of colonial India (3). Although the thirteen American colonies never experienced anything like the political and military domination India did, the extent of *cultural* colonization, from epistemology to aesthetics to dietetics, was much more comprehensive—partly because of the selfsame comparative benignity of the imperial regime's treatment of its American cousins. Indeed, it may be a rule of thumb for "second world" postcolonialism that it finds cultural colonization harder to resist: that such cases are particularly likely to manifest the "necessary *entanglement* of anti-colonial resistances within the colonialist machineries they seek to displace" (Slemon 39).[10]

2

For students of antebellum writing, the issue of American writers' cultural dependence upon vs. emancipation from Europe has come, at least since the 1960s,[11] to look like a side issue and, after about 1830, as a virtual nonissue. True, the tradition of Puritan legacy studies that flourished from the 1940s through the 1980s has fallen into decline as the emphasis of scholarship has shifted somewhat away from tracing the saga of (post)-Protestant culture to the interplay between that formation and its cultural and racial others; but this shift has if anything reinforced the impression, increasingly stressed by this tradition as Sacvan Bercovitch's ritual-of-consensus paradigm came to displace Perry Miller's declensionist paradigm as the preferred model for Puritan legacy studies,[12] of an incipient cultural normativity achieving enough dominance by the early nineteenth century to make Anglo-America's continuing umbilical tie to European culture seem uninterestingly epiphenomenal. This mentality reinforces the wishful view that any such cultural dependency was little more than a virus infecting the juvenilia of the antebellum canonical writers. I daresay that those of us who still refer our students to British reviewer Sydney Smith's dictum "In the four quarters of the globe, who reads an American book?" use it as a straw man rather than take it seriously as an ever-present anxiety and constituent shaping force in antebellum writing.

If so, consider Henry T. Tuckerman's *America and Her Commentators* (1864), still a useful barometer of the cultural self-consciousness of the American mid-Victorians. Tuckerman insists that Smith's dictum is "irrelevant and impertinent to-day," that in all major genres of writing have emerged "universally recognized and standard exemplars, of American origin, [that] now illustrate the genius and culture of the nation." But his project refutes him, preoccupied as it is with expounding upon how America has been anatomized as literary object rather than reborn as literary force. Tuckerman's argument that Americans are no longer mere culture consumers is quixotic and halfhearted. "The statistics of the book trade and the facts of individual culture," he argues, "prove that the master minds of British literature more directly and universally train and nurture the American than the English mind." This glosses over the statistics themselves (as late as 1876, the ratio of American book imports to exports stood at 10 to 1) and the consumer mentality that Tuckerman gamely tries to make the best of: that, owing to diffusion of education and the "distance that lends enchantment," "Shakespeare and Milton, Bacon and Wordsworth, Byron and Scott have been and are more generally known, appreciated, and loved, and have entered more deeply into the average intellectual life, on this than on the other side of the Atlantic" (Tuckerman 285–88). In short, U.S. cultural autonomy is proven by the fact that more copies of the English classics are bought and avidly read in the U.S. than in Britain.

Tuckerman does not draw a connection between how British classics "enchant" American readers and his repeated efforts to resist the influence of foreign travelers' representations of life in the United States. Yet his book, by its mere existence, dramatizes that the authority of European letters included an extensive discourse of America that Yankee writers had to reckon with. Although scholars have studied this body of travelers' reports for the better part of a century, and some of its distinguished examples are well known (notably Alexis de Tocqueville's *Democracy in America*), the significance of this prolific subgenre emerges more fully in light of recent colonial discourse studies, particularly of travel narrative.[13] During what came to be called the American literary "renaissance," the United States remained for many foreign commentators (especially the British), albeit diminishingly, a cultural outback—with the predictable connotations of exoticism, barbarism, and unstructuredness. This notwithstanding that no racial barrier separated most travelers from the dominant American racial group, and notwithstanding that European travelers were very well aware that *these* natives had the will and the technology to answer them back publicly in a European language. Indeed, American sensitiveness to foreign opinion was so keen that travelers often declared that it limited the frankness with which they could express themselves. At all events, it is clear that many nineteenth-century Euroamericans, like one politician who complained to geologist Charles Lyell, sincerely felt themselves relegated to banana republic status: "You class us with the South American republics; your embassadors [sic] to us come from Brazil and Mexico to Washington, and consider it a step in their advancement to go from the United States to . . . some second-rate German court" (1: 226).

For this there was much evidence. In particular, foreign visitors denied the U.S. civilizational refinement, the want of which was for Frances Trollope in *Domestic Manners of the Americans* the greatest national defect. Nineteenth-century travelers on the notorious American practice of tobacco chewing and spitting sound like V. S. Naipaul on Indian shitting.[14] European travelers acknowledged Yankee skill at practical calculation (deprecating it as part of the apparatus of American materialism), but tended to depict Americans as more irrational than rational, as an unphilosophical culture whatever its legislative genius: slapdash nation builders. They systematically denied that the nation had a high culture worthy of the name. ("If the national mind of America be judged of by its legislation," wrote Harriet Martineau, "it is of a very high order. . . . If the American nation be judged by its literature, it may be pronounced to have no mind at all") (Martineau 2: 200–201). They even denied the Yankees language, in the spirit of Rudyard Kipling's remark that "the American has no language," only "dialect, slang, provincialism, accent, and so forth" (Kipling 24).

It was common for foreign travelers to frame their accounts as narratives of disillusionment, to stress that they started with hopeful, even utopian, expectations of finding a model nation-in-the-making only to discover a backwater. Dickens, for example, starts on an upbeat note with a stimulating visit to Boston, but he gradually sours amid New York slums, Washington rowdiness, and an arduous trip to the interior that reaches a Conradian nadir during a steamboat voyage down the Ohio River. Dickens luridly evokes the dreary solitude ("For miles, and miles, and miles . . . unbroken by any human footstep"), the sudden ugly rent in the forest for a primitive cabin and straggling field "full of great unsightly stumps," and the malevolent tangle of fallen trees in the current ("their bleached arms start out . . . and seem to try to grasp the boat") (*American Notes* 159–60). But this is merely the "documentary" version, the equivalent of Conrad's Congo diaries. For purposes of Martin Chuzzlewit's ill-fated venture to "Eden," the *Heart of Darkness* equivalent, Dickens heightens the phantasmagoria: "On they toiled through great solitudes, where the trees upon the banks grew thick and close; and floated in the stream; and held up shrivelled arms from out the river's depths; and slid down from the margin of the land, half growing, half decaying, in the miry water. On through the weary day and melancholy night: beneath the burning sun, and in the mist and vapour of the evening: on until return appeared impossible, and restoration to their home a miserable dream" (*Martin Chuzzlewitt* 375).

Both Dickens and Tocqueville, each in his way, reckoned the United States a country of the future; but Tocqueville's estimate (that it represented the vanguard of the inevitable democratization of modern society afoot, willy-nilly, in Europe also) was less typical than Dickens' estimate of the U.S. as a crudely vigorous young country still a long way from maturity. Not surprisingly, Tuckerman lauded Tocqueville and deplored Dickens' "superficial and sneering" manner (130–31, 221). Yet Tocqueville himself exhibits perhaps the single most condescending colonializing gesture: overbearing confidence in classifying the traits of American character. "Americans of all ages, all conditions, and dispositions constantly form associations"; "the Americans are much more addicted to the use of general ideas than the English and entertain a much greater relish for them"; "the love of wealth is . . . to be traced, as either a principal or an accessory motive, at the bottom of all that the Americans do" (2: 114, 15, 240). Tocqueville's many shrewd hits should not blind us to the arrogance of this rhetoric of the magisterial generalization. One wonders, as when reading Foucault, whether Tocqueville felt a need to make magisterialism compensate for his theory of individual powerlessness to influence epistemic structure and drift. The imperial generalization, in any case, is a time-honored device for formulating natives, as Albert Memmi and others have pointed out.[15] Predictably, nothing discomfited British readers of American travel narrative more than when the Yankees turned the same device against them, as Emerson did in *English Traits*, acknowledging the *present* cultural and infrastructural inferiority of the United States but bracketing England as utilitarian, materialistic, intellectually stolid rather than progressive.

3

European travelers' reports rarely put (white) Americans in the same category as Africans or Asians: their native interlocutors were, after all, overwhelmingly of European stock, as well as energetic entrepreneurs of burgeoning economic and military potency, impressive for their efforts at general education if not for their high culture. But as a civilization, the United States of America was still comparatively barbarous, the frontier hinterland its presenting reality and its gentry (as Francis Grund stressed in *Aristocracy in America*) pathetic cardbord Europhiles. A thriving oral culture existed, but with scattered exceptions literary culture did not, and the most visible approximation to a literary class were American journalists, a disreputable lot.

The species of "domination" that this discourse expressed and reinforced during the antebellum period was certainly not of the same order as, say, modern manipulation of developing nations' regimes and economies by western oil companies, or the U.S. invasions of Mexico in the nineteenth-century and Cuba, Grenada, and Panama (to name but three examples) in the twentieth. That epoch of raw coercive imposition had clearly ended, albeit not long before, with the War of 1812; and even at its height imperial dominance of British America had never been tyrannous as such regimes go, notwithstanding the overheated rhetoric of the Declaration of Independence. In the literary-cultural sphere, however, the specter of neocolonialism loomed much larger both as a market reality for the publishing industry and at the level of internalized tastes and templates. Although an antebellum American merchant or military officer would have been nettled by the assumption of British cultural superiority without feeling greatly threatened by it, an aspiring writer—especially if this person were a moderately well-educated white male[16]—might have felt himself dismissed as little better than a Caliban.

With this as backdrop, we can better understand the terms under which Walt Whitman sought to give voice to American poetry in *Leaves of Grass*. The 1855 Preface starts with the super-confident image of America as the calm witness to the corpse of European tradition being "slowly borne from the eating and sleeping rooms of the house" (709). Because Whitman craftily adopts a pose of impassiveness, and because we are taught to classify this document firmly within the success story of U.S. literary independence, it takes an effort of will to realize that what Whitman has done is to make grotesque a trope from the Eurocentric repertoire, the *translatio studii*—the transfer of art and learning from Old World to New: a trope that had been invoked to underwrite colonization efforts and subsequently the hegemony of the late colonial gentry. This is a figure Whitman uses not just once but repeatedly, for example, in the 1871 "Song of the Exposition," which bumptiously summons the Muse to "migrate from Greece and Ionia," to "Placard 'Removed' and 'To Let' on the rocks of your snowy Parnassus," and envisions her wafting her way amid the "thud of machinery and shrill steam-whistle undismay'd," "Bluff'd not . . . by drain-pipe, gasometers, artificial fertilizers, / Smiling and pleas'd with palpable intent to stay,/ . . . install'd amid the kitchen ware!" (Whitman 709, 196, 198). The calculated grotesquerie that subverts traditional decorums while nominally observing them has a certain family resemblance, counter-intuitive though it might seem, to modern inversions of the Prospero-Caliban trope, as in George Lamming's autobiographical essays, *The Pleasures of Exile* and Aimé Cesaire's dramatic redaction *A Tempest*. For what Whitman has done in effect is to "Calibanize" *translatio studii*: to render it hairy and gross (reversing the stereotype of the colony as the place without culture) and thereby to reveal an ongoing struggle to extricate autochthonous forms of thought from old world categories, meaning not just rhetorical figures but also social figurations like the Americans-as-barbarians stereotype.

Even those who know about the history of *translatio studii* tend not to think this far, supposing (prematurely) that the trope must have become obsolete by the mid-nineteenth century and thinking (rightly) of Caliban as a figure who was elevated to hero status especially by third world and above all by Latin American intellectuals. Whitman's move was indeed certainly not identical to Césaire's: the specific linkage of "Caliban" to "Carib" and to indigenous oppressed peoples generally, to the end of designating "a copulative potential by way of the Atlantic system of slavery" (Spillers 6), is a modern transculturation of the image dating from the 1920s and 1930s. But Whitman anticipated it in effecting one of the first—if not the first—mid-19th century transculturation of "Caliban" in its then-standard European connotation, as a symbol of intellectual and cultural barbarity (as in Schopenhauer's dismissal of Hegel as an "intellectual Caliban") (1: xxi). When a British reviewer dismissed Whitman as "Caliban flinging down his logs, and setting himself to write a poem" (Murphy 60), the poet proceeded to select this among other excerpts to use as promotional material for the 1856 edition of *Leaves of Grass*. Ironically, when Latin American cultural critics themselves began deploying *Tempest* imagery fifty years later, they did so not only against Calibanism but specifically against blundering Yankee culture and might.[17]

Leaves of Grass grotesquifies *translatio studii* on a vaster scale in its bending and breaking of epic tradition.[18] This rewriting process reflects a resistance-deference syndrome that artists and scholars alike have found it hard to talk about coherently. Whitman by turns sought to eradicate old-world myth and to reinstate it ("Old Brahm I, and I Saturnius am") (443). The critic for whom the narrative of U.S. national differentiation is primary will be tempted to identify the former posture as more "authentic" or "progressive" than the latter, when in fact it was the creative irritant of their interaction that produced the unique result, an interaction in which the Eurocentric epic model figures as part of the empowerment as well as an object of attack.

James Fenimore Cooper's Leatherstocking is a related case. No vernacular hero has been more influential in U.S. literary history, with the possible exception of Huckleberry Finn, for whom Natty Bumppo helped prepare the way. Yet Bumppo was not, strictly speaking, an indigenous figure, though he can be traced to historical frontiersman prototypes, so much as a rewriting of the trope of the genteel protagonist cum vernacular sidekick in Scott's Waverley novels (e.g. Henry Morton and Cuddie Headrigg in *Old Mortality*), a configuration that indeed dates back to the inception of the "modern" novel in *Don Quixote*. Cooper's adaptation of this pattern was of landmark significance, providing U.S. literature's first compelling model of the vernacular hero; and this in turn helps accounts for Cooper's absorption as model and fellow-romancer in nineteenth and early twentieth-century Latin America (Sommer 140). Yet this breakthrough did not come easily to Cooper. He seems to have resolved to upend the Scottian hierarchy only during the process of composing *The Pioneers*, which begins squarely focused on the Oliver Edwards-Judge Temple melodrama and only gradually discovers that Natty is a more compelling character than either. Even at that, Cooper continues to require a gentlemanly Waverley figure and to labor over the proper mimetic level at which to peg Natty, whose speech, as Richard Bridgman remarks, "wobbles from one realm of usage to another," from racy slang to grand-manner cliché (Bridgman 67). As if to hold his incipient populism in check, Cooper sees to it that Natty retains his vassal status through the first four Leatherstocking tales; only after Cooper has reinvented him at his most decorous, in *The Deerslayer*, does he cease playing the factotum.

Natty's long subalternity, the *papier-maché* quality of his genteel charges like Oliver and Duncas Uncas Middleton, and the savagist machinery that increasingly motors his Mohican companion Chingachgook all can be thought of pejoratively as marks of "cultural colonization." But adaptation rather than extrication is after all precisely what postcolonial theory would lead one to expect.

A third exhibit to set beside Whitman and Cooper is Emerson's "The American Scholar," "our intellectual declaration of independence," as twentieth-century Americanists (following Emerson's friend and biographer Oliver Wendell Holmes) still like to call it. Its exordium contains Emerson's most famous literary nationalist aperçu: "Our day of dependence, our long apprenticeship to the learning of other lands, draws to a close." But when we examine the two specific signs of this, deferred until the end,

we find them presented as European-instigated trends only now on the verge of coming to fruition in the United States: the valorization of the humble and the familiar
("This idea has inspired the genius of Goldsmith, Burns, Cowper, and, in a newer
time, of Goethe, Wordsworth, and Carlyle") and the renewed respect accorded to the
individual person—which Emerson makes a point of emphasizing has not yet trickled
over to the U.S. (Emerson 1971, 52, 68–69). Unlike Tocqueville, he does not claim
the United States is in the vanguard of this international movement, though nothing
would have been easier given the nature of the occasion than for him to do so. It is as
if he has chosen to create national history in the image of his own belated intellectual
emergence, for which Coleridge much more than any American thinker provided the
scaffolding. Perhaps this explains why the literary nationalist theme, as Emerson han-
dles it, is so muted. He is at pains to unfold the scholar's triad of resources—nature,
books, and action—which in principle can be seen as a distinctly "new-world" recipe
(his emphasis being to devalue classical education, indeed formal study in general, and
to aggrandize direct noncosmopolitan experience and pragmatic application), yet he
does not explicitly characterize this regimen in cultural nationalist terms. Personal
self-reliance clearly interested Emerson more than national self-sufficiency.

Altogether, "The American Scholar" and Whitman's 1855 Preface might be taken
as the two poles between which the literary nationalism of elite antebellum culture
tends to oscillate: a vision of cultural emergence catalyzed by auspicious international
tendencies that the U.S. might be expected to develop further, vs. a vision of a scandal-
ously different American voice whose international precedents are more repressed,
but hardly deleted. In either case, "Europe" continues to exercise a weighty, conflict-
producing influence.

4

Closely related to the question of the models underlying literary practice is the
question of the audience to which the writing is directed. This has been a topic of
debate concerning the newer English literatures, which appear, in some interpretations, to represent national culture with international audiences in mind. For an initial
sense of what is at stake, consider this passage toward the start of Chinua Achebe's
Things Fall Apart, the first nonwestern text accepted into the Anglophone canon.
"Okoye said the next half a dozen sentences in proverbs. Among the Ibo the art of
conversation is regarded very highly, and proverbs are the palm-oil with which words
are eaten" (Achebe 10). Such expository rhetoric, common in African Anglophone
writing, raises such questions as: For whom is this passage written? Do Ibos need to
hear it? Do even Yoruba and Hausa readers need to hear it? Is Achebe mainly addressing a Euro-American audience, then? (He has denied this, but also emphasized that
"my audience is not limited to Nigeria. Anybody who is interested in the ideas I am
expounding is my audience.")[19] The rhetoric of this passage, anyhow, carefully negotiates the insider-outsider dualism by explicating ethnic custom while casting the explanation in Ibo form, as a proverb.

Americanists do not usually read antebellum texts as if the implied reader were other than cisatlantic; yet on reflection we know that is nonsense: Yankee writers keenly desired to be read abroad. The first words of Herman Melville's first book (the preface to *Typee*, written for publication in Murray's Colonial and Home Library series) were got up with British readership in mind, and the narrative is strategically sprinkled with familiarizing English place references (Cheltenham, Stonehenge, Westminster Abbey, etc.) (96, 154, 161). We know from Melville's letters and criticism that he was acutely aware of the problem of negotiating between ideologically disparate readerships, but no one has considered whether his doctrine (in "Hawthorne and His Mosses") that the great writer communicates to his ideal reader through double meanings which superficial readers are intended to miss might have been brought into focus partly by his position as a postcolonial writer, enforced at the start of his career by differential marketplace exigencies to cast his narrative one way for a British publisher who wanted facticity and another way for an American publisher anxious about Melville's anti-missionary satire (cf. Buell, "Melville," 219–21).

The textual marks of anticipating transcontinental readership are admittedly harder to identify than the absorption of foreign literary influences. Open-and-shut cases like the diplomatically vacillating essay on European travelers' accounts of the U.S. in Irving's *The Sketch Book* are rare. Direct evidence is usually limited to textual variants for which the responsibility is unclear (Did the author devise? advise? consent freely? grudgingly agree?) or to *ex cathedra* statements like Cooper's to a British publisher that *The Prairie* "contains nothing to offend an English reader," which do not in themselves prove that the work would have been written differently had the author designed it for a domestic readership alone (Cooper 1: 166). What we can assert positively is this. First, that some of the most provincially embedded texts of the period bear at least passing direct witness to anticipating foreign readers, like Thoreau's *Walden*, which starts by addressing fellow townspeople but ends by musing about whether "John [Bull] or Jonathan [the stereotypical Yankee] will realize all this" (Thoreau 333). And second, that the hypothesis of Yankees imagining foreign as well as native opinion, whatever their conscious expectation of literal readership, helps make sense of some otherwise puzzling effects. One such is Whitman's abrupt reconception of his persona between 1855 and 1856 as speaking not simply within and to North America but to the rest of the world, as in "Salut au Monde!" Another is the oddly extended sequence in *Moby-Dick* reporting the gam between the *Pequod* and the *Samuel Enderby*, and its aftermath (chs. 100–101).

James Snead remarks that Achebe's novels "provide an unexpectedly tricky reading experience for their western audience, using wild narrative stratagems to undermine national and racial illusions," such as "the almost casual manner in which they present African norms": with glossary apparatus incomplete, interjection of reminders of the Western reader's outsidership in the course of a cozily familiar-seeming, European-style realist narrative (Snead 241). For example, the guidebook dimension of the passage quoted above creates a deceptive degree of transparency for the western reader, inasmuch as its "we have a saying" formula is a common introductory formula in Ibo proverbial statement not remarked upon as such. The passage, then, maintains a certain code-switching covertness despite, indeed because of, its appearance of forthrightness. Melville uses narrative geniality in a somewhat analogous way.

The gam with the *Samuel Enderby* reworks a cross-cultural diagnosis often made by British travelers: that Yankees were grim workaholic zealots with no time for small talk. The chapter is clearly framed with national stereotypes in mind. It sketches the encounter between Ahab and Captain Boomer, or rather the garrulous byplay between Boomer and the ship's surgeon, so as to make the Englishmen seem like patronizing boobies, but then to seem to erase this prejudicialism through Ahab's hyper-impatient truculent overreaction, which makes fatuous English male joviality seem healthy by comparison. In the ensuing chapter, however, Ishmael gives a weird turn to the spirit of comic banter in paying mock-heroic homage to the firm of Enderby, which dispatched the first ships to hunt the sperm whale in the Pacific. In what looks like a digression but is actually a droll reflection on how Yankee whalers gained the competitive edge, Ishmael proceeds to report a later, more convivial gam with the *Samuel Enderby*, when he partook in a drunken feast "at midnight somewhere off the Patagonian coast" (444). Although Ishmael's restitution of good fellowship with his English counterparts atones *ex post facto* for Ahab's bad manners, in appearing to adapt obligingly to their code of hospitality, the maneuver also gives Melville license to have a Yankee's last laugh at the comparative amateurism of British whalemen not once but twice, thereby playing the Yankee trickster without unduly offending British readers. It is testimony to Melville's wiliness that the vigorous in-house censorship upon which his British publisher insisted, of religiously and culturally offensive matter in the manuscript of *The Whale* (resulting in the deletion of Chapter 25 on British coronation procedures, for example), left chapters 100–101 untouched.

The postcolonial discourse of dual address need not only take the form of "indigenous" motifs like Ibo proverbialism or Yankee tricksterism. Just as easily it can be produced by a cosmopolitan gesture Achebe's title allusion (to Yeats's "The Second Coming"), which (among other possible implications) relocates the crisis of modernity from the Eurocentric trauma of the Great War to the African trauma wrought by Europe's scramble for colonies, while making the point (reinforced by the powerful close, when the plot suddenly shrinks into a minor incident in the District Commissioner's intended memoir) that western readers are not likely to be able to do more than begin to be able to make that mental shift, though at least they can make a beginning. A fortuitous additional irony here is that Achebe knew that his domestic readership, e.g. Nigerian youth reading the standard English literature syllabus (to which *Things Fall Apart* was later added), would catch the allusion, whereas not more than a very few students in a typical group of contemporary Harvard undergraduates will think to connect the novel's title with the Yeats poem. Hawthorne practices a similar occulted cosmopolitanism at the end of *The Scarlet Letter*, when depicting in the hypothetical motto that the narrator says might have stood for a heraldic description of the appearance of the graves of Hester and Dimmesdale: "On a field sable, the letter A, gules." This reprocesses both the closing line of Andrew Marvell's "The Unfortunate Lover" and—even more pertinently—Scott's succinct diagnosis in the preface to his Waverley novels (wildly popular in the U.S.) of the difference between Scotland then and now (for our ancestors of the feudal era, wrath was colored gules; for the bourgeois era, when the institutions of civil society and moralism force the libido to express itself more obliquely, it is colored sable). Here too the esoteric hijacking of the canon: recentering and symbolically updating (though the plot dates back to an even earlier time) the Scottian scene of conflict of historical dispensations from late feudal Scotland to proto-Victorian Puritan New England, that even more remote outpost. Here too the nice additional fortuity of postcolonial cosmopolitanism producing almost total insouciance among modern readers.

5

The marks of postcolonial anxiety in the kind of U.S. writing under view are far more extensive than a short essay can cover. Here is a checklist of some of the most salient, in addition to what has already been noted.

1. *The semi-Americanization of the English language.* U.S. settler culture never faced this question in its most radical form, as put for example by Ngugi wa Thiong'o, who argues in *Decolonizing the Mind* and elsewhere that African literature should be written in the indigenous languages. Considering that English was the first language of a minority of the country's inhabitants in 1776, it is striking testimony to the cultural and political authority of Englishness in the U.S. that the option of linguistic pluralism was not more seriously discussed (cf. Shell 103–27)—though considering the examples of post-independence Nigeria (concerning which Achebe has declared that English has been crucial in keeping the country together) and India (where English persists as a medium of communication for the educated long after its abolition as national language) it is understandable that the U.S. should have institutionalized English from the start. Yet the weaker version of the linguistic indigenization argument (namely, how to creolize and neologize American English so that it spoke a voice of the culture distinct from the standardizing mother tongue) certainly does link writers like Cooper and Whitman and especially Twain with Amos Tutuola, Gabriel Okara, and Raja Rao, whose work sheds light on such subissues as the inextricability of "naturalness" and "artifice" in Whitman's diction and the inextricability of idealization and caricature in Cooper's vernacular heroes. Ashcroft, Griffiths, and Tiffin rightly remark that postcolonial literatures are "always written out of the tension between abrogation of the received English which speaks from the center, and the act of appropriation which brings it under the influence of a vernacular tongue" (Ashcroft et al. 39). That is a duality key to nineteenth-century U.S. writing as well.

In the early national period, one sees it especially in texts that counterpoint comic characters who speak in dialect with those who speak standard English, for example Colonel Manly versus his servant Jonathan in Royall Tyler's play *The Contrast*. At this stage, the vernacular is still clearly something of a national embarrassment, though a lively one. This is the Yankee equivalent of, say, the colloquial dramatic Indian-English monologues of Bombay poet Nissim Ezekiel:

> I am standing for peace and non-violence
> Why world is fighting fighting
> Why all people of world
> Are not following Mahatma Gandhi
> I am simply not understanding. (Ezekiel 22)

By the time of Thoreau and Whitman, the American inventiveness with language, through individual neologizing and provincial variant usages, that Tocqueville (as well as a number of U.S. intellectuals like George Perkins Marsh) considered one of the most "deplorable" consequences of democratization, had started to become positive aesthetic values (deTocqueville 2: 71; cf. Marsh 666–84). Thus Whitman could dare to take provocative aim simultaneously at the work ethic and English usage by introducing the verb "loafe" into literature for the first time and later, without any hint of parody at all, could exalt "the mossy scabs of the worm-fence" (Whitman 28, 33)— the latter a vernacular term for a typical practice of U.S. farmers that foreign visitors often singled out as particularly wasteful and ugly (Mesick, 161–62). Not that Whitman, in sometimes wishing to make the vulgar seem sublime, was prepared to forego literary English. His position, typical of Europhone postcolonial practice in this respect, was to justify an Americanization of English expression as the poetic way of the future on the ground that English itself was remarkable for its engraftment of other linguistic strains (Warren 5–69).

2. *Cultural hybridization*. Classic U.S. literary texts favor cross-cultural collages. Whitman's composite persona; Thoreau's hovering between the traditions of Puritan, Greco-Roman, Native American, and Oriental mythographies in *A Week* and *Walden*; Melville's multimythic elaboration of the whale symbol in tandem with presenting the *Pequod* as a kind of global village; Cooper's heteroglossic tapestry of six or seven different nationalities in *The Pioneers*. All these test and in some cases expand the limits of Crevecoeur's famous definition of "the American" as an amalgam of many (European) races. David Simpson persuasively argues, respecting Cooper, that Templeton's heteroglot character, each resident speaking his or her own peculiar dialect (except the Temple family, of course), registers the social fissures of still-experimental nationhood (Simpson 149–201);[20] and Cooper's practice can be set beside latter-day delineations of linguistic-cultural fissuring in post-independence societies as the *dramatis personae* of Wole Soyinka's in his play *The Road*, who shift about among standard English, pidgin, and American slanguage.[21] Likewise, Salman Rushdie's Saleem Sinai, who quixotically attempts to coordinate the voices of the hundreds of other Midnight's Children in his head, and G. V. Desani's racially and culturally syncretistic Mr. Haterr are comic analogues of Whitman's attempt to create "national" personae that will mirror the hybrid diversity of a nation in the making, a nation even more linguistically and culturally fissured than the United States of Whitman's day.

3. *The expectation that artists be responsible agents for achieving national liberation*, which in turn bespeaks an ambivalence toward art as specialization and toward the legitimacy of the aesthetic as such. Diagnoses of the strong utilitarian bias in U.S. literary thought—its legitimation of art as a vehicle for useful informational content and/or improving moral reflection—tends to get thought of by Americanists as a post-Puritan effect reinforced by Victorian moralism. Without rejecting this autochthonous line of explanation, one ought also take note of the fact that the conceptualization of art's mission in terms of socially urgent duty often runs strong in postcolonial societies elsewhere. Soyinka has called attention to the pressure upon postcolonial African writers to "postpone that unique reflection on experience and events which is what makes a writer—and constitute himself into a part of that machinery that will actually shape

events" (Soyinka 16), a call that he himself has at times heeded and eloquently fur-
thered both in activist memoirs like *The Man Died* and political drama like *Madmen
and Specialists* and *A Play of Giants*. Emerson wrestled with a similar-looking public/
private dilemma in "The American Scholar" and expressed his ambivalence about
sacrificing intellectual independence on the altar of activism even more pointedly later
on, even as he was making an intensified commitment to lend his voice to the antislavery movement (cf. Emerson 1995, 73–74). Anozie's statement that there "there
seemed to exist a genetic struggle between a . . . pursuit for its own sake and a
constantly intensive awareness of the social relevance of art" could apply almost as
well to Soyinka and to Emerson, though in fact it refers to Nigerian poet Christopher
Okigbo (Anozie 175), perhaps the closest approximation to a "pure aesthete" among
the major figures of the illustrious first contemporary generation of Nigeria's Anglophone literati, later killed as a soldier in the Biafran war.

   4. *The problem of "alien genres"*: Eurocentric genres that carry authority but seemingly imitable only upon sacrifice of cultural authority or upon condition of forcible
redefinition. I have already mentioned Whitman's "new-world" ambivalence toward
epic. But in the field of prose fiction particularly, there seems to be a correspondence
between the critique of the protagonist-centered reality novel by third-world intellectuals and complaints by the long-known nineteenth-century U.S. fictionists from Cooper to Hawthorne to James that the novel (i.e. traditional novel of manners) was
not transplantable to American soil. Conversely, some genres have seemed not only
transplantable with great ease but precisely tailored for the early U.S. and other new
nations. A prime example is my next and final topic, which deserves its own rubric
since it overspills the bounds of genre per se.

   5. *Post-European pastoral.* A recurring fascination with physical nature as subject,
symbol, and theater in which to act out rituals of maturity and perfection has long
been seen as a distinctive preoccupation with U.S. writers, not only white but also
Native American.[22] Mutatis mutandis the same can be said of Canadian and Australian
writing, although their versions of nature are (for more complicated reasons than
geography alone) less benign than ours; and a version of the same can be said of
some nonwestern writing also, despite manifest differences between the discourses of
European settlers and of non-European postcolonials whom Europe has otherized. The
most obvious analogue is Négritude, as well as other forms of cultural nationalism
that hold up a preurban, precolonial ideal order as a badge of distinctiveness.[23] Retrospective pastoralization of ancient tribal structures is a motif in U.S. antebellum writing also: in the more sentimentalized treatments of Puritan heritage and the old
plantation order, not to mention the even more vicarious sort of nostalgia represented
by savagist fantasies like Longfellow's *The Song of Hiawatha*. Perhaps this helps explain
why Thoreau simultaneously became addicted to nature, Native American ethnography, and New England antiquities. *Walden* and *The Scarlet Letter* are predictable complements in their mutual preocuupation with cultural origins.

   That naturism as cultural assertion can be symbiotic with naturism as neocolonial
residue is clear from a text like the sonnet addressed by William Cullen Bryant to his
friend the painter Thomas Cole, bound for Europe. Bryant imagines Cole bearing "to
Europe's strand

> A living image of thy native land,
> Such as on thy own glorious canvass lies;
> Lone lakes—savannahs where the bison rover—
> Rocks rich with summer garlands—solemn streams—
> Skies, where the desert eagle wheels and screams—
> Spring bloom and autumn blaze of boundless groves.

The sestet contrasts these pristine landscapes to the disadvantage of those of Europe, which bear "every where the trace of men"; but it also anxiously charges Cole not to be bewitched by them, but to "keep that earlier, wilder image bright!" Partly anticipating Whitman, Bryant reverses *translatio studii* by imagining Cole as an aesthetic errand-bearer to Europe, but the cautionary ending betrays anxiety as to whether his friend will keep the faith. In this Bryant acknowledges how much the two of them have already been affected by the European gravitational field. Cole, like other cisatlantic painters of the day, had been deeply influenced by the tropes of European Romantic landscape painting (Novak 226–73). As for Bryant, although his poem is replete with North American references (bison, eagle, and the fall colors that delighted European travelers), what most strikes a modern reader is its bondage to old-world language like "savannah" and "desert," and its unconsciously ironic choice of sonnet—a hypercivilized form if ever there was one—as the vehicle for enjoining the gospel of the "wilder image."

In an excellent study of landscape mimesis in the late eighteenth century, Robert Lawson-Peebles points out that cultural nationalist visions of a pastoralized America pulled "towards Europe and away from the facts of the American continent. Even the writers who attended closely to those facts shaped them so that they answered European criticisms, and in so doing they collaborated in a dream-world" (Lawson-Peebles 57). So here. It is as if "the American Wordsworth" (as Bryant was called according to a common U.S.-postcolonial nicknaming practice) had set out to play back to Coleridge an image of America just slightly (but not alarmingly) more feral than Coleridge had entertained thirty years before in *his* sonnet on "Pantisocracy," which envisions a rural valley in Pennsylvania purified of nightmare and neurosis.

In stressing the "dream-world" character of such pastoral visions, I certainly do not mean to discredit them; on the contrary, what strikes me especially is the power that they continue to exercise even today as mimetic and ideological instruments. No doubt they help account for the high degree of public environmental concern that now obtains in the U.S., despite notorious slippages between sentiment and practice. But in order to understand pastoral's power as cultural instrument, one needs also to understand the element of mimetic desire that has historically driven the pastoralizing impulse.

6. *Belatedness.* The source of post-European pastoral self-division is its element of belatedness; pastoral was inevitably fashioned to some extent as response to a preexisting Eurocentric dream about the colonial periphery. This instantiates a more pervasive postcolonial anxiety "about a perceived lack of authenticity in relation to place" (Masel 162). The scene may be rural or it may be urban, as in V. S. Naipaul's recollection of how

as a child in Trinidad I had projected everything I read onto the Trinidad landscape, the Trinidad countryside, the Port of Spain streets. (Even Dickens and London I incorporated into the streets of Port of Spain. Were the characters English, white people, or were they transformed into people I knew? A question like that is a little like asking whether one dreams in color or in back and white. But I think I transfered the Dickens characters to people I knew. Though with a half or a quarter of my mind I knew that Dickens was all English, yet my Dickens cast, the cast in my head, was multiracial.) (Naipaul 162)

Likewise, Thoreau's first summer's Walden journal sustains a mood of high excitement by repeatedly imagining the experience in epic terms, ancient Greece connoting for him, as for other Romantics, the morning of Western culture. In his encounter with the woodchopper in the "Visitors" chapter of *Walden*, Thoreau plays the kind of game Naipaul describes: loving and believing in the magnification that he halfway allows himself to realize is a game. Likewise he makes believe that the Walden region is "my lake country" (197).

For both Naipaul and Thoreau, the game of animating the provincial quotidian with imagery from the repertoire of metropolitan culture is of course class-specific (the elegant recreation of the cultivated person for whom Euroculture is the touchstone of local knowledge), but at all events this mentality involves at once tunnel vision and access of vision, vision of two opposite kinds: of the ordinary object, mystified as luminous; and of one's own imagination's tricks and needs.

6

The case of Thoreau, whose art is patently more homegrown than Bryant's, raises the question of when, if at all, the postcolonial moment in U.S. literary history can be said to have "ended." One way to resolve the issue is to appeal to historical moments: the Mexican War, gunboat diplomacy against Japan in 1853, the massacre at Wounded Knee, the invasion of Cuba in 1898, the first concerted attempt to display Yankee industrial might on a world stage at the Philadelphia Centennial Exposition of 1876. Alternatively, one might use foreign travel writing as the benchmark and point to the difference half a century seemed to make between Tocqueville and the highly respectful monumentalization of the U.S. by Lord Bryce in *The American Commonwealth* (1890), the most substantial late-century example of the genre. Or one might appeal to such fictive evidence as Mark Twain's imagination (in *The Connecticut Yankee*) of a Yankee-driven state of military and political superiority to an archaized Britain; or Melville's (in "Benito Cereno") of a Yankee entrepreneurialism counterpart to but more potent than a decadent Hispanic creole regime.

A more accurate answer to the "when" question, however, is that no clear answer can be given. On the one hand, "postcolonial" is from the start an objectionably flattening term since it coerces us to look at everything within an emerging cultural field as reactive to Europe, and this is patently not the case even for settler writing, much less for postcolonial nations like India with cultural roots stretching back millennia before European colonization. On the other hand, U.S. culture can be said to remain at least vestigially postcolonial so long as its citizens are impressed by the sound of an educated British accent, so long as there is no such thing as a distinctively U.S. cuisine apart from the hamburger and the hot dog, or—much more consequentially—so long as it treats white better than nonwhite.

This messiness is of no little interest in itself. For one thing, it is further evidence that "(post)colonial" and "imperial" are not discontinuous. There is of course plenty of evidence worldwide: that a country can be simultaneously postcolonial and imperial, as with Indonesia gobbling up East Timor or India overrunning Goa and imposing Hindi as national language over the protests of the south. In the case of the U.S., the dream of what might meaningfully be called empire as opposed to colony dates from the colonial period itself, and the self-conception of many American colonists including future founding fathers like Benjamin Franklin of participating in the consolidation of a greater British America. Indeed the founders took over this dream, most famously in Jefferson's slogan "Empire for Liberty." Nor did postcolonial anxiety imply abdication of it, indeed if anything the reverse. Cooper played the postcolonial to the extent that he quarreled with Scott's plot forms deferentially, but played the imperialist to the extent that his own narrative agendas reflected and perpetuated the romance of American expansionism, notwithstanding their critique of it. Whitman's insouciant proleptic lumping of "Kanada" under the sway of "America" (and at times the rest of the hemisphere too) is an even more blatant case. Small wonder, then, that Frederick Marryat, who as a British naval officer and author of juvenile adventure fiction helped to underwrite British expansionism, was told to his bemusement when visiting the United States in the 1830s that Britain need not exult over its superiority as an imperial power because the U.S. would soon pick up some colonies for itself.

It may be that the single most instructive dimensions of U.S. settler culture postcolonialism, instructive especially for Americanists but also perhaps for students of postcolonialism elsewhere, is this continuum between colonial and imperial mentalities. The evolution of the U.S. into the greatest world power, through a fortuitous combination of geographical and political circumstances, seems inextricably bound up in its antecedent history, as the creation of a colonial project: more specifically, with the identification of its own peculiar liberal democratic mission during the postcolonial period as a purified extension of the civilizational aims of that prior colonial project. Does this suggest that postcolonial anxiety if allowed to resolve and assert itself freely may tend chronically to seek not only freedom but dominance, both of one's internal minorities and of the rest of the world? To the extent that this is so, all the more reason for not allowing the cultural anxiety of the classic U.S. writers become lost from our critical narratives, be they sympathetic or disillusioned, of their rise to hegemony as the traditionally-acclaimed bearers and fomenters of U.S. literary tradition. For their anxiety, their very non-recognition of the certainty of their and their nation's future canonization, may prove their most compelling legacy after all.

Notes

This essay has been revised especially for this anthology. An earlier version was published in *American Literary History* 4.3 (Fall 1992): 411–42. We thank Oxford University Press for permission to reprint portions of the original essay.

1. Sharpe is representative in identifying U.S. postcoloniality exclusively with the history of "internal colonization" of minority groups.

2. Buell, "American Literary Emergence," rpt. Hutner. That previous version has been chastised as a "clumsy effort to colonize postcolonial theory" (Hulme 119, echoing Kaplan [21]) and for "rescind[ing] external, national, and even linguistic borders while implicitly holding fast to those internal boundaries that demarcate race, class, and gender differences" (Kutzinski 554). With these and other criticisms in mind, I have tried to correct previous errors and overstatements, although I continue to think that the primary source of strongly aversive reactions is epistème-driven reluctance on the part of what Schmidt and Singh loosely categorize as the "border studies" persuasion to entertain the very thought that the canonical U.S. white male writers might could have experienced a phase of cultural subalternity in any meaningful sense of the word—a position I continue to maintain. On the other hand, Porter (516–17) offers a critique of the essay more cogent to my mind on account of its greater willingness to entertain the possibility of the analogy between early 19th century U.S. cultural nationalism and other postcolonial cases.

3. R. Radikrishnan, for example, affirming that "no one historical angle can have a monopolistic hold over the possible elaborations of the 'postcolony,' " irenically counsels that "whoever joins the polemical dialogue [about what postcoloniality is or should be] should do so with a critical-sensitive awareness of the legitimacies of several other perspectives on the issue" (171).

4. As Mishra and Hodge point out (399ff), historically, "postcolonial" (or rather "postcolonial") seems to have begun as a neutral signifier to denote newly independent states, then to become associated specifically with anti-imperial currents in "third world" societies, then to become broadened again—especially by Europhone settler-culture critics—to apply to anti-imperialist currents more generally. The (re)extension of "postcolonial" was propagated most influentially by the study that occasioned Mishra's and Hodge's thoughtful essay-review: (Ashcroft, Griffiths, and Tiffin). The usage of "second world" is potentially confusing by reason of its association with the socialist as opposed to the "free world"—to which most "second world" postcolonial societies belong—but it has roots in the Renaissance-utopian conception of "new world," which informs what I call post-European pastoral below.

5. Although its ingredients have a long prehistory, the "imperialist" reading of U.S. cultural history has taken on new life since the Civil Rights movement of the 1960s and particularly since the Vietnam war, emerging first most saliently in the first book of Richard Slotkin's frontier trilogy (1973); achieving its quintessential "new historicist" expression in Jehlen, and its most seminal presentation (so far) of *fin-de-siècle* multiculturalist and Post-Cold-War orientations in Kaplan and Pease. Said (1993, pp. 282–303 and passim), is representative of post/colonial studies in its emphatic subscription to this narrative. Hardt and Negri impresses me as a particularly suggestive short account of imperial motifs in U.S. thought from a post-Marxist standpoint because of the distinctions it attempts (for the most part) to maintain between the permutations of U.S. ideology, ancient and modern imperialism, and "empire" in the authors' primary sense of supranational world order.

6. This was the basis of Ahmad's retort (rpt. 1992) to Jameson's lumping diagnosis of third-world writing as anti-colonial resistance (1986).

7. Bloom's statements begin with *Ringers* (1971) and proceed through a series of books culminating in *Agon* (1982). But the conceptual ghost of his hermeneutical machine is fully evident in Pearce.

8. Colacurcio (1991). Significant exceptions within this epochal cohort are Arac, Weisbuch, Chai, and Reynolds. Colacurcio's review treats the last two together with six other books (including one of my own) whose focus, however, is decisively cisatlantic: a selection typical of the U.S.-centripetalism of the decade.

9. Some particularly influential examples of each approach within American studies include Lowe, Gates, and Saldívar.

10. McClintock (89) claims categorically that "The United States, South Africa, Australia, Canada and New Zealand remain, in my view, break-away settler colonies that have not undergone decolonization, nor, with the exception of South Africa, are they likely to in the near future"—this specifically with reference to domination of minorities by the dominant culture.

11. Spencer's comprehensive critical history of early national cultural anxiety and assertion remains the standard codification.

12. The first chapter of Bercovitch (1978) lays out the grounds of difference succinctly.

13. The seminal text here of course is Said (1978). His argument that Europeans formulated a condescending discourse of the "other" region as a fascinating but inferior civilization broadly applies to antebellum travel narratives (and even more closely to American perceptions of how they were viewed by these). European commentators of course did not typically view (white) Americans as radically other, but their discourse certainly *was*, as Said writes of Orientalism, "premised upon exteriority," upon the amateur traveler or "expert" scholar constructing and explicating America "as an existential and as a moral fact" (20–21). Said's model been ramified, codified, and complicated by a next wave of studies more specifically directed to travel writing, Pratt and Spurr, most especially by taking into account the fragilities, fissures, and multilayeredness of traveler discourse, like the interplay of desire vs. domination, observation vs. intertextuality (cf. Behdad). Such complications too one sees in a number of the writers cited here: Martineau, Dickens, de Tocqueville, etc. Conversely, Euroamericans were often themselves both defensively anti-imperial and orientalizing at the same time, like Melville in *Typee*.

14. Naipaul: "Indians defecate everywhere. They defecate, mostly, beside the railroad tracks. But they also defecate on the beaches; they defecate on the river banks; they defecate on the streets; they never look for cover" (74). Compare this to Charles Dickens: "In the courts of law, the judge has his spittoon, the crier his, the witness his, and the prisoner his; while the jurymen and spectators are provided for, as so many men who in the course of nature must desire to spit incessantly" (*American Notes* 112–13). To put the (ex-)colony under the sign of filth was a common trope of colonial discourse (Spurr 76–91). For the postcolonial retort in kind, see Esty.

15. Memmi: "The colonized is never characterized in an individual manner; he is entitled only to drown in an anonymous collectivity ('They are this.' 'They are all the same.')" (85). Spurr 61–75 provides a succinct discussion of classifying procedures in colonial travel writing.

16. Although women writers of the period sometimes showed signs of postcolonial cultural anxiety and resistance (cf. Margaret Fuller's critical essays and Ellen Montgomery's exhibition of demurely insistent patriotism in her dialogues with the Lindsay family in Susan Warner's *Wide, Wide World*), generally they were much less burdened by a sense of national mission in their capacity as actors in the literary marketplace; and their absorption of European models was comparatively untroubled by the felt need to claim an American "difference." Cf. Walker for women poets and cf. for example Elizabeth Stoddard's Brontësque novel *The Morgesons* (1862) for a striking instance of adaptation of a transatlantic model whose will-to-difference seems to have virtually no cultural-nationalist agenda to it. African American writers of the period, for their part, deployed "Britain"—like "Canada"—as a site of comparative non-racism against which to measure U.S. culture and find it wanting. The very fact that it was suggested to Frederick Bailey that he rename himself Douglass (after a character in Walter Scott) was symptomatic of ongoing pervasive colonization of U.S. literary discourse by British models; but his decision to adopt the name cannot be explained on that ground (cf. McFeely 78).

17. The "blithe Latin American Ariel fighting off brutish North American Caliban" is Carlos Fuentes' shrewd though too offhanded characterization of the thrust of the most seminal Latin

text, José Enrique Rodó's *Ariel* (1900) (14). The complicated permutations of Caliban in Latin discourse are charted from a Marxist-Castroite standpoint in Retamar 3–45.

18. McWilliams 218–237 and passim convincingly argues that the United States succeeded in adapting epic models only by partially contorting them in parodistic ways.

19. Quoted in Egejuru 17.

20. See also Rosenwald's insightful discussion of Cooper's attempted mimesis of Native American language(s) in "American Anglophone Literature and Multilingual America" (329–35), an essay valuable (like the whole collection in which it appears) in emphasizing the *distinction* between the domains of "language" and "culture," which my analysis here tends to blur.

21. What Lewis Nkosi says of modern African Anglophone poetry's quest to define its path applies to Cooper's *Pioneers*: the "first requirement . . . was precisely to articulate . . . the heterogeneity of cultural experiences among which the poet had to pick his or her way" (Nkosi 151). He proceeds to quote from Abioseh Nicol's "African Easter," which starts with a nursery rhyme ("Ding, dong bell") and juxtaposes this with "matin bells," the cry of the muezzin, and "pagan drums"—an intercultural salad considerably more diverse than Cooper's Templeton, though the device of colliding vocabularies is similar.

22. To do full justice to this issue, it would obviously be necessary both to distinguish both between traditional "male" and "female" versions and between settler-culture and Native versions—without presenting either distinction as a simple dichotomy and recognizing too the historical shifts in the nature and degrees of difference.

23. I discuss settler culture pastoral and Négritude as allied although distinct postcolonial formations at some length in *Environmental Imagination* 53–82. See also Wasserman, an illuminating comparison of the construction of the two literary cultures in terms of an exotic environmental imaginary, first from without and then from within.

Bibliography

Achebe, Chinua. *Things Fall Apart*. Greenwich: Fawcett, 1959.

Ahmad, Aijaz. "Jameson's Rhetoric of Otherness and the 'National Allegory." *In Theory*. London: Verso, 1992. 95–122.

Anozie, Sunday. *Christopher Okigbo: Creative Rhetoric*. London: Evans, 1972.

Arac, Jonathan. *Commisioned Spirits: The Shaping of Social Motion in Dickens, Carlyle, Melville, and Hawthorne*. New Brunswick: Rutgers UP, 1979.

Ashcroft, Bill, Gareth Griffiths, and Helen Tiffin. *The Empire Writes Back: Theory and Practice in Post-colonial Literatures*. London: Routledge, 1989.

Behdad, Ali. *Belated Travelers: Orientalism in the Age of Colonial Dissolution*. Durham: Duke UP, 1994.

Bercovitch, Sacvan. *The American Jeremiad*. Madison: U of Wisconsin P, 1978.

Bloom, Harold. *Agon: Towards a Theory of Revisionism*. New York: Oxford UP, 1982.

———. *The Ringers in the Tower*. Chicago: U of Chicago P, 1971.

Bridgman, Richard. *The Colloquial Style in America*. New York: Oxford UP, 1960.

Buell, Lawrence. "American Literary Emergence as a Postcolonial Phenomenon," *American Literary History* 4 (1992): 511–442.

Buell, Lawrence. *The Environmental Imagination*. Cambridge: Harvard UP, 1995.

———. "Melville and the Question of American Decolonization." *American Literature* 64 (1992): 215–237.

Chai, Leon. *The Romantic Foundations of the American Renaissance*. Ithaca: Cornell UP, 1987.

Colacurcio, Michael. "The American-Renaissance Renaissance." *New England Quarterly*, 64 (1991): 445–493.

Cooper, James Fenimore. *Letters and Journals*. 6 vols. Ed. James Franklin Beard. Cambridge: Harvard UP, 1960–8.

de Tocqueville, Alexis. *Democracy in America*. Trans. Henry Reeve. Ed. Phillips Bradley. New York: Vintiage, 1945.

Dickens, Charles. *American Notes and Pictures from Italy*. London: Oxford UP, 1957.

———. *Martin Chuzzlewitt*. London: Oxford UP, 1966.

Egejuru, Phanuel. *Towards African Literary Independence: A Dialogue with Contemporary African Writers*. Westport: Greenwood, 1980.

Emerson, Ralph Waldo. *Emerson's Antislavery Writings*. Ed. Len Gougeon and Joel Myerson. New Haven: Yale UP, 1995.

———. *Nature, Addresses, Lectures*. Ed. Robert E. Spiller and Alfred R. Ferguson. Cambridge: Harvard UP, 1971.

Esty, Joshua. "Excremental Postcolonialism." *Contemporary Literature*. 40 (1998).

Ezekiel, Nissim. *Latter-Day Psalms*. Delhi: Oxford UP, 1982.

Gates, Henry Louis, Jr. *The Signifying Monkey*. New York: Oxford UP, 1988.

Gilroy, Paul. *The Black Atlantic: Modernity and Double Consciousness*. Cambridge: Harvard UP, 1993.

Hardt, Michael, and Antonio Negri. *Empire*. Cambridge: Harvard UP, forthcoming.

Hulme, Peter. "Including America." *Ariel*, 26 (1995): 117–23.

Hutner, Gordon, ed. *American Literature, American Culture*. New York: Oxford UP, 1998.

Jameson, Fredric. "Third-World Literature in the Era of Multinational Capitalism." *Social Text* 15 (1986): 65–88.

Jehlen, Myra. *American Incarnation*. Cambridge: Harvard UP, 1986.

Kaplan, Amy. " 'Left Alone with America.' " *Cultures of United States Imperialism*. Ed. Amy Kaplan and Donald E. Pease. Durham: Duke UP, 1993. 3–21.

Kipling, Rudyard. *American Notes*. New York: Arcadia, 1950.

Kutzinski, Vera M. "American Literary History as Spatial Practice," *American Literary History* 4 (1994): 550–557.

Lawson-Peebles, Robert. *Landscape and Written Expression in Revolutionary America: The World Turned Upside Down*. Cambridge: Cambridge UP, 1988.

Lowe, Lisa. *Immigrant Acts*. Durham: Duke UP, 1996.

Lyell, Charles. *A Second Visit to the United States of North America*. 2 vols. New York: Harper, 1849.

Marsh, George Perkins. *Lectures on the English Language*. 4th ed. New York: Scribner, 1854.

Martineau, Harriet. *Society in America*. 2 vols. New York: Saunders & Otley, 1837.

Masel, Carolyn. "Late Landings: reflections on belatedness in Australian and Canadian Literatures." *Recasting the World: Writing after Colonialism*. Ed. Jonathan White. Baltimore: Johns Hopkins UP, 1993. 161–189.

McClintock, Anne. "The Angel of Progress: Pitfalls of the Term 'Post-Colonialism.' " *Social Text* 31/32 (1992): 84–98.

McFeely, William S. *Frederick Douglass*. New York: Norton, 1979.

McWilliams, John P., Jr. *The American Epic: Transforming a Genre: 1770–1860*. Cambridge: Cambridge UP, 1989.

Melville, Herman. *Moby-Dick*. Ed. Harrison Hayford, hershel Parker, and G. Thomas Tanselle. Evanston: Northwestern University Press; Chicago: Newberry Library, 1988.

———. *Typee*. Ed. Harrison Hayford, Hershel Parker, and G. Thomas Tanselle. Evanston: Northwestern University Press; Chicago: Newberry Library, 1968.

Memmi, Albert. *The Colonizer and the Colonized.* Trans. Howard Greenfield. Boston: Beacon, 1965.

Mesick, Jane Louise. *The English Traveler in America, 1836–1860.* New York: Columbia UP, 1922.

Mishra, Vijay, and Rob Hodge. "What Is Post(-)colonialism?" *Textual Practice,* 5 (1991): 399–414.

Murphy, Francis, ed. *Walt Whitman: A Critical Anthology.* Baltimpre: Penguin, 1970.

Naipaul, V. S. *An Area of Darkness.* New York: Vintage, 1964.

———. *The Enigma of Arrival.* New York: Knopf, 1987.

Nandy, Ashis. *The Intimate Enemy: Loss and Recovery of Self Under Colonialism.* Delhi: Oxford UP, 1983.

Nkosi, Lewis. *Tasks and Masks: Themes and Styles of African Literature.* Essex: Longman, 1981.

Novak, Barbara. *Nature and Culture: American Landscape and Painting, 1825–1875.* New York: Oxford UP, 1980.

Pearce, Roy Harvey. *The Continuity of American Poetry.* Princeton: Princeton UP, 1961.

Porter, Carolyn. "What We Know We Don't Know: Remapping American Literary Studies." *American Literary History,* 6 (1994): 467–526.

Pratt, Mary louise. *Imperial Eyes.* London: Routledge, 1992.

Radikrishnan, R. *Diasporic Meditations: Between Home and Location.* Minneapolis: U of Minnesota P, 1996.

Rétamar, Fernández. *Caliban and Other Essays.* Trans. Edward Baker. Minneapolis: U of Minnesota P, 1989.

Reynolds, Larry J. *European Revolutions and the American Renaissance.* New Haven: Yale UP, 1988.

Rodó, José Enrique. *Ariel.* Trans. Margaret Sayers Peden. Prologue Carlos Fuentes. Austin: U of Texas P, 1988.

Rosenwald, Lawrence. "American Anglophone Literature and Multilingual America." *Multilingual America.* Ed. Werner Sollors. New York: New York UP, 1998. 327–347.

Said, Edward. *Culture and Imperialism.* New York: Knopf, 1993.

———. *Orientalism.* New York: Vintage, 1978.

Saldívar, José Davíd. *The Dialectics of Our America.* Durham: Duke UP, 1991.

Schopenhauer, Arthur. *The World as Will and Representation.* Trans. E. F. J. Payne. New York: Dover, 1969.

Sharpe, Jenny. "Is the United States Postcolonial? Transnationalism, Immigration, and Race," *Diaspora* 5 (1995): 181–199.

Shell, Marc. "Babel in America; or, the Politics of Language Diversity in the United States." *Critical Inquiry* 20 (1993): 103–127.

Shohat, Ella. "Notes on the 'Post-Colonial,' " *Social Text* 31/32 (1992): 99–113.

Simpson, David. *The Politics of American English, 1776–1850.* New York: Oxford UP, 1986.

Slemon, Stephen. "Unsettling the Empire: Resistance Theory for the Second World." *World Literature Written in English,* 30.2 (1990): 30–41.

Slotkin, Richard. *Regeneration Through Violence.* Middletown: Wesleyan UP, 1973.

Snead, James. "European Pedigrees/African Contagions: Nationality, Narrative, and Communality in Tutuola, Achebe, and Reed." *Nation and Narration.* Ed. Homi K. Bhabha. London: Routledge, 1990. 231–249.

Sommer, Doris. "Plagiarized Authenticity: Sarmiento's Cooper and Others." *Do the Americas Have a Common Literature?* Ed. Gustavo Pérez-Firmat. Durham: Duke UP, 1990. 130–155.

Soyinka, Wole. *Art, Dialogue and Outrage: Essays on Literature and Culture.* Ed. Biodun Jeyifo. Ibadan: New Horn, 1988.

Spencer, Benjamin. *The Quest for Nationality: An American Literary Campaign*. Syracuse: Syracuse UP, 1957.

Spengemann, William C. *A Mirror for Americanists*. Hanover: UP of New England, 1989.

Spillers, Hortense. "Who Cuts the Border?" *Comparative American Identities*. Ed. Hortense Spiller. London: Routledge, 1991. 1–25.

Spurr, David. *The Rhetoric of Empire*. Durham: Duke UP, 1994.

Thoreau, Henry David. *Walden*. Ed. J. Lyndon Shanley. Princeton: Princeton UP, 1973.

Tuckerman, Henry T. *America and Her Commentators*. New York: 1864.

Walker, Cheryl. *The Nightingale's Burden*. Bloomington: Indiana UP, 1982.

Warren, James Perrin. *Whitman's Language Experiment*. University Park: Pennsylvania State UP, 1990.

Wasserman, Renata R. Mautner. *Exotic Nations: Literature and Cultural Identity in the United States and Brazil, 1830–1930*. Ithaca: Cornell UP, 1994.

Weisbuch, Robert. *Atlantic Double-Cross*. Chicago: U of Chicago P, 1986.

Whitman, Walt. *Leaves of Grass: Comprehensive Reader's Edition*. Ed. Harold W. Blodgett and Sculley Bradley. New York: New York UP, 1965.

ROMANCING THE EMPIRE
The Embodiment of American Masculinity in the Popular Historical Novel of the 1890s

Amy Kaplan

In a speech urging the U.S. to annex the Philippines in 1900, Senator Albert Jeremiah Beveridge asked: "What does all this mean for every one of us?" and then readily answered: "It means opportunity for all the glorious young manhood of the republic—the most virile, ambitious, impatient, militant manhood the world has ever seen" (qtd. in Paterson 391). Not specifying the opportunities for particular actions, Beveridge implied tautologically that the empire offered the arena for American men to become what they already were, to enact their essential manhood before the eyes of a global audience. Although the Spanish-American War was viewed as a chivalric liberation of Cuba and the Philippines from a tyrannical old-world empire, Beveridge voiced an accompanying narrative: he welcomed the war's conquests as a rescue mission for American manhood, from the equally threatening forces of a modem industrial democracy.

A similar rescue mission was conducted on the pages of the popular historical romance, where thinly veiled American heroes pursued chivalric adventures in bygone eras. In the opening scene from the 1898 best-seller, *When Knighthood Was in Flower,* the heroine declares passionately upon her first sight of the hero fighting a duel: "For once I have found a real live man, full of manliness" (Major 27). In these novels, settings from European and American history function as the fictional equivalent of the Philippines for Beveridge, as the site where a man can reassert his "militant manhood," and where a woman serves as the eyes of the world.

Many contemporary readers linked the jingoistic clamor for foreign wars to what William Dean Howells called the "horrid tumult of the swashbuckler swashing on his buckler" in the 1890s (936). Looking back at his own youth, Henry Seidel Canby wrote in 1934, "Scott and the near-Scotts and the school-of-Scotts were such real determinants of inner life for readers brought up in the eighties and nineties that no one will ever understand the America of that day without reading and pondering upon not only *Ivanhoe,* but also To *Have and To Hold* and *Richard Carvel* and *Monsieur Beaucaire* and *Under the Red Robe"* (191–92). These novels, for Canby, linked the private psyche of the reader to the public enthusiasm for the Spanish-American War: "I cannot separate in my own memory the bands and cheering of '98, Hobson, Dewey, and manifest destiny in an expectant world, from the extravagant romanticism of the shallow, unphilosophical, unpsychological novels we had all been reading. One carried over into the other, and the same color was infused through both" (205). Overlooked by later critics in their characterization of the period as the "Age of Realism," historical romances, in fact, were the major best-sellers on the earliest published lists from 1895–1902, the period of heated national debates about America's imperial role.[1] Subsequent critical neglect has echoed Canby's ambivalence, which ascribes to the novels the power of determination while dismissing them as superficial.

An analogous contradiction informs the traditional diplomatic history of American imperialism, which attributes to public opinion the exorbitant power to provoke a war, whose significance is downplayed as a historical aberration. In both cases, popular culture—whether novels or newspapers—and the nationalism it expresses is blamed for and dismissed as hysterical excess. Critical treatments of the romance resemble historical approaches to the war as a nostalgic escape from modernity to the hardier life of the chivalric warrior, a collective form of blowing off steam. Yet such an approach reproduces the terms of imperialist discourse itself, while ignoring how nostalgia can abet modern imperial force and how an outworn genre can be refurbished to represent a new political context.[2]

A study of these novels can do more than revise literary history by including an overlooked chapter on popular texts. The extravagance that Canby dismisses—which goes beyond the imagined contours of American ideology—can provide access to the repressed political context of American imperialism, lurking in the background of cultural studies of the period. Foregrounding imperialism can suggest how the romance contributes to a broader cultural dynamic that simultaneously represents and renders invisible the politics of empire building.

In this article I argue that swashbuckling romances about knights errant offer a cognitive and libidinal map of U.S. geopolitics during the shift from continental conquest to overseas empire. By looking back with nostalgia at a lost wholeness, they create fanciful realms on which to project contemporary desires for unlimited global expansion. More than neat political allegories that transpose international conflict into chivalric heroism, the novels refigure the relation between masculinity and nationality in a changing international context.

The romance hero asserts his virility in more complex forms than the self-reliant frontier violence we might expect. The chivalric rescue narrative makes him dependent on the liberation and subjugation of the willing heroine, a composite figure for the subject and object of imperial power. Furthermore, his manhood is embodied through spectacles staged for the female gaze, to enlist American women in the traditional male realm of what Edward Said has called the "pleasures of imperialism" (27). Finally, I contend that both the spectacle of American manhood and nostalgia for the American past—in which the romance revival culminates—work to deny political agency and visibility to the subjects of the American empire.

1

THE DOUBLE DISCOURSE OF AMERICAN IMPERIALISM

Nationhood and manhood have long been intimately related in American history through the dynamic of territorial expansion. The frontier, where Frederick Jackson Turner located the formation of American individualism, became for later historians the site of conflict with Native Americans which forged the ideology of white masculinity. What happened to the link between nationality and masculinity when U.S. expansion shifted course from the continent to an overseas empire in the 1890s? The traditional explanation finds both nationalism and masculinity physically revitalized by imperial conquest. Congruence between the body and the state underlies the characterization of the period by Theodore Roosevelt's title, "The Strenuous Life," and the commonplace phrase, national "muscle-flexing," which deploys the body as a metaphor for international aggression. For revisionists, the contradictions that inhere in masculine regeneration on the frontier are exported and reproduced at the turn of the century in the confrontation with new "Indians" abroad. These explanations, however, demand reconsideration because they assume both a continuous history of expansion and a natural connection between the identification of the nation with the land and masculinity with the male body.[3]

Instead, a more complex double discourse of American imperialism emerges in the 1890s: politicians, intellectuals, and businessmen on both sides of the debate were redefining national power as *disembodied*—that is, divorced from contiguous territorial expansion. In the same period, and often the same breath, masculine identity was reconceived as *embodied*—that is, cultivated in the muscular robust physique.

The disembodiment of American nationalism can be seen in the much-heralded close of the frontier, which was inseparable from the call for open doors abroad. With the end of continental expansion, national power was no longer measured by the settlement and incorporation of new territory consolidated into a united state, but instead by the extension of vaster yet less tangible networks of international markets and political influence. Even the annexations of Hawaii and the Philippines were valued primarily as providing way stations en route to the fabled China markets, just as Cuba became the gateway to the Caribbean, itself the key to the isthmus that would become a canal and open the door to worldwide shipping. These islands, despite their bounded nature, became projections of the desire for an ever-growing expansion that seemed directed at noncorporeal objects. Disembodiment might describe the cultural fantasy underlying what historians have called the economically determined "informal empire," the desire for total control disentangled from direct political annexation.[4]

In fact, America's "New Empire," as Brooks Adams dubbed it, defined itself ideologically against the territorially based colonialism of the old European empires. While the frontier environment may have characterized the exceptional nature of America's past for Turner and his followers, the spatially unbounded quality of the "New Empire" promised to reconstitute national uniqueness. Thus, if, as Myra Jehlen has shown, Manifest Destiny "rests its case on the integrity of the continent," what she calls "incarnation," then the shift from continental to global expansion in the 1890s can be seen as a form of "disincarnation" (5).

In this light, the representation of American nationhood might undergo a "reincarnation" in the American man. The culture at large was in the process of redefining white middle-class masculinity from a republican quality of character based on self-control and social responsibility to a corporeal essence identified with the vigor and prowess of the individual male body.[5] Imperialist discourse drew on and reinforced this process, as Maurice Thompson testified: "The war has made startlingly clear how great a thing is physical health and strength. Probably no army and navy since the best days of the Roman Empire ever equaled ours man for man in the best results of athletic training" ("Vigorous" 619). Despite the evidence of war's physical ravages, caused by disease as much as combat, Thompson could continue, "In looking at our soldiers and sailors I was filled with admiration of their lithe and muscular forms and their show of virile health." This view reduces the empire to one among other rugged settings—the playing field, the boxing ring, the newly discovered wilderness—and relegates the war to one of the more vigorous activities—athletics, bicycling, weight lifting, hiking. Virility is less the means to the end of empire building than is empire the occasion for body-building, an inversion which ideologically effaces the violent conflict with foreign bodies on alien terrain. The discourse of American imperialism is therefore double, because it simultaneously delineates national power that is disembodied from territorial boundaries and re-embodied in the power of the male body.

The question remains, however, what links geographic disembodiment and masculine embodiment in the double discourse of American imperialism? Elaine Scarry's analysis of war suggests that an ideological spotlight on the individual body might concretize an otherwise abstract political struggle. If the political and territorial ends of John Hay's "splendid little war" seemed murky, the male body could thus provide an anchor in a sea of distended world power. The problem of conceptualizing American imperialism, however, lay less in its abstract political nature in the present than in its rupture with a vision of the past. Anti-imperialists opposed the forced annexation of noncontiguous islands as a radical departure from what they considered the organic growth of the nation. Furthermore, they protested such conquest as antithetical to America's democratic anticolonial tradition.

The discontinuity between the disembodied empire and the embodied man implicitly addresses the problem of how to make imperialism continuous with American history. In the introduction to his book, *Democracy and Empire* (1900), sociologist Franklin Giddings explicitly posed and resolved this contradiction: "The world has been accustomed to think of democracy and empire as antagonistic phenomena. It has assumed that democracy could be established only on the ruins of empire, and that the establishment of empire necessarily meant the overthrow of liberty by a triumphant reign of absolutism. Yet in our day we are witnessing the simultaneous development of both democracy and empire" (3). What Giddings saw as a distinctly modem development, others envisioned through the lens of nostalgia, which located the empire as the site for recuperating a primitive corporeal virility. Writers such as Frank Norris represented a historically changing construction of masculinity as no change at all but the return to a mythical origin: "[S]omewhere deep down in the heart of every Anglo-Saxon lies the predatory instinct of his Viking ancestors—an instinct that a thousand years of respectability and taxpaying have not quite succeeded in eliminating" (qtd. in Ziff 265). This instinctual self could only be recovered paradoxically on an externalized frontier remote from the U.S., whose internal national identity appeared threatened by the influx of nonAnglo-Saxon immigrants.

If the idea of an international empire seemed discordant with U.S. democracy, the representation of that empire in the primitive male body figured reassuringly as a return to a fundamental Anglo-Saxon heritage. In a period of the "New Woman," the "New South," and the "New Empire," the New White American Man was invented as a tradition, to use Hobsbawm's term (and unlike the others, as a tradition it remains tellingly unlabeled), as nothing new at all, but an enduring recoverable past.[6] Thus in the figure of a revitalized male body, geographic distension and overseas conquest figure as a temporal return to origins, literally as nostalgia, *nostos*, the return home.

Anthropologist Renato Rosaldo has recently defined "imperialist nostalgia" as the sentimental longing on the part of imperialist agents—government officials, missionaries, ethnographers—for the indigenous forms of life that they have had a hand in destroying. An inseparable element of imperialist nostalgia (which his own writing expresses) is not only for "the way they were," but also for "the way we were." In this discourse, the empire figures as the site where you can be all that you can no longer be at home—a "real live man"—where you can recover the autonomy denied by social forces of modernization, often aligned in this way of thinking with feminization. In the 1890s the lament for the close of the frontier loudly voiced such nostalgia for the formative crucible of American manhood; imperial expansion overseas offered a new frontier, where the essential American man could be reconstituted.[7]

Yet if the empire appeals to an antimodern desire to retrieve primitive origins, there is a counterdynamic at work as well. Rather than an untouched wilderness, the empire is represented as the setting where the primal man is staged as a highly theatrical spectacle by deploying the technologies of mass destruction and mass media he fled from at home. He proves his virility not in bloody contest with a native other, but by acting before the eyes of a domestic audience. This double dynamic of recovering the primitive and staging it in a hightech spectacle, of what Elliott Gorn in another context has called "controlled atavism" (224), was epitomized by Theodore Roosevelt, whose foray into the West to recover his health—literally to restore his body—and whose later adventures fighting in Cuba and hunting in Africa were manifestly theatrical. He highlighted his bodily vigor by purchasing custom-made authentic costumes from the tailors of New York, and he relied on the modem technology of photography to publicize his primitive image back home.[8] As his case suggests, the primitive male body proves to be as disembodied as the empire it represents; it becomes a highly constructed simulation. Rather than a bedrock reality underlying the veneer of corporate civilization, the male body becomes a layering of veneers.

The well-known biological metaphor justifying territorial expansion in the nineteenth century compared national growth to an organic body, which must continue to grow or die.[9] But the stable part of this metaphor—the body—was being destabilized in this period as an artfully composed spectacle. Thus the analogy between nationhood and manhood in the 1890s ultimately relies on their spectacular nature rather than their rooted physical organicism. Furthermore, the tension between the disembodied empire and the embodied American man is reproduced within the figure of masculinity itself, between nostalgia for the body and the spectacle of its display.

2
REVIVING THE ROMANCE

"The return to the romance," argued critic and novelist Maurice Thompson, "is simply a young, strong, virile generation pushing aside a flabby one. The little war we had with Spain did not do so much for us; the thing was already done by our schools, churches, gymnasiums, out-door sports; the war acted simply as a faucet through which our vigor began to act" ("Critics" 1920). To the athletic field and battlefield, Thompson added the revival of the historical novel, with its "distinction of large masculine power." Whereas Howells and Canby treated this revival as a collective regression into "the feverish exuberance of an unhealthy child," a view seconded by later critics, Thompson welcomed the historical romances with their "virile ancestry," not as antimodern regression, but as part of a progression suitable to America's new global role, "signs in the air of great world changes." To him, the return to the romance represented a step into the future: "[I]f the map of the world and the atmosphere of civilization are changing radically, a corresponding change in art should not be surprising." The revival of the romance turns a potential rupture with tradition into cultural and political continuity, a return to a healthier, more authentic American past.

The formulaic plot of the romance uncannily parallels the popular narrative of the Spanish-American War as a chivalric rescue mission that in turn rejuvenates the liberator. The historical romance opens with its own lament for the closed frontier, as the hero mopes, discontented with the dwarfed opportunities of his contemporary society. He then seeks adventure on a primitive frontier abroad, where he falls in love with a beautiful aristocratic woman, often the ruler of a kingdom and sometimes a genteel American. The hero, usually a disinherited or "natural" aristocrat, both saves the kingdom from falling to its barbaric enemies and thereby modernizes it and liberates the heroine from outdated class constraints by marrying her. The heroine of the novel, an athletically daring New Woman (often a Gibson girl in the illustrations), actively abets her own liberation by embracing the hero in marriage. At the end, the hero returns home with his bride, after relinquishing political control of the realm he has freed.

This formula is strikingly pliable to radically different settings and eras, from Richard Harding Davis's *Soldiers of Fortune* (1897), in which an American mercenary saves a fictional Latin American dictatorship from revolution and marries an upper-class American girl whose father owns mines there; to Charles Major's *When Knighthood Was in Flower* (1898), in which Brandon wins the heart of Mary Tudor and wrests her away from the power of the monarchy; to George Barr McCutcheon's *Graustark* (1901), set in a mythical medieval kingdom which a footloose American rescues from threatening neighbors to marry its princess; to Mary Johnston's *To Have and To Hold* (1900), in which a colonist of Jamestown, Virginia, saves a female ward of the King from the evil designs of Lord Carnal, while simultaneously defeating the last Indian attack on the colony. These four best-sellers, from which most of my examples are drawn, are characteristic of hundreds of novels which fit into four main categories: (1) the fewest are set in contemporary exotic arenas of the colonized world; (2) many more enact a kind of cultural imperialism by rewriting scenes from European history with identifiable Americanized heroes, from the fall of Rome to nineteenth-century Italy; (3) others similarly insert overt American heroes into the revision of a popular British genre set in mythical kingdoms, based on Stevenson's *Prince Otto* and Anthony Hope's *Prisoner of Zenda*; (4) this short-lived revival culminates in a proliferation of romances about American history, largely revolutionary and colonial, but also including the Civil War and Reconstruction. The modern Western, initiated in Owen Wister's *The Virginian,* I will suggest, finds its immediate genealogy in this genre, which reclaims the American West through the course of overseas empire.[10]

3
THE DISEMBODIED EMPIRE AND THE CLOSED FRONTIER

Not surprisingly, critics have viewed the historical romance primarily as a nostalgic retreat to a simplified past away from contemporary social strife at home and abroad.[11] To call these novels escapist, however, is not to show their avoidance of contemporary political discourse, but their reproduction of it. In the decade before the Spanish-American War, a politics of regulated escape was propounded by advocates of U.S. expansion, who believed that social and psychic pressures attendant upon the close of the frontier and the 1893 depression could be relieved by opening new frontiers abroad. Frederick Jackson Turner concluded his "Problem of the West" by endorsing overseas expansion as an inevitable solution: "For nearly three hundred years the dominant fact in American life has been expansion. With the settlement of the Pacific Coast and the occupation of the free lands, this movement has come to a check. That these energies of expansion will no longer operate would be a rash prediction; and the demands for a vigorous foreign policy, for an oceanic canal, for a revival of our power upon the seas, and for the extension of American influence to outlying islands and adjoining countries, are indications that the movement will continue" (296). Embedded in the discourse of closed space is the rhetoric of surplus energy that describes the overproduction of goods and the oversavings of capital as a physical pressure in need of release. Frank Norris compared this national surplus hemmed in by geographic boundaries to the undirected physical energy of "the boy shut indoors [who] finds his scope circumscribed and fills the whole place with the racket of his activity" (1184). Such destructive excess found outlet historically, according to Norris, only in the pursuit of more distant frontiers, either westward or in the eastern Crusades. The recent war in the Pacific and ensuing response to the Boxer Rebellion in China, he claimed, joined both trajectories in full circle around the globe.

Another ideologue of expansion, the Reverend Josiah Strong, revealed that American anxiety about the closed West may have had global dimensions that express fear of belatedness on the imperial stage, of the absence of those white spaces on the map impelling Marlow in *Heart of Darkness*. Strong warned that "there are no more new worlds. The unoccupied arable lands of the earth are limited and will soon be taken" (213). Yet in contrast to Lenin, who later foresaw international conflict as a result of a world that could only be "divided and subdivided," Strong turned crowded space into empty space, as he proclaimed that the Anglo-Saxon race in its highest form in the U.S. would yet transcend this geographic obstacle and, "to impress its institutions upon mankind, will spread itself over the earth" through its religious, cultural, and economic institutions. According to Strong, an escape for the excess "energy" galvanizing the Anglo-Saxon race was still available into a world infinitely malleable, if geographically limited, to be remade in the image of the United States.

The new historical romance directly addresses this anxiety about a world closed to expansion by remapping the world overcrowded with contesting powers to create new worlds out of old, which offer themselves for the taking. Howells, in fact, compared the novelist to the empire builder: "[I]maginary thrones, principalities and powers in a map of Europe which the novelist changed with more than Napoleonic ease, became the ready, the eager prey of English and American soldiers of fortune" (937). Most of these romances open by announcing the close of the frontier in the temporal form of the hero's lament for the lack of opportunity for past heroic adventure. This lament introduces the second crusade of *Via Crucis,* for example, which, in its commercialism and lack of heroism, seems a pale shadow of the first. This same complaint is directed against the Quaker father of Hugh Wynne, whose commercial bent, timid uprightness, and pacifism suffocate the young man, who welcomes the American Revolution as a return to the heroic valor of his Welsh ancestors. Even a novel set in colonial Jamestown starts with a sense of closed frontier as the hero daydreams of the good old days of Dale's laws, starvation, and bloody Indian battles. The present, by contrast, is hemmed in by peace with the Indians and the threat of domestication, in the form of a boatload of female settlers imported from England for marriage (Johnston, *To Have and To Hold,* ch. 1). If the novels as a genre offer a nostalgic retreat from late nineteenth-century America, they each open by reenacting this retreat, rendering the present of the novel as a closed space, longing for openness in the form of an even more distant virile past.

The most popular American version of this theme, *Graustark*, starts on a train home to the nation's capital from the clearly unromantic West. The upper-class hero, Lorry—bored with his routine life in Washington—has failed to find rejuvenation in a world where duels are outlawed and a stagecoach ride to save the heroine from missing her train devolves into a botched chivalric deed that appears to him as a parody of a dime novel. Only his pursuit of a mysterious Germanic princess reopens the possibilities of adventure foreclosed in the West. One of the first things Lorry learns upon arriving in Graustark, from another footloose American, is that the native men "fought like Sam Patch" (100), that they act like real cowboys on horseback, rather than the self-conscious parody which, as Frank Norris noted, the American West had become.

Part of the criticism of these romances as escapist is that they reflect America's provincial lack of interest in geopolitics (Knight 60–61). The novels, however, often present the same critique, and thus offer themselves as corrective lessons in world geography. Lorry, a world traveler, initially flaunts his ignorance of other lands: "his ideas of geography were jumbled and vague as if he had got them by studying labels on his hat-box" (13). This myopia, however, impedes his pursuit of the mysterious princess, when he tries to follow her to "one of those many infernal little kingdoms and principalities" somewhere east of Paris (91). After he finally locates Graustark on a Baedeker map, he is dismayed yet tantalized to find it "away off to the east," for "one would think barbarians existed there and not such people" as those "refined, cultivated, smart, rich" ones he met on the train (95). But such a duality is precisely the allure of Graustark, which in its medieval setting—complete with castle, tower, and dungeon—turns out to be attractively backward, with swarthy peasants in turbans, riding on horseback and brandishing swords. Yet like Twain's Camelot, Graustark also has the grace of an aristocratic civilization in its "air of antiquity," while its "guys are great on gallantry" (103).

The mythical kingdom of Graustark is typical of the settings of the historical romance, and, as an escape from the geopolitics of the 1890s, reveals the triadic structure shaping America's cognitive map of the world. Graustark has the overcivilized qualities of the European powers with which the U.S. was competing and the barbaric characteristics of the peoples it was trying to save and subdue. The romance conflates and makes exotic the threatening poles in contemporary political rhetoric of old-world "tyranny"—empire—and new-world "anarchy"—revolution—against which the U.S. intervenes and defines itself. In this respect the monarchy of Graustark resembles the republic of Olancho, "one of those little republics down there," in South America, in Richard Harding Davis's *Soldiers of Fortune*. In Olancho a gallant young Englishman dies defending his Spanish lady—the wife of the would-be dictator—against the threat of the Olanchan nationalists. As these noble but pathetic residues of the Spanish and English empires move offstage, the American hero, Clay, a civil engineer and abundantly decorated mercenary, can singlehandedly defeat the revolutionaries. The historical romance thus remaps a new world out of the ruins of a decayed empire and a thwarted revolution, and often merges the two in a single threat, as in the federation of Indian tribes—referred to as a "Southern Empire" in colonial Virginia of *To Have and To Hold*.

To rebuild these ruins, the American hero is offered the antiquated position of dictator or king, a job he laughingly declines, thus signifying the excess rather than absence of power. By marrying the heroine and bringing her home, he asserts a less direct and more complete control over the realm he has liberated. Lorry abandons the throne of Graustark to return to Washington; yet, in a gesture anticipating Woodrow Wilson, he bestows a democratic future on the monarchy by having its ancient noblemen vote to allow the princess to marry him; they conclude that in the absence of a masculine side of the noble family, "why not the bold, progressive, rich American" (396). After similarly declining the dictatorship of Olancho, Clay marries the daughter of the owner of the American mining company who employed him, on whose behalf he preserved the republic. *Soldiers of Fortune* ends on a ship with the hero returning to become a respectable "engineering expert," while he triumphantly points out lights on the distant horizon to his fiancée: "over there is the coast of Africa." In both cases, by refusing direct political power in favor of marriage, the heroes secure an even stronger hold overseas as they return home to the commercial corporate world they seemed to escape in foreign adventures.

Just as American political power is reinforced abroad by being renounced, the American hero can best prove his masculinity outside his national boundaries. The hero of *Soldiers of Fortune* becomes the ideal American man by virtue of his homeless-ness; his sentimental attachment to a home lies with the grave of his filibustering father. He divides the months of the year between his work of construction and de-struction in the outposts of the European empires, as a mercenary and engineer, and his vacation in Vienna, where he goes to imbibe high civilization. When Clay is saluted by an American marine at the end, he says proudly, "I have worn several uniforms since I was a boy, but never that of my own country" (335). It is striking that this representative American never lives there. Yet this absence, this refusal of national dress or place, is supposed to make him more authentically American than the uni-formed marine by rendering his country's qualities universal and self-evident in his own body.

Thus only in the release from geographic bounds can the U.S. secure the borders of its own identity. And this escape to a distant frontier is nostalgic in that it allows the American man to return home by becoming more fully himself. If Olancho and Graustark are escapees, they magically reopen that world which Strong sees closing down, a composite world of old and new, of barbarism and civilization, an "expectant world," in Canby's words, awaiting an influx of American might. Fantasies indeed, these novels enact the desire for infinite expansion without colonial annexation, total control through the abdication of political rule, the disembodiment of national power from geographical boundaries.

4
THE EMBODIED MAN AND THE NEW WOMAN

Masculinity freed of national boundaries at first glance appears a purely corporeal identity, materialized through the immersion in primal violence, as Lears has argued (119–24). The subject-position of the hero in these novels, however, lies at the con-junction of violent demonstrations of brute strength and a chivalric dedication to women, a commitment that sometimes leads to the renunciation of fighting in favor of love. When the hero of *Soldiers of Fortune* rides off with his beloved during a battle, he remarks, "I had forgotten. They have been having a revolution here" (306). He asserts his manliness through this nonchalance toward the male sphere of war, just as he asserts his Americanness by disavowing a uniform. Furthermore, this renunciation enhances his control by rendering the indigenous revolution insignificant background to his declaration of love.

The defeat of revolution, an implicit narrative in most of the novels, is displaced onto the more overt plot of rescue in which the hero saves the heroine from her own

environment. The romance splits the subjects of imperial power into gendered positions by which the heroine plays the part of the good Indian, siding with the forces of
progress, while her male counterparts resist as brutal savages. In fact, the measure of
their barbarism lies in their mistreatment of women. Both the backwardness and the
allure of all of these exotic cultures stem from their worship of women as objects of
chivalric adoration on the one hand, and the women's role as chattel to be married off
for political alliances on the other. The liberator frees the heroine from her outdated
role as item of exchange for a barbaric institution that makes "marriageable women
but commodities in statecraft" (Major 148). The hero undermines the feudal order
and supplants it with his own chivalry by liberating the heroine from this bondage.
He virtually acts out what Theodore Roosevelt claimed in 1910, for example, when
he lectured to Egyptian Moslems about the Christian respect for women as a mark of
superior civilization (Burton 190).

The women who are liberated in these novels have already in a sense saved themselves; by virtue of their love for the hero they have proven themselves ahead of their
time. Cast in the role of the New Woman—independent, self-reliant, and adventur-
ous—they often disguise themselves as men to plot the escape scenes, which the heroes
obediently act out. The heroine of *Richard Carvel* saves the hero from death in a British
prison, by disguising herself as a beggar. Even the heroine of *The Virginian,* a New
England schoolmarm, rescues the self-reliant hero from the wilderness, where he is
left wounded after a fight with Indians. The heroine's strong-willed passion, individualism, and activism show her out of place in her feudal or genteel environment. Mary
Tudor of *Knighthood* is described similarly as a self-willed "girl pitted against a body
of brutal men, two of them rulers of the two greatest nations on earth—rather heavy
odds, for one woman" (137). But Mary does beat the odds and marries Brandon
through her own machinations, with which he passively complies. Yet rather than run
away together to New Spain, as she had planned, her male disguise is exposed, and
this "sweet willful Mary" voluntarily "dropped out of history; a sure token that her
heart was her husband's throne; her soul his empire; her every wish his subject, and
her will, so masterful with others, the meek and lowly servant of her strong but gentle
lord and master" (248). Marriage is described here not simply in the rhetoric of political conquest, as we might expect, but in the language of political collaboration, the
language of desire. Voluntarily chosen by the woman, rather than forcibly imposed,
marriage represents the modem alternative to both empire and revolution.

The New Woman thus becomes a figure for imperial subjects of the "New Empire." The heroines prove their own modernity by at once freeing themselves from
traditional hierarchies and voluntarily subduing themselves to some "real live man,"
just as imperial subjects, like the loyal Olanchan general in *Soldiers of Fortune,* prove
their capacity for their own liberation through their alliance with American power.
The romance heroine plays a role like that described by Frantz Fanon in "Algeria
Unveiled": "In the colonialist program, it was the woman who was given the historic
mission of shaking up the Algerian man" (39). The romance heroines go one step
further in imperialist fantasy; they eclipse and supplant their colonized male counterparts.

In American mythology, this female role replays the Pocahontas myth, which was undergoing a revival in the popular culture of the 1890s.[12] In *To Have and To Hold,* Pocahontas has a constant allusive presence (after her death); her husband, Rolfe, is a companion of the hero, and her brother, a noble savage gracefully embracing his own doom, aids the British settlers in the final destruction of Indian resistance and thus the founding of the colony. In the figures of Pocahontas and the white heroines, these novels represent the female desire to be liberated from feudal and traditional bonds as the desire to be subjugated to modern power. The 1899 Schurman commission in the Philippines noted a similar desire in eroticized terms: "The very thing they yearn for is what of all others our Government will naturally desire to give them" (qtd. in Thompson et al. 117). Such a perfect fit is imagined between conqueror and conquered to erase any trace of conflict. Yet in the novels, this female desire to be liberated contains a potential threat to the man who saves her: "Such a woman as Mary" in *Knighthood* is called "dangerous, except in a state of complete subjection—but she was bound hand and foot in the silken meshes of her own weaving" (248). If these meshes are self—designed, can they be torn at will? That is the lurking threat in this fantasy of imperial collaboration; the position of the hero as chivalric rescuer makes him curiously reliant on maintaining the desire of his female subject.

The heroine, as a composite figure, has at least a double function: she feminizes colonial subjects and masculinizes American women. In the first case, the plot of rescue may shed light on a phenomenon often noted by historians, the abrupt shift in the American image of the Cubans and, to a lesser extent, the Filipinos, from heroic revolutionaries before the U.S. entry into the war against Spain to bedraggled "unmanly" bandits unworthy of their American allies.[13] When gender is taken into account in the narrative of rescue, this shift seems less extreme. Tales abounded in the popular press of outrages perpetrated by the Spanish against Cuban women, as in the alleged strip searches on the *Olivette,* or in the celebrated case of Evangelina Cosio y Cisneros, the "Cuban Joan of Arc," freed by a Hearst correspondent from a Spanish prison (Brown 95–102).

If the entry into the war was viewed as a chivalric rescue, then it is unsurprising that the Cubans and Filipinos could not be represented as men acting with autonomous agency for themselves or that they were viewed by Americans as lacking the "qualities which make for manhood" (qtd. in Pérez 204).[14] Not only did the conditions of guerrilla warfare shatter the image of the heroic soldier Americans expected to find, as historians have argued, but the feminized view of the Cubans as welcoming damsels in distress did not allow the Americans to represent them as subjects acting on their own accord. In a related context, McKinley justified the war against the Filipinos by chastising them for not acquiescing to the role of the rescued: "It is not a good time for the liberator to submit important questions concerning liberty and government to the liberated while they are engaged in shooting down their rescuers" (qtd. in Hilderbrand 44–45). To be liberated according to McKinley, means, as it does in the romances, to submit oneself to being rescued, not to make claims for self-government.

If the heroine is a model imperial subject by virtue of her combined rebellion against tradition and submissiveness to the modern order, she is similarly a model for the New American Woman. Many of the novels position the heroine against a more domestic or genteel counterpart, who, though attractive, is clearly an outdated and unsuitable match for the hero. Yet the "newness" of the heroine is often represented as a return to a more primitive and heroic past, as it is also for the hero. Even Maurice Thompson, who applauded the historical romance as a masculine revival of an older epic mode against the domestic novel, starts *Alice of Old Vincennes* with a prototypical New Woman represented as a type from hardier frontier days. Several novels, such as *Janice Meredith,* open with heroines reading romances illicitly, not to debunk a Bovary-like romanticism, but to fulfill their dreams with even more romantic adventures. The evidence of a female readership may prove Howells correct in his view that just as women were entering the arena of athletics and spectator sports, the romance was claiming the field of imperial adventure for women as readers (936).

The appeal of the historical romance to both female and male readers may suggest a way of reconsidering the representation of gender relations at the turn of the century. Advocates of masculine rejuvenation, such as Roosevelt, are usually seen to respond to the threat of the New Woman by urging a concomitant return of women to their traditional roles as homemakers and childbearers. In "The Strenuous Life" Roosevelt called not only for men to be more manly, but also for women to be more womanly by resuming their allegedly feared and rejected work of motherhood (6). These novels suggest a more complex pattern of recuperation—namely, that women are invited to imagine themselves participating in the adventures of empire as a means of rejecting traditional roles. The novels elicit the desire for liberation from domestic constraints through adventure and athletic activity, even as they channel that desire into the support of imperial conquest. By concluding with marriage, these works suggest that the home too can be recuperated by the empire, which channels women's dissent by reaffiliating them with their male counterparts. Roosevelt and his peers may have wished to send the New Woman straight home to bear more Anglo-Saxon children, but the romance offers a more circuitous—and perhaps more efficacious—route, via the course of overseas empire.

5

THE SPECTACLE OF MASCULINITY

In the chivalric rescue narrative, the hero must violently subdue a barbaric oppressor, whether treacherous Indians, British loyalists, Eastern Cossacks, or Latin American revolutionaries. Violence in the romance, however, is always framed by the theatrical display of the hero in conspicuously staged scenes, where the heroine serves as the chief spectator. On this fictional new frontier, physical rejuvenation does not emerge from bloody contests with a native other; the novels instead offer regeneration through a spectacle before the female gaze. This performance engineers the final defeat of the native insurgent by effacing his contesting agency.

Most violent acts in the novels are self-consciously performed for a female audience. The opening duel of *Knighthood,* the last act of violence in the book, focuses less on purgative bloodletting than on Mary's lovestruck stare. Even the climactic battle against the infidels in the remote Holy Land of *Via Crucis* takes place in front of female crusaders, whose queen declares to her knight in the midst of the fray, "Oh what a man You are! What a man" (363). Both cases relegate conflict with an enemy to a backdrop for the woman's act of witness, one that validates the hero's virility.

In some cases, the spectacle of masculinity preempts and displaces the necessity to engage directly in violence. Although Lorry leaves Washington exhausted and neurasthenic, he arrives with his friend in Graustark magically transformed into "two handsome, smooth-faced young Americans [who] were as men from another world, so utterly unlike their companions were they in personal appearance. They were taller, broader, and more powerfully built than the swarthy-faced men about them, and it was no wonder that the women allowed admiration to show in their eyes. . . . The two strangers were over six feet tall, broad-shouldered and athletic. They looked like giants among these Graustark men" (106–07). Without any physical exertion, the American men automatically recover their primal virility in a relation of difference, in contrast to the native men around them. This difference, however, is realized not through conflict with those men, but through the observation of the native women "who were eyeing them and commenting quite freely." At the end of the novel, Lorry luckily avoids a climactic duel (the one he was disappointed not to find out West), as his barbaric enemies conveniently plunge knives into one another. But he still saves the kingdom by unveiling the plots of conspiracies and declaring his love in a verbal pageant before a packed court.[15]

The theatrical quality of primitive nostalgia permeated other areas of contemporary physical culture as well. Thorstein Veblen in the chapter on "Modem Survivals of Prowess" in his *Theory of the Leisure Class* describes (quite sardonically) not just the atavistic qualities of sportsmanship, but also its marked histrionic appeal, the extravagant gestures of the white man hunting in his return to a wilderness, where make-believe and performance before a real or imagined audience become the focal point, rather than the kill itself. Theatricalized chivalry was in fact advocated by G. Stanley Hall, a psychologist and educator, in his book *Youth*. For him, one of the most important elements of athletics for adolescents is the attention of female spectators: "The presence of the fair sex gives tonicity to youth's muscles and tension to his arteries to a degree of which he is rarely conscious" (103). The youth exerts himself physically through contest with his peers in response to a teenage girl, "who performs her best service in the true role of sympathetic spectator rather than as fellow player" (104). The female spectator unleashes the brute in the man yet holds him in check. In the immensely popular novel *Ben-Hur*, dramatized on stage and in lavish outdoor spectacles, Ben Hur's beloved also figures as the audience for whom primitive violence is performed. She resists turning away from the chariot fight when she realizes: "An idea of joy there is in doing an heroic deed under the eyes of a multitude came to her, and she understood ever after how, at such times, the souls of men, in the frenzy of performance, laugh at death or forget it utterly" (359). The performative quality—rather than immersion in primitive violence—saves the actor from the fear of death, and redeems his masculinity, and the mass audience before whom he performs is represented by the female spectator.

The athletic arena, in which Veblen, Hall, and Wallace view the spectacle of masculinity, was often interchangeable with the imperial battlefield in contemporary discourse. "Jingoism is merely the lust of the spectator," wrote J. A. Hobson, journalist and theorist of imperialism, who also compared the emotions of the spectator aroused at a sporting event to those of the jingoist (215). The historical novel appeals to what Hobson calls "spectatorial lust" by positioning women in the role of the jingoist. When they are not actively rescuing the hero, they are more often watching him fight or perform. By turning women into spectators, the romance posits an additional collaborative relation with women in the constitution of masculinity and the establishment of empire. Moreover, if the heroine/spectator is a figure for the female reader, she suggests a redefinition of domesticity in relation to imperialism, not as a retreat from public space, but as a window or lens focused on masculine exploits abroad.[16] Furthermore, the presence of domestic viewers in the romance links these mass-marketed best-sellers to the strategic role of the mass-circulation newspapers in the culture of imperialism. By circulating imperial adventures into the American home, the novels incorporate domestic space into that imperial network, and work with the press, which, according to Strong, "transforms the earth into an audience room" (117).

In addition, these novels enact not just the lust of the spectator but the lust *for* a spectator, as described by Stephen Crane, a journalist, like Hobson, of turn-of-the-century imperial warfare. "When they go away to the fighting-ground," he wrote, "out of the sight, out of the hearing of the world known to them and are eager to perform feats of war in this new place they feel an absolute longing for a spectator. . . . None wanted to conceal from his left hand that his right hand was performing a manly and valiant thing" (171–72). The reference to hands splits the fighting male subject in two—the actor and spectator, who takes the form of the journalist, as panderer in the arousal of spectatorial lust: "The war correspondent arises, then, to become a sort of cheap telescope for the people at home; further still, there have been fights where the eyes of a solitary man were the eyes of the world; one spectator whose business it was to transfer, according to his ability, his visual impressions to other minds" (172). The focus of this passage shifts from the soldier and his enemy on the battlefield to the audience at home. While manliness is performed against the backdrop of remote frontiers, this spectacle does not fully materialize until it is broadcast by the media to a domestic audience.

This "absolute longing for a spectator" is dramatized in *Soldiers of Fortune,* during the full-scale battle against the revolutionaries which takes place significantly in the national theater. There a young American college boy's first experience of war reveals the importance of spectatorship on the battlefield. Although he first approaches the battle as an amusing collegiate football game, when he finds himself out front, "he felt neglected and very much alone. . . . [I]t struck him as being most absurd that strangers should stand up and try to kill one another, men who had so little in common that they did not even know one another's names. The soldiers who were fighting on his own side were equally unknown to him" (326). Rather than release the buried "predatory Viking" in the heat of the battle, his dislocation and loss of identity is mirrored in the anonymity of the soldiers on both sides. When the American enters the thick of fire, he is described as "continually winking and dodging, as though he were being taken by a flash-light photograph" (327). The fantasy of turning gunfire into the flash of a photograph recuperates his masculine identity, which is threatened by the violently inscrutable political affiliations of the imperial battlefield. Like Hall's adolescent athlete, whose muscles are made real by the gaze of his girlfriend, this soldier's sensation of being "shot" in a photograph recomposes a reassuring position as a fighting subject, which the presence of natives challenges.

This heightened dependence of the imperial adventurer on his domestic audience—the jingo—both enables and undercuts the image of the self-reliant white man alone in the wilderness by divorcing and sheltering him from the context in which he is fighting. Hobson notes a blindness paradoxically in the jingo as spectator, who gloats "over the perils, pains, and slaughter of fellow-men whom he does not know, but whose destruction he desires in a blind and artificially stimulated passion of hatred and revenge. In the Jingo all is concentrated on the hazard and blind fury of the fray" (215). Hobson's repetition of the word "blind" emphasizes (albeit in a romanticized view of fighting) that "respect for the personality of the enemies whose courage he must admit and whom he comes to realize as fellow-beings" is eliminated. Thus "spectatorial lust" effaces the agency of the enemy in battle by reorienting the terms of the conflict from the political struggle on the imperial battlefield to the relation between the colonizing soldier and his domestic audience.

The spotlight on the spectacle of American masculinity triangulated with the reporter and the domestic audience denies the existence of political resistance to imperialism, even in the act of war against those resistors. An oft-heard complaint in newspapers about the battlefields of Cuba and the Philippines was the invisibility of indigenous soldiers—both allies and enemies—who were literally hidden from view, by their "unconventional" guerrilla tactics. This invisibility also had to be produced ideologically, to deny Cubans and Filipinos representation as equal contestants in political struggle. The romance suggests that the spectacle of American masculinity in the gaze of the female spectator contributes to the disembodiment of the colonized soldier, by denying him political agency and by extension masculinity. His invisibility is also produced paradoxically by incorporating him as actor into the spectacle of combat.

The theatricalization of the chivalric warrior in these romantic novels was in some sense literally enacted on the battlefields of Cuba and the Philippines. In a scene that marked the end of the battle with Spain for Manila and the beginning of the three-year war against the Filipinos, the Americans faced a dilemma of how to enter the city, not in regard to combat strategy with Spain, whom they had already virtually defeated at sea, but in how to occupy Manila in a way that would allow them not to share the fruits of their victory with Aguinaldo's forces who had been battling the Spanish for years and who joined with the Americans in expectation of independence. So the American officer in command arranged secretly with the Spanish government of Manila to stage a mock battle, complete with the raising of the white flag (to be postponed in case of bad weather), in which the Spanish would surrender and the Americans would march into the city unaccompanied by their Filipino allies. As a military essayist explained, "our reason for this elaborate stage management seems obvious. It would keep the insurgents out of the city" (Millis 357). The Americans and Spanish colluded (as they did in the entry to Santiago, Cuba) in a theater of conquest and capitulation to exclude the Filipinos. Here the theatricalization of American power had an obvious intended effect of rendering colonized agency ineffectual. Yet an ironic consequence is that several Filipino troops mistook the theater for a real battle, and their shots generated rounds of shooting on both sides that gave unexpected reality to the "Battle of Manila." No wonder then that a reporter noted with surprise that the Filipino insurgents got their parts wrong, that they threw up trenches opposite the American outposts and "acted as if they were besieging us instead of being our 'friends' " (qtd. in Brown 427).

The historical romance makes overt the desire for unlimited control underlying such scenes of staged conquests, which are disrupted by the actions of imperial subjects who do not voluntarily adopt their allotted roles. The novels enact the American fantasy of global conquest without colonial annexation, what Albert Memmi called the ultimate imperial desire for a colony rid of the colonized (66). This disembodied empire projects imperial conflict as the dramatization of the male self before a domestic audience without a threatening contesting other. It strives to imagine conquest by effacing any element of conflict.

If the spectacle of American manhood has the political import of denying national agency to the conquered, this repression, however, can never be complete, for the theater itself is open to contest, to improvisation, as it was in Manila. Homi Bhabha has attributed a quality of mimicry to the colonized subject, which both subordinates him to imitation of his conquerors, yet yields a space for maneuver and mockery to subvert that identity. In the Battle of Manila, the Filipinos indeed mimicked their assigned theatrical roles by playing them for real. The imperialist agent, however, also engages in a form of mimicry in which he does not retrieve an embodied primal self, but assumes shifting theatrical roles which undermine his own agency. His need to turn gunfire into flashing camera lights fixes, destabilizes, and resocializes the identity of the "real live man," by making him contingent on the willing collaboration of the native actor playing a supporting role, and of the domestic spectator validating his image. With the close of the Western frontier, American masculinity turns to the "New Empire" to recuperate its Anglo-Saxon origins. But this same arena threatens that identity and retrieves the embodied male not in the longed-for primitive wholeness, but through fragmented spectacles in the gaze of the domestic audience. We only have to think of Theodore Roosevelt on San Juan Hill or Oliver North, today, to re-view them not as embodiments of primal white American manhood, but as highly theatrical and contingent spectacles produced by modern weapons and mass media, both more effective and more vulnerable for that dependence on the technologies they are meant to escape.[17]

6

BACK TO THE FUTURE

The spectacle's effacement of imperial subjects in the 1890s meant more specifically the denial of their revolutionary agency and national aspirations. The U.S. belatedly entered the international imperial arena on a double front: against the competition of European empire building, and equally opposed to the revolutionary anticolonial nationalist struggles in Latin America, the Pacific, and China. The revival of the romance registers this complex historical moment by culminating in a proliferation of novels about the American Revolution, which revive the notion of the anticolonial origins of the republic as the birth of future empire. Furthermore, they redefine and delimit the meaning of revolution to make it inaccessible to others. The historical romances of the 1890s "de-revolutionize" the revolution, in Michael Kammen's terms, not only to mitigate social conflict at home, as he argues, but also to repossess and neutralize the symbols of the American Revolution that served as a usable past for contemporary revolutions abroad (211; also chaps. 5 and 6).

Before the Spanish-American War, one of the major rhetorical figures deployed by Americans and Cubans in the U.S. to enlist support of the uprising against Spain was the analogy of the War of Independence. The Cuba Libre movement was legitimated as a reenactment of the American Revolution, as its general, Máximo Gomez, was compared to Washington, and its diplomat, Tomás Estrada Palma, to Ben Franklin. In the words of Congressman Sulzer, "Why they are just like us!" in emulating our revolution (qtd. in Pérez 197–99). In the immediate reaffiliations during and following the war, this analogy was rapidly dismantled in America, where it became more pressing to emphasize difference, that "they," unlike "us," were incapable of self-government to which revolution aspires. After the war, only anti-imperialists compared Aguinaldo of the Philippines to George Washington, a trope tantamount to treason in its betrayal of the American past, according to imperialists such as Senator Beveridge. Thus if the historical novels addressed an internal crisis of "cultural indirection" and social conflict, as Kammen argues, they also entered a contested terrain in international political culture, to dispossess others of the language of revolutionary aspirations.

A major tool in this struggle of dispossession was the representation of race (see Seaton). While politicians ridiculed the notion of a black or brown George Washington, the novel whitewashed the Revolution as an indisputably Anglo-Saxon heritage in novels by Winston Churchill and S. Weir Mitchell, Washington makes cameo appearances as the epitome of natural aristocracy and virility (demonstrated in one novel through his beating of a black slave out of spontaneous passion and anger).

Yet more effective a weapon than the direct representation of race in these novels is the nostalgic narrative of revolution as return to a fundamental Anglo-Saxon past. Revolution is recast as devolution, a recovery of origins in the figure of the masculine hero rather than a radical break with the past. These romances revile the British less for their tyrannical government than their degenerate profligacy, and the few glimpses of alternative political struggles—such as the Indian rebellion in *To Have and To Hold,* or nationalist revolution in *Soldiers of Fortune*—are always conflated with the degeneracy of the British or Spanish empires. The incipient Americans are represented as simply restoring a purer Anglo-Saxon family strain.

The culmination of the American Revolution in some novels results in the restoration of an inheritance, in *Richard Carvel,* for example, the hero retrieves his father's estate in Maryland. In *Hugh Wynne,* however, the problematic ownership of the ancestral estate in Wales—with which the novel opens—is never resolved; the question of land is made secondary to the recovery of manhood—Hugh Wynne's true heritage— from his commercial and pacifist Quaker father and degenerate British cousin. The Revolution as recovered heritage thus is at once divorced from European notions of landed inheritance and invested in the American man as the natural aristocrat. Revolution, in these novels, thus becomes a uniquely American heritage lodged firmly in the past, safe from the grasp of minorities and immigrants at home and anticolonial nationalists abroad.

If the historical romance rewrites the American Revolution through the lens of nostalgia for primitive origins, its recuperative potential is most fully realized in the figure of the Western cowboy. In his essay "The Evolution of the Cow-Puncher," Owen Wister portrays this quintessential American male as the atavistic reawakening of "slumbering untamed Saxon." Contrary to his title, Wister traces no evolution but instead a return to an essential identity, as "the knight and the cowboy are nothing but the same Saxon of different environments" (81). In this essay, originally entitled "The Course of Empire," Wister draws a continuous line not only between the knight and the cowboy, but between the West, now on the decline, and dawning American interests in the Pacific. Wister finds the same kernel of the Saxon man, who "has ruled the waves with his ship from that Viking time until yesterday at Samoa . . . from the tournament at Camelot to the round-up at Abilene" (81). When Wister writes *The Virginian* seven years later, the hero's lineage is already in place.

The modern Western—initiated by *The Virginian* in 1902—has an immediate genealogy in the popular historical novels of the 1890s and their romance of empire. By imagining contemporary American imperialism as the return to an original virile past, the historical romance reopens the closed frontier and reinvents the West as a space for fictional representation. Wister in his introduction explicitly labels his novel a "colonial romance," compares it to *Hugh Wynne,* and introduces it as a more realistic colonial romance than the frillier ones with "Chippendale Settees" (ix). Moreover, *The Virginian* recapitulates each feature of the romance delineated in this essay, easily substituting the Wyoming frontier for the mythical Graustark, the Latin American Olancho, or the Holy Land of the Crusaders. Wister's romance opens with its own nostalgia for the closed frontier, a "vanished world," where the Eastern narrator seeks physical rejuvenation. There the homeless and nameless Virginian embodies the national essence in his muscular beauty and animal prowess. Yet as Lee Mitchell has pointed out, this hero does not engage in the sharpshooting violence we have come to expect from the genre. Rather, he defeats a rebellion in a staged theatrical performance before an Eastern audience of travelers, and his physical vigor is composed in the narrator's feminized gaze.

The Virginian also asserts his virility through his chivalric attention to Molly, the genteel Vermont schoolteacher, who, like the other heroines, proves herself both as spectator and actor, rescuing the hero from Indians. In choosing the Virginian for a mate, she liberates herself from the traditional bonds of marrying to save her family financially, and she thereby proves herself worthy of her own more ancient revolutionary heritage. Her older aunt explains knowingly the heroine's attraction to the American hero, defining him tautologically, as does Senator Beveridge: "She wants a man that is a man" (163). The Western neither banishes woman from a rugged male terrain

(Tompkins) nor simply tames her (Mitchell); it co-opts her desires and includes her in its pleasures of romancing the empire.

If the historical romance starts with a nostalgic lament for the closed frontier, the revival of the genre collectively reopens that space of the West. Soon after the publication of *The Virginian,* the revival was on the wane, though not without injecting life into the modern Western. We are accustomed to think of the ways in which the Western frontier was violently exported to the "New Empire" in the Spanish-American War (and in later imperial wars of the twentieth century), in the form of soldiers—many of whom were veterans of Indian wars; social policy—the resettlement of native Filipinos according to the plans of Indian reservations; and vibrant symbols—Roosevelt's Rough Riders. Just as important, however, has been the way in which American imperialism reclaimed and galvanized the meaning of the West as the site of origins. The quintessential twentieth-century symbol of American nationhood—the lone self-reliant cowboy on the frontier—has endured parasitically by feeding on new outposts of the American empire. As the precursor of the modem Western, the historical novel of the 1890s romances the empire with a potent nostalgia that renders imperial conquest and the struggle for power over others as nothing more than the return home to the embodied American man.

Notes

The author would like to thank colleagues at Columbia, Dartmouth, Rutgers, and the University of Massachusetts, Amherst, for their thoughtful responses to an earlier version of this essay, and Ben Anderson, Dick Burt, Ann Fabian, Brook Thomas, Gauri Viswanathan, and Donald Weber for their helpful readings. The essay was originally published in *American Literary History* 2.4 (Winter 1990): 659–90. The editors of this anthology would like to thank Oxford University Press for permission to reprint.

1. Many novelists identified as naturalists and realists also wrote historical romances; e.g., Edith Wharton, *The Valley of Decision;* Sarah Orne Jewett, *The Tory Lover;* Frank Norris, *Yvernelle;* Booth Tarkington, *Monsieur Beaucaire;* and of course Twain's parodic romance, *A Connecticut Yankee in King Arthur's Court,* and his more romantic *Joan of Arc.* Stephen Crane at his death was contemplating a conventional historical romance about the American Revolution. A literary history of interpenetrating genres remains to be written.

2. This approach is almost too commonplace to document. For an influential formulation, see Hofstadter. The chapter in Higham includes imperialist adventure as one more form of antimodern muscularity. This is a good example of an influential cultural history that relegates imperialism to the margins, as does Lears. I argue against his view of the support for imperialism as an inadvertent consequence of the chivalric revival. For a recent rebuttal of the approach to American imperialism as antimodern nostalgia instead of modem rationalized force, see Axeen.

3. On masculinity and westward expansion see Rogin, *Fathers and Children;* Slotkin, *Regeneration Through Violence* and *The Fatal Environment;* Drinnon; and Takaki. All four analyses work within a common framework based on a model of repression that joins its political and psychoanalytical meaning. In these accounts white masculinity is constituted by denying its threatening features and projecting its "primitive" desires onto the colonized "others" who are conquered, and destroyed, in the process of expansion. Drinnon and Takaki extend their analysis

from westward to overseas expansion at the turn of the century and find the same dynamics at work in the later period.

4. The notion of an "informal empire" based on economic rather than territorial expansion has been propounded most thoroughly by Williams and LaFeber.

5. On the shift in the meaning of masculinity see Kett, Dubbert, Rotundo, and Gorn.

6. On the meaning of this term, see Hobsbawm and Ranger, chap. 1, and on the late nineteenth-century context in which the historical romance takes its place, see chap. 7.

7. The popular romance draws on a long tradition of this form of nostalgia in British and American literature from Prospero recuperating his authority while marooned on an island, to Robinson Crusoe acquiring his island estate, to Twain's mechanic in *Connecticut Yankee* becoming "Boss" of King Arthur's England, to Kurtz regressing to an atavistic horror in *Heart of Darkness*. In Rosaldo's account of his own first encounter with the Ilongots, the subject of his field work, he comments self-critically that he represented them in his journal as Hollywood Apaches in the Wild West. Yet he does not note that this nostalgia—even if ironic—was as much for reliving an American past, as for recovering the vanishing primitive. Like Theodore Roosevelt and his Rough Riders in Cuba, the contemporary anthropologist in the Philippines, by longing for the passing "other," can reimagine *himself* as primitive—a cowboy—mediated through the lens of mass media.

8. On Roosevelt's theatricality see Black, 3–5. This relation between nostalgia and spectacle links other case studies of the period and merits study as a general cultural phenomenon: Nash's influential study of the "Wilderness Cult" centers on an example of an individual survival in the wilderness staged as a media event; Rosenberg has shown that Buffalo Bill's international Wild West shows exported nostalgic values through technologically sophisticated productions (35–37); and Haraway has shown how the restoration of a vanishing Africa in the Museum of Natural History and of the great white hunter as a figure in that landscape was produced by the technologies of the gun and the camera.

9. For different national formulations of this analogy see, for example, Kern 224–40.

10. In addition to these four novels, I draw on a number of novels chosen, for the most part, from the best-seller lists reconstructed by Packett and by Mott. Additional sources can be found in Hart, chaps. 11 and 12, and Knight 14–20, 61–65. This list is representative and by no means exhaustive, not only because it excludes nonAmerican authors (the popular *Quo Vadis,* for example, by a Polish author, typifies the genre) nor because of the great numbers of such romances, but because this genre overlaps with so many others: regionalism, the Southern plantation romance, the costume romance, the adventure tale. The fewest examples of the first category, the exotic contemporary romance, occur in this period, a sparsity that needs consideration: Davis's *The King's Jackal* (1899) and his story "The Reporter Who Would be King." By the 1910s, however, many popular adventure tales (and movies) were set in imperial arenas, like the Tarzan tales and Frank Merriwell novels. In the second category are Lew Wallace, *Ben-Hur* (18 80), *The Prince of India* (1893); Francis Marion Crawford, *Via Crucis* (1898); S. Weir Mitchell, *The Adventures of François* (1898); Booth Tarkington, *Monsieur Beaucaire* (1899); Bertha Runkle, *The Helmet of Navarre* (1901). In the third are Davis, *Princess Aline* (1895); Harold McGrath, *Arms and the Woman* (1897) and *The Puppet Crown* (1900); McCutcheon, *Beverly of Graustark* (1904); Gertrude Atherton, *Rulers of Kings* (1904). In the last category are Mitchell, *Hugh Wynne: Free Quaker* (1898); Paul Leicester Ford, *Janice Meredith* (1899); Winston Churchill, *Richard Carvel* (1898); Maurice Thompson, *Alice of Old Vincennes* (1900). These novels will be cited parenthetically in the text.

11. As Howells put it, "the tarraddidles of the historical romancers" offered "a relief from the facts of the odious present" (936). See also Hart, Knight, Mott. The revival of Scott and of the martial ideal at large have been analyzed more acutely by Lears, as part of the patrician

rebellion against the routinization and weightlessness of bourgeois commercial life, a search for a primal authenticity by immersing the self in violence (Lears, chap. 3). Lears's antimodern argument, however, fits into a familiar paradigm of escape and nostalgia.

12. On the revival of Pocahontas as a national founding figure, see Banta 492–94. Pocahontas can also be found in Atherton's *Rulers of Kings,* as the name of the American hero's canoe; the name represents his early sentimental attachment to a maternal native wilderness, which he leaves to become ruler of Europe.

13. See Pérez, chaps. 10 and 11, and Linderman, chap. 5.

14. For a brief view of this image of Latinos in general as feminized and light skinned, see Hunt 58–62.

15. An important narrative inflection of this theatricality can be found in *Hugh Wynne.* Writing in the first person as a legacy for his heirs, the hero of the title quotes from his best friend's journal whenever he writes of his own duels or other belligerent acts, so that he can be seen by another in these poses. And this friend, uncommonly handsome, gentle, and unwarrior-like, is referred to throughout the novel as a "girl-boy." Here too masculine feats are given substance by the observation of a feminized figure, rather than narrated as an act of conflict.

16. The role of the woman as spectator has not yet been studied, I believe, in recent accounts of the representation of women and modern warfare, from which they most often are rendered separate—as beneficiaries of more freedom at home, victims of aggressive fantasies, or emblems of patriotic nationalism. See Gilbert 197–226, and Banta, chap. 12. Jeffords has powerfully analyzed the construction of the male body as spectacle in representations of Vietnam. Since she argues that these representations exclude women, blame them, or appropriate their powers, she does not consider their potential role as spectator or collaborator (ch. 1).

17. For a wide-ranging article on spectacle and the post-World War Two American empire, see Rogin, " 'Make My Day!' " Unfortunately this essay was published too recently for me to take account of its insights. It does confirm my sense that the spectacle has as much to hide—in its historical amnesia—as to display.

Works Cited

Axeen, David. " 'Heroes of the Engine Room': American 'Civilization' and the War with Spain." *American Quarterly* 36 (1984): 481–502.

Banta, Martha. *Imaging American Women.* New York: Columbia UP, 1987.

Bhabha, Homi. "Of Mimicry and Man: The Ambivalence of Colonial Discourse." *October* 28 (1984): 125–38.

Black, George. *The Good Neighbor: How the United States Wrote the History of Central America and the Caribbean.* New York: Pantheon, 1988.

Brown, Charles. *The Correspondents' War: Journalists in the Spanish-American War.* New York: Scribner's, 1967.

Burton, David H. *Theodore Roosevelt: Confident Imperialist.* Philadelphia: U of Pennsylvania P, 1969.

Canby, Henry Seidel. *The Age of Confidence: Life in the Nineties.* New York: Farrar, 1934.

Crane, Stephen. *The Third Violet and Active Service.* Ed. Fredson Bowers. Charlottesville: U of Virginia P, 1976.

Crawford, Francis Marion. *Via Crucis.* New York: American News, 1899.

Davis, Richard Harding. *Soldiers of Fortune.* 1897. New York: Scribner's, 1928.

Drinnon, Richard. *Facing West: The Metaphysics of Indian-Hating and Empire-Building.* New York: NAL, 1980.

Dubbert, Joe. *A Man's Place: Masculinity in Transition*. Englewood Cliffs, NJ: Prentice, 1979.

Fanon, Frantz. "Algeria Unveiled." *A Dying Colonialism*. New York: Grove, 1965. 35–67.

Giddings, Franklin Henry. *Democracy and Empire*. New York: Macmillan, 1900.

Gilbert, Sandra. "Soldier's Heart: Literary Men, Literary Women, and the Great War." *Behind the Lines: Gender and the Two World Wars*. Ed. Margaret Randolph Higgonet et al. New Haven: Yale UP, 1987. 197–226.

Gorn, Elliott. *The Manly Art: Bare Knuckle Prize Fighting in America*. Ithaca: Cornell UP, 1986.

Hall, G. Stanley. *Youth: Its Education, Regimen, and Hygiene*. New York: Appleton, 1906.

Haraway, Donna. "Teddy Bear Patriarchy: Taxidermy in the Garden of Eden, New York City, 1908–1936." *Social Text 11* (1984–85):20–64.

Hart, James D. *The Popular Book: A History of America's Literary Taste*. New York: Oxford UP, 1950.

Higham, John. "The Reorientation of American Culture in the 1890s." *Writing American History: Essays on Modern Scholarship*. Bloomington: U of Indiana P, 1973. 73–100.

Hilderbrand, Robert C. *Power and the People: Executive Management of Public Opinion in Foreign Affairs, 1897–1921*. Chapel Hill: U of North Carolina P, 1981.

Hobsbawm, Eric, and Terence Ranger, eds. *The Invention of Tradition*. Cambridge: Cambridge UP, 1983.

Hobson, J. A. *Imperialism: A Study*. 1902. Ann Arbor: U of Michigan P, 1972.

Hofstadter, Richard. "Manifest Destiny and the Philippines." *America in Crisis: Fourteen Crucial Episodes in American History*. Ed. Daniel Aaron. New York: Knopf, 1952. 173–200.

Howells, William Dean. "The New Historical Romances." *North American Review* Dec. 1900: 935–48.

Hunt, Michael. *Ideology and U. S. Foreign Policy*. New Haven: Yale UP, 1987.

Jeffords, Susan. *The Remasculinization of America: Gender and the Vietnam War*. Bloomington: Indiana UP, 1989.

Jehlen, Myra. *American Incarnation: The Individual, the Nation, and the Continent*. Cambridge: Harvard UP, 1986.

Johnston, Mary. *To Have and To Hold*. Boston: Houghton, 1900.

Kammen, Michael. *A Season of Youth: The American Revolution and the Historical Imagination*. New York: Knopf, 1978.

Kern, Stephen. *The Culture of Time and Space: 1880–1918*. Cambridge: Harvard UP, 1983.

Kett, Joseph. *Rites of Passage: Adolescence in America, 1790 to the Present*. New York: Basic, 1977.

Knight, Grant C. *The Strenuous Age in American Literature*. Chapel Hill: U of North Carolina P, 1954.

LaFeber, Walter. *The New Empire: An Interpretation of American Expansion, 1860–1898*. Ithaca: Cornell UP, 1963.

Lears, T. J. Jackson. "The Destructive Element: Modern Commercial Society and the Martial Ideal." *No Place of Grace: Antimodernism and the Transformation of American Culture, 1880–1920*. New York: Pantheon, 1981. 97–139.

Linderman, Gerald. *The Mirror of War: American Society and the Spanish-American War*. Ann Arbor: U of Michigan P, 1974.

McCutcheon, George Barr. *Graustark*. New York: Grosset-Dunlap, 1901.

Major, Charles. *When Knighthood Was in Flower*. Indianapolis: Bowen-Merril, 1898.

Memmi, Albert. *The Colonizer and the Colonized*. Boston: Beacon, 1965.

Millis, Walter. *The Martial Spirit*. Boston: Houghton, 1931.

Mitchell, Lee Clark. " 'When you call me that . . .': Tall Talk and Male Hegemony in *The Virginian*." *PMLA* 102 (1987): 66–77.

Mott, Frank Luther. *Golden Multitudes: The Story of Best Sellers in the United States*. New York: Macmillan, 1947.

Nash, Roderick. "Wilderness Cult." *Wilderness and the American Mind*. New Haven: Yale UP, 1982. 141–60.

Norris, Frank. "The Frontier Gone at Last." 1902. *Frank Norris: Novels and Essays*. New York: Library of America, 1986. 1183–90.

Packett, Alice Payne. *Seventy Years of Best Sellers, 1895–1965*. New York: Bowker, 1967.

Paterson, Thomas G., ed. "Senator Albert J. Beveridge's Salute to Imperialism, 1900." *Major Problems in American Foreign Policy: Documents and Essays. Vol. 1*. Lexington, MA: Heath, 1989. 389–91. 2 vols.

Pérez, Louis A. *Cuba Between Empires, 1878–1902*. Pittsburgh: U of Pittsburgh P, 1983.

Rogin, Michael. *Fathers and Children: Andrew Jackson and the Subjugation of the American Indian*. New York: Random, 1975.

——. " 'Make My Day!': Spectacle as Amnesia in Imperial Politics." *Representations* 29 (1990): 99–123.

Roosevelt, Theodore. "The Strenuous Life." *The Strenuous Life: Essays and Addresses*. New York: Scribner's, 1906. 3–22.

Rosaldo, Renato. "Imperialist Nostalgia." *Representations* 26 (1989): 107–22.

Rosenberg, Emily. *Spreading the American Dream: American Economic and Cultural Expansion, 1890–1945*. New York: Hill, 1982.

Rotundo, Edward Anthony. "Body and Soul: Changing Ideals of American Middle-Class Manhood, 1770–1920." *Journal of Social History* 16 (1983): 28–33.

Said, Edward. *"Kim*, The Pleasures of Imperialism." *Raritan* 8 (1987): 27–64.

Scarry, Elaine. "The Structure of War: The Juxtaposition of Injured Bodies and Unanchored Issues." *The Body in Pain: The Making and Unmaking of the World*. New York: Oxford UP, 1985. 60–157.

Seaton, Beverly. "A Pedigree for a New Century: The Colonial Experience in Popular Historical Novels, 1890–1910." *The Colonial Revival in America*. Ed. Alan Axelrod. New York: Norton, 1985. 278–93.

Slotkin, Richard. *The Fatal Environment: The Myth of the Frontier in the Age of Industrialization, 1800–1890*. New York: Atheneum, 1985.

——. *Regeneration Through Violence: The Mythology of the American Frontier, 1600–1860*. Middletown, CT: Wesleyan UP, 1973.

Strong, Josiah. *Our Country*. 1886. Cambridge: Harvard UP, 1963.

Takaki, Ronald. *Iron Cages: Race and Culture in Nineteenth-Century America*. New York: Knopf, 1979.

Thompson, James, et al. *Sentimental Imperialists: The American Experience in East Asia*. New York: Harper, 1981.

Thompson, Maurice. "The Critics and the Romancers." *Independent* 9 Aug. 1900: 1919–21.

——. "Vigorous Men, a Vigorous Nation." *Independent* 1 Sept. 1898: 609–11.

Tompkins, Jane. "West of Everything." *South Atlantic Quarterly* 86 (1987): 357–78.

Turner, Frederick Jackson. "The Problem of the West." *Atlantic Monthly* Sept. 1896: 289–97.

Veblen, Thorstein. "Modern Survivals of Prowess." *Theory of the Leisure Class*. 1899. New York: Penguin, 1981. 246–75.

Wallace, Lew. *Ben-Hur: A Tale of the Christ*. New York: Harper, 1880.

Williams, William Appleman. "The Age of Corporate Capitalism." *The Contours of American History*. Chicago: Quadrangle, 1966. 343–478.

Wister, Owen. "The Evolution of he Cow-Puncher." *My Dear Wister: The Frederick Remington—Owen Wister Letters*. Ed. Ben Merchant Vorpahl. Palo Alto: American West, 1973. 77–96.

——. *The Virginian*. 1902. New York: NAL, 1979.

Ziff, Larzer. *The American 1890s*. Lincoln: U of Nebraska P, 1966.

NEITHER FISH, FLESH, NOR FOWL
Race and Region in the Writings of Charles W. Chesnutt
Anne Fleischmann

The Supreme Court's decision in the 1896 *Plessy v. Ferguson* case is notorious for having sewn racial segregation into the fabric of American society. One of the decision's less obvious results was that it gave official sanction to the "one-drop" rule. That is, the *Plessy* ruling held that individual states could decide whether and how to classify citizens by race, and states which were so inclined could assert that any person with one black ancestor counted as black and was therefore subject to second-class citizenship. At its root, the *Plessy* decision was concerned with "racial purity"; between the Emancipation and 1896 the legal hierarchy that had elevated masters over slaves during slavery had been obliterated, and the "composite" race and attendant worries about "invisible blackness" threatened the South's de facto caste system which elevated whites over blacks. The supremacist *Plessy* holding put mixed-race citizens back "in their place." Though biracial identity had long been used by whites and blacks alike as the basis for local discriminations, *Plessy* defined for the nation a way of conceiving race that has persisted to this day. Ironically, the *Plessy* legacy has, up to now, affected the ways in which we have read and interpreted African American literature. In spite of our awareness of its absurdity, the one-drop rule has saturated our readings of African American authors and has contributed a nagging ahistorical quality to the project. In other words, we have been reading turn-of-the-century African American texts as if "race" has always been defined as it was by the justices who defined whiteness as inherently different and separate from blackness when they ruled on *Plessy*. The court's dichotomizing move might be explained by Abdul R. JanMohamed, who has argued that "colonialist fiction is generated predominantly by the ideological machinery of the manichean allegory" (102), the impermeable dichotomy between blackness and whiteness which spawns the racial stereotypes that make possible ideologies like "separate but equal." Recent post-colonial theoretical formulations can help us consider what biracial identity meant to the culture upon which the *Plessy* verdict was leveled; indeed, it is clear that we must re-examine racial classification as a problem to which turn-of-the-century authors, like Charles Chesnutt, were responding.

Virtually all of Chesnutt's works involve characters of mixed racial ancestry. While he was by no means the only author of his day to speculate on biracial existence, Chesnutt's ethnographic profiles of biracial communities invite us to consider the mixed-race character in an original light, as a new term in the discussion of African American literature. Previous interpretations of Chesnutt's work have largely misread the significance of his mixed-race characters, either by ignoring their existence—i.e., perceiving them as black—or by classifying Chesnutt's use of them as consistent with the "tragic mulatta" genre so popular in the late 19th-century. Earlier readings of Chesnutt's most widely anthologized short story, "The Wife of His Youth," have been inclined to consider the Groveland Blue Veins—Chesnutt's term for the Cleveland mixed-race socialites—not as a third race but as a group of upwardly mobile blacks who choose at the end to accept their black cultural heritage. This is an understandable tactic, given the dramatic and pervasive effect the one-drop rule has had on American race thinking. But when one considers the history of mixed-race peoples in America, "The Wife of His Youth" can be read more importantly as an allegory for the changing relationship between blacks and mixed-race peoples and between the free born and the freedmen during and after Reconstruction. Chesnutt's mixed society functions as a metaphor for the rejection of a two-race culture; as such, it also indicts segregation's color-coded "placing."

Two readings in particular illustrate the ways in which the significance of mixed race has been overlooked in "The Wife of His Youth." Werner Sollors reads "The Wife of His Youth" as a story about Mr. Ryder's choice between his "consent" identification, that is, his present, modern, "Americanized" identity, and his descent identification—his link with his "ethnic past" (Sollors 157). Sollors commits an interesting misreading of the text when he writes that Mr. Ryder "sides with the past against the future" (160), implying that "a previous condition of . . . rural slavery" (156) is his past. Yet Chesnutt takes pains to create in Mr. Ryder a character who is both "merlatter" and "free-bawn" (*Wife* 12). Casting Mr. Ryder as an ex-slave and ignoring his mixed-racial identity, Sollors sees images of ethnic association in the character and argues that the ethnic trappings of Chesnutt's stories are paradoxical—a way of using difference to take part in a collective American identity. But when Mr. Ryder is seen as the freeborn hybrid character he is, rather than as an erstwhile slave, his story is less about an individual's choice to identify with his descent culture than a story about the post-Civil War extinction of "mulatto" and "free born" as social and legal categories. Sollors's concept of descent, then, is not complex enough to describe Mr. Ryder, mixed racial identity during Reconstruction, or the changing nature of racial classification that was both the impetus for and the result of the Plessy decision.

In *To Wake the Nations: Race in the Making of American Literature*, Eric Sundquist approaches Chesnutt from the opposite camp. Sundquist argues that even in his urban tales of mixed race high society Chesnutt uses authentic African American cultural tropes and "even African retentions"—like conjuring and the cakewalk—to signify on the declining state of race relations during the post-Reconstruction era in which he lived (Sundquist 271). Sundquist believes Chesnutt's subtle focus on his African roots is meant to highlight his sense of difference and alienation from the mainstream. But which mainstream—black or white? Sundquist insists only on Chesnutt's alienation from the white mainstream, and at the base of his analysis is the essentialist notion that "the folk beliefs of African origin were contained somewhere in Chesnutt's own imaginative reservoir" (298). Without debating the merits of an essentialist stance, we might notice reverberations of *Plessy* in Sundquist's firm placing of Chesnutt and Mr. Ryder within a black folk tradition, taking part in the "symbolic past of [their] race" (299).

Of course, Sollors and Sundquist are not incorrect for privileging Mr. Ryder's African origins. The dramatic tension of the story itself arises from the fact that the Blue Veins are "more white than black." This description is meant to be physical as well as historical or temporal; their blue veins designate them as almost white physically and their concern with upward mobility and the absorption of their almost white group into the privileged "pure" white race by way of "passing" is the future for which Mr. Ryder and presumably the other Blue Veins ardently hope. This dramatic tension beckons us to read the text as a romance about race in which the black self, nearly extinguished or absorbed, is at the last moment resurrected and claimed. The threat of the whole race eventually "passing" is diffused at the end when by accepting Liza Jane the Blue Veins symbolically become black like her. But when in this romantic ending blackness is *not* erased, what *is* lost is the hybrid or mixed-race identity. In spite of their disagreement over Chesnutt's use of racial difference, Sollors and Sundquist assume Chesnutt and his mixed-race characters are grappling only with the legacy of an African American past rather than with the complex and separate issues that faced mixed-race peoples in the late 19th-century. We might use Homi K. Bhabha's theory of hybridity as a strategy for reading "The Wife of His Youth" with greater historical accuracy, problematizing rather than erasing the category of the racially hybrid character.

"The Wife of His Youth" is not a postcolonial text; that is, U.S. slavery is not equivalent to British colonialism and the post-slavery migration north that the story depicts is not the same as the post-colonial worlds of India, Africa, or the Caribbean. Nevertheless, because post-colonial texts and theories deal with intersections of races, classes and cultures, post-colonial theoretical strategies are available as models with which to re-read "The Wife of His Youth." Jenny Sharpe's helpful definition of the way post-colonial theories might apply to United States literature suggests that the term "postcolonial" can be used with respect to literature of the U.S. to designate "the presence of racial minorities and Third World immigrants." Sharpe argues that "given its history of imported slave and contract labor, continental expansion, and overseas imperialism, an implication of American culture in the postcolonial study of empires is perhaps long overdue" (Sharpe 181). Applying the concept of hybridity demands that one search for intersections between colonizer and colonized and locate the composite subject that stands between the dominant and the minority cultures. Such a theory, then, offers us a way to understand "The Wife of His Youth" that comes closer to solving the racial quandary of the story and its literary critical readings. Moreover, the history of mixed-race families in America as well as Chesnutt's own journals offer the basis for a significant revision of these previous readings of "The

Wife of His Youth." A closer look at biracial existence as a phenomenon separate and distinct from either "black" or "white" identity demonstrates that "The Wife of His Youth" is not so much a racial romance as it is an allegory for the disappearance of the biracial person as a social and legal entity during the darkest days of Jim Crow.

i

Certain conditions of late 19th-century biracial existence are well discussed. "The Wife of His Youth," for example, begins with a familiar portrait of a group of wealthy, professional biracial people who, because of the one-drop rule, occupy an interstitial space at the border of white society. Their existence, as "a little society of colored persons [whose] purpose it was to establish and maintain correct social standards among a people whose social condition presented almost unlimited room for improvement" (1), reflects what is well-known about biracial existence during the late 19th-century: their tentative social status in relation to the white community. Once defined as a third race and counted as such in the 1850 census, the antebellum "mulatto" elite was a group that had managed, for different reasons in different regions, to hold onto their partial membership in the dominant class in spite of the race prejudice and antipathy toward miscegenation that pervaded the South. As Joel Williamson points out, using a term borrowed from Chesnutt's novel of passing, *The House Behind the Cedars*, biracial Americans had originally been seen as a "new people,"[1] a group separate and distinct from black Americans. Between 1850 and 1915, however, this third race virtually disappeared from America's racial landscape. Williamson argues that after 1850, and particularly during Reconstruction, "mulatto communities . . . confronted an increasingly hostile white world implementing increasingly stringent rules against them in the form either of laws or of social pressures" (Williamson 62). Their response was to relinquish sympathy for the white world and form black alliances. As the white world "arrived at an almost total commitment to the one-drop rule," and as part of "a larger cultural fusion," comparatively privileged mixed-race individuals and freedmen were thrown together to tackle the task of racial uplift. Indeed, he writes, even wealthy "mulatto" families who had once owned slaves were now "fully identified in interest with the mass of colored people," though not at first willingly (Williamson 88).

Bent on establishing a segregated society, southern whites passed strict laws forbidding interracial marriage, naming the issue of such unions illegitimate. Racial identity became more than ever a legal category in cases like *Plessy v. Ferguson* as states decided what fraction of Negro blood constituted black identity, an identity which forbade its owner from centers of higher learning and cultural enrichment. The prevalence of the one-drop rule required light-skinned African-Americans to choose between identifying wholly with blacks or passing, which meant, in effect, entirely renouncing the black part of their heritage. In the South where "everyone knew his color and, hence, his place" (Williamson 99), biracial people had no official place.[2] Indeed, by 1890, census officials stopped counting mixed race people as a separate category and the nation became officially biracial.

In the black community, however, color and class distinctions remained. According to Willard Gatewood, "mulatto" aristocrats maintained a social distance from lower class blacks. "In a sense," as Gatewood says, "the aristocracy embraced a modified version of Booker T. Washington's famous hand and fingers analogy: in all things purely social the aristocrats tended to be as separate from other blacks as the fingers, yet one as the hand in all things for racial uplift" (28). Emancipation eradicated the social structure by which free blacks, who were usually of mixed parentage, maintained superiority over slaves, and the lines of the social hierarchy were subsequently redrawn after 1865. Emancipation produced a legion of new distinctions within the black community based on skin color, parentage, and legal status—slave or free—at birth. A family history worthy of aristocratic status "was in large measure bound up with blacks' experience with slavery—their place in the slave system, their role in opposing it, and the extent to which their families had been free from it" (Gatewood 9). Mulatto identity in the black community both before the Emancipation and after, then, had accorded its possessor a status that the white community had sought to deny by imposing the one drop rule. So even as southern society moved toward legal and social segregation, biracial identity and history—what we might call "biracial culture"—persisted.

Chesnutt's literary career spanned these years of racial redefinition within and outside the black community, and he uses the biracial character in his fiction to comment on the changing nature of racial identity during these years. Chesnutt's own experiences during this time shed some light on his use of the mixed race person as a literary construct. His highly written journal, which might be compared in its belletristic style to the autobiographies of Benjamin Franklin, Frederick Douglass, or Booker T. Washington, casts the mixed race character as a culturally placeless entity, a perception held not only by Chesnutt, but by his black and white acquaintances. In his 1881 journal Chesnutt described the feeling of a "poor white man" toward well-educated black men who, like Chesnutt, were light-skinned enough to pass for white. Chesnutt writes: "McL[aughlin] wound up with this declaration, which embodies the opinion of the South on the 'Negro Question.' 'Well he's a nigger; and with me a nigger is a nigger, and nothing in the world can make him anything else but a nigger' " (*Journals* 161). In a posthumous tribute to Chesnutt, W. E. B. Du Bois offered the contrary view. He said: "Chesnutt was of that group of white folk who because of a more or less remote Negro ancestor identified himself voluntarily with the darker group" (Render 30). This perception of mixed-race placelessness is reflected often in Chesnutt's journal as he describes his youthful attempts to place himself.

In 1875, the seventeen year-old Chesnutt writes of his estranging experiences as a light-skinned teacher among black freedmen. Searching for work in the country districts of North Carolina, Chesnutt arrives in a town called "Jonesville or Jonahsville, I don't know which" (*Journals* 59). The biblical allusion here makes sense in terms of Chesnutt's cultural misplacement; like Jonah who was instructed to preach in the wicked city of Nineveh, Chesnutt follows the call for racial uplift and ventures out into what to him is a cultural wilderness. He writes: "Where the 'ville' was I am not able to say, for there was but one house within nearly a half mile of the 'church' " (*Journals* 60). Clearly an "other" both racially and culturally, Chesnutt struggles to fit into a world in which the urban color prejudice he had grown accustomed to is reversed. At Jonesville, Chesnutt would be replacing a former teacher much maligned for favoring a light-skinned student. He writes, "I suppose they were prejudiced against her because she was yellow, for they are the blackest colored people up there that I ever saw" (*Journals* 60). Yet Chesnutt would like to achieve status on the basis of the color prejudice he is accustomed to; when accosted by "a high-headed gentleman of considerable color" who calls him, familiarly, " 'Uncle Chess,' " Chesnutt takes offense and remonstrates that he "was unaware of sustaining that relationship to him" (*Journals* 77).

Chesnutt doesn't get the Jonesville job, mainly because the church has no money to hire him, but he describes at length a conversation he has while there with a local white man and member of the school committee. This conversation reflects the way in which Chesnutt's biracial identity has left him placeless: "We arrived at once at Mr. Ayler's, and I immediately discovered that he was a German, and began a conversation in that language. He asked me my name, where I was educated, &c. He asked me what countryman was I, and when I told him I wanted a colored school he told me in Dutch [sic], which was unintelligible to my guide, that the white people wouldn't respect me if I taught a colored school. Said that the colored people ought to have colored, and the whites, white teachers. He even offered me the white public school which I respectfully declined" (*Journals* 61). Here we see both the ease with which Chesnutt could have passed and the class barrier which enabled him to identify more closely with well-educated whites than with poor blacks. The scene is almost anthropological or ethnographic in nature; Chesnutt is led by a native "guide" in an unknown region in which he meets a "countryman" with whom he can share a conversation in a common language. The fact that the "countryman," the man with whom Chesnutt can converse, is German and not a Southern white underscores Chesnutt's alienation from both black and white cultures and the extent to which his self-description as "neither fish[,] flesh, nor fowl—neither 'nigger', poor white, nor 'buckrah' " is apt (*Journals* 157). Chesnutt voluntarily passes in this scene because he does not advise the German of his error in assuming Chesnutt is white. But the scene also shows how mixed race people can be "misread," how their bodies become the sites of misapprehension and misplacement in a land where race is a social fiction, where a man considered black can be as fair as a man considered white.

ii

In Chesnutt's own history, then, one can see his concern with the disappearance of a hybrid identity, an identity which was neither black nor white. Indeed, internal and external factors prevented Chesnutt from asserting his membership in either the dominant or the subordinate class. And in "The Wife of His Youth," certainly, politics and sentiment allow the reader to champion Mr. Ryder's choice of 'Liza Jane over Molly Dixon and to read that choice as an appropriate and welcome privileging of his African connection. But to interpret his mixed race characters as struggling only with their black heritage, as Sollors and Sundquist do, is to overlook the position of the mixed race character during the 1890s and to ignore Chesnutt's condemnation of the two-race caste society in which he was living. The journals Chesnutt kept as a young man demonstrate his struggle to retain his hybrid identity in a culture that would cast him as black by default and allow him to be white only if he denied his heritage. His subsequent portrayals of mixed-race characters in "The Wife of His Youth" problematize the racial boundary drawing of the one-drop rule and the regional boundary drawing of programs such as Booker T. Washington's program of racial uplift that would accede to second-class citizenship for African Americans. In "Untragic Mulatto: Charles Chesnutt and the Discourse of Whiteness," Stephen Knadler argues that in his earliest political essays "Chesnutt was reinterpreting race as less a stigma against blacks, or an advantage for whites, than a cultural practice by which all are marked" (Knadler 426). Knadler illuminates Chesnutt's concern with what race means when he reports on Chesnutt's correspondence with George Washington Cable, who told Chesnutt that his own quadroon characters "really ask this question, 'What is a white man, What is a white woman'" (Knadler 427). Chesnutt also tries to rescue the mixed race character from his residence in a racial no-man's land and to re-place him in both the social and literary worlds, not as a tragic figure emblematic of racial strife but as a testimony to the possibility of racial hybridity. Chesnutt's biracial characters challenge the 19th-century racial definitions that opposed whiteness and blackness in a manichean allegory which made possible wide-spread prejudice and exclusion on the basis of racial difference.

Postcolonial theoretical constructions, such as Homi Bhabha's concept of hybridity, give us a way to describe Chesnutt's personal dilemma and the outcome of his story. Bhabha's complex redefinition of the relationship between the colonizer and the colonized imagines a middle ground or border upon which both colonial authority and native oppression are disrupted. Bhabha argues that "if the effect of colonial power is seen to be the *production* of hybridization rather than the noisy command of colonialist authority or the silent repression of native traditions, then an important change of perspective occurs" (Bhabha 173). This third space, which interrupts the polarity inscribed by the victor/victim, conqueror/conquered relationship, might work equally well to describe the racial hybrid or that which is lost by the end of "The Wife of His Youth." Though slavery cannot be equated with colonialism, the post-bellum era invites comparison with post-colonial situations because of the cultural syncretisms occasioned by the biological and cultural intermixing of master and slave, white and black. In places, the cultures of Africans, slaves, free-born African Americans and Europeans melded during the antebellum and post-war periods, creating a social and racial hierarchy that was both complex and dissimilar to a more simplistically imagined master/slave relationship. For this reason, though hybridity cannot function the same way in an American post-bellum context as it does in a European postcolonial one, articulating a space between oppressor and oppressed lets us read "The Wife of His Youth" without erasing the third term, the character of mixed races.

The notion of hybridity explains why Chesnutt imagines Ryder as a free-born African American man. Certainly this choice metaphorically reminds readers that a prior condition of freedom predates African enslavement. And, because Sam's freedom is discounted by 'Liza Jane's master in the early part of the story, this choice suggests the racial peril even free blacks lived under. Most importantly, however, that Mr. Ryder had always been free asserts a third position in the landscape of the story; in contradistinction to the positions of master and slave, Sam Taylor is neither-master-nor-slave. This third subject position foreshadows the hybrid identity Mr. Ryder later adopts.

Chesnutt emphasizes that the hybrid occupies a middle ground and stresses, from the outset, the "neither/nor" aspect of mixed-race existence. We might see in Mr. Ryder's complaints, for example, the problem of post-Civil War racial identity: "I have no race prejudice . . . but we people of mixed blood are ground between the upper and the nether millstone. Our fate lies between absorption by the white race and extinction in the black" (7). This statement bewails the prospect of the mixed race characters' disappearance and establishes their identity as a third race within the context of the story. Indeed, the Blue Veins choose to be neither white nor black; they are a group of light-skinned African Americans who choose not to pass for white but who could, given that "most of them would not have attracted even a casual glance because of any marked difference from white people" (18). At the same time, they refuse to admit dark-skinned ex-slaves to their group. The Blue Veins have, in effect, sustained their own racial identity and have fought for the color designation, neither white nor black, that attaches to it: "the society, though possessing a longer and more pretentious name, had been known far and wide as the 'Blue Vein Society,' and its members as the Blue Veins" (1–2). The narrator describes the society in the same geographic terms Chesnutt had used to describe his own search as a biracial person for *terra firma*—"the society was a life-boat, an anchor, a bulwark and a shield . . . to guide their people through the social wilderness" (2). Established as clearly separate from whites and blacks at the beginning of the story, the Blue Veins are a third race attempting to clear a space for themselves in the social turmoil that followed the Civil War. The end of the story, in which Mr. Ryder acknowledges the wife of his youth, articulates the impossibility of this project. The polarized, two-race world of the south, established in part by the *Plessy* decision, makes hybridity and syncretism impossible in the world of the story.

When read as a parable about race consciousness, Mr. Ryder's acknowledgment of 'Liza Jane, reinforced by the unanimous agreement of the Blue Veins, is apparently the morally right choice willingly made. When I teach "The Wife of His Youth," my students invariably see it as a story about one character's transformation from an acquisitive, class and race conscious snob to a man who "does the right thing." They buy, in other words, the romance of the ending. If one reads the story harboring a concern for the hybrid's difference, for the notion that the division between white and black need not be so sharply determined, and for evidence of the idea that Chesnutt advocated a multi-cultural, syncretic world view, "an important change of perspective occurs." Consider this: Mr. Ryder's choice is only overtly voluntary. A close look at the meeting between Mr. Ryder and 'Liza Jane demonstrates the extent to which this right choice has been orchestrated by forces beyond the control of the Blue Veins. Mr. Ryder's choice *seems* voluntary because of the obvious physical and class distinctions between himself and 'Liza Jane. No one—not the reader, not the Blue Veins, and not even 'Liza Jane herself—would have expected two such opposites to unite. In fact, though, Mr. Ryder and 'Liza Jane are linked not physically, but geographically. Their shared regional identity—that is, their Southern roots —forces their final union.

The raison d'etre of the Blue Veins is to avoid leveling, to maintain their position in the social hierarchy. Mr. Ryder, as their "dean," is pictured therefore as completely non-ethnic, as white as possible without actually being white. 'Liza Jane is imagined as his polar opposite—"black" in every aspect. Indeed, on the surface, 'Liza Jane could not be more different from Mr. Ryder; that he acknowledges her in spite of her difference is meant to show the heroism of his choice. 'Liza Jane is imagined as a throwback to slavery and as a personification of the hard but quaint rural life she has left behind. She is a picturesque curiosity, "a bit of the old plantation life, summoned up from the past by the wave of a magician's wand" (10). She is "little," "with very bright and restless eyes," "quite old, for her face was crossed with a hundred wrinkles." She has "short, gray wool" and "very black toothless gums," and she is dressed garishly (9–10). What Mr. Ryder loses for not being quite "as white as some of the Blue Veins," he makes up for in the refinement of his features, his sartorial conservatism, his nearly straight hair and his modern, urban life (3–4). Chesnutt's focus on his characters' physical features evidences the pervasive 19th-century concern with physicalized descriptions of racial qualities and testifies to the obsession with looking at and deciphering black and mixed-race bodies for the evidence or non-evidence of their racial "purity." But this focus also masks the similarities between 'Liza Jane and Mr. Ryder which are expressed in spatial or regional terms rather than in physical or social ones. This geographic coding draws the characters together and shows that Mr. Ryder's "choice" is governed by the 19th-century notion that fueled both Jim Crow and *Plessy*—that blacks should maintain their proper spatial and social "place."

Despite their physical and social differences, Mr. Ryder and 'Liza Jane share Southern regional markers. Mr. Ryder's rise to respectability has taken place in a distinctly urban setting, and his home, his passion for learning, his language, his white collar job, and his leisure activities all signal his rejection of his rural beginnings. But although Mr. Ryder can deny his rural roots, he cannot seem to deny his Southern ones. At the meeting scene, Mr. Ryder is sitting in "the shade of a vine," on the front porch of his own home (8). This image recalls a sharecropper in Chesnutt's journal who criticizes black teachers for "sitting in the shade" and reminds us of class distinctions in the black community. Certainly, the image casts Mr. Ryder as a member of the leisure class who maintains "an air of kindly patronage" (11) toward his lower-class visitor. But the image is odd because it is tinged with a Southern flavor despite the fact that the story is set in fictionalized Cleveland, an urban center of the Midwest and a Northern mecca for middle-class blacks fleeing the prejudice of the South. Mr. Ryder's porch inspires a vision of a cooling wisteria vine shading a large plantation gallery and portrays Mr. Ryder as an unreconstructed Southerner. Ostensibly, this is a positive image, showing how far Mr. Ryder has come to his current position of wealth and influence. But as Mr. Ryder asks 'Liza Jane to have a seat "behind the vine" we must wonder whether he is pulling her up into his world, as the story purports, or stepping down into hers, as history would suggest. Indeed, when Mr. Ryder retells 'Liza Jane's story to the Blue Veins he does so in the "same soft [Southern] dialect" (20) she used.

The meeting between Mr. Ryder and 'Liza Jane is a significant passing scene in which the usual objective for passing, that is, not to be recognized by whites as black, is redefined. Mr. Ryder passes, in the company of 'Liza Jane, a former slave, not for a white man but for someone who was never connected with nor threatened by slavery; he represents the Blue Veins who ignore slavery because it is a "servile origin of . . . grosser aspects" (3). But Mr. Ryder's need to pass here reminds us of how close he, and perhaps the other Blue Veins, has come to falling victim to slavery's grosser aspects. His flight from the South as a young man demonstrates how dangerous it was to be a free-born black or mixed-race person in the South in the years just prior to the Civil War, as light-skinned free blacks were stripped of rights and threatened with being sold into slavery. In other words, his destiny, in spite of his free birth and light skin, had been, during slavery, more closely linked to 'Liza Jane's than he acknowledges at their first meeting, when he passes for a Northerner unaffected by slavery. His transformation from Sam Taylor to Mr. Ryder, which is figured in images of travel and movement, shows that his destiny continues to be linked to hers even after Emancipation and even after he has acquired the stable identity of the propertied elite.

Mr. Ryder's attempts to modernize 'Liza Jane for her debut at the ball reflects how his fate is inextricably linked to hers. With his acknowledgment of the wife of his youth, Mr. Ryder renounces his desire to marry Mrs. Dixon, a light-skinned Northerner who by marrying Mr. Ryder "would help to further the upward process of absorption he had been wishing and waiting for" (8). Mrs. Dixon is, of course, another polar opposite of 'Liza Jane; she is nearly white, well-educated, refined, wealthy, and very young. To make his choice of 'Liza Jane over Mrs. Dixon seem more palatable, Mr. Ryder re-dresses 'Liza Jane for the ball, making her appear more refined. When she makes her appearance, she is "neatly dressed in gray" and wearing "the white cap of an elderly woman" (24). 'Liza Jane's new clothes, however, have less the effect of making her seem appropriate for the gathering and more the effect of distinguishing her from the other guests who are dressed in formal evening wear. While she may have lost the garish trappings of the slave mammy, her gray dress and white cap make her seem like a servant of another type.[3] In fact, 'Liza Jane looks suspiciously like an incarnation and an indictment of Booker T. Washington's program for racial uplift. She has been cleaned up and dressed up, but the fact that she stands mute in this scene, "trembling at the sudden plunge into this scene of brilliant gayety" (24) suggests that she remains in a servile position. That her fate has implications for the Blue Veins can be seen in the fact that Mr. Ryder has no choice but to accept her into his group with her servile qualities intact. Rather than showing the distinction between the Blue Veins and the freedmen, the acceptance of 'Liza Jane shows how both groups have very little control over the way they are perceived by the white world.

For example, Mr. Ryder's choice of name and his occupation reflect the futility of his attempts to advance toward full equality with whites. The name "Mr. Ryder" resonates with the *Plessy* decision which sanctioned segregation on the basis of race. "Mr. Ryder" can be read as a reference to the actual plaintiff, Homer Plessy, a mixed race train passenger who challenged the Jim Crow laws of Louisiana that had made race the ruling fact of life in the South. Walter Benn Michaels reminds us that Plessy was indistinguishable from a white man and thus of the "stunning incoherence" of the Supreme Court decision. As Michaels points out, the court argued that " 'legislation is powerless to eradicate racial instinct or to abolish distinctions based on physical differences,' but the question of what race Homer Plessy actually belonged to and so of what ineradicable racial instincts might be his could be determined only under the laws of the State of Louisiana" (Michaels 189).[4]

This formulation emphasizes the extent to which the *Plessy* decision was a sectional or regional controversy. In finding against Plessy, the Supreme Court restored sectional power lost to the South following the passage of the 14th and 15th amendments. Thus, as the question "what makes a white man white" became a legal issue, it also became a regional one. "The Wife of His Youth" reminds us of the idiocy of this decision in which one's racial designation and therefore one's rights and opportunities could differ from state to state, from region to region. Thus Mr. Ryder's movement through the story, his transformation from a shiftless Southern almost-slave to a prosperous, Northern, near-white, cannot be viewed optimistically. While he may be a member of the elite in his own Northern city, in his own club and in his own home, his equality under the *Plessy* law is possibly temporary and certainly restricted to those locales. As 'Liza Jane's change of clothing only trades one servile identity for another, Sam Taylor's change of name has not masked the ruling fact of his life—that even though he was born free and nearly-white, he cannot escape the fate of the Southern black.

In Mr. Ryder's name and in his occupation as "stationery clerk" for a railroad company, we see the dilemma of the mixed-race character post-Reconstruction. In light of *Plessy*, paradoxes abound. Mr. Ryder is not, in fact, allowed to ride on the same railroad car as whites and so he fits, in a punning way, his occupation as stationery clerk. The stability of his home ownership may represent his social rise, but the house's Southern trappings also show that he is hemmed in and limited by his racial and regional designations. The recognition scene between 'Liza Jane and Mr. Ryder reflects his untenable position. Mr. Ryder could, without being discovered, avoid acknowledging 'Liza Jane and so his eventual decision to do so can seem all the more heroic. And yet, when read in the context of the South's anxiety over "invisible blackness" and the *Plessy v. Ferguson* decision, the acknowledgment seems, short of passing as white, Mr. Ryder's only choice. Nationally sanctioned segregation on the basis of racial heritage forces his acknowledgment of 'Liza Jane and belies his statement to her that "their marriage was a slave marriage, and legally binding only if they chose to make it so after the war" (21). The "marriage" between blacks and mixed race people, between the free born and freedmen, is legally enforced after 1896 by *Plessy v. Ferguson*.

C. Vann Woodward suggests that the particular argument advanced by Plessy's attorney, Albion Tourgee, "illustrated the paradox that had from the start haunted the American attempt to reconcile strong color prejudice with equalitarian commitments." According to Woodward, Tourgee argued that Plessy had been deprived of property without due process of law. "The 'property' in question was the 'reputation of being white . . . the most valuable sort of property, being the master-key that unlocks the golden door of opportunity' " (Woodward 224).[5] This defense, of course, was specific to the biracial person who appeared white, for the visibly black man could claim ownership of no such "property." Obviously, this argument did not convince the Court, but it must have concerned Chesnutt. Neither Mr. Ryder's figurative property—his nearly white appearance and his free birth—nor his real property—his house—shield him from being associated with his "slave" past. The Blue Veins fear that admitting ex-slaves to their group would remind people of their "servile origin" (Wife 3); this reaction seems to refer directly to another of Tourgee's arguments against segregation, that it "perpetuated distinctions 'of a servile character, coincident with the institution of slavery'" (Woodward 225). We see here how Chesnutt uses "The Wife of His Youth" to weigh in against the *Plessy v. Ferguson* decision and its acquiescence to the South's drive to become a segregated society. When read in light of the *Plessy* case, Mr. Ryder's physical dissimilarities to 'Liza Jane become less a statement about class distinctions among blacks and more an indictment of the move to quantify "black" blood and restrict rights on that basis.

Thus, passing in "The Wife of His Youth," in all its guises, is at once a metaphor for placelessness, for the disappearance of "mulatto" as a racial or cultural category, and a metaphor for being "placed," unable to shed one's regional identity and its attendant constrictions. Mr. Ryder has passed from South to North, he has passed as a black man unconnected with the ravages of slavery, and he has even inadvertently passed in Groveland as white. But he cannot, ultimately, pass into a place of his own making. Even Mr. Ryder's northern piece of property cannot shelter him from being carried South, as it were, and associated with the servile, regional identity that is 'Liza Jane. Thus, Mr. Ryder's porch becomes a mirage, and we must see it as a false vision of the mixed-race character's social superiority over the freedman. This is perhaps the way 'Liza Jane sees it as she approaches from her hot, dusty journey. And 'Liza Jane, imagined at first by Mr. Ryder as the product of the magician's wand, becomes the reality; the hybrid character's connection with slavery and its vestiges—segregation and discrimination—cannot be denied.

Like many postcolonial texts, "The Wife of His Youth" reminds us in several ways that a history of oppression and subordination will continue to exert its power upon the cultures that follow it. When she appears at his porch, 'Liza Jane—one of slavery's vestiges—disrupts Mr. Ryder's "Dream of Fair Women," asserting herself into his imagination just as "the poet's fancy had called into being the gracious shapes of which Mr. Ryder had just been reading" (*Wife* 10). Startling Mr. Ryder out of his mimetic reverie, 'Liza Jane's presence erases the images of Tennyson's fair women and prompts Ryder to cast his lot with black identity rather than with the unattainable white identity embodied in the allusions to "pale Margaret" and Queen Guinevere. In Mr. Ryder's awakening and transformation, Chesnutt challenges what Bill Ashcroft, Gareth Griffiths and Helen Tiffin call "the mimicry of the centre proceeding from a desire not only to be accepted but to be adopted and absorbed" (Ashcroft 4). This reading interprets Mr. Ryder as a postcolonial subject who discards the ideology of self-hatred inscribed by his white oppressor. As plausible and inviting as it is, this reading oversimplifies the tangled relationship between Mr. Ryder and his erstwhile wife and therefore does a disservice to the complexity of Chesnutt's vision. In an equally compelling reading, the elision of Mr. Ryder's and the Blue Veins' hybrid identity is a tragedy because it reinscribes the same two race system of white dominance and black submission that orchestrated Mr. Ryder's self-hatred in the first place. Deeply concerned about the racial thinking that inspired the *Plessy v. Ferguson* decision, about Jim Crow and about the concessions to it advocated by Booker T. Washington's hand and fingers analogy,[6] Chesnutt wrote the following criticism of segregation to Washington in October of 1906. "I do not believe it possible for two races to subsist side by side without intermingling: experience has demonstrated this fact and there will be more experience along that line." By "experience" Chesnutt here refers both to social and conjugal racial mixing in general and to the outbreak of race-based violence at the turn-of-the-century that he had chronicled so forcefully in *The Marrow of Tradition*. Chesnutt's use of Mr. Ryder and the hybrid community in "The Wife of His Youth" questions the feasibility, the logic and the potential equality of a two-race society kept "separate but equal."

Notes

A version of this article will also appear in an upcoming issue of the *African American Review*; the editors would like to thank *AAR* and Indiana State University for permission to reprint.

1. Joel Williamson, *New People: Miscegenation and Mulattoes in the United States*. Tracing the emergence of the "mulatto elite" from its beginnings in the 17th-century through its gradual absorption into the Negro world following the Civil War, Williamson shows that the mixed race Southerner was "new" not only in terms of his mixed black and white ancestry but also in terms of his mixed cultural heritage and, given that he was neither a poor freedman nor a legitimate heir to the plantation class, his middle-class economic status.

2. The 19th-century association of race with place is well documented in George Fredrickson's *The Black Image in the White Mind: The Debate on Afro-American Character and Destiny 1817–1914*. Fredrickson traces the 19th-century defense of colonization, a defense which rested on ineradicable prejudice, fear of the "black peril," and the popular desire for racial homogeneity. His explanation of the forces behind Reconstruction can be used as a way to understand Chesnutt's sense of placelessness. Apparently believing that whites and blacks were biologically suited to inhabit different regions, Lincoln attempted to satisfy a constituency which favored racial homogeneity and, "during the first two years of the Civil War . . . labored to combine hesitant steps toward emancipation with a workable plan of colonization" (150). By 1864, however, the colonizationists' dream was eclipsed. "What had . . . happened . . . was that the Lincoln administration had adopted a deliberate policy designed to keep the freedmen in the South. V. Jacque Voegeli has demonstrated that the failure of colonization was followed by a political decision to do the next best thing as far as Northern opinion was concerned, namely, to institute a policy of 'employing and caring for blacks in the South' . . . which 'effectually sealed the vast majority of them in the region'" (166–67). Thus, national public policy reflected the South's drive to become a biracial society.

3. Clyde O. DeLand's illustration that accompanies the story depicts the moment when Mr. Ryder introduces 'Liza Jane to the assembled Blue Veins. In this drawing, 'Liza Jane's cap and the white piping on her dress look distinctly like a maid's uniform. Moreover, none of the Blue Veins in the picture is depicted as any whiter than 'Liza Jane. There would be no mistaking these folks for whites. These details suggest that to market the story it was necessary to portray mixed race people as black—the very state of affairs the story critiques.

4. Michaels's excerpts are from the *Plessy* decision which has been reprinted in Clark, *The*

South Since Reconstruction 155–167. See also Sundquist's chapter on *Plessy* and Mark Twain in *To Wake The Nations*.

5. Woodward quotes here from the brief Albion Tourgee filed with the Supreme Court in behalf of Plessy in October of 1895.

6. In his Atlanta Exposition Address, Booker T. Washington advocated segregation to his Southern white audience by making the following analogy: "In all things that are purely social we can be as separate as the fingers, yet one as the hand in all things essential to mutual progress" (Washington 129).

Works Cited

Ashcroft, Bill, Gareth Griffiths, Helen Tifflin. *The Empire Writes Back: Theory and Practice in Post-Colonial Literatures*. New York: Routledge, 1989.

Bhabha, Homi K. "Signs Taken for Wonders: Questions of Ambivalence and Authority under a Tree Outside Delhi, May 1817." *"Race," Writing, and Difference*. Ed. Henry Louis Gates, Jr. Chicago: U of Chicago P, 1985. 163–84.

Chesnutt, Charles W. *The Journals of Charles W. Chesnutt*. Ed. Richard Brodhead. Durham: Duke UP, 1993.

———. *The Wife of His Youth*. Ann Arbor: U of Michigan P, 1968.

Frederickson, George. *The Black Image in the White Mind: The Debate on Afro American Character and Destiny, 1817–1914*. New York: Harper and Row, 1971.

Gatewood, Willard B. *Aristocrats of Color: The Black Elite 1880–1920*. Bloomington: Indiana UP, 1990.

JanMohamed, Abdul R. "The Economy of Manichean Allegory: The Function of Racial Difference in Colonialist Literature." *"Race," Writing, and Difference*> Ed. Henry Louis Gates, Jr. Chicago: U of Chicago P, 1986.

Knadler, Stephen P. "Untragic Mulatto: Charles Chesnutt and the Discourse of Whiteness." *American Literary History* 8.3 (1996): 426–48.

Michaels, Walter Benn. "The Souls of White Folk." *Literature and the Body: Essays on Populations and Persons*. Ed. Elaine Scarry. Baltimore: Johns Hopkins UP, 1988.

Render, Sylvia Lyons. ed. *The Short Fiction of Charles W. Chesnutt*. Washington, D.C.: Howard UP, 1974.

Sharpe, Jenny. "Is the United States Postcolonial? Transnationalism, Immigration, and Race." *Diaspora* 4.2 (1995): 181–99.

Sollors, Werner. *Beyond Ethnicity: Consent and Descent in American Culture*. New York: Oxford UP, 1986.

Sundquist, Eric J. *To Wake the Nations: Race in the Making of American Literature*. Cambridge: Harvard UP, 1993.

Washington, Booker T. *Up From Slavery*. Oxford: Oxford UP, 1995.

Williamson, Joel. *The Crucible of Race: Black and White Relations in the American South Since Emancipation*. New York: Oxford UP, 1984.

———. *New People: Miscegenation and Mulattoes in the United States*. New York: Collier Macmillan, 1980.

Woodward, C. Vann. *American Counterpart: Slavery and Racism in the North-South Dialogue*. Boston: Little Brown, 1971.

POSTCOLONIALISM AFTER
W. E. B. DU BOIS

Kenneth Mostern

1
INTRODUCTION

My title suggests an absurdity: how, once we know that W. E. B. Du Bois' life as an intellectual overlaps almost perfectly with the period that we usually think of as the era of colonialism, could postcolonialism be anything other than "after W. E. B. Du Bois"? And if Du Bois has not, up until now, had any noticeable influence on the contemporary academic discourse called "postcoloniality", why refer to it as "after Du Bois", rather than after Fanon, or Foucault, or Heidegger?[1] Yet it is my contention that the absence of Du Bois' name from the contemporary discourse of "postcolonialism" helps to circumvent various issues that term ought to bring out: the genesis of the ambivalences said to be postcolonial, but which in fact have to do with 20th century colonialism in only the broadest sense; the rewriting of anti-imperialist history in a way that sidesteps marxism; and most strikingly, for me, how theorists of the contemporary academy continue to presume that the intellectual history of the African diaspora (and perhaps all non-European diasporas) is marginal to the task of theory construction.[2]

The first half of this paper will demonstrate that Homi Bhabha's definition of "postcolonial critique" in *The Location of Culture* applies unambiguously to Du Bois' 1903 volume *The Souls of Black Folk*. I don't believe that Bhabha, no strict historicist, would dispute such a characterization. Indeed, in a text which makes no reference to Du Bois until its final chapter, Bhabha practically recommends *Souls* as the direct precedent for his own book by quoting—in a book full of lengthy quotations— the following passage on his last page:

> So woefully unorganized is sociological knowledge that the meaning of progress, the meaning of swift and slow in human doing, and the limits of human perfectibility, are

veiled, unanswered sphinxes on the shores of science. Why should Aeschylus have sung two thousand years before Shakespeare was born? Why has civilization flourished in Europe and flickered, flamed and died in Africa? So long as the world stands meekly dumb before such questions, shall this nation proclaim its ignorance and unhallowed prejudices by denying freedom of opportunity to those who brought the Sorrow Songs to the Seas of the Mighty? (Bhabha 255; Du Bois 275)

This passage, positioned among the last paragraphs of both books, is itself both a double, mimetic in the sense that Bhabha develops throughout his book, and a reflection of the nonlinearity of historical time in cultural "development." As such, it both argues for and exemplifies the key temporal aspect of the definition of postcoloniality which Bhabha presents at the opening of his book:

Postcoloniality . . . is a salutary reminder of the persistent neo-colonial relations within the 'new' world order and the multinational division of labour. Such a perspective enables the authentication of histories of exploitation and the evolution of strategies of resistance. *Beyond this, however, postcolonial critique bears witness to those countries and communities . . . constituted . . . 'otherwise than modernity'. Such cultures of a postcolonial* contra-modernity *may be contingent to modernity, discontinuous or in contention with it, resistant to its oppressive, assimilationist technologies*; but they also deploy the cultural hybridity of their borderline conditions . . . (Bhabha 1994, 6, emphasis mine)

I will show that, in these terms, *The Souls of Black Folk* fulfills the entire definition of postcolonialism in nearly identical ways as *The Location of Culture* itself. By identifying the overlapping terminologies the two books use to describe cultures and psyches— doubling, ambivalence, hybridity, interdisciplaneity, migration, and national art—I argue that the the latter book should be read as a double of the former. To be clear: I am not claiming that postcolonialism provides us, at present, with a new framework for reading old Du Bois texts. I am claiming that the theoretical discourse Bhabha now calls "postcolonial critique" existed as early as 1903, and, since this is so, we must explain not only why it did, but also how the structure of the double represses this history by representing postcolonial discourse as "new".

Bhabha's work does not, of course, represent all positions in postcolonial theory. At least two other figures, Edward Said and Gayatri Spivak, are as widely identified with the field, and well-known attempts at definition have also been provided by Anthony Appiah, Gyan Prakesh, and others. At very least, Gayatri Spivak's suggestion that the "impossible 'no' to a structure, which one critiques, yet inhabits intimately, is the deconstructive philosophical position, and the everyday here and now named 'postcoloniality' is a case of it" (1993, 60) and therefore that "claiming catachreses from a space that one cannot not want to inhabit, and yet must criticize is, then, the deconstructive predicament of the postcolonial" (64) has been at least as influential a definition as Bhabha's. A longer paper would detail how Du Bois' *Dusk of Dawn* (1940), which I have examined at length elsewhere (Mostern 1996), performs similar work with regard to Spivak's definition, as *Souls* does with Bhabha's; this paper will indeed have cause to suggest at least one other parallel between Du Bois' and Spivak's work in its conclusion. Otherwise, it is a limitation of my work here that Bhabha will stand metonymically for what I take to be the dominant position in the field as presently constructed.

Because I understand my theoretical position as in part a development of the all-too-unknown work of the marxian Du Bois of *Dusk of Dawn* and other late work, I will end up explaining the appearance of the postcolonial double in terms quite distinct from Bhabha's. In particular, in the second half of this paper I will place certain of those concepts Bhabha considers most essential to postcolonialism inside two differing, but complimentary, descriptions of the contemporary intellectual field, by Cornel West and Pierre Bourdieu, who will permit me to treat "postcolonial/minority intellectuals" as a class fraction in determinate relation to other classes and fractions. In this reading, postcolonialism is, *precisely*, the experience of the migrant anti-systemic intellectual who is positioned so as to take advantage of the legal changes implied by the prefix "post"; it is not, by contrast, a term that appropriately describes either the "folk" or the "nation", which remain in a condition of superexploitation, neocolonization, and relegation to the reserve army of labor. Reference to key moments in the interpretation of *The Souls of Black Folk* since the 1960s will illustrate that African Americanists before me have also treated that work in these same terms. I will suggest in conclusion that since the later Du Bois is himself one of those earlier scholars who reinterpreted *Souls*, a course out of Bhabha's inadequate understanding of postcolonialism, which might give depth to—rather than doubling—his intellectual position[3] might begin with a substantial rereading of Du Bois' later work. Following Du Bois' path from his earlier double consciousness to his later spatially structured dialectical narrative, alternative possibilities for postcolonialism become possible.

2
CROSS-READING *THE SOULS OF BLACK FOLK* WITH *THE LOCATION OF CULTURE*

In its most abstract theoretical project, *The Souls of Black Folk* set out to do two related things: "it aspired to give the particular post-slavery experiences of western blacks a global significance" (Gilroy 1993, 126) and it was "an enterprise that involve[d] the application of philosophy to 'an historical interpretation of race relations'" by "present[ing] a mode of philosophizing that conjoins with the methodologies of the social sciences" (Adell 1994, 26). It is of more than passing significance to both Gilroy and Adell to insert these two Du Boisian intentions into a specifically European—in fact German—philosophical project, as a means of challenging the widespread assimilation of the Du Boisian problematic into a narrative of American pragmatism.[4] For Gilroy the fact that Du Bois travels to Germany and is fascinated over a long period with idealist theories of nationality he learned there,[5] and for Adell his repeated use of Hegelian rather than American pragmatic language suggest that the particular social position which leads to the formulation of double consciousness as a theory—"one ever feels his twoness—an American, a Negro" (Du Bois 1982 [1903], 45)—cannot be understood outside of a wider philosophical narrative. A more precise articulation of this would perhaps be that the experience of displacement and its articulation via specific forms of theoretical reflection are mutually reinforcing in Du Bois' work. Du Bois', then, is a strategy of juxtaposition which "recognize[s] that the problem of cultural interaction emerges only at the significatory boundaries of cultures" (Bhabha 1994, 34). It should not be surprising, given this description, that while Hegelian-idealist and postcolonial languages are usually seen to be at odds with one another, there are complicated and surprising ways in which Du Bois' arguments and Bhabha's arguments intersect. Indeed, one might see the move from *Souls* to *Location* as a move in which identical concerns, framed in overlapping terms, are juxtaposed to different theoretical networks that create new and perhaps *avant garde* syntheses in their own periods.[6] What follows is a description of the ways in which their arguments are similar.

Doubling and ambivalence. Perhaps the most obvious and most overarching point of convergence between Du Bois and Bhabha is their agreement that postslavery and postcolonial experience is particularly conducive to the generation of doubles. The generation of doubleness in Du Bois arises through the contradictory experience of simultaneous national identity, and racial domination within the nation, in the production of consciousness. If Hegelian consciousness is defined as the notion of itself, as Adell states (15), then it holds the same space for Du Bois that "theory", which "produce[s its] object of reference" (21), does for Bhabha.[7] Additionally, the particular doubleness of Du Bois' consciousness is produced in the set of educational institutions in which it is articulated, those which project the forms of human and/or racial striving which make consciousness possible to begin with; in this sense the production of this doubleness, in the postslavery setting, is inevitable and indeed desirable, in addition to being personally disorienting. Du Bois' polemic with Booker T. Washington may actually be read as an argument in favor of the increased production of double consciousness, so much so that in "On Booker T. Washington and Others" Du Bois is particular about labeling Washington's alternative vision of Negroes as the industrial laborers, craftsmen, and servants of a white republic, a "singleness of vision and thorough oneness with [its] age" (81). For Bhabha the "metropolitan site" (213) of a specifically postcolonial theory is then something which comes with a certain form of "aesthetic distance" (13) and "functions" to make the "political process double-edged" (26).[8] This serves to reinforce Du Bois' point that whatever the object being seen doubly, the position through which one sees it creates a constitutively different object than that seen by those placed more singularly. Gilroy, though not Bhabha, refers to this as "insight" (136).

Doubleness comes, in each narrative, with its particular affective component, ambivalence. For Du Bois as for Bhabha the opening question is not how to proceed politically, but how to describe a socially produced emotional state, the *feeling* of *being* a problem: "To the real question [everyone asks of me], How does it feel to be a problem? I answer seldom a word" (Du Bois 1982 [1903], 44).[9] For Du Bois, the ambivalence is produced by the moment in which the member of the dominant society actually notices him long enough to ask him a question—any question; while Bhabha, even more dramatically, derives his theory of ambivalence from issues internal to the colonizer in the act of colonization itself, regardless of the active form of recognition that Du Bois supposes. For example, in his well-known analysis of the stereotype, Bhabha makes a move that I continue to find surprising. Rather than "subject the representations of colonial power to a normalizing judgment", Bhabha's critique of the stereotype reads it from within to show how the stereotypical judgment is a fetish (ch. 3). That is, the stereotype is not defined by its divergence from the actual marginal or degraded body, but rather by its placement in a determinate position within the dominant person's network of possible desires. The colonized subject's desires are then presumed to be within this network constructed by the stereotype.[10] Du Bois' critique of racial paternalism does not happen in these precise terms, yet it is interesting to consider that Du Bois' specific claim about Washington's politics is not that Washington misrepresents the current reality of Negro life (though this could easily have been his strategy) but that he represses or silences certain "supplementary truths" (93) regarding the forms of Negro desire and expression. That is, Washington makes claims about the state of the Negro that are true, but contextualed via the workings of a fundamentally conservative ideology. Du Bois attempts to replace this conservative context with a practice of "striving", which, like mimicry in the colonial situation, leads postslavery politics to its necessary doubling and ultimately its hybridity.

Hybridity and interdisciplinarity. Hybridity is a term that it is difficult to speak of with a great deal of precision in Bhabha's work or in contemporary theory generally. For Bhabha it is generated first out of mimicry, and the inevitable loss that necessarily occurs in the performance of the mimic, such that the subversion of the original is produced without regard to the intention of the performer. Simultaneously hybridity has several other referents—the form of Bhabha's prose itself, in which lengthy quotations from people of every gender, nation, and ethnicity are juxtaposed upon one another to produce a sense of mimicry and singularity together; the thematic and formal contents of the contemporary multiethnic art Bhabha most likes to consider in his discussions of contemporary subversion; and the underlying justification for a "principled argument against political separatism of any colour" (27). The relation between any of these levels of hybridity is, I believe, considerably less clear in Bhabha than in Du Bois, who has no particular compunction about asserting that hybridity generates particular specificities that may under certain circumstances lead to the relative cultural autonomy of one group from another. In any event, it is possible to see that for Du Bois, throughout *Souls*, hybridity is itself the productive form of African American culture. Famously, Du Bois "sit[s] with Shakespeare and he winces not" (139); more significantly, in the final chapter of the book, it is the Fisk Jubilee Singers, who have taken the "low" folk tradition of the slave songs and the "high" artistic traditions of European concert performance and through their mutual elaboration have caused newness to enter the world, in Bhabha's phrase. The cultural forms of hybridity Bhabha continually cites are an update of this Du Boisian example.

Indeed, the most important form of hybridity that Du Bois and Bhabha share is their interdisciplinarity, though one's understanding of that interdisciplinarity may differ in the two cases based on the specific way that Bhabha defines this concept. Du Bois' work comes at the moment of the formation of sociology as a discipline within the U.S. academy; indeed, though he wanted to, he was not yet able to study that discipline at Harvard in the 1890s since it was not recognized there. Trained instead in the disciplines of philosophy, economics and history, themselves still in formation in the U.S. academy of the period, Du Bois structures *The Souls of Black Folk* as a series of essays which consistently address the overarching theme of the color line, but combining language and resources which cross the human sciences: if "Of Our Spiritual Strivings" is a take on Hegelian philosophy, subsequent essays take approaches which are self-consciously historical, ethnographic, economic, and art critical to produce a text which could only be located, in present terms, in "cultural studies". For all this, it is not clear whether this variance of object and approach would yet meet Bhabha's criteria of true interdisciplinarity: "To enter into the interdisciplinarity of texts means that we cannot contextualize the emergent cultural form by locating it in terms of some pre-given discursive causality or origin. . . . It is never simply the harmonious addition of contents or contexts that augment the positivity of a pre-given disciplinary or symbolic *presence*. In the restless drive for cultural translation, hybrid sites of meaning open up a cleavage in the language of culture . . ." (163). Houston Baker's reading of *The Souls of Black Folk* (Baker 1987, 58ff.) suggests that such a cleavage is precisely what is accomplished by Du Bois' insertion of musical staffs as dialogical commentary on his high cultural epigraphs, a moment where no one context can be given to understanding the content of the argument, but this reading has been sharply challenged by Adell (27–28), for whom the quantitative addition of disciplines in no way deconstructs disciplinary formations as such, and the presence of the musical staves is merely a conjoining rather than a dismantling of contexts. There is for Bhabha, however, no way of adjudicating between these theoretical procedures, because interdisciplinarity does not actually end the reign of the disciplines. In his introduction to "The Commitment to Theory," a chapter from which I have already quoted, Bhabha carefully distinguishes between the languages that might be appropriate to disciplinary study from those like his own which can be said to be properly interdisciplinary:

> I am convinced that, in the language of political economy, it is legitimate to represent the relations of exploitation and domination in the discursive division between the First and Third World, the North and the South. . . .
>
> What does demand further discussion is whether the 'new' languages of theoretical critique (semiotic, poststructuralist, deconstructionist and the rest) simply reflect those geographic divisions and influence. . . . I want to take my stand on the shifting margins of cultural displacement . . . and ask what the function of a committed theoretical perspective might be, once the cultural and historical hybridity of the postcolonial world is taken as the paradigmatic place of departure. (20–21)

What I hope I can suggest is not that the construction of interdisciplinarity in Du Bois and Bhabha is theoretically identical, but that adjusted for the variant historical contexts in which sociology was first emerging and now, when sociology is under the critique of cultural studies, it can be seen that each form of interdisciplinarity corresponds to the last phrase of this quote of Bhabha's: they each use "hybridity", which also appears in the previously quoted definition of "interdisciplinarity", "as the paradigmatic place of departure".

Migration and national art. Another way of saying this, broadly consistent with

Gilroy's approach to Du Bois, is that the phrase "place of departure" is doubled and ironized by its "place" being itself a migration—one might say that in both Du Bois and Bhabha one "departs" from the "departure" itself! Robert Stepto (1979, 67) is well-known for his analysis of the "symbolic geography" of north to south textualized by the New England born Atlanta University Professor Du Bois throughout *Souls*; it may be stated that the condition of possibility for Du Bois' hybrid narrative is the condition of movement between various social worlds, themselves able to be contextualized as well as understood in their singularity only on the condition of constant movement. The postslavery world, like the postcolonial world, is one with "no resting-place" (Du Bois, 49), one where people displaced across oceans as laboring migrants move themselves across vast territories from country to city (178), for various kinds of training (ch 6, *passim*), and, as most needs discussion, to tour with their art (ch 14, 265–67). All this movement, of course, starts with the "middle passage", understood in African American Studies since Du Bois as the first, and forced, migration; "middle passage" is the term transcoded in "DissemiNation" as Bhabha's metaphor for the activity of metaphor itself (139–40)!

The Fisk University Jubilee Singers are the people in *The Souls of Black Folk* who most suggest Homi Bhabha's principle of dissemination, for, closing the book, they are the artists who "formulate . . . the complex strategies of cultural identification and discursive address that function in the name of 'the people' or 'the nation' and make them the immanent subjects of a range of social and literary narratives" (Bhabha 1994, 140). In this final chapter, Du Bois opens with the scene of the concert in Nashville, where he has moved to attend college, in which he first sees the Singers perform the sorrow songs, which in their sacred guise become referred to as gospel, and in their secular guise, the blues. But if these songs are the precursors of these 20th century popular music forms, the Jubilee Singers themselves are of course the precursors of the contemporary migrant artist and intellectual class which uses the "ethnic" materials of its migration as well as its interpolation into dominant and/or middle class contexts in order to create the hybrid articulations that make up a text like *The Location of Culture*. That is, Du Bois famously comments about the sorrow songs that: "By fateful chance the Negro folk-song—the rhythmic cry of the slave—stands today not simply as the sole American music, but as the most beautiful expression of human experience born this side of the seas[,] . . . the singular spiritual heritage of the nation and the greatest gift of the Negro people" (265). The songs said to form this *national* heritage themselves are apprehended in a very specific context—that of the educated interpreter in the university concert hall. It is not that the songs, in their postslavery context of migratory labor are not already hybrid productions of the people, but that what makes them "representative" of the "people" is their displacement onto the field of "social and literary narratives" where "a tribe of interpreters of such metaphors" (Bhabha, 140–41) awaits them. Bhabha's full phrase is "there *must* be a tribe of interpreters of such metaphors" (my emphasis), which is to say, *us*, intellectuals who do cultural studies, for there to be a nation. Du Bois, notoriously, called this the talented tenth.

The Location of Culture is filled with the interpretation of poems, novels, and films by postcolonial artists, readings that look a good deal like Du Bois' reading of the

Jubilee Singers. "In such songs", Du Bois tells us, "the slave spoke to the (270); "They are Marx's reserve army of migrant labour who by speaking the foreignness of language split the patriotic voice of unisonance and become Nietzsche's mobile army of metaphors, metonyms and anthropomorphisms" (Bhabha, 164). These sentences themselves establish Du Bois and Bhabha as neither slave nor migrant laborer but authoritative agent of the making of art global. And while I certainly agree with Bhabha that his agency is institutional and generic rather than personal—this is, after all, what it is to be part of a postmodern tribe of interpreters rather than a member of a talented tenth—it nevertheless remains possible for the similarly institutionalized reader, like myself, also neither slave nor migrant laborer, to ask whether the narrative of Marx-become-Nietzsche, in practice, metaphorizes the differentially-constructed "folk" out of existence.[11]

3

POSTCOLONIALITY AS A CLASS CATEGORY

Cornel West's 1985 essay "The Dilemma of the Black Intellectual" continues to be a fine contemporary location for thinking through the meaning of the particular conjunction of Du Bois and Bhabha, which is in a different, but still quite obvious sense, also the conjunction of those two writers with West and this essay. West's essay starts with these words, in echo of Du Bois' analysis of double consciousness: "The contemporary black intellectual faces a grim predicament. Caught between an insolent American society and insouciant black community, the Afro-American who takes seriously the life of the mind inhabits an isolated and insulated world. This condition has little to do with the motives and intentions of black intellectuals; rather it is an objective situation created by circumstances not of their own choosing" (West 1985, 109). It is worth noting how with this extremely simple opening, West generates simultaneously the subjective problematic of double consciousness/hybridity, and also the objective problematic of the social interpolation of the subject, so that a relationship of determination is necessarily posited between double consciousness and a reading of objective conditions. In no way does this objectivity lead to one particular manifestation of double consciousness, and indeed in the second half of the essay West will outline four different ways African American intellectuals manifest double consciousness. It does, however, imply a particular form of the dialectic as a jumping off point for the analysis of the meaning of hybridity as such, one which notes that the intellectual her/himself occupies a particular location in the system of class stratification, as well as a particular and peculiar social activity: the life of the mind.

It is of course entirely conventional at this intellectual moment to see such a framework as part of the poststructuralist critique of representationality, and West's discussion of the impossibility of Black intellectuals' representing something constituted as "the black community", due to institutional positioning and the lack of a widespread support structure for anything resembling Gramscian "organicism" in intellectual work, is consistent with such a critique. But West's argument does not comfortably end with the critique of representation, because West continues to be aware of the implicatedness of black intellectual discourse with the social formation of "blackness" even after this critique has been performed. For one, he maintains that the fact that most black academics may not be "organic intellectuals" in no way makes the concept useless—indeed, he argues that the black preaching tradition and some black musical performance traditions may produce such organicism (114). Beyond this, however, West emphasizes the ways in which, in a white supremacist as well as an increasingly right-wing society, the activity of particular present black intellectuals will determine their reproduction in the future. In other words, the critique of political representation is not identical to the rejection of the possibility that something categorical is represented by the conjunction of "black" and "intellectual". Therefore there can be nothing problematic—no thing deserving "principled opposition"—about the building of institutions that support, promote, and theorize that conjunction.

What we must attempt to understand, then, in analyzing the class position of Du Bois, Bhabha, and West is the extent to which hybridity describes the differential experiences of intellectuals from dominant and nondominant cultural positions. Pierre Bourdieu has referred to intellectuals in general as "the dominated fraction of the dominant class" (Bourdieu 1984 [1979], 176). Bourdieu's description of intellectuals as members of the dominant class depends on the demonstration that cultural and symbolic relations, and not merely economic resources, form a variety of capital.[12] For African Americans, a sociologically determinate fragment which has never included a significant group of genuine bourgeoisie (in the more strictly marxian sense of extractors and beneficiaries of surplus-value), forms of cultural capital are especially important in the internal signification of "class" difference. Indeed, following E. Franklin Frazier's (1957) famous skewering of the "black bourgeoisie" as a bourgeoisie in name only, numerous black intellectuals have found it valuable, for the purpose of understanding their own social positions, to place their self-comprehension as "bourgeois" within strictly ironic constructions.[13]

To the extent that intellectuals in general are discontent with our relative lack of economic and social influence in regard to the holders of economic capital, our representation of reserve armies of labor as metaphors of revolution will proliferate. For those intellectuals of "other" natal communities,[14] whose double consciousness always already derives from identification processes that precede (as well as intersect) the project of becoming an intellectual, the attempt to forge a language of "national" or "cultural" connection will itself double what is already the psychic structure of their class-fragment. Simultaneously, John Guillory's discussion of how class categories and race/ethnicity (as well as gender) categories are constructed differently cannot be neglected: precisely because the socioeconomic space in which class is formed objectively is a differently located field from the sociopsychic space of race and gender, it is possible that a member of the dominant class might perform race/gender resistance by a process of wielding cultural capital against those without it. In the example most important to both Bourdieu and Guillory, this might be done through the investment in "canonicity", a specific value- and class-producing institution, into newly rediscovered literary texts. From my point of view, this is not necessarily avoidable; it is however possible to incorporate a theory of class reproduction which acknowledges theory's own productivity in the making of cultural capital into one's understanding of the politics of hybridity.[15]

Inasmuch as this analysis of actually existing hybridity applies identically to Du Bois' position in *The Souls of Black Folk* and Bhabha's in *The Location of Culture*, the objective position of the migrant professional class in the metropole at historical moments following one or another situation of oppressive dislocation—that is, slavery as well as colonialism—might be equally "postcolonial". (The colonialism of the contemporary world system dates, after all, to the 15th century.) What is key here is that double consciousness and ambivalence are not essentially products of the slave or colonial experience, which are quite different, but rather of the *post*slavery or *post*colonial experience of the educated middle classes, which are in many ways quite the same. The history of African-American and African-Caribbean *intellectuals* in the 19th and first half of the 20th centuries are therefore usefully reread with attention to this similar structural position; this history is related to and yet distinct from that of the pan-African proletariat.

This analysis permits us to examine the historical relationship of Du Bois' hybridity to other African-American theory, which will tell us in turn something about how hybridity hides its class origins. While I am unable to do a complete reading of the literature on Du Bois here, critical analyses of Du Boisian ambivalence have appeared during and since the movements of the 1960s, which like all serious movements for social change necessarily relied on the *non*ambivalent form of the demand. Here I can cite four examples, both overlapping and strikingly divergent in their implications: in *The Crisis of the Negro Intellectual* (Cruse 1984 [1967]), Harold Cruse argued that the tradition of speaking of Black political theorizing as occurring in some cyclical split between integrationist and segregationist tendencies has always been misleading in that it ignores the institutional position of those who were class positioned to integrate and gain intellectual assistance from the dominant society, and the large mass of African Americans, whose politics, whenever they become explicit, have tended to be separatist. The crisis for the intellectual is precisely that s/he must provide a kind of intelligent program that does not pretend to be built on mystifying notions of biological essence but which nevertheless makes use of existing popular separatist structures, because they provide the only possibility for racial justice for the group as a whole and not just opportunistic improvement in position for the intellectuals themselves. Robert Allen, a marxist of third worldist tendencies whose *Black Awakening in Capitalist America* (1990 [1972]) is the most significant book of African-American political theory which in my time as an academic I have never seen cited, argued in 1972 that Du Bois is an "excellent example of the ambivalence which afflicts middle-class black leaders. Du Bois once wrote that 'The Negro group has long been internally divided by dilemmas as to whether its striving upwards should be aimed at strengthening inner cultural and group bonds, both for intrinsic process and for offensive power against caste; or whether it should seek escape wherever and however possible into the surrounding American culture.' The middle-class black leader, particularly in times of social stress, personifies this dilemma" (99). Cruse's and Allen's positions are not identical, nor is it my intention to make them so: in fact, while both criticize the particular forms of Du Bois' ambivalence on this point, Cruse is more apt to see Du Bois as representing an integrationist tendency and Allen a nationalist one, something which is only possible because of the contradictory trajectory of Du Bois' career, to which I will turn below. But the significance of my lining them up will be further aided by two more contemporary quotes from theoretically inclined Black feminist academics, Gina Dent and Hortense Spillers, on the social status of ambivalence as a discourse:

> Double consciousness has always implied the articulation of two *identifiable* and *opposing* modes of consciousness: blackness and whiteness. In other words, it has remained inside the sphere of its invention: the twentieth century American color line. And because of this it has always hidden the ambiguous yet privileged national class position of the truly double-conscious. (Dent 1992, 18)

> But if by ambivalence we might mean that abeyance of closure, or *break* in the passage of syntagmatic movement from one more or less stable property to another, as in the radical disjuncture between "African" and "American", then ambivalence remains not only the privileged and arbitrary judgment of a postmodernist imperative, but also a strategy that names the new cultural situation as a *wounding*. (Spillers 1991, 54)

The ambivalent are always already present in the first world; the ambivalent are always already wounded. The ambivalent will tend to integrate, the ambivalent will tend to create their own closed community. I have provided four rather different possibilities for nuancing and elaborating theories of Black double consciousness in part to show just how complicated the effects of it are even from the point of view of those who assert its relative autonomy from other cultural contexts. At the same time, it should be possible to see the peculiar area of convergence in the quotes: the necessity of seeing Du Boisian argumentation, in the case of Dent and Spillers at its most clear-cut intersection with feminism/postcolonialism, as both structurally determined and as needing specification in race/class terms.[16] Ambivalence is always lived as ambivalence about something in particular, and may be not be productive from the point of view of the relatively unambivalent. Bhabha's ambivalent position, as a determinate update of Du Bois', is subject to all of these contextualizations.[17]

4
CONSEQUENCES FOR POSTCOLONIALISM: MARXIST

It should now be possible to understand the concluding evocation of *Souls* in *The Location of Culture*, with which I opened, as being simultaneously an identification within a class fraction, and also a representation of historical movement between the texts. As I have mentioned, there are real differences in the theory of agency between the notion of "leadership" which pervades Du Bois' modernism and that of "dissemination" which structures Bhabha's postmodernism. But this move is not merely one from a less correct to a more correct philosophical position, but also a move from an era of modern (imperial) to postmodern (global) subjectivity/capital—the actual constraints and conditions of agency really have shifted quantitatively and quite arguably qualitatively. This is, indeed, one of the key arguments of Frederic Jameson in

Postmodernism, or the Cultural Logic of Late Capitalism (Jameson 1991), that the shift to a dislocated subject which imagines agency as diffuse and therefore unwilling to choose specific identities for grounding politics is itself determined by actual changes in capitalism. More importantly, it is the precise reason why, in an earlier text (1981) Jameson argues that marxism forms "something like an ultimate *semantic* precondition for the intelligibility of literary and cultural texts" (75). Such an argument has been found offensive to previous scholars of race, ethnic and gender studies, in particular, and Jameson has said little that is helpful about these fields to indicate why those of us in them should take marxism seriously. For all that, Jameson's arguments may provide a backdrop (but *not* a guideline for future research) for leftist versions of race, ethnic and gender studies needing the material grounding of a dialectics that recognizes both the historical creation of the racial form of identity and the continual *change* in its subjective manifestations over time.

Marxism helps us to see that while minority discourse/postcolonialism/the discourse of hybridity is a discourse in which synchronic distinctions within class standpoints in a particular symbolic field are operative, it also stands among other, diachronic narratives, like those of technological change. The psychoanalytical ahistoricism of the discussion of racial stratification and caste—what Hortense Spillers calls "dominant symbolic activity [which] remains grounded in the originating metaphors of captivity and mutilation so that it is *as if* neither time nor history . . . shows movement" (1987, 68, my emphasis)—is misread by Bhabha, without the emphasized words, as a "new" historicism. History is evacuated, through the category of the double, making impossible a layered analysis that would demonstrate that Jameson's mode of production narrative and Spillers' psychoanalytic narrative stand in a determinate relation to one another. Arif Dirlik has provided the most substantive demonstration of the ways in which the current structure of global capitalism finally resembles that which Marx and Engels described in *The Communist Manifesto*: "The bourgeois has through its exploitation of the world market given a cosmopolitan character to production and consumption in every country. . . . In place of the old local and national seclusion and self-sufficiency, we have intercourse in ever direction, universal interdependence of nations. And as in material, so also in intellectual production. . . . National one-sidedness and narrow-mindedness become more and more impossible, and from the numerous national and local literatures, there arises a world literature . . ." (Marx and Engels, cited in Dirlik 1993, 137). In avoiding Marx, Bhabha avoids the question of to what extent his theory performs a particular moment of capitalist development, and thus ironically extends the liberal universalism of the early Du Bois' modernist, postslavery position. Only an adequate specification of our particular hybridities in both their synchronic and diachronic aspects (which is, ultimately, the unachievable representation of totality) will help us to understand the grounds of convergence and divergence between Du Bois and Bhabha.

5
CONSEQUENCES FOR POSTCOLONIALISM: IDENTITARIAN

Du Bois moved in the direction of precisely this analysis later in his own life, and the conclusion of this paper will explore the implications of Du Bois' subsequent career as both an argument for and exhibit of the need for African American Studies as such—which is to say that *contra* Bhabha, there can be no "principled argument *against* political separatism of any colour" (27).[18]

Du Bois is generally identified first of all as a writer engaged in a specifically American/postslavery political theory because he is always identified with his first, and most Americacentric, popular collection of essays. If you've read one book by Du Bois, it is *The Souls of Black Folk*, and if you've read only *The Souls of Black Folk* you've established him first of all as a writer about civil rights within the United States. Generations of nonmarxist African Americanists, indeed, have found it convenient to reinforce this notion, as it has been more advantageous for liberal Americans to imagine integration in the U.S., rather than third world proletarian solidarity, as a political project. Much of Du Bois' work is densely scholarly; his nonspecialist work is often eccentric and uneven, while his career as a so-called political leader (which he did not seek) was finally thwarted by the particular self-centeredness of his personality.[19] So there are several reasons why *Souls* is his only widely read book. Even *The Crisis*, the journal he edited for 25 years, saw its circulation fall dramatically in the 1920s when there were popular African American alternatives. For all this, those who have followed Du Bois' subsequent career as a theoretician—primarily U.S.-based marxists or social democrats—have noted that he stopped conceiving of the politics of race as a U.S.-civil rights (and thus integration) issue within a decade of the publication of *Souls*, and began his lengthy career as a Pan-Africanist organizer and one of the United States' first anti-imperialists. Indeed, in the sense in which marxism defined anti-imperialism for decades, Du Bois was the *very first* marxian theorist of anti-imperialism. His 1915 essay "The African Roots of the War" argues that 19th century imperialism was a solution to European banking and investment problems, and secondly a way for capital to make peace with a European 'labor aristocracy' (as Lenin called it) that would benefit from imperialism. This essay precedes Lenin's *Imperialism: The Highest Stage of Capitalism* by two years.

Now, the simple way to make this transformation seem politically suspect has been to refer to it in racialist terms—Du Bois was committed to a biological and cultural essentialism of Negro race and African descent and is therefore a precursor to the worst, and also the best, of Negritude. Eric Sundquist (1993) and Anthony Appiah (1986) present this case in different ways. This is a complicated issue, neither accurate nor entirely inaccurate, which deserves a level of attention that I have already given elsewhere (Mostern 1996). Here, I am interested in discussing something different, the horrible rewriting of the meaning of old fashioned Pan-African nationalism that has taken place in the last two decades. Angela Davis has remarked on this: "Contemporary representations of nationalism in African-American and diasporic popular culture are far too frequently reifications of a very contradictory project that had emancipatory moments leading beyond itself. For example, my own first major activist effort as a budding 'nationalist' was the construction of an alliance with Chicano students and progressive white students in San Diego for the purpose of the creation of a college we called Lumumba-Zapata" (Davis 1992, 323).[20] Frankly, if Du Bois was for a time a racialist, it does not matter, inasmuch as his most "nationalist" ideas of political alliance always looked beyond the category of African descent and towards a third worldist coalition politics.[21]

Thus while it is convenient to denounce Du Bois' 1940 *Dusk of Dawn: An Essay Toward an Autobiography of A Race Concept* as (a) essentialist (b) bizarrely separatist and (c) tied to a politics of representation, it should now be possible to specify the conditions which produce its specific analysis of separation and representation. In *Dusk*, Du Bois' intention is to explore, in the most complicated way he is able, the conditions which produced his political project before and after *The Souls of Black Folk*, the history of himself-as-intellectual. He discovers that he can do so can only by making sense of the determinations of a specific social identity, which he persists in calling Negro, still the most apt name he can find in 1940. These conditions could not but carry a specific sort of psychocultural valuation and a certain necessarily standpoint-oriented politics, not because his ideas were identical to those of other blacks, but because, he explains, once his complicated, hybrid-marxian, interdisciplinary arguments entered the realm of the social, his ideas were spontaneously understood (by himself and others) as *Negro ideas*. In this context the Du Bois of *Dusk* reads the hybrid cultural politics of *Souls* not as wrong or undesirable but as inadequate to the structural conditions (cultural, political and economic) that reproduce race relations both in the U.S., and, ever moreso, globally. It is thus his direct engagement with socialism after 1909, marxism after 1930, and of the anti-imperialist initiatives of which he is part in 1940, that lead him to advocate African American autonomist politics in the U.S. context as a stage (specifiable in space and time) in a global socialist movement. This politics is replicated in the structure of the book itself, in which his autobiographical narrative is located first within its field of local psychological motivation, which is then located in its national/racial context, and then located again more globally at the connected levels of racial imperialism and the international capitalist economy. It is the study of this last level—his adoption of the marxist analysis of the economy, now used also to recontextualize his earlier analyses of race in terms of the way cultural and aesthetic value is produced, which primarily occupies him at the moment of writing. *Dusk of Dawn*, for all its weaknesses and historical failings, attempts to provide a full elaboration of the interaction of social determinations under capitalist valuation at the economic, social/cultural, and psychological/affective levels: what Gayatri Spivak, extending Marx, calls the "Total or Expanded Form of Value" (76).

There is no contradiction between a broad marxian framework of analysis and the insistence on a carefully-defined, identitarian, practical intellectual politics. *Dusk*'s politics is identitarian in that it insists that national culture and economy, considered simultaneously in its relative autonomy and in its dialectical relation to a global whole, provide the resources and conditions for an effective opposition to certain oppressive power relations; it is marxian in its understanding that such a project is not uniquely liberatory, but to the extent that it works with anti-exploitative international movements, potentially contributes to the larger project of the critique and overthrow of capitalism. Postcolonialism, from *Souls* to *Location*, inasmuch as it represents the position of a determinate class fragment, provides a local analysis of part of this structure.

The call for precisely this kind of politics has most recently been made by Wahneema Lubiano in the context of her critique of a cultural studies that demands primary allegiance to hybridity, but finds its critical method in the texts of Europeans from the 1960s rather than Black Americans from the turn of the century. After rehearsing the argument that the "global" was not introduced to African American discourse recently, but is a key historical concern of Black intellectuals at least since Du Bois, and after further reminding us that the causes of Black separatism emerge from outside, not inside Black intellectual discourse (which then may make strategic use of the separatism, or not) Lubiano concludes: "It behooves us (Afro-Americanists) to try to make sure the world does not simplify Afro-American cultural production, does not rewrite Afro-American history or meta-commentary, does not leave us out of the discussion of ourselves" (76). The rewriting of postcolonialism and its relationship to U.S. ethnicity as a discourse always already after Du Bois, and not merely Fanon, Foucault, or Heidegger—even as a discourse to which Du Bois contributes not one, but several, evolving theoretical positions—is a fundamental place to take on such a project. Postcolonialism after Du Bois does not disappear, become nonhybrid or lose its ambivalence; it merely becomes specifically located at the particular juncture of race, class, and intellectual work, the complicated and multifarious spaces we inhabit, and by which we are identified.

Notes

Much thanks to Gina Dent, Colleen Lye, Rene Francisco Poitevin, Peter Schmidt, Bruce Simon, Amritjit Singh, and Yang Li-Chung, and my interlocutors at MLG-ICS 1996, all of whom commented about previous versions of this paper.

1. Ahmad (1995) notes that the present discourse concerning "postcolonialism" is not the first—in the 1970s a social science discourse making use of this this term appeared. I know of no other reference to this earlier discussion in recent writing. The existence of this earlier discussion—not its content, merely its existence—matters within this paper because in developing an argument concerning postcoloniality after Du Bois, I will also be developing an understanding of why the discussion of postcoloniality, or something closely resembling it, will recur among intellectuals regardless of changes in terminology or the historical memories of the participants.

2. With a small number of exceptions—most notably Sandra Adell, Nahum Chandler, and Paul Gilroy, all of whom are referred to below—those contemporary theorists who read Du Bois at all think of him as someone to be interpreted, not as a theoretician whose interpretations may themselves be of use.

3. In *The Location of Culture* the terms "double/depth" form a binary in which the prior term is consistently privileged as the psychic condition of cultural contact, and ultimately is used as one metaphor for textuality in general. See for example: "In place of the symbolic consciousness that gives the sign of identity its integrity and unity, its depth, we are faced with a dimension of doubling. . . . The space of doubling (not depth) is the very articulatory principle of discourse" (50). There is a sense in which my marxian position in this paper operates a reversal of Bhabha's binary by proposing to recontextualize (and thus give depth to) Bhabha's notion of psychic ambivalence within a totality of simultaneously possible psychoanalytic positions, but demonstrating this would require an entirely different paper.

4. The painstaking work of retracing the intellectual sources of Du Bois' early idealist dialectics—and its difference from James' pragmatism—has been done by Shamoon Zamir in

Dark Voices: W. E. B. Du Bois and American Thought, 1888–1903. Adell's careful philosophical argument about the relationship between Du Boisian and Hegelian double consciousness is the jumping off point of my argument here.

5. Indeed, Bismarkian authoritarian nationalism is perhaps the most damning thing Du Bois toyed with in his intellectual development, as Gilroy stresses.

6. In this sense there is nothing at all new about the prestige, on the one hand, and suspicion, on the other, of continental philosophy in the U.S. academy. My sense that regardless of the content of the philosophy being cited (i.e. my marxism, Bhabha or anyone's poststructuralism, Du Bois' German philosophy and sociology in the 1890s), continental philosophy in the U.S. occupies the same variety of cultural capital within the disciplines in the U.S., derives from my understandings of Pierre Bourdieu and especially the Bourdieuian John Guillory's *Cultural Capital* (1993). This is expanded below.

7. In Bhabha's discussion politics likewise produces its object of reference, so Hegelian consciousness may in fact provide a metaphor for all domains of activity; however, theory is specifically Bhabha's domain of activity in the analysis under discussion.

8. My sudden shifts in the reference to the double from throughout *Location* are necessitated by the need to link the different pieces in Bhabha's imaginary of doubleness.

9. Notwithstanding the well-known claim that Du Bois was a racial "essentialist", most commonly attributed to Anthony Appiah, I have demonstrated (1996) that in his mature work, like *Dusk of Dawn*, Du Bois' highly articulated analysis of racial positioning begins with such an existential description. Nahum Chandler (1996), in an important article which I read only after completing this paper, emphasizes that even from his earliest texts the very concept of "Negro" was dependent on a highly structured and multivalent attentiveness to that term's various discursive positionings (i.e. its binary with dominant constructions to whiteness), its psychic modes of being, and its construction through research projects and other forms of information retrieval. Chandler's analysis is also of particular relevance to the understanding of interdisciplineity in Du Bois (and ultimately Bhabha), which I take on below.

10. My understanding of the psychoanalytic fetish is derived from Zizek (1989, 49–53). Zizek's analysis here and elsewhere in the chapter "How Did Marx Invent the Symptom?" informs this paper inasmuch as it intersects the marxian and psychoanalytic concept of fetishism, describing via the former the economic history of contemporary ideology and via the latter its present moment of desire. My argument below that postcolonialism must be understood in both diachronous and synchronous terms is therefore parallel to Zizek's discussion.

11. Following Spivak, the subaltern position, descriptive of the remainder ("difference") of the population left after all those textually represented are counted, cannot (by definition) speak; this in no way means that there are not actual people in this remainder who suffer the consequences of capitalism. Read this way Bhabha's postcolonial critic continues to make civilization, however ironized, with documents of barbarism; on this please see Raymond Williams' analysis of Goldsmith's poem "The Deserted Village" (Williams, 1973, 74–79), paradigmatic for the understanding of all manner of aestheticist ideology in the past and theoreticist ideology in the present.

12. Bourdieu's elaborated argument regarding the homology in the expressed politics between members of the dominant fractions of each of the major classes of capitalism, as well as the dominated fractions, forms one of the implicit backdrops to this argument. See this entire section of *Distinction*, 175–208. Likewise, his suggestion that it is the literary field itself which reflects the class ambivalence of those who enter it (1995, 30) should not be neglected. Bourdieu's argument, not surprisingly, continues to be silent regarding the relationship of minority and dominant intellectuals within a given field.

13. This way of rethinking class categories is not the one taken by Resnick and Wolff (1987),

among authors often cited in *Rethinking Marxism*, for whom a marxian construction of class must be based only on the production of economic surplus value. Instead, in my conclusion I will suggest, with Spivak, that a working out of Marx's "Total (or Expanded) Form of Value" will require the comprehension of affective as well as economic labor-power, though actually providing a theory of value along these lines is well beyond the scope of this paper.

14. "Natal communities" is Hortense Spillers' characteristic and very precise term, throughout her essays for racial-cultural categories of origin. Spillers takes the term, which I assume it will be obvious is in no way "essentialist", from Christian (1979).

15. See Guillory (1993, 11). Please note that in making this absolutely correct argument Guillory's argument remains offensive to those who would take seriously race and gender studies in two separate ways: first, he presumes that the argument of all those who have discussed the necessity of race and gender studies has been for the expansion of the canon rather than the critique of the canon, which is entirely false and shows no widespread attentiveness to the debates within Ethnic Studies; and while he quite properly sees aesthetics as a socially determinate field the discussion of which cannot be eliminated through the critique of reification, he shows no similar interest in considering whether an analogous argument might be made about socially determinate race and gender.

On the subject of theory's position in the reproduction of class no one has yet been more articulate than Barbara Christian (1987). Need I add that this is not, and was not in 1987, an argument against theory, but an argument for the analysis of the production and dissemination of "theory"?

16. My use of race/class here is in no way intended as an avoidance of gender: the expanded version of this argument, which would explore Du Bois' masculinity in the context of black and postcolonial feminisms, is a necessary step. There is, unfortunately, no room for an adequate reading of *Dark Princess* (1928) in this paper.

17. Though my argument is very differently elaborated than those of previous scholars, analogous comments concerning the class and national position of Bhabha's work have been made by at least: Ahmad (1992, 1995); Dirlik (1994); JanMohamed (1986); Loomba (1994); McClintock (1994); Sharma (1995) and Mishra and Hodge (1994).

18. At the risk of belaboring the obvious: there can be no principled argument for political separatism either. Separation, like African American Studies, is always a tactical matter. However, at present—and as a white man in African American Studies—I consider the argument against all separatism as a danger which demands principled opposition. My detailed discussion of this point, and related ones addressing the development of Du Bois' career, appears in Mostern (1996).

19. "My leadership was always a leadership solely of ideas. I never was, nor ever will be, personally popular" (Du Bois, 1984 [1940], 303). We will of course disagree on this point, but as I see it you'd be self-centered too if you were the only person of your generation in the entire world who knew the particular range of things that you do (you know, like that Africa is central to the history of capital accumulation, and, for that matter, that capitalism creates "worlds" in the Wallersteinian sense), and everyone you encountered told you you were crazy for knowing them. I acknowledge, of course, that you'd have to be self-centered at the outset to learn what no one else in your generation knew, but isn't that the condition of being an intellectual?

20. Such reifications are in no way restricted to "popular culture", but are typical of academic writing about Pan-Africanism/Black nationalism/anti-imperialism.

21. This is most clearly the case in 1928's *Dark Princess*, in which the plausibility of political change for African Americans is intrinsically linked to a conspiracy of Asian and North African anti-colonialists. This novel is also, to my knowledge, the first representation of a romantic (and sexually explicit) relationship between persons of African and Asian Indian descent.

Works Cited

Adell, Sandra. *Double-Consciousness/Double Bind: Theoretical Issues in Twentieth Century Black Literature.* Urbana, IL: U of Illinois P, 1994.

Ahmad, Aijaz. "The Politics of Literary Postcoloniality." In *Race and Class* 36:3 (1995): 1–20.

———. *In Theory: Classes, Nations, Literatures.* New York: Verso, 1992.

Allen, Robert. *Black Awakening In Capitalist America.* Trenton, NJ: Africa World P, 1990 [1972].

Appiah, Anthony. "The Uncompleted Argument: Du Bois and the Illusion of Race." *"Race," Writing and Difference.* Ed. H. L. Gates. Jr. Chicago: U of Chicago P, 1986. 21–37.

Baker, Houston. *Modernism and the Harlem Renaissance.* Chicago: U of Chicago P, 1987.

Bhabha, Homi. *The Location of Culture.* New York: Routledge, 1994.

Bourdieu, Pierre. *The Rules of Art: Genesis and Structure of the Literary Field.* Stanford: Stanford UP, 1995 [1992].

———. *Distinction: A Social Critique of the Judgment of Taste.* Cambridge: Harvard UP, 1984 [1979].

———. *Outline of A Theory of Practice.* New York. Cambridge UP, 1977 [1972].

Chandler, Nahum. "The Economy of Desedimentation: W. E. B. Du Bois and the Discourses of the Negro." *Callaloo* 19:1 (1996): 78–93.

Christian, Barbara. "The Race for Theory." *Cultural Critique* 6 (1987): 51–63.

———. *Black Women Novelists: The Development of A Tradition.* Westport. CT: Greenwood, 1979.

Cruse, Harold. *The Crisis of the Negro Intellectual.* New York: Quill, 1984.

Davis, Angela. "Black Nationalism: The Sixties and the Nineties." *Black Popular Culture: A Project by Michelle Wallace.* Ed. G. Dent. Seattle: Bay Press, 1992. 317–24.

Dent, Gina. "Black Pleasure. Black Joy: An Introduction." *Black Popular Culture: A Project by Michelle Wallace.* Ed. G. Dent. Seattle: Bay Press, 1992. 1–19.

Dirlik, Arif. "The Postcolonial Aura: Third World Criticism in the Age of Global Capitalism." *Critical Inquiry* 20 (Winter 1994): 328–56.

———. "Post-Socialism/Flexible Production: Marxism in Contemporary Radicalism." *Polygraph* 6/7 (1993): 133–69.

Du Bois, W. E. B. *Dark Princess.* Jackson: UP of Mississippi, 1995 [1928].

———. *Dusk of Dawn: An Essay Toward An Autobiography of A Race Concept.* New Brunswick, NJ: Transaction, 1984 [1940].

———. *The Souls of Black Folk.* New York: New American Library, 1982 [1903].

Frazier, E. Franklin. *Black Bourgeoisie.* New York: Free Press, 1957.

Gilroy, Paul. *The Black Atlantic: Modernity and Double Consciousness.* Cambridge: Harvard UP, 1993.

Guillory, John. *Cultural Capital: The Problem of Literary Canon Formation.* Chicago: U of Chicago P, 1993.

Jameson, Fredric. *Postmodernism of the Cultural Logic of Late Capitalism.* Durham: Duke UP, 1991.

———. *The Political Unconscious: Narrative as a Socially Symbolic Act.* Ithaca: Cornell UP, 1981.

JanMohamed, Abdul. "The Economy of Manichean Allegory: The Function of Racial Difference in Colonialist Literature." *"Race," Writing and Difference.* Ed. H. L. Gates. Chicago: U of Chicago P, 1986. 78–106.

Loomba, Ania. "Overworlding the 'Third World'." *Colonial Discourse and Postcolonial Theory.* Ed. P. Williams and L. Chrisman. New York: Columbia UP, 1994. 305–23.

Lubiano, Wahneema. "Mapping the Interstices Between Afro-American Cultural Discourse and Cultural Studies: A Prolegomenon." *Callaloo* 19.1 (1996): 68–77.

McClintock, Anne. "The Angel of Progress: Pitfalls of the Term 'Postcolonialism.' " *Colonial*

Discourse and Postcolonial Theory. Ed. P. Williams and L. Chrisman. New York: Columbia UP, 1994. 291–304.

Mishra, Vijay, and Bob Hodge. "What is Post(-)colonialism?" *Colonial Discourse and Postcolonial Theory*. Ed. P. Williams and L. Chrisman. New York: Columbia UP, 1994. 276–90.

Mostern, Kenneth. "Three Theories of the Race of W. E. B. Du Bois." *Cultural Critique* 34 (1996): 27–63.

Resnick, Stephen, and Richard Wolff. *Knowledge and Class: A Marxian Critique of Political Economy*. Chicago: U of Chicago P, 1987.

Sharma, S. " 'What Culture Allows . . . What Structure Forecloses': Postcoloniality, Cultural Studies and Diaspora Writers." *Mediations* 19:1 (1995): 18–41.

Spillers, Hortense. "Moving On Down the Line: Variations on the African-American Sermon." *The Bounds of Race*. Ed. D. La Capra. Ithaca: Cornell UP, 1991. 39–71.

———. "Mama's Baby, Papa's Maybe: An American Grammar Book." *Diacritics* 17:2 (1987): 65–81.

Spivak, Gayatri. *Outside in the Teaching Machine*. New York: Routledge, 1993.

Stepto, Robert. *From Beyond the Veil: A Study of Afro-American Narrative*. Urbana: U of Illinois P, 1979.

West, Cornel. "The Dilemma of the Black Intellectual." *Cultural Critique* 1 (1985): 109–24.

Williams, Raymond. *The Country and the City*. New York: Oxford UP, 1973.

Zamir, Shamoon. *Dark Voices: W. E. B. Du Bois and American Thought, 1888–1903*. Chicago: U of Chicago P, 1995.

Zizek, Slavoj. *The Sublime Object of Ideology*. New York: Verso, 1989.

CONTEMPORARY CONTESTATIONS

HOW (!) IS AN INDIAN?
A Contest of Stories, Round 2
Jana Sequoya Magdaleno

The question of who and how is an Indian is an ongoing contest of stories in North America—a contest in many ways emblematic of global struggles to contain and control difference in modern societies.[1] It is emblematic not only because the figure of the American Indian symbolizes precisely such differences, nor because, especially in the late nineteenth century, it has come to signify the critical conscience of "modernity experienced as trouble" (Stuart Hall's phrase). Most importantly, it is emblematic because the contest of stories articulated on the figure of the American Indian precisely registers the global systemic effects of a shared historical process that "differentiates the world as it connects it" (Gupta and Ferguson 1992). This essay addresses the effects of that "difference-producing set of relations" at the local level of the United States, focusing on its social and cultural consequences for American Indians.

At stake for Native American peoples in general are the conditions of Indian identity within the encompassing national context. For the tribal nations, on the one hand, what is at issue in the Indian question is the possibility of consolidating autonomous political relationships to the federal and state governments. For those of Indian descent who are not tribally enrolled, on the other hand, the Indian question concerns the possibility of responding positively to the disarticulation of the histories we embody.

In the first instance, the possibilities inherent in tribal sovereignty are complicated by the paradox that the United States both suffers the tribes as testimony to its largess and exploits them as an internally constituted outside. Their ambiguous status as quasi-nations, virtually exempt from state regulation, prompted the leadership of even a prosperous tribe such as the Mescalero Apache, for example, to cast the homeland in the role of "willing host" to the nuclear waste industry.[2]

Such strategies to fortify a government-to-government relationship represents but one of many responses to multiple modes of subjugation, however. For those of Indian descent who are not tribally enrolled, the possibility of Indian identity is complicated

by the positions adopted both by our predecessors and our tribal nationalist contemporaries in response to US procedures of assimilation. Particularly during the first decades
of the twentieth century (and especially in the Southeastern region of the country), a
common response to policies that alternately sought to exterminate, eliminate, incar-
cerate and assimilate was to obliterate the evidence of Indian identity, even when that
meant self-annihilation.

Erasure of the site of control is no less the legacy of American Indian history than
is tribal enrollment. Yet under the pretext that our history began with the 1887
General Allotment Act (from which the tribal rolls derive), the new tribal nationalist
orthodoxy narrowly defines the category "Indian" as a political/legal entity for whom
genealogy is irrelevant. To adopt the position that if not enrolled, then not Indian, is
to forget that until quite recently the tribal roll was the preeminent sign of a colonized
identity.

The two poles of the spectrum of identity and identification implicit in the question
of who and how is an Indian are designated by Lakota philosopher Vine Deloria, Jr.,
as the "tribal" and the "ethnic" (Deloria and Lytle 1984). The former pertains to the
legal status of citizenship in two nations. The latter, to the dispersal characterized by
Edward Said as that great modern fact of diaspora. Regionally diverse, genetically
mixed, and politically various, as we are, the ethnic label is in many ways appropriate
for those of us who are not enrolled. That is, it accounts for the fact that American
Indian identification is (more or less) a function of indigenous descent, of corollary
(but diverse) relationships to westward expansion, and, in turn, of the ideological and
legal ramifications of that event. Yet because ethnicity suggests residual affiliations
which readily assimilate to the dominant Anglo-Saxon identity, it tends to belie the
"emotional continuity" that Deloria stresses, "must be recognized and considered seriously (Deloria and Lytle 245).

Given the rule of skepticism toward matters of emotion, however, it is expedient
to consider the tenacity of Indian identification in context of Raymond Williams's
cultural studies hypothesis of structures of feeling—"those social experiences still in
process, substantially connecting the generations [comprised of] particular linkages,
particular emphases and suppressions, particular deep starting points and conclusions
[with their] characteristic elements of impulse, restraint, and tone."[3] Indeed, Deloria's
recommendation of "some kind of determined and lasting cultural renewal [that] must
take place to help resolve the question of Indian identity in the modern world," depends on the possibility of articulating those "important mixed experiences," cited by
Williams. Even where such experience is but the index of that which can not be
assimilated to the official narratives of nationhood (be they tribal or federal), it nevertheless constitutes what is actually being lived in the register of identity. Yet in "the
struggle for authority and control of definitions" that Deloria considers the crux of
the North American Indian political arena (Deloria, "Comfortable Fictions" 399), the
anomalous experiences entailed in American Indian histories gives way to a fictitious
identity.

If we are to contravene the tendency to convert part to all or all to part, then
Native American writers must be particularly attentive to the multiple relationships
out of and into which we write. For in contrast to the range of Euroamerican identities,

self-evident to a degree in the dominant political and cultural institutions, the available meanings that constrain American Indian intervention in those institutions neither reflect nor adequately mediate the structures of feeling and modes of knowing that connect our generations.[4] Thus, the mixed experience that complicates my own use of pronouns is an effect of the subject-object under discussion—the relationship of narratives of identity and identification as they respond to, accommodate, and resist the master narratives of national culture.

The shifting standpoints of identity, identification, and affiliation at the outset of this essay, therefore, attempt to register the fact that each subject position occupied in respect to Indian and non-Indian identity has its own story to tell; each perspective is appraised by its other at the border of its particular discourse, along an axis of inside-outside. Both tribal and ethnic positions in the contest of stories, however, are immured in a double-bind: for who, what, when, and where can that Indian be, cast by the foundational stories of the United States as the timeless negative of the nation's own self-evident becoming? That projection, of course, was complicated by the presence of Indian peoples quite familiar with the ways of the encroaching society; it was complicated, too, by the resistance they offered to assimilation. However, the conflict between the figure of the Indian as national ancestor and the presence of Indian peoples defined as obstacle, and then—insofar as they retained tribal and ethnic identities—as residue, was concealed to an extent by the category of authenticity brought to bear in matters Native American. Invoked to neutralize the proliferation of levels of disjunction between the sign and its referent, the imaginary authentic Indian— whether of the Golden Age or demonic variety—is a colonial surrogate that casts into shadow our manifest presence and solicits our complicity in the negativity assigned us.

I

A striking example of the overshadowing power of the figure of the authentic Indian appears on the cover of the *Times Literary Supplement* (August 7, 1992). The full page (almost living) color reproduction of George Caitlin's early 19th century depiction of Buffalo Bull's Back Fat, head chief of the blood tribe, is clearly the spitting image of Indianness, and that manifest fact dictates the placement of the Indian question, "—revival or invention?"—in small letters beneath the boldface certification, "Native American," emblazoned across his porcupine quill breastplate. The portrait functions as a self-evident rejoinder to the Indian question, fetishizing that which is to be preserved under the rubric of cultural revitalization.

The *TLS* cover's repudiation of the after-effects of American Indian subjugation to the alien story thus graphically reproduces the discourse of Indianness. In so doing, however, it quite overrules the argument of its intended referent—Dell Hymes's perceptive discussion of Caitlin's project to "depict Indians untainted by civilization." Hymes's review, entitled, "Indian Identities: What It Was and Is to Be a Native American," argues that since "frames of reference for interpretation are inherently unstable" [as an effect of shifting ideological standpoints], '[h]ow to tell and show the story [of Native Americans] is more than ever contested" (3). Indeed, the discrepancy between the cover and its referent attests to the determining factor in that contest: the tendency of popular representations, in general, to constitute an autonomous level of hyper-reality that supercedes the merely existent. The *TLS* cover, in particular, complies with the colonial surrogate by reducing the genealogical, political, and legal complexities of cultural transformation and judicial constructions of identity to the binary terms of a moral antithesis. As an effect of the discourse of authenticity encoded in the thesis—revival (of essential Indianness), the antithesis—invention (of a spurious identity), denies to those of Native American descent the conditions of modern identity-formation celebrated as freedom by the general citizenry throughout the history of the United States.

The problem, of course, is that the material conditions of being Indian have changed over time, while the images of Indianness have not. Thus, a more adequate rendering of Indian identity would articulate its retention in the teeth of modern history—those lived relationships to the dominant social formation in which, as Fredric Jameson observes, "the traditional or 'natural' unities, social forms, human relations, cultural events, even religious systems, are systematically broken up in order to be reconstructed more efficiently, in the form of new post-natural processes or mechanisms" (1981). As Fanon remarked of that systematic disruption and reconstruction, the process achieves domination at the personal level by "blurring the identity of the colonized" (1963).

However efficient for the institutions it serves, those mechanisms of breakdown and assimilation contribute significantly to the problem of identity that has emerged as a central concern of modern Indian discourse—a problem to which the conservative Lakota newspaper, *Indian Country Today,* attests: " 'Who is Indian?' Smithsonian wants to know" (1993). Avis Little Eagle asserts that the question is "one of the larger issues facing board members of the National Museum of the American Indians." In consultation with interested tribal representatives the museum attempted to set "standards [that] are going to affect other museums as well as educational institutions." According to Professor Ray Apodaca, a participant from Laguna, Pueblo, "A definition would be helpful in religious matters, art, politics and education." Although he feels it is unfortunate that, "when we define it someone is going to be left out," he nonetheless agrees with Dr. Bea Medicine of Standing Rock, who maintains that, "Some resolution has to be made and it is something the museum has to confront." Apodaca confirms her recommendation, declaring, "We can't leave it undefined," because "There are too many charlatans, fakes, wannabes and has beens."

The discourse of authenticity in which these American Indian scholars participate is continuous with that carried on sixty years earlier by Indian Commissioner John Collier and Senator Howard Wheeler, both of whom embraced the position that unless a standard of blood-quantum was set, "all sorts of people are going to come in and claim that they should be put on the tribal roles." Their objective—to "get rid of the Indian problem rather than add to it"—was formalized in the language of the Indian Reorganization Act of 1934 (Deloria and Lytle 138).

It is remarkable that contemporary American Indian interventions in the discourse of Indianness resonate so precisely with the terms and interests of federal regulation of the Native American population. Although the earlier position proceeds from the exigencies of federal administration and the subsequent from the project to confirm the national imagination of Indianness, both reflect the requirements of a national apparatus concerned with questions of authenticity in the interests of categorical formalization. Both occasions, that is to point out, mirror the constitutive principle of the museum—an institution that at once corresponds to and mediates the symbolic function of the figure of the Indian as an icon of the past.

During the last decade of the nineteenth century the same principle sanctioned concerted federal and tribal efforts to control the question of who and how is an Indian. Among the more vexed results was the "Indian Arts and Crafts Act of 1990" (Public Law 101–644), which provided that anyone not meeting the technical definition of "Indian" (that is, not a member of a federally recognized tribe), who "offers to display for sale or to sell any good [. . .] which suggests it is Indian produced," would receive penalties of up to one million dollars in fines and fifteen years in federal prison. First time offenders are to be fined $250,000 dollars or face five years in prison.

The law is particularly unfair to California Indian artists. Since many of their tribes lack the mandatory federal or state recognition, they are not included in the official definition of Indian. Also excluded are those of American Indian descent who have not become enrolled members of their tribe for political, religious or personal reasons, including the common experience of removal from our families. Thus the work of internationally renowned Cherokee artist, Jimmie Durham, for example, cannot be represented as "Indian produced." Although Durham was born into the Cherokee Wolf clan and raised by parents who considered themselves to be traditionals, Durham is not Indian according to the criteria of the Act because he refused to register as such with the federal government. Despite the fact that he is a former American Indian Movement (AIM) activist and a founder-director of the International Treaty Council who worked in that capacity at the United Nations from 1974–1980, it would be illegal to sell Durham's art as American Indian.

This dubious legislation of the contest of stories has prompted even *The Wall Street Journal* to protest that the Act "criminalizes the selling of Indian art not made by Indians." However, *Indian Country Today* attributes the position of the *Journal* to the "arrogance and ignorance on Wall Street." Editor Tim Giago admonishes that "It is inevitable when fighting for specific Indian rights that some individuals will fall through the cracks. But should the entire Indian art community be shortchanged and placed in jeopardy because of these few?" (26 November 1992, A-4). The detail that "falls through the cracks" of Mr. Giago's question, of course, concerns the "jeopardy" in which undocumented American Indians are placed "because of these few" imposters who, according to Giago, "have been making life difficult for genuine, enrolled Indian artisans."

Federal and tribal efforts to reduce the category American Indian to a legal entity (in fact, a corporate formation) for whom genealogy is irrelevant is in part, a political response to the proliferation of Indian identity and identification celebrated by N. Scott Momaday's manifesto of the imaginary Indian, "An Indian is an idea a given man has of himself" (1970). Aside from its basis in the growing American Indian population, that proliferation is an effect of popular fantasies of Indianness. For the most part, of course, the given man does not imagine Indianness in terms of ordinary

Indian people; it is the hyper-reality of the colonial surrogate—that is, the figure of the Indian as a national retro-spectacle that appeals to him. By much the same process of imagination, the most accessible Indian fantasy for the given middle-class white woman is the benevolent spirit guide which apparently has a particular interest in that disaffected personage.

(A humorous instance of the "given man's" idea of Indianness is recounted by a Taos friend: among the visitors to the Pueblo who earnestly try to emulate Indian ways—right down to the comical gestures that community satirists adopt to foil them—Renee tells of a young white woman who assumed the bent posture and halting gait of those she determined to be the authentic Indians—the elderly Taos women.)

Although the figure of the authentic Indian is a figment of the popular imagination, it nevertheless has real consequences for contemporary American Indian peoples. Among the most obvious of these is that we must respond to the question of Indian identity in terms that position us in a double-bind. As an effect of the paradoxical injunction entailed by the figure of the American Indian (that is, if Indian, then not contemporary; hence, if contemporary, then not Indian), we ourselves have come to internalize the discourse of authenticity by which our lived histories are construed as invalid.

Many American Indians must therefore contend with accusations of being "not Indian" when, for whatever reason, they have aroused the ire of their own tribes, as well as of other American Indians. Writer Sherman Alexie, an enrolled member of the Spokane, for example, publicly admits that, "There is a lot of infighting, Indian against Indian. Even among writers, there's a lot of that" (*Bloomsbury Review*). Although he was born and raised (mostly) on that reservation, he confesses to "catching a lot of crap because of the success I'm having. About whether I'm really Indian or not. How traditional I am."

Most significant among the real consequences of the imaginary figure of the authentic Indian, however, is its function as a red-herring, one might say. For by inducing American Indians to continually question who is and is not an Indian, it misdirects awareness from the mechanisms and processes of domination discussed by Fanon and Jameson. Accordingly, even our own versions of who and how is an Indian are not so much the antithesis of the colonial surrogate as its echo. The problem is not a trivial one. For we cannot take a stand on imaginary ground.

The echo nevertheless reflects upon its source, and in reflection is a degree of refraction, as demonstrated by one of the earliest recorded interventions in the discourse of Indianness. Precisely because the name by which they were called implied an elusive and threatening presence "beyond the pale" of the colonizing system, Native American adoption of the name—"Indian"—accommodated the performance of an indigenous critique. That critical reflection was remarked by Roger Williams, founder of the state of Rhode Island, in his 1643 treatise on the language of America: "They have often asked me, why we call them Indians, Natives, &c. And understanding the reason, they will call themselves Indians, in opposition to English, &c."[5]

The name "Indian" is thus rooted not only in New World fantasies of lost origins, but also in contested material transactions between the colonizing self and the colonized other, figured as the New and the Old. Implicit in that figuration was the image of the Vanishing American (the polar opposite of the New Englander). Accordingly, when our bicultural forbears became obsolete as active intermediaries between the unmapped wilderness and the civilizing market, the fledgling economy of manifest destiny sold the concept of the Indian as Art before the product was on the streets, both figuratively and literally. In the earliest commodity form of the colonial surrogate, tribal remnants of westward expansion were befeathered, furred, and frozen in attitudes of sorrowful nobility. The resulting icon, a reflection at once of land and soul, represented an ideal integral to the New World self-image: all the wilderness that had been overcome, all the wildness waiting in the heart, ready to spring into action should the occasion demand (and occasions continue to demand: sporting occasions, occasions of warfare; confrontations between right and wrong, good and evil). Although the displacement and control of that sorrowful wildness seemed to the young republic a guarantee of its future, the contest with uncertainty was won at a certain cost. For freedom is not to be thought of as cheap; sacrifices must be made. As an emblem of the cost, the Vanishing American represents that which is necessarily superseded. It is out of time, and therefore out of place. Envisioned against the ideal of democracy—conceived as an unending process of becoming, the finality of the Vanishing American constitutes both the authenticating sign of Indianness and an alibi for national usurpation of the territorial and cultural space indicated by that sign.

Under the auspices of legal, educational, aesthetic, and popular representations, then, colonizing imperatives are in many instances not "post" but ongoing. In so far as American Indians have been defined generically in terms of the past (but whose?) by tellers of tall and self-serving tales, whatever our own standpoints in the contest of stories (and they will be many according to tribal and family histories), our presence in relationship to those terms must necessarily be equivocal. For our sense of who we are in relation to the majority society, as well as our judgment of other Indian-identified people, is conditioned by what continues to be at stake in the question of who and how is an Indian—the replacement of traditional Native American structures of identity with those of Euroamerica. The part of the colonial surrogate is thus to substitute pathos for the irony that the discourse of authenticity confers on matters Indian.

Despite assertions to the contrary, however, the conditions of Indian identity have indeed changed over time. Many of those changes are directly related to differing degrees of access to land and resources among American Indian peoples, as well as to corresponding restrictions on traditional religious and economic practices which depend on such access. Real (as distinct from imaginary authentic) answers to the question of "how" is an Indian therefore must depend in part on whether one is Indian in the city or the country; whether in the ways of tradition or of modernization; whether drawing more on old or on new cultural influences.

But the question of "who" is an Indian is subject to other conditions as well, and these are indirectly related to federal restrictions on non-capital intensive access to the land. For it is one of the paradoxes of democratic government that without the appearance of homogeneous political identity—an identity, that is to say, constituted in terms of the dominant system of representation—that the issues crucial to Native

Americans cannot be heard. It is at this impasse, then, that American Indian writers must become particularly inventive.

II

The genre of Native American fiction is exemplified by the work of N. Scott Momaday and Leslie Marmon Silko in the 1960s and 1970s. These syncretic works created great public and academic interest, to the extent that both authors are now included in most standard American anthologies. For all that the poetry, novels, and autobiographies of these two writers resonate with the growing movement in the schools and universities to reclaim the standpoints of those who have much at stake but little say in North American culture and society, they continue to inspire new generations of writers and to encourage critical interventions in the discourse of Indianness.

Although the work of Momaday and Silko are stylistically different, they share many similarities: both are concerned with the recuperation of indigenous sources of identity, and towards that end both draw upon tribal oral stories. Most significantly for a consideration of the relationship of these writers to the discourse of authenticity expressed in the moral antinomy, "revival or invention," the first novels of both incorporate elements of traditional sacred story cycles. That practice, however, raises an ethical question vis-à-vis the particular communities of which these authors write.[6]

It is a question that arises from the dual social contexts of these syncretic texts, yet which tends to be answered in terms of academic interests. Because for the most part neither the university nor the mainstream reading public has regarded ethical considerations as relevant to the category of fiction, critical commentary has tended to follow the lead of the authors in effacing the communal sanctions that restrict the use of sacred oral stories in traditional tribal communities. This essay, therefore, is part of an ongoing project to include in discussions of contemporary Native American literature not only the canonical esthetics of the privileged imagination mediated by ethnographic material, but a sense of responsibility to the lived relationships in which culture functions as a connected way of life—connected, that is, to varied modes of continuity, emergence, and, yes, invention.

Surely to many Indian-identified students it seems ironic at best that academic commentary on these works cites the literary incorporation of fragments of sacred story as evidence that they are authentically American Indian. The problem, of course, is precisely one of context: what is misuse in relation to the sacred cultures of particular tribal communities, is just that which for the secular humanist culture of Euroamerica evokes the atmosphere of authenticity. In defense of that marketable commodity, moreover, protests offered in the interests of the former are dismissed as impertinent by appeal to the category of aesthetics. The prerogative of a cross-cultural preserve, exempt from accountability to the tribal communities whose world-views it purports to represent, is justified in the name of fiction. Such dismissive strategies are perhaps an institutionalized residue of the nostalgic idea of the Vanishing Indian. Certainly they highlight the difference between traditional American Indian social goals and those of the majority culture.

That effective difference between the two ways of having stories (that is, culture) is increasingly a matter of public record as tribal spokespeople on behalf of traditional ethos are finding their voices in cross-cultural forums. Among many examples is an article published in the Northern Arizona University newspaper *The Lumberjack* in which Hopi tribal leader Vernon Masayesva protests that "as a people we are studied as artifacts." Director of Hopi cultural preservation, Leigh Jenkins, explains that, "The conflict arises when non-Indians want to preserve the Hopi culture by means of publishing their secrets" (1 February, 1991).

In the context of the university, Jenkins assertion that, "the tribe would prefer to lose its traditions," may be perceived as self-destructive for all parties to the contest of stories. Nevertheless, the limits of academic freedom to interfere with ways of life based upon a different system of cultural values and practices is similarly asserted when Vine Deloria, Jr. protests that, "Indian students are being trained to view themselves and their cultures in the terms prescribed by university 'experts' rather than in the traditional terms of the tribal elders." Because, according to Deloria's observations, "The process automatically sets the members of Indian communities at odds with one another," he concludes that "it is not only a travesty of scholarship but is absolutely devastating to Indian societies" (1988).

The alarm sounded by Masayesva, Jenkins, and Deloria refers to the fact that since many American Indian communities and traditions have been shattered, the young must reinvent viable conditions of being Indian. And because that reinvention entails the recuperation of cultural fragments from many sources, including archive material that is most often the purview of non-Indian "experts," the dangers to which they point will be mitigated by a teacher whose knowledge is well grounded in a Native American community. The preferred teacher of Indian students would be one who has internalized the perspectives of a particular Native American culture, as well as of the dominant society. The best teacher for American Indian students, that is, would be fully bicultural. The problem of training young Indians in the critical issues of their own cultures thus becomes one of gaining informed perspectives on, in James Clifford's phrase, "the predicament of culture," from the standpoint of more traditional American Indian social goals, rather than from those of Euroamerica.

Traditional Native American social goals are in many ways different from the general aims of the majority culture, and foremost among these differences is the function and meaning of culture itself. While experiences of cultural difference and assimilation are processes that inform both American Indian and non-Indian societies, Indians are more likely to designate culture as a system of alignment with the shifting conditions of the environment. Whether those conditions are elemental, geographical, spiritual, or social, the system of alignment allocated to the abstract category of culture by the West is embodied for American Indians in the living members of the community. However in contrast to the secular humanist celebration of the creative capacities of the individual (and the sovereign individual is itself, of course, a cultural response to a particular set of political and economic circumstances), traditional American Indian cultural identities are not centered in the ego. Instead, as is often remarked, an Indian cultural identity is centered in the interdependent system of relationships between the sacred beings manifest in the surroundings, including the elements and the other life forms of the region. Rather than defining culture against the nonhuman realm as do Judeo-Christian and secular-humanist traditions, those raised in (or more influenced by) American Indian traditions are thus more likely to point to familiar geographical features—the hill or river, for instance, and say, "That is our culture."

Traditional American Indian social goals, then, differ from those of modern Euroamerica in their positive identification with ancestral events, customs, and values; and these are preserved in story and song, ritual and ceremony, as well as in the daily practices of the members. Yet most crucially, cultural identity is sustained by the territorial features of the homeplace. Thus, when those geographical embodiments of culture are banished from our lives as a National Sacrifice area, for example, the social system organized around their symbolic meaning is effectively sacrificed as well. By the same token, when the places that define Native Americans as a people are exploited for their material resources, our sense of identity is proportionately impoverished. This is what is at stake in the contest of stories for American Indians, both tribal and ethnic.

A geocentric sense of identity may be understood from Western standpoints if it is considered in light of similar self-confirmation in reference to classical Greece, for example (or, as for my French-Welsh grandmother avows, to gay Paris). Just as Euroamerican cultural traditions—embodied in its literature and art, located in its museums and libraries—depend on access to those institutions, so indigenous cultural practices depend on physical access to the places in which the tribal traditions are embodied. Thus, for all that the threat of cultural extinction has been mitigated by contemporary American Indian literature, that creative—indeed inventive—response to the dominant society's depredation against the environment entails its own series of paradoxes.

Modern literary forms of cultural revitalization are paradoxical forms in that they are necessarily not constituted in the cultural terms of the traditions which they would vitalize. "Necessarily not," that is, because they belong to the cultural logic of the colonizing story—a logic of space rather than of place. Of space, in that the technologies of mechanical reproduction and electronic transmission are inherently centrifugal, expansive and assimilative technologies. At the same time as they foster the atomized individual by insulating that entity from the human and geophysical environment, they promote the expansion of its domain. Therein, of course, is their value. And that value conforms to the principle of esthetic representation as a movement away from the particular (deemed to be idiosyncratic) to the general (considered to be representative and accessible).

In contrast, the social role of traditional tribal story is to gather together the members of the society in communal place. For in order to hear the stories which tell them who they are, dispersed members of the tribal community must return to their elders. And in order to receive the tribal knowledge embedded in the traditional stories, they must submit to the social terms of which the stories are a vital part. Communal sanctions against committing the oral stories to print thus counter the disintegrative tendencies of the dominant society, encouraging the reintegration of acculturated (or deculturated) Indians with the community. Thus, these differences between ways of having stories have powerful consequences for each society.

Approaches to cultural revitalization that are benevolent in the context of the academy can therefore have negative consequences for the culture they would preserve, as Masayesva, Jenkins, and Deloria contend. Yet not only may well-meaning academics disparage as superstitious the objections of Mr. Masayesva or dismiss as irrelevant the warnings of social critics like Vine Deloria, Jr., but authors and scholars of Native American literature may unwittingly denigrate the social goals of American Indian cultures by subordinating them to the dominant representational esthetics of displacement, substitution, and generalization. The figure of the authentic Indian is a case in point: although it is meant to celebrate a version of the Native American past, it nevertheless trivializes the histories we actually embody.

It is important to bear in mind, therefore, that just as the dominant society has internalized elements of Indianness (principally as symbolically loaded images), so American Indians have internalized many of the ideological premises that sanction the dominance of the encompassing nation. Moreover, just as Indians have always adopted elements of the dominant society that they find useful, so modern American Indian communities—despite their relatively conservative cultural principles— adapt global technologies to their purposes. Thus, the distinction that I am elaborating between ways of having stories in no sense implies that Indian identities are constituted outside the field of contemporary social conditions, as the discourse of authentic Indianness would have it. On the contrary, as an effect of the shared historical process that, as Gupta and Ferguson so elegantly declare, "differentiates the world as it connects it," the various forms of domination and erasure to which Native American societies have been (and continue to be) subject are common experiences for both native and non-native populations. Mindful of the shared conditions such experiences entail, then, I will proceed to engage (in a necessarily general way) the particular social contexts of the Native American communities upon which Momaday's *House Made of Dawn* and Silko's *Ceremony* draw.

While a common aim of tribal communities is to persist and to flourish as self-determining formations within the institutional structures of American society, most are tenuously poised against the assimilative pressures of those institutions: whether constituted by Western ideas of education or of economic necessity; by ever changing federal Indian policies and the corollary interdiction of traditional practices, or by the systematic devastation of ancestral land bases, the influences of global capitalism and its institutional expressions pervade most tribal communities as fully as they do non-Indian social formations.

An important factor in the permeability of modern tribal formations, moreover, is the extensive practice of "mixed" marriage—a matter which itself reflects paradoxically on the idea of the racial basis of Indianness. Since most Native American communities define members on the basis of kinship affiliations and social acuity rather than blood quantum, the key to being American Indian in terms of a given community is in the degree of incorporation into the social network of that community. Thus, a "fullblood" may be thoroughly acculturated to the dominant society, while a "mixed-blood" may identify and function entirely as a member of a tribal group that has assimilated biological non-Indians over generations.[7] Although kinship ties promote porous tribal boundaries, the Pueblos depicted in *House Made of Dawn* and *Ceremony* tend to be exclusive rather than inclusive communities. Indeed, the tendency toward a defensively organized cohesiveness may be a protective response to centuries of Spanish and then U.S. colonialism.[8]

Although the more conservative Pueblo communities are perhaps less internally divided by the influences of mainstream society than many others, there is nevertheless a tension along the lines of revitalizing tradition and selective modernization—imprecise terms which signify the divergent social principles which I have attempted to clarify. Those disparate influences and social goals are differently engaged, of course, according to the relative material and social bases of regional tribal communities. As customary values and practices are altered by the influences and institutions of the dominant formation, some members carry on the traditional ways while others are more inclined to the margins of the community, nearer to mainstream culture. (The spatial metaphor of center-periphery understood from the tribal perspective registers asymmetrical relationships to antithetical conceptions of power: traditionally based resources of power and knowledge, on the one hand, are symbolically encoded in ritual and oral traditions; dominant resources, on the other, are transmitted through state and church. Both positions entail problems of access: the traditional center restricts specialized knowledge through clan and gender roles; the modernizing sector of tribal communities follows the dominant society's model of qualification based on formal testing and informal gatekeeping.)

In general, then, the traditional American Indian social order is penetrated by way of the legal and health-care systems, while the more permeable periphery enters the mainstream of the dominant society through state and parochial educational systems. The latter prepares the way for a normative American identity, internalized through increasing identification with the homogenizing influences of popular entertainment and advertising. Indeed, it is indicative of the crisis for Native American identity in this contest of stories that the Indian children who grew up with the genre of American frontier movies identified with the cowboy hero rather than with the Indian antagonists; of course, they could not recognize themselves in the mirror image of the authentic Indian.

The relationship of both Momaday and Silko to the tribal communities in which their first novels are set is similar, then, in that—as their autobiographical writings attest—both were raised in families with strong connections to the dominant society's educational and economic practices, and somewhat peripheral relationships with the tribal communities among whom they lived.[9] Both thus write from the perspectives of the dual cultural contexts which this essay has regarded as being at odds in significant ways. Their articulation of those disparate social goals and differently empowered social conditions, moreover, mediates the changing configurations of identity occurring simultaneously in tribal and dominant cultures. Both Momaday and Silko, that is, creatively engage the global social and cultural forces contending for dominance within the tribal societies of which they write, as well as those of the mainstream reading public for whom they write.

Yet for all that the tribally based aspects of these works—as distinct from those based in the esthetic values of the dominant culture—are at odds with the more traditional ethos that they (partially) represent, both *House Made of Dawn* and *Ceremony* must be considered not only as contemporary adaptations of Native American story-telling (the interpretive strategy that most often accompanied their early reception). They must be considered as well in the more ambiguous light of the overlay of one set of social values by another. In particular, they must be considered in relationship to the counterculture movement of the '60s and '70s when many young white, mid-dle-class Americans began looking for alternatives to orthodox forms of spirituality. Since the canonical status of both novels is more than incidental to that context, rather than attempting to position them within a tribal ethos that becomes exoticized by the quest for authenticity (quite a tempting prospect for non-Indian academics), they may be more accurately understood in relation to the common experiences of contemporary North America. That is to consider that the mixed-blood or "halfbreed"[10] subject positions articulated by these syncretic works reflect not only the authors' somewhat equivocal relationship to the tribal communities of which they write, but most impor-tantly, they reflect the existential condition of the mainstream reader.

Precisely because the mixedblood protagonist depicted by these early works is mar-ginal to both tribal and dominant formations, the figure affords the disaffected reader an accessible (albeit male gendered) structure of identification. As the mainstream reader's agent in a threatening but attractive scenario that at once mirrors and dis-places the reader's real circumstances, the mixedblood protagonist symbolically re-forms the conditions of their common alienation. Hence the emphasis of early commentary on the healing functions of Silko's *Ceremony*, for example. If for no other reason than that these protagonists are constituted by the postmodern condition of partiality, they are particularly adapted to mediate the global-systemic effects of the "difference producing set of relations" in which the mainstream reader also partici-pates. Emphasis on the commonality of the conditions negotiated by these protago-nists (if not the specific circumstances in which those conditions are encountered) avoids the Orientalizing strategies of legitimation engendered by the question, "What is Indian about these works?"

Moreover, their consideration in light of shared historical conditions would lend critical support to the objections of Silko and others to the classification of their works as Native American.[11] For these hybrid forms register an ambiguous sign of Indian-ness—a fossilized trace of numinous passage, perhaps, though certainly not the mystic critter itself. (A certain resemblance to the infamous Trickster suggests itself in this regard. Indeed, this essay got its title from a tricky teller of tales at a recent powwow: Two Mescalero Apaches were hanging out in a park, said Lorenzo Baca, when they were approached by a hippie speaking what he believed to be their native tongue. "How!" said the hippie to the Indians. Coyote looked at his friend, Ramon, and said "What?" Ramon looked back and said "Where?" Coyote asked "Who?" Ramon, "Why?" The hippie walked away muttering "Wow!").

Similarly, the early syncretic works of Momaday and Silko articulate a paradoxical presence defined by a crucial absence in the general currency of representations: they invoke familiar images of the exotic, while giving the comfortable a peculiar twist. They may raise the Art level a notch beyond our comfort zone, as—according to some tastes—in Momaday's earliest work. Then again, fragments of the sacred may be recuperated from the already alienated context of anthropological archives—a sort of textual necrophilia. But whatever it is, it is not what it appears to be.

To pursue the authentic Indian in this forest of ambiguity is to go astray. For the interpretive project of American literary criticism must contend with an unreadable sign not unlike that legendary inscription carved into a tree in the abandoned Roanoke colony—a sign composed only of the local Indian name for a neighboring tribe, a sign that would seem to indicate adversity, yet not punctuated by the agreed upon sign of distress. That sign—of what if not of distress?—was perhaps the first move toward such literature.

The category of Native American fiction may be clarified by placing it within the theoretical framework of colonial discourse. The mixed-blood protagonist in its ideal form—a form to be taken with a grain of salt—articulates a range of emergent subjectivities generated by colonial dependency and postcolonial dissolution. Because the position belongs to neither side of the boundary that constitutes its condition of partiality, it is able to both mediate and negate the relation of opposition between colonizer and colonized.

Ceremony's motif of the spotted and the commingled is a metaphor for the new categories of meaning that proceed from the dissolution of the old oppositions. That metaphor is personified by the various protagonists whose genealogical ambiguity is evidenced by green or yellow eyes. It also structures the narrative of the hero's progress from a fragmented condition to an ever more inclusive standpoint. The structure of *Ceremony* thus replicates the Hegelian dialectic as a development of higher level syntheses from the confrontation of opposites. The same principle is established as the prerogative of Tayo's dual racial heritage: "I'm a half-breed. I'll be the first to say it. I'll speak for both sides" (43).

The representative status Silko ascribes to the "half-breed" figure counters the reifying tendency exemplified by the *Times Literary Supplement*'s version of the Indian question—"revival or invention?" *Ceremony* inverts that moral antinomy, assigning cultural authenticity to the racially hybrid position. Its affirmation of Indian identity as both revival *and* invention renders a generally accessible structure of identification for the mainstream reader: the hero's initially uncertain status with respect to the tribal community reflects that of the reader. By the same token, the tribal aspect that positions the half-breed as potentially a full member of the community signifies a colorful loophole exiting reader alienation from the dominant society.

Certainly, the preeminence Silko accords the half-breed figure redresses the depiction of Indian identity as a relic of the national past. However, the relationship of the figure to the dominant culture is difficult to decide when considered in light of its prior inscriptions in colonial literary discourse. It is counterintuitive, of course, to consider an icon of the multicultural project in terms of Matthew Arnold's formulation of a colonial elite, produced from the synthesis of Anglo-Saxon and Celtic racial "types," whose vocation it is to infuse the dominant aesthetic sensibility with a sense of mystery.

Nevertheless, it must be remarked that the structure of privilege Silko maps onto *Ceremony*'s mixed blood protagonist echoes Arnold's prescription for assimilating native

Irish literature to the dominant currents of Anglo-Saxon culture (with a capital "C"). The question is whether that echo reflects critically or affirmatively on the transfer of values from the subordinate to the mainstream of culture.

American Indian creative literature is presumed to emerge from the perspective of indigenous critique of the dominant society, as does Silko's *Almanac* (despite her public protests that the work "has no political intent," (Silko interview, 1992). At the narrative level, *Ceremony* conforms to that expectation, and critical commentary celebrates the work as exemplary of an "Indian" revitalization movement.

Yet the disposable position of the fullblood antagonist, Emo, complicates that judgment. The bearer not of culture, but of the witchery (a practice that is inconsistent with his particular tribal background), Emo is bound by precisely the circumstances that Tayo is able to transcend by virtue of his doubleness: "no boundaries, only transitions through all distances and time."

Tayo's healing, on the one hand, depends on his ability to transcend and thus to "speak for both sides" of the colonizer/colonized dyad; that achievement consists in his recuperation of an ethical standpoint recalling the old "universal subject" affirmed by both Arnold and Silko as the more "accessible" form.[12] Conversely, the cultural degeneracy of the fullblood antagonist, Emo, recalls Fanon's description of the colonized native who, "is declared insensible to ethics; he represents not only the absence of values, but also the negation of values" (41).

The grain of salt with which *Ceremony*'s mixedblood figure must be taken, then, consists in its equivocal relationship to an indigenous population already disparaged by its prior representation as a primitive stage in the universal development of civilization. Its mission to secure a more accessible structure of identification precisely replicates the canonical strategy of representation as generalization (*vorstellung*) from a particular, and therefore limited instance, figured by the Navajo healer, old Ku'oosh. More problematically, its mission to supersede and then to take the place of the circumscribed position renders representation as substitution (*vertreten*) by which the dominance of the dominant culture is achieved. If the mixedblood subject is not to thus write itself over the less privileged positions alongside which it would take its ethical stand—if it is not, that is, to emerge as a new form of an old mode of domination—cultural mediators must be mindful of both the ambivalence and the advantage of the positions we occupy.

Aside from the literary arena, however, ambivalence tends to overshadow advantage. In Mexico and the Americas to the south, and to varying degrees in Canada, the category of the mestizo or the métis refers to historically cohesive cultures. To the north and south, then, they have developed socially stable mixed identities. In North America, on the contrary, pressures for assimilation tend to produce fragmentation and dispersal of identity rather than cohesiveness. Though the American Indian half-breed experience in the United States is an often painful one (as Paula Gunn Allen's essay "A Stranger in My Own Life" recounts), the mixed-blood position here refers as much to contemporary resistance to nationalistic meltdown as to quantum of Indian "blood". In any case, the latter may be difficult to determine due to the powerful assimilative pressures exerted against our predecessors. Racism, internalized as self-hatred, institutionalized as political and economic restriction, inclined our mixed-blood parents (speaking of my Chickasaw father, born in Oklahoma in 1914) to the denial of Indian heritage. Because it was considered a stigma until very recently, many of us embody a genealogical blank, filled with secondhand bits of information, partially uncovered tracks, fragments of photos in which we strain to recognize our own features and those of our children. My father believed all this was his gift to me: "You won't have to worry about that," was all he would say when I asked.

Our predecessors were ambivalent. Caught between the lines of powerfully contending stories of origin and aim, they attempted to blend into the anonymous niches between, in Bhabha's phrase, "almost, but not quite; (not white)." That legacy is as determining for us mixed-bloods as was the more forthright horror of those who were rounded up and confined to reservations, or the resignation of others allotted eighty acres of poor land in exchange for a way of life that had long satisfied and sustained them.

Yet even moving nearer to the main currents of the dominant society, we will be hard pressed to find anyone who considers his or her identity to be appropriately integrated within the available social structures. Without a doubt, therefore, syncretic tribal literature presents new possibilities of relationship to both the biosphere (battered, as it is by the new world order) and to the self (similarly scarred, since part and parcel of that order).[13] From the point of view of the tribes on which it is based, however, when the Native American tribal novel renders the aura of authenticity by means of culturally proscribed narratives, it immediately becomes unrepresentative of the very communities it is taken to represent. As Masayesva, Jenkins, and Deloria have indicated, the colonial quest for authenticity then becomes an ethical question of transgression against the object of its pursuit.

The Prologue of Leslie Marmon Silko's *Ceremony* positions the reader at the crux of those contesting ways of having stories. However, the conflict between creational and recreational ethos is apparently mitigated by the narrator-author's assertion that her relationship to the novel we are reading is continuous with Thought-Woman's creation of the world: "Thought-Woman, the spider, named all things and as she named them they appeared," the clan-story begins. Shifting to the recreational provenance of the reader ("no boundaries, only transitions"), the narrator announces, "She is sitting in her room thinking of a story now. I'm telling you the story she is thinking" (1).

As an effect of the cultural authority implied by that narrative transaction, the framing device seems quite transparent: the narrator's identification with the Laguna creatrix authorizes the novel's representation of the Laguna Pueblo oral tradition. Rather than constituting an object of critical inquiry in relation to its ostensible referent—the traditional Laguna, therefore, the assimilation of sacred to secular standpoints is generally not recognized as such.[14]

The transition of authority is particularly smooth for readers immersed in the dominant culture's ways of having stories because it occurs undercover of a series of displacements that enacts the historical emergence and cultural consolidation of the individual ego from the matrix of communal identity. Indeed, the narrator's rendition of that ego emergence precisely replicates the strategy of canonical representation as *vertreten*—as the substitution of the author function for the proscribed conditions communal storytelling. The substitution of typographic for topographic sites of knowledge and power as well as the corollary insertion of the autonomous individual into Laguna creational story is thus generally received in the normative terms of Western individuation.

However, that mode of reception may not be far off the mark. It goes astray not so much in reading through the lens of the dominant culture as in its attempt to corroborate that culture's quest for authenticity in matters Indian. For even though critical commentary on *Ceremony* celebrates its recuperation of the mixedblood position from the literary scorn of the nineteenth century, the important mixed experiences articulated by that bicultural positionality tend to be paradoxically subordinated to the prevailing ideas of authentic Indianness. For the most part, it must be emphasized, those ideas do not so much reflect the object onto which they are projected as the displaced concerns of the dominant culture.

Foremost among those ideas, of course, is that of the spiritual authority of the American Indian. Accordingly, early commentary inclined toward the view that reading Silko's first novel in itself comprised a healing ceremony, an opinion which reflects both *Ceremony*'s desired effect and the longing of disenchanted Americans to restore the spiritual dimension of experience to their daily world. That longing for spiritual authority (however compromised by intellectual training) tended to overrule the contradiction of "telling" these sacred story fragments within the recreational context of the novel form, even for scholars otherwise sensitive to the incongruity between those competing ways of having stories.[15]

The Prologue invites that response not only by transferring the structure of authority from traditional Pueblo to dominant standpoints, but by excluding the real position of the reader from its system of representation. It must exclude that position because, in contrast to the sacred-effect of *Ceremony*'s narrative about tribal ways of having stories, actual access to sacred material presupposes conditions that are difficult to honor within the secular context in which the novel circulates. As a member of the Santa Clara Pueblo remarks to anthropologist Nancy Scheper-Hughes's, "This kind of cultural knowledge is not for casual use. If it is distributed casually, the power goes out of it, and Destruction Day comes closer" (1987). The Prologue reduces the conflicts between sacred and secular ethos to an allegory of good and evil in which its representation of the sacred is the privileged term of the opposition. In so doing, *Ceremony*'s Prologue exerts pressures against readings that might escape those terms. In particular, it hinders recognition of the multivalence of the accusatory sign: "Their evil is mighty but it can't stand up to our stories. So they try to destroy the stories, let the stories be confused or forgotten" (2).

Although the reader may not immediately register the multiple referents of that sign, our role as guardian of imperiled tradition nevertheless entails a degree of cognitive dissonance. For to assume that role, we must suppress awareness that it is a reversal of our actual position vis-à-vis the tribal community to which the possessive "our stories" seems to refer. That is, if the clan story fragments included in *Ceremony* retain their sacred function for Pueblo life, a function which is threatened by "they [who] try to destroy the stories/let the stories be confused or forgotten," then the problem which the Prologue introduces, that of protecting the stories (and hence the social relations they entail), is not resolved but confirmed by their literary incorporation.

From the standpoint of those interests with which it addresses us—the standpoint of the more traditional among the Laguna—the reader's identification with the possessive "our" thus entails a double-bind: the recreational context in which our defense of the clan stories is constituted is a context in many respects emblematic of precisely those depredations against which we are to guard them.

In order to recover the critical perspectives foreclosed by the binary terms of *Ceremony's* framing device, therefore, it is necessary to consider the multidirectional structure of recrimination underlying the Prologue's accusatory sign: As the foregoing argument suggests, its most concrete referent is none other than we readers. For if the possessive "our" refers to the clan whose stories these are, then "they who would let the stories be confused or forgotten," is we who assimilate them to the dominant cultural ethos. At this level of analysis, we discern the cognitive dissonance that paradoxically consolidates our identification with the narrator. For in taking up the dual positions of identity and identification offered by the Prologue, we have become enmeshed in a process of displacement and substitution that reverses our real relationship to its ostensible referent. We have inadvertently confused our own ways of having stories, that is, with those that exclude us precisely in the interests of Laguna identity.

Recognition of the reader's part in the confusion of the clan stories with the autonomous relations of Western literature allows us to discern a still more disconcerting axis of the Prologue's accusatory sign: it also rebukes those who resist that confusion by restricting the context in which the clan stories circulate. It implicates those for whom "they aren't just entertainment." That is, the traditional Laguna.

The structure of recrimination thus returns to the contesting relations between tribal and ethnic positions in the dominant culture's imagination of Indianness. For by collapsing the perspectives of those who are inside and we who are outside the context of traditional sanctions into an internally divided identity (a form which itself mirrors the colonized subject) we silence crucial aspects of those tribal traditions we would reclaim. In place of the real differences between the ways of having story is then only that disjunctive space—the arena of the colonial surrogate—where Indian identity becomes a question that goes with the territory.

Notes

1. An earlier version of this essay was published in *New Voices in Native American Literary Criticism*, edited by Arnold Krupat (Washington, DC: Smithsonian Institution Press, copyright © 1993). Used by permission of the publisher. We thank Smithsonian Institution Press for permission to reprint portions of this earlier essay.

2. I argue this point in " 'A ruse is a ruse is a ruse . . .': Trope Tricks: The Symbolic Functions of the Figure of the Indian for the Modern Imagination" (Ph.D. Dissertation, Stanford University, 1996).

3. Williams explains that the term is "concerned with meanings and values as they are actively lived and felt . . . a social experience which is still in process, often indeed not yet

recognized as social but taken to be private, idiosyncratic, and even isolating, but which . . . has its emergent, connecting, and dominant characteristics (*Marxism and Literature* 132).

4. In order to designate this distinction, I will use the term "traditional" in the way it is generally used by American Indians to indicate the differences between the progressive factions within tribal communities and those seeking to retain or revitalize the cultural worldviews and practices that sustained collective identity prior to conquest, relocation, and internalization of the ideological systems and structures of the dominant society. The distinction between the two becomes an opposition at the level of politics when modernizing factions are closely associated with federal policies to capitalize and usurp control of tribal land bases. Yet that political opposition can be subordinated to the resilient system of cultural practices that is signified by American Indian invocations of the term "tradition." Thus, the traditional spiritual orientation is, under pressure of modernizing forces, itself a political position in resistance to those forces. Although the more conservative enclaves within many tribal communities tend to be the most economically impoverished, precisely because their goal is not a Western-style economic expansion but the survival to the seventh generation of their ways of having stories, their spiritual practices constitute an invaluable resource for assuring the continuity of perspectives able to counter the commodification of every value characteristic of late capitalism.

5. See *A Key Into the Language of America; Or, An Help to the Language of the Natives in That Part of America Called New-England*, in Berkhoffer 15.

6. Paula Gunn Allen has criticized the practice in "Special Problems in Teaching Leslie Marmon Silko's *Ceremony*."

7. The ideology of race, of course, derives from medieval Europe, where it functioned to secure the nobility's control of increasing peasant and mercantile pressures. America's indigenous peoples appropriated and transposed that cohesive strategy in order to resist the assimilative pressures of colonization. Hence, the notion of "blue blood" is adapted by Indian-identified peoples as the valorization of "red blood." While the tropological basis of the notion of mixed-blood must be remarked and the irony of its use registered, it is well to keep in mind the brute facts of colonization within which the signifier "mixedblood" functions. Indeed, tribal assimilation of the offspring of mixed marriages varies widely among Indian communities and even among the same tribe on a regional basis. For instance, the Lakota word *Iyeska*, in contemporary usage conveys for some a strongly pejorative attitude toward mixedbloods, while for others, it retains traces of its earlier sense of "translator" as an agent of communication between the sacred and the human worlds.

8. A. LaVonne Ruoff-Brown writes of the bicultural orientation of the Laguna Pueblo resulting from its history of penetration by Spanish and then American forms of domination and regulation is addressed in *MELUS* 5 (1978). Ruoff-Brown cites Elsie Clews Parsons' account of the history of Laguna : "Laguna was the first of the Pueblos to Americanize through intermarriage [. . .] and Silko's great grandfather, Robert Marmon, led the Americanization faction, resulting in the exodus of the traditional Laguna to Mesita and then to Isleta" (2–3). However, Tony and Wilma Purley of Mesita, caution that it is a mistake to apply both the notion of relative Americanization and the counter-notion of resistance to the cultural situation of the main village at Laguna. They point out that although all the villages partake of television and other mainstream cultural forms, such incorporation constitutes, in practice, not the Americanization of the Pueblos but, instead, the Indianization of dominant cultural forms. Thus, they contend that rather than resistance to the structures of modernization, the Pueblos incorporate them into the old traditions. Nevertheless, the village "has its secrets" that outsiders should respect (but have notoriously betrayed).

9. Momaday, one might assume, identifies more particularly with the Kiowa of his paternal heritage than with the Jemez Pueblo and Navajo depicted in *House Made of Dawn*. Yet he also

deeply identifies with the latter as he observes in *The Names*: "My parents lived and taught at the Jemez Day School for more than a quarter of a century. It was my home from the time I was twelve until I ventured out to seek my fortune in the world. My most vivid and cherished boyhood memories are centered upon that place" (117–118).

10. The term "half-breed" is commonly used by Native Americans of mixed descent both as an affirmation and as a pejorative appellation (legitimating, by contrast, those whose identities are less ambiguously constituted). In its affirmative function, it belongs to the same category of resistance as that earlier designation—Indian—adopted by indigenous peoples to assert their sense of difference from those who wielded the name against them.

11. For example, during an interview shortly after the publication of *Ceremony*, Dexter Fisher asked Silko if she would "distinguish Native American literature from other literature, like black literature, for example?" She protests that such distinctions are not particularly relevant to her work: "I think that what writers, storytellers, and poets have to say necessarily goes beyond such trivial boundaries as origin." Her attitude toward applying the categories of race and ethnicity to literary works is made even more clear by her warning that, "There's also the danger of demeaning literature when you label certain books by saying this is black, this is Native American, and then, this is just writing. That's what's going on now, and I don't like it."

12. During her interview with Fisher, Silko affirms the canonical form of representation, particularly the version recommended by nineteenth century literary critic and theorist of "high culture," Matthew Arnold: "I would say that good literature has to be accessible. It's incredibly narcissistic to be otherwise. Artists can't work with a chip on their shoulders. And that's what has happened to a lot of feminists. Politics can ruin anything ." Both categories of the particular (i.e., ethnicity and gender) evidently function for Silko as the negative pole of Arnold's pre-scribed "mainstream," a construct that she here designates the "accessible." However, she quali-fies her indictment of the intrusion of politics into the aesthetic domain: "Politics in the most crass sense—rally around the banner kind. I'm political, but I'm political in my stories. That's different." Silko does not explain the difference that she asserts except by implication, restating her previous assertion: "I think the work should be accessible, and that's the challenge and the task of the teller—to make accessible perceptions that the people need." In the same vein, when the interviewer asked how she feels about being generically classified as a Native American writer, like many other major American Indian writers, she responds, "I just see my self as a writer."

13. Paula Gunn Allen designates these syncretic novels, in which the protagonist is mixed-blood or half breed, "tribal narratives" in contrast with the category of Western fiction (*The Sacred Hoop*, "Whose Dream Is This Anyway?").

14. A notable exception to that rule is Paula Gunn Allen's "Special Problems in Teaching Leslie Marmon Silko's *Ceremony*."

15. N. Scott Momaday declares that, "Leslie Marmon Silko's novel is [. . .] more precisely a telling, the celebration of a tradition and form that are older than the novel as such" ("The Man Made of Words," 1979). The quote is canonized by Alan R. Velie in *Four American Literary Masters* (1982) and proclaimed on the cover of recent editions of *Ceremony*. However, celebration of Native American storytelling in the novel form seems to overlook the fact that the story-telling effect was also a conventional device of nineteenth century French and English novels.

Works Cited

Allen, Paula Gunn. *The Sacred Hoop: Recovering the Feminine in American Indian Traditions*. Boston: Beacon P, 1986.

————. "Special Problems in Teaching Leslie Marmon Silko's *Ceremony." The American Indian Quarterly: Journal of American Indian Studies* 14.4 (1990): 379–86.

Arnold, Matthew. *The Complete Prose Works of Mathew Arnold.* Vol. 3: Lectures, Essays, and Criticism. Ed. R. H. Super. Ann Arbor: U of Michigan P, 1962.

Art in America (February 1993).

Baca, Lorenzo. *Songs, Poems and Lies.* Cassette tape of oral performance at a powwow. Stanford, California. May 1990.

Berkhoffer, Robert F., Jr.. *The White Man's Indian.* New York: Vintage, 1979.

Bloomsbury Review (May/June 1994).

Clifford, James. *The Predicament of Culture: Ethnography, Literature, and Art.* Cambridge: Harvard UP, 1988.

Deloria, Vine , Jr., and Clifford Lytle. *The Nations Within: The Past and Future of American Indian Sovereignty.* New York: Pantheon Books, 1984.

————. "Comfortable Fictions and the Struggle for Turf: An Essay Review of *The Invented Indian: Cultural Fictions and Government Policies.* Edited by James A. Clifton. New Brunswick: Transaction Publishers, 1990." *The American Indian Quarterly: Journal of American Indian Studies* 16.3 (Summer 1992): 397–410.

Fanon, Frantz. *A Dying Colonialism.* Trans. Haakon Chevalier. New York: Grove P, 1965.

Fisher, Dexter. "Stories and Their Tellers: A Conversation with Leslie Marmon Silko." *The Third Woman: Minority Women Writers of the United States.* Boston: Houghton Mifflin, 1980. 18–23.

Gupta, Akhil, and James Ferguson. "Beyond 'Culture': Space, Identity, and the Politics of Difference." *Cultural Anthropology* 7.1 (February 1992). 6–23.

Hall, Stuart. "Ethnicity: Identity and Difference. *Radical America* 23:4.

Hobson, Geary. *The Remembered Earth: An Anthology of Contemporary Native American Literature.* Albuquerque: U of New Mexico P, 1980.

Hymes, Dell. "Indian Identities: What It Was and Is to Be a Native American." *Times Literary Supplement* (7 August 1992). 1, 3.

The Lakota Times/Indian Country Today (26 November 1992).

Lumberjack [newspaper]. Northern Arizon University. 1 February 1991.

Momaday, N. Scott. *House Made of Dawn.* New York: Harper and Row, 1968.

————. *The Names.* New York: Harper Colophon Books, 1977.

News From Native California (Fall 1991).

Ruoff-Brown, A. LaVonne. "Ritual and Renewal: Keres Traditions in the Short Fiction of Leslie Silko." *MELUS* 5 (1978): 3–17.

Sequoya, Jana. "A ruse is a ruse is a ruse . . ." *Trope Tricks: The Symbolic Functions of the Figure of the Indian for the Modern Imagination.* Ph.D. Dissertation, Stanford University, 1996.

————. "How (!) Is An Indian: A Contest of Stories." *New Voices in Native American Literary Criticism.* Ed. Arnold Krupat. Washington, DC: Smithsonian Institution P, 1993.

Scheper-Hughes, Nancy. "The Best Of Two Worlds, The Worst Of Two Worlds: Reflections on Culture and Field Work among the Rural Irish and Pueblo Indians." *Comparative Studies in Society and History* 29 (1987): 56–75.

Silko, Leslie Marmon. *Ceremony.* New York: Viking, 1977.

————. "Storyteller" [Interview]. Marilyn Moss, interviewer. *Los Angeles Times. Village View* section. January 24, 1992. 20–21.

Wilden, Anthony. *System and Structure.* London and New York: Tavistock P, 1980.

Williams, Raymond. *Marxism and Literature.* Oxford: Oxford UP, 1977.

Velie, Alan R. *Four American Indian Literary Masters.* Norman: U of Oklahoma P, 1982.

REVISIONING OUR KUMBLAS
Transforming Feminist and Nationalist Agendas in Three Caribbean Women's Texts

Rhonda Cobham

A bizarre logic connects the typical nationalist (usually male) creative writer to mainstream feminist (typically white) writers and/or critics. For each, an engagement with marginality in the terms laid out by the dominant culture is an important point of departure and there is a temptation to claim a utopian space beyond the imperatives of any socio-symbolic contract as the right of the marginalized subject. But in each case this structure risks repeating the anthrocentrism of the hierarchy it assails. Ultimately it asserts the humanity of the new subject at the expense of some other group. Caribbean women share with these feminist and nationalist writers a number of literary agendas common to modernist writing in the twentieth century. They include the search for an identity that acknowledges or transcends the fragmentation and alienation of modern life, a concern with origins, and a questioning of the psychological needs and cultural myths which drive such searches. Like their feminist sisters elsewhere in the modern world, Caribbean women frequently have turned inward to examine their personal experience as a way of naming the issues they deem pertinent to their search for a language and an identity. Like male writers in other postcolonial cultures, Caribbean women writers also look beyond themselves to the indigenous cultures of their region as a rich source of metaphor.

The challenge for the modern feminist writer in the Caribbean, however, has not been merely to assert her colonized subject's humanity, or to create a feminist counter culture. Either option entails conforming to a system that positions self at the center and marginalizes others, or subscribes indirectly to a passive notion of original innocence. Furthermore, such strategies have been constructed traditionally in relation to a humanist hierarchy in which the Black/colonial woman invariably occupied the lowest rung. Rather than claiming the non-space of ultimate victim or constructing an Other in relation to which her claims to humanity may be judged (animals, flowers, machines? One wonders what would be left!), the Caribbean woman writer has had to look for ways to accommodate her subjectivity as well as that of her oppressors: to write "without claim to an original language before violation" or a "founding myth of original wholeness" (Haraway 94); to confront the whole notion of otherness and the allocation along racial or gender lines of specific properties and values.

In the discussion which follows I have isolated four aspects of the literary project which the writers Erna Brodber, Paule Marshall and Merle Hodge successfully transform in their novels. They are the text's structure, its representation of feminine attributes and sexual identities, its inscription of the maternal role, and its reconfiguration of the descent into madness. Some of these strategies have counterparts in the writing of other marginalized groups as well as in the work of so-called postmodern critics within the "mainstream" tradition. Throughout the essay, but particularly in its conclusion, I have tried to map some of the intersections between the perspectives of the writers I discuss and these other traditions and to examine the implications of my own claims for the uniqueness of these strategies.

I

Merle Hodge's *Crick Crack, Monkey* (1970) is the earliest published of the three novels discussed here. It appeared far in advance of any recognizably feminist Caribbean tradition and until recently was Hodge's only published novel. *Crick Crack, Monkey* shares with the nationalist novels of the late 1960s and early 1970s a sense of postcolonial angst, even despair. Nevertheless, in its construction of female roles and in the way in which its structure revises the terrain upon which quest narratives like Lamming's *In the Castle of My Skin* are constructed, Hodge's novel transforms the narrative conventions by which it is contained. Erna Brodber's *Jane and Louisa Will Soon Come Home* (1980) represents the culmination of many of the trends that I wish to consider. It makes sustained use of Creole language patterns and narrative structure to explore the kinds of intellectual ideas commonly associated with "erudite" writers like Lamming, Harris, and Walcott. Brodber's novel opens ways back to the texts of these canonical Caribbean writers and their male protagonists, whose reintegration is an important dimension of her writer's project. Many of the issues raised in Hodge's novel are resolved in Paule Marshall's *Praisesong for the Widow* (1983). Although Marshall is usually considered an African-American writer, I have used her novel here as a representative Caribbean text because of its Caribbean setting and its continuities with the work of Hodge and Brodber. In addition, the ideas developed here could be used profitably in reading the work of many African-American women writers, whose position vis-à-vis mainstream feminism and the writing of Black nationalists is comparable in many respects to that of the Caribbean woman writer.

The titles of all three novels point immediately to a shared quality at the heart of their aesthetic—their reliance on orature for the symbols and organizing principles within their narratives. The phrase "crick-crack monkey" is part of a call and response chanted at the end of folk tales in the southern Caribbean:

> Storyteller: Crick-crack!
> Listeners: Monkey brek 'e back
> On a rotten pomerac.

"Crick-crack" probably imitates the sound of a branch breaking as the self-opinionated monkey falls out of the tree and slips on the skin of a pomerac fruit. But the literal meaning of the phrase is less important than its symbolic function as a marker separating the fantasy world of the story from the "real" world of the storyteller and her audience. The child protagonist, Tee, shouts this response to end the Anancy stories her grandmother tells during holidays in the countryside where, the novel suggests, an earlier world survives, whose magic has not yet been deformed by the demands of growing up. But the tag is also used in the novel by city youths as a means of challenging the stories told by Manhattan, a member of their circle who claims to be an expert on the American way of life:

> When the fellows were in a tolerant mood they would let Manhatt'n tell of his encounter with the sheriff in Dodge City and how he outdrew him. . . . But when one day someone maliciously murmured "Crick-crack!" at the end of one of these accounts in perfect Western drawl, Manhatt'n in his rage forgot to screw up his mouth to one side before starting to speak. "Crick-crack yu mother! Is true whe ah tell yu—yu blasted jealous it ain' you! Crick-crack? Ah go crick-crack yu stones gi'yu!" Manhatt'n was seen rather less at the bridge after that. (Hodge 7)

Hodge deploys the deflationary technique associated with the tag in other contexts to emphasize the hiatus between fantasy and reality in the options open to Tee. Thus, Aunt Beatrice's fantasy world of respectability and pseudo-whiteness is undermined when Tee's younger brother, Toddan, shatters the prim tea-time idyll with his earthy insistence that he must make "ca-ca." Tee's raucous, big-hearted Tante, is undermined by similar devices, in spite of the positive, caring values which distinguish her from Aunt Beatrice. Sexual independence in Tante's life has degenerated into sexual promiscuity; freedom from social taboos has degenerated into alcoholism. This is why the decision of one of her older wards, Mikey, to fight for her honor on the street touches Tante so profoundly. Mikey's intervention on her behalf is his answer to the "crick-crack" challenge of the boys on the bridge to the myth of Tante's respectability. However, his heroic stance does not change the fact that Tante's lifestyle is in many respects as unauthentic as that of Aunt Beatrice and that it offers Tee no viable alternative in her search for a role model.

Hodge's use of the crick-crack motif in overt and covert forms as a central ordering technique anticipates the dilemma at the heart of Marshall's *Praisesong*, to which the protagonist, Avey, gives voice: "Would it have been possible to have done both? That is, to have wrested, as they had done over all these years, the means needed to rescue them from Halsey Street and to see the children through, while preserving, safeguarding, treasuring those things that had come down to them over the generations, which had defined them in a particular way?" (Marshall 139). *Crick Crack* resembles the novels of many male Caribbean writers in that it offers us no way of resolving the contradiction between sterile middle-class fantasy and sordid lower-class reality. But the fact that Hodge sets up the problem by recourse to an oral form suggests that its resolution may be achieved through the folklore associated with Tee's grandmother. This is the spoor followed in Marshall's more fully developed narrative. For the time being, however, it is important to note that Hodge uses the crick-crack tag self-reflexively, to provide the deep structure of the text and to critique the narrative to which it gives shape.

"Jane and Louisa will soon come home" is the opening line of a popular ring game played throughout the Anglophone Caribbean. Players form a circle around one girl, singing:

> Jane and Louisa will soon come home
> Soon come home, soon come home
> Jane and Louisa will soon come home
> Into this beautiful garden

The rhythm of the song suggests a stately minuet. The player in the middle picks a partner from the ring while singing the next verse, which starts "My dear will you allow me to pluck a rose." During the third verse, "My dear will you allow me to waltz with you," the partners perform a dance that is imitated by the rest of the circle. The fourth verse repeats the first verse, completing the cycle, while the first player rejoins the ring and a new partner enters to waltz with the remaining player in its center.

Lines from the song provide headings for the sections of Brodber's novel. They give the reader familiar with the game a key to the pattern of development in what, to the uninitiated, may seem a confusing, even structureless work. In the first section, "My Dear Will You Allow Me," we enter into the inhibitions and taboos that circumscribe the life of the protagonist, Nellie. They consist of half-veiled threats, contained in proverbs and partially understood anecdotes, which create in the child a fear of con-tamination and prevent her from interacting socially or sexually with her community once she reaches puberty. Section II, "To Waltz With You," describes Nellie's brief flirtation with so-called liberated sexuality and a desiccated, theoretical version of radical politics, from which she emerges after significant trauma into renewed social interaction when she attends a dance in a tenement yard. In Section III, entitled "Into This Beautiful Garden," Nellie begins to explore the garden of her past, so that by the last section, "Jane and Louisa Will Soon Come Home," she is ready for the journey back to self and community implied in the title of this section and the novel.

Folk songs, sayings and stories that Nellie at first only partially understands are threaded through the narrative, creating a series of interlocking metaphors. They sustain the novel's movement through alienation and disintegration toward fresh possibil-ities of reconciliation. Central to this movement is the story of the kumbla, a protective but disfiguring narrative device that Anancy uses as a code in order to trick the Sea King out of stealing his only son, Tucumba. In the Anancy story, as Brodber tells it, Anancy bargains for his life with the Sea King by offering the King his five "worthless" sons in exchange for free passage back to the land. In reality, Anancy has only one son, whom he presents to the King and his shortsighted tally keeper over and over in different disguises. Each presentation is heightened by Anancy's vituperative comments on his son which always end "Yu Face fava—go eena kumbla" (you are despicable—get out of my sight). This is actually Tucumba's cue to slip away and change his disguise. Eventually the King agrees to allow the last of the sons presented to row Anancy back to the shore and in this way Anancy and Tucumba make their escape (Brodber 124–28).

In the novel the kumbla, this "round seamless calabash that protects you without caring" (Brodber 123), becomes a symbol for the manifold strategies by which Black women throughout the ages have ensured their own survival and that of the race. Nellie's kumbla of respectability saves her from "spoiling" herself and ensures her academic success. However, as the novel goes on to demonstrate, "[t]he trouble with the kumbla is the getting out of the kumbla. If you dwell too long in it, it makes you delicate, [i]t makes you an albino: skin white but not by genes" (Brodber 130). Tia Maria, the family's Black progenitress, wills her own disappearance from the family tree in order to improve the social chances of her mulatto children. She pays for this act ultimately with her sanity, but some of her children make good. Nellie's shame-dispensing Aunt Becca, a more severe version of Tee's Aunt Beatrice, in *Crick Crack,* improves her family's status when she aborts her child by Mass Tammy in order to "keep herself" for marriage to the village school teacher. Her self-directed violence leaves her barren and childless, although her well-appointed home provides Nellie with a safe haven from which to embark on her education. The price Nellie pays for her own successful kumbla of primness and academic dedication is sexual frigidity and social alienation. However, her education and social status provide her with the reflective space she needs to begin rewriting her history. In each of these situations the power and potential for oppression of the wider society are claimed as part of the heritage or kumbla of the women themselves. Consequently, their capacity for good or ill is acted out within the psyche of each woman rather than being externalized onto a third party. No single actor remains purely an agent of good or of evil nor is any character, male or female, merely victim or victor.

The spiral structure of the folk song that frames the narrative ensures that each generation, while going back to the beginning of the sequence, does so with a new partner: a new set of resources and inhibitions, which are based on accretions from the past but which constantly describe a movement onward to new contexts and possibilities. The geometry of this structure erases the distinction between linear time and cyclic time inherent in the Hegelian notion of Africa as outside of history[1] but equally present in the nostalgic backward glance to a period of "primitive communism" before the reification of the subject in Jameson's work[2] or the celebration of cyclic, Black time as apposite to linear white time in the work of a critic like Bonnie J. Barthold.[3] In Brodber's figure, cyclic and linear patterns cannot be separately identified and extricated from the pattern she weaves and the reader must accept the possibilities and limitations of both forms as well as the new combinations suggested by their creative tension.

Like Erna Brodber, Paule Marshall uses snatches from various songs as chapter and section headings within her narrative. In addition to music and orature, she also employs dance as a metaphorical device. *Praisesong* is set on the island of Tatem, South

Carolina, in the city of New York, and on the tiny Caribbean dependency of Carriacou. There are songs of praise connected with each of these settings that provide a frame- work for the middle-aged African-American woman, Avey, in her search for identity. They include the shouts used by the Tatem church members, whose intricate, shuffling dances Avey remembers watching on holiday visits to her Great Aunt Cuney. Then there are the Blues songs and spirituals shared by Avey and her husband in the private dance sessions of their early, poverty-stricken years, before the struggle for education and better living conditions for their children turn Avey and Jay into upstate New York versions of Aunt Becca and Aunt Beatrice. Finally, there are the ceremonial chants used during the annual meeting on Carriacou when out-islanders living over- seas return to their tiny island to greet their ancestors and dance out the steps signify- ing their African "nations." Through her involvement with each of these songs, dances and settings, Avey is able to reconcile the various facets of her experience and reformu- late her attitude toward herself as a woman and as a descendant of Africans. The structure of the novel reenacts the structure of a dance or jazz improvisation, moving between the linear narrative of Avey's long day and the remembered melodies of her Tatem childhood which thread their way through her consciousness with ever-increas- ing clarity until the final, grand movement on Carriacou. This structure allows the reader to experience a sense of fulfillment at the end of the tale although the storyline remains open-ended and incomplete. We have only the vaguest notion of what Avey will do with her new-found selfhood but we expect if will take up the theme melody of the shuffling dance in infinitely innovative sequences.

The association of orature, children's games and dance with female protagonists is hardly novel, as Black women often have been represented by Black nationalist writers as handing on oral rather than written cultural forms. What is new is the way in which the women writers discussed here integrate this specifically female body of tradition into the structure of the novel. Like the boy G in Lamming's *Castle*, each protagonist embarks on a journey in search of a self in relation to a submerged aspect of her cultural community. Structurally, however, unlike the questing hero of the male writer, the folk culture in relation to which the heroine's alienation is measured is also the source or potential source of her redemption. Instead of allowing the literary form of the romance and its latter-day equivalent, the existentialist narrative, to define and marginalize the culture of Black women as outside of time, and historically redundant, that culture itself becomes a structuring agent, providing the ambience through which modern problems like alienation and the loss of authenticity are articulated. Where G, with the reader, observes the folk culture of his community from the outside, with the respect accorded a soon-to-be extinct species, Nellie, Avey and, to a lesser extent, Tee, experience this culture from the inside and are therefore in a position to change its meaning and direction for themselves and for those before and after them.

The Caribbean women writers' insistence on the presence of aggression and nega- tion in the lives of their protagonists, while affirming their potential for initiating change, differentiates their work also from all but the most experimental mainstream feminist writers. Patriarchy and colonialism may be the bogeymen, but the stories make it clear that the women themselves have participated in reproducing the system, and that the power they now possess to challenge that system has often been won by their complicity within it.[4] Brodber's metaphor of the kumbla is perhaps the most striking of the symbols for this process, enhanced as it is by the context of the spiral form which the ring game gives to the novel as a whole. Thus women are not merely the disfigured victims of the Patriarchy, doomed to reproduce their own oppression. They are also active players in the ongoing game, with a chance each time the wheel turns to change their partners and alter the steps of the dance.

The perspective has its Caribbean male equivalent in the apocalyptic vision of the Guyanese novelist Wilson Harris, whose concept of "backward resurrection" calls into question the whole notion that historical or individual progress is dependent on movement forward, whether it be through conquest or personal victory. From this perspective, even the most abject death may lead backwards to a new beginning. Contemporary feminist science fiction produced beyond the region seems also to embrace this possibility. In Joanna Russ's *The Female Man*, the four J's, as they move back and forth along the time-space continuum, must deal with the reality that even the most progressive versions of themselves which they encounter may incorporate aspects of human nature deemed inimical to their gender interests in earlier worlds.

For the Caribbean women writers discussed here, however, the consequences of this difference in approach are at once profound and unexpected. Other revisionist writers have often found that self-assertion may mean defining oneself in apposition to the values associated with the dominant culture. Thus, for the feminist theorist Hélène Cixous, if male power is focused and penetrative, the feminine principle must celebrate the dispersed nature of pleasure. Similarly, for the proponents of Negritude, if white culture is synonymous with rationality, Black culture must validate pure intuition. Such categories are often self-fulfilling, reproducing the very hierarchies whose values they seem to assail. But even where feminist writers portray women invading the economic and cultural space traditionally dominated by men—the pulpit, the work place, the sports field, the marriage bed—they often end up displacing other qualities associated with the feminine and reinforcing the idea that certain human activities are incompatible within a single personality.

Alice Walker touches on a related issue in her review of Jean McMahon Humez's *Gifts of Power: The Writings of Rebecca Jackson*. While praising the work's reclamation of the life and work of this nineteenth century Black woman preacher, she criticizes the ease with which Jackson's feminist biographer equates her subject's strength, innovativeness and independence with a lesbian lifestyle, for which no direct historical data is given or presumed necessary (Walker 79). The issue here is not so much whether or not Jackson was a better person for being or not being a lesbian, but whether the identities and values associated with a lesbian identity, as defined for instance in Adrienne Rich's essay on "Compulsory Heterosexuality," only can be imagined outside of a heterosexual identity. One encounters the same assumption in some works of feminist science fiction that repeatedly posit female utopias in which strong, decisive women have dispensed with their biological functions, as if there were a necessary correlation between cultural roles of inferiority and heterosexuality or childbirth.

Part of the problem is that within Western literary discourse female biology has functioned for so long as such a powerful metaphor for female weakness and oppression that it is just much easier to jettison it completely as the utopian writers do, or invest it with mystic power within a separatist universe, than to grapple with the creation of new, integrative images. One thinks for example, of Sherry Ortner's classic argument that "female is to male as nan the course of its development subtly begins to take on the dualisms it purports to critique."[5] But, as Donna Haraway points out, "the political struggle is to see from both perspectives at once because each reveals both dominations and possibilities unimaginable from the other vantage point" (Haraway 71).

II

Caribbean women writers have a cultural precedent for eroding boundaries between gendered attributes. Historically, the Black woman in the New World has always been associated with such qualities as physical strength, sexual independence and economic resourcefulness.[6] These associations are a consequence of her status as nonperson (and therefore non-woman) during slavery but, like the kumblas of Brodber's vision, the disfigurement functioned dialectically to protect and extend purportedly African traditions of female independence and physical prowess.[7] During the early twentieth century many Caribbean writers experimented with literary strategies for representing these "masculine" traits. The barrack-yard stories of the *Beacon* magazines published in Trinidad during the 1930s, Claude McKay's Caribbean prose and poetry, and the popular novels of H. G. de Lisser provide a range of examples of this kind of protagonist.[8] The value judgments the male writers make about their female subjects differ dramatically, depending on the author's social class and cultural sympathies. Nevertheless such figures allowed the writers to imagine women as androgynous or heterosexual in terms of their sexuality but functionally masculine by Western standards in terms of their gender attributes. The existence of these literary representations acknowledges the tenacity with which the first generation of Black women after emancipation fought for the right to an independent and emotionally satisfying existence for themselves.[9] Their disappearance from later Caribbean fiction, or their truncation into stereotypes in the work of the nationalist writers of the 1950s and 1960s did not mean such women ceased to exist. Rather, it reflects the ambivalence of the emergent Black elite, from whose ranks the nationalist writers were drawn, about their connection with a female tradition so at odds with the normative gender roles of their new class.

Contemporary Caribbean women writers have been able to appropriate purportedly masculine prerogatives for their female characters by drawing on the legacy of those Caribbean women, whose strength and independence so fascinated and perplexed an earlier generation of Caribbean male writers. In each of the novels discussed in this essay, powerful, older women provide the protagonists with their most vital link to alternative perspectives on the roles of women as individuals and members of the community. In *Crick Crack*, Tee's grandmother is the only character whose self-narrative remains unchallenged—in fact it is she who teaches the children to voice the "Crick-crack" response with which they confront the unauthentic roles offered them by the wider society. Although she is the dispenser of nurture, toolum, and sugar cakes, Ma Henrietta is described as "a strong, bony woman who did not smile unnecessarily, her lower jaw set at an angle that did not brook opposition or argument" (Hodge 13). Ma Henrietta passes on to Tee the oral traditions of her African heritage while teaching the child respect for nature and the elements. She also holds the secret of Tee's African name, handed down from her great-grandmother of whom Tee is held to be the reincarnation. In keeping with the novel's inconclusive ending, Tee never learns this secret name, as by the time her grandmother is ready to impart it, the child has moved out of the ambit of the older woman's influence. Ma Henrietta's function as a "masculine" role model for Tee is emphasized in such details as the way her grandchildren imitate their grandmother's style of dressing in the "jumble sale" cast-offs of her dead husband; their induction through her into the strenuous work of farming and marketing, and their unreflective imitation, like "spattered acolytes" (Hodge 18) of her private rituals, such as the trek she makes after every storm to the swollen river.

The continuities between Hodge's text and Paule Marshall's transformative approach to gender-bound social roles in *Praisesong* is so marked, one is tempted to speculate that Marshall set out deliberately to actualize the potential suggested in the relationship between Tee and Ma Henrietta in her presentation of Avey and Great Aunt Cuney. The image of priest and acolyte, the emphasis on functional clothing and physical strength as specifically feminine attributes and the older woman's communion with nature as a facet of the shared memory of the race are given overt symbolic significance in the following passage describing the preparation for the ritual treks to lbo landing that the child makes with her aunt each time she visits Talem Island:

> At least twice a week her great-aunt (who resembled the trees in her straight, large-boned mass and height) would take the field hat down from its nail on the door and solemnly place it over her headtie and braids. With equal ceremony she would then draw around her the two belts she and the other women of her age in Tatem always put on when going out: one belt at the waist of their plain, longskirted dresses, and the other (this one worn in the belief that it gave them extra strength) strapped low around their hips like the belt for a sword or a gun holster. "Avatara." There was never any need to call her, because Avey, keeping out of sight behind the old woman, would have already followed suit, girding her non-existent hips with a second belt (an imaginary one) and placing—with the same studied ceremony—a smaller version of the field hat (which was real) on her head. . . . Thus attired, they would set out, her great-aunt forging ahead in her dead husband's old brogans, which on her feet turned into seven league boots, while Avey, to keep up, often had to play a silent game of Take a Giant Step with herself. (Marshall 32–33)

In her version of this scene, Marshall takes pains to connect what could be dismissed in Hodge's description as personal, masculine-derived eccentricities of style to a female dress code, within which strength and dexterity with weapons are desirable traits. Even the cast-off men's shoes are invested with added female power, rather than investing their female wearer with male strength.

Like Ma Henrietta's trek to the swollen river, Aunt Cuney's pilgrimage ends at the river's edge. But instead of silent contemplation she shows Avey the spot where slaves were disembarked, and from which, according to tradition, one group of Ibo slaves had simply walked back to Africa. Avey's questioning of the legend's authority temporarily breaks the bond between her and the older woman, as it reveals she has missed the connection with an African past that the legend maintains. But she has learned enough to reconnect with this vision forty years later in Carriacou. Significantly, the protagonist in Marshall's novel does inherit the name of her slave ancestor, Avatara, of whom, like Tee in *Crick Crack*, she is considered a reincarnation.

Hodge and Marshall both use specific references to an African heritage to underpin their construction of an alternative set of gender attributes for their female figures. Indeed it is significant that the typical "masculine" female in these novels is usually a woman past childbearing age when, according to many West African traditions, the gender distinction between men and women no longer matters. The age bias in the African precedent suggests that there may be a stronger correlation than I have allowed between this literary strategy and the desexualizing of characters in the work of feminist science fiction writers, or the use of lesbian and androgenous figures to challenge conventional notions of heterosexual femininity. But again, the difference lies in the way the Caribbean texts implode boundaries between potentially competing versions of sexuality. In the Caribbean stories, conflicting gender attributes or identities are merged or held in creative tension rather than erasing each other. At the end of *Praisesong,* for example, Avey's search for identity, which has involved a reaffirmation of her sexual and emotional ties to her former husband, reaches its symbolic climax when she achieves an orgasm in response to the touch of her female masseuse (Marshall 223–24).[10] Conversely, near the end of *Jane and Louisa,* when Nellie makes the predictable heterosexual advance of gratitude to her friend and mentor, Baba, he refuses to take on the role of heterosexual lover. As he puts it: "I fear you offer yourself because you don't want you" (Brodber 71). His words challenge Nellie to confront her sexuality in relation to her own needs rather than in response to conventional constructions of the feminine role.

The connection between the African cultural legacy and the creation of alternative representations of female sexuality and social identity is mediated by myth, rather than by reference to specific present-day or historical African communities, many of which have been oppressively patriarchal. Because of their distance in historical time and geographical space from Africa, Caribbean writers can select those aspects of a remembered culture which undermine the values of the dominant culture most effectively. Consequently, they are able to base their rejection of patriarchal models on a fictive affinity with an entire civilization rather than retreating into an exclusively female subculture. On the other hand, the historicity of the connection between Africa and the New World and the continued existence of a different view of women's attributes within Caribbean folk culture and early Caribbean writing lend an aura of realism or at least aesthetic inevitability to what could otherwise be read as a utopian celebration of women's strength. Mainstream feminist writers by contrast often must strain after similar effects in their creation of futuristic utopias or their rehabilitation of an earlier, pre-patriarchal society.

III

It would seem that Caribbean writers have developed a foolproof literary mechanism for reaffirming selfhood and community. Certainly, in the works of several male nationalist writers, the African heritage in its symbolic association with the female has functioned as the philosopher's stone of social reaffirmation. But the women writers' commitment to the reclamation of her own personhood as well as that of her oppressors resists the construction of false utopias. The strength invested in Caribbean women is recognized as a source of both good and evil in each of the novels under consideration.[11] Ma Henrietta's firm jaw and masculine stride find their echo in the terrifying rectitude of Aunt Beatrice as well as the disciplinary excesses of Tante. The strength and determination Avey evinces in fighting her way out of the ghetto are the same qualities that make it possible for her to repress her affection for her husband and corset the unspoken yearnings of forty sterile years. We have seen how these patterns are repeated in the powerful kumblas Nellie's foremothers construct for themselves and their daughters. How then to avoid the familiar heresy that the very pathology of this strength is responsible for the emasculation of the Black male and the impoverishment of Afro-Caribbean culture?

Caribbean women writers have responded to this challenge by redefining the notion of motherhood itself. In none of the three novels under consideration is the heroine's mother or the heroine's role as mother a central or pivotal issue. Tee's mother dies in childbirth at the beginning of *Crick Crack, Monkey*. The mothers of the heroines in the two other novels are given minor roles. In both cases, the reality of their sexual needs and the straightforward biological factors of reproduction rather than any association with the social aspects of mothering inform the way they are seen by their daughters.[12] Avey, watching her parents dance during the Hudson River boat trip, is suddenly suffused with the knowledge that "it was out of this holding and clasping, out of the cut-eyes and the private smiles that she and her brothers had come" (Marshall 190). In *Jane and Louisa*, Nellie at eight years old is able to divine that her mother's swollen belly is in some way connected to the day that her parents had bathed together in the same wash pan (Brodber 96).

Rather than celebrating the maternal in themselves or acting out their victimization as daughters, the symbolic arena of conflict between mother and daughter is removed from the realm of individual psychoanalysis and worked out in terms of community.[13] In this way the writers rupture the seemingly inevitable link between biological and social mothering. Maternal caring, involving nurture, discipline and unconditional affection, normally associated with the mother, is provided in all three narratives by an assortment of Aunts, grandparents, godmothers, elderly neighbors and youthful, often unemployed male family connections. Avey's Great Aunt Cuney and Aunts Becca and Beatrice spring immediately to mind, but so too does Mikey, Tante's half-grown ward who acts as comforter and protector to Tee and Toddan. The classic womb images evoked by the physical closeness of the children and the young man as he transports them to school on his bicycle and by the association of their moments together with water as they cool off in the river on a hot day with "Mikey cruising around in the deep part with one lazy eye on [them]" (Hodge 6), constitute

some of the most unambiguously positive representations of nurturing that we encounter in Hodge's occasionally desolate narrative.

A similar relationship exists between Nellie and Mass Mehiah in *Jane and Louisa*.
The description of their interaction is redolent with sights, sounds and smells commonly associated with maternal dialogue:

> I loved Mass Stanley and nobody seemed to mind. There were pimento trees in his yard
> growing out of rocks. And the rocks were peculiar too. They were full of holes. You had
> to walk carefully for if you stubbed your toe, it was liable to get stuck and break off
> altogether. And the rocks had a smell. Sometimes of coffee and tobacco and sometimes
> of sweet soap as if Miss Sada washed them. . . . They liked to have me creeping into
> their house too. I would walk in and sit at the doorway and Mass Stanley, smoking his
> pipe in his rocking chair by the door, would crinkle his eyes and start talking to me.
> (Brodber 103)

Such fictive scenarios coincide closely with the reality of the extended family as it
exists in New World Black communities, where migration, crowded living conditions,
long working hours for women and relatively high rates of death in childbirth severely
limit the probability that any child grows up in a one-to-one relationship with both
its biological parents.[14] In addition, children must often live away from home to attend
school and the notion of kin is less a matter of blood ties than of shared exigency.
However, none of this is viewed in these novels as deviancy from the norm. On the
contrary, once again an actual cultural precedent, which in this case necessitates the
separation of social and biological aspects of mothering, is used as the basis for an
alternative vision. The novels contrast the wide network of social support and interaction such a system provides with the efforts of some of the girls' kin to lock them into
monolithic, emotionally overcharged relationships with specific mother figures. Tee's
violent reaction to Aunt Beatrice's attempt to create a special bond of sentiment
between them during the family vacation at the seaside, is a case in point (Hodge 93).
Conversely, Avey's sensation during the Hudson River boat-trip of being linked by
invisible silken threads streaming out of her navel with all family members and friends
on the boat is one of the most positive memories she takes with her into adult life
(Marshall 190).

In keeping with the comparatively denser symbolic structure of *Jane and Louisa*,
social mothering in Nellie's community is presented in a variety of situations, involving many other children besides the protagonists. Baba's upbringing by his grandparents, Mass Stanley and Miss Elsada is a typical example. Having acted out the
standard Oedipal conflict between himself and his son, Mass Mehiah finds himself
saddled with the upbringing of this son's illegitimate offspring, Baba, who has been
abandoned by both his natural parents. Rather than being drawn as a child under a
curse, Baba is presented as a special gift whose presence heals the cycles of oedipal
frustration within his grandfather's household (Brodber 110). Brodber presents the
complex interaction between parenting and community in synchronic and diachronic
terms. Thus, the beautiful garden into which Nellie's Great Aunt Alice leads h r is
planted with family members, past and present, all of whom have contributed to the
strengths and weaknesses which are part of Nellie's psyche. The intricate weave of

relationships finds its profoundest symbol in the dance that Nellie watches all the adults in her community perform at the village fair (Brodber 101–2). Its continuous exchange of partners is reminiscent of the children's game for which the novel is named, but it also re-enacts the way in which the seemingly arbitrary patterns of kinship and nurturing in Nellie's community weave an intricate web of social possibilities similar to the silken threads of Avey's Hudson River boat trip experience.

IV

In narratives about so-called marginal groups, madness or socially deviant behavior is a common strategy for representing a character's rejection of the roles assigned by the dominant culture. In works like Charlotte Perkins Gilman's short story, "The Yellow Wallpaper," or Richard Wright's *Native Son*, the price the protagonist pays for such acts of defiance is often the ultimate one of self-destruction. Alternatively, where the protagonist survives the trauma of insanity—as happens in Sylvia Plath's *The Bell Jar* or V.S. Naipaul's *The Mimic Men*, the worlds to which they return often are places in which their irreversible social isolation seems inevitable. In the novels of Caribbean women, mental breakdowns also occur but they seldom mark the final position of the protagonist at the end of the story. Rather, they are used as emotionally releasing devices which help the female protagonist articulate her sense of social inadequacy and spiritual deprivation.[15] This therapeutic aspect of the psychological crisis is reinforced by its association with the possession and healing rituals of African syncretic religious traditions so widespread in the New World.

Within this context the moment of breakdown is not a moment of isolation but a moment of contact: with the ancestral past, with the community, and with the self. For Avey in *Praisesong* the dark night of the soul occurs when she relives the trauma of the Middle Passage on the boat journey between Grenada and Carriacou. Respectable, middle-aged matron that she is, she at first experiences her gross retching out of her stomach's contents as the ultimate indignity. Her incontinence and hallucinations mark a violent rupture with her role of corseted respectability as a wealthy widow. But even as she plumbs the depths of psychic and physical disintegration, she becomes aware of soothing female voices and hands which help her through this traumatic rebirth:

> They held her. Hedging her around with their bodies—one stout and solid, the other lean, almost fleshless but with a wiry strength—they tried cushioning her as much as possible from the repeated shocks of the turbulence. . . . Their lips close to her ears they spoke to her, soothing low-pitched words which only sought to comfort and reassure her, but which from their tone seemed to approve of what was happening. "Bon," they murmured as the gouts of churned up, liquefied food erupted repeatedly, staining for a moment the white spume on the waves below. "Bon," they whispered at the loud hawking she was helpless to control and at the slime hanging out of her mouth. "Bon" at the stench. (Marshall 205)

The healing bath and massage to which Avey submits herself in the aftermath of the experience on the boat recalls the laying on of hands within Christian and neo-

African religious traditions. Subsequently, Avey participates in the island rituals, purged, cleansed and anointed; a fitting vessel for the spirits of the ancestors. If we compare this scene to the vomiting scene in *The Bell Jar,* the contrast between the two literary renditions of similar situations is thrown into relief. In Plath's novel, each of the girls who succumb to food poisoning, after a banquet intended to groom them for the social roles they are about to take on, throws up in a separate cubicle. Afterwards each is placed in an identical bed and given an identical present. Plath's strategy dramatizes the girls' atomization and isolation in a world that can even reduce revolt to a commodity. But it leaves her reader with no outlet for the anger, victimization or sense of hopelessness it evokes.[16]

Nellie's psychic crisis in *Jane and Louisa* occurs after her radical intellectual lover is consumed by the fervor of his social vision and becomes a human torch. The first time she allows herself to weep for him, Nellie is overwhelmed by the direct physical support she receives from the inhabitants of the tenement yard whom she had formerly patronized or avoided. As she says: "it was a new experience to have people hugging me and drying my tears" (Brodber 54). However, she is not yet ready to let go of her inhibitions. Her neurosis continues to be inward directed, taking the form of pathological scratching, walking in ever tighter circles and finally climaxing in a sense of levitation after which she loses consciousness. As she emerges from her coma, Nellie begins to register the sounds of human life around her for the first time: "In my six weeks of convalescence, I could hear their shuffling in the kitchen and assumed they were fat women. Heard the jingle of the toilet chain and heard the rush of water. Heard the slam of the dominoes and could imagine the men with cigarettes illicitly and precariously propped at the side of their mouths" (Brodber 73). The night she finally feels confident enough to brave the dance hall alone, these sounds merge into a seamless fabric of humanity in which the lines of demarcation between human bodies are no longer of importance. Here, too, the metaphor is one of physical and spiritual rebirth; Nellie's crossing of the threshold into the dance hall becomes a movement through a human archway or birth canal that ushers her into the "beautiful garden" of her family's past. The description of this moment recalls the human tunnel through which religious initiates are passed when they "catch the spirit": "as my eyes became accustomed to the lighting, I realized that a part of the round, represented the hunched shoulders of men sitting on what must be a verandah rail, rounding their shoulders, to keep their balance or protect their beer bottles between their legs. As my eyes traversed the round of their backs, I could make out a wooden arch. Experience told me that this must be the entrance and that there must be a gateman. I was right about the first, but there was no gateman. There was no formal rite of passage" (Brodber 74).[17]

Male Caribbean writers who make use of psychic crisis in their work as a marker of their protagonists' most extreme point of alienation or defiance are seldom able to achieve transformative resolutions of this nature when their protagonists are also male. However, both Claude McKay in *Banana Bottom* (1933) and George Lamming in *Season of Adventure* (1962) submit their female protagonists to immersion in religious rituals of possession as a way of indicating a moment of interface between a middle-class elite and their lower class origins. Derek Walcott in *Dream on Monkey Mountain*

(1970) and Edward Braithwaite in *Mother Poem* (1977) also use female figures as guides for their protagonists through the labyrinths of their personal hells, but this latter strategy has its obvious parallels in traditional male quest narratives.

V

Living in a world "without history" or with a history too brutal to contemplate, speaking in the language of the colonizer from within the psyche of the colonized, Caribbean writers more than most have had to find ways to accommodate paradox, not merely in order to create but in order to survive. Some writers, like V.S. Naipaul, have chosen to identify primarily with an idealized European sense of order. Others, like Kamau Brathwaite, have searched for ways to articulate the Caribbean reality based on identification with Africa. Still others, like Derek Walcott, George Lamming and Wilson Harris, have reveled in the terror and promise of the open-ended Caribbean social experiment and have looked for ways of transforming this into satisfying aesthetic forms. The women writers bring to this tradition an awareness of gender as a factor in this dynamic. Through their gendered prism they envisage new possibilities within Caribbean Creole culture, some of which build on the work of their male counterparts.

Paradoxically, and in contrast to both cultural nationalist and radical feminist writers, the women writers discussed here seem singularly committed to that oldest of female/colonial responsibilities of maintaining and renewing the sociosymbolic order. Their acceptance of responsibility for the system that reproduces their oppression, their appropriation of structural patterns that have been used by such unlikely benefactors as Hegel and the Romantics, as well as their implied rejection of most forms of separatist politics, could be read as a revisionist attempt to create a space for themselves within the dominant discourse. Spivak suggests as much in defining what she sees as the limits of Jean Rhys's challenge to colonial discourse in *The Wide Sargasso Sea*: "Attempts to construct the 'Third World Woman' as a signifier remind us that the hegemonic definition of literature is itself caught within the history of imperialism. A full literary reinscription cannot easily flourish in the imperialist fracture of discontinuity, covered over by an alien legal system masquerading as Law as such, an alien ideology established as only Truth, and a set of human sciences busy establishing the 'native' as self-consolidating Other" (Spivak 273).

This is one of the risks the strategies I have described carry with them. To it one could add a tendency to idealize the folk culture. All the three novelists discussed are members of that Black middle-class strata of women who have benefitted from the intersection of class, racial and sexual bias. The kumblas that have protected them for long enough to allow them to consolidate their status before turning to interrogate it, do not exist for the majority of their lower-class sisters. Although both lower-class and middle-class women in the Caribbean use folk forms to structure their narratives in ways that few male writers achieve, there are stark differences between the middle-class writer's apprehension of the folk culture and that of a group like the Jamaican theatre collective, Sistren, most of whose members are drawn from the ranks of the urban poor. In Sistren's play, *Bellywoman Bangarang*, for example, ring games like "Bull inna di Pen and Im Caan get out" are used to create images of imprisonment and cyclic frustration rather than the constantly transforming spirals of Brodber's vision or the intricate unfolding of Marshall's jazz-like sequences.[18]

The narrative and metaphorical experiments of the writers discussed, however, deliberately thematize these representational limitations, so that the texts themselves, like Brodber's kumblas, come to function as a potential critique of the process they embody. Their openness to the possibility of subversion, while constantly working towards the consolidation of a functioning sociosymbolic order, differentiates their work from the deconstructive strategies available to writers and critics within Western discourse, where the unraveling of the dominant discourse is often represented as synonymous with the breakdown of all social order. This angst-ridden premonition of chaos is present to a degree in *Crick Crack, Monkey,* where the alternatives offered by both Tante and Aunt Beatrice are discredited and Tee is left without a name. Only the existence of texts like *Praisesong* and *Jane and Louisa* makes it possible for us to "read" retrospectively such characters as Mikey and Tee's Great Grandmother as marking vestigial possibilities for social transformation in Hodge's novel. The contribution the Caribbean women's texts make to feminist and nationalist discursive traditions is precisely this possibility of imagining new categories to describe and account for familiar tensions and hierarchies. By presenting such categories as fluid and provisional the writers urge us to envision a social order capable of containing without necessarily erasing both extremes within the dualistic frameworks through which we have learned to apprehend our reality.

Notes

This essay has been revised especially for this anthology. An earlier version of the essay appeared in *Callaloo* 16.1 (1993): 44–64. We are grateful to the editor of *Callaloo*, Charles Rowell, and to Johns Hopkins University Press for permission to reprint portions of the earlier essay.

1. Ironically, Hegel's own representation of history makes use of a similar spiral metaphor, by which "culture" (static, repetitive) interacts with "progress" (linear, positivist) to produce self-reflection and therefore "History." However, Hegel found it necessary to locate the hypothetical limit of his paradigm (culture *without* progress) in an actual geographical space, Africa, thus negating the possibility of "culture" ever interacting with "progress" in his understanding of an African society. James Snead's essay, "Repetition as a Figure of Black Culture," contains a useful discussion of the implications of this position for a reading of African-American culture.

2. Dowling tries hard to rescue Jameson from this idealization of primitive societies in his study of *Jameson, Althusser and Marx* (21–22), but ultimately I think he fails. By positing primitive communism as a "form of life" rather than an economic stage or mode of production, Jameson comes close to investing some ur-primitive society with the status of life before violation—a society with a claim to a "language before desire" (Haraway 94). Kristeva's strictures on the political dangers of imagining a-topias in her essay on "Women's Time" seem relevant here.

3. The seductive symmetry of Barthold's readings is most effective when she looks at African-American texts which partake of both forms of temporality. When she tries to set up

moments within African texts in purely cyclic terms, her paradigm fits less easily on her readings.

4. A similar gesture may be observed in Deborah King's work on African-American women. In her essay "Multiple Jeopardy, Multiple Consciousness: The Context of a Black Feminist Ideology," she tries to account for the statistically quantifiable paradox that while Black women as a group are the worst paid category of persons in American society, "the returns of post- secondary education, a college degree or higher are greater for Black females than for white females while among those with less than a college degree, Black females earn less than white females. A similar pattern is not found among males" (King 81).

5. Ortner's interest in origins rather than process is characteristic of the historical moment in the 1970s at which her essay was written. However, she seems not to have thought it necessary to interrogate the ethnocentric position from which mankind's relationship with nature is assumed to be a matter of establishing control, an assumption that lies at the heart of the system of hierarchies she sets out to compare. It is not impossible to read her argument as saying "this is what happens to females when the relationship between man and nature is taken as hierarchical," but in fact, since most people in Western cultures take this view of nature as a given, many women have read Ortner as confirming their worst fears about the "natural" inevitability of their second-class status.

6. For a discussion of this historical reconstitution of Black female identity in American slave society see Chapter 1, "The Legacy of Slavery: Standards for a New Womanhood," in Angela Davis' *Woman, Race and Class*.

7. Jameson reminds us in *The Political Unconscious* that "the dynamic of reification . . . is a complex one in which the traditional or 'natural' unities, social forms, human relations, cultural events, even religious systems are systematically broken up in order to be reconstructed more efficiently, in the form of new post natural processes or mechanisms; but in which, at the same time, these new isolated broken bits and pieces of the old unities acquire a certain autonomy of their own, a semi-autonomous coherence which, not merely a reflex of capitalist reification and rationalization, also in some measure serves to compensate for the dehumanization of experience reification brings with it and to rectify the otherwise intolerable effects of the new process" (Jameson 63).

8. For fuller discussions of the representation of women in early Jamaican and Trinidadian writing, respectively, see Rhonda Cobham, "Women in Jamaican Literature," and the sections on the barrack-yard stories in Reinhard Sander's *The Trinidad Awakening*.

9. In "Profile of the Jamaican Free Woman," Erna Brodber, in her other role as social anthropologist, analyzes a sample of life histories of the first generation of free born women, part of the oldest generation of women still alive in Jamaica in the early 1960s. Brodber characterizes their distinctive traits as "emotional accommodation" (the ability to adjust without trauma to changing domestic units and/or relationships), independence and authority. Brodber interviewed only those women who had survived to a ripe old age, but her observations about their cohort are corroborated by early twentieth-century observers. In his documentary *Black Jamaica* (1899), W. P. Livingstone, a Scottish-born journalist, singles out the independent spirit of the Black Jamaican woman as one of the two major obstacles—the other being Obeah—in the path of Christian missionaries attempting to "civilize" the former slaves.

10. Marshall's use of a lesbian moment of contact as a positive image in this novel must be read as a deliberate departure from the almost homophobic correlation between homosexuality and cultural alienation in her earlier novel, *The Chosen Place, The Timeless People*.

11. The paradoxical promise and terror of Caribbean women's power, despite their social oppression, was raised as a central issue in several of the papers presented by Caribbean women at the first symposium on Women in Caribbean Culture (Bridgetown, Barbados, July 1981). It

is characteristic of the perceptual difference between feminists in the Caribbean and in Western societies that, where the latter must often start by setting in perspective the historic weakness of women, Caribbean women start by qualifying and critically assessing their fabled strength.

12. In privileging *The Mother-Daughter Plot*, ignored and erased within patriarchal discourse, Marianne Hirsch notes that the Anglo American women whose texts she examines "write within literary conventions that define the feminine only in relation to the masculine as object or obstacle" and that even while they develop emancipatory strategies such female texts "act out the frustrations engendered by these limited possibilities." Hirsch remains uneasy with the way in which such assumptions force her to operate within a psychoanalytical framework that takes the father-mother-child triad of the nuclear family as its normative base. She registers her reservations in her reading of the relationships in Morrison's *Beloved* which, as she points out, refuse to dissolve themselves into neat groups of threes. Although Hirsch accepts that such triads structure, perforce, her own analysis, she longs "for a space in which maternal subjectivities could be articulated and for the means of politicizing the psychological and the familiar" goals which she acknowledges conflict with certain basic psychoanalytical assumptions (Hirsch 10). My aim here is not to challenge the necessity or value of such reinscriptions of the maternal, but rather to suggest ways in which the texts I consider begin to create that space beyond triangulated desire for which Hirsch longs.

13. One could claim that the writers perform on the text of their society the same kind of rereading that Jameson speaks of in relation to Deleuze in *The Political Unconscious* where he takes up Deleuze's argument about the way in which a psychological ur-narrative may be imposed by a critic operating within the present social milieu in reading practically any text. The writers I describe here make the reverse move, as they displace the psychoanalytical narrative of desire for the mother with one of desire for reintegration into the community from which their protagonists have been separated by colonization and elitism. Consequently, they are able to give their account of the same series of narrated events a completely different meaning.

14. See Olive Senior's *Working Miracles* for a detailed description of strategies for coping with child rearing and sharing responsibilities among Caribbean women.

15. The writers' transformation of the symbolic meaning of madness is particularly radical when one keeps in mind, as Lawrence Fisher points out in *Colonial Madness,* his study of the social construction of madness in Barbados, that madness in Caribbean society generally is perceived as the ultimate form of ostracism from the social contract. Furthermore, it is associated with violence and idleness (strongly tabooed behaviors in the former slave colonies); with "studiation" (the affliction of those who think too independently or continuously about life's contradictions, or who try too hard to improve their status through education); and Obeah—the ultimate negative signifier for the region's discredited African cultures. However, not all Caribbean women writers make use of this strategy. Novelists like Joan Riley in *The Unbelonging* and Jamaica Kincaid in *Annie John* are much closer to Naipaul and Plath respectively in their depiction of mental breakdown as a prelude to social alienation.

16. Plath's inability to imagine a social situation that would make re-entry into community possible creates certain structural limitations for her narrative and leads ultimately to her channeling the girls' anger into the racist scapegoating of a Black warder at the mental hospital where her protagonist is incarcerated. It also leads to an unrelieved negativity in the protagonist's perception of her relationship to her mother.

17. This must be the only occasion in a literary text where the entry of a solitary female into what must be the Caribbean equivalent of a college frat party becomes the occasion for a feminist metaphor of rebirth!

18. For a discussion of this difference in perspective in the work of Sistren see my essay, " 'A Wha Kind a Pen Dis?' The Function of Ritual Frameworks in Sistren's *Bellywoman Bangarang.*"

Works Cited

Barthold, Bonnie J. *Black Time: Fiction of Africa, the Caribbean and the United States.* New Haven: Yale University Press, 1981.

Brathwaite, Edward. *Mother Poem.* London: Oxford University Press, 1978.

Brodber, Erna. *Jane and Louisa Will Soon Come Home.* London: New Beacon Books, 1980.

―――. "Profile of the Jamaican Free Woman." Paper presented at the Institute for Social and Economic Research, University of the West Indies, Mona, Jamaica: May, 1980.

―――. " 'A Wha Kind a Pen Dis?' The Function of Ritual Frameworks in Sistren's *Bellywoman Bangarang.*" *Theater Research International* 15.3 (1990).

―――. "Women in Jamaican Literature." *The Creative Writer and West Indian Society: Jamaica 1900–1950.* Ann Arbor, Michigan: University Microfilms, 1983, no. 8720091. 195–252.

Cott, Nancy. "Comment on Karen Offen's 'Defining Feminism: A Comparative Historical Approach.' " *Signs* 15.1 (Winter, 1989): 203–5.

Davis, Angela. *Women, Race and Class.* New York: Random House, 1981.

Dowling, William C. *Jameson, Althusser, Marx: An Introduction to the Political Unconscious.* Ithaca: Cornell University Press, 1984.

DuBois, Ellen Carol. "Comment on Karen Offen's 'Defining Feminism: A Comparative Historical Approach.' " *Signs* 15.1 (Winter, 1989): 195–97.

Fisher, Lawrence. *Colonial Madness: Mental Health in the Barbadian Social Order.* New Brunswick, NJ: Rutgers University Press, 1985.

Haraway, Donna. "Manifesto for Cyborgs." *Socialist Review* 15.2 (March/April 1985): 65–107.

Harris, Wilson. "Tradition and the West Indian Writer." *Tradition, the Writer and Society: Critical Essays.* London: New Beacon Books, 1967. 28–47.

Hirsch, Marianne. *The Mother-Daughter Plot: Narrative, Psychoanalysis, Feminism.* Bloomington, IN: Indiana University Press, 1989.

Hodge, Merle. *Crick Crack, Monkey* (1970). London: Heinemann Caribbean Writers Series, 1981.

Hope, Margaret (ed.). *Journey in the Shaping: Proceedings of the First Symposium on Women in Caribbean Culture—July 24, 1981.* Cave Hill, Barbados: Women and Development Project, 1981.

Jameson, Fredric. *The Political Unconscious: Narrative as a Socially Symbolic Act.* Ithaca: Cornell University Press, 1981.

Kincaid, Jamaica. *Annie John.* New York: Farrar, Straus, Giroux, 1985.

King, Deborah. "Multiple Jeopardy, Multiple Consciousness: The Context of a Black Feminist Ideology." *Feminist Theory in Practice and Process.* Ed. Michelene Malson, et al. Chicago: University of Chicago Press, 1989. 75–106.

Kristeva, Julia. "Women's Time." Trans. Alice Jardine and Harry Blake. *Signs* 7.1 (Autumn, 1981): 13–35.

Lamming, George. *In the Castle of My Skin.* London: Secker and Warburg, 1953.

―――. *Season of Adventure.* London: Michael Joseph, 1960.

Livingstone, W. P. *Black Jamaica.* London: Low Marston & Co. Ltd., 1899.

Marshall, Paule. *Praisesong for the Widow.* New York: E. P. Dutton, 1984.

McKay, Claude. *Banana Bottom.* New York: Harper and Row, 1933.

Naipaul, V. S. *The Mimic Men.* London: André Deutsch, 1967.

Offen, Karen. "Defining Feminism: A Comparative Historical Approach." *Signs* 14:1 (Autumn 1988): 119–57.

―――. "Response to Ellen DuBois." *Signs* 15.1 (Winter, 1989): 198–201.

―――. "Response to Nancy Cott." *Signs* 15.1 (Winter, 1989): 206–9.

Ortner, Sherry B. "Is Female to Male as Nature Is to Culture?" *Woman, Culture, and Society*, Ed.

Michelle Rosaldo and Louise Lamphere. Stanford, CA: Stanford University Press, 1974. 67–87.

Plath, Sylvia. *The Bell Jar*. New York: Harper and Row, 1971.

Rich, Adrienne. "Compulsory Heterosexuality and Lesbian Existence." *Signs* 5.4 (1980): 631–60.

Riley, Joan. *The Unbelonging*. London: Women's Press, 1985.

Russ, Joanna. *The Female Man*. New York: Bantam Books, 1975.

Sander, Reinhard. *The Trinidad Awakening: West Indian Literature of the 1930s*. Westport, CT: Greenwood Press, 1988.

Senior, Olive. *Working Miracles: Women of the English Speaking Caribbean*. Barbados: Women in the Caribbean Project ISER, 1989.

Snead, James. "Repetition as a Figure of Black Culture." *Black Literature and Literary Theory*. Ed. Henry Louis Gates, Jr. New York: Methuen, 1984. 59–79.

Spivak, Gayatri. "Three Women's Texts and a Critique of Imperialism." *Race, Writing and Difference*. Ed. Henry Louis Gates, Jr. Chicago: University of Chicago Press, 1986. 262–79.

Walcott, Derek. *Dream on Monkey Mountain and Other Plays*. New York: Farrar, Straus and Giroux, 1970.

Walker, Alice. "Review of Gifts of Power: The Writings of Rebecca Jackson." *In Search of Our Mother's Gardens: Womanist Prose*. London: The Women's Press, 1984. 71–82.

ARAB-AMERICANS AND THE MEANINGS OF RACE

Lisa Suhair Majaj

Race . . . now functions as a metaphor so necessary to the construction of Americanness that it rivals the old pseudo-scientific and class-informed racisms whose dynamics we are more used to deciphering. . . . American means white.

—Toni Morrison (47)

For better or for worse, without a clear racial identity a North American is in danger of having no identity.

—Howard Winant (3)

No one today is purely *one* thing. Labels like Indian, or woman, or Muslim, or American are not more than starting-points, which if followed into actual experience for only a moment are quickly left behind . . . just as human beings make their own history, they also make their cultures and ethnic identities.

—Edward Said, *Culture and Imperialism*, 336

What does "race" mean to Arab-Americans? This question takes on increasing significance at the present time as Arab-Americans, excluded from the rosters of minorities of color as well as of white ethnic groups, debate whether to lobby for a categorization as "Arab" or "Middle Eastern" or to continue to struggle for inclusion as white Americans on other than merely "honorary" grounds.[1] Like other immigrant groups at various historical junctures, Arab Americans occupy a contested and unclear space within American racial and cultural discourse.[2] Although classified as "white" by current government definitions, they are conspicuously absent from discussions of white ethnicity, and are popularly perceived as non-white. Such liminality has profound implications for Arab-Americans as they attempt to assert a public identity, claim a voice within the American multiculture, and take collective action on issues of

320

common concern. It also makes clear the inability of prevailing American models of racial and ethnic classifications to fully account for the diversity of the American multiculture.

CONTESTED CATEGORIES

Underlying the current status of Arab-Americans is a history of inconsistent racialization. Although individual Arabs had traveled to the United States since before the beginning of the nation, Arabic-speaking immigration did not begin in earnest until the late nineteenth century. From the early days of their immigration there was much confusion over how to classify Arabic-speaking immigrants. As historian Alixa Naff notes, the immigrants—largely Eastern-rite Christians from Mount Lebanon, at that time part of Ottoman-controlled "Greater Syria" (present-day Syria, Lebanon and Israel/Palestine) were considered an "enigma" and viewed with mingled curiosity and derision (14). Initially classified on immigration forms under the category "Turkey in Asia" or "other Asians" (Naff 109), they were subsequently termed "Syrians" by immigration officials, and adopted this nomenclature themselves, finding their more familiar categories of identification, according to familial, village or religious affiliation, of little relevance in the American context. Meanwhile, they were also characterized through a variety of derogatory racial terms, including "nigger," "dago," and "sheeny" (Naff 250–51). While the immigrants' strong pride in their own cultural identity to some extent allowed them to shrug off such negative characterization as a case of "mistaken identity," the repercussions could nonetheless be serious.[3]

Arabic-speaking immigrants also had to contend with nativist rhetoric from government officials and scholars—rhetoric that was particularly worrisome within the context of legislative and judicial debates about immigration and naturalization. The Naturalization Act of 1790 had granted the right of citizenship to what it termed "free white persons." However, the definition of "white" remained a subject of intense debate. By 1899 the Bureau of Immigration had begun "to distinguish Syrians and Palestinians by 'race' from other Turkish subjects, considering them Caucasian" (Naff 109). But after 1906 immigrants from western Asia became caught up in new naturalization laws basing eligibility for citizenship on non-Asiatic identity. In 1910, Syrians, Palestinians, Turks, Armenians, and others were classified as "Asiatic" by the U.S. Census Bureau. In 1911 the Bureau of Immigration and Naturalization ordered court clerks to "reject applications for first papers from 'aliens who were neither white persons nor persons of African birth and descent' " (Naff 253)—a ruling that targeted "Asiatics" for exclusion. A series of court cases ensued, known as the "prerequisite cases," in which petitions for naturalization were challenged and in some instances denied on the basis of whether or not petitioners qualified as "white." These cases not only decided the fate of individual immigrants, but also set precedents for the inclusion or exclusion of entire ethnic groups.[4]

At stake in these cases were competing and sometimes contradictory definitions of "whiteness." As Ian F. Haney Lopez notes, "The courts had to establish by law whether, for example, a petitioner's race was to be measured by skin color, facial features, national origin, language, culture, ancestry, the speculations of scientists, popular opinion, or some combination of these factors. Moreover, the courts also had to decide which of these or other factors would govern in the inevitable cases where the various indices of race contradicted one another" (2). The definition of whiteness was particularly an issue in the case of immigrants from south and west Asia, such as Arabs and Indians, whose darker complexion set them at odds with popular perceptions of whiteness. Although such groups were scientifically identified as Caucasian, their popular perception as nonwhite was so persuasive that courts were willing to privilege common knowledge over scientific evidence when the two were at odds, thereby upholding politically motivated assumptions about the meaning of "whiteness." [5]

This schism between scientific evidence and popular perception played a significant role in the series of prerequisite cases involving Arab applicants between 1909 and 1915 and again in the 1940s, in which courts declared Arab applicants to be variously white and non-white.[6] At stake in the cases were these questions: whether Arabs are "white" in color; whether Arabs are Asian or Caucasian; whether whiteness is determined by race, color, geography, culture or religion; and whether there is an intrinsic connection between Caucasian identity and whiteness. The answers that emerged illustrate the contradictory and politicized meanings of race during this period of nativist xenophobia and generalized anxiety about American identity.

The arguments presented as rationale for challenging the right of Arabic-speaking applicants to naturalization included dark skin color, origin on the continent of Asia, distance (literal and metaphorical) from European culture, and cultural and geographical proximity to Islam. Despite—or perhaps because of—the difficulty of defining "whiteness," the courts' decisions were frequently made on the grounds of commonsense assumptions about race: judges were more likely to deem lighter-skinned applicants worthy of naturalization, and to deny naturalization to darker-skinned immigrants even when attributing rejection to other reasons. For instance, applicant Faras Shahid, described by the court as "walnut or somewhat darker than is the usual mulatto" (*Ex Parte Shahid* 813), and applicant George Dow, described as "darker than the usual person of white European descent" (*Ex Parte Dow* 487) were both initially excluded from naturalization, while applicant Tom Ellis, described as Semitic but "a markedly white type of the race," was admitted (see Ferris 4).

However, "whiteness" was understood to involve not just racial appearance and skin color, but also geographical, cultural, linguistic and religious factors. Under the "white person" prerequisite, immigrants whose cultural background and place of origin seemed to have proximity to Europe were more likely to be judged admissible than those whose cultural background and place of origin were perceived as alien to European culture. Thus, although the judge who excluded George Dow presented a discourse on the relative coloration of different west Asian peoples, he ultimately argued that in cases of ambiguous coloration "whiteness" must be construed on the basis of general affiliation with European identity. If an applicant from Syria "cannot rest on complexion," he asserted, he "must find other grounds . . . to establish any community of race with the European races assuming those last to be the white race" (*In Re Dow* 363).

Intrinsic to this European "community of race" was Christian identity. Although most of the early Arab immigrants were in fact Christian, this fact was obscured by the popular confusion between Arabs and Muslims. Islamic culture was viewed as diametrically opposed to western European culture, and, in a conflation of religious and racial identity, was construed as intrinsically non-white.[7] In asserting their claims to "whiteness" and American citizenship, Syrian immigrants therefore tended to stress their Christian identity and their historical, geographical and religious relationship to the Holy Land, and to accentuate their distance from Islam. It comes as no surprise, for instance, that during Dow's rehearing one of the arguments presented on his behalf was that the Syrians' "connection through all times with the peoples to whom the Jewish and Christian peoples owed their religion, made it inconceivable that the Statute could be intended to exclude them" (*In Re Dow* 357). But even though non-Christian identity weighed heavily *against* applicants seeking naturalization, the link between Christian identity and whiteness was viewed as insufficient grounds for inclusion. Indeed, arguments for naturalization on the grounds of an intrinsic Syrian connection to the birthplace of Christianity were dismissed as "emotional" and having "no place in the judicial interpretation of a statute" (*Ex Parte Shahid* 816).

Although the prerequisite cases had various outcomes, most of the cases before 1920 were eventually resolved in favor of the applicants. As a result, scholars have viewed the prerequisite controversy as an anomalous period in a relatively straightforward Arab-American history of assimilation (e.g. Naff 259). Indeed, the official classification of Arabic-speaking immigrants as "white" seemed ensured by a 1917 decision of the Congress that drew the longitudinal and latitudinal lines of Asian exclusion along boundaries that situated immigrants from Greater Syria within the space of "whiteness" and Americn citizenship (see Ferris 22–4). This inclusion seemed solidified by the 1920 census, which identified Syrians and Palestinians, separately, under the category "Foreign-born white population" (Naff 117).[8]

However, the link between western, European, Christian identity and "whiteness," and the importance of this link in defining American identity, persisted. So too did the connection between non-European, non-Christian and non-white identity. A 1942 case denying naturalization to a Yemeni applicant, Ahmed Hassan, made clear the extent to which "whiteness" continued to be interpreted as a characteristic of European Christians but not of non-Europeans or non-Christians. "Apart from the dark skin of the Arabs," the judge argued, "it is well known that they are a part of the Mohammedan world and that a wide gulf separates their culture from that of the predominantly Christian peoples of Europe" (In Re *Ahmed Hassan* 845). Although affiliation to Christianity had earlier been held irrelevant as a rationale for inclusion of Arabs, in this case non-Christian cultural identity was viewed as convincing rationale for exclusion. In contrast, the judge noted that certain (non-Arab) applicants might be judged suitable for American citizenship on the basis of their relationship to Christian Europe. Although voicing "serious doubt as to whether any peoples of Asiatic stock could be considered white persons within the meaning of the statue," he noted that Armenians could be considered "white" because they were Christian and were geographically closer to Europe (In Re *Ahmed Hassan* 845).[9] Through such reasoning, markers of religion were assimilated into the geographical construction of race, with

Islam relegated to the opposite side of the geographical boundary separating white, western Christian Europe from non-white, eastern, non-Christian Asia.[10]

The continuing association between western identity and whiteness also played a role, with different results, in a 1944 case that granted naturalization to an Arab applicant. In this case the judge argued that Arabs could be considered "white"—not in and of themselves, but because they had historically served as *transmitters* of western civilization. The basis for inclusion as white, the judge held, turned upon "whether the petitioner is a member of one of the 'races [(a)] inhabiting Europe or [(b)] living along the shores of the Mediterranean' or [(c)], perhaps, is a member of a race of 'Asiatics whose long contiguity to European nations and assimilation with their culture has caused them to be thought of as of the same general characteristics' " (*Ex Parte Mohriez* 943). In contrast to earlier courts that had argued the distance of Arabs from European culture, this judge held that Arabs had accrued sufficient whiteness through their role in transmitting European civilization to be considered white. As he stated, "the Arab people stand as one of the chief channels by which the traditions of white Europe, especially the ancient Greek traditions, have been carried into the present" and therefore "the Arab passes muster as a white person" (*Ex Parte Mohriez* 943).

This ruling marked the end of explicit challenges on racial grounds to the suitability of Arab immigrants for naturalization. However, the question of racial classification reemerged in a 1987 discrimination case filed by an Iraqi professor charging that he had been denied tenure on the basis of being of "Arabian race" (*Saint Francis College v. Al-Khazraji* 604). The case, filed under civil rights statute 42 U.S.C. Section 1981, was initially thrown out of court because the civil rights statute assumes a non-white plaintiff. However, the Supreme Court subsequently determined that "although Arabs are Caucasians under current racial classifications, Congress, when it passed what is now [Section] 1981, did not limit its protections to those who today would be considered members of a race different from the defendant's . . . at a minimum, [Section] 1981 reaches discrimination directed against an individual because he or she is genetically part of an ethnically and physiognomically distinctive subgrouping of *homo sapiens*" (*Saint Francis College* 604). As Therese Saliba notes, the ruling not only "supports the claim of an 'Arabian race' within the arbitrary construction of racial categories" but also challenges existing racial categories—for "once 'Arabs' as a category are included in racial politics, it is not in addition to already familiar groups of people of color covered under Affirmative Action, but rather, their inclusion leads to a dismantling of those categories" (Saliba 312).

Informing such legal debates both in the early period and at the present time are historical discourses of Orientalism and heathenism that situate non-Europeans and non-whites as uncivilized and inferior to white, Christian Europeans. As Edward Said has cogently demonstrated, Orientalism, functioning as a "system of knowledge" filtering the Orient into Western consciousness, has perpetuated "the idea of European identity as a superior one in comparison with all the non-European peoples and cultures" (*Orientalism* 5–7). In the Orientalist worldview, the West is "rational, developed, humane, superior," while the Orient is "aberrant, undeveloped, inferior" (Said, *Orientalism* 300). Islam fares particularly badly in Orientalist portrayals; historically represented as a "menace" to the west and to Christianity, it has more recently been caricatured as the epitome of barbarism, repression and irrational political violence, supplanting communism as the new enemy of the "civilized" west.

American views of Arabs also draw on the racially inflected "civilized/heathen" schism that historically opposed white American colonists to native peoples, immigrants and enslaved Africans. As the definition of "American" became equated with the characteristics of whiteness, Christianity, European/Anglo Saxon origin and "civilization," other groups were both racialized and hierarchically ranked in relationship to these characteristics.[11] Immigrants whose tenuous racial status compromised their ability to assimilate into white America often sought to move up the racial scale, and hence accentuate their claim to American identity, by distancing themselves from people of color. For instance, in their bid for acceptance in the American context, Irish and Italian immigrants sought to put as much distance as possible between themselves and African Americans.[12] Similarly, Arabic-speaking immigrants, recognizing that perceptions of "whiteness" turned upon relative distance from the "darker" end of the racial spectrum, anxiously sought to assert their difference from blacks. For instance, in a 1929 Florida incident involving the lynching of a Syrian man after a car accident (see "Syrian and Wife Killed in Florida"), the Syrian immigrant community responded not only with outrage, but also with a defensive attempt to assert their "whiteness." A letter published in a Syrian immigrant journal declaimed, "The Syrian is not a Negro whom Southerners feel they are justified in lynching when he is suspected of an attack on a white woman. The Syrian is a civilized white man who has excellent traditions and a glorious historical background" ("Has the Syrian Become a Negro" 42). While racist, such responses also made clear the immigrants' anxieties about their own racial identification in a context where to be non-white had serious consequences. As one immigrant journal warned: "*Al-Hoda* is of the opinion that the Syrians should proceed with extreme caution in this matter. . . . A certain feeling of prejudice undeniably exists against the Syrians in some parts of the South and any rash action on their part might tend to aggravate matters unnecessarily" ("Syrian and Wife Killed in Florida" 47–48).

At the same time, the anomalous location of Arabs within the binary framework of American race relations sometimes positioned immigrants outside of this framework altogether. For instance, Egyptian students in racially segregated regions of the U.S. during the 1950s and early 1960s found that their foreignness often set them outside of the black-white racial dynamics that might otherwise have relegated them to a disadvantageous sphere. Despite their dark skin, they were welcomed as "foreign students" and assigned to "white" schools (Morsy 184). Similarly, Lebanese Catholics in racially-segregated Protestant Birmingham were able to sidestep some of the implications of being "colored" in the segregated south because their Catholic identity set them apart from both black and white Protestants (Conklin and Faires 80).[13]

In the contemporary period, perceptions of and attitudes toward Arabs draw not only upon Orientalist discourse and traditional racism, but also on what has been described as "political racism" (Samhan). Political racism is distinguishable from earlier, nativist strands of racism by a focus on Arab-oriented political activity, particularly activity related to the Palestinian struggle for national rights (Samhan 16). Post-WWII political events—the 1948 creation of the state of Israel, the corresponding dispossession of the Palestinians and the military response of Arab states, the 1967 Arab-Israeli war, the 1973 Arab-Israeli war, the oil boycott of the 1970s, the Israeli invasion of Lebanon in 1982, the 1990–91 Gulf Crisis, and incidents of violence, whether or not carried out by Arabs (e.g. the 1995 bombing of the Oklahoma City Federal Building, perpetrated by a white European-American but initially attributed to Arabs)—have resulted in a climate of hostility toward Arab Americans in general and politically active individuals in particular.[14] Arab-American offices, homes and religious centers have been bombed and vandalized, and individuals have been threatened, beaten and murdered in politically-motivated assaults.[15] In 1985, following the murder of Alex Odeh, the west coast regional director of the American-Arab Anti-Discrimination Committee (ADC), FBI director William Webster warned that Arab-Americans and others advocating "Arab points of view have come within the zone of danger" (quoted in Abraham 165).

At the same time, however, federal government agencies have also played a role in targeting Arab Americans. As Helen Samhan notes, "While Arab American first amendment rights to speak and assemble are protected by the Constitution, government agencies in varying degrees have often abused those rights in the name of security against terrorism" (17). A striking example may be seen in the case of the "LA Eight"—the seven Palestinians and one Kenyan arrested in Los Angeles on January 26, 1987, incarcerated and publicly labeled a "terrorist threat" for legitimate First Amendment activities, who remain under threat of deportation at the present time (Abraham 199–203; Naber 7). Since the passage of the 1996 Anti-Terrorism Bill, targeting of Arab-Americans has increased. In addition to being subjected to special scrutiny at airports and other public places, Arab-Americans have been singled out by the bill's provisions for arrest and detention on the basis of secret evidence. It cannot pass notice that *all* of the detainees imprisoned on "secret evidence" to date (25 by January 1999), who face deportation without being allowed to know either the charges levied against them or the identity of their accusers, are of Arab or Muslim identity.[16]

Given these realities, whether or not Arabs are viewed as "white" or "non-white" matters both discursively and pragmatically. Classification and nomenclature play a role in community visibility, political power and access to resources, as well as in the ability to claim protection from discrimination. Governmental classifications that include Arab Americans within the majority white population have not protected Arab Americans from targeting on the basis of ethnicity. Rather, demographic research would arguably show that this group has "suffered historic, pervasive discrimination like other minority groups" (Gregory Nojeim, quoted in *ADC Times*, Aug-Sept. 1994: 11.) Categorization as "white" not only obscures this history of discrimination, but makes it difficult to collect accurate statistics on Arab Americans and to assess their needs.[17] Classification as white also makes Arab Americans culturally invisible, creates contradictions for dark-skinned Arabs who are not socially perceived as "white,"[18] and glosses over disparities between governmental as well as popular treatment of Arabs and Europeans in the American context (for instance, unequal access to the right of immigration).

The implications of this schism between official classification and popular perception emerge with particular clarity at moments of crisis, such as the 1995 Oklahoma Federal Building bombing, carried out by the European-American Timothy McVeigh. In the wake of the bombing, government officials identified the suspects as "white males." Surprised reporters, who had immediately raised the specter of Arab/Muslim terrorism, queried whether this identification excluded Middle Easterners. [19] Their disconcertion made clear their assumption that "white" and "Middle Eastern"—and by extension, "American" and "Arab," "American" and "terrorist"—are mutually exclusive categories. Moreover, popular opinion clearly supported such views: despite the lack of evidence pointing toward Arab perpetrators, ordinary Arab-Americans across the country were harassed, threatened, assaulted and abused in the days following the bombing.[20]

Such incidents have convinced many Arab-Americans that the designation "white," with its implications of mainstream status, does not reflect the reality of their experiences. As a result, Arab-American community leaders have begun lobbying for a specific racial or ethnic classification, even as they remain divided over whether to work towards legal identification as "Arab-Americans" or as "Middle-Eastern-Americans" (an identification that would include not just Arabs but also Iranians, Turks, Armenians and others).[21] At the time of the 1990 census, national Arab-American organizations launched a concerted campaign to encourage Arab Americans to answer the ancestry question on the "long form" by writing in an Arab country of origin, rather than identifying as "white" or by a religious designation.[22] And in 1994, following the decision of the Federal Office of Management and Budget to review the categories used for collecting data on race and ethnicity in preparation for the 2000 census, the Arab American Institute held discussions on the question of minority status (Naber 11–12).

The increasing turn to panethnic identification among Arab Americans has been encouraged by factors specific to the Arab-American community, including on-going immigration from Arab countries, the increasing proportion of Muslims among Arab Americans, and the growing politicization of Arab-Americans in response to both domestic and international events. However, it also reflects the general reliance in the American context on panethnic models of racial organization. As many scholars have argued, race, far from being a "biological" category, is "an unstable and 'decentered' complex of social meanings constantly being transformed by political struggle"(Omi and Winant 55), a fact that has long been evident in the shifting classifications of the U.S. census.[23] The current white-Black-Hispanic-Asian-American Indian pentagon[24] formalized during the Nixon era is a product of this political struggle between state-level ordering and community efforts to "claim or rearticulate identity" (Frankenberg 12). While panethnic categorization blurs distinctions between groups, it also helps minority groups to find a third space between specific ethnic identification and the binary opposition of black/white relations (Winant 60).[25] Recognizing this, Arab-Americans, like other groups, have increasingly turned to panethnic delineation to confront their identity "in a political environment of heightened racial consciousness and mobilization" (Winant 61).

LITERARY REFLECTIONS

Arab American literature both reflects and is situated within this history of contested racial categories. Literary texts from the first half of the century make clear the anxieties of Arab-Americans as they struggled for inclusion as "white" Americans. Aware of their contested racial, legal and social status in the American context, early Arab-American authors tended to emphasize those aspects of their identities more likely to gain acceptance by white Americans, and to distance themselves from those elements of Arab culture viewed as particularly foreign and less readily assimilable. In particular, they stressed their Christian identity, their geographical origin in the "Holy Land," and their "spirituality," employing biblical rhetoric and religious parallels in their attempt to engage American readers and familiarize the "exotic," while at the same time seeking to distance themselves from Islam.

A typical example of such strategic representation may be found in the work of the Lebanese immigrant writer, Reverend Abraham Mitrie Rihbany. In his autobiography *A Far Journey,* Rihbany draws heavily on biblical themes, structuring his text along the pattern of scriptural discourse and proclaiming the immediacy and relevance of biblical events to life in the modern-day Middle East. Although his religious profession predisposed him to the use of such parallels, his emphasis on Christian imagery and language may also have had a pragmatic, historically situated rationale. Rihbany's text was published in 1914, the same year in which George Dow was refused American citizenship, spurring the Arab-American community to various efforts in the attempt to prove their "white" identity.[26] In stressing his Christian identity and his intrinsic connection to the Holy Land, Rihbany sought to make the point that Syrian immigrants were not simply the recipients of American largesse, but had something of great value to offer to their new country: an ancient spiritual heritage. In a later book, *Wise Men From the East and From the West* (1922), Rihbany expounded on this argument. The Syrians, he argued, with their "deep reverence for moral and spiritual ideals" and their intrinsic Christian heritage, were not only "justly classed with the civilized peoples" (241–2) but also had the responsibility to impart this spirituality to the west: "The Oriental must never cease to teach his Occidental brother, nor ever allow himself to forget his own great spiritual maxims which have guided the course of his life for so many centuries (301).

At the same time as authors stressed their connection to Christianity, however, they also engaged in a careful distancing from Islam, viewed in the American context as the antithesis of all that was Christian, western and white. This strategy paralleled efforts by many Arab-Americans to accentuate their "whiteness" by dissociating themselves from blacks. In *A Far Journey,* for instance, Rihbany describes the childhood injunctions he received upon going to Beirut: "I was not to gaze curiously at the Mohammedans, whom I knew by their white turbans. They considered us *kuffar* (infidels) and enemies of the faith; therefore they were ever ready for the slightest provocation to beat or even kill us"(81). His description not only made clear the difference between Muslims and Christians, it also played upon stereotypes of Muslims (here called by the inaccurate American term "Mohammedans") as violent. Similarly, in

Wise Men Rihbany refers to Muslims as "the traditional enemy of my people" (243–4). In so doing he implicitly aligns himself and other Christian Syrians with Christianity, Europe and the west—despite his acknowledgement that "we Christians of Syria and all the Arabic-speaking countries, although of various origins, have always loved to call ourselves Arabs" (243).[27]

In addition to using Christian identity to assert their intrinsic affinity to white American society, Arab-American authors also made strategic use of the "exoticism" of their Holy Land origin. In so doing, they drew upon the overlapping paradigms of racial essentialism, assimilation and cultural pluralism that structured cultural interaction in the American context. While the essentialism that viewed races and ethnic groups as totally distinct set Arabs apart from European Americans, it also allowed them to assert their "uniqueness" (transposed onto a cultural and spiritual plane) as exotic emissaries from the Holy Land. At the same time, however, the assimilation paradigm held out the possibility of melding into American society, particularly given their similarities, as Christian Caucasians, with white Americans. By valorizing elements of their heritage viewed as compatible with American values, therefore, Syrian Christian immigrants were able to delineate themselves as both different *and* white.

As the century progressed, the strident assimilation pressures characterizing the early decades of the twentieth century gave way to a greater focus on cultural pluralism, and to a humanism characterized by the stance that different races and groups were "all the same under the skin." However, these shifts notwithstanding, Arab-Americans found that "American" continued to mean Christian, European, western, and white, and that they were still located outside of this definitions. Meanwhile, the orientalist stereotypes of Arabs held such sway that ordinary Arab-Americans were often viewed as not "exotic" enough to be "authentic."

Consider, for instance, the humorous autobiography *Which Way To Mecca, Jack*, published in 1960 by Lebanese-American William Blatty. Although Blatty seeks in this text to affirm both his Lebanese and his American identity, his autobiography makes clear that challenging American racial hierarchies is as difficult as challenging orientalist stereotypes. Despite Blatty's longing to fit in as a white American, for instance, his childhood desire is more limited: he wishes simply to be mistaken for a minority slightly higher on the racial hierarchy. "How I envied the Irish boys their snub noses, their pale skins," he writes. "But . . . I was usually content to look forward to the now-and-then occasions when someone would call me 'dago' or 'wop,' for at least the Italians were a majority minority" (29).

In addition to failing to pass muster as a white person, Blatty also fails to meet orientalist expectations of what an "Arab" is. Attempting to get a part in the movie *The Ten Commandments*, he is rejected for not looking "authentic" enough, for he has blue, not brown, eyes. He subsequently takes revenge on Hollywood: disguising himself as an "Arab prince," he is wined and dined by an establishment that fawns over "royalty." But he can only achieve this by cariacaturing Arabs, drawing on every orientalist stereotype imaginable in order to prove his "authenticity." As critic Evelyn Shakir points out, it is clear that "Hollywood has embraced not William Blatty, Arab-American, but . . . a personification of its own romantic (and essentially Orientalist) fantasies about the East. To win the favor of an industry that trades in images, he has had to turn himself into a cartoon Arab" ("Coming of Age" 68).

Whether through tactics of assimilation or through the strategic deployment of exoticism, writers such as Rihbany and Blatty sought not to unsettle the racial categories of white America so much as to find acceptance within them. In contrast, however, contemporary Arab-American writers increasingly seek to challenge established cultural and racial boundaries in their articulation of Arab-American identity, and to assert their identity on their own terms. Lebanese American Lawrence Joseph,[28] Jordanian American Diana Abu-Jaber,[29] and Egyptian American Pauline Kaldas[30] provide examples of contemporary writers' efforts to grapple more directly with the racialization and politicization of Arab-American experience and to assert their Arab-American identity without apology.

In his poetry and prose, Lawrence Joseph simultaneously claims and critiques his Arab identity, even as he makes clear that the Arab-American experience must be situated within a broader American context of black-white racial tension. Consider, for instance, Joseph's poem "Sand Nigger," a poem that Arab-Americans frequently invest with iconic status (*Curriculum Vitae* 27–9). The poem not only evokes the complexity of Arab-American identity, but also probes the racial and cultural boundaries that delineate, situate and inform this identity. It begins with familiar markers of ethnicity—food, place names, familial intimacies; emblems easily recuperated into the paradigm of ethnic assimilation and "white ethnicity." But instead of inscribing ethnicity at a transitional site between ethnic past and American future—the strategy by which ethnic writers so often seek to contain markers of difference and seek to accrue "whiteness"—Joseph instead reconstitutes ethnicity at the fault lines of racial and intercommunal tensions: family quarrels, war in the Middle East, anti-Arab discrimination, the violence and poverty of Detroit. In so doing he insists on the need to move beyond nostalgia to a grappling with racialization and violence in contemporary Arab-American experience.

Indeed, despite the community's classification as "white," Arab-American literature increasingly explores issues of racialization and violence. In a story titled "At the Continental Divide," Jordanian-American writer Diana Abu-Jaber depicts a newly arrived Jordanian immigrant, Jamil, whose dark skin, foreignness, and ambiguous sexual identity make him the target of a policeman's rage. The policeman, whose epithets are described as "brand[ing] Jamil's skin," snarls, "Oh, A-rab, one of *them*. Worse than niggers aren't you? Kill your own babies and mothers, bomb planes with Americans on them . . . A-rab scum" (147). The physical beating that follows parallels this "branding," reinscribing Jamil's "non-white" identity onto his body in definitive terms.

However, Abu-Jaber makes clear that the response to such violent racial inscription should not be the assertion of "whiteness." While some Arab-Americans might be able to "pass," others, marked by their dark skin and hair as well as by their Arab names, are pragmatically unable to do so. Besides, the cultural pressures toward assimilation enact their own kind of violence. As Abu-Jaber writers elsewhere, "Lighten the hair, thin the lips, change the name, cover the dress, hammer down the accent, stash away the strange gods, the poetry, the ancient disturbing pointless old stories. Smash it all down flat" ("Arabs and the Break in the Text," 132).

Indeed, contemporary Arab-American literature increasingly probes the ways in which classification as "white" serves not as a mode of inclusion but as a form of erasure. Consider, for instance, the poem "Exotic" by Egyptian-American poet Pauline Kaldas. Beginning with an invocation of markers of "exotic" beauty, the poem explores the ways in which Arab women are excluded from "white" American identity, yet simultaneously recuperated into its domain through a neocolonial gesture of possession. Dark enough to be "interesting," yet white enough to be "safe," the Egyptian woman in the poem presents what Kaldas terms an "also permitted" alternative to the mainstream "golden beauty" (168). But such "permissible" difference turns not only upon exoticism but also upon the safety of categorization. The woman is surrounded by a swirl of voices that attempt to define and contain her in an ethnic kaleidoscope: "'Qué pasa niña?'/'Hey baby!'/'What are you—Lebanese, Armenian, Spanish, Puerto Rican, Italian, Mexican/c'mon what are you?'/'You're either Spanish or Italian.'" By invoking ready-made slots of identification, these efforts at containment ward off an actual engagement with the complexity of difference. As Kaldas writes, "The square edges me as it extends *White/includes People from North Africa and the Middle East*" (168).

The classification tensions evoked in Kaldas' poem are not dissimilar from the tensions around race that informed the prerequisite cases earlier in the century. As in those court cases, here too Arab identity challenges the boundaries of available racial and ethnic classification, contained only by exclusion or by extending the meanings of whiteness. But while the definition of individual Arabs as "non-white" in the early period reflected a politics of exclusion, the contemporary location of "Arab" in the square of "white" is felt by many Arab-Americans to obscure Arab American realities, silencing them through a strategy of containment and rendering them invisible.[31]

The inadequacy of the category "white" to account for Arab-American experience is reflected in Kaldas' poem through images of food and embodiment that spill bodily over the square's demarcation lines. "White?" she queries. "As fava beans stirred green with olive oil/falafel fried sesame seeds burned black/baklava and basboosa the aroma browned crisp in the oven/White is not my breasts growing at nine/ . . . not my last menstruation at sixty (168–9). But official categories recuperate this bodily excess, containing it within the bounds of exoticism: the ethnic food aisle in the grocery store, the glass cases displaying mummies. Next to the identification box, which holds only a precise, anonymous X, the speaker writes her name. But her "guttural kha script/twirl[s] into ABC"; her body, its excesses contained, is wound by "lengths of cloth/mummy encased in glass" (169). If figurations of race are modes of scripting the embodied self, whiteness here is written in standardized typeset. Converted into "the exotic," the speaker is commodified: the poem ends with the sardonic invitation, "taste a color not confined/by the squares" (169).

This recognition that Arabs constitute a "color not confined by the squares" underlies the growing search among Arab-Americans for categories of identification able to account for their realities. As Edward Said has written, "No one today is purely *one* thing. Labels like Indian, or woman, or Muslim, or American are not more than starting-points, which if followed into actual experience for only a moment are quickly left behind" (*Culture and Imperialism*, 336). The debate among Arab-Americans over how to identify—as Arab, as Middle Eastern, as Asian or North African—comes together with the community's internal diversity—religious, national, cultural and ideological—to underscore the inadequacy of rigid categories of identification.

In response, Arab-Americans are beginning to explore alternative modes of self-representation. Consider, for example, Diana Abu-Jaber's novel *Arabian Jazz*. In this novel, Abu-Jaber explores the identification options open to her protagonist, Jemorah, daughter of a Jordanian father and a white American mother. Not quite at home in either her Arab or her American contexts, Jemorah struggles to find a place for herself, but for much of the novel remains confused and stymied by her mixed identity. An interchange with her employer Portia brings to a crescendo these tensions. For Portia, the "good white blood" running in Jemorah's veins from her American mother has been contaminated by her Arab father who "[isn't] any better than Negroes" (294). But this Arab "taint" (294) is, for Portia, nonetheless recuperable into a framework of white ethnicity. As Portia tells Jemorah, "I've noticed that in certain lights it's worse than in others. . . . Now, if you were to change your name, make it Italian maybe, or even Greek, that might help some. . . . We'll try putting some pink lipstick on you, maybe lightening your hair, make you *American*" (295). Recoiling from such bigotry, Jemorah turns instead to her Arab identity, announcing her intention to marry an Arab cousin and move to Jordan. But Abu-Jaber makes clear that such dualistic thinking is not a solution either. As Jemorah's cousin points out, "You're torn in two. You get two looks at a world. You may never have a perfect fit, but you see far more than most ever do. Why not accept it?" (330). Indeed, the novel turns in its final passage to a metaphor of jazz, positing cultural cross-over and improvisation as an alternative to unitary identification.

While early Arab-Americans sought to claim a space within white American culture through strategies of assimilation and strategic deployment of exoticism, contemporary Arab-Americans increasingly seek to affirm their identities without minimizing complexity, and to claim a classification adequate to their experiences. Situated at boundaries delineated by racial and political pressures, Arab-Americans seek to challenge what Ruth Frankenberg terms the "color evasiveness" and "power-evasiveness" of paradigms of assimilation and race-neutrality (14). But as Therese Saliba notes, "It is unclear how long we will inhabit this space of ambiguity which often excludes us from both mainstream and marginalized groups. And it is unclear when and if we will enter an age of "post-ethnicity" in which racialized relations will no longer be a considerable political factor in determining representation" (316).[32] These ambiguities inform and delineate cultural production. As Arab-American writers probe the contradictions of their identities, they give voice to what Lebanese-American writer David Williams terms the "double legacy" of Arab-Americans, a heritage borne, in Williams' words, "the way, you might say, a camel carries water" (*Traveling Mercies* 67).

Notes

1. On the term "honorary whiteness" see Joseph Massad in "Palestinians and the Limits of Racialized Discourse" and Soheir Morsy in "Beyond the Honorary 'White' Classification of Egyptians: Societal Identity in Historical Context."

2. In *Racial Formation in the United States* Richard Omi and Howard Winant use Arabs as their example of groups "whose racial category is ambiguous at present" (162, note 3).

3. For example, a Syrian merchant in an Oklahoma town was warned by the Ku Klux Klan to "keep away from the town at the risk of economic boycott and his own life," while the store of another Syrian merchant "was burned down soon after he received a threat by mail ordering him to move away from the town." (See Shadid, "Syria for the Syrians" 23–24).

4. Ian F. Haney Lopez provides a compelling analysis of these cases in *White by Law: The Legal Construction of Race.*

5. See Haney Lopez 5–9 for a discussion of the clash between common knowledge and scientific evidence.

6. Arab applicants were declared white in 1909 and 1910, non-white in 1913 and 1914, white in 1915, nonwhite in 1942, and white in 1944.

7. Nadine Naber terms this conflation the "racialization of religion" (8).

8. Although Naff cites the 1929 census this seems to be an error. See also Hitti, who notes that "In the reports of the fourteenth decennial census of 1920, the Syrians were for the first time treated as a separate people" (page 19 note 1).

9. Indeed, in a 1909 case involving an Armenian applicant, the circuit court judge held that the applicant should be granted citizenship because Armenians may readily become westernized and Europeanized, and because "history has shown that Christianity in the near East has generally manifested a sympathy with Europe rather than with Asia as a whole" (*In Re Halladjian*).

10. Such racialization of geography and culture, while particularly glaring in the case of Arabs and Muslims, reflected the general tenor of the times. As Omi and Winant point out, in the wake of 19th century political and ideological struggles over the racial classification of Southern Europeans, Irish, and Jews, "Nativism was only effectively curbed by the institutionalization of a racial order that drew the color line *around,* rather than *within,* Europe" (65).

11. For instance, Mexicans in California were considered "half civilized" because they spoke a romance language, were Christian, had been "Europeanized" through their colonization by Spain, and were racially assimilable because of their "mixed-blood" ancestry (Almaguer 54).

12. Southern Italian immigrants, considered "tainted" by the "dusk of Saracenic or Berber ancestors showing in their cheeks" (a telling reflection of attitudes toward Middle Eastern peoples) and made to sit with black congregants in church, separated themselves from black Americans as much as possible (Orsi 318). Similarly, Irish immigrants attempted to facilitate their own transformation from "Irish" to "American" by positioning themselves in opposition to blacks (Takaki 151).

13. However, such "honorary" white status was not always reliable. Soheir Morsy points out that although some Egyptians in the U.S. were exempted from classification as non-white on the basis of being foreign, others were denied housing, told to sit in the back of the bus, and refused service in restaurants, "often after long consultations among waitresses who were audibly debating our racial identity" (184–5).

14. Nabeel Abraham argues that contemporary anti-Arab discrimination and hate crimes are rooted in three sources: traditional racism; politically-motivated racism, and jingoistic racism. The first, arising when Arabs are ethnically visible, is evident throughout the history of Arabs in the U.S. The second, linked to the Arab-Israeli conflict, is ideologically motivated and targets individuals who support Palestinian and other Arab causes. The third arises in the context of international unrest such as hijackings and military conflict, and involves a knee-jerk lashing out at "the enemy." See his discussion in "Anti-Arab Racism and Violence in the United States."

15. See Abraham for a detailed account of such incidents.

16. See ADC Times 19,5 (August/September 1998): 4.

17. For instance, ADC has reported that, "Due to the absence of federal, state or local guidelines requesting census data on Arab Americans, the National Education Association (NEA) does not include Arab Americans in discussions of multiculturalism in school curricula ("The 2000 Census: Will We Count?").

18. In an incident reported to ADC, a Palestinian American girl was forbidden from attending her school prom with *either* a black *or* a white date. She was allegedly told by her teacher, "You're a foreigner. Go with someone who has the same features as you" (ADC mailing, fall 1994.)

19. Press conference with U. S Attorney General Janet Reno, April 20, 1995.

20. Two hundred twenty-two incidents were reported to ADC during the three-day period immediately following the bombing. In one incident, a pregnant Arab American woman lost her baby when her house was attacked by angry mobs. The *1995 Report on Anti-Arab Racism* states that the woman "huddled in the bathroom with her two children as angry crowds grew outside, throwing stones and other objects at her house. Believing the loud noises were gunshots and terrified for her children, she began hemorrhaging. Shortly thereafter, her child was stillborn" (Khoury, Ramadan and Wingfield 4).

21. The category "Arab American" has been proposed by the American-Arab Anti-Discrimination Commmittee (ADC), while the Arab American Institute (AAI) has lobbied for the category "Middle Eastern." Other possible modes of classification include identifying West Asian Arabs as Asian-American and North African Arabs as African American. However, while such categorizations have the advantage of fitting Arabs into existing classifications, they privilege geography over culture as the basis for identification, accentuate the invisibility of Arabs as they become subsumed within these larger groups, and risk dividing a community still struggling for unity.

22. Given the diverse ways in which Arabs identify themselves, there were fears that Arab-Americans who wrote in such answers as "Maronite" or "Muslim" would not be tabulated, resulting in an undercount of Arab Americans—something that virtually all Arab American scholars agree occurred anyway.

23. See Sharon M. Lee's discussion of census classifications in "Racial Classifications in the US Census: 1890–1990."

24. This framework was first promulgated in a 1977 Office of Management and Budget circular, "Race and Ethnic Standards for Federal Statistics and Administrative Reporting" (see Sanjek 109). David Hollinger notes that the issuing of this directive was "the single event most responsible for the lines that separate one bloc from another" (33).

25. For instance, although the category "Asian-American" obscures the linguistic, cultural, historical, and national distinctions between immigrants from different Asian countries, it also makes it possible for immigrants from these diverse countries to take action on issues that affect them *as Asians,* such as "exclusionary immigration laws, restrictive naturalization laws, labor market segregation, and patterns of ghettoization by a polity and culture that treated all Asians as alike" (Winant 60).

26. For instance, in preparation for Dow's rehearing, a volume titled *Origin of the Modern Syrian* was produced, asserting and documenting the Syrian claim to "whiteness" (see Suleiman, "Early Arab-Americans" 44–45.)

27. Other Arab-American writers of the pre-WWII period, such as Salom Rizk and Michael Shadid, similarly invoke the specter of Muslim hostility toward Christians, taking care to distance themselves from cultural elements associated with Islam. See Rizk's *Syrian Yankee* (57) and Shadid's *Crusading Doctor* (21–22). While not all Syrian-Americans spoke in such negative terms of Islam—the prolific writer Ameen Rihani was a noticeable exception—the tendency to

do so suggests their awareness that association with Islam might problematize attempts to claim American identity. Michael Suleiman writes of a similar phenomenon in the bilingual (Arabic/English) study *The Origin of the Modern Syrian*, published in an attempt to prove the Caucasian origin of Arabs and hence their suitability for American citizenship. While the text includes lists of notable Semites, only the Arabic section of the text includes the Prophet Muhammad; the English section omits the Prophet, in what appears to be a deliberate strategy. (See Suleiman , "Early Arab-Americans"44–45.)

28. Lawrence Joseph is the author of the poetry collections *Shouting at No One, Curriculum Vitae* and *Before Our Eyes*, and of the prose volume *Lawyerland: What Lawyers Talk About When They Talk About Law*.

29. Abu-Jaber is author of the novel *Arabian Jazz*, of essays and short stories, and of the forthcoming novel *Memories of Birth*.

30. Pauline Kaldas' poetry has appeared in *Lift Magazine, Michigan Review, Food for Our Grandmothers, The Space Between Our Footsteps* and in a special Arab-American issue of *Jusoor*. She is the author of *Egyptian Compass*, a poetry collection (unpublished).

31. As Joanna Kadi writes in the introduction to *Food For Our Grandmothers*, "One reason it's hard to find an accurate name [for Americans and Canadians of Arab, North African and Middle Eastern origin] has to do with our invisibility. It's tough to name a group when most people aren't aware the group exists" (xix).

32. Despite Arab-American lobbying efforts for a separate racial/ethnic category with the federal government, and despite acknowledgement by the Federal Office of Management and Budget that classifying Arab-Americans as "white" is problematic, on the 2000 census Arabs and Middle Easterners will still be classified as "white" (Naber 12).

Works Cited

Abu-Jaber, Diana. *Arabian Jazz*. New York: Harcourt Brace, 1993.

———. "Arabs and the Break in the Text." *Scars: American Poetry in the Face of Violence*. Ed. Cynthia Dubin Edelberg. Tuscaloosa and London: University of Alabama Press, 1995. 130–33.

Abu-Jaber, Diana. "At the Continental Divide." *Writer's Forum* 17 (Fall 1991): 130–53.

Abraham, Nabeel. "Anti-Arab Racism and Violence in the United States." *The Development of Arab-American Identity*. Ed. Ernest McCarus. Ann Arbor: University of Michigan Press, 1994. 155–214.

Almaguer, Tomas. *Racial Fault Lines: The Historical Origins of White Supremacy in California*. Berkeley and Los Angeles: University of California Press, 1994.

ADC Times, Aug-Sept. 1994.

Blatty, William. *Which Way to Mecca, Jack?* New York: Geis, 1960.

Conklin, Nancy Faires, and Nora Faires. "'Colored' and Catholic: The Lebanese in Birmingham, Alabama." *Crossing the Waters: Arabic-Speaking Immigrants to the United States Before 1940*. Ed. Eric J. Hooglund. Washington, D.C. and London: Smithsonian Institution Press, 1987. 69–84.

Dow v. United States. 226 *Federal Reporter*. Sept. 14, 1915.

Ex Parte Dow. 211 *Federal Reporter*. Feb. 18, 1914.

Ex Parte Mohriez. 54 *Federal Supplement* 1500. April 13, 1994.

Ex Parte Shahid. 205 Federal Reporter. June 24, 1913.

Ferris, Joseph W. "Syrian Naturalization Question in the United States: Part 1." *The Syrian World* 2, 8 (Feb.1928): 3–11.

————. "Syrian Naturalization Question in the United States: Part 2." *The Syrian World* 2, 9 (March 1928): 18–22.

Frankenberg, Ruth. *White Women, Race Matters: The Social Construction of Whiteness*. Minneapolis: University of Minnesota Press, 1993.

"Has the Syrian Become a Negro." *Ash-Shaab*, New York, May 24, 1929. Reprinted in *Syrian World* III, 12 (June 1929): 42.

Haney Lopez, Ian F. *White By Law: The Legal Construction of Race*. New York and London: New York University Press, 1996.

Hitti, Philip. *The Syrians in America*. New York: George Doran Co. 1924.

Hollinger, David A. *Postethnic America: Beyond Multiculturalism*. New York: Basic Books, 1995.

In Re Dow. 213 *Federal Reporter*. April 15, 1914.

In Re Halladjian. 174 F. 834. Dec. 24, 1909.

In Re Ahmed Hassan. 48 *Federal Supplement* 843. Dec. 15, 1942.

Joseph, Lawrence. *Before Our Eyes*. New York: Farrar, Straus and Giroux, 1993.

————. *Curriculum Vitae*. Pittsburgh: University of Pittsburgh Press, 1988.

————. *Lawyerland: What Lawyers Talk About When They Talk About Law*. New York: Farrar Straus and Giroux, 1997.

————. *Shouting at No One*. Pittsburgh: University of Pittsburgh Press, 1988.

Kadi, Joanna. *Food For Our Grandmothers: Writings by Arab-American and Arab-Canadian Feminists*. Boston: South End Press, 1994.

Kaldas, Pauline. "Exotic." *Lift* No.3 (July 1990): 26. Reprinted in *Food for Our Grandmothers: Writings by Arab-American and Arab-Canadian Feminists*. Boston: South End Press, 1994. 168–69.

Khoury, Ghada, Mary Ramadan, and Marvin Wingfield (preparers). *1995 Report on Anti-Arab Racism: Hate Crimes, Discrimination and Defamation of Arab Americans*. ADC Special Report. Washington D.C.: ADC Research Institute, 1996.

Lee, Sharon M. "Racial Classifications in the US Census: 1890–1990." *Ethnic and Racial Studies* 16, 1 (January 1993): 75–94.

Massad, Joseph. "Palestinians and the Limits of Racialized Discourse." *Social Text* 34 (1993): 94–114.

Morrison, Toni. *Playing in the Dark: Whiteness and the Literary Imagination*. Cambridge, MA: Harvard University Press, 1992.

Morsy, Soheir. "Beyond the Honorary 'White' Classification of Egyptians: Societal Identity in Historical Context." *Race*. Ed. Steven Gregory and Roger Sanjek. New Brunswick, New Jersey: Rutgers University Press, 1994. 175–98.

Naber, Nadine. "Arab-American In/Visibility." *AAUG Monitor* 13, 3 (December 1998). 1–16.

Naff, Alixa. *Becoming American: The Early Arab Immigrant Experience*. Carbondale and Edwardsville: Southern Illinois University Press, 1985.

Omi, Michael and Howard Winant. *Racial Formation in the United States from the 1960s to the 1990s*. New York and London: Routledge, 1994.

Orsi, Robert. "The Religious Boundaries of an Inbetween People: Street Feste and the Problem of the Dark-skinned Other in Italian Harlem, 1920–1990." *American Quarterly* 44 (1992): 313–47.

Rihbany, Abraham Mitrie. *A Far Journey*. Boston: Houghton Mifflin, 1914.

Rizk, Salom. *Syrian Yankee*. Garden City, New York: Doubleday and Co., 1943.

Said, Edward. *Culture and Imperialism*. New York: Alfred A. Knopf, 1993.

————. *Orientalism*. New York: Vintage, 1978.

Saint Francis College v. Al-Khazraji, 481 U.S. 604 (1986).

Saliba, Therese. "Resisting Invisibility: Arab Americans in Academia and Activism." *Arabs in*

America: Building a New Future. Ed. Michael Suleiman. Philadelphia: Temple University Press, 1999. 304–19.

Samhan, Helen. "Politics and Exclusion: The Arab American Experience." *Journal of Palestine Studies* XVI, 2 (Winter 1987): 11–28.

Sanjek, Roger. "Intermarriage and the Future of Races in the United States." *Race*. Ed. Steven Gregory and Roger Sanjek. New Brunswick, New Jersey: Rutgers University Press, 1994. 103–30.

Shadid, Michael. *Crusading Doctor*. Boston: Meador, 1956.

———. "Syria for the Syrians." *Syrian World* I, 8 (February 1927): 21–24.

Shakir, Evelyn. *Bint Arab: Arab and Arab American Women in the United States*. Westport, CT and London: Praeger, 1997.

———. "Coming of Age: Arab American Literature." *Ethnic Forum* 13, 2–14, 1: 63–88.

Suleiman, Michael. "Early Arab-Americans: The Search for Identity." *Crossing the Waters: Arabic-Speaking Immigrants to the United States Before 1940*. Ed. Eric J. Hooglund. Washington, D.C. and London: Smithsonian Institution Press, 1987. 37–54.

———, ed. *Arabs in America: Building a New Future*. Philadelphia: Temple University Press, 1999.

"Syrian and Wife Killed in Florida." *Syrian World* III, 12 (June 1929): 45–48.

Takaki, Ronald. *A Different Mirror: A History of Multicultural America*. Boston, Toronto and London: Little, Brown and Company, 1993.

"The 2000 Census: Will We Count?" *ADC Times*, May-June 1995: 12.

Williams, David. *Traveling Mercies*. Cambridge, MA: Alice James Books, 1993.

Winant, Howard. *Racial Conditions*. Minneapolis and London: University of Minnesota Press, 1994.

BROKEN ENGLISH MEMORIES
Languages of the Trans-Colony

Juan Flores

Historical memory is an active, creative force, not just a receptacle for storing the dead weight of times gone by. *Memory* has been associated, since its earliest usages, with the act of inscribing, engraving, or, in a sense that carries over into our own electronic times, "re-cording" (*grabar*). It is not so much the record itself as the putting-on-record, the gathering and sorting of materials from the past in accordance with the needs and interests of the present. Remembering thus always involves selecting and shaping, constituting out of what was something new that never was yet now assuredly is, in the imaginary of the present, and in the memory of the future. And the process of memory is open, without closure or conclusion: the struggle to (re-)establish continuities and to tell the "whole" story only uncovers new breaks and new exclusions.

It is in the terms of such weighty verities that the well-known critic and Princeton professor Arcadio Díaz-Quiñones ponders the condition of contemporary Puerto Rican culture. In *La memoria rota* (1993), his much-discussed collection of essays from the 1980s and early 1990s, Díaz-Quiñones identifies the most glaring lapses in Puerto Rican historical memory, the ruptures and repressions which have left present-day public discourse devoid of any recognizable field of critical reference. The "broken memory" that he attributes to the current generation is rooted in centuries of imperial mutilation of social consciousness, culminating in his own lived memory in the triumphalist rhetoric of progress and modernization of the mid-century years. His point about the present, end-of-the-century condition is that even though the persuasiveness of that populist, accommodationist narrative seems to have waned definitively, the historical gaps grounding those earlier hegemonies remain largely unfilled. Despite Díaz-Quiñones' emphatic disclaimer of all "totalizing" presumptions and of any intention to set forth a "rigorous theory," *La memoria rota*, loosely unified around the suggestive metaphor of the broken memory, may well turn out to be the book of the

338

decade in Puerto Rican cultural theory, the 1990s counterpart to José Luis González' *El país de cuatro pisos* of the 1980s, or René Marqués' *El puertorriqueño dócil* of the 1960s, or Antonio S. Pedreira's *Insularismo* of the 1930s.

Díaz-Quiñones' critical eye ranges widely over Puerto Rican political and literary history; his familiarity with the particular national landscape is enriched by continual references to congruent and kindred concerns of other cultural theorists, from Theodor Adorno to Frantz Fanon, from Edward Said to Angel Rama. Rhetorically, the disjunctures he signals in the official story of the national culture take the form of euphemisms having the effect of minimizing the abruptness and violence of imposed historical change, most notably European colonization, centuries of slavery, U.S. occupation, the ideological decimation of the independence and socialist movements, and mass emigration to the U.S. He shows how the dominant memory needs to sweeten the pill of colonial power and constantly to construct and refurbish the illusion of internal harmony, compliance, consensus. Emotionally charged catch-words like *family, symphony of progress* and *cultural affirmation* hide the seams and muffle the discord that make up the real fabric of the society, which without these comforting mythologies appear as an intricate patch-work of contending claims and social meanings. In *La memoria rota*, the very concept of "the national"—what it means to "be" Puerto Rican—has become a battlefield in the ongoing struggle for interpretive power.

One exclusion to which Díaz-Quiñones draws repeated attention—perhaps the most pronounced break in collective memory—is the emigrant Puerto Rican community in the United States. The exodus of Puerto Ricans between the late 1940s and the early 1960s, an integral and orchestrated part of the country's passage into "modernity," is still occluded from the national history; in another new essay, "Puerto Rico: Cultura, memoria y diáspora" (1994), Díaz-Quiñones even cites two recent history text books, *Historia general de Puerto Rico* (1986), by Fernando Picó, and *La historia de Puerto Rico* (1987), by Blanca Silvestrini and María Dolores Luque de Sánchez, neither of which devotes more than a few pages to the emigrant Puerto Rican community. With all of its revisionist correctives to the colonial, class, gender and racial biases of the traditional narrative of the nation, the "new historiography" which has gained such prestigious intellectual ground since the 1970s continues to present that "other half" of the Puerto Rican population as just that, an "other" lurking in the wings of the main national drama. Puerto Ricans *en el destierro*, or simply *de allá*, persist as a footnote, sympathetic at best but ultimately dismissive and uncomprehending.

To its immense credit, *La memoria rota* places the life of Puerto Ricans in the U.S. squarely on the agenda of contemporary historical analysis. Díaz-Quiñones' insistence no doubt is fueled by his many years of living and working in New Jersey. He points up the long reach of collective experience back to the late nineteenth century and acknowledges the many other writers and thinkers who have recognized its importance, such as Bernardo Vega, César Andreu Iglesias and José Luis González. More than merely filling in historical blanks that they have left, though, Díaz-Quiñones asserts the central, constitutive role of Puerto Ricans in the U.S. in the making and breaking of the Puerto Rican nation in the twentieth century. His allusions to other contemporary theorists of diasporic, transnational identity, such as Said, Partha Chatterjee, and Renato Rosaldo, serve him well in contextualizing that dramatic divide in modern-day Puerto Rican history. Far from unique or exceptional, the cultural disjunctures, ambiguities, and re-connections undergone by Puerto Ricans in both localities are paradigmatic of experiences familiar to more and more people, and nations, of the world.

Yet for all his stitching and patching, Díaz-Quiñones still leaves the Puerto Rican broken memory in need of serious repair. It is not enough to point to the break and glue the pieces together by mentioning forgotten names and events. The seams and borders of national experience need to be understood not as absences or vacuums but as sites of new meanings and relations. Here again, as in the exclusionary vision Díaz-Quiñones would transcend, the Puerto Rican community in the U.S. still appears as an extension of discourses based on the island, its history an appendage of "the" national history, with no evident contours or dynamic in its own right. To attend to the "break" that migration has meant in Puerto Rican history, it is necessary to remember the whole national "project" from the perspectives of the breaking-point itself, from aboard the *guagua aérea*.[1]

Remembering in Puerto Rican today inherently involves a dual vision, a communication where languages bifurcate and re-combine. Puerto Rican memories are mixed-code memories, lodged at the points where English breaks Spanish and Spanish breaks English. The act of memory defies uniformity; it undermines the privilege typically accorded either of the sundered fragments—Spanish or English, *acá* or *allá*—over the living relation between them, as evidenced in the rupture itself. On this point the metaphor of Puerto Rico's broken memory, and the elegant arguments that sustain it, backs away from its deeper theoretical implications.

2

A people's memory and sense of collective continuity is broken not only by the abrupt, imposed course of historical events themselves, but by the exclusionary discourses that accompany and legitimate them. Thus, while the massive emigration of the Puerto Rican population to the United States has involved a geographical and cultural divide unprecedented in the national history, it is the dismissive rhetoric of "assimilation" and "cultural genocide" which has effected the glaring omission of Puerto Rican life in the United States from the historical record. In *La memoria rota* Arcadio Díaz-Quiñones repeatedly takes this ideological agenda to task, and reinstates creative agency and continuity in the cultural experience of the emigrant community.

In one of the most moving passages in the lead essay "La vida inclemente," Díaz-Quiñones argues that "los emigrantes fortalecían—de una manera imprevista por el discurso excluyente de algunos sectores de las élites puertorriqueñas—la necesidad de conservar identidades, y, de hecho, la necesidad de fijar nuevas descripciones de la identidad." [the emigrant reinforced—in a manner unforeseen by the exclusionary discourse of some sectors of the Puerto Rican elite—the need to maintain identities, and even the need to form new descriptions of identity]. Rather than leave the Island behind and forget about their homeland, "había en aquellas comunidades puertorriqueñas la posibilidad de un nuevo futuro que exigía conservar ciertos lugares reales y simbólicos, una nueva valoración de la geografía insular, de sus ríos y lomas, de sus barrios." [in those Puerto Rican communities there existed the possibility of a new future that required the preservation of certain real and symbolic places and that lent a new value to the geography of the island, its rivers and hills, and its barrios] (50–1). Geographic separation and distance, rather than deadening all sense of community and cultural origins, may have the contrary effect of heightening the collective awareness of belonging and affirmation. Referring to Edward Said's accounts of life in present-day Palestinian communities, Díaz-Quiñones contends that "la *pertenencia*, el sentido de 'hogar' y comunidad, se afirma sobre todo en la distancia, con la incertidumbre del lugar. Ello explica, quizás, por qué se puede dar la paradójica situación de que algunos en Guaynabo desprecian su cultura, mientras que otros, en Filadelfia, la defienden con pasión" [the sense of belonging, a feeling for 'home' and community, is affirmed with the strongest emphasis from a distance, when there is an uncertainty as to place. Perhaps this goes to explain the paradoxical situation that people, say in Guaynabo, can take their culture for granted, while others in Philadelphia defend it passionately].

The accuracy of the "paradoxical" inversion of geographical location and cultural belonging resounds in the countless tales of emigrants feeling more Puerto Rican than ever when in the New York setting; in the flourishing of *bomba y plena* and *música jíbara* groups in all of the emigrant neighborhoods, from Hartford to Lorain, Ohio, from Hawaii to Perth Amboy, in the fashioning of Island-style *casitas* in the abandoned lots of the South Bronx and Williamsburg, Brooklyn. The contrasting attitudes toward cultural continuity find dramatic expression in much of the literary and artistic work by Puerto Ricans in the United States, most forcefully perhaps in Tato Laviera's memorable poem "nuyorican," from the volume *AmeRícan*. The title identifies, in English, the speaker of the poem, a monologue addressed by an irate New York Puerto Rican, in Spanish, to his lost island homeland. "Nuyorica" is an impassioned plea by a son of the migration to his beloved "puerto rico" not to forget why he was born "nativo en otras tierras" and to be aware of the real play of cultural loyalties:

> yo peleo por tí puerto rico, ¿sabes?
> Yo me defiendo por tu nombre, ¿sabes?
> Entro en tu isla, me siento extraño, ¿sabes?
> Entro a buscar más y más, ¿sabes?
> Pero tú con tus calumnias,
> me niegas tu sonrisa
> me siento mal, agallao
> yo soy tu hijo,
> de una migración
> pecado forzado,
> me mandaste a nacer natico en otras tierras
> por qué, porque éramos pobres, ¿verdad?
> Porque tú querías vaciarte de tu gente pobre,
> ahora regreso, con un corazón boricua, y tú,
> me desprecias, me miras mal, me atacas mi hablar,
> mientras comes mcdonalds en discotecas americanas,

y no pude bailarla salsa en san juan, la que yo
bailo en mis barrios llenos de todas tus costumbres,
así que, si tú no me quieres, pues yo tengo
un puerto rico sabrosísimo en que buscar refugio
en nueva york, y en muchos otros callejones
que honran tu presencia, preservando todos
tus valores, así que, no me
hagas sufrir, ¿sabes?

[i fight for you, puerto rico, you know?
I defend myself for your name, you know?
I enter your island, i feel foreign, you know?
I enter searching for more and more, you know?
but you, with your insults,
you deny me your smile,
i feel bad, indignant.
I am your son,
of a migration,
a sin forced on me,
you sent me to be born a native of other lands.
why? because we were poor, right?
because you wanted to empty yourself of poor people.
Now i return, with a boricua heart, an you,
you scorn me, you look askance, you attack the way i speak,
while you're out there eating mcdonalds in american discotheques,
and i couldn't even dance salsa in san juan, which i
can dance in my neighborhoods full of your customs.
So that, if you don't want me, well, i have
a delicious puerto rico where i can seek refuge
in new york, and in lots of other alleyways
that honor your presence, preserving all
of your values, so that, please, don't make
me suffer, you know?]

Such texts, structured for their emotional force around the clash between an imaginary and a "real" Puerto Rico, and between jarring identity claims of "here" and
"there," abound in "Nuyorican" literature. Works by Sandra María Esteves and Victor
Hernández Cruz, Edward Rivera and Esmeralda Santiago, show that "la memoria
rota" is the site not merely of exclusion and fragmentation but also of new meanings
and identity. They attest to the act of memory at the break itself and thereby move
from the pieces of broken memory to the creative practice of "breaking memory."
Discontinuity, rather than a threat to cultural survival and inclusion, helps us critically
examine prevailing continuities and imagine and create new ones. Homi Bhabha, for
whom Díaz-Quiñones expresses great admiration in *La memoria rota*, provides an excellent description of ironically privileged positionality "at the break." Inspired by Said's
move from Foucault to the scene of the Palestinian struggle, "from the Left Bank to
the West Bank," Bhabha speaks in a recent interview of

the possibilities of being, somehow, *in between*, of occupying an interstitial space that was not fully governed by the recognizable traditions from which you came. For the interaction or overdetermination often produces another third space. It does not necessarily produce some higher, more inclusive, or representative reality. Instead, it opens up a space that is skeptical of cultural totalization, of notions of identity which depend for their authority on being 'originary," or concepts of culture which depend for their value on being pure, or of tradition, which depends for its effectivity on being continuous. A space where, to put it very simply, I saw great political and poetic and conceptual value in forms of cultural identification which subverted authority, not by claiming their total difference from it, but were able to actually use authorized images, and turn them against themselves to reveal a different history. And I saw this little figure of subversion intervening in the interstices, as being different from the big critical battalions that always wanted to have a dominating authority, opposed by an equally subordinated agency: victim and oppressor, sparsely and starkly blocked out. (*Migration and Identity* 190)

The experience of being "in between," so deeply familiar to Puerto Ricans in the United States, thus harbors the possibility of an intricate politics of freedom and resistance. Understood in this way as a kind of phenomenology or philosophy of experiential space, the "break" appears as both a limit and a breaking of the limit. The "third space" and "little figure of subversion" identified by Bhabha summon the notion of transgression and its constant crossing of lines and demarcated limits. In *Language, Counter-Memory, Practice*, Foucault describes this relation between transgression and limit: "Transgression is an action which involves the limit, that narrow zone of a line where it displays the flash of its passage, but perhaps also its entire trajectory, even its origin; it is likely that transgression has its entire space in the line it crosses" (33–34).

Rather than negate the limit by crossing it, transgression foregrounds and mediates contrasts by illuminating the spaces on either side of the limit. In a striking metaphor, Foucault suggests that the relationship between the limit and its transgression "is like a flash of lightning in the night which . . . gives a dense and black intensity to the night it denies, which lights up the night from the inside, from top to bottom, and yet owes to the dark the stark clarity of its manifestation"(34).

Such insights from contemporary cultural theory point up the need to appreciate the complexity of Puerto Rico's "broken memory" from the vantage point of those living "in between," in the space of the "break" itself. Sandra María Esteves gives voice to this complexity in the opening lines of her poem "Not Neither":

> Being Puertorriqueña
> Americana
> Born in the Bronx, not really jíbara
> Not really hablando bien
> but yet, not Gringa either
> Pero ni portorra, pero sí portorra too
> Pero ni que what am I? (*Tropical Rains* 26)

Occupying and transgressing the limit can be baffling, bewildering to the point of existential anguish, yet facing up to the confounding reality can allow for a newfound sense of confidence and identity. Esmeralda Santiago, for one, after years of jostling and juggling between Puerto Rican and U.S. parts of her life, has finally "learned to insist on my peculiar brand of Puerto Rican identity. One not bound by geographical, linguistic or behavioral boundaries, but rather, by a deep identification with a place, a people and a culture which, in spite of appearances, define my behavior and determine the rhythms of my days. An identity in which I've forgiven myself for having to look up a recipe for 'arroz on pollo' in a Puerto Rican cookbook meant for people who don't know a 'sombrero' from a 'sofrito'" ("The Puerto Rican Stew" 34, 36).

In what language do we remember? Is it the language we use when we speak with friends and family in our everyday lives? Or does our choice of a language of memory involve a transposition, a translation in the literal sense of moving across: *trasladar*, "de un lado a otro" [from one side to the other]? For Puerto Ricans, half of whom may be on either "side" at any given time, a symbiosis between language and place, and between identity and memory, is especially salient today. Spanish, English, Spanglish, all in the plural and in lower case, make for an abundant reservoir of expressive codes with which to relate (to) the past. For language is not only the supreme mnemonic medium, the vehicle for the transmission of memory; fifty years of Puerto Rican history have shown that language can also be the site and theme of historical action, the locus of contention over issues of identity and community that reach far beyond our preference for, or reliance on, this or that word or grammar. "La memoria rota," the fragmenting of Puerto Rican historical memory as a result of selective privileges and suppressions, makes its most palpable appearance as "la lengua rota," or, as Antonio Martorell puts it in his inspired performance piece, "la lengua mechada" [stuffed tongue].[2]

In his essay "La política del olvido" (1991), Arcadio Díaz-Quiñones shows that it is not necessary to accept the inaccurate, colonially charged claim that Puerto Rico is a "bilingual nation" in order to stand in equally critical opposition to the officialization of Spanish as the national language. For while the annexationist impulse behind the bilingual-nation idea is evident, Díaz-Quiñones recognizes the "Spanish-only" campaign as no more than chronic recourse of the autonomist leaders (in this case then-governor Rafael Hernández Colón) in their most desperate moments of opportunism. "Qué alcance tiene la definición del idioma *único*," he asks, "ante la hibridez y mezcla del español, del inglés y del spanglish que se oye en Bayamón, Puerto Nuevo o en Union City? Las élites puertorriqueñas defienden, con razón, su bilingüismo, que les permite leer a Toni Morrison o a Faulkner, y acceder a la alta cultura del Metropolitan Museum o el New York City Ballet, y, claro, a Wall Street. La diáspora de emigrantes puertorriqueños ha ido mezclando su lengua, una vez más, en sus continuos viajes de ida y vuelta" [What can be gained from defining an *only* language in the face of the hybridity and mixing of Spanish, English , and Spanglish that one hears spoken in Bayamón, Puerto Nuevo, or Union City? The Puerto Rican elites have good reason to defend their bilingualism: it allows them to read Toni Morrison or Faulkner and partake of the high culture of the Metropolitan Museum or the New York City Ballet, and of course Wall Street. The diaspora of Puerto Rican emigrants has been mixing their languages over and over, in their continual trip back and forth]. New York, Díaz-Quiñones reminds us, has been a Caribbean and Puerto Rican city for over a century now, witness to and deeply influenced by the lives and writings, the songs and struggles, of many illustrious Puerto Ricans, along with Cubans of the prominence of José Martí and Celia Cruz. "Yo prefiero la hibridez de las nacionalizaciones" [I prefer the hybridity of nationalities], he continues, and concludes his reflections on the politics of language with the challenging question, addressed toward Puerto Ricans on both sides of the linguistic divide: "¿Tendremos nosotros la capacidad para descolonizar nuestro imaginario, salir de la niebla colonial de que habló Hostos, sin renunciar a este revolú que nos identifica?" [Will we have the capacity to decolonize our imaginary, to take leave of the colonial fog that Hostos spoke of without relinquishing that special "mess" that identifies us?].

When it comes to language, "este revolú que nos identifica" amounts to a veritable stew, if such a tired and overloaded expression may be pardoned in the interest of differentiating the dynamic of blending and multiple intersection from notions of transition, transfer, interference, or even back and forth movement. It's a *sancocho* whose ingredients include, as Esmeralda Santiago has learned, *sofrito* and not sombreros, because it is not random, much less a sign of confusion and incoherence, as the "English or Español Only-ists" would have it. On closer look, bilingualism as practiced by Puerto Ricans on both sides of *el charco*, but especially by the half "over here," constitutes an intricate tactic and strategy of response and assertion, with deep poetic and political implications. "Broken" English, "broken" Spanish, English and Spanish "breaking" (into) each other—who with any contact at all with Puerto Ricans can fail to hear the semantic micro-politics at play in usages like "Cógelo con take it easy!" or "No problema," or in the bent meanings in the use of words like *anyway, o.k.., foquin* or *bro-ther* in a Spanish context, or *pero, verdad, este* or *mira* when speaking English? Whether the primary code is Spanish or English, colloquial Puerto Rican is characterized by its porousness, its undermining and breaking, of the authority of monolingual discourse. Collective memory and identity find their appropriate articulation in this lively, "macaronic" sensibility, where the mixed-code vernacular voice responds in both directions to the imposition of official, standard constructs of "the" national language. Puerto Rican dreams are "broken English dreams," as Pedro Pietri announced in one of his signature poems from the early 1970s (*Puerto Rican Obituary* 12–16). The cultural idiom of many Puerto Ricans and other Latinos in the U.S., their language of expression and fantasy, is captured well in the title of the forthcoming book by the Cuban American cultural critic Coco Fusco, who calls her essays on "cultural fusion in the Americas" *English Is Broken Here*.

Yet as fluid as this interlingual practice may be, there is still a here and a there. Its being "translocal" does not erase the efficacy of "locus"; boundaries of difference and distance remain, most obviously in relation to place and location. Geography is the richest metaphorical field for the politics of linguistic and cultural breaking; the contrast between here and there permeates the idiom, from everyday speech to the lingo of popular songs to twists and turns of bilingual poetry. The there is not only imaginary; it is acknowledged and even thematized as imaginary. The imaginary there and then serves as an accessible foil to the intensity of lived presence, and often, as in the poetry of Sandra María Esteves and Victor Hernández Cruz, becomes a resource for self-discovery and political insight.

Tato Laviera takes this locational counterpoint as the structuring principle of his dramatic poem "migración," where the lyrics of the proverbially nostalgic ballad "En mi viejo San Juan" share the same lines and stanzas with the words, also in Spanish, of a Puerto Rican on the frozen winter streets of the Lower East Side as he reflects on the death of the song's composer, Noel Estrada. Eventually, the emotionally laden chords of "En mi viejo San Juan," often considered the anthem of the Puerto Rican and Latin American emigrant, bring out the sun and, as they resound in barbershops and night-spots in El Barrio, play their consoling yet challenging role in the familiar here and now. This sharp dramatic interplay between two cultural places, the quoted there and the unmediated physical here, allows for a new mode of identity-formation freed from the categorical fixity of place. In his essay "Migratorias," the critic Julio Ramos concludes his comments on Laviera's "migración" by speaking of a practical, "portable" identity: "Porque se trata, precisamente, de un modo de concebir la identidad que escabulle las redes topográficas y las categorías duras de la territorialidad y su metaforización telúrica. En Laviera la raíz es si acaso el fundamento citado, reinscrito, por el silbido de una canción. Raíces portátiles, dispuestos al uso de una ética corriente, basada en las prácticas de la identidad, en la identidad como práctica del juicio en el viaje" [It is a way of conceiving identity that defies the usual topographical connections, along with rigid categories of territoriality and their telluric metaphorization. In Laviera, "roots" may amount to that foundation as a citation, reinscribed as the syllable of a song. Roots that are portable, disposed to use in a "mainstream ethic," based on practices of identity, on identity as practice of judgment in the course of traveling] (Ramos 60).

The themes of spatial, historical and linguistic counterpoint are joined by Laviera in his remarkable poem "melao" in *Mainstream Ethics (éthica corriente)*, which enacts paradigmatically what I have been calling broken English and Spanish memories:

> melao was nineteen years old
> when he arrived from santurce
> spanish speaking streets
>
> melao is thirty-nine years old
> in new york still speaking
> santurce spanish streets
>
> melaíto his son now answered
> in black american soul english talk
> with native plena sounds
> and primitive urban salsa beats
>
> somehow melao was not concerned
> at the neighborly criticism
> of his son's disparate sounding
> talk
>
> melao remembered he was criticized
> back in puerto rico for speaking
> arrabal black spanish
> in the required english class

> melao knew that if anybody
> called his son american
> they would shout puertorro
> in english and spanish
> meaning i am puerto rican
> coming from yo soy boricua
> i am a jíbaro
> dual mixtures
> of melao and melaíto's
> spanglish speaking son
> así es la cosa papá (27)

Though the narrative voice is in English, Spanish words, sounds and meanings burst through the monolingual seams; every shift in geographic and biographical reference undermines the "official" status of either language standard. Close and repeated reading reveals a vernacular Spanish subtext that explodes at the end but collides and colludes with English semantics in the dead center of the poem. The centrally placed word *disparate*, spelled the same in both languages, also "means" in both languages, but the simultaneous meanings are not the same. The concealed (Spanish) phonetics harbors a repressed signification, and the poetics of convergence and divergence underlies an everyday politics of the break in cultural and historical memory.

"La memoria rota," evocative image of the fragmentation of Puerto Rican historical consciousness, is thus most appropriate, especially as it refers to the migratory experience, when reimagined as an active process of breaking and re-membering. Arcadio Díaz-Quiñones has succeeded in placing those lapses and exclusions indelibly on the contemporary intellectual agenda and has signaled the attendant political implications of a needed historical revision. But for Puerto Rican memory to be "repaired," for it to assume greater coherence and continuity, its incoherences and discontinuities must be probed as they manifest themselves in lived experience and expression. "Ese revolú que nos identifica," the elusive mortar of Puerto Rican cultural identity, appears as a magnetic field of unity and diversity, relations and translations. Puerto Rican memory gets "unbroken" by melao, and by melaito, his "disparate sounding" son, and by "melaito's spanglish speaking son" when he affirms his "dual mixture" by proclaiming, "así es la cosa papá."

Notes

An earlier version of this essay appeared in *Modern Language Quarterly* 57.2 (June 1996): 381–95; the revised essay printed here is from Juan Flores' *From Bomba to Hip Hop: Puerto Rican Culture and Latino Identity* (Columbia University Press, 2000). Republished with permission of Columbia University Press, 562 W. 113th St., New York NY 10025. Republished portions of "Broken English Memories" reproduced by permission of the publisher via Copyright Clearance Center, Inc.

1. The title of Luis Rafael Sánchez's story, "La guagua aérea" [The air bus], has become proverbial for the commuter status of Puerto Rican culture.

2. Martorell's performance-installation was first presented at the International Colloquium on the Contemporary Social Imaginary, held at the University of Puerto Rico in February 1991. The text, "Imalabra II," appears in *Coloquio internacional sobre el imaginario social contemporáneo*, ed. de Jesús et al, 161–64. What Martorell means by "la lengua mechada" (as in "carne mechada," meat that has been larded and stuffed) becomes clear in the following sentence: "Nuestra lengua, querrámoslo o no, está mechada y requetemechada con otras lenguas y con imágenes soñadas, recordadas, olvidadas, combatidas, rendidas, victoriosas y subversivas que versadas o en verso, prosaicas o procaces, silentes o sin lentes, encarnadas o bernejas, berrendas o virulentas dan sabor y grosor a nuestro apetito, estensión a nuestras ansias, caricia a nuestra hambre." [Like it or not, our tongue (language) has been stuffed and stuffed to the gills with other languages and with images which were dreamed up, remembered, forgotten, combated, surrendered, victorious and subversive, well versed or in verse, prosaic or precocious, silenced or no-lensed, incarnate or inchoate, tame or tempestuous, lending flavor and fullness to our appetite, length to our longing, endearment to our hunger].

Works Cited

Bhabha, Homi. "Between Identities: Homi Bhabha Interviewed by Paul Thompson." *Migration and Identity*. Ed. Rina Benmayor and Andor Skotnes. Oxford: Oxford UP, 1994). ———
———.

Díaz-Quiñones, Arcadio. "Puerto Rico: Cultura, memoria y diáspora." *Tercer Milenio*1 (1994): 11–19.
———. *La memoria rota: Ensayos sobre cultura y política*. Río Piedras, P.R.: Ediciones Huracán, 1993.

Esteves, Sandra María. *Tropical Rains: A Bilingual Downpour*. New York: African Caribbean Poetry Theater, 1984.

Foucault, Michel. *Language, Counter-Memory, Practice: Selected Essays and Interviews*. Ed. Donald F. Bouchard. Ithaca: Cornell UP, 1977.

Fusco, Coco. *English Is Broken Here: Notes on Cultural Fusion in the Americas*. New York: New P, 1995.

Laviera, Tato. *AmeRícan*. Houston: Arte Público, 1985.
———. *Mainstream Ethics (ética corriente)*. Houston: Arte Público, 1988.

Martorell, Antonio. "Imalabra II." *Coloquio internacional sobre el imaginario social contemporáneo*. Ed. Nydza Correa de Jesús, Heidi Figueroa Sarriera, and María Milagros López. Río Piedras: Universidad de Puerto Rico, n.d. 161–64.

Pietri, Pedro. *Puerto Rican Obituary*. New York: Monthly Review P, 1973.

Ramos, Julio. "Migratorias." *Las culturas de fin de siglo en América Latina*. Ed. Josefina Ludmer. Buenos Aires: Beatriz Viterbo, 1994. 52–61.

Sánchez, Luis Rafael. "La guagua aérea" [The air bus]. Trans. Diana Vélez. *Village Voice* 24 January 1984. ———

Santiago, Esmeralda. "The Puerto Rican Stew." *New York Times Magazine*, 18 December 1994. 34, 36.

"BORN-AGAIN FILIPINO"
Filipino American Identity and Asian Panethnicity

Leny Mendoza Strobel

B ehind the "new face" of the Filipino American community in the mid-1990s are significant phenomena around cultural identity and Asian panethnic consciousness that need to be articulated. Our presence within Asian American Studies needs to be expanded beyond the Bulosan and Philip Vera Cruz generation, the literary contributions of the "flip" generation, and the oral history books by Cordova (1983), Vallangca (1987), and more recently, Espiritu (1995). While there is an emerging body of scholarly work, the post-1965 community is yet to be extensively studied. The numerous materials generated in the last ten years by the community itself, such as the Filipino American Experience Research Project at San Francisco State University, newspapers and magazines, television programs, and cultural productions, have not been theorized in academic texts although they have been the subject of internal community discussions.[1]

In this article I focus on the discourse on Filipino American cultural identity and the implications for Asian American panethnic consciousness. I emphasize the concerns of post-1965 Filipino Americans who comprise 65 percent of the community. The concerns of this group are markedly different from earlier immigrants. Those who arrived between 1965 to the late 1970s were called the "brain drain" generation because this was the first large group of professionals and highly skilled technical workers to migrate to the United States. The percentage of professionals who arrived between 1966–74 was between 60–70 percent (Steinberg, 1981, p.273). This immigration was largely the result of the "pull" of perceived economic opportunities in the U.S. (which was embedded in the American-patterned educational system and the dominance of American popular culture in the Philippines). The "push" factor was the political and economic crisis under the dictatorship of then-president Marcos. Immigration, therefore, was natural for this group whose education, values, and career aspirations were shaped by their colonial experience.

The classical paradigm of immigration is the assimilation model. This model sees the achievement of immigrants as dependent on their human capital, motivations, values, and talents. It further assumes the weakening and/or disappearance of traits and bonds of ethnicity as generations are absorbed into mainstream society (Morawska, 1990). If this model were applied to post-1965 Filipino immigration, it would obscure the role of structural and historical determinants of immigration, such as the Philippines/U.S. colonial relationship and the global capitalist system that influences the movement of peoples from poor to the affluent countries. It would also obscure the importance of the historical timing of Filipino immigrants' arrival in the U.S. and the formation of large ethnic enclaves. All these factors, along with the discussion of identity issues, should be considered as the context for understanding where Filipino Americans are located within the Asian panethnic framework. This article, however, is limited to the study of the formation of cultural identity and the development of Asian panethnic consciousness among post-1965 Filipino Americans.

In northern California, the large Filipino communities are located in Vallejo, Daly City, San Francisco, Union City, Fremont, and South Francisco. Of the 276,000 Filipinos who arrived between 1965–76, two-thirds were professionals and skilled or semi-skilled immigrants from urban areas and the middle classes, and between twenty to forty years old. Many arrived with young children or started families soon after their arrival. According to a recent study based on the 1990 Census, the median age of U.S.-born Filipino Americans, which comprise 35 percent, or 505, 988, of the total population, is 14.1 years (Cruz, 1994). This accounts for the surge in population of Filipino American college students today.

Espiritu's book (1992), *Asian American Panethnicity*, cites the limited Filipino American participation in pan-Asian organizations and relates it to the perception of power relations within the Asian community, the perceived cultural "distance" of Filipinos from other Asian Americans, and the predominantly immigrant composition of the Filipino community. In this article, I present a new perspective for understanding the post-1965 Filipino American experience. We want to be understood on our own terms, based on our own political, historical, and cultural realities—all of which shape our perceptions of, responses towards, and commitment to Asian panethnicity.

Efren Padilla, professor of sociology at California State University at Hayward, speaks for many when he states: "We are not against Asian panethnicity if it means political coalition building. Culturally, what we would like to know is: what are we in the imagination of the Chinese, Japanese, and other Asian Americans? The Chinese see themselves as the Middle Kingdom and everyone else is barbarian or foreigner. Do they see us as "sons of the yellow emperor, too"? And if they do, are we willing to accept that definition? We aren't. So, who do we say we are? What is our story?"

FOCUS OF STUDY: THE "BORN-AGAIN FILIPINO" EXPERIENCE

My involvement with the *Samahan sa Sikolohiyang Pilipino* (Association for Filipino Psychology) since 1992 has allowed me to observe an emerging phenomenon in our community, which one student has called the "born-again Filipino" experience[2]. The association is composed of Filipino American academics, researchers, and cultural workers who are interested in studying indigenous culture and psychology and its implication for cultural identity. In 1992, Virgilio Enriquez, founder of *Sikolohiyang Pilipino* in the Philippines, convened the first conference in the U.S. at UC Berkeley. Subsequent conferences were held at University of San Francisco, San Francisco State University, and California State University at Hayward. Enriquez himself traveled and lectured to various sites in the U.S. on the topic of Filipino Indigenous Psychology, its concepts and methods, its vision and goal as a psychology for the liberation Filipino colonial consciousness, until his untimely death in 1994. The various dialogues that have since emerged around the U.S. among Filipino American scholars, community and cultural workers, mental health and public health professionals center on the theme of Filipino American identity and how indigenous psychology might inform its formation and how this formation is at the same time tied to the political, economic and sociocultural context of Filipinos in the U.S.

What I have come to label as the process of cultural identity formation among Filipino American college students and some community and cultural workers is the attempt to comprehend the interrelatedness of: 1) the need for Philippine historical and cultural knowledge, 2) the function of personal memory, and 3) the consequences of language loss. These variables are needed to understand how Filipino/Filipino American (colonial) identities were constructed from the outside. To re-invent or re-imagine our cultural identity as "indigenization from within" (Enriquez, 1994) is to create alternative narratives and in so doing transform the understanding of the immigrant experience beyond the classical assimilation model. As a result of this project, I have observed that re-invented cultural forms, practices and new narratives are emerging from several locations within our community and that this process of identity formation is an important aspect of our decolonization work.

My study, through the participatory research method—or its Filipino equivalent, *pagtatanung-tanong* (Pe-Pua, 1990), which literally means, "to ask questions repeatedly"—focuses on college students and several community organizations in northern California. The participants are from UC Berkeley (UCB), San Francisco State University (SFSU), City College of San Francisco (CCSF), Sonoma State University (SSU), UD Davis (UCD), and California Polytechnic University at San Luis Obispo. For the past five years I have given lectures to student and community groups, conducted dialogues and interviews, and used open-ended survey questionnaires on the topic of decolonization and cultural identity. In these settings, I have had in depth dialogues with over a hundred participants. I also organized numerous symposia on related topics with visiting scholars from the Philippines. A symposium on Filipino Americans and Asian American Panethnicity was held in December 1995[3]. I had extensive discussions with Luz de Leon, director of Philippine Resource Center and the Filipino American Arts Exposition, and e-mail discussions on panethnicity with E. San Juan Jr., Professor, Ethnic Studies, Washington State University; Larry Shinagawa, Professor of Ethnic Studies, Sonoma State University; and Filipino National Artist in Literature, N. V. M. Gonzalez.

Participatory research is influenced by the work of Paulo Freire on education for critical consciousness and social justice. *Pagtatanung-tanong* is a Filipino indigenous research method developed as a way to understand the common folk (*tao*). More important, it is an attempt to articulate a people's experience in their own language and voice through stories, myths, folkloric traditions, and cultural practices. In this sense it is an emancipatory project.

Pagtatanung-tanong includes *kuwentuhan* (story telling), *usap-usapan* (small talk), *padalaw-dalaw* (casual visits), phone conversations, e-mail talk, and even *tsismis* (gossip as an informal and indirect way of communication, of passing on information through a third party when one avoids face-to-face confrontation)—all of which the researcher synthesizes through the process of *pagninilay* (reflection). The underlying framework is the Filipino value of *pakiramdam*: "the non-verbal inner process where all the senses, the intellect included, are opened to admit all the factors of a particular event or circumstance . . . mulled together in what appears to be an intuitive process" (Obusan, 1995).

I have positioned myself in that space between academia and the community because I realize the need to make sure that theory and practice inform each other. This article is a result of collaborative work amongst the participants in this study.

The development of pan-Asian identity among post-1965 Filipino Americans is complicated and intertwined not only with the history of Asians in the U.S. but the legacy of American colonialism and its impact on the self-perception of Filipino Americans. E. San Juan, Jr. says that the work that needs to be done is to find the substance in the Filipino American "form", and reinventing the Filipino in the United States, articulating her silence and invisibility. In order to do this, Filipino Americans must come to an understanding of the effects of ideology on the Filipino psyche; how we are rendered as gendered, classed, ethnic agents within the framework of racial formation in the U.S. (San Juan, 1992). This project requires a historical consciousness that challenges the master narratives that have defined the Filipino from the outside. In this regard, Filipino-specific cultural resources are useful for constructing an identity "from within."

In the following pages, I articulate the perspective of a segment of the Filipino American community, which has experienced the process of redefinition. If the face of our community has changed in the last twenty years, what do we want others to know about us? This is the question that we struggled to answer together. In the process of formulating an answer, we told stories, ate *sinigang*, *lumpia*, and *halo-halo*, laughed ourselves to tears, and sighed and pointed fingers as to who should sit down and write an "academic" text so that we could become visible to "others" – Asian Americans, other ethnic groups, and the dominating white culture. As Filipino American community and cultural advocate, Luz de Leon says to other Asian Americans: "You cannot claim us if you don't know us."

FINDINGS AND ANALYSIS[4]

The participants in this study primarily identify themselves as Filipinos in America and Filipino Americans. Only a few consider themselves Americans with Filipino backgrounds or claim to be "other." They identify as Asian Americans in certain circumstances, but it is usually not their primary identification.

> Michelle: I think it's much easier to claim a Filipino American identity when there is a background on Filipino history and culture. For instance, if you travel to high schools that have Filipino clubs or large population of Filipino students . . . the Filipino clubs do facilitate in forming this Filipino American identity. College in general is a major time of identity development that can contribute to other "born-again" situations (religion, for example). Currently, I represent Asian Pacific Islander Students for Affirmative Action and have participated in other Asian coalition meetings. I use the affiliation to demonstrate how the topic extends to other ethnicities and the diversity of the Asian population. I will most often call myself Fil Am. If I identify as Asian Am, it will be to represent an Asian Am or API group/organization or to bring an Asian representation in a group that has very few Asians.

Narratives like Michelle's, a graduate of UC Berkeley and the former editor of *maganda,* a magazine produced by Filipino students from UCB, may not differ greatly from the earlier experience (pre-1965) of Filipino Americans in their emphasis on the need to know about Philippines history and culture and the need to be part of the pan-Asian framework. Without this knowledge, the claim to being Filipino American is mere "form" without substance.

Abe Ignacio grew up in the 60s and 70s and identified as Asian American because he knew little about being Filipino and because, according to him, there were only a few Chinese, Japanese and Filipinos in his school, so they formed an Asian club. They petitioned their high school for an Asian American history class because the club members felt "there was camaraderie as Asian American not as Filipino or Japanese."

For Mary Ann Tabor, being born in the U.S. and growing up in the 40s and 50s means talking about her lack of Filipino cultural knowledge. "My Chinese friends all had to go to Chinese school, they all had to speak their mother tongue and yet it never happened in the Filipino community in those years. I didn't have the pressure to speak Tagalog and I am wondering now and I wish I had a little of that pressure."

For Michelle, Abe, and Mary Ann, Filipino indigenous knowledge was not available until recently. This does not mean, however, that Filipino Americans did not have a sense of cultural identity. It simply means that what they felt and lived everyday was not affirmed by their external environment and remained nameless. U.S. society heavily depends on textbook knowledge in naming people's experiences. When Filipino Americans do not find themselves or their history in school texts, they doubt the validity of their experiences. In my lectures on indigenous cultural values, student responses range from, "now I understand why my parents are . . . " or "oh, I have always done (cultural practice) but I didn't know it is culturally Filipino, I thought it was just me."

In the 70s, our community began to articulate the idea of a Filipino national and cultural identity on the basis of our experiences in the U.S. However, according to Helen Toribio of the Filipino American National Historical Society who also teaches Filipino American and Asian American studies at City College of San Francisco, there was a gap between the growing new immigrant population and the U.S. born. Language was a major divisive issue because knowledge of Filipino language was used as indicator of national and ethnic identity. Mary Ann Tabor adds that what was also missing for the U.S.-born was the Philippine perspective. "Our teachers were ourselves and not professors from the Philippines." Moreover, the big influx of "brain drain" immigrants in the 70s didn't help in defining a Filipino American cultural identity, according to Toribio, because "their own national identity as Filipinos didn't seem to be consolidated."

The political events in the U.S. in the 60s and 70s also shaped the experiences of the U.S.-born. Many second and third generation activists became part of the Third World strike and the anti-war movement in coalition with Asian Americans and other ethnic groups. However, one activist who went to the Philippines to join the anti-Marcos movement and came back to the U.S. in the mid-80s observed that during this period few Filipino American institutions developed because there was little organizing at the grassroots level. Instead, Filipino Americans joined the Asian Law Caucus, Asian Health Services and other pan-Asian agencies. By the early 1970s, the Filipino American community's face had begun to change due to the large influx of immigrants, but the methods of creating community institutions used by U.S.-born Filipinos did not adequately address the cultural nuances of the immigrant population. An immigrant leader who wishes to remain anonymous said, ". . . we (immigrant community) are being blamed for the lack of political, economic, and social clout, for being invisible, because they (U.S.-born Filipinos) take the position of 'I understand the community better than you do and you did not follow me therefore you are wrong.' The bottom line is, don't blame the masses for their lack of political education. If the U.S.-born denigrates the immigrant experience, if the immigrant feels patronized, he will not be interested in panethnicity, with Filipinos or other Asians."

This activist feels that the cultural divide in the 90s is being bridged through political and cultural education on both sides. Political education for new immigrant and the U.S.-born promotes both the development of Filipino American identity and pan-Asian awareness. On this relationship, Luz de Leon says,

> . . . the Asian Americans like the Chinese and Japanese, even Koreans, who have already developed traditions here and who may no longer need the source there (the homeland) must understand that we still need the source (Philippines). Before Filipino immigrants develop consciousness as Asian Americans, they must undergo political education; if nobody educates them, they will remain stereotypical or racist. Even though they may have the same experience as other Asian Americans, if no one explains and raises their level of awareness, there will not be a common consciousness.

The "Philippines as a source" for developing a Filipino American identity needs to be understood in the context of our colonial history, diaspora experience, and our efforts towards decolonization. The immigrant and the U.S.-born must see their experiences as part of the same thread that sews our history together. This weaving together of history is articulated by many college students who now find themselves as a critical mass, poised to shape the future of our community. This "Philippines as a source" functions as part of Filipino America's operative culture. This is manifest through the various forms (via email, listserves, cultural exchange programs, visiting scholar programs) of lively exchanges between scholars, artists, cultural workers, environmental workers in the Philippines and their counterparts in the U.S. More and more Filipino American students are participating in short-term and long term study programs in the Philippines; Philippine artists are collaborating with Filipino American artists.

But there is also a decolonizing phase that provides a framework for understanding our status as Filipino Americans who are, at the same time, on the outside and inside the category of Asian Americans. This adds another perspective for understanding why Filipino Americans may not seem quick to assume a pan-Asian identity. What is the basis of identity as Asian American? Is it primarily political? What is the impact of the perceived "cultural distance" of Filipino Americans from other Asian Americans that still allows them to claim Filipinos as Asians? Political coalition-building can be constrained by perceived cultural distance. For example, conversations with participants in this study about Asian panethnicity reflect their "sense of affinity" with Southeast Asians, both as newly arrived immigrants and as post-colonial subjects. One participant mentioned that his perception is that those who appropriate Asian America come from northeast Asian culture—the Chinese, the Japanese and Korean; below the equator, the identity is more regional and therefore, "fragmented."

N. V. M. Gonzalez states that the perception of Filipinos as "lacking in great cultural traditions when compared to China and Japan" is based on positionality. "What if Filipinos began to see themselves and their homeland as the center? How would the narrative change? What if we began to claim a central position to our myths and folkloric traditions, written and unwritten, how would that change the perception? Colonialism is like a jacket we have been wearing; if we take it off, we'll be alright."

It is this attempt to "take off the jacket of colonialism" that is beginning to take hold of our community. In 1993, I had written a personal narrative on "becoming a split Filipina subject" (Strobel, 1993) where I trace the consequences of colonization on my psyche. In putting together the "patchwork" pieces of my self as shaped by my family's history—our Protestant religion, our associations with the U.S. military installations where my father and later, my older sisters worked, the American missionaries, Peace Corps volunteers—I was able to make sense of the feelings of alienation and confusion that assaulted me once I arrived in the U.S. This "making sense" was made possible by my return to my memories as I searched for signs of the repressed indigenous consciousness. I read Filipino history, philosophy and psychology from the critical perspective of Filipino social scientists and therein found the courage to affirm the strength of our indigenous imagination. From this location, I was able to respond to the overdetermination of colonial master narratives in my life.

In the late 1990s, a literary renaissance is happening; never before have Filipino American writers and artists been more prolific. What is more notable is that the themes of new books and publications, poetry slams, oral literary scene are marked by decolonizing efforts—a "returning of borrowed tongues" (Carbo,1995), so to speak. In addition to Jessica Hagedorn (1990, 1993a, 1993b) and N. V. M. Gonzalez (1996, 1997), some of the newly published writers are: Peter Bacho (1997), Ruth Mabanglo (1999), Marianne Villanueva (1991), Eileen Tabios (1998), Cecilia Manguerra-Brainard (1991, 1993, 1994). Bino Realuyo's *Umbrella Country* (1999) is published by Ballantine Books and has received critical acclaim. Likewise, community arts—poetry slams, websites for arts and literature, cultural events—flourish across the U.S. with the visible linkage to similar events in the Philippine scene and among Filipinos in the diaspora. This decolonizing trend is a significant marker in the continuous but uneven presence of Filipino literature and the arts within Asian America and in the U.S. in general[5].

THE IDENTITY FORMATION OF FILIPINO AMERICAN COLLEGE STUDENTS

The discourse of today's Filipino American college students focuses on decolonization and indigenization. I define decolonization as the process of undoing the effects of colonization on the Filipino psyche by recognizing the master narratives that constructed colonial identity and replacing them with indigenous narratives. The term "indigenous" is used here to refer to worldviews, values, beliefs, and practices that define Filipino-ness. The sources of these narratives come mainly from cultural or tribal communities, which resisted colonization and were therefore able to maintain their indigenous cultures.

The development of indigenous psychology as an academic discipline in the Philippines in the last twenty-five years is based on research conducted in these communities and the *tao's* (folk)ways, her sense of self and place in the world as equal to everyone else. This secure sense of identity is quite contrary to the colonial identity of Filipinos who found themselves on the elite-side of the cultural divide that is a product of colonization. Decolonization, therefore, is primarily a psychological process; it is *not* a literal return to a primordial or precolonial culture or identity. For Filipino Americans, its consequences are not limited to consciousness transformation but to a broader change in behavior, attitudes, and perspective. Indigenization is the attempt to reclaim cultural values through constructs derived from language-based research. It is a process of centering the Filipino self as a reference to the "other" without creating rigid boundaries between one's self and the other. After all, the Filipino concept of self, or *kapwa*, refers to a shared sense of inner self, or "I am a part of you and you are a part of me." Indigenization is a departure from the western-imposed psychological models that were used to explain Filipino cultural identity in the past. Virgilio Enriquez (1990) states that colonized peoples tend to be characterized as inadequate approximations of people from presumably better cultures. Labels placed on so-called Filipino values were borrowed from the English and Spanish language, so that in using the colonizer's perspective we fail to understand the indigenous ways of perceiving.

This development of decolonizing discourse in the social sciences and humanities in the Philippines has influenced the discourse within the Filipino American community in the 1990s. As this perspective is integrated into community discussions, it provides a medium for the articulation of cultural identity that is rooted in indigenous consciousness.

Most of the post-1965 "brain drain" immigrants had no access to this academic discourse. It is their children who are now college students who use this knowledge to redefine their identity. They call themselves "born-again Filipinos." They write in *alibata,* the ancient alphabet still used by the Mangyan tribe in the Philippines; they sport *alibata* tattoos that say *"kayumanggi"* (brown skin) *or taga-ilog* (Tagalog, or "from the river"); they learn *kali* and *escrima* (indigenous martial arts); they write poetry in Pilipino and do research on the anti-colonial resistance movements. Through e-mail they circulate lists of "what makes a truly Filipino home," referring to the folkloric traditions and cultural practices brought over the U.S. Student groups print t-shirts with indigenous images framed by quotations from Jose Rizal, the national hero, and proverbs like *"Ang hindi marunong lumingon sa kanyang pinanggalingan ay hindi makakar-ating sa paroroonan"* (Whoever does not look back to where he came from will not get to where he is going). Immigrants to the U.S. from the indigenous groups like the Bontoc, Ifugao, Banawe, Agra, Kalinga (BIBAK) and their U.S. born children are reviving their rituals and traditions and are being performed at community events. In the East Coast, a Filipino dance group, *Kinding Sindaw,* is led by a Maranao princess, Potri Ranka Manis who is a nurse-by-day and artist-by-night, keeping Maranao and Muslim dances and traditions as close to their original forms as possible.

In all these practices, the students realize the important role of Filipino language/s as a bearer of cultural meanings. In a survey I conducted in the Fall of 1993 among Filipino American students enrolled in a Tagalog class at UC Berkeley, their motivation for learning or re-learning the language was related to their desire to understand and rediscover their ethnic roots. Tagalog classes are also in demand today at the high school level.[6]

The desire to learn and maintain the Filipino language/s and other cultural forms becomes the means by which students explore the Filipino part of their identity, creating new narratives that decenter notions of cultural inferiority based on master narratives that portray Filipinos as either having a "damaged culture" or none at all. In the process, they also create a new discourse that implicates U.S. imperialism and colonialism in the Philippines. The discourse questions their miseducation in the U.S., which until recently didn't teach them about the psychic and epistemic violent consequences of American presence in the Philippines at the turn of the century.

These indigenous narratives can be problematic if they are misunderstood as expressions of an "authentic or pure" pre-colonial culture. However, when they are seen as "useful fictions," their function in the re-imagining of cultural identity is empowering (Rosaldo, 1989, p. 217). For Filipino American immigrants the re/presentation of indigenous narratives and traditions in community events and cultural productions become a journey for remembering and re-membering of the fragments of the past; for U.S.-born Filipinos it is a journey of discovery of the parent Filipino culture. It is the process of journey-ing itself that creates new liberating meaning as history, traditions, and personal memories of "homeland" are integrated into consciousness.

At this phase of decolonization, it may be easy to identify with Asian America solely on political grounds but according to N. V. M. Gonzalez, a pan-Asian identity is problematic because "an obstacle arises in the equally strong, if not more attractive, possibility of cultural intervention from the Philippines itself, to disturb the unity you want to form. Your sense of home says, 'no you cannot do this really.' You may do it with one foot but not with both feet."

NARRATIVES

The narratives of students show the attempt to construct an identity through the weaving of historical knowledge and personal memory, and to articulate a Filipino voice from the oral character of the language. The following narrative is about the role that a mother's selective memory played in denying her daughter access to her own cultural identity and history.

> Clarissa: . . . Now my question is—how do I go about learning my mother's history? I feel that it is something that I must do because there is such a gap, an ocean, separating me from her most of the time . . . I used to hate it when she would accuse me of being too "American." But now I realize that is true . . . How can I be more "Filipino" when I don't know anything about what that means? I think that a lot of the anger in her remarks came from within. I know that in some way she realizes that she's contributed to my behavior and what she thinks is my lack of "Filipino-ness" . . . I want to be able to say that I am Filipino American and know what that means . . . if my mother could find it within herself to face up to her memories, to acquire that capacity of recall and recognition, it would be a great benefit to myself as well as the rest of my family.

Other narratives show how access to historical knowledge (Filipino American and Philippine history) enables participants to reconstruct personal history and bridge the generation gap with Philippine-born parents.

> Jaime: When I say "lost in America," I am referring to the fact that although I was proud to be Filipino I really didn't know anything about Filipino history in the PI and in the U.S. None of these things were taught to me in school or in the home. It seemed everyone in my family was working all the time. They were working hard toward a better life and I was swept up in the idealisms of the American dream, much like the Manongs of the first wave. After four years of studying psychology from a Eurocentric point of view at SFSU, I decided to spend my last year in college taking other courses to broaden my perspective. I enrolled in various Asian American courses and soon found myself swimming in a sea of knowledge completely new yet utterly familiar. I felt like I had quenched a thirst that I never knew I had. My view of America as one big happy family was shattered in an instant. And I had to rebuild my view of America through the knowledge that I was absorbing. And it was through these courses and the PACE organization that I really begun to understand the concept of colonial mentality. It was not until I began to recognize my own ethnic identity struggles that I realized that the rift between my family and myself was a result of these issues. Upon this realization I began to open up more of myself toward my parents. And this is a process that is still beginning to unfold.

> Che-che: How can I call myself Filipino if I do not know history? I think my parents didn't want me to learn about the Philippines because they'd rather I learned what I'm getting here. They wanted me to assimilate so that I don't have to suffer. In college, I

am being awakened. I'm learning about civil rights. I think we must recognize that Filipinos are oppressed. There are things more important than the material.

Tess wrote this as a letter to her mother: At this point in my life I struggle to find out the folklore of my people's past. It is through this oral tradition of ours that I can investigate into the psyche of my brothers and sisters. I continue to do this through school events and functions, through lectures, books, and conversations with others concerned. That is why I am never home. I am searching for me. Now that I have the opportunities to search for my identity, I want to be able to hear the stories you heard from your mother and father. Growing up I always felt as though there was a hint of shame in you for being Filipino. I see in you how society has molded an "assimilated" Filipino woman. I say this in quotes because I know through all your put downs and comments about people, at heart you will always be a Filipina. I refuse to forget where I come from. Filipinos are great and resilient people. I want to somehow pass this on to my children.

The narratives are representative of the "voice" that is emerging among college students. The narrators weave personal memory and historical knowledge in a critical language that has learned to question the dominant narratives learned from their parents and the educational system. When there is a lack of knowledge about Filipino colonial history, the narratives reflect a narrowing of perception and understanding to the realm of the personal, unable to take into consideration the way personal experiences are shaped by historical and political constructions. Furthermore, the lack of knowledge prevents them from understanding how racism and other oppressive ideologies construct and limit the experience of ethnic groups in the U.S.

In a discussion with students from Sonoma State University, I asked them to talk about the factors that led to their parents' immigration to the U.S., and their answers ranged from "I am not sure," to "economic reasons," and "to join the U.S. Navy." In becoming aware that their narratives have not taken into account the larger political and historical context that shaped immigration, they begin a journey of re-discovery, or re-construction of ethnic/cultural identity, by attending lectures, civil rights rallies, and community sociocultural functions. Their involvements often also lead to a deeper search into their personal memory banks and critical questioning of the contexts that have shaped their parents' immigrant experience and their own identity. This process is often painful and emotional. Feelings of shame, guilt, anger, confusion, may rise to the level of awareness. It takes time, energy and peer support to deal with these emotions; to mine them for new meanings and to find the language and knowledge with which to construct new narratives. Eventually, the students who work through this decolonization process are also the students who commit themselves to working in the community in various capacities—as volunteers, community workers, youth counselors, advocates, artists, and writers (Strobel 1996).

Padilla (1994; 1998) proposes another framework for cultural identity formation that parallels the indigenous approach. He calls it a "return to the folkloric." This is a component of the folkloric-colonial-diasporic matrix, with the folkloric representing the precolonial culture symbolized by the self-sufficient and organic *barangay* (village) and the autonomous *datu* (chief). It is based on close family ties, kinship and blood relationship, and devotion, hospitality, and collective spirit nourish it. The colonial matrix (Hispanic and American colonialism) produced the Filipino elite who created a cultural divide (the elite versus the folk). As an inorganic and rationalistic product, the colonial matrix destroyed social solidarity and promoted alienated individualism, basically producing a caste system. The diasporic matrix or the spread of Filipinos to every part of the world today, bears the mark of the folkloric parent. The diaspora can be perceived as a by-product of "limited vision of mendicancy, (and a reminder that) Filipinos did not forget the ways of the folks. Taken as a whole, neither the internal or external polemics against Filipino culture, nor the numerous news and articles on Philippine corruption . . . have noticeably prejudiced the humility and will of many Filipinos to redeem and recover themselves" (Padilla 1998, 249). According to Padilla, the presence of folkloric traditions among Filipino Americans symbolizes a form of reverse colonialism, not in the imperial sense but in a more naturalistic sense of colony-building. Affirming folkloric traditions, encouraging the recovery of myths, folktales, proverbs, songs, dances, and art forms, and presenting these in their "authentic" or re-invented Filipino American form deepens the cultural knowledge of the community.

When college students in this study weave their understanding of historical, political and social formation (both in the Philippines and the U.S.), with indigenous knowledge and integrate these psychologically, the results are akin to what Lugones (1990) calls the overcoming of "arrogant perception." This can bridge the cultural divide, the class differences, and intergenerational conflicts within the family and the community. This is evident in the emerging theme of the "born again" experience: *Pilipino kahit saan, kahit kailan* ("we are all Filipinos, anytime, anywhere").

This discovery could also facilitate "traveling" to other Asian American worlds, thus developing a pan-ethnic consciousness. The ability to "travel" playfully into other "worlds" is grounded in a newly found sense of strength and pride in Filipino-ness. But whether Filipino Americans' travel to other Asian American worlds is playful or not depends on whether the latter welcomes the traveler.

IMPLICATIONS FOR PANETHNICITY: LOOKING BACK WHILE MOVING FORWARD

Does decolonization and indigenization represent a primordialist, essentialist, na-tivistic, and therefore, problematic approach to cultural identity formation in the age of borderlands and playful world travelling? How can the "return to the indigenous" be good for panethnic consciousness in the long run?

If the key indicators of pan-Asian consciousness include self-identification, membership in pan-Asian organizations, and friendship and marriage patterns, then post-1965 Filipino Americans' identification with Asian America is weak. But if the development of pan-ethnic consciousness is seen within the context of a group's transcultur-ation (Pratt, 1992, 1–11), then Filipino Americans need not be judged by the same indicators used for Chinese and Japanese Americans.

However, the existing criteria for panethnicity are met by some segments of our community, namely, second and third generation Filipino Americans. Their identification as Asian Americans is based more on political than cultural reasons. Yet, even in political coalitions, Filipino Americans find themselves marginalized.

"When are you (Filipino Americans) going to get your act together?" William Tamayo of Asian Law Caucus mentioned this often-asked question by other Asian Americans in his keynote address at the 1992 Association for Asian American Studies Conference in San Jose, California. Until recently, there was this perception of our community as not "having its act together." But as we decolonize ourselves and begin to create our narratives, we also begin to question the criteria for panethnicity which subtly imitates the criteria for assimilation in the U.S., i.e., locating the problem in the Filipino American community's culture and values and not implicating the structures that impose themselves on us.

As a community that is emerging from invisibility and marginalization and as a largely newly-arrived immigrant group, Filipino Americans are in the process of: 1) developing community institutions that would make access to indigenous knowledge and narratives of decolonization available not just to academics but to all sectors of the community, and 2) bridging the gap between academic and community discourse. This would facilitate a dialogue that would support our ability to interface with other Asian communities. Luz de Leon of Philippine Resource Center states: "Other Asian Americans must accept the cultural specificity of our work if we are to become full participating partner in Asian America. When we are asserting our specificity, we are making sure that the term Asian America is inclusive; and it should not be perceived as 'lacking in broad view,' i.e., 'you are not like us,' when compared to the hegemonic groups within Asian America."

Panethnicity is only possible when we understand each other's communities and cultures, de Leon says, and that "you must know the community from the ground up because it will tell you many things." An immigrant Filipino may not develop panethnic consciousness until she understands her location. Sometimes she won't feel she belongs until she has a green card, has become a citizen, or becomes culturally competent. Cultural competence can mean knowing when to be Filipino American or Asian American or even multicultural; having an understanding and awareness of racism; having a political perspective; or something as simple as knowing when to speak Pilipino and when to use "standard" English.

SITES OF PANETHNICITY WITHIN THE
FILIPINO AMERICAN COMMUNITY

Can Filipino Americans re-root their identity in the indigenous/folkloric while at the same time developing a panethnic consciousness? Can one inform the other? Can the movement be simultaneous? Who is leading this movement?

In certain cities with large Filipino Americans such as Vallejo, Daly City or Union City, Filipino high schools students are often perceived as either Asian American "model minority" or "gang members." The successful students easily appropriate the

Asian American (model minority) identity but upon entering college, they find that Asian identity refers mainly to Chinese, Korean, and Japanese Americans and not to Filipino Americans. This is one of the triggering events of the search for Filipino cultural identity. The process of identity formation then becomes a full-time preoccupation, with Asian paenthnic consciousness taking a back seat. However, these students also recognize the political significance of pan-Asian coalitions and they participate in projects which are inclusive and which do not marginalize Filipino American interests.[7]

The results of *pagtatanung-tanong* with San Francisco State University and UC Berkeley students reveals that whenever there is a small Filipino population in a high school, Filipino Americans will likely identify as Asian American. Even when there is a large Filipino population but no education component about Philippine and Filipino American history, the claim of students to Filipino Americanness is still only form without substance.

The perception that Filipino Americans do not have a clear sense of national or cultural/ethnic identity has been perpetuated and circulated by narratives that were written by others. N. V. M. Gonzalez says,

> The literary achievements of early Filipinos, such as the Manobo epic, *Agyu,* the oral art forms such as *balagtasan,* have not been honored because of the weight of the educational system that was imposed on us. The foreign writers minimized these things. To them they were artifacts, to us they were living things. That part of our history has to be written. Our traditions have not been expressed by this generation, by us, who has found itself suddenly vocal but tongue-tied. Our problem is the carrot and the stick, the stick of poverty and the carrot of affluence. That is why it appears that we are neither here nor there.

Even as Filipino Americans look back to the Philippines-as-source they are also moving forward. A good case study in the development of panethnicity is in the area of cultural production. In northern California, the 1994–95 Filipino American Arts Exposition (FAAE), a project of the Philippine Resource Center (PRC), presented a month-long exhibit of Filipino American arts and culture held at Yerba Buena Gardens in San Francisco. The exposition was a "celebration as well as an artistic interrogation of the community and its struggle for cultural equity." It attempted to bridge the cultural divide between U.S.-born Filipinos and immigrants while at the same time situating our community within a multicultural landscape. This exposition was led by U.S.-born artists and cultural activists who see their work as a continuation of their cultural activism in the Philippines. But the working body of volunteers is mostly college students. In struggling for cultural equity in the U.S., exposition organizers view the strengthening of the parent indigenous culture as a necessary phase. This is the simultaneous movement of "looking back while moving forward." This cultural production brings in resource persons from the Philippines who are experts in indigenous traditions. These exchanges also engage these scholars in the discourse of what it means to be a transnational and transcultural Filipino.

The Executive Director of PRC, Luz de Leon, states:

The exposition . . . is at this point, culturally specific, i.e., Filipino American. The Expo's themes last year and this year are aimed at deepening the cultural knowledge of Filipino Americans. We need this as a grounding, as a source of strength that can enable us to carve out our space in a multicultural setting. We want to move from being a self-blaming, self-flagellating community to a community with a critical perspective that we can bring to bear on complex issues. And to a vision of what the community can and should be. As a multicultural produciton, we want to create palpable cultural symbols and traditions that will not only speak to Filipino Americans but to non Filipino Americans as well. We need to ask how we can do this without nostalgia and objectification of our own culture.

We want to address the issue of Asian American panethnicity by asking how our cultural productions can respond to the question of Filipino American identity within the Asian American rubric; how do we create linkages, coalitions, dialogues to answer these? If Asian America is to become a truly multicultural site where all Asian groups have space and representation, we should be able to look at the political power plays that create "superior" vs. "inferior" polarities. Filipino Americans must address these from a position of rootedness in a culturally-specific identity.

More recent panethnic collaboration is demonstrated by a 1998 FAAE and PRC cultural production. The theatre production of *Sisa*, a play based on the heroine in Jose Rizal's novel *Noli Me Tangere*, was staged as a Japanese Noh drama at the Theatre Yugen in San Francisco. Filipino playwright Amelia Lapena Bonifacio, Filipino drama director Christ Millado and Noh drama director Yuriko Doi of Theater Yugen, and the cast from the Filipino American theatre group, Teatro ng Tanan (TNT, or Theater for Everyone) had a successful run in San Francisco even as a work-in-progress. This production combined the noh-drama form with the *pasyon* (a Filipino lenten ritual of narrating the Christ story through song) resulting in a new theatre form. This immersion in each other's history and theater traditions demonstrates the creative and productive potential of "playful traveling" into each other's worlds. The successful reception of this novel collaboration surprised both its producers and its multicultural audience. The full-length finished work will be premiered in San Francisco on April 1999.[8]

Even as the Exposition highlighted the "way of the folk" in its early cultural productions, today Filipino American artists are also experimenting with contemporary forms in the popular culture such as hip-hop. The tradition of the Pilipino Cultural Night (Gonzalves, 1995) on college campuses now includes not only the folkloric showcase of Filipino dances and music, it may also incorporate skits with social or political content, modern dance, stand-up comedy, hip-hop, and R and B music—as Filipino-nuanced performances.

Wilma Consul, a performance artist and artistic director of TNT, draws her wealth of materials from Asian America as well as Latino sources. She has performed with the Asian American comedy group, 18 Mighty Mountain Warriors, as well as Latino Theater Lab, and Culture Clash. However, Consul is better known for her one-woman show where she plays the role of Manang (wife of a Filipino farm laborer in the 1930s-40s) and the lead role in *Sisa*.

Another site, the 1999 Asian American Film Festival in San Francisco included films by Filipino film-makers, most notably Marilou Diaz-Abaya's *Sa Pusod ng Dagat* (In the Navel of the Sea) and *Rizal*. The former is about indigenous traditions in contemporary Philippine village life and the latter is a biography of the Philippine national hero, Jose Rizal. As an Asian-panethnic festival, both Filipino American and Asian American audiences have the opportunity to learn about Filipino indigenous cultures and values.

This need to become visible to ourselves precedes the capacity to do bordercrossing or world traveling to other Asian American worlds. The premise is that the more we know about our parent culture and ourselves the more respect and appreciation we can have for each other and other Asian Americans. When the Expo pushed its visibility into the mainstream and the multicultural arena, many Filipino Americans were surprised. *"Ah, puwede pala yon!"* (Oh, I didn't know it could be done that way!). Filipino American identity no longer suffers from facelessness and it is this presence and particularity that may unsettle the definitions of Asian Americanness. Asian panethnicity is a tapestry of colors, and those who claim to be stalwarts of panethnicity must know the history of those they label. That's how arrogance is resisted.

The deepening of cultural knowledge enables Filipino Americans to connect with Asia through the recognition of parallel traditions, beliefs, and value systems, based on filial/familial relations, and relationship with nature and ancestral spirits. Even though it may seem problematic to refer back to cultural patterning that hints of essentialism, there is an undeniable intuited linkage with Asian traditions that Filipino Americans recognize. The question of panethnicity might benefit from this articulation of shared cultural influences and values that are still deeply felt in our Asian American lives. This perspective can also expand the context for panethnic coalitions beyond the existing basis of shared political and historical experiences in the U.S., to a recognition of the long connection between the Philippines and its Asian neighbors. However, while some cultural workers express an optimism in this potential of shared cultural heritage, it is also problematic because of the temptation to exoticize and commodify our Asian-ness for a white audience thirsty for the "exotic other". Fortunately, cultural activists who are also politically astute recognize the trap of essentializing cultural traditions.

"But what are we in the imagination of the Chinese and Japanese Americans?" Padilla's question is begging for an answer. N. V. M. Gonzalez again states that the Filipino American presence in America is only one of the "functions of a venturing race in search of hope; wherever there is hope, there is a Filipino. All of the Asian Americans are really 'hope immigrants' but they are not accepting that, but once they do, then they will see that we are all brothers/sisters. But maybe the fact that many second, third, or fourth generation Asian Americans no longer have that attachment to their homelands, will have a say on whether or not this can be a basis for panethnicity." E. San Juan, Jr. (1992) writes that of all the Asian American groups, the Filipino community is "perhaps the only one most obsessed with the impossible desire of returning to the homeland, whether in reality or fantasy (123)." To San Juan, to invoke the claim of bottomless hybridity would be to remain complicitous with the continuing "civilizing mission" of the U.S.; that the only way to develop a critical sensibility that can address unequal power relations is through an understanding of history and global processes. This recuperation of attachment to the homeland can be recognized as prerequisite to the development of panethnic consciousness.[9]

CONCLUSION

I have emphasized the importance of recognizing the role of the "return to the indigenous/folkloric" movement in decolonizing our consciousness. But I also emphasize the simultaneity of our movement—it is looking back and moving forward, a crisscrossing. A Filipino word, *salpukan,* paints the image of clashing, of hitting with an impact and diverging in different directions, but the parts are held together within a wide boundary—which is an apt metaphor for the crisscrossing/clashing of borders. The movement is multilingual, transnational and transcultural. As such, Asian panethnicity becomes one of the many borders that Filipino Americans cross strategically on a daily basis.

Can other Asian communities who have established viable communities and secured leadership role within Asian America, and, therefore, have effectively positioned themselves at the center of the Asian rubric, create a space for Filipino Americans? Who will benefit from this decentering of Asian America? What would it mean to overcome "arrogant perceptions" within the Asian community, given the competitive society we live in and given the limited resources we fight over? A Filipino American who has worked with several pan-Asian agencies says:

> My personal experience with pan-Asian groups has generally been positive in the sense that my presence was welcome and my voice was heard. However, I always felt like a minority within a minority. In that sense, Filipino inclusion in pan-Asian groups often was token and less them empowering because those who ran pan-Asian groups were almost always Chinese or Japanese American. To get a sense of the predominance of Chinese and Japanese Americans in pan-Asian organizations, you need only to look at their top management and the make-up of their board of directors. I think you could go through each pan-Asian organization one by one, review their staff and board, and see how small the Filipino representations—if it exists at all.[10]

Overcoming the perceived "arrogance" means that pan-Asian leaders and organizations need to create more opportunities for dialogue; discuss panethnicity issues beyond political coalition building; discuss how ethnic-specific cultural productions can be supported by pan-Asian organizations. Maybe pan-Asian organizations can invite Filipino American college students to work as interns. A pan-Asian dialogue must also bring to the table the issue of power relations, tokenism, and sharing power. Furthermore, the boundaries of panethnicity should go beyond common history of oppression in the U.S., decentering victimhood without minimizing the importance of the traditions of resistance.

Trinh Minh-ha (1990) writes that there need not be conflict in our differences—that, in fact, we do not own anything, not even what we create. How could this Buddhist-like way of thinking help us in creating a panethnic consciousness? This is also the indigenous Filipino way of seeing the interdependence and interrelatedness of human beings and all of creation. The inclusive "we"(*tayo* in Tagalog) replaces the exclusive "we" (*kami*) in recognition of this interconnectedness; there is no inside/outside duality in *tayo*. Although it is an abstract philosophy, it behooves us to think about the conceptualization of panethnicity not only in its economic, political, and sociocultural implications, but also in ways that widen these borders. The artist who waxes lyrical and mythical about political issues may sound naïve or fatalistic but he probably knows more about being a prisoner of hope than most of us do. A Filipino poet-philosopher, Fr. Bert Alejo, wrote:

> *Totoo, ang aking kalayaan ay nakasalalay sa sariling galaw ng aking loob. Subalit posible lamang ito sa loob ng isang daigdig na mayroon akong kasama, sapagkat kung ako lang, hindi ko alam kung hanggang saan ang aking abot. Kailangan kong mamulat na hindi ako nag-iisa, na kahit anong mangyari, meron akong kapiling na kapanalig na kapwa ko na nagnanasang magpakatao at lumaya ring tulad ko.* (115)

> (True, my freedom lies within me. But this would only be possible if I lived in a world where I am with others who want to be fully human and free. I need to know that I am not alone, I need to know that I can count on my fellow beings).[11]

Notes

This article has been revised and updated especially for this anthology. An earlier version appeared in *Amerasia Journal* 22.2 (1996): 31–53. We thank the editor of *Amerasia Journal*, Russell Leong, for permission to reprint.

1. The Filipino American Experience Research Project: A Journey of Rediscovery, 1565–1965, is now in CD-ROM format and available through San Francisco State University Asian American Studies Program (Prof. Dan Gonzales and Alex Fabros, Jr.). The CD-ROM contains volumes on the Filipino American Military Experience, Filipino American Newspaper Collection, Filipino American Photo Collection, Personal Papers and Documents. There are also at least a half-dozen community newspapers in the Bay Area alone, which cover both Philippine news and local Filipino American news. A 24-hour cable channel, *The Filipino Channel,* has thousands of subscribers. There are locally produced television shows with a cultural and political focus such as Manila, Manila, and *Pinoy Pa Rin*. A monthly magazine, *Filipinas*, tries to maintain a balanced and critical perspective on social and political issues affecting Filipino Americans. For a recent historical bibliography and a two-volume collection of essays on the Philippines and the US, see Raul Ebio (1998) and dela Cruz—particularly the essays in dela Cruz by August Espiritu (on N. V. M. Gonzalez) and by Steffi San Buenaventura (for her discussion of the "crossings" between Filipinos and other American ethnic groups, e.g. African Americans, Native Americans, as part of the 'underside' of the colonial narrative). Selected earlier texts providing essential background include Ileto, Rafael, Campomanes, Gonzalez's *Work on the Mountain,* Campomanes' and Gonzalez joint survey (1997), as well as San Juan's work cited below.

2. In 1993, a student from San Francisco State University said: "My vision for the future is a room full of Filipino Americans asking each other, 'and when were you born again as a Filipino'?" The expression, "born-again" Filipino has since circulated amongst college students.

3. The 1995 Filipino Americans and Asian American Panethnicity symposium was attended by N. V. M. Gonzalez, professor emeritus and National Philippine Artist in Literature

awardee, California State University at Hayward (CSUH) and Narita Gonzalez; Efren Padilla, sociology professor, CSUH; Helen Toribio, City College of San Francisco/Asian American Studies, Filipino American National Historical Society (FANHS), and Filipino Civil Rights Advocates (FILCRA); Abraham Ignacio, FANHS and and FILCRA; Luz de Leon, Executive Director of the Philippine Resource Center; Carmen Kirk and David Brady, Sikolohiyang Pilipino; Mary Ann Tabor, doctoral candidate, University of San Francisco. Unless specified, all subsequent quotations in the essay by Efren Padilla, N. V. M. Gonzalez, and Luz de Leon are from this symposium.

4. In this section, I have combined the results of several inter-related studies that I have conducted from 1993 to 1998 through *pagtatanung-tanong*; these are part of an on-going project. The first names of participants whose statements are quoted here are from U.C. Berkeley, San Francisco State University, Sonoma State University. Participants whose full names are mentioned here have given their permission. Unless otherwise identified, interview quotations elsewhere in this essay are from this project's archives.

5. For a critical and historical perspective on the state of Filipino American literature, see Campomanes, O. and Gonzalez, N. V. M., "Filipino American Literature," in *An Interethnic Companion to Asian American Literature* (1997). A popular website and listserve that discuss literature and the arts: http://www.uni.edu/webfiles/faculty/gotera.html and FILIPINOARTS-L@ HOME.EASE.LSOFT.COM. The discussion in these groups may often include topics relevant to Filipinos in the diaspora and to Filipinos in the Philippines; as such they are transnational in scope.

6. Tagalog is the base of the national language, Filipino. Union High School in Union City, California has recently offered Tagalog classes. Classes are also offered at Balboa High School in San Francisco as well as Skyline Community College. More Tagalog classes and Filipino Amerian Studies courses are in demand as Filipino American college students express a need to re-learn the language and history, e.g. at Santa Clara University, University of San Francisco.

7. Dialogues with Larry Shinagawa, Associate Professor, American Multicultural Studies Deparment at Sonoma State University, advisor to Asian and Pacific Islander Organization (APIO) and co-advisor to Filipino American Students of SSU.

8. Interview with Luz de Leon, Executive Director, Philippine Resource Center, and Wilma Consul, Artistic Director, Teatro ng Tanan (TNT).

9. See San Juan's critique on the "cult of panethnicity" as he "rejects liberal ideology of market-oriented pluralistic society where individuals follow the 'American Dream' path." He is also critical of post-colonial anti-essentialism when it's "anathema to collective self-discovery" of Filipinos in the process of decolonization. San Juan's position is that the Filipino is not post-colonial yet and to reject Filipino values as "essentialist" can lead to the mere pastiche of hybridity. He opts for the development of critical sensibility that translates into oppositional and transgressive practice. (San Juan, 1992, 97–130). See also his "Postcolonial Theory Versus Philippine Reality: The Challenge of Third World Resistance Culture to Global Capitalism."

10. Statement by a participant in the December 1995 symposium (see footnote 3) who did not want to be identified.

11. Alejo's book, *Tao Po!Tuloy! Isang Landas ng Pagunawa sa Loob ng Tao* (1990), is written in Pilipino and is a study of the concept of "loob," which means "inner core of being." "Loob" is related to "pakikiramdam" (deep empathy/compassion) and "pakikipagkapwa" (I and the other are one)—these, according to Alejo and Enriquez, are core Filipino values. This articulation differs from earlier theories about Filipino cultural values as being based on "hiya" (shame), "utang na loob" (debt of gratitude), and "pakikisama" (smooth interpersonal relations).

Works Cited

Alejo, A. *Tao Po! Tuloy! Isang Landas sa Pagunawa sa Loob ng Tao*. Manila: Office of Research and Publications, Ateneo de Manila University, 1990.

Bacho, P. *Dark Blue Suit and other stories*. Seattle: U of Washington P, 1997.

Campomanes, O. "The New Empire's Forgetful and Forgotten Citizens: Unrepresentability and Unassimilability in Filipino American Postcolonialities." *Critical Mass: A Journal of Asian American Cultural Criticism* 2.2 (1995): 145–200.

———, and N. V. M. Gonzalez, "Filipino American Literature." *An Interethnic Companion to Asian American Literature*. Ed. King-Kok Cheung. Cambridge UP, 1997. 62–124.

Carbo, N., ed. *Returning Borrowed Tongues: An Anthology of Filipino and Filipino American Poetry*. Minneapolis: Coffee House P, 1995.

Cordova, F. Filipinos: Forgotten Asian Americans. Seattle: Demonstration Project for Asian Americans, 1983.

Cruz, R. C. "How Far Have We Come?" *Filipinas*. October 1994: 40–44.

dela Cruz, Enrique, ed. *Essays into American Empire in the Philippines: Part I— Legacies, Heroes, and Identities. Part II—Culture, Community, and Capital*. Two volumes. Los Angeles: UCLA Asian American Studies Center P, 1998.

Ebio, Raul, ed., et al. *Pilipino America at the Crossroads: 100 Years of United States-Philippines Relations* [A Bibliography]. Los Angeles: UCLA Asian American Studies Center P, 1998.

Enriquez, V. *From Colonial to Liberation Psychology: The Philippine Experience*. Manila: De La Salle UP, 1994.

———, ed. *Indigenous Psychology: A Book of Readings*. Quezon City, Philippines: Philippine Research and Training House, 1990.

Espiritu, Y. L. *Asian American Panethnicity*. Philadelphia: Temple UP, 1992.

———. *Filipino American Lives*. Philadelphia: Temple UP, 1995.

Gonzalez, N. V. M. *A Grammar of Dreams*. Quezon City, Philippines: U of the Philippines P, 1997.

———. *The Novel of Justice*. Quezon City, Philippines: Anvil Publishing, 1996.

———. *Work on the Mountain*. Quezon City, Philippines: U of the Philippines P, 1995.

Gonzalves, T. "The Show Must Go On: Production Notes on the Pilipino Cultural Night." *Critical Mass: A Journal of Asian American Cultural Criticism*, 2.2 (1995): 129–44.

Hagedorn, J. *Danger and Beauty*. New York: Penguin Books, 1993a.

———. *Dogeaters*. New York: Pantheon, 1990.

———, ed. *Charlie Chan is Dead: An Anthology of Contemporary Asian American Fiction*. New York: Penguin Books, 1993b.

Ileto, R. *Pasyon and Revolution: Popular Movements in the Philippines: 1840–1910*. Manila: Ateneo de Manila University P, 1979.

Mabanglo, R. *Invitation to the Imperialist: Poems*. Honolulu: U of Hawaii P, 1999.

Manguerra-Brainard, C. *Pilipino Woman in America*. Quezon City, Philippines: New Day, 1991.

———, ed. *Fiction by Filipinos in America*. Quezon City, Philippines: New Day, 1993.

———. *When the Rainbow Goddess Wept*. New York: Dutton, 1994.

Minh-Ha, T. "Not Like You/Like You: Post-colonial Women and the Interlocking Quesitons of Identity and Difference." *Making Face, Making Soul: Creative and Critical Perspectives by Women of Color*. Ed. Gloria Anzaldua. San Francisco: Aunt Lute Books, 1990. 371–75.

Morawska, E. "The Sociology and Historiography of Immigration." *Immigration Reconsidered: History, Sociology, and Politics*. Ed. V. Yans-McLaughlin. New York: Oxford UP, 1990. 187–238.

Obusan, T. "A *Hiyang* Approach." *Pamamaraan: Indigenous Knowledge and Evolving Research Paradigms*. Quezon City: University of the Philippines, Asian Center, 1995. 89–110.

Padilla, E. "Reverse Colonialism: A Theoretical Inquiry into the Social Reconstruction of the Filipino Community in the New World." Paper presented at the Annual Conference of the American Association for Filipino Psychology. San Francisco State University, 1994.

——. *The New Filipino Story*. Dubuque, IA: Kendall/Hunt Publishing, 1998.

Pe-Pua, R. "*Pagtatanung-tanong*: A Method for Cross-cultural Research." *Indigenous Psychology: A Book of Readings*. Ed. V. Enriquez. Quezon City: Philippine Research and Training House, 1990. 231–49.

Pratt, M. *Imperial Eyes: Travel Writing and Transculturation*. London and New York: Routledge, 1992.

Rafael, V. *Contracting Colonialism: Translation and Christian Conversion in Tagalog Society Under Early Spanish Rule*. Manila: Ateneo de Manila UP, 1988.

Realuyo, B. *The Umbrella County*. New York: Ballantine Books, 1999.

Rosaldo, R. *Culture and Truth: The Remaking of Social Analysis*. Boston: Beacon P, 1989.

San Juan, E., Jr. *Racial Formations/Critical Transformations: Articulations of Power in Ethnic and Racial Studies in the United States*. New Jersey and London: Humanities Press, 1992.

——. "Postcolonial Theory Versus Philippine Reality: The Challenge of Third World Resistance Culture to Global Capitalism." http://www.boondocks.com/centennial

Steinberg, S. *The Ethnic Myth: Race, Ethnicity, and Class in America*. Boston: Beacon P, 1981.

Strobel, L. "A Personal Story: Becoming a Split Filipina Subject." *Amerasia Journal* 19:3 (1993): 117–29.

——. "Coming Full Circle: Narratives of Decolonization Among Post-1965 Filipino Americans." *Filipino Americans: Transformation and Identity*. Thousand Oaks, Ca: Sage Publications, 1997: 62–79.

Tabios, E. *Beyond Life Sentences*. Pasig, Philippines: Anvil Publishing, 1998.

Vallangca, C. *The Second Wave: Pinoy, Pinay*. San Francisco: Strawberry Hill P, 1987.

Villanueva, M. *Ginseng and Other Tales from Manila*. Corvalis, Or: Calyx Books, 1991.

SOUTH ASIAN
AMERICAN LITERATURE
"Off the Turnpike"
of Asian America

Lavina Dhingra Shankar and Rajini Srikanth

How is the increasing presence of postcolonial diasporics—such as the South Asians—in the United States changing the definition of Asian America/n, and hence altering ethnic American literature?[1] For the purposes of census classification and enumeration, South Asians are now considered Asian American. While some South Asian Americans are comfortable with an Asian American identification, there are many who consciously and actively "dis-identify"[2] themselves from this ethno-racial category. As we have argued in our critical anthology *A Part, Yet Apart: South Asians in Asian America* (1998), part of this disidentification stems from the recognition by South Asian Americans that Asian American social and cultural spaces have histori-cally been dominated by literary artists and scholars of East Asian ancestry—that is, those originating primarily from China, Japan, and Korea—even though South Asians were among the earliest immigrants to the United States in the nineteenth century, and today South Asian Americans outnumber the Japanese Americans and are compa-rable in their percentage among Asian Americans to Korean Americans.[3]

Highlighting the ambivalent position of postcolonial South Asians within Asian American literary and cultural studies, this essay attempts to locate four writers and their works within the rubric of the U.S. ethnic canon: Shani Mootoo, Tahira Naqvi, Agha Shahid Ali, and Abraham Verghese.[4] We concur with Ketu Katrak that "the category 'South Asian American' does not indicate a monolithic whole, but rather a collection of differences" (192–3), and recognize that the category "Asian American" is itself painfully fraught with internal fissures. Nevertheless, we endorse Susan Koshy's view that however conflicted these terms, "'Asian American' [and may we add 'South Asian American'] offers us a rubric that we cannot not use" (342).

Asian American literature grew out of the imperatives of the ethnic movements of the 1960s and the 1970s. Even when turn-of-the-century writers, such as Sui Sin Far, have been brought into the scope of this territory, it has been so through a retrospective analysis of their works in light of the paradigms articulated during those ethnic movements. U.S. ethnicity—despite Werner Sollors' attempt to declare all Americans, including Yankees, as ethnics (20–39)—carries with it an unmistakable stamp of the racial "Other." Ethnic literature, as it is understood in the United States, is expected, both by the dominant culture and by minority cultures, to focus on certain themes— among these, discrimination, double consciousness, search for individual and group identity, examination of ethnic heritage, reclamation of silenced personal and communal history, resistance to exclusion from mainstream socio-political institutions, and the empowerment of victims. These themes emerged against the backdrop of the U.S. sociopolitical landscape; ethnic writers reflect the general desire of their communities to be considered full and equal participants in the fabric of American life. Postcolonial South Asian writers living and publishing in the United States have complicated these expectations due to the tension within Asian American studies on whether the writers and their protagonists identify themselves as postcolonial exilic, expatriated Asians in America, or as ethnic Americans of Asian descent.[5] South Asians' writing frequently exhibits a tendency to render the United States not as the central stage on which the action of their texts unfold, but as only one site of relevance amidst a number of possible locations worldwide. The nation-state of the U.S. recedes into the background, and membership within the American polity is not typically a central concern. Both tendencies—the concurrent invocation of other homelands and the relative lack of concern with issues of citizenship and belonging within the U. S. civic structure— have inhibited the easy incorporation of writing by South Asian Americans into the domain of Asian American literature.

Historically, Asian American literary scholars have responded to the difficult and complex issues raised by the South Asian presence by choosing to sidestep this group. Early scholarship in Asian American literary studies—for example, Elaine H. Kim's *Asian American Literature* (1982) and the anthology *Aiiieeeee!* (1974) edited by Frank Chin and others—had focused exclusively on East Asian writers to map out Asian American literature.[6] Such scholarship not only resulted in an erasure of the South Asian presence in Asian American literature but also of their immigration history. Although King-Kok Cheung's and Stan Yogi's valuable *Asian American Literature: An Annotated Bibliography* (1988)—in which the South Asian section is based primarily on *Indian Literature in English* (1981), ed. A. Singh, R. Verma, I. Joshi—included some South Asian writers, Elaine Kim's essay "Asian American Literature," published in the *Columbia Literary History of the United States* (1988), nonchalantly excluded the writings of South Asians.

In her major work, *Immigrant Acts* (1996), Lisa Lowe seems to rectify Elaine Kim's erroneous description of Indians and Pakistanis as "very new population groups" (xiii)—which was Kim's stated rationalization for excluding literature by South and Southeast Asians, in her *Asian American Literature: An Introduction to the Writings and Their Social Context* (1982). Although Lowe doesn't go so far as to specifically name Kim's earlier mis-classification, she seems to refer to it in the language of her disclaimer: "Immigrants from South Asia are not a 'new' group, having come to the United States since the late nineteenth century" (199). This acknowledgment of the earlier erasure of South Asian American history, and the ensuing brief comment on the changing position of South Asians within Asian America, seems gracious, if overdue. However, what makes this inclusion appear ex-orbitant (outside the main text's orbit), is that it occurs in a footnote! Of course, one might agree with Jacques Derrida that footnotes are critical, and that the marginal is central here.

One South Asian writer who has been almost universally adopted—or, who has, shall we say, adopted America with much eagerness—is Bharati Mukherjee.[7] Despite the unwavering critiques by South Asian American readers of Mukherjee's problematic identity politics and of her inaccurate, exoticized representations of an imaginary, ahistorical India, her 1989 novel *Jasmine*, has become an iconic South Asian American text among most non-South Asian scholars. Many of Mukherjee's South Asian critics believe that the writer has calculated well that the majority of the American reading public's knowledge of non-western geographies and cultures is so limited that she can pass as "authentic" her inadequately researched representations of South Asian regions and populations she too is largely unfamiliar with. To consider two recent examples of her representative status as an Asian American, Bharati Mukherjee is the only writer of South Asian descent included in the critical collection *Asian-American Women Writers* (1997), edited by Harold Bloom, and a HarperCollins anthology, *Asian American Literature* (1996), edited by Shawn Wong.

Demographic changes within Asian America in the last two decades have necessitated the re-thinking of a U.S.-centric paradigm of Asian American literature. The fastest growing populations have been the Filipinos, Southeast Asians and South Asians and, as Stephen Sumida has suggested, these are the populations most interested in seeing how their once colonized ancestral or home nations are faring as independent political entities.[8] Thus, it is no surprise to find among these groups strong ties to their original homelands and to see these extra-U.S. ties reflected in the literature. Transnationalism is a palpable reality for these groups, a mode of being. Even when no physical travel to home or ancestral countries takes place, current technological developments enable the maintaining and nurturing of emotional connections (cricket matches, for instance, being beamed via satellite to restaurants in New York) (Vardarajan 24g; Appadurai, *Modernity* 10). Andrew Lam has remarked that Vietnamese American youngsters use the CD-ROMs to learn about Vietnamese culture and history. The length of stay in the United States is not a reliable indicator of U.S.-centrism for South and Southeast Asians, if the current trends are any clue to the trajectory of allegiance. In part, the histories of South and Southeast Asia have involved colonial powers other than the United States; it is not surprising, therefore, to find these diverse influences impinging on the lives of South and Southeast Asians within the United States or to recognize that time will not significantly diminish this interest given the relative ease with which many immigrants can today maintain global diasporic networks.[9] The diasporic experiences of many individuals of Asian descent in the United States and the resulting multiplicity of cultural/national influences is problematizing a simple acceptance of the United States as home. The effectiveness of Asian America as an emotional site of belonging for these postcolonial immigrants also appears to be in question. Given these demographic realities, Susan Koshy has accurately characterized the field of Asian American studies as "inhabit[ing] the highly unstable temporality of the 'about-to- be'" (315). We would argue that

South Asian American literature offers a unique vantage point from which to view and comprehend this critical time of flux within the Asian American and North American demographic landscape.

Even as early as 1993, the publication of a special issue of *Amerasia Journal* (Volume 19.3) devoted to the question of the changing Asian American subject is evidence that the discipline had already begun to acknowledge the presence of transnational forces that could not be ignored. Shirley Lim reminds us in a recent essay "Immigration and Diaspora" (1997) that "the shift from 'writing produced by U.S. writers of Asian descent' to 'writing produced by members of a diasporic group' . . . carries ideological, political, and institutional consequences" (290). It is not clear whether Lim's remarks are made in response to Sau-ling Wong's much cited essay (reprinted in this volume with a new prefatory note), as she doesn't refer to Wong's essay. Lim does, however, mention Wong's caution against "an uncritical adoption of a diasporic perspective" (290) in a paper entitled "Going Diasporic? Concepts and Constituencies in Asian American Literature," delivered by Wong at the University of California, Santa Barbara, in 1993. Lim's own recent memoir, *Among the White Moon Faces* (1997), offers convincing evidence of the varied cultural and national influences that are central to her writing and her scholarship—born and raised in Malaysia and employed intermittently in Singapore where her mother lived, Lim records her interactions with the Muslim, Hindu, Christian, and Buddhist communities in both countries and describes the multiplicity of peoples and cultures—Malaysian Muslims, Malaysian Chinese, Singapore Chinese, Malaysian Indians, Malaysian British—that had a significant impact on her life. Even after she has made a life for herself in the United States, she remains actively connected to Malaysia and Singapore.

Such diasporic and transnational realities have finally been acknowledged, for instance, in the dramatic increase in the number of panels and sessions dedicated to the representation of marginalized postcolonial Asian Americans, such as the Vietnamese, Filipino, and South Asian Americans at the April 1999 annual convention in Philadelphia of the Association of Asian American Studies. This self-conscious reexamination of the field's paradigms follows the escalating critiques over the past five years of the internal hegemonies within Asian American Studies. One such reexamination includes the Pilot Proposal for dealing with the peripheral position of such groups at a seminar hosted by New York University in December 1998, in which both of us were invited to participate. In recent years, certain forums such as the Asian American Writers Workshop in New York City have enlarged the vision of Asian American studies by including postcolonial writers of South Asian, Southeast Asian and Filipino/a American descent in their projects. The Temple University Press Series edited by David Palumbo-Liu, Sucheng Chan, and Michael Omi has also been attentive to previously neglected Asian groups.

Sau-ling Wong reminds readers that although ideas of nationhood may seem anachronistic in the current postmodern age of refugee and labor migration and transnational capital, keeping a focus on the nation state is essential to ensuring full membership in a participatory democracy.[10] Jinqi Ling echoes Wong in the introductory chapter to his recently published book, *Narrating Nationalisms* (an in-depth study of selected writings by Frank Chin, Louis Chu, Maxine Hong Kingston, and John Okada)

(1998). Ling acknowledges the problematic nature of the early Asian Americanists' cultural nationalism—epitomized by Frank Chin et. al's assertion, in the introduction to *Aiiieeeee!* (1974) that "Asian American" referred to "Filipino-, Chinese-, and Japanese-Americans, American born and raised, who got their China and Japan from the radio, off the silver screen, from television, out of comic books" (vii). While recognizing the undeniable current presence of transnational and diasporic forces, Ling—like Sau-ling Wong—nonetheless writes against de-emphasizing the United States. Still, Koshy's position that "it is often impossible fully to understand and respond to the local without a comprehension of global forces and institutions" (341) is borne out in such situations as the Asian Campaign Finance "scandal." United States foreign policy with respect to China and the U.S.'s still active suspicion of and anxiety regarding Communism renders every Chinese American a potential threat to the integrity of the nation state (Wang, 1998). Thus, it would appear naïve to ignore the extent to which every Asian American is already de-nationalized. Similarly, Kandice Chuh writes perceptively that the idea of "transnation," or allegiance to the nation of origin—defined by Arjun Appadurai as a delocalized diasporic collectivity of people who "retain a special ideological link to a putative place of origin" (*Modernism* 172)—is not always a matter of choice. One is purported to belong to a "transnation," whether or not one does in reality. Just as African Americans are racially defined regardless of their own self-definition, Asian immigrants are often viewed even today as "not Americans," as belonging to another nation. Speaking of the Japanese American internment, Chuh says, "Investigation of narratives of internment makes it clear that state apparatuses worked to delineate a Japanese transnation by means of manipulating mechanisms of U.S. citizenship, and thus exposes a coercive element in this transnation formation" (94). Min Song observes that perhaps the recent interest within Asian American studies in the subject of diaspora is a result of the realization that the role of the immigrant (as the individual who has severed ties with the land of origin to enter into a contract with America) is never unequivocally available to the Asian American.[11] Many South Asians, who are domiciled in North America, exhibit what Shirley Lim defines as the "exilic" as opposed to the "immigrant" sensibility: "The exilic experience, like that of immigration, is the condition of voluntary or involuntary separation from one's place of birth; but, unlike immigration, this physical separation is offset by continued bonds to the lost homeland, together with nonintegration into the affiliative order in which the exilic subject is contingently placed" (296). According to Chuh and Song, the nonintegration into the affiliative order is not always voluntary. Diaspora can no longer be ignored within Asian American studies. R. Radhakrishnan has rightly observed that

> If "ethnicity" is to be realized both as an "itself" and as a powerful factor in the negotiation of the putative mainstream identity, it must necessarily be rooted in more than one history: that of the present location and that of its past. . . . Particularly, in the American context, it is of the utmost importance that a variety of emerging postcolonial-diasporic ethnicities (Asian-American, Latina, Chinese-American, Chicano, etc.) establish themselves "relationally" with the twin purpose of affirming themselves and demystifying the so-called "mainstream." But this task is unthinkable unless ethnicity is coordinated as a "critical elsewhere" in active relationship with the status quo. (766)

Postcolonial theorists such as Gayatri Chakravorty Spivak, Ella Shohat, and Jenny Sharpe, among others, have pointed out that the United States is globally implicated (especially in view of its "superpower" status) in neocolonial enterprises. Therefore, globally-conscious South Asians might feel impelled not only to critique the U.S. role in world affairs, but also to challenge their native lands on, say, human rights or environmental infringements.[12] South Asian Americans' occupation of the interstitial spaces created by postcoloniality, diaspora, transnationalism, and multiple and ever-shifting "borderlines"—what Homi Bhabha describes as the "third space" of "cultural hybridity [which] gives rise to something different, something new and unrecognisable, a new area of negotiation of meaning and representation" ("The Third Space" 211)—has intensified the urgent need to reconfigure the Asian American literary terrain. N. V. M. Gonzales's term, "fusion of migrancy and exile" (82) used to describe Filipino/a American literature is also applicable to South Asian American literature.[13]

II

The four South Asian writers of diverse backgrounds on whom we focus in this essay—Shani Mootoo, Tahira Naqvi, Agha Shahid Ali, and Abraham Verghese—all push in different ways against the U.S.-centrism of American ethnic literature. In addition, Ali's and Verghese's texts offer no easy ethnic markers, provoking thereby an examination of multiculturalism and identity politics in its current stage of conflicted and contested imperatives.

Shani Mootoo was born in Dublin, Ireland, to parents of Indian origin, was raised by grandparents in Trinidad, and currently lives in Vancouver, Canada. So, within her life experience both "postcoloniality" and (Asian) "American-ness" have been conjoined. In her remarkably variegated history, she resembles many South Asians who, in the words of Parminder Bhachu, are "twice, thrice, and quadruple migrant" (224), from Canada, Latin America, U.K., the Caribbean, and Africa. We include Mootoo in our discussion to broaden the scope of "America" to encompass the Caribbean and Canada and to draw attention to the complex array of national and cultural influences on diasporic South Asians. Mootoo's writing intersects also with queer studies; her work is particularly relevant to discussions of ethnic authenticity and to issues of heterosexuality and patriarchy in diasporic communities. In her short story "Out on Main Street," the title story of her collection *Out on Main Street and Other Stories* (1993), Mootoo writes both humorously and poignantly of the displacement of a lesbian Indo-Trinidadian couple in Canada. The two women feel themselves to be inadequate Indians—"kitchen Indians," merely—because they are the descendants of great-grandparents who came as indentured laborers from India to Trinidad. Neither woman has any direct experience of India. The narrator describes their awkwardness:

> I used to think I was a Hindu *par excellence* until I come up here and see real flesh and blood Indian from India. Up here [in Canada], I learning 'bout all kind a custom and food and music and clothes dat we never see or hear 'bout in good ole Trinidad. Is de next best thing to going to India, in truth, oui! But Indian store clerk on Main Street doh have no patience with us, specially when we talking English to dem. Yuh ask dem

a question in English and dey insist on giving de answer in Hindi or Punjabi or Urdu or Gujarati. How I suppose to know de difference even! And den dey look at yuh disdainful disdainful—like yuh disloyal, like yuh is a traitor. (47–48)

The young women's authenticity as Indians is constantly under question; they do not speak any Indian language, and, when they enter the Indian Canadian store "Kush Valley Sweets,"[14] they exhibit their unfamiliarity with the specific names of Indian desserts, calling them only by the generic term, "Meethai." The salesman behind the counter underscores the narrator's inauthenticity with his response: "These are all meethai, Miss. Meethai is Sweets. Where are you from"(51)? His disdain reminds the narrator that she and her partner are "cultural bastards" (51), that she is a "bastard-ized Indian" (52). In a fit of pique, she declares, "all a we in Trinidad is cultural bastards, Janet, all a we. *Toutes bagailles*! Chinese people, Black people, White people, Syrian, Lebanese. I looking forward to de day I find out dat place inside me where I am nothing else but Trinidadian, whatever dat could turn out to be" (52). In that final remark, the narrator reveals that she does not fully belong anywhere—not in Trinidad, not in Canada, and certainly not in India because she can never demonstrate her authentic Indian-ness. Her displacement and sense of isolation are made more complete when it becomes evident that she is gay. A woman in the store who had only just recently joined in a gesture of solidarity with the narrator turns away and makes a face "dat look like it was in de presence of a very foul smell" (57). Gayatri Gopinath observes that "current articulations of diaspora tend to replicate and indeed rely upon conventional ideologies of gender and sexuality; . . . certain bodies (queer and/or female) are rendered invisible or marked as other" (121). Women are imagined, she says, as "reproducers (both literally and metaphorically) of 'culture' and commu-nity" (121). The mother daughter team of Shamita Dasgupta and Sayantani Dasgupta also speak of the pressures on women in diasporic communities to become preservers and reproducers of authentic ancestral culture. They observe, "Besides being bearers of culture, mothers are positioned as monitors of their daughters' conduct, and their punishment for disregarding the community's dictates is to be identified as 'bad moth-ers.' Daughters, on the other hand, are even more restricted within the community's prescriptions, and their transgressions are deemed gross betrayals of the culture" (193). Given these expectations, homosexuality further alienates an individual from the post-colonial diasporic or ethnic community.[15]

Tahira Naqvi's tragic-comic story "All Is Not Lost" (1995) captures both the desire to preserve the homeland culture and the inevitable assaults on it in the new country. Naqvi's writing career follows an easy-to-understand path of gradually increasing en-gagement with the United States as a site of new selfhood and developing identity. Naqvi, who was born in Iran to Pakistani parents, spent her childhood in Pakistan, and has lived in the U.S. for nearly three decades, explains that "my writing, which began with a focus on the immigrant experience, has now branched off into the 'Asian experience.' It has in turn contributed to an understanding of my Pakistani American/ Asian American self" (145). Naqvi, who is compiling a collection of her short stories, *Memories of a Lahore Childhood*, has gained critical repute not only through her collection, *Attar of Roses and Other Stories from Pakistan* (1995), but also for her translations of renowned Urdu writers such as Sadat Hassan Manto, Hijab Imtiaz Ali, and Ismat Chugtai. Naqvi's story "All Is Not Lost" describes the intergenerational conflict between the rebellious, second-generation Pakistani Americans like Maryam, and the conservative, older first-generation immigrants, like her parents and their Aunt Sakina. While the elders desperately attempt to preserve their "native" cultural values, and the family's respect among the Pakistani American community—which is signified through their daughters' virginity and ability to preserve their authentic purity and "Pakistani-ness"—the Americanized Maryam disregards traditional mores and chooses to marry a Euro-American man. For Aunt Sakina, the fault lies in South Asians' choice of their new homeland: "'If these fools had stayed in their own country,' she continued despondently, 'none of this would have happened. Why did they leave Pakistan and come to settle in a country where your daughters are not safe from Umreekan boys?'" (148).

The narrator's tongue-in-cheek tone underscores the ironies inherent in the immigrant family's attempt to reconcile their Islamic heritage and past with their present "Umreekan" reality. With exaggerated seriousness, the narrator describes the family's fall from grace, since, before the occurrence of what is perceived as the community tragedy, Maryam's mother had been admired as the ideal role-model for all Pakistani American mothers who, ironically, "watched her with reverence and awe and a hope, voiced openly, that they too could do their job as well as she had done hers" (146).

> She had taken her daughter to weekend Islamic classes, she made sure the girl fasted and said her prayers regularly, she even went so far as to tell Maryam to carry a plastic glass in her bag so that if she had to use a ladies' bathroom somewhere, she'd not be put out for lack of a container of water. Such pains the woman had taken, and now this. And the weekly Islamic class, in turn, had done all it could to enforce the ideas of a woman's place and the need for her to protect herself against the evil ways of those to whom modesty was just a joke. (146–7)

By relating the parents' (almost absurdly) melodramatic reaction —Parveen behaves as if someone had died, and the enraged Shahid threatens to kill his prospective son-in-law—which follows Maryam's threats to elope, Naqvi's narrator's ironic tone critiques the patriarchal ideology and (mis)education of the Islamic classes Maryam had been subjected to by the mullahs, "intrepid counselors who uprooted themselves from their native lands to come to America in order to keep [others'] children in the fold" (147). The final reconciliation occurs when the young man, Jerry Noggles, is converted to Islam and renamed Tariq Hasan. While Aunt Sakina laments the shame brought by Maryam, not only upon the extended family but also the entire Pakistani American community, by marrying a man who is not circumcised, her niece Fatima who is most closely identified with the narratorial perspective, justifies the situation by stating that, hence, ironically, by the family's immigrating to the U.S.— as the story's title suggests—"all is not lost" (154). As Naqvi's narrative tone and voice suggests, the first-generation immigrants such as Aunt Sakina, and Maryam's hypersensitive parents, steeped in ancient traditions, and pathetically failing in their attempts to protect their children from being sullied by America and to preserve a pure and authentic "Pakistani-ness," become the objects of the reader's humor, if not, ridicule. As Naqvi clearly delineates, second-generation postcolonials in the U.S. such as Maryam, despite their traditional Asian upbringing at home, live through their choices and actions on ethnic borderlines as the new (Asian) Americans.

Agha Shahid Ali's poetry, however, does not so readily capitulate to the category Asian American. He calls himself a Kashmiri-American-Kashmiri. In the double hyphenation (evocative of the distinction made by Arjun Appadurai in his essay "The Heart of Whiteness"), Ali reveals that the "American" is not the end-point of his identity, not the destination of his being. Placed as it is, between the two hyphens, the "American" implies that from his position in America, Ali is able to understand the kind of Kashmiri he was before his arrival here and the Kashmiri he has become living on U.S. soil. Cleverly, he suggests that America takes him back to Kashmir. This sentiment, that America facilitates a return to a previous homeland, is found in the following excerpt from a longer poem aptly titled "In Search of Evanescence," from which we have borrowed the phrase "off the turnpike" in the title of our essay. Here, Ali explains how, crossing the exit to Calcutta, in Ohio, he hadn't realized that he had "begun mapping America, the city limits/ of Evanescence now everywhere" (39):

> When in Route 80 in Ohio
> I came across an exit
> to Calcutta
> the temptation to write a poem
> led me past the exit
> so I could say
> India always exists
> off the turnpikes
> of America (41)

Not only does this poem brilliantly evoke India in the physical and geographical markers of America, but it also implies that real living, meaningful existence, takes place off the turnpike—away from the frenetic motion that is America—and in India, in the little towns and communities to which those exits lead. The title of the collection in which this poem appears is, not inappropriately, *A Nostalgist's Map of America.*

In the same poem, Ali takes readers on a journey driving through the American midwest and southwest—Pennsylvania, Ohio, and Arizona—to the railway platform at Howrah on the banks of the river Ganges, in Calcutta, India. Before the poem ends, the exilic poet-persona's (or his alter-ego/dying/dead? friend Phil's?) tortured cries about the loss of homes, streets, addresses, postcards, family, and friends, is poignantly presented in an italicised section, addressed directly in the poet's name:

> Shahid, you never
> found Evanescence
>
> . . . .
>
> You didn't throw away
> addresses from which
> streets
> departed. There's
> no one who you know
> in this world. (56–8)

Ali thus powerfully re-presents the desperate loneliness and alienation of the postcolonial immigrant who, as a result of colonization, can no longer live in the native homeland, and yet despondently searches for new communities (including those of homoerotic love) in the neocolonial metropolis he now inhabits physically, while constantly seeking familiar signs of forsaken familial neighborhoods, streets, and addresses. Finally, Ali's allusions to and brilliant play on Emily Dickinson's poem about the presence of the global in the local—#1463 ("A route of Evanescence . . . ")—furthers his theme of evanescent crossings of his Kashmiri-Indian-U.S. landscapes and memories and cultural traditions, losses and (re)discoveries of self and community.[16]

In the poem "Snow on the Desert," Ali once again evokes the homeland. Here, after dropping his sister off at Tucson International Airport, the speaker declares,

> As I drove back to the foothills, the fog
> shut its doors behind me on the Alvernon,
> and I breathed the dried seas
> the earth had lost,
> their forsaken shores. And I remembered
> another moment that refers only to itself:
> in New Delhi one night
> as Begum Akhtar sang, the lights went out. (103)

The physicality of his presence in America evokes the memories of a past that is invested with the palpability of the present. He compares that earlier moment in Delhi to the present one in Arizona, almost conflating the two homes:

> like this turning dark
> of fog, a moment when only a lost sea
> can be heard, a time
> to recollect
> every shadow, everything the earth was losing,
> a time to think of everything the earth
> and I had lost, of all
> that I would lose,
> of all that I was losing. (104–105)

The repetition of the verb "to lose" in its various conjugations refers not only to the earlier home that has been lost, but also to the present home that is also being lost, and future ones that will be lost again.

An earlier poem, "Postcard from Kashmir" (1987), also potently captures the personal and communal losses as well as the cultural and spatial displacement that many first-generation South Asian Americans experience:

> Kashmir shrinks into my mailbox,
> my home a neat four by six inches.
>   I always loved neatness. Now I hold
>   the half-inch Himalayas in my hand.
> This is home. And this is the closest
> I'll ever be to home.
> (*The Half-Inch Himalayas,* 1)

Notice, however, that despite the yearning for home that the poem records, there is also the definite suggestion that home is transportable—in this instance, through a postcard, and, by extension, the reader is led to understand, through one's writing, through a poem.

The co-existent feeling of homelessness and the desire to claim some physical, emotional, and psychical territory, in new homelands is thus seen in much of the collection *A Nostalgist's Map of America* (1991). Like Abraham Verghese—who is discussed next in this essay—Ali, too, is looking for his "own country," and when he can't find it, he tries to create it in his mind. Ali has probably been ignored as an Asian American writer because his poems neither ethnicize his self-presentation nor focus on his persecution as a member of an American minority. Ali's poetry thus helps raise important questions about the tensions within postcoloniality and U.S. ethnicity: What precludes a postcolonial poet living in the U.S. from being considered an (Asian) American, too? Why must the commodification of one's ethnicity be a prerequisite for a postcolonial writer to be classified as an (ethnic) American?

Like most of Agha Shahid Ali's poetry, Abraham Verghese's memoir, *My Own Country: A Doctor's Story of a Town and Its People in the Age of AIDS* (1994), does not focus on ethnicity per se; there is a reason that the title makes no mention of his Indian American heritage. This is not primarily a narrative about the experience of being an Indian American doctor in a small town. Rather, the memoir delivers what its title promises: a doctor keenly observing and recording the experiences of his AIDS patients in rural Tennessee—in Johnson City—a setting in which AIDS had never been imagined. That the observing and narrating doctor is Indian American seems incidental. Ethnicity is not invisible in Verghese's memoir, but it dots the landscape at widely spaced intervals. It makes its appearance largely in the early pages of the text, as Verghese tells us about the various inner-city hospitals at which he interviewed for a residency: "As I crisscrossed the country, in search of a residency slot, . . . I was amazed by the number and variety of foreign interns and residents I met in these hospitals. I overheard snatches of Urdu, Tagalog, Hindi, Tamil, Spanish, Portugese, Farsi, and Arabic. Some hospitals were largely Indian in flavor, others largely Filipino. Still others were predominantly Latin or East European" (19). Later, as a full-fledged doctor, he decides that he will avoid these ethnic enclaves: "What was the point of coming to America to train if I wound up in a little Bombay or a little Manila?" Verghese asks (20). Lest we condemn him for his disdain of ethnic settings, we should keep in mind that Verghese's description of these ethnically staffed hospitals as "urban war zones" speaks to a reality in which doctors from foreign countries who choose to stay in the big cities find themselves having to work in hospitals that U.S.-graduated doctors shun for being too unsafe. Knowing that as a foreign medical graduate (he grew up in Ethiopia, but completed his medical degree in India), he will have few options available to him, Verghese decides to take up a job in rural Tennessee.

South Asian American readers have embraced the book for its unequivocal demonstration of the value of the South Asian presence in America. It is possible that South Asian American doctors in the many small rural communities in the United States see it as vindication of their endurance in environments in which they are visibly and culturally different from the majority (read Euro-American) residents.[17] Verghese's book says to them that they, too, as physicians can find their own country in these rural American settings. Verghese's relationship with other Indian American doctors is a complicated one; in the memoir he suggests that many of them don't understand his desire to work with AIDS patients, even as they accept him as one of their own. Yet, in his minimally ethnic stance and self-presentation, they see perhaps not so much an erasure of their own ethnicity as Indian Americans but a confirmation that ethnicity can be subsumed by work, that labor can suspend ethnic "Othering." While their hope may be valid, one should not be oblivious to the gaps in their reasoning. It is as *doctors* that these (middle- and upper-class immigrants) find membership in small-town America, not as South Asians *per se*; those employed in less prestigious jobs do not so readily become incorporated.

The other aspects of Verghese's text that test the parameters of ethnic writing are the near absence of "blackness," in particular, and race, in general, in the memoir. Given that he grew up in Africa, one could reasonably expect from Verghese an awareness of race. In this context, one cannot help but think of Toni Morrison who, in *Playing in the Dark* (38), views "blackness" as the unstated and unarticulated background against which "whiteness" often defines itself in the U.S. (and, we might add, "brown-ness" as well). At a recent reading in Boston of his second memoir, *The Tennis Partner* (1998), Verghese revealed that it was only after he moved to El Paso, that he became sensitized to his brown-ness. Could it be, perhaps, that in Verghese's Tennessee perspective we have an instance of Frantz Fanon's "white mask" as a means of survival? But once in Texas, amongst the large Hispanic population, Verghese acknowledged that he became fully aware of how different he must have seemed to the white majority in Tennessee.

A related issue is Verghese's non-adversarial depiction of white Southern culture. "The people I met in Johnson City would, unlike those in a big city, trust a stranger almost to the point of stupidity" (38) he says. One wonders whether he is, in truth, talking about the South. But Verghese insists that the most palpable discrimination that he experienced was in Boston (23). Perhaps Verghese, with appropriate forms of "cultural capital"—a Westernized education, the ability to play tennis, drink beer, and play the guitar—was able to enter into the fabric of the Johnson City community and become "one of the boys." Is it this empathetic representation of the majority culture that has made it difficult for Asian American scholars to consider Verghese's text for discussion?

In *Immigrant Acts*, Lisa Lowe considers the importance of Asian American studies as "an oppositional site from which to contest the educational apparatus that reproduces and continues to be organized by Western culturalist, as well as developmental, narratives" (38). Lowe cites Martin Carnoy in calling for the discipline to become "'an exploitable political space for those willing to engage in the struggle for change'" (40). The critical word in her articulation of the Asian American agenda is "oppositional."

It would appear at first glance that Verghese's limitation is that he is insufficiently politicized, and that he does not interrogate the power structures of his profession. He is, one could argue, content to be the "healer" and concentrate on easing his patients' pain, and he does not openly challenge the conditions that give rise to the inadequate

medical resources available to his patients. Yet, Verghese is seen as an activist by those
who work with AIDS patients, and he has been invited many times to speak on the
complexities of delivering rural health care. The book itself is not without its critique
of the medical bureaucracy and big money. For instance, here is his description of an
encounter with a well-known infectious disease specialist at a conference in Los
Angeles, a man "who wore the latest Italian suits, silk ties, and thousand-dollar shoes"
and of whom it was said that "no pharmaceutical company would dare launch a new
antibiotic compound in North America without getting his endorsement":

> he [the specialist] was telling several of us of a major grant for AIDS care that his division
> had received. I was curious to know exactly how he managed to run such a huge AIDS
> clinic in a big city? What were the logistics? I knew that he was rarely in his office
> because he was so often on the road, almost an itinerant lecturer. . . . Who sees the
> patients, I asked. He lowered his voice and looking around conspiratorially said: "What
> you have to do is hire 'drones' to do the day-to-day clinical work. You can't possibly be
> running down from your office to see every clinic patient who shows up on a nonclinic
> day with high fever or seizures." (224)

Verghese, shocked by the specialist's response, informs his readers that the drones
were probably "Indians, Pakistanis, Koreans, Filipinos, Middle Easterners—all doctors
with visa problems and the need to remain in a 'training' situation till they could
make the switch from a J1 visa to an immigrant visa" (224).

Should Verghese have pushed further the point about the exploitation of immigrant
medical labor? Would it have mattered if he had?[18] Perhaps not. In an Asian American
Studies or Ethnic Studies paradigm of opposition, one does not typically register outrage at overworked immigrant medical labor with the same vehemence reserved for
the exploitation of migrant farmworkers, garment workers, and taxicab drivers. Perhaps the problem in the academy is that we define activism too narrowly. It is entirely
possible to be a socially conscious doctor or an activist lawyer. As educators, we would
do well to pay attention to narrow constructions of activism, even if we do so with
alertness to class lines.

An immigrant who is a doctor, who plays tennis, drives a Datsun Z, and who
accompanies his wife, however reluctantly, to look for a house to purchase is not the
stuff of oppositional literature. Verghese does not fit the role of an ethnic victim, a
deprived racial being. What is under siege in this book is not race, not ethnicity, but
sickness—a particularly virulent sickness. AIDS has become a national emergency,
and perhaps Verghese's memoir has received the attention it has only because of its
subject matter. To invalidate his text within the context of ethnic literature, however,
is to risk commodifying the ethnic experience. Garrett Hongo sarcastically reminds us
that there is an unstated litmus test for consideration as an Asian American writer:
"traits of bitterness and anger in a kind of political activist model" (4).

III

There are complex expectations placed upon most North American writers who
are not from the majority Euro-American culture. More pernicious than these expecta-

tions (both by the majority culture and the members of the author's ethnic or racial group) is the commodification of ethnicity that underpins and sustains them— exemplified blatantly in 1997 by the publisher's inclusion of spice packets in review copies of Chitra Divakaruni's second novel, *The Mistress of Spices*. In his introduction to *The Ethnic Canon* (1995), David Palumbo-Liu makes the point tellingly in inviting a careful critique of a too-easy implementation of multiculturalism:

> Within the specific domain of current uses of multiculturalism within the academy, the reading of ethnic literature may be taken as an occasion for the negotiation of difference, the fusion of horizons, and the "recovery" of equilibrium that creates social subjectivities now "educated" as to the proper negotiations of race, ethnicity, gender, and class. . . . The point of such readings of ethnic literature is therefore to "understand" difference as a general phenomenon and subsume it under categories *that do not radically obstruct the smooth functioning of social apparatuses*. (11, emphasis added)

Gayatri Chakravorty Spivak too has directed her warning against a fetishizing of identity to the "ethnics" themselves. She cautions that ethnic enclaves can become "artificial and affectively supportive subsocieties that, claiming to preserve the ethnos of culture or origin move further and further away from the vicissitudes and transformations of the nation or group of origin" (279). The most eloquent call for going beyond the ethnic comes from Sucheta Mazumdar, in her Afterword "Identity Politics and the Politics of Identity" (1996) to *Contours of the Heart*. She challenges ethnic (in this case South Asian American/Canadian) writing to look outward, beyond the boundaries of the ethnic community, insisting on its moral obligation to do so: "[D]oes my identity have to be constructed by what I have inherited and not by what I have struggled to make of myself? Am I doubly doomed by my genes and country of ancestral origin? Or do politics and struggle for social change, for social justice for all—not just the people with whom one may share an ancestral affinity—matter at all" (469)?

We are by no means suggesting the superfluity of "ethnic" themes. As long as racial "Othering" continues, as long as power differentials exist to devalue the contributions of ethnic minorities, a focus on traditional ethnic issues will be necessary and central to asserting one's presence and claiming political and literary space. Examining South Asian American literature, thus, provides a new critical lens from which to re-map Asian American literature to match the demographic realities of postcolonial diasporas. While in the past it might have been easier to bypass South Asians' writing in discussing Asian American literature, today these British postcolonial subjects invite accommodation within a reconfigured ethnic American paradigm, and assert their claim to be acknowledged as both Asian and American. That their position is complex we readily acknowledge. The equivocal position of South Asian American literature within Asian American studies epitomizes many South Asians' desire to be a part of, and yet remain apart from the rest of Asian America.

Notes

1. The phrase "Off the Turnpike" in our title comes from Agha Shahid Ali's *A Nostalgist's Map of America* (41), discussed later in this essay. For a brief history of the changing names with

which South Asians have been idenitified in the U.S. since their first immigration in the nine-teenth century, see Lavina Shankar's essay, "The Limits of (South Asian) Names and Labels: Postcolonial or Asian American?" The term "South Asian" refers to people from the seven countries in the Subcontinent, i.e., India, Pakistan, Bangladesh, Nepal, Bhutan, Sri Lanka, and the Maldives. As our discussion of Shani Mootoo in this essay suggests, "South Asian" as an ethno-racial category, would arguably include Asian Indians from other parts of the world including East Africa, Trinidad and Guyana.

2. Lisa Lowe uses the term in her *Immigrant Acts* (1997): "the demand that Asian immi-grants identify as U.S. national subjects simultaneously produces alienations and disidentifica-tions out of which critical subjectivities emerge" (16–17). At the New York University seminar on the marginalization of South Asians within Asian American Studies, Anupama Rao applied the term specifically to South Asians (1998).

3. The 2000 census is not out yet. The figures can be roughly calculated, however, given the rates of immigration for each nationality between 1994 and 1996. The 1990 census identi-fies only Asian Indians within the South Asian category. The actual numbers of South Asians are obviously higher than the figure for Asian Indians. The 1990 census figures for Chinese, Filipino, Asian Indians, Vietnamese, Koreans and Japanese are as follows: Chinese 1,645,472; Filipino 1,406,770; Japanese 847,562; Asian Indian 815,447. (This figure does not include Pakistanis, Bangladeshis, Sri Lankans, and Nepalese or people of South Asian descent from countries such as Fiji, Surinam, Guyana, and Trinidad); Korean 798,849; Vietnamese 614,547. The immigration rates from these countries in 1994, 1995, and 1996 are as follows: Of the 804,416 immigrants from all countries in 1994, 6.7% Philippines, 4.3% India, 6.7% China, 5.1% Vietnam, 2.0% Korea, 1.1% Pakistan, 0.4% Bangladesh. Of the 720,461 total immi-grants in 1995, Philippines 7.1%, India 4.8%, China 4.9%, Vietnam 5.8%, Korea 2.2%, Paki-stan 1.4%, Bangladesh 0.8%. Of the 915,900 total immigrants in 1996, Philippines 6.1%, India 4.9%, China 4.6%, Vietnam 4.6%, Korea 2.0%, Pakistan 1.4%, Bangladesh 0.9%. No-tice that Japan is not even listed in the census immigration figures, suggesting the low rates of migration from Japan to the U.S. and affirming that the Japanese American population is not increasing in significant numbers. Check website http://www.ins.usdoj.gov/stats/annual/fy98/1005.html for more up-to-date figures.

4. See especially David Palumbo-Liu's collection of essays, *The Ethnic Canon*, whose title testifies that once-marginalized literatures have now established their own set of canonical writers.

5. For an extended discussion on the distinction between South Asians' "postcolonial" and "Asian American" identifications and the ensuing "partitions" within the academy, see Lavina Shankar's essay "The Limits of (South Asian) Names and Labels: Postcolonial or Asian Ameri-can?" (1998). For a different if more controversial view of these issues, see Bharati Mukherjee, "Immigrant Writing: Give Us Our Maximalists" (1988).

6. Some of the examples of such South Asian exclusion have emerged in our phone conver-sations of February 1999 with Amritjit Singh; Frank Chin et. al. refused to include South Asians even in their revised edition *The Big Aiiieeeee!* (1991). In 1993, when asked in a phone interview about this omission by Gulshan Kataria (a Visiting Fulbright Scholar from Punjabi University, Patiala, India), Chin justified this exclusion in terms of his unfamiliarity with the sensibility and literature of India, erasing the "Asian American" presence of South Asians in North America. When asked specifically about Bharati Mukherjee, he pointed out that she regarded herself as a Caucasian and "that is OK by me." (Amritjit Singh is in possession of an audio cassette of this interview).

In her preface to *Reading Asian American Literature* (1993), Sau-ling C. Wong thanks Ronald Takaki for advising her to include Asian Indian writers in her study, and yet her minimal mention of South Asians is apparently an afterthought. Wong mentions Bharati Mukherjee briefly, but there is little attempt to work any South Asian writers into her central paradigm of Necessity and Extravagance. While Wong understandably makes a special case for the inclusion of a Canadian text such as Joy Kogawa's *Obasan* within "Asian American Literature" (16–17), she appears quite unaware of the strong South Asian voices in Canadian writing such as M. G. Vassanji, Rohinton Mistry, Sam Selvon, Cyril Dabydeen and others. Even Michael Ondaatje is arguably a South Asian Canadian.

Also, there are now numerous South Asians writing in the U.S. other than Mukherjee— including Meena Alexander, Chitra Divakaruni, Sara Suleri, Bapsi Sidhwa, Shauna Singh Baldwin, Indran Amirthanayagam, and Roshni Rustomji-Kerns. For an extensive list of contemporary South Asian American writers and texts, see Lavina Shankar and Rajini Srikanth, "Closing the Gap? South Asians Challenge Asian American Studies" (1998). See also Nelson (1992 and 1993) and Knippling.

7. For a more detailed analysis of Mukherjee's "claiming of America," see Lavina Shankar's essays "The Limits of (South Asian) Names and Labels" (1998), and "Activism, Feminisms, and Americanization in Bharati Mukherjee's *Wife* and *Jasmine*" (1995).

8. Conversation with Stephen Sumida at East of California Conference, Association of Asian American Studies, Ann Arbor, Michigan, October 1998.

9. Of course, this ability to maintain such connections does depend on one's socioeconomic class status, as Sau-ling Wong has reminded us in her essay, "Denationalization Reconsidered." It assumes that one can afford to access the internet, satellite t.v., and other such resources.

10. A revised version of Wong's essay appears for the first time in this volume.

11. Min Song made this observation at a talk he delivered at Tufts University on January 21, 1999, on Korean American literature.

12. We are grateful to Amritjit Singh for making this point.

13. Leny Mendoza Strobel's essay in this volume raises similar issues on Filipino/a American identity.

14. "Kush" which sounds like "Khush," in Hindi, means gay (i.e., happy) and is a code word in the South Asian gay and lesbian community to refer to homosexuality.

15. See, for instance, Rajini Srikanth's "Gender and Images of Home in the Asian American Diaspora: A Socio-Literary Reading of Some Asian American Works." On March 8, 1996, in her keynote address to the national meeting of SASA (South Asian Student Association), Urvashi Vaid—author of *Virtual Equality* (1995)—articulated how as a young law student she depended almost entirely for emotional and social support upon the gay and lesbian community in Boston but was now much more interested in exploring her South Asian identity.

16. We thank Peter Schmidt for bringing Ali's allusion to Dickinson to our attention.

17. See especially Lavina Melwani. See also *The Twilight Hour* by Udaya Kabadi, an Indian American physician in Iowa.

18. Verghese takes up this issue in greater detail in his essay, "The Cowpath to America," *New Yorker*, June 23 & 30, 1997: 70–88.

Works Cited

Ali, Agha Shahid. *The Half-Inch Himalayas*. Hanover, NH: Wesleyan UP, 1987.

———. *A Nostalgist's Map of America*. New York: Norton, 1991.

Appadurai, Arjun. *Modernity at Large*. Minneapolis: U of Minnesota P, 1996.

———. "The Heart of Whiteness." *Callaloo* 16.4 (1993): 796–807.

Bhabha, Homi. "The Third Space." *Identity: Community, Culture, Difference.* Ed. Jonathan Rutherford. London: Lawrence & Wishart, 1990. 207–21.

Bhachu, Parminder K. *Twice-Born Migrants.* New York: Tavistock, 1985.

Bloom, Harold, ed. *Asian-American Women Writers.* Broomall, PA: Chelsea House, 1997.

Cheung, King-Kok, ed. *An Interethnic Companion to Asian American Literature.* Cambridge: Cambridge UP, 1997.

———, and Stan Yogi, *Asian American Literature: An Annotated Bibliography.* New York: MLA.

Chin, Frank, Jeffrey Paul Chan, Lawson Fusao Inada, and Shawn Hsu Wong, eds. *Aiiieeeee! An Anthology of Asian-American Writers.* Washington, D.C.: Howard UP, 1974.

———, eds. *The Big Aiiieeeee! An Anthology of Asian-American Writers.* Second Edition. New York: NAL/Dutton, 1991.

Chuh, Kandice. "Transnationalism and Its Pasts." *Public Culture* 9 (1996): 93–112.

Dasgupta, Shamita Das, and Sayantani DasGupta. "Bringing Up Baby: Raising a 'Third World' Daughter in the 'First World.'" *Dragon Ladies: Asian American Feminists Breathe Fire.* Ed. Sonia Shah. Boston: South End P, 1997. 182–99.

Fanon, Frantz. *Black Skin, White Masks.* New York: Grove/Atlantic, 1989.

Gonzales, N. V. M., and Oscar V. Campomanes. "Filipino American Literature." Cheung: 62–124.

Gopinath, Gayatri. "Funny Boys and Girls: Notes on a Queer South Asian Planet." *Asian American Sexualities: Dimensions of the Gay and Lesbian Experience.* Ed. Russell Leong. New York: Routledge, 1996. 119–27.

Hongo, Garrett. "Asian American Literature: Questions of Identity." *Amerasia Journal.* 20.3 (1994):1–8.

Kabadi, Udaya. *The Twilight Hour.* New York: Vantage, 1998.

Katrak, Ketu. "South Asian American Literature." Cheung: 192–218.

Kim, Elaine H. *Asian American Literature: An Introduction To The Writings and Their Social Contexts.* Philadelphia: Temple UP, 1982.

Koshy, Susan. "The Fiction of Asian American Literature." *Yale Journal of Criticism* 9.2 (1996): 315–46.

Knippling, Alpana Sharma, ed. *New Immigrant Literatures in the US: A Sourcebook to Our Multicultural Heritage.* Westport, CT: Greenwood, 1996.

Lam, Andrew. "Vietnamese Americans Discover the Rice Field in the Microchip." *Pacific News Service,* September 27, 1995.

Lim, Shirley Geok-lin. *Among the White Moon Faces: An Asian American Memoir of Homelands.* New York: Feminist P, 1997.

———. "Immigration and Diaspora." Cheung: 289–311.

Ling, Jinqi. *Narrating Nationalisms: Ideology and Form in Asian American Literature.* New York: Oxford UP, 1998.

Lowe, Lisa. *Immigrant Acts.* Durham: Duke UP, 1996.

Mazumdar, Sucheta. "Afterword: Identity Politics and the Politics of Identity." *Contours of the Heart: South Asians Map North America.* Ed. Sunaina Maira and Rajini Srikanth. New York: Asian American Writers Workshop, 1996. 461–69.

Melwani, Lavina. "Call of the Country." *India Today International.* Sept. 14, 1998: 24c-24e.

Mootoo, Shani. "Out on Main Street." *Out on Main Street and Other Stories.* Vancouver: PGang Publishers, 1993.

Morrison, Toni. *Playing in the Dark.* New York: Norton, 1992.

Mukherjee, Bharati. "Immigrant Writing: Give Us Our Maximalists." *New York Times Book Review.* August 28, 1988.

Naqvi, Tahira. "All Is Not Lost." *Living in America: Poetry and Fiction by South Asian American Writers* Ed. Roshni Rustomji-Kerns. Boulder: Westview P, 1995: 145–54.

Nelson, Emmanuel, ed. *Writers of the Indian Diaspora: A Bio-Bibliographical Critical Sourcebook*. Westport, CT: Greenwood, 1993.

———, ed. *Reworlding: The Literature of the Indian Diaspora*. Westport, CT: Greenwood, 1992.

Palumbo-Liu, David. Introduction. *The Ethnic Canon: Histories, Institutions, and Interventions*. Ed. David Palumbo-Liu. Minneapolis: U of Minnesota P, 1995. 1–27.

Radhakrishnan, R. "Postcoloniality and the Boundaries of Identity." *Callaloo* 16.4 (Fall 1993):750–71.

Shankar, Lavina Dhingra. "The Limits of (South Asian) Names and Labels: Postcolonial or Asian American?" Shankar and Srikanth, *A Part, Yet Apart*: 49–66.

———. "Activism, 'Feminisms,' and Americanization in Bharati Mukherjee's *Wife* and *Jasmine*." *Critical Mass: A Journal of Asian American Cultural Criticism*. 3.1 (Winter 1995): 61–84.

——— and Rajini Srikanth, eds. *A Part, Yet Apart: South Asians in Asian America*. Philadelphia, Temple UP, 1998.

———, eds. Introduction. "Closing the Gap? South Asians Challenge Asian American Studies." *A Part, Yet Apart*. 1–22.

Sharpe, Jenny. "Is the United States Postcolonial? Transnationalism, Immigration, and Race." *Diaspora*. 4.2 (1995): 181–99.

Shohat, Ella. "Notes on the 'Post-colonial.'" *Social Text* 31/32 (1992): 99–113.

Singh, Amritjit, Rajira Verma, and Irene Joshi, eds. *Indian Literature in English, 1827–1979: A Guide to Information Sources*. Detroit: Gale Research Company, 1981.

Sollors, Werner. *Beyond Ethnicity: Consent and Descent in American Culture*. New York: Oxford UP, 1986.

Spivak, Gayatri Chakravorty. *Outside in the Teaching Machine*. New York: Routledge, 1993.

Srikanth, Rajini. "Gender and Images of Home in the Asian American Diaspora: A Socio-Literary Reading of Some Asian American Works." *Critical Mass: A Journal of Asian American Criticism*. 2.1 (Winter 1994):147–81.

Vaid, Urvashi. *Virtual Equality: The Mainstreaming of Gay and Lesbian Liberation*. New York: Anchor/Doubleday, 1995.

Vardarajan, Tunku. "A Lonely Planet: Cricket Subtly Ghettoes Its Desi Fans in the US." *India Today International*. February 22, 1999: 24.

Verghese, Abraham. *My Own Country: A Doctor's Story of a Town and Its People in the Age of AIDS*. New York: Simon and Schuster, 1994.

———. "The Cowpath to America." *The New Yorker*. June 23 and 30, 1997: 70–88.

———. *The Tennis Partner: A Doctor's Story of Friendship and Loss*. New York: HarperCollins, 1998.

Wang, L. Ling-chi. "Race, Class, Citizenship, and Extraterritoriality: Asian Americans and the 1996 Campaign Finance Scandal." *Amerasia Journal* 24.1: 1–21.

Wong, Sau-ling. "Denationalization Reconsidered: Asian American Cultural Criticism at a Theoretical Crossroads" *Amerasia Journal* 21.1 & 2 (1995): 1–27.

———. *Reading Asian American Literature: From Necessity to Extravagance*. Princeton: Princeton UP, 1993.

Wong, Shawn, ed. *Asian American Literature: A Brief Introduction and Anthology*. New York: HarperCollins, 1996.

CAN YOU GO HOME AGAIN?

Transgression and Transformation in African-American Women's and Chicana Literary Practice

Inés Salazar

It is a sinful pleasure, this willing transgression of a line, which takes one into new awareness, a secret, lonely, and tabooed world—to survive the transgression is terrifying and addictive. To know that everything has changed and yet nothing has changed; and in leaping the chasm of this impossible division of self, a discovery of the self surviving, still well, still strong, and, as a curious consequence, renewed.

—Patricia Williams (129–130)

What does it mean for women of color to participate in "feminist" revisions of the meaning of community given their self-conscious invocation of race or ethnicity as a simultaneous and no less important facet of identity than gender? Moreover, how does a condition of diaspora shape the meaning of community, especially for Chicanas and African-American women? Historically, the situation of physical and cultural displacement has engendered an acute desire to secure a stable sense of "home," albeit often in ways that challenge prevailing conceptions of community. However, as the Black and Chicano movements of the late 1960s and early 1970s demonstrate, the impetus to establish respective autonomous homelands also often has been coupled with the reinforcement of patriarchal values. Women were expected to support male leaders and to produce and nurture the next generation. Moreover, while much of the women's movement of the same period was centered on eradicating patriarchal inequality, it also largely alienated women of color for its tendency to view women as an undifferentiated class. Nevertheless, as their writings during the period bear witness, many African-American women and Chicanas actively contested the demand for subordination within their movements and critiqued the shortsightedness and even latent racism of the women's movement. The key question thus becomes how do these and other acts of transgression help to transform existing cultural practices into a new vision of community that isn't predicated on a totalizing unity or harmony? *The Shorter Oxford English Dictionary* defines the verb to transgress as "to go beyond the limits prescribed by (a law, command, etc.); to break, violate, infringe, trespass against" (2356). Much of the literature of women of color represents acts of transgression as necessary to the enterprise of change and transformation, for as the epigraph by Patricia Williams suggests, engaging in transgressive behavior potentially builds new worlds. Specifically, the representation of figures of transgression provides a model for the reconfiguring of community and self as an ongoing dialectic.

Toni Morrison's *Sula,* through its representation of the novel's eponymous character, implicitly argues for transgression as a crucial means to enact change and transformation. In doing so, *Sula* never seeks to resolve the tension between the yearning for independent selfhood and the pull of communal ties and thus questions the value and nature of community as a key "feminine" concept in much feminist writing.[1] I thus would like to read the novel's implications about self and community against Iris Marion Young's piece, "The Ideal of Community and the Politics of Difference" because she makes a similar critique of conventionally feminist notions of community.

Young argues that feminist thought and practice has typically held up the ideal of community in opposition to "the alienation and individualism we find hegemonic in capitalist patriarchal society" (300). She goes on to say that as a result many feminists have embraced the notion of "mutual identification and mutual affirmation" and thus have found "conflict or respectful distance suspect" (300). She thus maintains that certain feminists' definition of community often "helps reproduce their homogeneity." If the feminist groups to which Young refers reproduce their homogeneity, what qualities are constitutive of that homogeneity? The unstated, but implicit assumption is that this subject of feminism is white, middle class and heterosexual. "A woman in a feminist group that seeks to affirm mutual identification will feel and be doubly excluded if by virtue of her being different in race, class, culture, or sexuality she does not identify with the others nor they with her" (301). Thus, although Young's overall point is well-taken, she makes the all-too-common mistake of privileging so-called mainstream feminist thought at the expense of that produced by women of color.

In *Sula,* the community of the "Bottom" is able to accommodate both Sula and Shadrack, the psychologically and physically wounded World War I veteran, even as it fails fully to understand them. Such an arrangement effectively decenters the community as the focal point of meaning and organization for its subjects. Sula's actions in the novel constitute a bold attempt not merely to wrest agency for herself and to live on her own terms but to render existing social frameworks null and void. As Morrison herself has said, Sula is "new world black and new world woman extracting choice from choicelessness, responding inventively to found things" ("Unspeakable" 25). Sula's death at an early age suggests both that the world is not ready for the nature of her transgression and that Sula herself, in her desire to make herself *sui generis,* has underestimated the ineluctable tie between self and community.

Ultimately, the need for Sula's difference or transgressive behavior is most forcefully demonstrated by the effect she has on the community. Sula's difference sets her apart from and engenders the community's transformation. "Their conviction of Sula's evil changed them in accountable yet mysterious ways. Once the source of their personal misfortune was identified, they had leave to protect one another" (*Sula* 117). Notably, after Sula's death the residents of the Bottom revert to their former ways. Similarly, by the end of the novel, it is clear that the "Bottom" has been a source of sustenance, now lost, for many in the community. "Maybe (the Bottom) hadn't been a community, but it had been a place. Now there weren't any places left, just separate houses with separate televisions and separate telephones and less and less dropping by" (166). The passage thus also undermines a Western idea of progress based on bourgeois individualism.

While such feminist notions of community as those Young cites also reject bourgeois individualism, the idea of unity is largely derived from a Western idea of harmony or consensus that spurns dissent, sometimes violently. In contrast, a model of African-American dialogic communication, exemplified by call-and-response, underlies Morrison's vision of community, as manifested by the "Bottom."[2] Moreover, I read Sula's thwarted creative impulses in terms of a Black feminist critique embedded in Morrison's depiction of the community, which essentially rejects the concept of mutual identification both because it denies the differences between African-American men and women and privileges unity above the need for agency for all African-Americans, including women. As Patricia Hill Collins has noted eloquently,

> Black feminist thought's emphasis on the ongoing interplay between Black women's oppression and Black women's activism presents a matrix of domination as responsive to human agency. Such thought views the world as a dynamic place where the goal is not merely to survive or to fit in or to cope; rather, it becomes a place where we feel ownership and accountability. The existence of Afrocentric feminist thought suggests there is always choice, and power to act, no matter how bleak the situation may appear to be. Viewing the world as one in the making raises the issue of individual responsibility for bringing about change. It also shows that while individual empowerment is key, only collective action can effectively generate lasting social transformation of political and economic institutions. (237)

The emphasis on individual responsibility and self-accountability reflects an appreciation for the basic separateness between subjects even as they come together in the collective pursuit of liberation. The desirability of individual agency no doubt stems from a historical legacy of denied humanity, which has resulted in an understanding that a community's vitality is dependent on healthy subjects propelled by a sense of purpose that is simultaneously individualized and collective. A Black feminist perspective on the relationship between self and community undermines not only the dichotomies on which Western Culture rests but the opposition between individualism and community embraced by much feminist thought. As Young persuasively argues, this opposition is "integral to modern political theory and is not an alternative to it" (306).

She continues: "The opposition individualism/community receives one of its expressions in bourgeois culture in the opposition between masculinity and femininity. The culture identifies masculinity with the values associated with individualism—self-sufficiency, competition, separation, the formal equality of rights. The culture identifies femininity, on the other hand, with the values associated with community-effective relations of care, mutual aid, and cooperation." Again, Young invokes culture as well as femininity and masculinity in universal and transhistorical terms that, in fact, reflect post-Enlightenment, western values not generally applied to African-American women and men. There is therefore no reason for a Black feminist conception of community to valorize those qualities of the "feminine" from which African-American women have largely been excluded. In rejecting a facile opposition between self and community, Black feminist thought undermines what Young calls "shared subjectivity," that is, the ability of subjects to experience one another's subjectivities through mutual understanding and knowledge. She astutely refutes this idea on the grounds that it presupposes a subject that is transparent to itself, for only such a subject would be able fully to understand other subjects. Young offers as an alternative a kind of utopian urban space characterized by social differentiation and coupled with a de-emphasis on face-to-face relations.

> In the city strangers live side by side in public places, giving to and receiving from one another social and aesthetic products, often mediated by a huge chain of interactions. This instantiates social relations as difference in the sense of an understanding of groups and cultures that are different, with exchanging or overlapping interactions that do not issue in community, yet which prevent them from being outside of one another. The social differentiation of the city also provides a positive inexhaustibility of human relations. The possibility always exists of becoming acquainted with new and different people, with different cultural and social experiences; the possibility always exists for new groups to form or emerge around specific interests. (319)

Young unwittingly relies on the same logic for which she derides political theorists who valorize transparent community relations. That is, she posits a communal space as achieved, a kind of telos that exists as the end of history, her expectation of new group formations notwithstanding. Moreover, she invokes small groups or subgroups as a means of personal identification within the parameters of the city, thereby reinstantiating the kind of communal configuration she purports to disavow.

As yet another alternative, I would like to propose a model based on the promise contained in the "theoretical" underpinnings in *Sula*, which implicitly supports the invocation of race and gender as unifying categories for the purposes of empowerment within a context that respectfully differentiates among various subject-positions. In *Sula*, the apparent linchpin to such an effort is the ability to create one's self subjec-t(ively) through aesthetic practice. The implication is that through aesthetic pursuits, the subject engages in the ongoing process of mediating between one's self and the community. In this way, community has no end, but is instead continuously reexamined and defined against and for its subjects. What we need are conceptions of community to carry us through the present and into the future, not an imagined vision of an achieved future. It is thus that Hortense Spillers emphasizes the "urgency to perceive 'community' as an analogue on the shifting subject-position," adding that the " 'natal community' is a portable space, as movable a feast as oneself. We are in its midst wherever we are" (72). Spillers displays an understanding that a displaced people cannot rely solely on a sharply demarcated physical space, such as Young's city, to shape a sense of community.

Once we accept the premise that self and community are mutually contingent terms, how do we then figure community? More specifically what does it mean for marginalized, displaced peoples and more specifically, women, to invoke community? Finally, what role do cultural practices play in shaping and maintaining a sense of community?

The emphasis on creative expression within the African-American and Chicano/a literary traditions as a means of self-making, not in an individuated way but within the context of community, has its basis in the experience of diaspora. This condition has resulted in the need to cultivate a sense of cultural continuity that transcends a dislocation from material roots. As Houston A. Baker, Jr. has argued: "Africans uprooted from ancestral soil, stripped of material culture, and victimized by brutal contact with various European nations were compelled not only to maintain their cultural heritage at a *meta* (as opposed to a material) level but also to apprehend the operative metaphysics of various alien cultures. Primary to their survival was the work of *consciousness*, of nonmaterial transactions" (38). People of Mexican origin were themselves divested of much of their material culture following the forced annexation of roughly one-third of Mexico's lands in the mid-nineteenth century. Ramón Saldívar has coined the term counterdiaspora to refer to the peculiar phenomenon of being displaced culturally as well as geographically within the borders of one's own former territories. After the annexation was formalized in 1848, Mexican settlers, now U.S. citizens under terms of the treaty of Guadalupe Hidalgo, who remained north of the new border "not only lost their family and communal lands but became subject to racial and political discrimination as well as cultural erosion. Their eventual second-class status set the pattern for later treatment of Mexican immigrants" (García 1). Moreover, both African-Americans and people of Mexican origin have exhibited patterns of migration to areas in which they have not typically resided. For example, Blacks began to migrate to Northern cities in large numbers from the South beginning in 1915. Similarly, people of Mexican origin have migrated to the Midwest and even places further east in ever-increasing numbers.

Such a situation gives rise to creative expression that privileges the process itself of making and re-making culture rather than one whose goal is to fashion an artifact that reflects a cultural frame of reference that is already assumed. In short, the point is not to reify particular cultural tendencies or characteristics. Cultural expression in this case becomes a continuously unfolding enterprise that, as Ramón Saldívar has suggested, creates aesthetic worlds anew and at the same time properly acknowledges the weight of a repressed collective history. In a manner that mirrors the dialectic between self and community, the contemporary literary expression of African-American women and Chicanas by and large negotiates a delicate balance between long-standing historical traditions and the need to make culture responsive to ever-shifting realities. What role does transgression, that is, an oppositional embodiment of difference, play in the remaking of communal forms and practices? Thus, what types of textual strategies inform a literary practice that embodies the principles outlined above?

Sandra Cisneros's *The House on Mango Street* centers on the Chicana adolescent narrator's growing rebellion not only against sexist and racist norms but against broader materialist economic and political structures that underlie the oppression of women of color in particular. Thus, the feminist vision that emerges from the book is one that implicitly indicts and seeks to transform larger political, social, economic as well as cultural forces. In this way, the book engages in a strong critique of marriage that doesn't merely and stereotypically lay the blame on macho Latino men. While the book represents the pain and terror of domestic violence, it also poignantly explores the misguided hope that the women of the narrator's community often place on marriage given the lack of educational and economic opportunities that would grant them some autonomy. In advocating broader opportunities for women of color, however, the book emphatically rejects a conception of upward mobility that is largely self-directed. The *House on Mango Street* provides a complex examination of the external and internal forces that shape the lives of women of color and a vision of empowerment based on the dialectic between self and community much as Toni Morrison's *Sula* does. Therefore, the narrator transgresses both against the norms for women that prevail within her community as well as against the myth of the American Dream, that cornerstone of bourgeois American individualism. As such the book also redefines the parameters of the autobiographical form as I will discuss.

The House on Mango Street implicitly addresses the question, "Why write?" Is the enterprise of writing ever really a wholly private pursuit or is writing always implicated in larger discursive, social, and even political practices? The tensions that underlie Cinseros's exploration of the role of discourse and more specifically literature in our society echo Langston Hughes's lament in his 1940 autobiography *The Big Sea* that "The ordinary Negroes hadn't heard of the Negro Renaissance. And if they had, it hadn't raised their wages any" (228). Nevertheless, both apparently write out of an irrepressible conviction that the pursuit of writing is ultimately essential if often a terribly complicated business. The operative question then becomes how and to what aim do we write. (*The House on Mango Street*, structured as a collection of discrete but related vignettes, illuminates the role that discourse can play either in obscuring or in elucidating this relationship between the private and public.)

Significantly, the book opens with the narrator's initial confrontation with the discursive and structural forces that shape her life as an adolescent Mexican-American growing up in Chicago. In that first vignette also entitled "The House on Mango Street," Esperanza Cordero recalls that when her family is still living in a rented house on Loomis Street, a nun from her school approaches her as she plays outside her home. In a shift reminiscent of W. E. B. Du Bois's notion of double consciousness, Esperanza suddenly views her surroundings through the prism of the nun's perspective and feels ashamed.[3]

> The laundromat downstairs had been boarded up because it had been robbed two days before and the owner had painted on the wood YES WE'RE OPEN so as not to lose business.
> "Where do you live?" she asked.
> "There," I said pointing up to the third floor.
> "You live *there*?"
> *There*. I had to look to where she had pointed—the third floor, the paint peeling, wooden bars Papa had nailed on the windows so we wouldn't fall out. You live *there*?

The way she said it made me feel like nothing. *There.* I lived *there.* I nodded. (Mango 4–5)

Esperanza experiences self-alienation, engendering a sense of absence, as if she has ceased to exist. However, she turns the now empty signifier "I" into a desire to change her material circumstances and thus presumably remake herself: "I knew then I had to have a house. A real house. One I could point to" (5). Unfortunately, she goes on, the house that her family has purchased since that encounter, a house with "bricks . . . crumbling in places and . . . (a) front door so swollen you have to push hard to get in . . ." "isn't it" (4–5). This impetus for a "real house" that doesn't arouse shame leads Esperanza on a metaphysical journey, undertaken through her writing, that allows her to achieve a more comprehensive cognition not just of her situation but of the other members of her community, in particular the women. The book articulates Esperanza's struggle to decide whether she wants to or even can act in a purely private, individuated way. If her first impulse it to equate her family's inability to acquire "the house we'd thought we'd get," one with "real stairs, not hallway stairs, but stairs inside like the houses on T.V." to a personal failure, the very act of writing results in a profound reevaluation of her and her community's circumstances. Esperanza's narrative instead goes on to expose the failure of the public sphere as when she describes her decision to procure part-time employment because "The Catholic high school cost a lot, and Papa said nobody went to public school unless you wanted to turn out bad" (53). Moreover, once she secures a position at a photo processing lab, she "just did what I was told" (54), and finds herself the target of sexual harassment from one her co-workers.

This ongoing effort to re-evaluate the forces that shape her life, in turn, culminates in a blueprint for a vision of collective change that Esperanza articulates in one of the later vignettes, when she states, "One day I'll own my own house, but I won't forget who I am or where I came from. Passing bums will ask, Can I come in? I'll offer them the attic, ask them to stay, because I know what it is to be without a house" (87). Her apparently unselfconscious use of the typically pejorative term "bums" reflects that young Esperanza is already entangled in prevailing discursive practices. Yet, the narrator's identification with the "bums" and their condition and her incipient vision of a more inclusive community speaks to the marked shift in Esperanza's consciousness and the emergence of an acute sensibility. Moreover, the book as a whole demonstrates the powerful potential for writing to make a difference, to effect change. At the same time, Cisneros emphatically elides any utopian or even naively optimistic impulses by interweaving stories of women who lack the material and personal resources to acquire the cognition that Esperanza does.

The narrator devotes one of her vignettes to Minerva, who is only slightly older than Esperanza, but has two children and an abusive, largely absent husband. Interestingly, Minerva also writes poems, "on little pieces of paper that she folds over and over and holds in her hands a long time, little pieces of paper that smell like a dime" (84). In contrast to Esperanza, for Minerva writing is means of survival and nothing more. Despite Esperanza's gestures of friendship ("She lets me read her poems, I read her mine."), she expresses a desperate sense of helplessness. "I don't know which way

she'll go. There is nothing *I* can do" (85). The ironic emphasis on "I" is suggestive of
the inherent limitations of individual action alone. This vignette also underscores that
however much the practice of writing contributes to the development of Esperanza's
heightened consciousness, that activity in and of itself can change neither her nor
Minerva's material situation. The contrast between Esperanza's and Minerva's relationship to writing is also highly telling. At best, writing for Minerva provides an
outlet for her personal anguish and a connection to a sympathetic friend, while Esperanza, although disadvantaged in numerous ways, has the comparative luxury of supportive parents actively trying to secure whatever opportunities they can for their
daughter. As a result of this disparity, perhaps, Minerva is mired in recording and
living the "same story" (85), as Esperanza points out. Meanwhile, Esperanza begins
to assert the confidence to challenge prevailing narratives about love, romance, and
marriage, for example, and inaugurate new ones specific to her experiences as a Chicana.

I thus read *The House on Mango Street* as an autobiography that consciously decenters
the subject-narrator in order to explore the material and discursive underpinnings of
the sociosymbolic contract for the *community* of women of color. This links the enterprise of writing one's own story to political praxis. In its appropriation of aesthetic
practice as an instrument to remake the self, that is, to construct a sense of self in
opposition to hegemonic cultural configurations, *The House on Mango Street* supports
the viability of individual agency. This possibility, the book implicitly argues, is, contingent, however, on one's place figuratively and literally. The very title of Cinseros's
book serves to emphasize the importance of place in providing a sense of cultural and
personal demarcation. The use of the word "mango," which of course refers to a widely
available and very popular fruit in Mexico and other parts of Latin America, telegraphs
the Latino diaspora, a historical process that has been under way since the mid-nineteenth century. The word "mango" also signals the irreversible "Latinization" of urban
American centers, some, like Chicago, far from the U.S.-Mexico border; finally,
"mango" alludes to the material boundaries that are defined by race and class within
urban spaces. Esperanza herself is unfamiliar with this history; she describes only a
sense of personal deprivation because even in her family's new home "everybody has
to share a bedroom" (4). But for readers of the book, the fictional Mango Street alludes
to an all-too-real but suppressed history of people of Mexican origin as Esperanza's
discomfortingly poignant insistence that she doesn't live in a "real" house suggests.
The invisibility of that history and the people linked to it reinforces what Jonathan
Arac has referred to as "our enmeshment in representation" (xx). If Esperanza can
assert that she doesn't live in a "real" house or that she'd like "a name more like the
real me, the one nobody sees," the underlying reason is that Esperanza and people
like her have largely been either unrepresented or misrepresented within the popular
American imagination. Cisneros herself has recalled that until she enrolled in the
famed Iowa Writers' Workshop "I had never felt my home, family, and neighborhood
unique or worthy of writing about" ("Ghosts and Voices" 72). In an echo of the
opening pages of *The House on Mango Street*, Cisneros states that at Iowa "I only knew
that for the first time in my life I felt 'other' " ("Ghosts and Voices" 72). She thus

experienced a sense of urgency to write about that which "(s)urely my classmates knew nothing about. . ." ("Ghosts and Voices" 73).

The trope of "Mango" therefore encapsulates that complex history that might and should be available to Esperanza under different circumstances. The history of Mexican-Americans in Chicago is one that dates back to the 1920s when significant numbers of Mexicans and Mexican-Americans were recruited to work in Chicago's steel mills, stock yards, and railroads to support this nation's industrial expansion. Notably, this population's willingness to migrate stemmed both from the impoverished and otherwise difficult conditions many Mexican-Americans faced in the Southwest and the policies of Mexico's dictator Porfirio Diaz, which by 1910 rendered 97 percent of all rural families within Mexico landless. Furthermore, his central industrial policy was to encourage foreign investment with the result that most sectors of the nonagenarian economy came to be controlled by foreign, mainly U.S., interests. Although many of those early residents, citizen and non-citizen alike, were forcibly and illegally repatriated back to Mexico during the Great Depression, the number of people of Mexican origin in Chicago has continued to grow and currently constitute the metropolitan area's fastest growing population. The underlying story of Mango is also that of segregation and discrimination resulting in Mexican-Americans, as well as Blacks, typically having to pay much more in rent than European immigrants and for substandard housing at that.

While this specific history is never explicitly articulated in *The House on Mango Street*, the representation of Esperanza's struggle advocates the view that she needs to engage the structures that underlie her existence. In terms of form, the book begins much like a *bildungsroman*. Cisneros goes beyond borrowing this tradition, however, by rejecting a strictly retrospective narrative voice. Instead, the collection of vignettes seek to represent the process itself by which Esperanza arrives at an understanding of her discursive and material inscription as a subject and how she subsequently seeks to resist and reshape the codified boundaries of that subjectivity.

Although the book does begin in a retrospective voice ("But what I remember most is moving a lot"), its usage is quickly rendered ambiguous when the narrator shifts to a simple present tense ("The House on Mango Street is ours, and we don't have to pay rent to anybody . . ."). It can longer be assumed that the narrator is reflecting back on events in the distant past. This change undermines the reader's expectation that the book conveys a familiar narrative of personal discovery and growth told from a comfortable distance. The use of a young narrator who has not fully "theorized" the various subject positions she occupies allows Cisneros to interrogate the discursive inscription of identity. In Esperanza's case, she occupies a space at the interstices between American and Mexican cultures as they are popularly represented. It is appropriate that as a young woman who has not yet been exposed to a politicized discourse of empowerment, she does not refer to herself as a Chicana. Yet her ruminations in the story "My Name," on the different meanings of her name in English and Spanish, and her desire to rename herself suggest an incipient impulse toward a Chicana subjectivity. Esperanza's gesture underscores both the constructedness of subjectivity and more importantly, its contingence on one's perceived relationship to the material world. As the Chicana cultural critic Norma Alarcón has noted,

"The name Chicana is not a name that women (or men) are born to or with, as is often the case with "Mexican," but rather it is consciously assumed" ("Chicana Feminism" 250).

An extended analysis of the vignette demonstrates how Cisneros develops these themes. She begins, "In English my name means hope. In Spanish it means too many letters. It means sadness, it means waiting" (10–11). Although hope is a literal translation of "esperanza," the narrator makes it clear that the English word "hope" does not fully convey the meaning of her name, which is derived from the Spanish verb "esperar," which means to wait for as well as to hope. This difference thus becomes a metaphor for cultural difference. In English, hope conveys an unbridled American optimism alien to Esperanza and her family as working class people of color whose version of the American Dream is only fulfilled ironically—through ownership of a house that the narrator feels she can't point to with pride.

Esperanza's Mexican heritage, metonymically represented by her great-grandmother, after whom she was named, embodies the underlying possibility of disappointment contained within hope. The senior Esperanza was literally forced into marriage, an outrageous insult from which she seems never to have recovered. "She looked out the window all her life, the way so many women sit their sadness on an elbow" (11). Nevertheless, the younger Esperanza expresses a certain admiration for her ancestor's alleged spiritedness. "I would've liked to have known her, a wild horse of a woman, so wild she wouldn't marry. Until my great-grandfather threw a sack over her head and carried her off. Just like that, as if she were a fancy chandelier. That's the way he did it" (11). The narrative implies that whatever sense of independence the senior Esperanza possessed was effectively stamped out by the patriarchal rule of law. Her great-grandmother's fate leads Esperanza to ruminate, "I have inherited her name, but I don't want to inherit her place by the window" (11). Esperanza's wish to escape the oppression of patriarchy does not constitute a rejection of her great-grandmother per se, or even of her Mexican heritage, but of overdetermined definitions of culture that do not allow for contradiction or difference. Esperanza likewise feels a sense of dislocation within mainstream American culture. "At school they say my name funny as if the syllables were made out of tin and hurt the roof of your mouth. But in Spanish my name is made out of a softer something, like silver. . ." (11). Esperanza thus exists in a borderlands between Mexico and the U.S. as sites of *imagined* common cultures.

This situation gives rise to Esperanza's desire to "baptize myself under a new name, a name more like the real me, the one nobody sees" (11). The "real me, the one nobody sees" functions as a critique of American culture's insistence on frequently representing difference in terms that simultaneously render it visible and invisible in ahistorical ways. Difference is visible as a distinguishing mark of sometimes negatively encoded physical and/or cultural traits; difference also signifies invisibility in contemporary models of diversity that embrace difference for its own sake, effectively eliding considerations of the specific histories of oppressed peoples in this country and their continued inscription into asymmetrical relations of power. Esperanza therefore christens herself "ZeZe the X" as a means of rejecting her ascribed place within existing cultural configurations. The stories thus go beyond mapping out how Esperanza achieves "cognition of a situation for herself" (Alarcón, "The Theoretical Subject(s)" 39), for she rejects the terms of subjectivity available to her and instead suggests that cultural practices need to be redefined in order for her to be able to assert an alternative subject position. The "real me" thus also signifies a grounding of the self within a cultural specificity that is largely unseen and unacknowledged, suggesting a new form of subjectivity that never achieves stasis or completion but is potentially politically empowering because it is contingent on culturally specific practices that reflect constantly shifting realities.

The story "Red Clowns" demonstrates in brutally stark terms the oppressive effects of negative discursive constructions of difference. Reading Esperanza's sexual assault by several presumably white boys only within the context of a sexual economy governed by male power ignores the significance of race in this narrative. One implication of the story is that Esperanza is an easy and natural target because she is not white. "The one who grabbed me by the arm, he wouldn't let me go. He said I love you, Spanish girl, I love you, and pressed his sour mouth to mine" (100). She is not just a girl, but a Spanish girl, a term that simultaneously objectifies her in racial as well as sexual terms and denies her specific cultural history. Calling Esperanza or any Latina "Spanish" implicitly excludes her from dominant discursive practices, which is signified by the English language. The sharp demarcation between "Spanish" and "English" also linguistically enacts the Mexico-U.S. border as the site of historical amnesia, for the border has been naturalized to the point that it masks the illegal war launched by the U.S. in the mid-nineteenth century for the expressed purpose of annexing more than one-third of Mexico's land.

The term "Spanish girl" also encapsulates the disjuncture between Esperanza's discursive formation as an oppressed, racialized woman and the dominant, popular narratives of romantic love. "They all lied. All the books and magazines, everything that told it wrong. Only his dirty fingernails against my skin, only his sour smell again" (100). The failed promise of these narratives does not mean, of course, that they do not hold sway in the lives of many young girls and women, which only underscores the need for alternative narratives. Esperanza's writing constitutes just such a cultural intervention, from which she has derived a sense of personal empowerment by the end of the collection. "I put it down on paper and then the ghost does not ache so much. I write it down and Mango says goodbye sometimes. She does not hold me with both arms. She sets me free" (110).

Underlying Cisneros's appropriation of aesthetic practice as a means of human development is an engagement with the possibility of a subjectivity that traverses a differentiated "We." In strategic terms, I place her aesthetics within a dual cultural imperative: the larger one of the Western tradition and the more specific one of Chicano cultural nationalism. On the one hand, she rejects the subject(ive) form of the western tradition, which would seek to deny difference, while adopting the notion that aesthetic practice is personally enabling. On the other hand, she rejects the reliance of Chicano cultural nationalism on an essential revolutionary subject while simultaneously embracing the movement's premise that art should occupy an important role in political and social transformation.

This dialectic between personal and collective empowerment is also reflected in Cisneros's own narrative of the development of her mission as a writer and activist.

> When I left Iowa I went to work directly in the Chicano barrio as a teacher to high school dropouts. I didn't have time to write the three years I worked there, but it was an important time for my political development. . . . But I soon grew tired of not having time to write. I left the alternative high school and took a job at my alma mater, Loyola University of Chicago I worked as an administrative assistant—mostly as a college recruiter and counselor for minority and disadvantaged students. From this experience of listening to young Latinas whose problems were so great, I felt helpless. I was moved to do something to change their lives, ours, mine. I did the only thing I knew how. I wrote. ("Do You Know Me" 78)

The phrase "their lives, ours, mine" delineates a linguistic progression that brackets community between differentiated, but related, ethnic female subjects. It is clear that Cisneros views herself neither as synonymous with her young students nor as singularly separate. In addition, the placement of "ours" as the middle term serves to challenge the idea that a community is merely the sum of its members; rather, the central position implies that a community constitutes its own material reality shaped by ideological and social forces, which in turn, influence subject-formation.

Toni Cade Bambara's novel *The Salt Eaters* and Helena María Viramontes's short story, "The Moths" represent the possibilities for transformation through female-centered spiritual practices. The spiritual realm functions not only as a necessary site for female rebellion but underscores the ways in which cultural practices embedded in patriarchy actually transgress against women, making their own transgressive behavior imperative.

For peoples who have experienced diaspora, the impetus to protect a particular cultural heritage needs to be conducted at a nonmaterial level, that is, at a level that transcends a particular geographic location or access to tangible materials or products that constitute the currency of daily cultural life. It is thus appropriate, even inevitable, that discursive practice, initially manifested in an oral tradition, would become and continue to function as a primary means of maintaining, disseminating and remaking cultural traditions.[4]

The dislocation experienced by African-Americans and Chicanas/os occurred at the level of the psyche, rendering "the work of *consciousness*" a means of cultural and even physical survival. In this way, the nature of being itself cannot be assumed, which means that the creation and nurturing of selfhood, individually and collectively, represents a fundamental pursuit of African-American and Chicana/o cultural practice. As an ongoing pursuit that remains very much alive, what cultural markers link its current manifestation to that of earlier periods? Also how are those markers appropriated and transformed by women writers of color and to what end?

Continuing his argument of the importance of the nonmaterial in Afro-American culture, Baker writes: "The primacy of nonmaterial transactions in the African's initial negotiations of slavery and the slave trade led to privileging of the roles and figures of medicine men, *griots*, conjurers, priests, and priestesses" (38). Baker goes on to suggest that the primacy of the spiritual in Afro-American culture is linked to the necessity for diasporic Africans "to seek a personal, spiritual assurance of worth" given that the philosophical and social framework of the time denied them their very humanity. In a similar vein, Norma Alarcón has noted that a Chicana feminist discourse invokes Aztec goddesses such as Coatlicue, Cihuacoatl, and Ixtacihuatl both to give voice to a repressed collective female history and to represent a process of self-making that consciously resists the framework of western culture. Alarcón thus cites Gloria Anzaldúa and her evocation of "La Herencia de Coatlicue/The Coatlicue State." The state, Alarcón writes, "is paradoxically, an ongoing process, a continuous effort of consciousness to make 'sense' of it all" ("Chicana Feminism" 252).

The evocation of spiritual figures and practices within African-American and Chicana cultures thus displays three fundamental functions. The first is personal affirmation outside the framework of western cultural paradigms. Secondly, cultural and geographical dislocation requires a nonmaterial means to maintain historical remembrance and cultural continuity in the face of potential erasure. Finally, and perhaps most importantly, the emphasis on the spiritual signals a process of transformation that signifies the always unfolding negotiation between the collective and the subject; and between the preservation of the past and the requirements of the present. Furthermore, the long-standing association between women and spirituality allows African-American women and Chicanas both to transgress and to lay claim to their cultural inheritance. We thus find ourselves come full circle, for while the conditions of diaspora necessitate a reliance of nonmaterial transactions, they are pursued to elicit material changes.

As a creative act, this process of transformation also finds expression within the contemporary literature of African-American women and Chicanas. Here, this legacy of spirituality manifests itself in what I refer to as interrelated tropes of healing and wholeness. These tropes serve not only as metaphors for the dialectic between self and community but reflect and shape the textual strategies that Toni Cade Bambara and Helena María Viramontes make.

> Words are to be taken seriously. I try to take seriously acts of language. Words set things in motion. I've seen them doing it. Words set up atmospheres, electrical fields, charges. I've felt them doing it. Words conjure.

—Toni Cade Bambara ("What It Is" 163)

Although Bambara in the above quotation mirrors a post-structuralist view of language as material, I would like instead to elicit the ways in which her view of language comes out of African-American culture and thus expands on post-structuralist theory. The African-American literary tradition was constituted in the foreknowledge that discourse has material ramifications. The worlds rendered within aesthetic practice are therefore neither strictly immanent nor mere reflections of a discretely separate and extant reality. This insight also informs Bambara's conception of language, which she claims "sets things in motion." In referring to "acts of language," she suggests that writing is a potential site of agency for the subject, in particular the marginalized subject. Moreover, her invocation of "atmospheres, electrical fields, charges" implies that the act of writing has consequences that extend far beyond the writing subject.

In keeping with an African-American literary tradition, writing is always already a collective enterprise the purpose of which is to remake the world.

This transformative function of African-American literature has translated into the appropriation of western discursive forms in culturally specific ways. Bambara uses "conjure" in a way that recalls long-standing spiritual practices, in particular those that have been the domain of women, within African-American culture.[5] If African-American culture was founded from the need to rely on extra-discursive media, such as the oral and the spiritual, then contemporary African-American literature still incorporates these older forms as a means of historical remembrance and resistance to western discursive practices.

In Toni Cade Bambara's novel *The Salt Eaters*, the dual impetus to remember the past and to remake the present is represented in the character of Minnie Ransom, a folk medicine healer, for as a magician and cultural guardian, she traffics in creativity and history. Her ministering to Velma Henry, a Black feminist activist who has tried to commit suicide, forms the book's "literal-metaphoric center," to quote Gloria Hull (217). Literal because the healing itself, which takes place in less than two hours, constitutes the core action in a book that lacks a traditional, linear plot. Indeed, Bambara interweaves narratives of the past, present, and future into her novel. Superficially, the book narrates the activities of many of fictional Claybourne, Georgia's residents as well as numerous visitors on the very day Velma and Minnie are engaged in a time-honored ritual of survival. The book's much more ambitious project, however, is to render a picture of the whole community—that is, its history, present, and potential—through its individual members and their particular pasts, presents, and futures.

Bambara's narrative thus represents community not as a fixed entity whose contours can be presumed but as organic. The community derives its "life" from its members, whose individual histories intersect with one another and with a shared history based on broader categories, such as race and gender, that transcend the borders of Claybourne. The novel's scope is thus both sweeping and intensely personal. In this way it becomes impossible to reduce the community, whether it is Claybourne or African-Americans as a whole, merely to a set of descriptive characteristics. Community is also those intangible facets of history, both as experienced by individual subjects and the community as a whole, the traces of which are borne by the present and thus must be taken into account to shape the future. The novel thus decenters community, by which I mean that community is not figured as existing prior to its subjects. Within a post-structuralist discourse the notion that subjects do not exist *a priori* culture is by now commonplace. Not as much attention has been accorded, however, to the ways in which subjects shape culture. Bereft of their cultural moorings and denied an assigned role in the formation of American culture, diasporic Africans intuitively understood that culture had to be made by and through its subjects in a kind of dialectical oscillation that privileges neither half of the equation.

In this way, the act of healing that opens and closes the book serves as a metaphoric center for the process of bringing together community and subjects. The effort to make Velma well parallels the process of healing that Bambara envisions for the community as a whole. The question, mouthed by Minnie, that opens the book—"Are you sure, sweetheart, that you want to be well?" (3) thus resonates throughout the entire book. Furthermore, Velma's own skepticism about this endeavor mirrors Claybourne's own potential dislocation from its history and relationship to African-American cultural practices, in particular spiritual practices that assign women a central role in the making of communal forms. Velma's transgressive attempt to commit suicide mirrors the community's transgression against women in denying them a primary role in the contemporary struggle for liberation.

> Velma blinked. Was ole Minnie trying to hypnotize her, mesmerize her? Minnie Ransom, the legendary spinster of Claybourne, Georgia, spinning out a song, drawing *her* of all people up. Velma the swift; Velma the elusive; Velma who had never mastered the kicks, punches and defense blocks, but who had down cold the art of being not there when the blow came. Velma caught, caught up in the weave of the song Minnie was humming, of the shawl, of the threads, of the silvery tendrils that extended from the healer's neck and hands and disappeared into the sheen of the sunlight. (4)

Velma barely recognizes, let alone appreciates Minnie's spiritual gifts, which would serve to establish a continuity to Velma's past and to her relationship with the community both in the local sense of Claybourne and the larger sense of African-American culture. The sarcasm that underlines the phrase "legendary spinster" and the emphasis on her in the phrase "drawing *her* of all people up" reinforces Velma's disdain. Even more importantly, the emphasis on *her* conveys Velma's alienation from her nonmaterial cultural ties; in other words, she has lost her way spiritually. In using the free indirect style as a narrational strategy, Bambara also allows the reader to discern that Velma herself is unaware of this lapse and stubbornly clings to a view of herself as utterly independent. This independence has in turn cost her the ability to protect herself: "Velma who had never mastered the kicks, punches and defense blocks. . . . " As her friend Jan, also a spiritualist, proclaims, "The drive for invulnerability usually leaves us totally vulnerable" (216).

The distinction between the material and the nonmaterial is important, for Velma is a committed activist who has put considerable energy into various causes. Her fatigue and sense of alienation are evident in a lengthy sequence that recounts her memory of a somewhat rancorous meeting at the Academy of Seven Arts, the town's community center. During this memory she lapses into yet an earlier memory of a Civil Rights march that she has completed, dirty and exhausted, her hands and feet swollen.

> Velma had gone up to the hotel, her shoes dangling around her neck, her clipboard in the ache of her left arm. She'd hitched but mostly walked, keeping her eyes strictly off her swollen feet. Gone up the hotel to make some calls—find another doctor locate the support group to bring food and aspirin, phone in the press notices, try to locate James's group that had gone to meet with King in D.C.
>
> She was hanging on to the counter with both hands, nails splitting, the phone too heavy to consider handling without a deep intake of breath and resolve. She could barely stand up, much less focus on the clipboard and flip pages. And behind her the easy

laughter, that familiar voice. On those dulcet tones. And she looked into the mirror. The speaker and his cronies and the women, those women, coming down the corridor. (38)

The offhand reference to the Rev. Martin Luther King, Jr. not only connects her to the history of the Civil Right Movement, but more importantly, emphasizes the ongoing, prosaic, even mundane, character of the struggle for liberation. The suggestion is that Velma, a tireless grass-roots worker who wills herself to replace an ill doctor before taking care of her own needs, is just as vital to the community, if not more so, than a man accorded the stature of a leader. The community is not embodied in any one person, and the success of social movements has always been contingent on the efforts of Velma and others like her. The passage also shows that within an ongoing struggle for African-American liberation taking care of one's self spiritually is perhaps the fundamental revolutionary act. In her desire to serve her community, Velma has indeed lived "history," but has nevertheless neglected the spiritual negotiations that have sustained her people for over 400 years. The community as a whole, however, has also participated in neglecting its legacy, for in casting liberation in masculinist terms, it has ignored the long history of African-American women as leaders. Thus, Velma, the text suggests, is right to challenge the patriarchal values embodied by members of her community. However, she has overlooked the viability of woman-centered spiritual practices as a means by which to supplant patriarchy.

The effort to render Velma whole is predicated on linking her political commitment with the nonmaterial, sustaining, and women-centered aspects of African-American culture. The function of healing is the achievement of wholeness, of a state of balance. As in Anzaldúa's "The Coatlicue State," the state of wholeness does not signify stasis but a process of cultural genealogy and continuous transformation both for the community and its subjects. Such an endeavor, the narrative implies, is not easy, but necessary. "Just so's you're sure, sweetheart, and ready to be healed, cause wholeness is no trifling matter. A lot of weight when you're well," Minnie cautions Velma during the course of the healing (10). The word "weight" conveys substance and implies that culture is substantive and material to political struggle. The use of weight here also suggests that culture needs to be cultivated, looked after, to retain its meaning. Likewise, the political struggle has no meaning without a sense of cultural roots and purpose. Marginalized, displaced peoples especially need to anchor their personal and collective identities as well as activities in vernacular cultural practices, for they provide the means to resist the negative ascription of difference imposed by the western tradition. Finally, Minnie's words convey the message that such work is not easy. Near the end of the novel, the narrative projects into Velma's future with her recollecting the healing episode. "And years hence she would laugh remembering she'd thought *that* was an ordeal. She didn't know the half of it. Of what awaited her in years to come" (278).

Diana Fuss has suggested that "like the female subject, the Afro-American subject (who may also be female) *begins* fragmented and dispersed, begins with a double-consciousness, as Du Bois would say" (95). I would say that this fragmentation stems from the dislocation African-Americans have historically experienced from the dominant culture, which fuels the creation of an alternative culture. In post-structuralist terms, Afro-American culture has always intuitively recognized the fallacy of the terms of western identity; in a sense African-Americans have always existed as decentered subjects.

It is too facile, I believe, to maintain, as Fuss suggests, that for African-Americans this state of fragmentation becomes something to be overcome rather than celebrated. Instead, Afro-American culture posits a third alternative: wholeness, which signifies an ongoing synchrony between self and community, rather than either a totalizing unity or alienation. In Bambara's narrative, community signifies not just the members of a group with whom one identifies, but that patchwork of shared cultural practices that constitute the repository of a collective memory; at same time, these practices are malleable, responsive to particular contingencies over place and time, lending to culture an improvisational quality. It is in this manner that subjects derive agency through cultural practices.

Minnie's healing talents represent both an ancient and constantly evolving art form through which Velma simultaneously reconnects with herself and with her community. These two enterprises cannot be separated, for self and community are mutually contingent. Within this framework, knowing one's self is dependent on knowing one's cultural roots. For this reason, *The Salt Eaters* privileges a non-western epistemology that rejects a western metaphysics of presence. What is "real" and therefore, knowable in *The Salt Eaters* often occupies a liminal space between the material and the immaterial, most notably, in the figure of Old Wife, Minnie's spirit guide, now dead, but very much a presence in the narrative. Making no distinction between the corporeal and incorporeal, Minnie calls on Old Wife to assist her in the healing process. Within the narrative they converse with each other, unbeknownst to the spectators in attendance, as if they both occupied concrete space.

> Nothing much changed since (Old Wife) passed. Old Wife's complexion was still like mutton suet and brown gravy congealed on a plate. She was still slack jawed. The harelip was as deep a gouge as ever. Nothing much to recommend her, or to signal she was special. "You'd think they'da fixed that lip," Minnie muttering to herself, sitting down on the ledge she'd built during her apprenticeship. A fountain made from ceramic pipes she'd thought much too lovely to be laid underground conducting sewerage. A pause to view the water, to watch the fishes glinting shots of shine around the pool, the aromas from the right wafting past like a brushstroke in a cartoon. (51)

Bambara's treatment of the spiritual as real reflects a Black feminist literary practice that seeks to redefine the parameters of reality in representational terms. The "real side" of Afro-American life, its consciousness, has remained largely invisible to mainstream culture. Bambara's narrative astonishes because she is deliberately signifying, in the African-American sense (Gates 286), on classical literary realism. This act of repetition and reversal effectively transforms the form, making it responsive to the specificities of Afro-American culture.

But in staking a claim for literary practice as potentially proactive and transformative,[6] Bambara is also acutely aware of the need to remain anchored in long-standing cultural practices. The injunction to remain historically and culturally connected is manifested in the title of the novel itself, which invokes a folk custom of treating a snake bite by ingesting salt and applying a salt poultice to the wound. Metaphorically, eating salt refers to the process of transformation in the face of domination and poten- tial destruction. As Bambara has said, "To struggle, to develop, one needs to master ways to neutralize poisons. 'Salt' also keeps the parable of Lot's Wife to the fore. Without a belief in the capacity for transformation, one can become ossified" ("What It Is" 166).

During the course of the healing, Velma becomes culturally and historically recon- nected when she remembers an incident in which M'Dear Sophie treated a snake bite to her husband Daddy Dolphy with salt.

> At some point in her life she was sure Douglass, Tubman, the slave narratives, the songs, the fables, Delaney, Ida Wells, Blyden, DuBois, Garvey, the singers, her parents, Malcolm, Coltrane, the poets, her comrades, her godmother, her neighbors, had taught her that (salt eating as a folk cure). Thought she knew how to build immunity to the sting of the serpent that turned would-be cells, could-be cadres into cargo cults. . . . Thought the workers of the sixties had pulled the Family safely out of range of the serpents fangs so the workers of the seventies could drain the poisons, repair the damaged tissues, retrain the heartworks, realign the spine. Thought the vaccine offered by all the theorists and activists and clear thinkers and doers of the warrior clan would take. But amnesia had set it anyhow. (258)

Velma, however, overcomes that amnesia, and Bambara's novel represents an effort to overturn that amnesia at a much broader level by expanding the boundaries of cultural practice.

In the short story, "The Moths," the Chicana writer Helena Maria Viramontes also approaches matters of the spirit as another, vital plane of reality. Unlike Bambara, however, who explores the conjunction between Family and family, that is, between the condition of the race as a whole and the personal relationships that constitute daily life, Viramontes focuses on family relations at the more personal level. This tendency does not mean that larger cultural processes and practices are immaterial. Rather, Viramontes is interested in examining how cultural processes function in the lives of particular Chicanas. Yet, in examining through fiction the role of culture, she both critiques existing practices and suggests an alternative vision of the Chicana commu- nity.

"The Moths" is narrated in the first person as the memory of an unnamed Chicana's powerful, transformative experience with her *abuelita*, or grandmother. The narrator recalls being asked to help her grandmother, who is in the final stages of terminal cancer. This 14-year-old girl thus finds herself taking on the role her grandmother had filled. The difference is that the narrator was successfully healed; her grandmother will die. "Abuelita had pulled me through the rages of scarlet fever by placing, remov- ing and replacing potato slices on the temples of my forehead" (23). The opening paragraph thus announces that the narrator's grandmother traffics in folk medicine, which also signals her function as a cultural guardian. In effect, by requesting her granddaughter's assistance, Abuelita is passing on this role to her.

However, like Velma, the narrator is skeptical about Abuelita's healing powers. "I even went so far as to doubt the power of Abuelita's slices, the slices she said absorbed my fever. 'You're still alive, aren't you?' Abuelita snapped back, her pasty gray eye beaming at me and burning holes in my suspicions" (23). The implication underlying Abuelita's retort is that her restorative powers are real. Still, the narrator's skepticism betrays an assertiveness and independence that, the story suggests, make up a necessary form of transgression for a Chicana community. "I wasn't even pretty or nice like my older sisters and I just couldn't handle the fineries of crocheting or embroidery and I always pricked my fingers or knotted my colored threads time and time again while my sisters laughed and called me bull hands with their cute waterlike voices" (23). The narrator rebels against the cultural paradigm of woman as passively feminine, a response her Abuelita seems to respect and wants to cultivate. The use of the word "bull," reinforces her rejection of a stereotypical female role. Her grandmother, recognizing that she has more important work to accomplish with her hands than crocheting or embroidering, "made a balm out of dried moth wings and Vicks and rubbed my hands, shaped them back to size and it was the strangest feeling. Like bones melting. Like sun shining through the darkness of your eyelids. I didn't mind helping Abuelita after that, so Amá (the narrator's mother) would always send me over to her" (23–34). Abuelita shapes the narrator's hands back to size not to do woman's work in the traditional sense but to prepare her to inherit the cultural practices that constitute an alternative, anti-patriarchal tradition. The receipt of this legacy will transform the narrator, as the phrase "bones melting" suggests, just as she will begin to transform these older cultural forms in an incipient Chicana feminist gesture. Moth wings, a symbol of death and hence, change, also signify this potential transformation.

This conjoining of moth's wings and Vicks to make a healing balm juxtaposes the old and the new and the spiritual and the mundane. The implication is that for Chicanos/as and Afro-Americans, cultural practices, even, or perhaps especially, of spiritual, nonmaterial nature, are always rooted in daily lived experiences. The relevance of culture to the "real" is encapsulated in the juxtaposition of the similes "like bones melting" and "like sun shining through the darkness of your eyelids." The first signifies the balm's recuperative effect on the narrator's psyche, while the second signifies the physical, more prosaic relief the balm provides.

This bringing together of the psyche and the physical equates healing with the process of becoming whole, much as *The Salt Eaters* does. Again, culture's sustaining powers cannot be divorced from everyday life. For the narrator, Abuelita as a cultural guardian provides that sustenance, in no small part because her home represents a refuge from the narrator's difficult and even oppressive home life. "I always felt (Abuelita's) gray eye on me. It made me feel, in a strange sort of way, safe and guarded and not alone. Like God was supposed to make you feel" (24).

The narrator contrasts the spirituality her grandmother represents with that of the Roman Catholic Church, which she associates with an empty solitude and even lifelessness. "Across the street from Jay's Market there was a chapel. After I cleaned my fingernails, I looked up at the high ceiling. I had forgotten the vastness of these places, the coolness of the marble pillars and the frozen statues with blank eyes. I was alone. I knew why I had never returned" (25). Her grandmother's home, which is teeming with the life of the jasmine, heliotrope, cilantro, and hierbabuena she cultivates in red

Hills Brothers coffee cans, provides the personal, cultural and spiritual connection for which she yearns. "The roots would burst out of the rusted coffee cans and search for a place to connect. I would then feed the seedlings with water" (24).

The narrative also associates the oppressiveness of the Church with Apá, the narrator's father.

> He would pound his hands on the table, rocking the sugar dish or spilling a cup of coffee and scream that if I didn't go to mass every Sunday to save my goddamn sinning soul, then I had no reason to go out of the house, period. Punto final. He would grab my arm and dig his nail into me to make sure I understood the importance of catechism. Did he make himself clear? Then he strategically directed his anger at Amá for her lousy way of bringing up daughters, being disrespectful and unbelieving, and my older sisters would pull me aside and tell me if I didn't get to mass right this minute, they were all going to kick the holy shit out of me. (25)

The phrase "Punto Final" conveys that Apá believes he is the final authority on this matter, but her mother's role in maintaining his patriarchal authority is made clear. She is the designated cultural guardian, but not of an underground female spirituality, like Abuelita. Her sisters are also being schooled in this role and mimic their father's abusive behavior. Because domination is upheld through the dissemination of cultural practices, the narrator's potential redemption depends on her openly rebelling against these practices and positing alternatives. The narrative further implies, however, that this intervention cannot spring up *sui generis*, but must have a basis in Mexican/Chicano culture, in particular as it is more positively embodied by Abuelita.

The feminism that underlies the narrative is not one based on pure opposition; rather, it seeks to recover those aspects of Mexican/Chicano culture that are sustaining for women. In this way, Abuelita performs an alternative Sunday ritual that is no less spiritual than a Catholic mass. "Abuelita lifted the burnt chiles from the fire and sprinkled water on them until the skins began to separate" (26). She prepares the chile with a solemn respect that echoes reverence for the act of transubstantiation of bread and wine during Mass.

Abuelita's offer of an alternative spirituality enables the narrator to inherit her grandmother's cultural practices when the time comes. Thus, when Abuelita dies, the narrator automatically and seamlessly adopts the role of spiritual caretaker. "From the cabinet I got a tin basin, filled it with lukewarm water and carried it carefully to the room. I want to the linen closet and took out some modest bleached white towels. With the sacredness of a priest preparing his vestments, I unfolded the towels one by one on my shoulders. I removed the sheets and blankets from her bed and peeled off her thick flannel nightgown. I toweled her puzzled face, stretching out the wrinkles, removing the coils of her neck, toweled her shoulders and breasts" (27).

The narrator consciously appropriates the traditionally male role of the priest in a manner that not only constitutes her own remaking but extends the possibilities available to Abuelita. This act of self-healing resonates with a collective potential that parallels Gloria Anzaldúa's own appropriation of the priest's role to fashion what she calls a new mestiza consciousness. "*La mestiza* has gone from being the sacrificial goat to becoming the officiating priestess at the crossroads" (80). The crossroads is a metaphor for the Chicana's need to negotiate across several cultures: the Anglo, the Mexican and the Chicano. The mestiza, whose mixed race status, connotes hybridity, sifts, culls and chooses from the various cultures according to her needs to produce an alternative culture, exemplified by Chicana feminism.

It is a Chicana feminist discourse that recuperates the tarnished image of La Malinche, Hernan Cortés's mistress, as a traitor to her race, a scapegoat for oppression, which is a legacy that has been inherited by her daughters; instead, Chicana feminism holds her up as a model of resilience and rebirth. Chicana feminism also locates La Virgen de Guadalupe/The Virgin of Guadalupe, the Catholic patron saint of Mexico, within an indigenous spiritual tradition, emphasizing her role as defender, traditionally open only to male figures.[7]

The adoption of a priestly role thus simultaneously places the narrator of "The Moths" both within long-standing traditions of female resistance by Mexican-origin women and a more contemporary Chicana feminist discourse. In keeping with Viramontes's narrative focus on the personal, the process of healing and self-healing also brings the narrator closer to her own grandmother and mother, establishing a relationship between the smaller community of the family and the broader one of women of color. The narrator's spiritual redemption is contingent on her taking her place within a community of women even as she strives to change its contours. Intuitively, she senses that this is a difficult task, and thus experiences the weight of loneliness upon her grandmother's death. "The water in the tub overflowed and poured onto the tile of the floor. Then the moths came. Small, gray ones that came from her soul and out through her mouth fluttering to light, circling the dull light bulb of the bathroom. Dying is lonely and I wanted to go to where the moths were, stay with her and plant chayotes whose vines would crawl up her fingers and into the clouds; I wanted to rest my head on her chest with her stroking my hair, telling me about the moths that lay within the soul and slowly eat the spirit up" (28). Viramontes's notion of spirituality as a source of personal and collective redemption is not rooted in facile optimism. The "moths that lay within the soul and slowly eat the spirit up" signify that the process of becoming healed and whole is an arduous one. ("The bathroom was filled with moths, and for the first time in a long time I cried, rocking us, crying for her, for me, for Amá, the sobs emerging from the depths of anguish, the misery of feeling half born. . ." [28].) The anguish and the feeling of being half born suggest that the narrator has only just begun that process. Nevertheless, by the end of the story she has accepted her grandmother's legacy and begun to participate in the cycle of making and remaking the boundaries of cultural inscription for the Chicana community. "There, there, I said to Abuelita, rocking us gently, there, there" (28). Like Velma, the narrator of "The Moths" discovers that in engaging in necessary, transgressive behavior she has a legacy of such previous activity on which to draw and expand.

The dream of wholeness that is manifest in African-American and Chicana cultures represent in part a desire to exploit, but not resolve, the dialectic between self and community. Within this scheme, the self is neither singular nor a mere reflection of the community at large. Instead, the effort to achieve wholeness, itself a paradox, for wholeness is never finally achieved but remains a process, is an attempt to heal the dislocation engendered by the diasporic condition. Part of that process entails recovery and reconstruction, that is, recuperating those cultural practices from the past that have sustained the community in its condition of diaspora and rendering a history that has been suppressed. Reconstruction also refers to the process of recreating long-standing cultural forms to accommodate shifting realities. In large measure, this is the enterprise in which Black and Chicana feminisms are involved.

Notes

This essay was written especially for this anthology.

1. I am indebted to Prof. Sandra E. Drake for helping me to clarify my thinking on this topic.

2. Morrison herself has likened her technique as based on a model of call and response.

The Afro-American novel "should try deliberately to make you stand up and make you feel something profoundly in the same way that a Black preacher requires his congregation to speak, to join him in the sermon, to behave in a certain way, to stand up and to weep and to cry and to accede or to change and to modify—to expand on the sermon that is being delivered. In the same way that a musician's music is enhanced when there is a response from the audience. Now in a book, which closes after all—it's of some importance to me to try to make that connection—to try to make that happen also. And, having at my disposal only the letters of the alphabet and some punctuation, I have to provide the places and spaces so that the reader can participate." ("Rootedness: The Ancestor as Foundation" 341)

3. The passage reads:

After the Egyptian and Indian, the Greek and Roman, the Teuton and Mongolian, the Negro is a sort of seventh son, born with a veil, and gifted with second-sight in this American world,—a world which yields him no true self-consciousness, but only lets him see himself through the revelation of the other world. It is a peculiar sensation, this double-consciousness, this sense of always looking at one's self through the eyes of others, of measuring one's soul by the tape of a world that looks on in amused contempt and pity. One ever feels his two-ness,—an American, a Negro; two souls, two thoughts, two unreconciled strivings; two warring ideals in one dark body, whose dogged strength alone keeps it from being torn asunder.

4. For excellent discussions of this oral tradition, see Levine, and Paredes.

5. See, for example, Teish, and Hurston.

6. Bambara has said, "Writing is one of the ways I participate in the struggle—one of the ways I help to keep vibrant and resilient that vision that has kept the Family going on. Through writing I attempt to celebrate that tradition of resistance, attempt to tap Black potential, and try to join the chorus of voices that argues exploitation and misery are neither inevitable nor necessary. Writing is one of the ways I participate in the transformation—one of the ways I practice the commitment to explore bodies of knowledge for the usable wisdoms they yield" ("What It Is I Think I'm Doing Anyhow" 154).

7. See Chabram-Dernersesian.

Works Cited

Alarcón, Norma. "Chicana Feminism: In the Tracks of 'the' Native Woman." *Cultural Studies* 4.3 (1990): 248–56.

————. "The Theoretical Subject(s) of *This Bridge Called My Back* and Anglo-American Feminism." *Criticism in the Borderlands: Studies in Chicano Literature, Culture, and Ideology.* Eds. Hector Calderón and José David Saldívar. Durham, N.C. and London: Duke UP, 1991. 28–39.

Anzaldúa, Gloria. *Borderlands/La Frontera: The New Mestiza.* San Francisco: Spinsters/Aunt Lute, 1987.

Arac, Jonathan. Introduction. *Postmodernism and Politics.* Ed. Arac. Minneapolis: U of Minnesota P, 1986. ix–lviii.

Baker, Jr., Houston A. *Workings of the Spirit: The Poetics of Afro-American Women's Writing.* Chicago: U of Chicago P, 1991.

Bambara, Toni Cade. "What It Is I Think I'm Doing Anyhow." *The Writer on Her Work.* Ed. Janet Sternburg. New York: W. W. Norton, 1980. 153–68.

————. *The Salt Eaters.* 1980. New York: Vintage, 1981.

Chabram-Dernersesian, Angie. "I Throw Punches for My Race, but I Don't Want to Be a Man: Writing Us—Chica-nos (Girls/Us)/Chicanas—into the Movement Script." *Cultural Studies.* Ed. Lawrence Grossberg, Cary Nelson, and Paula A. Treichler. New York: Routledge, 1992. 81–95.

Cisneros, Sandra. "Do You Know Me? I Wrote *The House on Mango Street.*" *The Americas Review* 15.1 (1987): 78.

————. "Ghosts and Voices: Writing from Obsession." *The Americas Review* 15.1 (1987): 72.

————. *The House on Mango Street.* 1984. New York: Vintage, 1989.

Collins, Patricia Hill. *Black Feminist Thought: Knowledge, Consciousness, and the Politics of Empowerment.* 1990. New York: Routledge, 1991.

Du Bois, W. E. B. *The Souls of Black Folk.* New York: Penguin, 1989.

Fuss, Diana. *Essentially Speaking: Feminism, Nature and Difference.* New York: Routledge, 1989.

García, Mario T. *Desert Immigrants: The Mexicans of El Paso, 1880–1920.* New Haven: Yale UP, 1981.

Gates, Jr., Henry Louis. *The Signifying Monkey: A Theory of African-American Literary Criticism.* Oxford: Oxford UP, 1988.

Hughes, Langston. *The Big Sea.* 1940. New York: Hill and Wang, 1993.

Hull, Gloria T. "'What It Is I Think She's Doing Anyhow:' A Reading of Toni Cade Bambara's *The Salt Eaters.*" *Conjuring: Black Women, Fiction, and Literary Tradition.* Ed. Marjorie Pryse and Hortense Spillers. Bloomington: Indiana UP, 1985. 216–31.

Hurston, Zora Neale. *Mules and Men.* Bloomington: Indiana UP, 1978.

Levine, Lawrence W. *Black Culture and Black Consciousness.* New York: Oxford UP, 1977.

Little, William, H. W. Fowler, and Jessie Coulson, eds. *The Shorter Oxford English Dictionary on Historical Principles.* Prepared by 1973. Oxford: Oxford UP, 1985.

Morrison, Toni. "Unspeakable Things Unspoken: The Afro-American Presence in American Literature." *Michigan Quarterly Review* 28.1 (1989): 1–34.

————. "Rootedness: The Ancestor as Foundation." *Black Women Writers (1950–1980).* Ed. Mari Evans. Garden City, New York, 1984. 340–45.

————. *Sula.* New York: New American Library, 1973.

Paredes, Américo. "The Folk Base of Chicano Literature." *Modern Chicano Writers: A Collection of Critical Essays.* Ed. Joseph Sommers and Tomàs Ybarra-Frausto. Englewood Cliffs, N.J.: Prentice-Hall, 1979. 4–17.

————. *"With His Pistol in His Hand": A Border Ballad and Its Hero.* Austin: U of Texas P, 1958.

Spillers, Hortense. "Response to Deborah McDowell." *Afro-American Literary Study in the 1990s.* Ed. Houston A. Baker, Jr. and Patricia Redmond (Chicago: U of Chicago P, 1989), 71–73.

Teish, Luisah. "Women's Spirituality: A Household Act." *Homegirls: A Black Feminist Anthology.* Ed. Barbara Smith. New York: Kitchen Table, 1983. 331–35.

Viramontes, Helena María. "The Moths." *The Moths and Other Stories.* Houston: Arte Público P, 1985. 23.

Williams, Patricia. *The Alchemy of Race and Rights: Diary of a Law Professor.* Cambridge, Mass.: Harvard UP, 1991.

Young, Iris Marion. "The Ideal of Community and the Politics of Difference." *Feminism/Postmodernism.* Ed. Linda J. Nicholson. New York: Routledge, 1990.

HYBRIDITY IN THE AMERICAS
Reading Condé, Mukherjee, and Hawthorne

Bruce Simon

If there is one word postcolonial theory has disseminated throughout the U.S. academy and beyond, that word is hybridity. Yet as hybridity's currency becomes ever more widespread, familiarity with debates surrounding the term has become increasingly uneven. In the decade and a half since Homi Bhabha inaugurated hybridity's academic popularity in the United States, no other word—with the possible exception of "postcolonial" itself—has come under such scrutiny and critique.[1] Indeed, critical engagement with hybridity—which began with arguments by such critics as Abdul JanMohamed, Benita Parry, Robert Young, and Anne McClintock—has become so pronounced in recent years that it has resulted in the publication of an anthology devoted to the subject. *Debating Cultural Hybridity* (edited by Werbner and Modood), which features the work of European sociologists and anthropologists, is only the latest testament to the transatlantic scope and political stakes of recent efforts to theorize hybridity.[2] And yet, despite such a vigorous, cross-disciplinary, and international debate in and around postcolonial studies, awareness of the debate's parameters and implications lags behind the spread of the term that occasions it.

For instance, many of us interested in transforming the assumptions and institutions that shape Americanists' everyday practices have been turning to a peculiarly inflected version of "hybridity" to advance our claims. Without attempting either to defend the "purity" of hybridity's intellectual origins or to celebrate the U.S. academy's "hybridization" of the concept, I examine in this essay how those of us working in the field of race and American literature have engaged hybridity.[3] Given that Americanists (like myself) are relative latecomers to debates that began in other places and fields, our work provides a fruitful site for examining what happens to hybridity as it travels. What do Americanists mean when we write or say "hybridity"? What difference have the debates in postcolonial studies made in and to the research, pedagogy, and curricula that go under the name of American Studies?

By raising these questions, I mean to suggest that considering the stakes of the hybridity debates can be a valuable way of thinking the relation of (and relations among) such disparate but overlapping intellectual projects as American, American Indian, African American, Latin American, Chicano/a, Asian American, and postcolonial studies, studies of migrations, diasporas, nationality, and globality, of the extended Caribbean, of the Black Atlantic, of the New World, of the literatures of the Americas (to name just a few).[4] By responding to these questions, I intend to provide both a perspective on the relation between American and postcolonial studies and an example of how Americanists can engage the hybridity debates. I do this in particular by examining some of the ways in which Maryse Condé's *I, Tituba, Black Witch of Salem* and Bharati Mukherjee's *The Holder of the World* respond to Nathaniel Hawthorne's *The Scarlet Letter*. In doing so, I focus on Condé's and Mukherjee's quite different literary treatments of hybridity in the Americas and reflections on American (literary) history. My goal in offering these readings is to identify and discuss some of the most urgent theoretical, pedagogical, and curricular problems and questions that the hybridity debates have opened up, particularly for American Studies. How are we to read hybridity in the Americas? And what is at stake in contemporary deployments of—and debates over—hybridity?

HYBRID AMERICA?

Examining how recent works on race and American literature are identified, framed, and marketed to prospective readers is a fitting way to begin analyzing how "hybridity" is theorized in contemporary American literary studies. Consider, for example, the rhetoric on display in the blurb on the back cover of the collection, *Criticism and the Color Line: Desegregating American Literary Studies*, edited by Henry Wonham. Although not necessarily representative of the claims and arguments of the contributors (and in fact explicitly questioned in several of the essays), this rhetoric nevertheless represents one quite popular version of what Americanists mean by "hybridity":

> This volume celebrates the hybridity of American literary culture by examining the dynamic relationship between "mainstream" and African-American expressive traditions in America. Over the last several decades and more, students and scholars of American literary history have tended to emphasize the distinctiveness of the nation's many ethnic and cultural traditions. The contributors to this collection, no matter how varied their points of view on other matters, are less interested in racial and cultural distinctiveness than in the complex interaction of black and white voices in American writing. Engaging the work of writers from Edgar Allan Poe and Frederick Douglass to Gertrude Stein and Richard Wright, they concur in treating the color line as a site of cultural mutation where American identities are produced, not diluted, through acts of cultural exchange. The book develops new research into the rich, contentious, yet thoroughly pluralistic cultural milieu that is American literature.

Hybridity, in this account, is the name for a desegregated American literary studies.[5] Hybridity is the name for a "rich, contentious, yet thoroughly pluralistic" American literary culture. Hybridity is defined as a challenge to notions of cultural separatism and purity, as a "dynamic relationship between 'mainstream' and African-American expressive traditions" and as a "complex interaction of black and white voices in American writing." Hybridity, pluralism, and America are insistently lined up as mutually defining and practically synonymous terms in this passage. In the face of its overriding emphasis on culture, questions of politics or economics drop quietly out of the picture. Even the color line is no longer a site of political and economic exclusions and discriminations, but rather a site where hybridity happens, where a "cultural mutation" in which "American identities are produced, not diluted, through acts of cultural exchange" takes place. The back cover blurb implies that the proper response to such hybridity is celebration.

Many critics have been astounded at the facility with which hybridity can be assimilated to a model of pluralist nationalism and used as a signifier of ethnic diversity and cultural pluralism that connotes a power-blind celebration of multiplicity and difference. David Palumbo-Liu, for instance, argues that "the notion of a universal hybridization of all of us in the postmodern age seems a particular modification of the melting pot ideology"; he goes on to question the efficacy of what he sees as an attempt to revalue a term used to devalue mixedness:

> "hybrid" has a particularly disturbing history in the United States; it was popularized by the eugenics movement, a movement that authorized the forced sterilization of over twenty thousand Americans by the mid-1930s, the exclusion and deportation of countless Asians, and the proliferation of antimiscegenation laws (many still on the books) based on a violent aversion to the idea of hybridity. . . . Now, obviously the current use of the word, "hybrid" is taken precisely to reclaim and rehabilitate the notion of mixedness. However, this revisionist act seems to me to be facilitated much too smoothly, as if material history provided no point of resistance or counterpressure. (62, 59)

Palumbo-Liu challenges those who believe that simply celebrating hybridization as cultural pluralism in action is sufficient. Yet as compelling as his critique of such rhetoric is, he misses an opportunity to explore intersections between Asian Americanist and postcolonialist work by assuming that this pluralist version of hybridity is the only one.[6] To see what this assumption passes over, we must turn to earlier debates over hybridity in postcolonial studies, which begin from quite different assumptions than Americanist debates between those who would identify hybridity with America and those who would identify America with aversion to hybridity. Considering this earlier set of debates over Homi Bhabha's reading of the politics of the "English book" in colonial India can also help us better understand the significance of Mukherjee's and Condé's responses to *The Scarlet Letter* and more accurately gauge hybridity's relevance to and potential impact on American Studies.

HYBRIDITY AND ITS DISCONTENTS; OR, RE(-)CITING THE ENGLISH BOOK

Robert Young has pursued a similar approach as Palumbo-Liu's genealogical critique, but where Palumbo-Liu stops in the early twentieth century, Young pursues hybridity's origins to nineteenth-century racial science. In so doing, he corrects the assumption that hybridity means mixedness by distinguishing between two versions of cultural hybridity—"fusion" (or "merging" or "creolization," which involves "the creation of a new form") and "dialectical articulation" (or "dialogization" or "carnivalization," which produces "a radical heterogeneity, discontinuity, the permanent revolution of forms") (23–25). Yet Young insists that, however double its conceptual structure, hybridity still reveals the "connections between the racist categories of the past and contemporary cultural discourse" (27). According to Young, "'Hybrid' is the nineteenth century's word. But it has become our own again. In the nineteenth century it was used to refer to a physiological phenomenon; in the twentieth century it has become reactivated to describe a cultural one. While cultural factors determined its physiological status, the use of hybridity today prompts questions about the ways in which contemporary thinking has broken absolutely with the racialized formulations of the past" (6). And yet Young's own formulations also prompt questions: given the ongoing workings of racialized and racializing social formations in the present, is it even possible—much less desirable—to break *absolutely* with the past's racialized formulations? Could an uninterrogated ideology of color-blindness be informing his critique of the use of hybridity today?[7] Young seems to believe that rehearsing hybridity's centrality to nineteenth-century scientific racism is enough to support his claim that the term "may be used in different ways, given different inflections and apparently discrete references, but it always reiterates and reinforces the dynamics of the same conflictual economy whose tensions and divisions it reenacts in its own antithetical structure" (27). Oddly enough, however, although his stated aim is to trace "the strange and disquieting ramifications of [hybridity's] complex, forgotten past," Young hardly hesitates before announcing, "We shall not here be examining in any further detail the complex procedures of contemporary accounts of cultural hybridity" (27). But how can one trace the *ramifications* of hybridity's genealogy without attending as closely to contemporary accounts of cultural hybridity as to its past, however complex or forgotten?[8]

Besides these logical difficulties, there is a larger problem to the genealogical critiques of hybridity epitomized by Palumbo-Liu and Young. Perhaps because they limit their research to the nineteenth and twentieth centuries, they seem unaware that scientific racism's use of hybridity was itself a rearticulation of an earlier usage. According to Jack Forbes, " 'Hybrid' formerly referred to almost any type of mixture including that between 'wild' and 'tame' or between 'citizen' and 'stranger.' *Mestizo* commenced its history as an equivalent of 'hybrid' and originally was applicable to animals as well as humans, and to mixture that was religious, ethnic or cultural as well as 'racial.' . . . But in the nineteenth century, and especially after the US Civil War, greater and greater emphasis was placed upon wholly biological or 'racial' categorization and differentiation in North America" (268–69). Forbes's carefully historicized research implies that the current emphasis on cultural hybridization, rather than insufficiently breaking with racial science, might instead be something of a return to an older usage. Thus, although there is much to be said for Young's larger argument— particularly his cogent criticisms of today's dominant account of race into culture, his persuasive demonstration that postcolonialists must take into account specifically

American ideologies of race, his intensive exploration of the mutual interarticulations of race, culture, sexuality, and desire in nineteenth-century transatlantic Anglo-American culture, and the compelling cautionary tale he tells about the limits of dehistoricized anti-essentialism—still, in the end, Young fails to treat the important questions he raises as anything more than rhetorical.

To his credit, Young does specifically engage the most important contemporary rearticulation of hybridity, Homi Bhabha's "Signs Taken for Wonders," when he writes that "Bakhtin's intentional hybrid has been transformed by Bhabha into an active moment of challenge and resistance against a dominant cultural power" (22–23). But it is in the way he engages Bhabha elsewhere in his chapter that he makes a widely-shared but questionable assumption. When he implies that Bhabha may be included among those who, in "deconstructing . . . essentialist notions of race today," may only be "repeating the past [rather] than distancing ourselves from it or providing a critique of it" (27), he puts a new twist on an old criticism of Bhabha—namely, that he only attempts the deconstruction of the colonizer's discourse. Benita Parry was one of the first to argue that Bhabha participates in a poststructuralist program "marked by the exorbitation of discourse and a related incuriosity about the enabling socio-economic and political institutions and other forms of social praxis" (43). Parry offers a still-unsurpassed summary of Bhabha's theorization of hybridity and a sympathetic assessment of his project: "Bhabha's theorizing succeeds in making visible those moments when colonial discourse, already disturbed at its source by a doubleness of enunciation, is further subverted by the object of its address; when the scenario written by colonialism is given a performance by the native that estranges and undermines the colonialist script." But in the end Parry considers the moments he reveals to be merely a "textual insurrection against the discourse of colonial authority" (42). In a similar vein, Rey Chow sarcastically suggests that were we to follow Bhabha's program, "All we would need to do would be to continue to study—to deconstruct—the rich and ambivalent language of the imperialist!" (35). Although Parry credits Bhabha with revealing acts of native insurgency against colonial discourse and Chow charges Bhabha with conflating subaltern agency with the doubleness and ambivalence of the colonialist's writing, both seem to agree that he pays too much attention to colonialist language and discourse, to the exclusion of more important arenas of social antagonism and struggle.[9]

As interesting and productive as the larger questions raised by the hybridity debates are—questions about the relations between ambivalence and hybridity in Bhabha's work, between voice and agency in postcolonial studies, and between the discursive and non-discursive in contemporary theory—I must put them aside here in order to question the assumption shared by Young, Parry, and Chow that Bhabha's theorization of hybridity is merely deconstruction exported to the colonies. Instead, I would argue that Bhabha's project is a challenge to the limits and blind spots of certain French variants of poststructuralism and an attempt to transform them. A brief survey of "Signs Taken for Wonders" lends some support to this reading. Bhabha explicitly differs from Derrida's consideration of transparency and presence (108–10), challenges "current avant-garde orthodoxy" (109), mocks "theorists who engage in the battle for 'power' but do so only as purists of difference" (111), cautions against misreadings of hybridity as a celebration "of the joyous power of the signifier" (112), and distinguishes hybridity from Derridean deconstruction (115) and from "Lacan's vel" (116, 119). Those who understand Bhabha's project simply as linguistic idealism or apolitical formalism often pass over his attempts to turn the poststructuralist project into a site of contestation; he may be much more of a strategic thinker than his critics have recognized.[10]

This point is worth emphasizing in some detail; it is not just a matter of attending to the specific ways in which Bhabha deploys hybridity or to the performative as well as constative elements of his theorizing (as important as these are), but it is also a matter of identifying the strengths and limitations of his version of hybridity (the problems it addresses and the questions it raises). It is too often forgotten that "Signs Taken for Wonders" is above all a meditation on a certain "scene in the cultural writings of English colonialism": "the sudden, fortuitous discovery of the English book" (102).[11] In restaging this scene, Bhabha's aim is to uncover the "conflictual moment of colonialist intervention" usually clothed in "myths of origin and discovery" and the "constitutive discourse of exemplum and imitation," as well as to show how the "texts of the civilizing mission" get put to other uses in the colonial contest (105). Attending to the thread that links hybridity with the English book in Bhabha's essay can help us understand the stakes of the hybridity debates. What this link and these debates ask us to consider is the difference between reciting the English book and re-citing it, and the difference this difference might make.

What does the English book stand for in Bhabha's argument? With what is it associated? According to Bhabha, the scene of the English book's discovery "inaugurates a literature of empire" (102) and "sustains the discipline of Commonwealth history and its epigone, Commonwealth literature" (105). This scene's emergence coincides with a shift in the East India Company's policies from an "'Orientalist' educational practice" to a "much more interventionist and 'interpellative'" strategy of conversion (105), a strategy that entailed the "colonial construction of the cultural" as "the site of the civilizing mission" (114). The English book, that is, stands for the emergence of a new colonial conjuncture in the early nineteenth century (one that, according to Bhabha, still influences the configuration of contemporary literary studies). At the same time, Bhabha associates the English book with "effects of power" (108), "the inscription of strategies of individuation and domination" (108), "questions of authority" (109), "regulation of spaces and places," (109), "mode[s] of governance" (109), and "modes of discrimination" (111). According to Bhabha, then, the English book is metaphorically and metonymically shot through with power—both under nineteenth-century English colonialism and under the rubric of Commonwealth literature—so much so that it becomes a mode and medium of power, the power of colonial discourse.[12]

To what end does Bhabha link the scene of the discovery of the English book with the "exercise of colonialist authority" (111)? His aim is to demonstrate that this scene—which might seem to establish "a measure of mimesis and a mode of civil authority and order" and thus to "suggest the triumph of the writ of colonialist power" (107)—can be read otherwise, as a "strategy of address . . . not a proposal that you cannot positively refuse" (109). "If the appearance of the English book is read as the production of colonial hybridity," Bhabha writes, "then it no longer simply commands authority" (113). From the perspective of the colonialist, that is, the very media of the civilizing mission become estranged from their origins, the very tools of English cultural imperialism become uncannily (in)effective, so that it becomes difficult to tell what work they are doing and for whom. The English book, once the unquestioned "symbol of national authority," has been revalued as the ambivalent "sign of colonial difference" (114).

Yet this is no cause for unmitigated celebration. Certainly, Bhabha argues that the discourse of English colonialism necessarily exceeded the essentialism it appealed to in order to underwrite "the presence of authority as an immediate mimetic effect" (111). To be sure, he emphasizes that even the more aggressive colonialist authority that emerged in the early nineteenth century could not simply command or repress, but instead "require[d] the production of differentiations, individuations, identity effects[,] . . . modes of discrimination (cultural, racial, administrative . . .) that disallow a stable unitary assumption of collectivity" (111). But all this means is that socio-political conditions in India prevented English colonialists from relying on old means of domination. That the practice of English colonialism demonstrates the limits of essentialism is of small solace when we consider, with Bhabha, that "the effect of colonial power is . . . the production of hybridization" (112). That is, colonial power works precisely through the "articulation of 'differentiatory,' discriminatory differences" (111–12); the business of colonialism is the production of hybrid subjectivities. Hybridity is constituted (although not fully determined) by colonial power: "the colonial hybrid is the articulation of the ambivalent space where the rite of power is enacted on the site of desire, making its objects at once disciplinary and disseminatory" (112).

But this is not the end of the story. For while hybridity is "the sign of the productivity of colonial power, its shifting forces and fixities," it is also "the name for the strategic reversal of the process of domination through disavowal[,] . . . a form of subversion . . . that turns the discursive conditions of dominance into the grounds of intervention" (112). Because the knowledges of colonial authority are deprived of their full presence, they "may be articulated with forms of 'native' knowledges or faced with those discriminated subjects which they must rule but can no longer represent. . . . This may lead, as in the case of the natives outside Delhi, to questions of authority that the authorities—the Bible included—cannot answer" (115). By emphasizing "the subversive character of the native questions" in the closing pages of his argument (116–22), Bhabha closes on the note of native resistance, the unexpected interrogation of the English book in the midst of the civilizing mission. Re-citing the book introduces a colonial difference: "Hybridity is a problematic of colonial representation and individuation that reverses the effects of the colonialist disavowal, so that other 'denied' knowledges enter upon the dominant discourse and estrange the basis of its authority—its rules of recognition" (114). Thus, even as the English book is intimately involved in the production of hybridity (as a "partial presence, a [strategic] device in a specific colonial engagement, an appurtenance of authority" [114–15]), it also becomes hybridized and becomes a site of contestation at the same time.

Bhabha's re-citation of the scene of the appearance or discovery of the English book, then, aims to disclose the intricate ways in which power is at work and at stake under colonialism, the ways it is both challenged by and implicated in hybridity. By restaging this oft-repeated scene—performing another variation on it, citing it in a new context—Bhabha calls on us to attend as closely to what he is doing as to what he is describing. What he describes asks us to consider the difference between reciting the English book and re-citing it, as well as the difference this difference—if it exists—makes (if any). And what he enacts is itself a repetition of that which he describes. In other words, Bhabha both describes and enacts hybridity in "Signs Taken for Wonders." In much the same way that the Indian natives' questions resulted in and took advantage of the hybridization of the English book, the questions Bhabha poses attempt the hybridization of French theory.

And yet, even if understood as conscious deployment rather than unconscious repetition, as strategic intervention rather than theoreticist formalism, Bhabha's rearticulation of hybridity is still open to question. In fact, the debate over Bhabha's theorizing of hybridity has made three questions in particular unavoidable today. What if, much as English colonialists in the early nineteenth century fetishized the English book as a symbol of national authority, U.S. academics in the late twentieth century may be in danger of fetishizing the hybridization of the Anglo/American book as a sign of political resistance? What are hybridity's political valences in the age of transnational capital, a conjuncture in which "globalization," not "the civilizing mission," is the dominant narrative in the ongoing (neo)colonial construction of the cultural? And what does it mean to translate hybridity from its colonial context, to redeploy a term with such a checkered past—and what responsibilities might such acts of translation and rearticulation entail?

To read Maryse Condé's *I, Tituba, Black Witch of Salem* and Bharati Mukherjee's *The Holder of the World* in relation to Nathaniel Hawthorne's *The Scarlet Letter* is to confront these questions directly. How? First, both Condé and Mukherjee have been identified with hybridity in the course of their careers. Timothy Brennan, for instance, argues that Mukherjee has issued a "declaration of cultural 'hybridity'—a hybridity claimed to offer certain advantages in negotiating the collisions of language, race and art in a world of disparate peoples comprising a single, if not exactly unified, world" (35). Similarly, many critics have attempted to situate Condé in Caribbean literary debates over *antillanité* and *créolité*, or demonstrated the ways her works challenge and exceed such classifications. Second, and more important, Condé's and Mukherjee's novels put the various meanings and histories of hybridity into dialogue, even as each enacts a different version of cultural hybridity. Thus, an attempt to discern the cultural work the two novels do—which necessarily includes but is not limited to their authors' positions and interventions in the hybridity debates—can help us formulate our own answers to the truly open and pressing questions those debates have raised.

Hybridizing Hawthorne; Or, Rewriting the New English Book

Maryse Condé's sixth novel, *I, Tituba, Black Witch of Salem*, was originally published in 1986 as *Moi, Tituba, sorcière . . . Noire de Salem*. Translated into English in 1992 by

Condé's husband, Richard Philcox, *Tituba* is the narrative of a slave, told by herself, from her conception on board an English slave ship en route to Barbados in the late 1600s, to her persecution as both a slave and a witch in Puritan New England, her friendship with Hawthorne's Hester Prynne, her execution in Barbados for fomenting a slave rebellion, and beyond.[13] Bharati Mukherjee's fourth novel, *The Holder of the World*, published in 1993, is the life story of a late-seventeenth-century Puritan woman who travels to England and colonial India and back to the American colonies, as told by Beigh Masters, a current-day daughter of the Puritans, who closes her narrative with a disquisition on the origins of *The Scarlet Letter*.[14] What does it mean to claim—as we might be tempted to—that Condé's *I, Tituba, Black Witch of Salem* and Mukherjee's *The Holder of the World* hybridize Hawthorne? Is it possible and desirable to translate Bhabha's deployment of hybridity to the terrain of the Americas? How might the hybridity debates in postcolonial studies enable Americanists to rethink what it means for Condé and Mukherjee to engage *The Scarlet Letter*?

Before the hybridity debates, it might have been sufficient simply to celebrate how Condé and Mukherjee bring issues of slavery, colonialism, race, gender, sexuality, and power to bear on American colonial history that Hawthorne either was unwilling or unable to address, or addressed obliquely or directly, but in limited ways. Condé and Mukherjee's interrogations of such notions as the "errand into the wilderness" and the "Puritan origins of the American self" could be read as showing the Puritan tradition in American letters to be only one among many, a kind of immigrant literature of its own. Their novels could be said to be recovering silenced perspectives and reimagining American history from the perspective of the disenfranchised. It is not that these readings are wrong—and, indeed, I will be making such claims in the course of this section—but that now, in the wake of the hybridity debates, it is incumbent upon us to ask finer-tuned questions: what are the differences between Condé's and Mukherjee's rewritings of Hawthorne? what versions of hybridity do we find in their novels? and what difference do these differences make? In short, it is not simply *that* Condé and Mukherjee hybridize Hawthorne but *how* and *to what ends* they do so that is the most important line of inquiry today.

Let me very schematically indicate some of the major differences between the novels. Conde's novel examines a north-south divide; Mukherjee's an east-west one. Where *Tituba* explores the links between Puritan New England and the Anglophone West Indies by emphasizing slavery in the Americas, *Holder* links seventeenth-century New England with seventeenth-century India by focusing on the span of the British empire. Although both novelists use the wanderings of their protagonists to move their narratives across the divides they each emphasize, Condé brings to the foreground the presence of blacks in New England, while Mukherjee exploits the ambiguity of the phrase, "Puritans and Indians." Where Condé rewrites the history of the Salem witch trials to put racism at its core, Mukherjee rewrites both American literary history and the origins of national independence to emphasize Indian influences. On the question of representing America, Condé strategically accepts the thesis of the Puritan origins of the American self in order to emphasize continuities of racism in the U.S. By showing Puritans suppressing others on the basis of race, gender, and religion, she argues that not much has changed in three hundred years in terms of

U.S. racism.[15] By contrast, Mukherjee hybridizes the origins of America, refusing to accept the thesis of an unalloyed Puritan origin. In so doing, she resituates Puritans as subjects for immigrant literature and rewrites the captivity narrative at the same time.[16]

One of the more striking differences between the two novels is the divergent uses to which Condé and Mukherjee put the first person point-of-view, the most obvious revision of the third-person voice in *The Scarlet Letter*. Both first-person narrators have a strong sense of needing to redress historical distortions, invisibilities, and silences, but that is where the similarities end. Tituba proleptically rails against her exclusion from the historical record:

> It seemed that I was gradually being forgotten. I felt that I would only be mentioned in passing in these Salem witchcraft trials about which so much would be written later, trials that would arouse the curiosity and pity of generations to come as the greatest testimony of a superstitious and barbarous age. There would be mention here and there of "a slave originating from the West Indies and probably practicing 'hoodoo.'" There would be no mention of my age or my personality, I would be ignored. As early as the end of the seventeenth century, petitions would be circulated, judgments made, rehabilitating the victims, restoring their honor, and returning their property to their descendants. I would never be included! Tituba would be condemned forever! There would never, ever, be a careful, sensitive biography recreating my life and its suffering. (110)

Tituba's prediction of this "future injustice" is confirmed and made a symbol of the history of slavery by the spirit of her foster father Yao, who in Cesairean fashion tells her: "Our memory will have to be covered in blood. . . . Our memories will have to float to the surface like water lilies" (165). By contrast, Mukherjee's narrator, Beigh Masters, sets out to redress the misrepresentations of "a person undreamed of in Puritan society" (59): "Most books take a racy interest in a white divorcée, more rumor than fact, who consorted with a Hindu noble. They call her an adventuress of obscure origins, a pirate's wife who comes off less well than the socially prominent Sarah Bradley, widow of the hanged William Kidd" (258). Beigh's reasons for reconstructing Hannah's history are intensely personal—the asset hunter is involved with Venn Iyer, a virtual reality pioneer from India—and, as she puts it, she and Venn "remember what happened to Hannah Easton Fitch Legge a.k.a. the Bibi from Salem so that we may predict what will happen to us within our lifetime" (91). Where Condé lets Tituba tell her own story, Mukherjee's emphasis is as much on the one reconstructing the history as on the reconstructed historical figure. Where Condé's project is to reimagine the life and voice of a black woman born to slavery, Mukherjee's is to reconceptualize whiteness.

Furthermore, where Condé wants Tituba's tale to be representative of the hidden history of slavery, Mukherjee wants Beigh's narrative to represent and enact a difference in New England letters. Condé expressly tries to retell the story of the Salem witch trials from Tituba's perspective, reshaping the conventions of the African-American slave narrative in the process. Her efforts to signify on the tradition of black first-person narrative are ironically emphasized in the American edition of *Tituba*, which contains not only an author's note from Maryse Condé (in which she implies that she is taking the position of an abolitionist ghostwriter to Tituba's escaped slave), but also an authenticating letter from none other than Angela Davis (ix-xi).[17] To top it off, the first paragraph contains one of the most famous and repeated clauses in all of African American writing, "I was born" (3). Like Condé, Mukherjee is out to rewrite American colonial history, but where Condé retells the story of the Salem witch trials by signifying on the conventions of the slave narrative, Mukherjee is much more interested in subverting colonialist historiography—and an entire tradition of New England letters—from within. Beigh Masters names Rowlandson, Hawthorne, and Pynchon at various points in the narrative, cites two versions of a Puritan hymn, and merges this literary tradition with adventure tales and Indian mythology. Mukherjee's blending of the captivity narrative with the story of Sita emphasizes cross-cultural continuities between East and West, whereas Condé's telling the story of the Salem witch trials through the conventions of the slave narrative displaces the colonialist historiographical tradition.[18]

But far and away the clearest distinction between the two novels is the divergent uses to which they put Hawthorne's protagonist, Hester Prynne. In *Tituba*, Hester is an unashamedly anachronistic figure—a kind of caricature of "global sisterhood" white American feminists—even as she becomes one of Tituba's only close friends, one whose suicide affects her deeply.[19] Hence, at the same moment Condé remains quite faithful to Hawthorne—whose ambivalence (at best) toward antebellum feminists and reformers shaped his portrayal of the ostensibly seventeenth-century Hester—she also takes up one of the most famous characters in American literature cavalierly and, in effect, kills her off. Although Hester reappears after her death as one of Tituba's "invisibles," and although Tituba's narrative closes with a vision of the two spirits remaining "on her side of the ocean," pursuing related but separate liberationist projects (178), Hester is but one of many people Tituba encounters in her hemispheric travels, neither more nor less important than Abena, Yao, Mama Yaya, John Indian, Susanna Endicott, Samuel and Elizabeth Parris, Benjamin Cohen d'Azevedo, Christopher, and Iphegene. Making Hester a stand-in for rehearsing tensions between white feminists and women of color is the clearest possible signal that Condé is not interested in inscribing herself in the American literary canon, but is instead selectively appropriating various literary traditions and incorporating them into her own revisionary interventions into Afro-diasporic literature.

By contrast, Mukherjee invokes Hawthorne's Hester in order to claim New England and American literary traditions as her own. At the simplest level, she has Hannah and Jadav Singh face a similar choice as Hester and Dimmesdale in *The Scarlet Letter*—whether to flee West or not—although this time the suggested flight is *from* "Indian" territory, rather than *to* it. At another level, Mukherjee's narrator Beigh Masters asks at the end of *Holder*, "Who can blame Nathaniel Hawthorne for shying away from the real story of the brave Salem mother and her illegitimate daughter?" (284). In Beigh's reconstruction of American (literary) history, Hawthorne picked up stories of Rebecca, Hannah, and their children from his grandfather, the seafaring Joseph Hathorne (the son of the very witchcraft judge who had made a cameo appearance in *Tituba*), who heard the story of her life from Hannah's own mouth. Thus,

Mukherjee makes the characters whose lives her narrator reconstructs the historical sources of Hawthorne's Hester Prynne and Pearl—both the Rebecca/Hannah and White Pearl/Black Pearl relationships in *Holder* parallel the Hester/Pearl relationship in *The Scarlet Letter*. Hence Hester is a combination of Rebecca and Hannah, and Pearl of the women the town gossips named White Pearl and Black Pearl (284). Mukherjee puts hybridity as miscegenation at the core of *The Scarlet Letter*.[20]

But Mukherjee is not content to draw on a Hawthornean scene or posit her characters as two of the more-than-New England sources of *The Scarlet Letter*, for in *Holder*, she also encodes "Hester" as a floating signifier disclosing complicated desires. "Hester" is the name of Hannah's closest friend in colonial Salem. Hester Manning, who dies early in the novel under mysterious circumstances, "would only go halfway round the world with [Hannah's future husband, Gabriel Legge], the tiresome, well-trod half, to England" (68).[21] "Hester" is also the name Hannah gives to her closest friend in Fort St. Sebastian, the Hindu woman who first appears as Hannah's servant with the name Bhagmati, whose name we discover was bestowed by her former master and lover, the Englishman Henry Hedges. The woman born Bindu Bashini is buried as Hester Hedges (97), with, as we discover with Beigh at the end of the novel, the most perfect diamond in the world—the Emperor's Tear—hidden in her body.[22]

This scene is crucial to Mukherjee's project in *Holder*, for it gets to the heart, so to speak, of her linking of Puritan and Indian traditions. Thanks to Venn, Beigh Masters is able to enter virtual reality in search of the Emperor's Tear; she returns as Bindu Bashini/Bhagmati/Hester in the middle of the final battle between the Mughal emperor Aurangzeb and Hannah's lover, Raja Jadav Singh. This is a surprise—throughout her narrative Beigh had overtly identified with Hannah, yet when push comes to shove, she returns as the Hindu woman with the Puritan name. Taking on the role of the self-immolating subject, Beigh/Bindu Bashini/Bhagmati/Hester commits suicide in the middle of the battlefield, taking the Emperor's Tear "with" her to "her" grave, where, Beigh is certain when she comes out of VR, it still lies. What remains is an interesting chain of interlinked and layered figures: the actual author, Bharati Mukherjee, tells a story through the voice of the "fictional" Beigh Masters, who in "virtual reality" appears as a "historical" Hindu woman, Bindu Bashini/Bhagmati, is addressed as "Hester" by Hannah, and calls Hannah her "Pearl." It is thus no coincidence that Bharati Mukherjee and Beigh Masters not only share the same initials, but also part of a last name (Mukherjee means "master of liberation"). The tangled chains of projection and identification in this last scene demonstrate the ways that hybridity for Mukherjee is always a matter of desire, ambivalence, and the blurring and crossing of borders.

The multiple referential passage in which Beigh Masters claims that Hawthorne was only able to "touch and briefly bring alive the first letter of an alphabet of hope and of horror stretching out, and back to the uttermost shores" emblematizes Mukherjee's hybridizing narrative strategy (286). On the one hand, the Salem Bibi appropriates the Puritan form of punishment, reinscribing Hawthorne's "first letter of an alphabet of hope and of horror" in the process: "When she bathed, she tattooed a pink alphabet of guilt all over her body with the fibrous roots Bhagmati had taught her to use as cleansing agents" (230). On the other, Masters's "uttermost shores"

takes us back to the two versions of the psalm which made such an impact on the
twelve-year-old Hannah:

*Aske thou of me, and I will give the Heathen for thy lot; and of the earth thou shalt possess the
utmost coasts abroad* (The Bay Psalm Book of 1640).

*Desire of me, and I shall give thee the heathen for thine inheritance; and the utmost parts of the
earth for thy possession* (Psalms 2:8) (43).

Masters muses, "Ask or desire—what's the difference, anyway? Except. Except that
'ask' suggests aggression and self-righteousness. It seems like a clash of the sexes, a
triumph of pioneer virility. . . . Did Philip's Wampanoag warriors and Rebecca's Nipmuc lover suffer as they went from 'inheritance' to 'lot' in Puritan vocabulary?" (43–
44). Not only does Masters read the politics of gender and race between the lines of
these early articulations of manifest destiny, she also considers the sampler Hannah
created to illustrate these lines to be "the first native American response to a world
that could be African or Indian or anything not American" (44). Masters celebrates
Hannah's talent for—precisely—hybridity: the appropriation of a form meant to be
prayed to and to prove one's marriageability as instead "the embodiment of desire"
(44), so that even "at bedtimes when she knelt by it to pray, it shot the familiar virtues
she prayed for—humility, gratitude, meekness—with a pagan iridescence" (45).
Twice, then, Masters implicitly compares Hawthorne's "morbid introspection into
guilt and repression" with the desire, energy, and vibrancy of Hannah's art, inspired
by both a vision and an experience of the Orient, and finds it lacking (286). Thus
the judgment of his own countrywoman condemns Hawthorne—Hannah is a truer
American, truer because more hybrid. That Hannah and her daughter Pearl Singh
also agitate for American independence is the final touch, literalizing Mukherjee's
theme of the Puritan-Indian origins of the American self.

It might seem, then, that the major difference between *Tituba* and *Holder* is in their
relation to and uses of hybridity. That is, it would be plausible to argue that Condé
resists white hegemony through an expressly liberationist account of the Salem witch
trials—emphasizing slave resistance, agency, and world-view, and putting the witch
trials in the larger context of her protagonist's travels through the Americas—where
Mukherjee is out to diversify American history, to rewrite the American book, to
refigure New England colonial history and literature. Yet this kind of reading passes
over the subtle workings of Condé's engagement with hybridity. It is not that one
novel is about hybridity and the other is not; it is that the novels differ most fundamentally in their deployments of hybridity.

Although Condé, like Mukherjee, focuses on interracial desire—Tituba and her
Jewish lover Benjamin Cohen d'Azevedo join Hannah and Jadav Singh, Rebecca and
her Nipmuc lover, and Beigh and Venn in demonstrating that hybridity (in the nineteenth-century sense of amalgamation or miscegenation) does not preclude love—she
does not romanticize the material conditions of the production of hybridity under
slavery: "Abena, my mother, was raped by an English sailor on the deck of Christ the
King one day in the year 16** while the ship was sailing for Barbados. I was born
from this act of aggression. From this act of hatred and contempt" (3). Hybridity is

never an unmitigated good in Condé's fictional universe; rather, it is the product of what Gayatri Chakravorty Spivak has called "enabling violation," which leaves the hybrid subject trying to "change something that one is obliged to inhabit."[23]

Condé also thematizes cultural hybridity. In the epigraph to *Tituba*, she cites the Puritan poet John Harrington, whose verse—"Death is a porte whereby we pass to joye;/Lyfe is a lake that drowneth all in payne" (vii)—expresses an African cosmology that Tituba herself espouses. For instance, Tituba matter-of-factly reports on the aftermath of a fatal beating: "They buried him at the foot of a majagua tree. Then everyone rejoiced because at least one of us had been delivered and was on his way home" (7). In a similar vein, Benjamin Cohen d'Azevedo's daughter speaks to him and Tituba from the spirit world, saying, "Death is in truth the greatest fulfillment" (135). But even as Tituba treats the death of Mama Yaya, her protector and mentor, philosophically—"I did not cry when I buried her. I knew I was not alone and that three spirits were now watching over me" (10)—in the course of the narrative we discover Tituba to be so deeply affected by the deaths of her loved ones, Abena and Hester in particular, that she without hesitation describes her future disappearance from the historical record as "more cruel than death itself" (110). African and Puritan attitudes toward death cross, intersect, and migrate in *Tituba*.

Beyond these thematizations of hybridity as sexual or cultural amalgamation, Condé's narrative strategy itself is triply hybrid. By bringing alternative epistemologies and value systems to bear on Puritan and Anglo assumptions, Condé effectively turns the "discursive conditions of dominance into the grounds of intervention"—one of Bhabha's definitions of hybridity.[24] As Jeanne Garane explains: "Contrary to Ann Petry, whose Tituba possesses no supernatural abilities, Condé embraces the accusation, and makes it the very space from which Tituba opposes both patriarchal colonial discourse and cultural imperialism" (157).[25] Those unfamiliar with Condé's writings might be tempted to interpret this move as supplanting a kind of Eurocentrism with a kind of Afrocentrism, but witchcraft, it turns out, is the very engine—and emblem—of hybridity in *Tituba*. Tituba learns her craft from an old woman whose husband and two sons had been tortured and executed for instigating a slave revolt: "She was not an Ashanti like my mother and Yao, but a Nago from the coast, whose name, Yetunde, had been creolized into Mama Yaya" (9). "Under her guidance," Tituba continues, "I attempted bold hybrids, cross-breeding the *passiflorinde* with the *prune taureau*, the poisonous *pomme cythère* with the surette, and the *azalée-des-azalées* with the *persulfureuse*" (11). What the Nago healer teaches Tituba is the practice of hybridity. After Tituba accompanies John Indian to Puritan New England, she finds herself following Mama Yaya's proverb—"When you get to the blind man's country, close both eyes" (54)—and hybridizing her practice of witchcraft still further: "What was I going to do in this unknown and inhospitable land across the sea? I decided to make substitutions. A maple tree whose foliage was turning red would do for a silk-cotton tree. Glossy, spiny holly leaves would replace the Guinea grass. Yellow, odorless flowers would do for the *salapertuis*, the panacea for all the body's ills, which only grows in the foothills back home" (45). Cross-breeding, making substitutions, this is what witchcraft is all about in *Tituba*. Yet Condé has planted an additional intricate joke in these scenes, for the *passiflorinde*, the *prune taureau*, the *azalée-des-azalées*, the *persulfur-*

euse, and the *salapertuis* are each, according to the novel's glossary, "a literary invention by the author" (185–186).[26] Not only is there always mixing and substituting going on in *Tituba,* but it turns out that the "originals" being mixed are usually inventions. Hybridity, for Condé, is not simply the mixture of opposites but also the exposure of the myth that pure opposites exist in the first place.

Even as I emphasize Condé's deployments of hybridity in *Tituba,* I do not want to underplay the extent to which Mukherjee is, at times, interrogating hybridity in *Holder.* Recall, after all, that Hannah's sampler is literally made possible by colonialism, for its threads come from "Bandar Abbas, Batavia, Bimlipatam" (44). Thus, when Beigh Masters says that "The result is, for me, one of the great colonial samplers" (44), Mukherjee may be doing something much different than endorsing her narrator's appreciation of a fine collector's item. What's more, it is Hannah's foster parents' "aborigiphobic son" Thomas—the man to whom "Hannah's education was wholly entrusted"—who frames her sampler "in the finest cherrywood left over from the chest he had made for the fearsome old magistrate, the twisted John Hathorne (whose excesses in the witch trials would so torment his descendant, Nathaniel Hawthorne)" (39, 43, 45). Thus, what Beigh recognizes as Hannah's strategy of hybridity is both made possible by the world system of colonial exchange and is literally framed in the Americas by the representatives of a racist and repressive colonialist regime, a regime, it turns out, for whom sentiments expressed by White and Black Pearl (such as "We are Americans to freedom born") were "considered advantageous to the maintenance of social order" (285). What remains open to question in these implicit critiques of hybridity is whether Mukherjee sees the American Revolution that Hannah and Pearl advocate as a break with or as a continuation of Anglocentric colonialism. If Hannah's sampler is the first "native American" response to the world's diversity, then Mukherjee seems to be implying that the hybridity it represents and enacts can and should be freed from the repressive frame that surrounds it.[27] By putting emphasis on Beigh's recognition that Hannah's "pure vision . . . has now become commodified," surviving only in "the private collection of a Hollywood mogul, son of a Dachau survivor," Mukherjee has created in the history of Hannah's sampler an emblem of a potentially revolutionary yet actually embedded and commodified hybridity (44, 45).[28]

If this is so, then even Mukherjee's interrogative moments are not directed at hybridity, but at the ways it has been misrecognized, repressed, and commodified in America. Although Condé, too, posits cultural hybridity as an alternative to a racist Puritan regime, she refuses to romanticize it, instead linking hybridization with the rape of black women under slavery. Thus, although the two novelists have addressed every aspect of the hybridity debates—the conjunction and co-production of culture and power, hybridity as an ambivalent strategy of resistance and as an unruly product of colonialism, the links between cultural hybridity and hybridity as a synonym for amalgamation or miscegenation, the question of hybridity in the Americas—they have done so from different positions and to different ends. Condé aims at hybridizing African American, and Mukherjee, New England, literary traditions. Condé theorizes opposition and hybridity together, where Mukherjee relates hybridity to personal transformation. Slavery drops out of Mukherjee's exploration of Puritan-Indian connections, where a shared experience of hybridization by marginalized seventeenth-century characters becomes a prelude to information-age America. For Condé, by contrast, the enslaved African woman in the New World is the figure and emblem of hybridity-as-condition-and-survival-strategy. Condé and Mukherjee also differ in their takes on the relation between hybridity and America; where Condé sees the U.S. as consistently rejecting hybridity (and imprisoning those who do not do so), Mukherjee sees hybridity as both America's (rejected) past and its (possible) future. In short, Mukherjee's recasting of Americanization as hybridization and Condé's attempt to articulate cultural hybridity with a radical view of New World history and with oppositional politics each represent and enact different versions of hybridity. So what is at stake in these differences? How do Condé's and Mukherjee's creative reinscriptions comment on the state of American Studies and on the hybridity debates?

HYBRIDITY AND PEDAGOGY; OR, RETHINKING AMERICAN STUDIES

Perhaps the best way to approach the question of hybridity's stakes is through the problematic of pedagogy. After all, Bhabha's "Signs Taken for Wonders" charts a shift in English pedagogical strategy in early nineteenth-century India. So what is the relation between pedagogy and hybridity today? By considering what work we can do in teaching *Tituba* and *Holder* with *The Scarlet Letter*, and by analyzing the representations of pedagogy in the novels, we can begin to think through the curricular and institutional issues Condé's and Mukherjee's rewritings of *The Scarlet Letter* and the hybridity debates have raised.

How, where, and whether we teach *Holder* and *Tituba* matters.[29] Take the problem of symmetrical reversal in Mukherjee's novel. Clearly, *Holder* reverses the pattern set in Mukherjee's earlier works, where a wide range of immigrants come to America and survive violent and rapid changes on their way to becoming American ethnics. This time, it's white women experiencing diversity and self-transformation—Beigh Masters reconstructs the life story of a Puritan woman who goes from being called Hannah Easton to Hannah Fitch to Hannah Legge to Salem Bibi to Mukta to Precious-as-Pearl to White Pearl. What is the status of this reversal of Mukherjee's typical transformation plot? To be sure, *Holder* provides evidence of an ambitious literary project—to sequentially inhabit and transform several traditions of writing, including expatriate/diasporic Indian-English writing, Canadian and American immigrant literatures, multiethnic literatures, and, now, New England letters.[30] But does *Holder* remain open to the same kind of critiques earlier works like *Jasmine* and *The Middleman and Other Stories* have elicited? Is Mukherjee's applying the pattern of violent mutability from her earlier works to the experiences of a white Puritan woman an adequate answer to charges that she orientalizes Indian history, exoticizes non-European immigrants, evades ethico-political issues, elides specificity, struggle, and conflict, naturalizes her privilege, and homogenizes different differences?[31]

One reading of *Holder* would suggest that Mukherjee's strategy of reversal repeats many of the same problems of her earlier fiction. In fact, it would be quite easy to read the novel as a form of diversity management, a way of encouraging student readers to overcome their fears of change and difference, a way of promoting the

pleasures of multiculturalism in predominantly white institutions of higher education.[32] Consider the different stages of Hannah's experience of the world that Beigh
identifies. Hannah changes from being a "pure product of her time and place, her
marriage and training, exposed to a range of experience that would be extreme even
in today's world, but none of it, consciously, had sunk in or affected her outer behavior" (220), to experiencing a "moment's sharp awareness, *My God, they're alive!*" upon
realizing suddenly that "Bhagmati had had a vital life, distinct from waiting on *firangi*
households" (222), and finally to realizing, when she is with Jadav Singh: "how inap-
propriate it was in India—how fatal—to cling, as White Towns tenaciously did, to
Europe's rules. She was no longer the woman she had been in Salem or London. The
qsbas and villages of Roopconda bore no resemblance to the fading, phantom landscapes where she'd lived in Old and New England. Everything was in flux on the
Coromandel coastline. The survivor is the one who improvises, not follows, the rules
(234). Given this progression, many readers will find it no surprise that the one quality
of Hannah's that Beigh most admires and that makes Hannah "entirely our contemporary in mood and sensibility" is "the sheer pleasure she took in the world's variety"
(104). It is entirely plausible to read *Holder* as a paean to pluralism, a celebration of
diversity.

On the other hand, an alternative reading of *Holder* would attempt to contextualize
and historicize Beigh's brief discussions of colonialism, to frame Mukherjee's impres-
sionistic globalization of the question of colonial history. Such a reading could discuss
the ways Mukherjee links issues of race, hygiene, and economics: "It was proven that
the most profitable factories—trading posts—were those that enforced the rules of
order and cleanliness" (99).[33] It could explore how Holder illustrates the materiality
of desire: "Fort St. George, Fort St. Sebastian, Fort St. Joseph, Fort St. Luke: they are
monuments to stern-souled, gouty-toed and chilblained Englishmen's sudden submission to the flame-tipped arrows of a dark-skinned Eros. Love dictates the pattern of
streets and walls; its aftermath invites demographic upheaval" (105).[34] Above all, it
could flesh out Beigh's contrasts between English colonialism in the Americas and in
India: "Perhaps, beguiled by the fecundity, the can't-miss promise of preexistent riches
like gold and jewels, the British in India felt no compulsion to search long and hard,
as they had in the New World, for ideal harbors and salubrious settings. They had
not come to India in order to breed and colonize, or even to convert. They were here
to plunder" (99). After all, Beigh first views 1690s India through the lens of capitalist
booms in the United States of the 1890s, 1920s, and 1980s (101), but later reverses
the analogy when it becomes clear (due to her own virtual meeting with Hannah) that
Venn's VR scheme works: "They'll miniaturize it, pump up its power, and twenty
years from now little girls in Burma will be working on assembly lines turning out
time-space laser disks. Venn and Jay will pocket their awards, MIT will prosper on
the patent and maybe buy out Harvard, and the rest belongs to the heirs of the
Coromandel factors, the franchisers and marketers jockeying for market share" (278).
In this reading, that is, *Holder* might actually provide an opportunity to examine
continuities between the history of colonialism and contemporary strategies of flexible
accumulation.[35] Perhaps Mukherjee's emphasis on the hybrid individual who takes

pleasure in the world's diversity is the only alternative she can envision to an economic system that may be the true holder of the world in her imagination.[36]

Condé's reenvisioning of Tituba's life raises a similar problem of historiography and pedagogy, for Americanists have built a strong case that the historical Tituba was neither black nor a witch. Chadwick Hansen, Robert Morsberger, and Bernard Rosenthal have traced the transformation of Tituba in the historical record from being a Carib Indian practitioner of English magic, to a half-Indian, half-black practitioner of Indian magic, to a "Negro practicing voodoo" (Hansen 3).[37] Most recently, Elaine Breslaw has argued that the most plausible account of Tituba's origins has her as an Arawak captured by a European raiding party in Guiana and brought to Barbados as a slave (3–62).[38] Similarly, noting that stories associating Tituba with witchcraft or voodoo did not emerge until the nineteenth century, Rosenthal argues that "Tituba remains in our mythology as the dark woman, the alien, who enters the Puritan world and plunges it into chaos. The myth of dark Tituba recapitulates with an American tint the myth of original sin, the archetypal tale of the woman as progenitor of evils to come" (13–14). Hansen draws a lesson for white liberals from these myths about Tituba: "We are not free of racism, and we will not be free of it until we recognize, among other things, that beliefs and practices which we regard as superstitious do not necessarily have racial boundaries—until we recognize, in short, that witchcraft, when it is found in New England, is more likely to be English in origin than Indian or Negro" (12). Does Condé's novel simply reinscribe these nineteenth-century narratives and reinforce liberal racism?

Only if *Tituba* is read as a counter-history making a strong claim to referentiality, rather than a challenge to an entire historiographical tradition, can this question be answered in the affirmative. Condé stresses that "For me *Tituba* is not a historical novel. *Tituba* is just the opposite of a historical novel. I was not interested at all in what her real life could have been" (Scarboro 200–01). Her narrative strategy in *Tituba*, that is, is not to correct the historical record, but instead to reorient it. Condé's Tituba—half-English, half-Ashanti, with a name invented by her step-father, brought up and educated by a Nago, married to a half-Arawak, half-Nago slave named John Indian, and practitioner of a "witchcraft" which is itself triply hybridized—negotiates her hybrid subjectivity as she negotiates the cultural, social, economic, and political realities of slavery and colonialism in the New World. Condé does not turn away from the task of exposing and critiquing the kinds of white racism Hansen indicts, but she starts from an assumption of hybridity, not pure, easily recognizable identity. Where Hansen and Morsberger assume that what is behind Tituba's transformations is historical revisionism, Condé calls into question what they assume to be the facts of the case.[39] The point is not to engage in a futile debate over whether Tituba was "really" "red" or "black," but to recognize, with Angela Davis, that "When Tituba takes her place in the history of the Salem witch trials, the recorded history of that era—and indeed the entire history of the colonization process—is revealed to be seriously flawed" (x).[40] Whatever Tituba's racial identity as it would be understood today, Davis suggests, the point is that the Salem witch trials are not only of local or national significance, but are inextricably imbricated with a colonial system that extends throughout the New World.

Condé and Mukherjee do not only implicitly point the way to research and courses that put New England and the U.S. in an international frame, but they also put serious pedagogical issues on the table, for it is not simply a question of how to teach their novels, but to what ends we teach them. The representations of pedagogy in *Holder* and *Tituba* suggest that the stakes here are high. After all, Mukherjee emphasizes that her Puritan protagonist's "education was wholly entrusted" to a recent convert to the metaphysics of Indian-hating who literally frames Hannah's hybrid art (43). And Condé puts a scene of torture and rape precisely in pedagogical terms; according to the Puritan ministers who set out to extract from Tituba a confession and a denunciation of her accomplices, they need her testimony even though others have already made such accusations because "Children talk in childish ways. We shall soon teach them not to forget the important points. And you'll be the first lesson" (91). Mukherjee opposes Hannah's hybridity to Thomas Fitch's racist pedagogy. Condé emphasizes that the disciplining of Tituba (and by implication the production and containment of hybridity) is an object lesson in the reproduction of Puritan social relations.

Even as they suggest the wider stakes of pedagogy, both novelists also suggest alternatives to the pedagogy of Thomas Fitch and Samuel Parris. Condé locates hybridity in the Americas and through Tituba calls for a pedagogy of the oppressed: "I am hardening men's hearts to fight. I am nourishing them with dreams of liberty. Of victory. I have been behind every revolt. Every insurrection. Every act of disobedience" (175). From the spirit world Tituba chooses her own daughter and teaches her how to read hybridity: "I teach her to look for the invisible shapes in the world, the crisscross of communications, and the signs and the symbols" (177). Where Condé's mock-epic folk heroine of the West Indies practices a liberationist pedagogy, Mukherjee implicitly valorizes a non-racist pedagogy that would recognize and celebrate America's repressed hybridity. Consider Beigh's reflection on the origins of her interest in Hannah's story: "Asa Brownledge's American Puritans seminar at Yale . . . set in motion a hunger for connectedness, a belief that with sufficient passion and intelligence we can deconstruct the barriers of time and geography. Maybe that led, circuitously, to Venn. And to the Salem Bibi and the tangled lines of India and New England" (11). Mukherjee here brings out continuities between the thesis of the monocultural origins of the American self and multiculturalism. Mukherjee's novel attempts to posit a connection between efforts to remap "American culture" today and older models of American Studies.

How we evaluate this connection has serious consequences. For if American Studies can be thought of as institutionalizing the discovery of the non-English book, then Condé's and Mukherjee's efforts can be read in at least two ways—as a move to hybridize the American book by re-citing it, or as a move to take its place as the new non-English book so suddenly and fortuitously discovered. On the one hand, Condé and Mukherjee's hybridizing of Hawthorne can be modeled on the subversive questions that Bhabha's natives direct to the English book. It is no coincidence, after all, that Condé and Mukherjee went to Hawthorne, for few other writers have stood for American literature in quite the same way—and few have enjoyed the near-continuous institutional backing that Hawthorne has. From the publication of *The Scarlet Letter* on, he was trumpeted as America's first major literary contribution to the (Anglo/ American) world, taken up by influential New England publishing houses, memorialized both before and after his death, appropriated by nineteenth-century New England educational institutions, and seized upon by the twentieth-century academy as a classic American author. Hawthorne's theorizing about the romance became the basis for the "symbolic-romance" school that dominated American Studies for the decades leading up to and following World War II.[41] In a sense, Hawthorne—and *The Scarlet Letter* in particular—can be thought of as symbols of New England literary hegemony over American literature.[42] *The Scarlet Letter* has been a "new English book" for a very long time. To consider the limits of this book and create counter-narratives is an important and necessary project.[43]

And yet, given Bhabha's emphasis on the colonial production of hybridization, I also want to raise the possibility that Condé's and Mukherjee's novels can themselves take on a similar function as the English book does in Bhabha's argument. If part of the aim of education in the early twentieth century was to Americanize recent immigrants and their children through the invention of a New England tradition of letters, and if by mid-century academics in higher education had adjusted this project to the needs of a Cold War culture of consensus, then it is quite possible that contemporary critiques of these projects might lead Americanists to be relatively uncritical toward a quite plausible alternative to it: the notion of a global cultural hybridity.[44] Americanists who take up this idea without engaging the ideas of Bhabha and his critics can simply assimilate "hybridity" to notions of "pluralism" or "diversity" and thereby reinscribe the key tenets of the ideology of Americanization in their analyses of global formations, movements, and struggles. Americanist engagements with multiculturalism and postcolonialism, that is, can all too easily become another form of diversity management. By the same token, if the recent and long overdue attention to and respect for African-American and ethnic studies has begun to lead to something like the "diversification" of American Studies, then Americanists' responses to the incredible boom of postcolonial studies might become something akin to "globalization." The economic resonances of these phrases should be troubling. Diversification and globalization are something like capitalist doubles of what most universities now claim to take as somewhat troublesome but on the whole untroubling goods—respect for diversity and global awareness. Perhaps this doubling suggests that the halting efforts of American universities to institute multiculturalism are not separable from the ongoing transnationalization of capital and financialization of the globe.[45]

What, then, are we to do if adding *Tituba* and *Holder* to an already-constituted pluralist model could be to reinscribe the ideology of Americanization, while making them the core of a hybrid, transnational literary studies may be to help inscribe an ideology of globalization? Taking this question seriously does not commit us to a determinist account of hybridity's significance or a reductionist reading of Condé's and Mukherjee's fiction. With regard to the former issue, Gyan Prakash reminds us that although capital itself works through a hybridizing logic, it does not have absolute power: "To recognize that hybridization does not mean resistance to capital's expansion but constitutes its ambivalent and uncertain mode of expansion is to acknowledge that globalization is a differentiated and differentiating structure. It operates in unevenness, and it proceeds by domesticating difference. . . . Clearly, the international-ization of capital . . . produces new forms of unevenness, inequality, difference, and discrimination. The very same process, however, also renders capitalism open to subal-tern pressures, to the pressure exerted by the forms and forces it subordinates."[46]

Similarly, if hybridity in the nineteenth century entailed the "strategic reversal of the process of domination through disavowal" that was the civilizing mission, then a similar effort to turn the "discursive conditions of dominance into the grounds of intervention" might be one way of responding to today's globalizing mission. This is not to say that hybridity is the only game in town, that it is above critique, or that it is always the best way of achieving political effects in all circumstances. It is only to say that we should neither ignore it nor foreclose its effects in our ethico-political analyses, even as we acknowledge that it can never become the political version of Condé's *salapertuis*, the panacea for all the body politic's ills. This is where the latter issue—how to read *Tituba* and *Holder* attentively—returns, in the context of the cur-ricular and institutional future of American Studies. For to inquire into the relations between hybridity and pedagogy, as we have been doing, is to put the question of the nation on the table. What kind of American Studies would we need in order to take seriously Condé's and Mukherjee's interventions into the hybridity debates? How should American Studies conceptualize the relationships among its pedagogical strate-gies and institutional structures, the movements of global capital, and the future of the nation-state? Can there be, to borrow from Bhabha's "DissemiNation," a peda-gogy that, in breaking with nationalist narratives that are based upon "the continuist, accumulative temporality of the pedagogical" (145), is not simply a celebration of global capitalism?

Responding to these questions would require us to treat hybridity not as a melting pot, not as acculturation, not as diversity, not as multiculturalism (neither a pluralism nor a relativism), not as syncretism, not as creolization, not as *mestizaje*, not as *métissage* (neither amalgamation nor miscegenation). Rather, it would mean treating hybridity as an invitation to consider the ways in which cultural politics matters, the ways that global power relations continue to construct the cultural. It would mean taking hy-bridity as an opportunity to rethink our own responsibilities as we develop new ways of organizing contemporary literary studies.

Notes

For their careful readings and constructive criticisms of earlier drafts of this essay, I am grateful to Anthony Alessandrini, Eduardo Cadava, Wendy Chun, Mike Davis, Judith Jackson Fossett, Donna Jones, Gavin Jones, Wahneema Lubiano, Kenneth Mostern, Arnold Rampersad, and Noliwe Rooks. For feedback on lectures based on this essay, I thank the audience at the "Haw-thorne and/as Postcolonialism" panel organized by Mark Kemp at the 1995 NEMLA confer-ence, the English department at the University of Missouri at Kansas City, and my colleagues at SUNY Fredonia, particularly Bob Deming. Special thanks to Lynne Dahlgren for pointing me toward *The Holder of the World*, and to Wendy, Tony, and Kenny for going well above and beyond the call of duty and friendship in their comments and support.

1. On "hybridity," see in particular Bhabha 102–22; Busia; Farred; and Kawash 1–22, 210–18. For commentaries on "postcolonial," see Loomba; Mishra and Hodge; Appiah; Mc-Clintock, "Angel"; Shohat; Frankenberg and Mani; Miyoshi; Radhakrishnan; Dirlik; Ahmad; Kumar; Dayal, "Postcolonialism's"; Hall, "When"; Prakash, "Who's."

2. I discuss the various critiques of hybridity and of Bhabha in more detail later in the essay. See JanMohamed, esp. 78–80; Parry, esp. 43; McClintock, *Imperial*, esp. 67–68; Young, *Colonial*, esp. 22–28; Young, *White*, 141–56; Werbner and Modood (especially essays by Werbner and Papastergiadis, which provide valuable overviews, and by Friedman, van der Veer, and Hutnyk, which provide particularly sharp critiques); Brah and Coombes; and Moreiras.

3. For overviews of studies of race and American culture, see Fishkin; Moon and Davidson; Wonham. Most of these studies were inspired by or are responses to Morrison's "Unspeakable Things Unspoken" and *Playing in the Dark*, both of which may be read as responses to earlier rethinkings of "American culture" by such authors as W. E. B. Du Bois, Richard Wright, Ralph Ellison, James Baldwin, and Albert Murray.

4. Exploring the parallels, intersections, exchanges, cross-fertilizations, and tensions among these fields—not to mention their conditions of intellectual production and political repercussions—is necessarily a collective project, one that is only just beginning. For an exemplary program for comparative literature and American Studies in the age of transnational capital, see Spivak, *Outside*, 255–84; for assessments of relations between African American and postcolonial studies, see duCille and Boyce Davies, *Black*, 80–112; for consideration of "postcolonialism" in the Americas, see Klor de Alva and Sharpe; and for major statements by Americanists see Kaplan and Pease (especially essays by Kaplan, Pease, Jehlen, Viswanathan, Rafael, and Saldívar), Porter, Sundquist (especially essays by Romero, Dayan, Pérez-Torres, and Cheyfitz), Pease, Jay, esp. 169–213, and the works cited in note 3.

5. Desegregated, by implication, through a choice against critical self-segregation, rather than through a consideration of criticism as an institution still feeling the effect of long-held habits of exclusion. It should be noted that Paul Lauter's praise of the collection emphasizes the latter vision of desegregation, focusing on "the protracted struggle . . . not only to integrate 'American literature' but to reconstruct critical practices which even today sustain cultural segregation."

6. For an example of his work that doesn't miss this appointment, see Palumbo-Liu, *Ethnic*, 1–27. See also Shankar.

7. For cogent criticisms of certain versions of "color-blindness," see P. Williams; Omi and Winant 113–59; Peller; Gotanda; Crenshaw.

8. By using the word "ramifications," Young combines the two senses of "consequence" and "outgrowth," thereby merging logical and historical narratives of progression; by doing this, he reinforces his emphasis on postcolonial theory's repetition of scientific racism. In practice, however, Young substitutes an analysis of the logical consequences of hybridity's nineteenth-century uses for the kind of close genealogical scrutiny that would actually make his case that twentieth-century rearticulations of hybridity are some sort of outgrowth of those earlier uses. In trying to avoid the dangers of historicism, Young not only risks an idealist argument about the significance today of nineteenth-century uses of hybridity but also obscures his implicit argument that the impact of racist practices and discourses must be understood in terms of trauma. The term "ramifications," that is, works against the most interesting thrust of his argument; namely, that the relation of present to past should not be understood in terms of "consequence" or "outgrowth" but instead as "traumatic repetition." However, Young fails to consider the possibility that some sort of repetition may be the only way of transforming the impact of trauma; for such consideration, see Butler, esp. 15, 23–24, 36–37, 157–63. For a cogent critique of Young, see Hall, "When."

9. For a series of important interventions that respond to Parry's concerns about "textual insurrection" and the "exorbitation of discourse," see the work of Wahneema Lubiano, including "Shuckin,'" "Black," and "Like."

10. Where Bhabha usually is read as an American-style poststructuralist, Abena Busia reminds us that the essays that appear in *The Location of Culture* were written from within Black British Cultural Studies and thus that Bhabha should be read in relation to Stuart Hall, Paul Gilroy, Hazel Carby, and the other writers in *The Empire Strikes Back*. Thanks to Tony Alessandrini for sharing Busia's important observations with me; for his own views on this matter, see "Humanism." See also Prakash, "Who's," 197–201.

11. Bhabha's examples of this scene are drawn from the colonial archive, as well as from novels by Joseph Conrad and V. S. Naipaul. See Lubiano, "Shuckin,'" 182, for a useful explication of Bhabha's emphasis on this scene.

12. For an another exposition of "colonial discourse as an apparatus of power," see Bhabha 70–71.

13. For articles that address Condé's career and narrative strategies, see Clark, "Developing Diaspora Literacy: Allusion in Maryse Condé's *Hérémakhonon*" and "Developing Diaspora Literacy and *Marasa* Consciousness"; Smith; Herndon; Shelton; Spear; and Wylie. For articles on *Tituba*, see Scarboro; Manzor-Coats; Mudimbé-Boyi; Dukats, "A Narrative"; Arnold; and Garane. Late in the revision process, I came across Dukats "The Hybrid," which anticipates several of my arguments, even as hybridity is read through Toni Morrison's rather than Homi Bhabha's work.

14. Studies on Mukherjee's writings that have directly influenced me and to which I respond include: Knippling; Grewal; Dayal, "Creating"; Sharma; Stone; Buell, 198–211; Pfeil; Ruppel; and Alessandrini, "Politicizing." In the course of revising this essay, I came across several recent articles that examine *Holder*, including Iyer, Rajan, and Hsiao.

15. In an interview with Scarboro, Condé said: "Writing *Tituba* was an opportunity to express my feelings about present-day America. I wanted to imply that in terms of narrow-mindedness, hypocrisy, and racism, little has changed since the days of the Puritans" (Scarboro 207). Earlier, she had said: "I could not have written the book if I had not been in America, because I had to breathe the American air, understand what white American society is, and look at white faces to portray some of the characters in *Tituba*" (Clark, "'I Have Made Peace,'" 129–30). Mukherjee, by contrast, is well known for asserting that racism is more virulent in Canada than the United States, although in *Holder* she does address U.S. racism explicitly ("Two Ways," 21, 35–39).

16. Perhaps unintentionally, then, she situates herself in another American tradition, that of black writers appropriating the captivity narrative; see Zafar, Sekora, and Montgomery.

17. It is difficult to tell if this structure was intentional on Condé's part, or if it was an unintended consequence of the marketing of an author from the Francophone West Indies for American audiences (Condé herself is cagey on this question). In a similar vein, Manzor-Coats has discussed the politics of the various covers of Condé's novels (737–39) and Mudimbé-Boyi has suggested links between Condé's assumed position as Tituba's interlocutor and Latin American *testimonios* (752–54).

18. On Mukherjee's rewriting of the captivity narrative, see in particular Iyer, and Hsiao 224–26.

19. On this point, see Garane, who links Hester to western feminism in both its global sisterhood and radical separatist modes and emphasizes the difference between "western feminist rejection of the patronym and the process of naming as empowerment in the context of the diaspora" (160–63); Manzor-Coats argues that "the encounter is a parody of contemporary Anglo-feminist liberal discourse," exposing the ways Hester treats Tituba as a native informant,

and adds that Condé is also parodying feminist separatists, specifically Monique Wittig (742–43); Shelton references Helene Cixous's and Catherine Clément's take on the witch in her discussion of *Tituba* (720). I would add that the figure of John Indian—who exploits mimicry for survival and personal gain, and who eventually pretends to be persecuted by witches, thereby effectively ending his relationship with Tituba—might also be an implicit critique of Luce Irigaray's notion of mimicry. Condé could well be suggesting that in the context of slavery, black men can more easily make use of this strategy, and it might actually work against black women.

20. Compare Mukherjee's practice here with Grossman and Brickhouse. Hawthorne himself often dwelled on the subject of amalgamation in his notebooks and fiction; see *Centenary Edition* 8: 122, 502–03; 23: 146; the flower imagery in "Rappaccini's Daughter" and *The House of the Seven Gables*; *The Marble Faun*.

21. Of course, Hawthorne's Hester does go halfway around the world—and, like Hannah, returns to New England. In addition, Manning was Hawthorne's mother's maiden name; Nina Baym points out that Elizabeth Clarke Manning's first child was born "barely seven months after . . . her parents' marriage," and speculates that the Hathorne family's reaction could have provided a model for the opening scaffold scene of *The Scarlet Letter* (40–41). As the essay in which this claim appeared was first published in 1982, there is no doubt that Mukherjee could have had access to this suggested link between Hester and Manning.

22. Much can be done by comparing Mukherjee's use of "the Emperor's Tear" with Hawthorne's use of "the Great Carbuncle" (435–49). For a highly suggestive commentary on Hawthorne's story, see Colacurcio, *Province*, 510–13.

23. I take these phrases from Spivak, "Who," 283 and *The Post-colonial Critic*, 72, respectively. See also her Translator's Preface and Afterword to Mahasweta Devi's *Imaginary Maps* (esp. 197 with respect to hybridity and xxvii–xxviii with respect to gender). The figure of Mary Oraon in Devi's "The Hunt" is crucial here, and bears comparison with Tituba (Devi 1–17).

24. Compare Bhabha's notion of hybridity as political strategy with Ernesto Laclau's discussion of "necessary surfaces of inscription within which *any* hegemonic alternative has to be constructed" ("Totalitarianism," 92).

25. Dukats, however, shows that Tituba's actual powers are small compared to the Cesairean hero's—a reminder of the difference gender makes ("The Hybrid," 337).

26. Condé repeatedly emphasizes the importance of humor and parody to her project; see Scarboro 201, 212.

27. In signifying on the story of George Washington and the cherry tree as well, Mukherjee suggests that the racist framing of American hybridity is a lie, a distortion of the Founding Fathers' vision masquerading as the truth. This helps explain her contention in a recent interview: "I want people to realise we—people like me—are all here to stay and we are all 100 percent American, in our different ways" (Faulk, "No Hyphenation"). Mukherjee is recasting Americanization as hybridization. Her celebration of Americanization as "fluidity, self-invention, blue jeans and T-shirts" and as "cultural and psychological 'mongrelization'" in "Two Ways" bears comparison with Bourne and Yúdice.

28. Thanks to Tony Alessandrini for pointing out the framing (personal correspondence, 10 October 1996) and Bob Deming for pointing out the hanging (personal conversation, 6 November 1998) of Hannah's sampler.

29. In what follows, I build upon Manzor-Coats's observation that *Tituba* is largely taught in women's, not African American, studies programs and her criticism of "the ways in which texts by women of color form an integral part of the political economy of the university while women-of-color scholars are still relevantly absent from this economy" (739).

30. On Mukherjee's career, see Sharma; Stone 215–16; Buell 207–08; and Hsiao 224–26. Her newest novel, *Leave It to Me*, was released too late for consideration here.

31. On these points, see Knippling 146–50; Grewal 181–96; and Pfeil 201–02, 205–06.

32. Diversity management is not limited to the academic world; for analyses, see *Social Text* 44 (1995); Palumbo-Liu's, *The Ethnic*, 1–27; Davis, "Gender." For considerations of the politics of different versions of multiculturalism, see Carby; Mohan; Newfield; Rouse; Eisenstein; and Lubiano, "Like."

33. On this topic, see McClintock, *Imperial*, 207–31.

34. On this topic, see Young, *Colonial*, 159–82.

35. On flexible accumulation, see Harvey 121–97; Sivanandan 169–95; Rowbotham and Mitter; Appelbaum; Bonacich; Walker; and Mohanty.

36. Mukherjee has made her own investments in this border-crossing version of hybridity clear in an interview, while describing the Mughal miniature that apparently inspired the novel: "A European woman in Mughal court dress at Aurangzeb's court, a caged bird at her feet. I feel as if I'm looking at a pre-incarnation of myself, when the voyage to India had to be made in creaky ships, a woman who chose not to stay in the ghetto of her white world, but somehow went out, Indianised herself" (Faulk, "No Hyphenation"). That Mukherjee describes Hannah in precisely the same terms as she describes her own process of Americanization (in "Two Ways") indicates that she considers both kinds of border crossings to be symmetrical and easily substitutable. As these comments should indicate, I do not disagree with Rajan's scathing critique of Mukherjee, but I would add that the work of teaching does not necessarily have to limit itself to identifying and endorsing an author's vision.

37. See in particular Hansen; Morsberger; and Rosenthal 10–31.

38. See especially 12, 41, and 205n41 for Breslaw's emphasis on cultural and sexual intermixture between Africans and Indians in Barbados. Despite two careless references to Condé that suggest she hasn't read *Tituba* (202n4, 219n13), many of Breslaw's historical reconstructions are actually quite similar to Condé's account of Tituba in New England.

39. On this point, see Garane 153–55, 163. As Rosenthal argues, "[U]ncovering what happened in the witchcraft episode becomes a textual problem—one of narration, of weighing competing narratives against each other for their reliability, at getting under the stated texts to the best versions of what might have occurred" (27).

40. For a related argument, see Hall, "When," 249–50.

41. See Graff 209–25.

42. On these matters, see Baym 81–101, Brodhead, and Spanos; see also Bérubé 203–24. For an exploration of the issues Hawthorne's preeminence has raised for later writers, see Budick.

43. In this sense, *Tituba* and *Holder* intersect with the small but significant number of recent "postcolonial" readings of Hawthorne. See Kemp; Mackenzie, "Hawthorne's *Roger Malvin's Burial*: A Postcolonial Reading," "American and/or Post-Colonial Studies and *The Scarlet Letter*," and "Colonization and Decolonization in *The Blithedale Romance*"; plus Luedtke.

44. On the turn-of-the-century United States, see Baym 81–101; on mid-century America, see Spanos. See also Jay 136–213, esp. 146–57, 178–80; Bérubé 226–28; Graff 209–25; and Russell Reising 49–91. For a spirited and insightful defense of the New England tradition, regionally (re)conceived, see Colacurcio 1–25.

45. Gayatri Chakravorty Spivak has been raising these kinds of questions about multiculturalism and globalization for years. The most best-known example is "Can," but see also "Who" and "Questions," as well as the range of her readings of Marx and value: "Marx after Derrida," "Scattered Speculations," "Speculations on Reading Marx," "Poststructuralism," "In the New World Order," "Supplementing Marxism," and "More on 'Imperialism Today.'" Stuart Hall is

also working to bring postcolonial studies and critiques of globalization into dialogue; in addition to "When," see also "Local" and "Old." See also Garcia Canclini and Moreiras.

46. Prakash, "Who's," 199; see also Pieterse.

Works Cited

Ahmad, Aijaz. "The Politics of Literary Postcoloniality." *Race & Class* 36.3 (1995): 1–20.

Alessandrini, Anthony. "Humanism in Question: Fanon and Said." Ray and Schwartz (forthcoming).

———. "Politicizing Postcolonialism and Multiculturalism: On Comparing Mahasweta Devi and Bharati Mukherjee." *Michigan Feminist Studies* 10 (1995–1996): 1–25.

———. "The Politics of Literary Postcoloniality." *Race & Class* 36.3 (1995): 1–20.

Alexander, M. Jacqui, and Chandra Talpade Mohanty, eds. *Feminist Genealogies, Colonial Legacies, Democratic Futures*. NY: Routledge, 1997.

Appelbaum, Richard. "Multiculturalism and Flexibility: Some New Directions in Global Capitalism." Gordon and Newfield 297–316.

Appiah, Kwame Anthony. "Is the Post- in Postmodernism the Post- in Postcolonial?" *Critical Inquiry* 17 (1991): 336–57.

Arnold, A. James. "The Novelist as Critic." *World Literature Today* 67 (1993): 711–16.

Attridge, Derek, Geoff Bennington, and Robert Young, eds. *Post-Structuralism and the Question of History*. Cambridge: Cambridge UP, 1987.

Baym, Nina. *Feminism and American Literary History: Essays*. New Brunswick: Rutgers UP, 1992.

Bérubé, Michael. *Public Access: Literary Theory and American Cultural Politics*. NY: Verso, 1994.

Bhabha, Homi. *The Location of Culture*. NY: Routledge, 1994.

Bonacich, Edna. "The Class Question in Global Capitalism: The Case of the Los Angeles Garment Industry." Gordon and Newfield 317–29.

Bourne, Randolph. "Trans-National America." *Atlantic Monthly* (July 1916): 86–97.

Boyce Davies, Carole, and Elaine Savory Fido, eds. *Out of the Kumbla: Caribbean Women and Literature*. Trenton: Africa World P, 1990.

Boyce Davies, Carole, ed. *Moving Beyond Boundaries, Volume 2: Black Women's Diasporas*. London: Pluto P, 1995.

———. *Black Women, Writing and Identity: Migrations of the Subject*. NY: Routledge, 1994.

Brah, Avtar, and Annie Coombes, eds. *From Miscegenation to Hybridity? Re-thinking the Syncretic, the Cross-Cultural and the Cosmopolitan in Culture, Science, and Politics*. NY: Routledge, 1998.

Brennan, Timothy. *Salman Rushdie and the Third World: Myths of the Nation*. London: Macmillan, 1989.

Breslaw, Elaine. *Tituba, Reluctant Witch of Salem: Devilish Indians and Puritan Fantasies*. NY: NYU P, 1996.

Brickhouse, Anna. "Hawthorne in the Americas: Frances Calderón de la Barca, Octavio Paz, and the Mexican Genealogy of 'Rappaccini's Daughter.'" *PMLA* 113 (1998): 227–42.

Brodhead, Richard. *The School of Hawthorne*. NY: Oxford UP, 1986.

Budick, Emily Miller. *Engendering Romance: Woman Writers and the Hawthorne Tradition 1850–1990*. New Haven: Yale UP, 1994.

Buell, Frederick. *National Culture and the New Global System*. Baltimore: Johns Hopkins UP, 1994.

Busia, Abena. "Performance, Transcription and the Languages of the Self: Interrogating Identity as a 'Post-Colonial' Poet." James and Busia 203–13.

Butler, Judith. *Excitable Speech: A Politics of the Performative*. NY: Routledge, 1997.

Cain, William. *Philosophical Approaches to Literature: New Essays on Nineteenth- and Twentieth-Century Texts.* Lewisberg: Bucknell UP, 1983.

Callari, Antonio, Stephen Cullenberg, and Carole Biewener, eds. *Marxism in the Postmodern Age: Confronting the New World Order.* NY: Guilford P, 1994.

Canclini, Nestor Garcia. *Hybrid Cultures: Strategies for Entering and Leaving Modernity,* trans. Christopher Chiapari and Silvia Lopez. Minneapolis: U of Minnesota P, 1995.

Carby, Hazel. "The Multicultural Wars." Dent 187–99.

Chambers, Iain, and Lidia Curti. *The Post-Colonial Question: Common Skies, Divided Horizons.* NY: Routledge, 1996.

Charvat, William, et al., eds. *The Centenary Edition of the Works of Nathaniel Hawthorne.* 23 vols. Columbus: Ohio State UP, 1962–.

Chow, Rey. *Writing Diaspora: Tactics of Intervention in Contemporary Cultural Studies.* Bloomington: Indiana UP, 1993.

Clark, Vèvè. " 'I Have Made Peace with My Island': An Interview with Maryse Condé." *Callaloo* 12.1 (1989): 86–133.

———. "Developing Diaspora Literacy and *Marasa* Consciousness." Spillers 40–61.

———. "Developing Diaspora Literacy: Allusion in Maryse Condé's *Hérémakhonon.*" Boyce Davies and Fido 303–19.

Colacurcio, Michael. *Doctrine and Difference: Essays in the Literature of New England.* NY: Routledge, 1997.

———. *The Province of Piety: Moral History in Hawthorne's Early Tales.* 1984. Durham: Duke UP, 1995.

Collier, Peter, and Helga Geyer-Ryan, eds. *Literary Theory Today.* Cambridge: Polity P, 1990.

Condé, Maryse. *I, Tituba, Black Witch of Salem.* 1986. Trans. Richard Philcox. NY: Ballantine, 1992.

Crenshaw, Kimberlé, Neil Gotanda, Gary Peller, and Kendall Thomas, eds. *Critical Race Theory: The Key Writings that Formed the Movement.* NY: New P, 1995.

Crenshaw, Kimberlé. "Color-Blindness, History, and the Law." Lubiano, *House* 280–88.

Davis, Angela. "Gender, Class, and Multiculturalism: Rethinking 'Race' Politics." Gordon and Newfield 40–48.

———. Foreword. Condé, Maryse. *I, Tituba, Black Witch of Salem.* 1986. Trans. Richard Philcox. NY: Ballantine, 1992. ix-xi.

Dayal, Samir. "Creating, Preserving, Destroying: Violence in Bharati Mukherjee's *Jasmine.*" Nelson 65–88.

———. "Postcolonialism's Possibilities: Subcontinental Diasporic Intervention." *Cultural Critique* 33 (Spring 1996): 113–49.

Dent, Gina, ed. *Black Popular Culture: A Project by Michele Wallace.* Seattle: Bay P, 1992.

Devi, Mahasweta. *Imaginary Maps.* Trans. Gayatri Chakravorty Spivak. NY: Routledge, 1995.

Dirlik, Arif. "The Postcolonial Aura: Third World Criticism in the Age of Global Capital." *Critical Inquiry* 20 (1994): 328–56.

duCille, Ann. "Postcolonialism and Afrocentricity: Discourse and Dat Course." Sollors and Diedrich 28–41.

Dukats, Mara. "A Narrative of Violated Maternity: *Moi, Tituba, sorcière . . . Noire de Salem.*" *World Literature Today* 67 (1993): 745–50.

———. "The Hybrid Terrain of Literary Imagination: Maryse Condé's Black Witch of Salem, Nathaniel Hawthorne's Hester Prynne, and Aimé Cesaire's Heroic Poetic Voice." Myrsiades and McGuire 325–40.

Eisenstein, Zillah. *Hatreds: Racialized and Sexualized Conflicts in the 21st Century.* NY: Routledge, 1996.

Farred, Grant. " 'Not Like Women at All': Black Female Subjectivity in Lauretta Ngcobo's *And They Didn't Die.*" *Genders* 16 (Spring 1993): 94–112.

Faulk, Tina. "No Hyphenation for Mukherjee." *New Straits Times* 9 April 1997.

Featherstone, Mike, Scott Lash, and Roland Robertson, eds. *Global Modernities.* Thousand Oaks: Sage, 1995.

Fishkin, Shelley Fisher. "Interrogating 'Whiteness,' Complicating 'Blackness': Remapping American Culture." *American Quarterly* 47 (1995): 428–66.

Forbes, Jack. *Black Africans and Native Americans: Color, Race and Caste in the Evolution of Red-Black Peoples.* Cambridge: Basil Blackwell, 1988.

Frankenberg, Ruth, and Lata Mani. "Crosscurrents, Crosstalk: Race, 'Postcoloniality,' and the Politics of Location." *Cultural Studies* 7 (1993): 292–310.

Garane, Jeanne. "History, Identity and the Constitution of the Female Subject: Maryse Condé's *Tituba.*" Boyce Davies, *Moving* 153–64.

Gates, Henry Louis, Jr., ed. *"Race," Writing, and Difference.* Chicago: U of Chicago P, 1986.

Gordon, Avery, and Christopher Newfield, eds. *Mapping Multiculturalism.* Minneapolis: U of Minnesota P, 1996.

Gotanda, Neil. "A Critique of 'Our Constitution Is Color-Blind.' " Crenshaw, Gotanda, Peller, and Thomas 257–75.

Graff, Gerald. *Professing Literature: An Institutional History.* Chicago: U of Chicago P, 1987.

Grewal, Gurleen. "Born Again American: The Immigrant Consciousness in *Jasmine.*" Nelson 181–96.

Grewal, Inderpal, and Caren Kaplan, eds. *Scattered Hegemonies: Postmodernity and Transnational Feminist Practices.* Minneapolis: U of Minnesota P, 1994.

Grossman, Jay. "'A' is for Abolition?: Race, Authorship, *The Scarlet Letter.*" *Textual Practice* 7 (1993): 13–30.

Hall, Stuart. "Old and New Identities, Old and New Ethnicities." King 41–68.

———. "The Local and the Global: Globalization and Ethnicity." King 19–40.

———. "When Was 'The Post-Colonial'? Thinking at the Limit." Chambers and Curti 242–60.

Hansen, Chadwick. "The Metamorphosis of Tituba, or Why American Intellectuals Can't Tell an Indian Witch from a Negro." *New England Quarterly* 47 (1974): 3–12.

Harvey, David. *The Condition of Postmodernity.* Cambridge: Basil Blackwell, 1989.

Hawthorne, Nathaniel. "Rappaccini's Daughter." Pearce 975–1005.

———. "The Great Carbuncle." Pearce 435–49.

———. *Nathaniel Hawthorne: Novels.* Ed. Millicent Bell. NY: Library of America, 1983.

———. *Nathaniel Hawthorne: Tales and Sketches.* Ed. Roy Harvey Pearce. NY: Library of America, 1982.

———. *The House of the Seven Gables.* Bell 347–627.

———. *The Marble Faun.* Bell 850–1242.

———. *The Scarlet Letter.* Bell 115–345.

Herndon, Gerise. "Gender Construction and Neocolonialism." *World Literature Today* 67 (1993): 731–36.

Hsiao, Ruth Yu. "A World Apart: A Reading of South Asian American Literature." Shankar and Srikanth 217–234.

Iyer, Nalini. "American/Indian: Metaphors of the Self in Bharati Mukherjee's *The Holder of the World.*" *ARIEL* 27.4 (October 1996): 29–44.

James, Stanlie, and Abena Busia, eds. *Theorizing Black Feminisms: The Visionary Pragmatism of Black Women.* NY: Routledge, 1993.

JanMohamed, Abdul. "The Economy of Manichean Allegory: The Function of Racial Difference in Colonialist Literature." Gates 78–106.

Jay, Gregory. *American Literature and the Culture Wars*. Ithaca: Cornell UP, 1997.

Kaplan, Amy, and Donald Pease, eds. *Cultures of United States Imperialism*. Durham: Duke UP, 1993.

Kawash, Samira. *Dislocating the Color Line: Identity, Hybridity, and Singularity in African-American Literature*. Stanford: Stanford UP, 1997.

Kemp, Mark. "*The Marble Faun* and American Postcolonial Ambivalence." *Modern Fiction Studies* 43.1 (1997): 209–36.

King, Anthony, ed. *Culture, Globalization and the World-System: Contemporary Conditions for the Representation of Identity*. Minneapolis: U of Minnesota P, 1997.

Klor de Alva, J. Jorge. "The Postcolonization of the (Latin) American Experience: A Reconsideration of 'Colonialism,' 'Postcolonialism,' and 'Mestizaje.'" Prakash, *After* 241–75.

Knippling, Alpana Sharma. "Toward an Investigation of the Subaltern in Bharati Mukherjee's *The Middleman and Other Stories* and *Jasmine*." Nelson 143–59.

Kruger, Barbara, and Phil Mariani, eds. *Remaking History*. Seattle: Bay P, 1989.

Kumar, Amitava. "Postcoloniality: Field Notes." *the minnesota review* n.s. 41–42 (1995): 271–79.

Laclau, Ernesto. "Totalitarianism and Moral Indignation." *diacritics* 20.3 (fall 1990): 88–95.

Loomba, Ania. "Overworlding the Third World." *Oxford Literary Review* 13 (1991): 164–91.

Looser, Devoney, and E. Ann Kaplan. *Generations: Academic Feminists in Dialogue*. Minneapolis: U of Minnesota P, 1997.

Lubiano, Wahneema, ed. *The House That Race Built: Black Americans, U.S. Terrain*. NY: Pantheon, 1997.

———. "Black Ladies, Welfare Queens, and State Minstrels: Ideological War by Narrative Means." Morrison, *Race-ing* 323–63.

———. "Like Being Mugged by a Metaphor: Multiculturalism and State Narratives." Gordon and Newfield 64–75.

———. "Shuckin' Off the African-American Native Other: What's 'Po-Mo' Got to Do with It?" *Cultural Critique* 18 (1991): 149–86.

Luedtke, Luther. *Nathaniel Hawthorne and the Romance of the Orient*. Bloomington: Indiana UP, 1989.

Mackenzie, Manfred. "American and/or Post-Colonial Studies and *The Scarlet Letter*." *Australasian Journal of American Studies* 13.2 (December 1994): 17–33.

———. "Colonization and Decolonization in *The Blithedale Romance*." *University of Toronto Quarterly* 62.4 (Summer 1993): 504–21.

———. "Hawthorne's *Roger Malvin's Burial*: A Postcolonial Reading." *New Literary History* 27.3 (Summer 1996): 459–72.

Magnus, Bernd, and Stephen Cullenberg, eds. *Whither Marxism? Global Crises in International Perspective*. NY: Routledge, 1995.

Manzor-Coats, Lillian. "Of Witches and Other Things: Maryse Condé's Challenges to Feminist Discourse." *World Literature Today* 67 (1993): 737–44.

McClintock, Anne. "The Angel of Progress: Pitfalls of the Term 'Post-Colonialism.'" *Social Text* 31/32 (1992): 84–98.

———. *Imperial Leather: Race, Gender and Sexuality in the Colonial Contest*. NY: Routledge, 1995.

Mishra, Vijay, and Bob Hodge. "What Is Post(-)colonialism?" *Textual Practice* 5 (1991): 399–414.

Miyoshi, Masao. "A Borderless World? From Colonialism to Transnationalism and the Decline of the Nation-State." *Critical Inquiry* 19 (1993): 726–51.

Mohan, Rajeswari. "Multiculturalism in the Nineties: Pitfalls and Possibilities." Newfield and Strickland 372–88.

Mohanty, Chandra Talpade. "Women Workers and Capitalist Scripts: Ideologies of Domination, Common Interests, and the Politics of Solidarity." Alexander and Mohanty 3–29.

Montgomery, Benilde. "Recapturing John Marrant." Shuffelton 105–115.

Moon, Michael, and Cathy Davidson, eds. *Subjects and Citizens: Nation, Race, and Gender from Oroonoko to Anita Hill*. Durham: Duke UP, 1995.

Moreiras, Alberto. "Hybridity and Double Consciousness." *Cultural Studies* 13.3 (July 1999): 373–407.

Morrison, Toni, ed. *Race-ing Justice, En-gendering Power: Essays on Anita Hill, Clarence Thomas, and the Construction of Social Reality*. NY: Pantheon, 1992.

Morrison, Toni. "Unspeakable Things Unspoken: The Afro-American Presence in American Literature." *Michigan Quarterly Review* 28 (Winter 1989): 1–34.

———. *Playing in the Dark: Whiteness and the Literary Imagination*. Cambridge: Harvard UP, 1992.

Morsberger, Robert. "The Further Transformation of Tituba." *New England Quarterly* 47 (1974): 456–58.

Mudimbé-Boyi, Elisabeth. "Giving a Voice to Tituba: The Death of the Author?" *World Literature Today* 67 (1993): 751–56.

Mukherjee, Bharati. "Two Ways to Belong to America." *New York Times* 22 September 1996.

———. *The Holder of the World*. NY: Ballantine, 1993.

Myrsiades, Kostas, and Jerry McGuire, eds. *Order and Partialities: Theory, Pedagogy, and the "Postcolonial."* Albany: SUNY P, 1995.

Nelson, Cary, and Lawrence Grossberg, eds. *Marxism and the Interpretation of Culture*. Urbana: U of Illinois P, 1988.

Nelson, Emmanuel, ed. *Bharati Mukherjee: Critical Perspectives*. NY: Garland, 1993.

Newfield, Christopher, and Ronald Strickland, eds. *After Political Correctness: The Humanities and Society in the 1990s*. Boulder: Westview P, 1995.

Newfield, Christopher. "What Was 'Political Correctness'? Race, the Right, and Managerial Democracy in the Humanities." J. Williams 109–45.

Omi, Michael, and Howard Winant. *Racial Formation in the United States: From the 1960s to the 1990s*. 2nd ed. NY: Routledge, 1994.

Palumbo-Liu, David, ed. *The Ethnic Canon: Histories, Institutions, and Interventions*. Minneapolis: U of Minnesota P, 1995.

———. "Theory and the Subject of Asian American Studies." *Amerasia Journal* 21.1–2 (1995): 55–65.

Parry, Benita. "Problems in Current Theories of Colonial Discourse." *Oxford Literary Review* 9.1–2 (1987): 27–57.

Pease, Donald. "National Narratives, Postnational Narration." *Modern Fiction Studies* 43 (1997): 1–23.

Peller, Gary. "Race Consciousness." Crenshaw, Gotanda, Peller, and Thomas 127–58.

Pfeil, Fred. "No Basta Teorizar: In-Difference to Solidarity in Contemporary Fiction, Theory, and Practice." Grewal and Kaplan 197–230.

Pieterse, Jan Nederveen. "Globalization as Hybridization." Featherstone, Lash, and Robinson 45–68.

Porter, Carolyn. "What We Know That We Don't Know: Remapping American Literary History." *American Literary History* 6 (1994): 467–526.

Prakash, Gyan, ed. *After Colonialism: Imperial Histories and Postcolonial Displacements*. Princeton: Princeton UP, 1995.

————. "Who's Afraid of Postcoloniality?" *Social Text* 49 (Winter 1996): 187–203.

Radhakrishnan, R. "Postcoloniality and the Boundaries of Identity." *Callaloo* 16.4 (1993): 750–71.

Rajan, Gita. "Fissuring Time, Suturing Space: Reading Bharati Mukherjee's *The Holder of the World*." Looser and Kaplan 288–308.

Ray, Sangeeta, and Henry Schwartz, eds. *A Companion to Postcolonial Studies*. Cambridge: Basil Blackwell, forthcoming.

Reising, Russell. *The Unusable Past: Theory and the Study of American Literature*. NY: Methuen, 1986.

Rosenthal, Bernard. *Salem Story: Reading the Witch Trials of 1692*. Cambridge: Cambridge UP, 1993.

Rouse, Roger. "Thinking through Transnationalism: Notes on the Cultural Politics of Class Relations in the Contemporary United States." *Public Culture* 7 (1995): 353–402.

Rowbotham, Sheila, and Swasti Mitter, eds. *Dignity and Daily Bread: New Forms of Economic Organizing among Poor Women in the Third World and the First*. NY: Routledge, 1994.

Ruppel, F. Timothy. "'Re-inventing Ourselves a Million Times': Narrative, Desire, and Identity in Bharati Mukherjee's *Jasmine*." Myrsiades and McGuire 391–407.

Scarboro, Ann Armstrong. Afterword. Condé 187–225.

Sekora, John. "Red, White, and Black: Indian Captivities, Colonial Printers, and the Early African-American Narrative." Shuffelton 92–104.

Shankar, Lavina Dhingra, and Rajini Srikanth, eds. *A Part, Yet Apart: South Asians in Asian America*. Philadelphia: Temple UP, 1998.

Shankar, Lavina Dhingra. "The Limits of (South Asian) Names and Labels: Postcolonial or Asian American?" Shankar and Srikanth 49–66.

Sharma, Maya Manju. "The Inner World of Bharati Mukherjee: From Expatriate to Immigrant." Nelson 3–22.

Sharpe, Jenny. "Is the United States Postcolonial? Transnationalism, Immigration, and Race." *Diaspora* 4.2 (1995): 181–99.

Shelton, Marie-Denise. "Condé: The Politics of Gender and Identity." *World Literature Today* 67 (1993): 717–22.

Shohat, Ella. "Notes on the 'Post-Colonial.'" *Social Text* 31/32 (1992): 99–113.

Shuffelton, Frank, ed. *A Mixed Race: Ethnicity in Early America*. NY: Oxford UP, 1993.

Sivanandan, A. *Communities of Resistance: Writings on Black Struggles for Socialism*. NY: Verso, 1990.

Smith, Arlette. "The Semiotics of Exile in Maryse Condé's Fictional Works." *Callaloo* 14 (1991): 381–88.

Sollors, Werner, and Maria Diedrich, eds. *The Black Columbiad: Defining Moments in African American Literature and Culture*. Cambridge: Harvard UP, 1994.

Spanos, William. *The Errant Art of* Moby-Dick: *The Canon, the Cold War, and the Struggle for American Studies*. Durham: Duke UP, 1995.

Spear, Thomas. "Individual Quests and Collective History." *World Literature Today* 67 (1993): 723–30.

Spillers, Hortense, ed. *Comparative American Identities*. NY: Routledge, 1991.

Spivak, Gayatri Chakravorty. "Can the Subaltern Speak?" Nelson and Grossberg 271–313.

————. "In the New World Order: A Speech." Callari, Cullenberg, and Biewener 89–97.

————. "Marx after Derrida." Cain 227–46.

————. "More on 'Imperialism Today.'" *Against the Current* 63 (July/August 1996): 20–21.

————. "Poststructuralism, Marginality, Postcoloniality, and Value." Collier and Geyer-Ryan 219–44.

————. "Questions of Multi-culturalism." *The Post-colonial Critic* 59–66.

————. "Scattered Speculations on the Question of Value." *diacritics* 15.4 (winter 1985): 73–93.

————. "Speculations on Reading Marx: After Reading Derrida." Attridge, Bennington, and Young 30–62.

————. "Supplementing Marxism." Bernd and Cullenberg 109–19.

————. "Who Claims Alterity?" Kruger and Mariani 269–92.

————. *Outside in the Teaching Machine.* NY: Routledge, 1993.

————. *The Post-colonial Critic: Interviews, Strategies, Dialogues.* Ed. Sarah Harasym. NY: Routledge, 1990.

————. Translator's Preface and Afterword. Devi xxiii–xxix, 197–205.

Stone, Carole. "The Short Fictions of Bernard Malamud and Bharati Mukherjee." Nelson 213–26.

Sundquist, Eric, ed. "American Literary History: The Next Century." *American Literature* 67 (1995): 793–853.

Walker, Richard. "California's Collision of Race and Class." *Representations* 55 (1996): 163–83.

Werbner, Pnina, and Tariq Modood, eds. *Debating Cultural Hybridity: Multi-Cultural Identities and the Politics of Anti-Racism.* London: Zed, 1997.

Williams, Jeffrey. *PC Wars: Politics and Theory in the Academy.* NY: Routledge, 1995.

Williams, Patricia. *The Alchemy of Race and Rights: Diary of a Law Professor.* Cambridge: Harvard UP, 1991.

Wonham, Henry, ed. *Criticism and the Color Line: Desegregating American Literary Studies.* New Brunswick: Rutgers UP, 1996.

Wylie, Hal. "The Cosmopolitan Condé, or Unscrambling the Words." *World Literature Today* 67 (1993): 763–68.

Young, Robert. *Colonial Desire: Hybridity in Theory, Culture and Race.* NY: Routledge, 1995.

————. *White Mythologies: Writing History and the West.* NY: Routledge, 1990.

Yúdice, George. "We Are *Not* the World." *Social Text* 31/32 (1992): 202–16.

Zafar, Rafia. "Capturing the Captivity: African Americans Among the Puritans." *MELUS* 17.2 (Summer 1991–1992): 19–35.

CONTRIBUTORS' NOTES

PETER SCHMIDT teaches U.S. literature and history at Swarthmore College and has written a book on William Carlos Williams and a prize-winning book on Eudora Welty. Most recently he has published Web essays on Thomas Pynchon's *Mason & Dixon*; "On Ruins and Prophecy" treating Pannini, Poussin, and the Napoleon-sponsored *Description d'Egypt*; plus a number of other pieces on undead Elvis, Frank Sinatra's "ethnic" hair, John Cage's *Rolywholyover*, computer and video games, and *Xena: Warrior Princess* (see www.swarthmore.edu/Humanities/pschmid1/essays). He is now working on *Briar Patch: Migration and Return in Southern U.S. Fiction*, a literary history that incorporates some current postcolonial and diaspora theory.

AMRITJIT SINGH, Professor of English at Rhode Island College, has recently edited reprint editions of *The Color Curtain* and *Black Power* by Richard Wright. His other publications include the following co-edited volumes: *The Magic Circle of Henry James* (1989); *The Harlem Renaissance: Revaluations* (1989); *Memory, Narrative, and Identity: New Essays in Ethnic American Literatures* (1994); *Conversations with Ralph Ellison* (1995); *Conversations with Ishmael Reed* (1995); and *Memory and Cultural Politics: New Approaches to Ethnic American Literatures* (1996).

LAWRENCE BUELL is John P. Marquand Professor of English at Harvard University and author of *Literary Transcendentalism*, *New England Literary Culture* and *The Environmental Imagination*, among other books and articles on U.S. literary history. One of his projects-in-progress is a book focusing on post-Civil War literary and cultural discourses, including conflicting postcolonial formations.

RHONDA COBHAM is an Associate Professor of English at Amherst College, Massachusetts, specializing in African American and Caribbean literatures. She has published

445

articles on Nuruddin Farah, Ismith Khan, modern Nigerian fiction, and the Jamaican Sistren collective.

ANNE FLEISCHMANN is a lecturer in English at the University of California, Davis, where she teaches American literature and writing. Her current project, of which the present essay is a part, is a study of the intersections of race and region—scenes of racialized contact—in late nineteenth-century American fiction.

JUAN FLORES is Professor in the Department of Black and Puerto Rican Studies and also Director of the Center for Puerto Rican Studies at Hunter College, CUNY. He is the author of *The Insular Vision* (winner *Casa de las Americas* award) and *Divided Borders: Essays on Puerto Rican Identity*; translator of *Memoirs of Bernardo Vega*; and co-editor of *On Edge: The Crisis of Latin American Culture*. His newest book is *From Bomba to Hip Hop: Puerto Rican Culture and Latino Identity* (Columbia University Press, 2000).

MAE G. HENDERSON is Professor of English at the University of North Carolina at Chapel Hill. She is author of numerous articles on literature, theory, and cultural studies, including "Speaking in Tongues: Dialogics, Dialectics, and the Black Woman Writer's Literary Tradition," originally published in Cheryl Wall's *Changing Our Own Words* (Rutgers University Press, 1989). Professor Henderson is also co-editor of the five-volume *Antislavery Newspapers and Periodicals: An Annotated Index of Letters, 1617–1871* (1980), and editor of *Borders, Boundaries, and Frames: Essays in Cultural Criticism and Cultural Studies* (Routledge, 1993). Her collection, *Speaking in Tongues: Reading Black Women Writing,* is forthcoming from Oxford.

AMY KAPLAN teaches English and American Studies at Mt. Holyoke College. She is the author of *The Social Construction of American Realism* (Chicago UP, 1988). She wrote the introduction, "Left Alone with America," for *Cultures of United States Imperialism*, the anthology she co-edited with Donald Pease (Duke UP, 1993). She is currently completing *The Anarchy of Empire in American Culture* (Harvard UP, forthcoming).

MAUREEN KONKLE is Assistant Professor of English at the University of Missouri, Columbia. She is currently working on a book manuscript, "The Epistemology of the Treaty: Colonialism and the Emergence of Native Writing in English, 1768–1868," and teaches courses in early American literature, nineteenth-century American literature, colonialism in North America and the U.S., and Native literature.

ARNOLD KRUPAT teaches at Sarah Lawrence College and has published widely on Native American literature and history. Selected writings include "America's Histories" (in *American Literary History*, 1998); *The Turn to the Native: Studies in Criticism and Culture* (U of Nebraska P, 1996); *Native American Autobiography: An Anthology* (U of Wisconsin P, 1994); *New Voices in Native American Literary Criticism* (Smithsonian P, 1993); *Ethnocriticism: Ethnography, History, Literature* (U of California P, 1992); *The Voice in the Margin: Native American Literature and the Canon* (U of California P, 1989); and *"I Tell You Now": Autobiographical Essays by Native American Writers*, edited with

Brian Swann (U of Nebraska P, 1987). He is also the author of a novel: *Woodsmen; or, Thoreau and the Indians* (U of Oklahoma P, 1994).

JANA SEQUOYA MAGDALENO is the author of a number of articles on Native American literatures and cultures, including "Telling the Difference: Representations of Identity in the Discourse of Indianness" in *The Ethnic Canon: Histories, Institutions, and Interventions* edited by David Palumbo-Liu (U of Minnesota P, 1995). A co-editor with Hertha Dawn Wong of *Contemporary Native American Women's Short Story Writing* (Oxford UP, 2000), she was a University of California President's Postcolonial Fellow in the English Department at Berkeley from 1996 to 1998.

LISA SUHAIR MAJAJ was a Visiting Scholar in Women's Studies at Northeastern University for 1998–99. She has co-edited, with Amal Amireh, a collection entitled *Going Global: Reception of Third World Women Writers* (Garland, 2000). Her articles include "Arab-American Literature and the Politics of Memory," in *Memory and Cultural Politics: New Essays in American Ethnic Literatures*, ed. Amritjit Singh, Joseph Skerrett, and Robert E. Hogan (Northeastern UP, 1995), and "Arab-American Ethnicity: Locations, Coalitions and Cultural Negotiations," in *Arabs in America: Building a New Future*, ed. Michael Suleiman (Temple University Press, 1999).

KENNETH MOSTERN is Assistant Professor of English at the University of Tennessee. He is author of *Autobiography and Black Identity Politics* (Cambridge UP, 1999), and has published work in *Cultural Critique, MELUS, International Journal of Comparative Race and Ethnic Studies*, and *Between Borders: Pedagogy and the Politics of Cultural Studies*. He is now working on a book on W. E. B. Du Bois and contemporary critical theory.

RAFAEL PÉREZ-TORRES is an associate professor of English at UCLA. He studies the connection between contemporary literature and social configurations of race, ethnicity and gender and has published articles on postmodernism, multiculturalism, and such contemporary American authors as Toni Morrison, John Rechy and Luis Rafael Sánchez. His recent work focuses on *mestizaje* and the Chicana/o cultural imagination. In addition to the book *Movements in Chicano Poetry: Against Myths, Against Margins* (Cambridge University Press, 1995), his recent publications include "Chicano Ethnicity, Cultural Hybridity, the Mestizo Voice" (*American Literature* 70.1) and "Nomads and Migrants— Negotiating a Multicultural Postmodernism" (*Latinos and Education: A Critical Reader*, Antonia Darder et al., eds.). His current project is a book-length study of the relationship between ethics and the aesthetics of Chicano fiction.

CARLA L. PETERSON is a professor of English, Comparative Literature, Women's Studies, and American Studies at the University of Maryland-College Park. Recipient of fellowships from the American Council of Learned Societies, the American Association of University Women, and the National Research Council's Postdoctoral Fellowship Program for Minorities, she is the author of *"Doers of the Word": African American Women Speakers and Writers in the North, 1830–1880* (Oxford UP, 1995; paper, Rutgers UP, 1998) and several essays on race, class, and gender in the writings of women writers such as Pauline Hopkins, Gertrude Stein, Frances E. W. Harper, and Charlotte Forten.

LAVINA DHINGRA SHANKAR teaches English at Bates College, in Maine. She teaches courses in South Asian Literature, Asian American Women Writers, and Postcolonial Literature and Theory. With Rajini Srikanth she has co-edited *A Part Yet Apart: South Asians in Asian America* (Temple UP, 1998), an interdisciplinary anthology of critical essays. Previous publications include essays in *Teaching What You're Not: Identity Politics in Higher Education* and *Multiculturalism and Representation*. She is working on two book-length projects—oral narratives of early Indian American immigrants who entered the U.S. before 1965; and an analysis of the cultural production and racial construction of Uday Shankar's dance-dramas in the U.S. and U.K. from 1920–1970.

BRUCE SIMON is an assistant professor of English at SUNY Fredonia and a general editor of the web journal *Workplace* (www.workplace-gsc.com). His published articles have appeared in *Race Consciousness: African-American Studies for the New Century* and *The Social Construction of Race and Ethnicity in the United States*. He is teaching courses in American, African American, and world literature, completing a book manuscript entitled *American Studies and the Race for Hawthorne*, and co-editing a collection of essays on race and trauma.

RAJINI SRIKANTH teaches in the English department at the University of Massachusetts Boston. She is co-editor of the award-winning anthology *Contours of the Heart: South Asians Map North America* (Rutgers, 1996), a collection of poetry, fiction, essays, and photography by first- and second-generation South Asian Americans/Canadians. With Lavina Dhingra Shankar, she is co-editor of *A Part Yet Apart: South Asians in Asian America* (Temple UP, 1998). Her research interests and publications are in Asian American literature, including South Asian American literature and writing in the South Asian diaspora; literature of the American South; Native American literature; whiteness studies; and South Asian American political participation. Her essay "Identity and Admission into the Political Game: The Indian American Community Signs Up" is forthcoming in *Amerasia Journal*. She is currently co-editing a literary collection titled *White Women in Racialized Spaces*.

LENY MENDOZA STROBEL teaches at Sonoma State University in the Hutchins School of Liberal Studies and American Multicultural Studies Department. With Roshni Rustomji-Kerns and Rajini Srikanth, she is co-editor of *Geography of Encounters: People of Asian Descent in the Americas.* (Rowman and Littlefield, 1999). Articles include "You Can Go Home Again: Reimagining Filipino Identity" in *Paterson Literary Review* 27 (1998); and "Coming Full Circle: Narratives of Decolonization Among Post-1965 Filipino Americans" in *Filipino Americans: Transformation and Identity* (Ed. Maria P. P. Root; Thousand Oaks, Ca: Sage Publications, Inc.). See also http://www.newfilipina.com.

SAU-LING CYNTHIA WONG is Professor of Asian American Studies and Ethnic Studies in the Department of Ethnic Studies, University of California, Berkeley. She has published extensively on various aspects of Asian American, especially Chinese American, literature and culture, including gender and sexuality, Chinese-language immigrant and diasporic literature, reception and canon formation, and autobiography—including essays in King-Kok Cheung's *An Interethnic Companion to Asian American Literature* (Cambridge UP, 1997) and Sidonie Smith's *Women, Autobiography, Theory: A Reader* (Wisconsin UP, 1998). She is the author of *Reading Asian American Literature: From Necessity to Extravagance* (Princeton UP, 1993) and editor of *Maxine Hong Kingston's "A Woman Warrior": A Casebook* (Oxford UP, 1999); and with Stephen H. Sumida she is co-editor of *A Resource Guide to Asian American Literature* (Modern Language Association, forthcoming).

NAME INDEX

Abraham, Nabeel, 333 n 14, 333 n 15
Abu-Jaber, Diana, 330, 332, 335 n 29
Achebe, Chinua, 20, 23, 205–07
Acuña, Rodolfo, 45 n 3, 119 n 4
Adams, Brooks, xv, 222
Adell, Sandra, 45 n 1, 260, 263, 272 n 2
Adorno, Theodor, 339
Aguilar-San Juan, Karin, 142 n 8
Ahmad, Aijaz, 25, 50 n 18, 50–51 n 19, 52 n 25, 53 n 29, 144 n 23, 214 n 6, 272 n 1, 274 n 17, 433 n 1
Alarcón, Daniel Coper, 55 n 3, 114
Alarcón, Norma, 396–97, 400
Alejo, (Father) Bert, 366, 367 n 11
Alessandrini, Anthony, 434 n 10, 434 n 14, 435 n 28
Alexander, Meena: Fault Lines, 28; The Shock of Arrival, 28, 34, 385 n 6
Alexie, Sherman, 83, 284
Ali, Agha Shahid, 370, 375, 378–80, 383 n 1, 385 n 16
Ali, Hijab Imtiaz, 377
Allen, Paula Gunn, 36, 267, 293, 297 n 6, 298 n 13, 298 n 14
Allen, Robert, 267
Allen, Theodore W., 36
Amin, Shahid, 26
Amirthanayagam, Indran, 385 n 6

Amos, Daniel, 171 n 24
Anand, Mulk Raj, 35, 55 n 34
Anderson, Benedict, 46–47 n 6, 53–54 n 30
Andrews, William L., 179, 193 n 1
Anthony, Michael, 28
Anzaldúa, Gloria, 13, 30–31, 41, 46 n 6, 116–17, 400, 403, 406, 407
Apess, William, xiii–xiv, 151–75, 169 n 12; Eulogy on King Philip, 152, 153, 158–66; Indian Nullification of the Unconstitutional Laws of Massachusetts, 151, 164, 165
Apodaca, Ray, 282
Appadurai, Arjun, 29, 30, 40, 56 n 39, 372
Appelbaum, Richard, 436 n 35
Appiah, Kwame Anthony, 17–19, 22, 52–53 n 27, 79–82, 86, 89, 168 n 9, 270, 273 n 9, 433 n 1; In My Father's House, 23, 75
Arac, Jonathan, 214 n 8, 395
Arnold, David, 26
Arnold, Matthew, 292–93, 298 n 12
Arteaga, Alfred, 45 n 3, 47 n 9
Asad, Talal, 76–78, 91 n 7
Asante, Molefe, 22
Ashcroft, Bill, 17–19, 25, 28, 32, 33, 45 n 3, 52 n 27, 54 n 31, 73, 208, 214 n 4, 255
Ashwill, Gary, 167 n 4
Atherton, Gertrude, 240 n 8, 241 n 12
Austen, Jane, 19–21; Mansfield Park, 20

451

Babb, Valerie, 36
Bacho, P., x, xix
Bacon, Francis, 200
Baker, Houston A., Jr., 99–100, 102 n 1,
    392, 399–400
Bakhtin, Mikhail, 166 n 2, 177
Balce-Corres, Nerrisa, 143 n 25
Baldwin, James, 12, 99, 433 n 3
Baldwin, Shauna Singh, 385 n 6
Balibar, Etienne, 41, 53–54 n 30
Bambara, Toni Cade, xix–xx, 3, 45 n 1, 400,
    411; *The Salt Eaters*, 399, 401–06, 409 n 6
Banks, Marcus, 46 n 3
Banta, Martha, 241 n 16
Barksdale, Richard, 96
Barrera, Mario, 107
Barron, Pepe, 110
Barthold, Bonnie J., 304, 315 n 3
Bass, Jack, 101
Baym, Nina, 435 n 21, 436 n 44
Bell, Bernard, 45 n 1
Bell, Betty Louise, 83, 86, 91 n 17
Bell, Daniel, 48 n 10
Benjamin, Walter, 3, 76
Bercovitch, Sacvan, 200, 215 n 12
Bernhard, Sandra, 38
Berubé, Michael, 436 n 42
Beveridge, Albert Jeremiah (Senator), 220,
    238
Bevis, William, 86, 92 n 18
Bhabha, Homi, xvi, xix, 23–24, 37, 50 n 18,
    52 n 27, 53–54 n 30, 182, 236, 246, 250,
    258–64, 272 n 4, 273 n 7, 273 n 9, 273 n
    11, 274 n 17, 342–43, 412, 414, 416–19,
    431, 432, 433 n 1, 433 n 2, 434 n 11, 434 n
    13; *Location of Culture*, 258–65, 267–69,
    272, 434 n 10; *Migration and Identity*, 343,
    348
Bhachu, Parminder, 375
Bigler, Ellen, 47 n 9
Bishara, Azmi, 39, 56 n 38
Black, George, 240 n 8
Black Hawk, 164
Blassingame, John B., 101
Blatty, William, 329–30
Blauner, Robert, 45 n 3
Bloom, Allan, 9
Bloom, Harold, 198, 214 n 7, 372
Blyden, Edward, 405

Boas, Frantz, 91 n 17
Boehmer, Elleke, 18, 20–21, 50 n 17
Bonacich, Edna, 436 n 35
Bongie, Chris, 22, 52 n 27
Boudinot, Elias, 169 n 12
Bourdieu, Pierre, 260, 266, 273 n 6, 273 n 12
Bourne, Randolph, viii, 12, 30, 46 n 5, 435 n
    27
Bracey, John H., 45 n 3
Brady, David, 367 n 3
Brah, Avtar, 433 n 2
Braithwaite, Kamau Edward, 314
Branch, Taylor, 56 n 42
Brent, Linda. *See* Jacobs, Harriet
Breslaw, Elaine, 429
Brickhouse, Anna, 435 n 20
Bright, Charles C., 163
Brinton, Daniel, 75
Brodhead, Richard, 436 n 42
Brodber, Erna, xvii, 301, 304, 306, 309–15,
    316 n 9
Brodkin, Karen, 55 n 36
Brown, A. Lavonne, 167 n 4, 297 n 8
Brown, John, 190
Brown, William Wells, *Clotel or The President's
    Daughter*, 184–85
Bruce, Dickson, 45 n 1
Bryant, William Cullen, xiv, 210–11
Bryce, Lord, 212
Buell, Frederick, 53–54 n 30, 143 n 13, 143 n
    22
Buell, Lawrence, xiv, xvii, 29, 45 n 3, 206,
    214 n 2, 436 n 30
Burns, Robert, 205
Busia, Abena, 434 n 10
Butler, Judith, 52 n 25, 433 n 8
Butler-Evans, Elliott, 139
Byron, George Gordon, Lord, 200

Cable, George Washington, 250
Cabral, Amilcar, 20
Caitlin, George, 281
Calderón, Hector, 47 n 9
Callahan, John, 100
Campomanes, Oscar, 129, 137–38, 143 n 16,
    366 n 1, 367 n 5
Canby, Henry Seidel, 220–21, 225, 229
Canclini, Nestor Garcia, 436–37 n 45
Carby, Hazel, 17, 188

Carlyle, Thomas, 205
Carnes, Mark, 190
Carnoy, Martin, 381
Carr, A. L., 83
Carroll, Lewis, 81
Cather, Willa, 37
Cayton, Horace, 99
Césaire, Aimé, 12, 16–17, 20, 203
Cha, Theresa Hak Kyung, 139
Chabram-Dernersesian, Angie, 409 n 7
Chai, Leon, 214 n 8
Chan, Jeffrey Paul, 142 n 5
Chan, Sucheng, 373
Chand, Prem, 35, 55 n 34
Chandler, Nahum, 101, 272 n 2, 273 n 9
Chang, Elaine K., 46 n 6
Chatterjee, Partha, 26, 32, 50–51 n 19, 56 n 39, 339
Chauhan, P. S., 51 n 21
Cheney, Harriet Vaughn Foster, 170 n 19
Chesnutt, Charles W., xv–xvi, 30, 244–57; "The Future American," viii; Uncle Julius Stories, 35; "The Wife of His Youth," 245–47, 250, 254
Cheung, King-Kok, 47 n 9, 129, 142 n 7, 371
Chew, Shirley, 50 n 18
Cheyfitz, Eric, 90 n 3, 168 n 11, 433 n 4
Chief Pokagon, 12, 13
Child, Lydia Maria, 12, 176, 180–81, 184–93
Chin, Frank, 142 n 5, 371, 373–74, 384 n 6
Chin, Vincent, 126
Chow, Rey, 52 n 25, 54 n 30, 416
Chris, Laura, 18
Chrisman, Laura, 55 n 33
Christian, Barbara, 17, 144 n 30, 274 n 14, 274 n 15
Chu, Louis, 373
Chugtai, Ismat, 377
Chuh, Kandice, 124, 374
Chun, Wendy Hui Kyong, 125
Churchill, Ward, 152, 167 n 6
Churchill, Winston (novelist), 237, 240 n 10
Cisneros, Evangelina Cosio y, 231
Cisneros, Sandra, *The House on Mango Street*, 392–99
Cixous, Helene, 306, 435 n 19
Clement, Catherine, 435 n 19

Clark, Vévé, 434 n 15
Clifford, James, 39, 40, 45 n 3, 53–54 n 30, 77
Cobham, Rhonda, xvii, 316 n 8
Coetzee, J. M., 35
Colacurcio, Michael, 198, 214 n 8
Coleridge, Samuel Taylor, 205, 211
Collier, John (Commissioner), 282
Collins, Patricia Hill, 390
Colón, Don Diego, 74
Colón, Rafael Hernández, 344
Coltrane, John, 405
Columbus, Christopher, 74
Condé, Maryse, xx; *Tituba, the Black Witch of Salem*, 412, 413, 419–32
Conklin, Nancy Faire, 325
Conrad, Joseph, 87, 177, 434 n 11; *Heart of Darkness*, 201, 227, 240 n 7
Consul, Wilma, 363
Cook-Lynn, Elizabeth, 89–90, 90 n 2, 152, 167 n 6, 168 n 9
Coombes, Anne, 433 n 2
Coombs, Isaac, 171 n 24
Cooper, Anna Julia, 99
Cooper, James Fenimore, xiv, 204, 206, 209, 216 n 21
Cordova, Filipinos F., xviii, 349
Cowper, William, xiv, 205
Crane, Stephen, 234, 239 n 1
Crawford, Francis Marion, 240 n 10
Crenshaw, Kimberle, 433 n 7
Crevecoeur, Hector St. John de, 9–10
Crouch, Stanley, 49 n 11
Cruse, Harold, 267–68
Cruz, Celia, 345
Cruz, Philip Vera, xviii, 349–50
Cruz, Victor Hernández, 340, 345
Cuesta, Jorge, 110

Dabydeen, Cyril, 384–85 n 6
Dangaremba, Tsitsi, 28
Daniels, Jessie, 55–56 n 36
Dannenberg, Anne Marie, 167 n 4
DasGupta, Sayantani, 374
Dasgupta, Shamita, 374
Davidson, Cathy N., 193 n 8, 193 n 11, 433 n 3
Davies, Carol Boyce, 17, 433 n 4
Davis, Allen F., 46 n 5

Davis, Angela, 99, 144n 29, 270, 316n 6, 436n 32

Davis, John (Governor), 171n 25

Davis, Richard Harding, xv, 225, 228–31, 234–35, 240n 10

Dayal, Samir, 434n 14

de Burton, María Ámparo Ruiz, 12

De Forest, John, 75

de Leon, Luz, 352, 354, 362, 367n 3, 367n 8

de Lisser, H. G., 307

de Tocqueville, Alexis, ix, 200, 202, 205, 212, 215n 13

DeHart, Evelyn Hu, 133

DeLand, Clyde O., 256n 3

Delany, Martin R., 405; *Blake*, 189–91, 194n 12

Deleuze, Gilles, 119n 5, 317n 13

Delgado, Richard, 55–56n 36

Deloria, Vine, Jr., 152–54, 166n 1, 167n 6, 167n 7, 280, 282, 287, 289

Demott, Benjamin, 46n 5

Dent, Gina, 268

Derrida, Jacques, 25, 27, 46–47n 6, 372, 416–17

Desmond, Jane, 45n 2

Dexter, Lincoln, 170n 18

Dhaliwal, Amarpal K., 53–54n 30

Diawara, Manthia, 97–99, 102

Díaz, Porfirio, 396

Diaz-Abaya, Marilou, 364

Díaz-Quiñones, Arcadio, xviii, 338–48

Dick, Bruce, 55n 35

Dickens, Charles, 201–02, 215n 13, 215n 14

Dickinson, Emily, 379, 385n 16

Dimock, Wai-chee, 45n 3

Dionne, E. J., Jr., 48n 10

Dirlik, Arif, 50n 18, 56n 39, 73, 92n 21, 122–23, 142n 9, 269, 274n 17, 433n 1

Dissanayake, Wimal, 45n 2

Divakaruni, Chitra, 383, 385n 6

Dixon, John, 91n 7

Doi, Yuriko, 363

Dominguez, Virginia, 36, 45n 2

Dorris, Michael, 83

Douglass, Frederick, 53–54n 30, 198, 215n 16, 405, 413

Dow, George, 322, 334n 26

Drake, Alexander, 160

Drake, Samuel Gardner, 160–61, 169n 14, 170n 18

Drake, Sandra E., 409n 1

Drinnon, Richard, 49n 14, 88, 239n 3

D'Souza, Dinesh, 49n 11

Du Bois, W. E. B., viii, 3, 12–13, 20–21, 30, 35, 44, 45n 1, 46n 5, 50n 17, 53–54n 30, 96, 98, 248, 393, 403, 405, 409n 3, 433n 3; *Dark Princess*, 274n 16, 274n 21; *Dusk at Dawn: An Essay Toward an Autobiography of Race Concept*, 259, 271–72, 273n 9; *The Souls of Black Folk*, xvi, 21, 44, 98, 258–72, 409n 3

Duany, Jorge, 13

Dubbert, Joe, 240n 5

duCille, Ann, 433n 4

Dukats, Mara, 434n 13, 435n 25

Durham, Jimmie, 283

During, Simon, 19, 22, 28

Dyer, Richard, 55n 36

Eagleton, Terry, 15, 53n 29

Early, Gerald, 45n 1

Eastes, Sandra María, 342–43, 345, 348

Eaton, Edith Maude, 370

Eliot, George, 198

Eliot, John, 163

Eliot, T. S., 21, 91n 17

Elizondo, Sergio, 115, 117

Ellington, Duke, 9, 29, 35

Ellis, Tom, 322

Ellison, Ralph, 53–54n 30, 99, 433n 3; *Invisible Man*, 36–37

Emerson, Ralph Waldo, 197–98, 205, 210

Engels, Friedrich, 269

Enriquez, Virgilio, 351

Erdrich, Louise, 83

Espiritu, August, xviii, 349–50, 366n 1

Esteves, Sandra María, 340–41, 345

Estrada, Noel, 346

Ethington, Philip J., 49–50n 15

Everett, Edward, 153, 156–58, 161–63, 168–69n 12, 170n 21

Ezekiel, Nissim, 208

Fairchild, H. P., 46n 5

Faires, Nora, 325

Fanon, Frantz, 12, 17, 20, 26, 38, 50n 17,

51 n 20, 54 n 33, 107–09, 230, 258, 272, 282, 339, 381
Faulk, Tina, 436 n 36
Faulkner, William, 91 n 17, 344
Ferguson, 279, 289
Ferris, Joseph, 323
Feuer, Lewis, 102 n 1
Fine, Michelle, 46–47 n 6, 55 n 36
Fish, Phineas, 171 n 25
Fisher, Dexter, 298 n 11, 298 n 12
Fisher, Lawrence, 317 n 15
Fisher, Philip, 49 n 11
Fishkin, Shelley Fisher, 433 n 3
Fitch, Thomas, 430
Fleishmann, Anne, xv
Flores, Juan, xviii, 14
Forbes, Jack, 415
Ford, Paul Leicester, 240 n 10
Foster, Frances Smith, 193 n 3
Foucault, Michel, 16, 27, 47 n 16, 258, 272, 342–43, 348
Fox, Robert Elliot, 17, 55 n 36
Franco, Jean, 55 n 33
Frankenburg, Ruth, 35, 55 n 36, 327, 433 n 1
Franklin, Benjamin, 9, 213, 237
Franklin, John Hope, 12, 96
Frazier, E. Franklin, 46–47 n 6, 49 n 14, 99, 266
Frederickson, George, 257 n 2
Friedman, Thomas L., 39
Friere, Paulo, 351
Frye, Northrop, 81
Fuchs, Lawrence, 49 n 11
Fuentes, Carlos, 215 n 17
Fukuyama, Francis, 6, 9–10, 39, 48 n 10
Fuller, Margaret, 215 n 16
Fusco, Coco, 345, 348
Fuss, Diana, 403–04

Gandhi, Leela, 26, 27, 51 n 19
Garane, Jeanne, 425, 434 n 13, 434 n 19, 436 n 39
Gardner, Eric, 193 n 10
Garrison, William Lloyd, 182
Garvey, Marcus, 20–21, 55 n 36, 405
Gates, Henry Louis, Jr., 17, 51 n 20, 55 n 35, 99–100, 188, 193 n 5, 215 n 9, 404
Gatewood, Willard, 248

Geertz, Clifford, 56 n 37
George, Rosemary Marangoly, 53 n 29
Ghosh, Amitav, 50 n 18
Giago, Tim, 283
Giddings, Franklin, xv, 223
Gilbert, Sandra, 241 n 16
Giles, Paul, 53–54 n 30
Gilman, Charlotte Perkins, 312
Gilroy, Paul, 17, 21–22, 45 n 1, 51–52 n 23, 54 n 30, 100, 132–33, 198, 260–61, 264, 272 n 2, 273 n 3, 434 n 10; *The Black Atlantic*, 20–21, 198
Gingrich, Newt, 141
Giroux, Henry, 46 n 6, 55–56 n 36
Gitlin, Todd, 48 n 10
Glancy, Diane, 83–86
Glass, Lauren, 49 n 12
Gleason, Phillip, 46 n 5
Goethe, Johann, 205
Goldberg, David Theo, 55 n 36
Goldsmith, Oliver, 205, 273
Gómez-Peña, Guillermo, 46 n 6, 115–16
Gómez-Quiñones, Juan, 112, 119 n 2
Gonzales, N. V. M., 351, 355, 357, 361, 364, 366 n 1, 366 n 3, 367 n 5, 375
Gonzales, Rodolfo "Corky," 108
Gonzales, Sylvia, 112
González, Deena, 119 n 1
González, José Luis, 339
González, Narita, xix, 367 n 7
Gopinath, Gayatri, 125, 376
Gordimer, Nadine, 35
Gorn, Elliott, 224, 240 n 5
Gossett, Thomas Y., 55–56 n 36
Gotanda, Neil, 433 n 7
Graff, Gerald, 436 n 41, 436 n 44
Graham, Maryemma, 37
Gramsci, Antonio, 16, 26–27, 97, 265
Grant, Bruce, 142 n 9
Graulich, Melody, 91 n 15
Greenblatt, Stephen, 74
Grewal, Gurleen, 434 n 14, 436 n 31
Grewal, Inderpal, 17, 39, 46 n 3, 50 n 16, 52 n 25, 53–54 n 30, 55 n 33, 132, 138
Griffiths, Gareth, 17–19, 22, 23, 25, 28, 32, 33, 45 n 3, 52 n 27, 54 n 31, 73, 75, 79, 81–82, 86, 89, 208, 214 n 4, 255, 273 n 9, 433 n 1
Gross, Elizabeth, 27

Grossman, Jay, 435 n 20

Grund, Francis, 202

Guattari, Felix, 119 n 5

Gubar, Susan, 55 n 36

Guha, Ranajit, 26, 52 n 25

Guillory, John, 167 n 5, 266, 273 n 6, 274 n 15

Gupta, Akhil, 279, 289

Guzman, Ralph, 119 n 4

Hagedorn, Jessica, xix, 132, 134, 137, 355

Hall, G. Stanley, 233

Hall, Stuart, 8, 17, 31, 39, 45–46 n 3, 53 n 29, 53–54 n 30, 95, 101, 138, 279, 433 n 1, 433 n 8, 436 n 40, 436–37 n 45

Hallet, Benjamin, 171 n 23

Handlin, Oscar, 6, 9, 12, 14–15, 49–50 n 15

Haney Lopez, Ian F., 36, 55 n 36, 321–22, 333 n 4, 333 n 5

Hansen, Chadwick, 436 n 37

Haraway, Donna, 315 n 1

Hardiman, David, 26

Harding, Vincent, 95–97, 102

Harper, Francis E. W., 12, 35

Harring, Sidney L., 159, 167 n 7

Harrington, John, 425

Harris, Cheryl, 55–56 n 36

Harris, Wilson, 301, 306, 314

Hart, James D., 240 n 11

Harvey, David, 436 n 35

Hassan, Ahmed, 323

Hawthorne, Nathaniel, 170 n 14, 197, 207, 210, 413–37; The Scarlet Letter, xx, 198

Hay, John, 223

Hegel, Georg Wilhelm Friedrich, 9–10, 39, 260–61, 263, 273 n 4, 304, 314, 315 n 1

Heidegger, Martin, 258, 272

Hellwig, David, 51 n 22

Hemingway, Ernest, 37

Henderson, Mae G., xii

Henderson, Stephen, 100

Henry, Gordon, 83

Herder, Johann Gottfried von, 75

Herskovits, Melville, 12

Hicks, D. Emily, 46 n 6

Higham, John, 51 n 22, 239 n 2

Hill, Mike, 55 n 36

Hillerman, Tony, 91 n 14

Hing, Bill Ong, 142 n 8

Hirsch, Marianne, 317 n 12

Hitti, Philip, 333 n 8

Hobsbawm, Eric, 240 n 6

Hobson, J. A., 234

Hodge, Merle, xvii, 214 n 4, 274 n 17, 433 n 1; Crick Crack, Monkey, 301–02, 308–09, 311

Hofstadter, Richard, 239 n 2

Hogan, Robert E., 28–29, 46 n 5, 49 n 12

Hollinger, David, 6, 49 n 11, 334 n 24

Hongo, Garrett, 382

hooks, bell, 17, 99, 193 n 2; Black Looks, 38; Outlaw Culture, 34

Hope, Anthony, 226

Hopkins, Pauline, 177

Howells, William Dean, 220, 225, 227, 240 n 11

Hsiao, Ruth, 434 n 14

Huang, John, 126

Hubbard, William, 163, 170 n 14

Huggins, Nathan, 101

Hughes, Langston, 35, 393

Hull, Gloria, 401

Humez, Jean McMahon, 306

Huntington, Samuel, 39

Hurston, Zora Neale, 35, 99, 409 n 5

Hutcheon, Linda, 17

Hutchinson, George, 49 n 12

Hymes, Dell, 78, 281

Iglesias, César Andreu, 339

Ignacio, Abraham, 353, 367 n 3

Ignatiev, Noel, 36, 55 n 36

Inada, Lawson Fusao, 142 n 5

Irving, Washington, 206

Iyer, Nalini, 434 n 14, 434 n 18

Jackson, Andrew, 163, 169 n 12, 306

Jackson, Rebecca, 306

Jacobs, Harriet, 176–95, 198; Incidents in the Life of a Slave Girl, 185–86

Jaimes, Annette, 90, 92 n 24

James, C. L. R., 12, 21, 53–54 n 30

James, Colin, 142 n 9

James, Henry, 197, 210

Jameson, Frederic, 43, 48 n 10, 49 n 13, 50–51 n 19, 53–54 n 30, 91 n 11, 268–69, 282, 304, 315 n 2, 316 n 7, 317 n 13

JanMohammed, Abdul, 17, 40, 46 n 6, 142 n 4, 167 n 8, 244, 274 n 17, 412, 433 n 2
Jay, Gregory, 433 n 4
Jefferies, Leonard, 22
Jefferson, Thomas, 9, 45 n 3, 184
Jehlen, Myra, 222, 433 n 4
Jenkins, Leigh, 287, 289
Jewett, Sarah Orne, 239 n 1
Johnson, Charles, 56 n 42
Johnson, David E., 46 n 6, 47 n 9, 55 n 33
Johnson, Pauline, 91 n 12
Johnston, Mary, xv, 225–31
Jones, Gayl, 99–100, 102 n 3
Jordan, June, 56 n 42
Joseph, Lawrence, 330, 335 n 28
Joshi, Irene, 371
Joyce, James, 21, 81
Juárez, Benito, 111
Julien, Isaac, 101

Kabadi, Udaya, 385 n 17
Kabotie, Michael, 77
Kadi, Joanna, 334 n 31
Kaldas, Pauline, 331, 335 n 30
Kallen, Horace, 12, 46 n 5
Kammen, Michael, 237
Kandiyoti, Deniz, 55 n 33
Kaplan, Amy, xv, xvii, 29, 45 n 3, 46 n 5, 49 n 13, 55 n 33, 214 n 5, 433 n 4
Kaplan, Caren, 17, 39, 50 n 16, 52 n 25, 53–54 n 30, 55 n 33
Kataria, Gulshan, 384 n 6
Katrak, Ketu, 17, 53–54 n 30, 55 n 33, 370
Kazin, Alfred, viii
Keats, John, 198
Kemp, Mark, 436 n 43
Kern, Stephen, 240 n 9
Kett, Joseph, 240 n 5
Khoury, Ghada, 334 n 20
Kiang, Peter, 143 n 27
Kim, Elaine, 123, 129, 137, 139, 371
Kincaid, Jamaica, 317 n 15
Kincheloe, Joe L., 55 n 6
King, Deborah, 316 n 4
King, Martin Luther, Jr., 56 n 42, 403
King, Rodney, 139
Kingston, Maxine Hong, 142 n 6, 373
Kipling, Rudyard, 19, 201
Kirk, Carmen, 367 n 3

Kissinger, Henry, 88
Klor de Alva, Jorge, 109, 113
Knadler, Stephen, 250
Knight, Grant C., 240 n 11
Knippling, Alpana Sharma, 385 n 6, 434 n 14, 436 n 31
Kogawa, Joy, 385 n 6
Kolodny, Annette, 47 n 9
Konkle, Maureen, xiii, xvii
Koshy, Susan, 56 n 37, 123, 370, 372
Kristeva, Julia, 315 n 2
Kroeber, Karl, 166 n 1
Krupat, Arnold, xi–xii, xvi–xvii, 29, 90 n 5, 91 n 6, 164–65, 166 n 1–2, 167 n 9, 167 n 9, 296 n 1
Kuhn, Thomas, 102 n 1

Labarthe, Elyette, 109, 112
Lacan, Jacques, 417
Laclau, Ernesto, 118, 119 n 6, 435 n 24
LaFeber, Walter, 240 n 4
Lam, Andrew, 372
Lamming, George, 203, 301, 305, 314
Lan, Nguyen Ngoe, 143 n 27
Landry, Donna, 25, 27, 52 n 25
Larson, Charles, 166 n 2
Lasch, Christopher, 48 n 10
Lauter, Paul, 433 n 5
Lavie, Smardar, 45 n 2
Laviera, Tato, 341, 346, 348
Lawson-Peebles, Robert, 211
Lazarre, Jane, 55–56 n 36
Leal, Luis, 110–12
Lears, T. J. Jackson, 239 n 2, 240 n 11
Lee, Ang, 130
Lee, Sharon M., 334 n 23
Lee, Spike, 22
Lejeune, Phillippe, 193 n 7
Lemke, Sieglinde, 22, 53–54 n 30
Lenin, Vladimir, 227, 270
Lenz, Guenter, 46 n 5
Leong, Russell, 122, 134, 143 n 19
Levine, Lawrence, 100, 185, 409 n 4
Levitt, Theodore, 39, 56 n 37
Li, David, 125
Lienhardt, Godfrey, 77
Lim, Shirley, 129, 373–74
Limbaugh, Rush, 141
Lincoln, Kenneth, 166 n 2, 170 n 18

Linderman, Gerald, 240 n 13
Ling, Amy, 129
Ling, Janqi, 373–74
Lipsitz, George, 42, 47 n 8, 56 n 42, 99, 102
Little Eagle, Avis, 282
Littlefield, Daniel F., Jr., 167 n 6, 167 n 9
Liu, Eric, 49 n 11, 126
Liu, Haiming, 130
Livingstone, W. P., 316 n 9
Lloyd, David, 17
Locke, Alain, 21, 50 n 17, 99
Longfellow, Henry Wadsworth, 210
Loomba, Ania, 18, 54 n 33, 274 n 17
Lopez, Ian F. Haney. *See* Haney Lopez, Ian F.
Lorde, Audre, 55 n 35
Louis, Adrian, 83
L'Ouverture, Pierre Toussaint, 190
Lowe, Lisa, xiii, 17, 31, 33, 40, 47 n 9, 123–
    24, 133, 136–37, 143 n 22, 143 n 23,
    215 n 9, 371, 381, 384 n 2
Lubiano, Wahneema, 271–72, 436 n 32
Luedtke, Luther, 436 n 43
Lugo, Alejandro, 46 n 6
Lumumba, Patrice, 270
Lye, Colleen, 144 n 32
Lyell, Charles, 201
Lytle, Clifford M., 154, 167 n 7, 280, 282

Mabanglo, Ruth, xix, 355
Macaulay, Thomas, ix, 24
McBride, James, 55–56 n 36
McClintock, Anne, 40, 45 n 2, 54 n 33, 197,
    215 n 10, 274 n 17, 412, 433 n 1, 433 n 2,
    436 n 33
McCutcheon, George Barr, xv, 225, 227–28,
    233, 240 n 10
McGrath, Harold, 240 n 10
McKay, Claude, 21, 51 n 21, 307, 313
McKinley, William, 231
MacLean, Gerald, 25, 27, 52 n 25
McLean, Justice John, 156, 161
McLoughlin, William, 170–71 n 23
McNickle, D'Arcy, 91 n 12
McQuaid, Kim, 170 n 17
McVeigh, Timothy, 327
McWilliams, John P., Jr., 216 n 18
Magadaleno, Jana Sequoya. *See* Sequoya Ma-
    gadaleno, Jana
Majaj, Lisa, xvii–xviii

Major, Charles, 225
Manguerra-Brainard, Cecilia, xix, 355–56
Mann, Harveen Sachdeva, 34–35, 54 n 31
Manning, Elizabeth Clark, 435 n 21
Mansfield, Katherine, 21
Manto, Sadat Hassan, 377
Manzor-Coats, Lillian, 434 n 15, 435 n 29
Marable, Manning, 177
Marcos, Ferdinand, 143 n 25, 349
Marcus, Alan, 46 n 4
Marcus, George, 77
Marley, Bob, 53–54 n 30
Marmon, Robert, 297 n 8
Marqués, René, 339
Marryat, Frederick, 213
Marsh, George Perkins, 209
Marshall, John Justice, 154–59, 169 n 10
Marshall, Paule, xvii, 301–02, 304, 308, 309,
    312, 315, 316 n 10
Marston, Charles, 171 n 25
Martí, José, viii, 12–13, 30, 345
Martineau, Harriet, 215 n 13
Martorell, Antonio, 344, 348 n 2
Marvell, Andrew, 207
Marx, Karl, 269–71
Masayesva, Vernon, 287, 289
Massad, Joseph, 332 n 1
Massey, Douglass, 119 n 3
Masters, Beigh, 422
Matthews, John Joseph, 91 n 12
Matthiessen, F. O., 197
Mattina, Anthony, 76
Mazumdar, Sucheta, 43, 128, 131, 383
Medicine, Bea, 282
Melville, Herman, xiv, 37, 197–98, 206, 212,
    215 n 13
Melwani, Lavina, 385 n 17
Memmi, Albert, 215 n 15, 236
Mercer, Kobena, 101
Merriwell, Frank, 240 n 10
Meyer, John R., 177
Michaels, Walter Benn, 49 n 12, 253, 256 n 4
Michaelsen, Scott, 46 n 6, 47 n 9
Miller, Perry, 200
Milton, John, 197, 200
Minh-ha, Trinh T., 17, 33, 365; *A Tale of Love*
    (film), 34
Mishra, Vijay, 54 n 31, 214 n 4, 274 n 17,
    433 n 1

Mistry, Rohinton, 17, 384–85 n 6
Mitchell, S. Weir, 237, 240 n 10
Mitter, Swasti, 436 n 35
Miyoshi, Masao, 53–54 n 30, 433 n 1
Moallem, Minoo, 54–55 n 33
Modood, Tariq, 433 n 2
Mohan, Rajeswari, 436 n 32
Mohanty, Chandra Talpade, 17, 25, 33, 54 n
    32, 55 n 33, 132–33, 436 n 35
Mohanty, Satya, 17
Momaday, N. Scott, 91 n 13, 283, 286, 290–
    92, 297 n 9, 298 n 15; *The House Made of
    Dawn*, 78–83, 289–93
Monhanram, Radhika, 31, 53 n 29
Montgomery, Benilde, 434 n 16
Montgomery, Ellen, 215 n 16
Montoya, José, 113
Moon, Michael, 433 n 3
Mootoo, Shani, xix, 370, 375
Moreiras, Alberto, 433 n 2, 436–37 n 45
Morris, Nomi, 56 n 38, 56 n 39
Morrison, Toni, 317 n 12, 320, 344, 389–90,
    393, 409 n 2, 433 n 3, 434 n 13; *The Bluest
    Eye*, 37; *Playing in the Dark*, 36–37, 381,
    433 n 3; *Sula*, xix–xx, 389–91, 393
Morsberger, Robert, 436 n 37
Morsy, Soheir, 325, 333 n 13
Mortorell, Antonio, 348 n 2
Mostern, Kenneth, xvi, 21, 270, 274 n 18
Mott, Frank Luther, 240 n 11
Mufti, Aamir, 45 n 2, 54 n 33
Mukherjee, Arun, 17, 54 n 31
Mukherjee, Bharati, xx, 372, 384–85 n 6,
    385 n 7; *The Holder of the World*, 413, 419,
    421–37; *Jasmine*, 372
Mukherjee, Meenakshi, 50 n 18
Mura, David, 134
Murray, Albert, 99, 433 n 3
Murray, David, 78, 90 n 3, 167 n 4
Myrdal, Günnar, 6, 9, 12, 53–54 n 30

Naber, Nadine, 327, 333 n 7, 335 n 32
Naff, Alixa, 321, 333 n 8
Naipaul, V. S., 24, 28, 211–12, 215 n 14,
    312, 314, 317 n 15, 434 n 11
Najmi, Samina, 55–56 n 36
Nakamura, Lisa, 125
Naqvi, Tahira, xix, 370, 375–78
Narayan, Kirin, 41

Narayan, R. K., 28
Nash, Gerald D., 49 n 13, 194 n 13
Nelson, Emmanuel, 385 n 6
Newfield, Christopher, 436 n 32
Newitz, Annalee, 55–56 n 36
Ngugi, Thiong'o wa, 22
Nicol, Abioseh, 216 n 21
Nielsen, Donald M., 170 n 17
Nietzsche, Friedrich, 23
Nkosi, Lewis, 28, 216 n 21
Nkrumah, Kwame, 19
Nojeim, Gregory, 327
Nonini, Donald, 125
Norris, Frank, 223, 226, 227, 239 n 1
North, Oliver, 236

Obregón, Alvaro, 110
O'Connell, Barry, 164, 165, 167 n 4, 170 n
    21
Odeh, Alex, 326
Okada, John, 373
Okara, Gabriel, 208
Okihiro, Gary, 15, 56 n 42
Omi, Michael, 7, 45 n 3, 47 n 8, 122, 327,
    332–33 n 2, 333 n 10, 373, 433 n 7
Ondaatje, Michael, 17, 384–85 n 6
Ong, Aihwa, 125, 135
Ortiz, Alfonzo, 3
Ortiz, Simon J., 77, 152, 167 n 6
Ortner, Sherry, 307, 316 n 5
Oskinson, John Milton, 91 n 12
Ouologuem, Yambo, 79, 89
Ow, Jeffrey, 125
Owens, Louis, 82–83, 86, 91 n 13, 166 n 2

Packett, Alice Payne, 241 n 10
Padilla, Efrin, 350, 358–60, 367 n 3
Padilla, Genero, 111
Palma, Tomás Estrada, 237
Palumbo-Liu, David, xiii, 125, 126, 143 n 17,
    143 n 20, 373, 383, 384 n 4, 413–15,
    433 n 6, 436 n 32
Pandey, Gyan, 26
Panniwitz, Rudolph, 76
Paredes, Américo, 12, 14, 47 n 6, 49 n 14
Park, Louisa, 169 n 12
Park, Robert, 12, 46–47 n 6, 49 n 14
Parris, Samuel, 430
Parry, Benita, 25, 52–53 n 27, 412, 416

Parsons, Elsie Clews, 297 n 8
Paul, Pope John, II, 92 n 19
Paz, Octavio, 110–11
Pearce, Roy Harvey, 49 n 14, 88, 198
Pease, Donald, 45 n 3, 46 n 5, 50 n 15, 214 n
    5, 433 n 4
Pedreira, Antonio S., 339
Peller, Gary, 433 n 7
Penn, W. S., 83–84, 86
Pérez, Louis A., 241 n 13
Pérez-Torres, Rafael, xii–xiii, 433 n 4
Peterson, Carla, xiv
Peyer, Bernd C., 167 n 4
Pfeil, Fred, 434 n 14, 436 n 31
Philcox, Richard, 420
Philip, King, 160–61
Phillips, Caryl, 17
Phillips, Kevin, 55 n 36
Pieterse, Jan Nederveen, 437 n 46
Pietri, Pedro, 345, 348
Pilipino, Sikolohiyang, 367 n 3
Pittman, John, 9
Plath, Sylvia, 312, 313, 317 n 15, 317 n 16
Poe, Edgar Allan, 37, 198, 413
Porter, Carolyn, 45 n 2, 214 n 2, 433 n 4
Porter, Dorothy, 99
Post, Amy, 181
Pound, Ezra, 21
Power, Susan, 83
Prakash, Gyan, 259, 433 n 1, 434 n 10, 437 n
    46
Pratt, Mary Louise, 46–47 n 6, 215 n 13
Proust, Marcel, 91 n 17
Puar, Jasbir, 125
Purley, Tony, 297 n 8
Purley, Wilma, 297 n 8
Pynchon, Thomas, 422

Quiñones, Arcadio Díaz, 338–48

Radhakrishnan, R., 39, 124, 214 n 3, 374,
    433 n 1
Rai, Amit S., 125
Rajan, Gita, 31, 53 n 29, 434 n 14, 436 n 36
Rama, Angel, 339
Ramadan, Mary, 334 n 20
Ramsey, Jarold, 166 n 1
Ramos, Julio, 346
Ranger, Terence, 240 n 6

Rao, Anupama, 384 n 2
Rao, Raja, 21, 208
Ray, Satyajit, 55 n 34
Realuyo, Bino, xix, 356
Redding, J. Saunders, 96
Reddy, Maureen, 55–56 n 36
Reed, Ishmael, 55 n 35
Reising, Russell, 436 n 44
Reno, Janet, 334 n 19
Resnick, Stephen, 273–74 n 13
Rétamar, Fernández, 88
Reynolds, Larry J., 214 n 8
Rhys, Jean, 21, 314
Rich, Adrienne, 306
Ridgeway, James, 55–56 n 36
Rihbany, Abraham Mitrie (Reverend),
    328–30
Riley, Joan, 317 n 15
Rivera, Edward, 342
Rivkin, Julie, 51–52 n 23
Rizal, José, 363
Rizk, Salom, 334 n 27
Robertson, William, 169 n 16
Robinson, Armstead, 101
Rodo, José Enrique, 216 n 17
Roediger, David, 55–56 n 36
Rogin, Michael, 239 n 3, 240 n 17
Roman, David, 119 n 1
Roosevelt, Theodore, 222, 224, 230, 236,
    239, 240 n 7, 240 n 8
Rosaldo, Renato, 29, 46–47 n 6, 224, 339
Rosenberg, Emily, 240 n 8
Rosenthal, Bernard, 436 n 37, 436 n 39
Rosenwald, Lawrence, 216 n 20
Ross, Edward, 46 n 5
Rotundo, Edward Anthony, 240 n 5
Rouse, Roger, 436 n 32
Rowbotham, Sheila, 436 n 35
Rowe, John Carlos, 47–48 n 9
Rowlandson, Mary, 161, 422
Rumpel, Steve, 143 n 28
Runkle, Bertha, 240 n 10
Ruoff, A. Lavonne Brown, 167 n 4
Ruppel, F. Timothy, 434 n 14
Rushdie, Salman, 17, 22, 24, 132, 209
Russ, Joanna, 306
Rustomji-Kerns, Roshni, 385 n 6
Ryan, Michael, 51–52 n 23

Sáenz, Benjamin Alire, 46 n 6
Safran, William, 107
Said, Edward, 3, 16–17, 19–20, 25, 27, 39,
    40, 44, 51–52 n 23, 54 n 30, 88, 132, 153,
    167 n 8, 215 n 13, 221, 259, 320, 324,
    331–32, 339, 341–42; *Culture and Imperi-
    alism*, 19–20; *Orientalism*, 16–17, 49–50 n
    19, 167 n 8
Salazar, Inés, xix
Saldívar, José David, 17, 31, 46 n 6, 47 n 9,
    49 n 14, 133, 215 n 9, 433 n 4
Saldívar, Ramón, 392
Saliba, Theresa, 324
Samhan, Helen, 326
San Juan, E., Jr., 40, 45 n 3, 137, 351–52,
    367 n 9
Sánchez, George, 14, 29, 49 n 15
Sánchez, Luis Rafael, 347 n 1, 348
Sánchez, Maria Dolores Luque de, 339
Sánchez-Eppler, Karen, 183
Sander, Reinhard, 316 n 8
Sandoval, Chela, 112
Santiago, Esmeralda, 342–43, 345, 348
Sayre, Gordon, 167 n 4
Scarberry-Garcia, Susan, 91 n 13
Scarboro, Ann Armstrong, 434 n 15
Scheckel, Susan, 168 n 11
Scheper-Hughes, Nancy, 295
Schlesinger, Arthur J., Jr., 6, 9, 10, 48 n 10
Schmidt, Peter, 386 n 16
Schoolcraft, Henry Rowe, 166 n 1
Schubnell, Matthias, 91 n 13
Schueller, Malini Johar, 45 n 3
Schuyler, George S., 35–36, 46 n 4
Scott, Sir Walter, 200, 207–08, 215 n 16,
    220, 240 n 11
Sekora, John, 434 n 16
Selvon, Sam, 384–85 n 6
Sembene, Ousmane, 23
Sen, Amartya, 56 n 39
Senghor, Leopold Sedar, 20, 23, 52 n 24
Senior, Olive, 317 n 14
Sequeira, Isaac, 46 n 4
Sequoya Magadaleno, Jana, xvi
Shadid, Michael, 333 n 3, 334 n 27
Shahid, Faras, 322
Shakespeare, William, 81, 197, 200; *The
    Tempest*, 203–04
Shakir, Evelyn, 329

Shankar, Lavina Dhingra, xix, 43, 47 n 9,
    385 n 6, 433 n 6
Shankman, Arnold, 51 n 22
Sharma, Maya Manju, 434 n 14, 436 n 30
Sharma, S., 274 n 17
Sharpe, Jenny, 45 n 3, 55 n 33, 214 n 1, 246,
    375
Sheehan, Richard Lee, 143 n 27
Shelton, Marie-Denise, 435 n 19
Shklovsky, R. Viktor, 97
Shi, Zhongx-in, 142 n 9
Shimakawa, Karen, 124
Shinagawa, Larry, 351
Shohat, Ella, 45 n 2, 54 n 33, 197, 375, 433 n
    1
Sidhwa, Bapsi, 385 n 6
Silko, Leslie Marmon, xii, 78–82, 88–90,
    92 n 20, 92 n 21, 166 n 2, 286, 290, 298 n
    12, 298 n 15; *Almanac of the Dead*, 79, 293;
    Ceremony, 78–83, 87, 91 n 16, 289–96,
    297 n 6, 298 n 14, 298 n 15; *Storyteller*, 85
Silvestrini, Blanca, 339
Simon, Bruce, xx
Singh, Amritjit, 28–29, 37, 38, 45 n 1, 46 n
    4, 46 n 5, 49 n 12, 51 n 21, 55 n 35, 371,
    384–85 n 6, 385 n 12
Singh, Nikhil Pal, 53–54 n 30
Sinha, Mrinalini, 32
Sivanandan, A., 436 n 35
Skerrett, Joseph T., Jr., 28–29, 46 n 5, 49 n
    12
Skidmore, Max J., 46 n 4
Slotkin, Richard, 49 n 14, 214 n 5, 239 n 3
Smith, Henry Nash, 49 n 14
Smith, Paul, 178
Smith, Sydney, 200
Smith, Valerie, 193 n 5
Snead, James, 206, 315 n 1
Snelling, William Joseph, 151, 164–65,
    170 n 22
Sollors, Werner, 6, 10–11, 47 n 9, 49 n 12,
    245–46; *Beyond Ethnicity*, 48–49 n 11, 49 n
    12, 371; "A Critique of Cultural Plural-
    ism," 48–49, 49 n 12
Song, Min, 385 n 11
Sowell, Thomas, 10, 48 n 10
Soyinka, Wole, 23, 52 n 24, 209–10
Spanos, William V., 47–48 n 9, 436 n 44
Spencer, Benjamin, 215 n 11

Spengemann, William, 198

Spillers, Hortense, 47n9, 99, 183, 193n9, 268, 274n14, 391

Spivak, Gayatri Chakravorty, xiii, xvi, 17, 25–27, 40–41, 45–46n3, 50n16, 50n 19, 52n26, 52n27, 53n28, 54n30, 56n 41, 259, 271, 273n11, 273–74n13, 314, 375, 383, 425, 433n4, 435n23, 436n 45; "Can the Subaltern Speak?," 26–27, 167n8; *A Critique of Postcolonial Reason,* 25–27; *In Other Worlds,* 25, 56n37; *Outside in the Teaching Machine,* 25, 56n39, 433n 4; *The Post-Colonial Critic,* 25, 53n28; "Rani of Sirmur," 167n8

Spurr, David, 215n13

Srikanth, Rajini, ix, xix, 43, 47n9, 55n36, 56n36, 385n6, 385n15

Standish, Miles, 162

Steele, Shelby, 6

Stefancic, Jean, 55–56n36

Stein, Gertrude, 413

Steinberg, Stephen, 49n12

Stephens, Gregory, 46–47n6, 49n12, 53–54n30

Stepto, Robert B., 264

Stevens, Wallace, 81

Stevenson, Robert Louis, 226

Stoddard, Elizabeth, 215n16

Stone, Carole, 434n14, 436n30

Stowe, Harriet Beecher, 181, 185, 188, 194n 12

Strobel, Leny Mendoza, xviii–xix, 355, 385n 13

Strong, Josiah (Reverend), 226

Sui Sin Far. *See* Eaton, Edith Maude

Suleri, Sara, 17, 32, 54n32, 385n6

Sumida, Stephen, 45n3, 372, 385n8

Sundquist, Eric, xv, 167n4, 245–46, 249, 270, 433n4

Susman, Warren I., 49n13

Swann, Brian, 74–75, 90n3, 166n1

Swedenberg, Ted, 45n2

Tabios, Eileen, xix, 355

Tabor, Mary Ann, 353–54, 367n3

Takagi, Dana, 122

Takaki, Ronald, 47n9, 56n42, 239n3, 384n6

Tapahonso, Luci, 77

Tarkington, Booth, 239n1, 240n10

Teish, Lusiah, 409n5

Tennyson, Alfred, Lord, 198

Tensuan, Theresa, 137

Theo, David, 55n36

Thomas, Brook, 49n13

Thompson, Maurice, 223, 225, 232, 240n10

Thoreau, Henry David, xiv, 197–98, 206, 209, 212

Tiffin, Helen, 17–19, 22, 23, 25, 28, 32, 33, 45n3, 52n27, 54n31, 73, 75, 79, 81–82, 86, 89, 208, 214n4, 255, 273n9, 433n1

Tomasky, Michael, 48n10

Tomlinson, John, 78, 91n8

Toribio, Helen, 367n3

Tourgée, Albion, 35, 254, 257n5

Trollope, Francis, 201

Tubman, Harriet, 405

Tucker, Mark, 9

Tuckerman, Henry T., 200, 202

Tudor, Mary, 225, 230

Turner, Darwin T., 96

Turner, Frederick Jackson, viii, 4–6, 9–13, 30, 46–47n6, 48n10, 49n13, 222, 226

Turner, Nat, 190

Tutola, Amos, 208

Twain, Mark, xv, 37, 208, 228–29, 239n1, 240n7

Tyler, Royall, 208

Vallangca, C., xviii, 349

van der Veer, Peter, 433n2

Varadharajan, Asha, 167n8

Vassanji, M. G., 17, 384–85n6

Vaughan, Alden T., 167n7

Veblen, Thorstein, 233

Vega, Bernardo, 339

Velie, Alan, 90n1, 166n2, 298n15

Verghese, Abraham, xix, 375, 380–82, 385n 18

Verma, Rajiva, 371

Vesey, Denmark, 190

Villa, Pancho, 111

Villanueva, Marianne, xix, 355

Viramontes, Helena María, xix–xx; "The Moths," 399, 400, 405–08

Visawanathan, Gauri, 17, 433n4

Vizenor, Gerald, 78–83, 89–90, 91 n 10,
92 n 19, 152, 167 n 6; *Heirs of Columbus*,
79, 92 n 22, 92 n 23; *Manifest Manners*,
92 n 22
Voegeli, V. Jacque, 256 n 2

Wacker, R. Fred, 46–47 n 6
Walcott, Derek, 301, 313–14
Wald, Alan, 49 n 12
Wald, Patricia, 41, 45 n 2, 53–54 n 30
Walder, Dennis, 18, 53 n 29
Walker, Alice, 306
Walker, Cheryl, 13, 48 n 9, 102 n 2, 167 n 4,
436 n 35
Walker, Richard, 143 n 29, 436 n 35
Wall, Cheryl, 102 n 2
Wallace, Lew, 233, 240 n 10
Wallace, Michele, 99
Wallerstein, Immanuel, 41, 53–54 n 30
Wang, L. Ling-Chi, 126, 140–41
Wang, Peter, 136
Ware, Caroline F., 46 n 5
Warrior, Robert Allen, 152, 167 n 6, 168 n 9
Washington, Booker T., 248, 250, 253,
257 n 6, 261
Washington, George, 161, 237, 435 n 27
Washington, Madison, 190
Washington, Mary Helen, 56 n 40
Wasserman, Renata R. Mautner, 216 n 23
Waters, Mary C., 49 n 11
Watts, Steven, 51 n 19
Webb, Frank J., *The Garies and Their Friends*,
176, 177, 191–92
Webb, Walter Prescott, 12, 49 n 14
Webster, Daniel, 163, 170 n 21
Webster, William, 326
Weisbuch, Robert, 214 n 8
Welch, James, 81–82, 86
Wella, Ida B., 405
Werbner, Pnina, 433 n 2
Wesley, Charles, 99
West, Cornel, 53–54 n 30, 96–98, 102, 260,
265–66
Wharton, Edith, 239 n 1
Wheeler, Howard (Senator), 282
White, Barbara A., 193 n 10
White, G. Edward, 158, 159, 168 n 10, 170 n
15

Whitman, Walt, xiv, 197, 208–11
Wiget, Andrew, 166 n 1
Williams, Patricia, 55 n 33, 55–56 n 36,
388–89, 433 n 7
Williams, Raymond, 240 n 4, 273 n 11, 280,
296 n 3
Williams, Roger, 284
Williams, Shirley Anne, 99–100
Williamson, Joel, 247, 256 n 1
Wilson, Harriet, *Our Nig*, 177, 186–89
Wilson, Rob, 45 n 2, 142 n 9
Winant, Howard, 7, 45 n 3, 47 n 8, 320, 327,
332–33 n 2, 333 n 10, 334 n 25
Wingfield, Marvin, 334 n 20
Wise, Gene, 46 n 5
Wister, Owen, xv, 226, 230, 238–39
Wolff, Richard, 273–74 n 13
Wong, Sau-ling C., xiii, 49 n 12, 373, 384–
85 n 6, 385 n 9
Wong, Shawn, 142 n 5, 372
Wong, Shelley, 129
Wonham, Henry, 433 n 3
Woodson, Carter, 12, 96, 99
Woodward, C. Vann, 254, 257 n 5
Woolf, Virginia, 21, 87, 91 n 17, 143 n 14
Wordsworth, William, 200, 205
Wray, Matt, 55–56 n 36
Wright, James, 91 n 14
Wright, Richard, 12, 23, 35, 99, 312, 413,
433 n 3

X, Malcolm, 405

Yarborough, Richard, 193 n 1
Yeats, William Butler, 207
Yellin, Jean Fagan, 193 n 5
Yogi, Stan, 371
Young Bear, Ray, 77
Young, Iris Marion, 389–91
Young, Robert J. M., 24–25, 412–16, 433 n
2, 433 n 8, 436 n 34
Yudice, George, 435 n 27

Zafar, Rajia, 47–48 n 9, 434 n 16
Zamir, Shamoon, 272–73 n 4
Zapata, Emiliano, 111, 270
Zepeda, Ofelia, 77
Zizek, Slavoj, 273 n 10

Subject Index

Acculturation, 10, 288–89. *See also* Assimilation

Africa/African(s), 22–23, 79–80, 139, 202, 304–07, 309–10, 312–13, 315–16

African American(s), 3, 7, 10–11, 16, 20–22, 24, 29–30, 33–38, 42, 44, 95–102, 139, 244–76, 324, 381, 392, 413; and cultural studies, 95–102, 315, 404; literary tradition, 36–37, 95–102, 315; nationalism, 110, 190, 274n 20; novel in the nineteenth century, 44–57, 176–95; and postcolonial studies, 258–76, 433n 4; and underdevelopment 178–84; and whiteness studies, 35–38; women, 301, 316; women writers, 176–95, 388–411

African American Studies, 95–102, 198, 274n 21

AIDS, 380–82

Algeria, 19

Alienation, 300, 304, 317, 379

Ambivalence, 261–62, 267–68, 273n 12

American Imperialism, xv, 5, 226–29, 236–37, 352; double discourse of, 222–25; and female gaze, 232–34; and historical novel/romance, 221, 226–29; "informal empire," 222; and "Manifest Destiny," 88; and masculinity, 221, 229–36; and the Philippines, 220, 235–36; and the Spanish-American War, 220, 235–37. *See also* Colonialism

American Indian Movement (AIM), 283

American Studies, 28, 46n 15, 49n 13, 412–14, 427, 430–32. *See also* U.S. Studies

American Studies Association (ASA), 56n 40; Radical Caucus, 46n 5; National American Studies Faculty (NASF), 46n 5

American Studies *v.* U.S. Studies, 45n 2

American-Arab Anti-Discrimination Committee (ADC), 326, 334n 16–18, 334n 20–21

Androgyny, 307, 309. *See also* Gender; Lesbianism

"Anti-imperial Translation" (Krupat), 167, 167–68n 9. *See also* Language; Translation

Anti-terrorism Bill, 326. *See also* Legislation (U.S.)

Arab Americans, 320–37

Arab-American Institute (AAI), 334n 21

Asian American(s), 7, 14, 28–29, 31–34, 38, 42–43, 122–44, 344–67, 370–85; and Asians, 129–32. *See also* Chinese American(s); Filipino-Americans; Indian-Americans (Asian Indians); Pan-Asian Ethnicity; Pakistani-American(s); South Asian American(s)

Asian American Studies, 122–44, 198, 370–85

465

Asian American Studies *v.* Asian-American
    Studies, 131
Assimilation, vii–ix, 3–45, 46 n 4, 49 n 12,
    105, 114, 279–96, 297 n 7, 358
Australia, 210
Authenticity, 23, 33, 42, 54 n 32, 281, 282,
    284, 285, 289, 290, 292, 294, 295, 329,
    375–78
Autobiography, 177–78, 271, 290, 393–99
Aztlán, 103–19

Back-to-Africa Movement, 21
Bandung Conference, vii
Barbados, 316–17 n 11, 317 n 15, 436 n 38.
    See also Caribbean, the
Before Columbus Foundation, 55 n 35
Bengal, 32
Biracial Identity, 82, 244–49, 255. *See also*
    Half-Breed Figure; Hybridity; Mestizaje/
    Mestizo; Tragic Mulatta/o
Black Arts Movement (U.S.), 95, 100
Black Atlantic, the, 20–22, 133, 198, 413
Black Capitalism, 190, 192
Black Panthers, 100
Black Power, 100
Blues, 305. *See also* Jazz; "Sorrow Songs"
Border(s)/Borderlands, 5–8, 30, 47 n 7, 50 n
    15, 103–05, 114, 116–19, 281, 375, 378
Borders School, xi, 3–8, 11, 38–45, 46 n 5,
    47 n 7, 47–48 n 9, 50 n 15. *See also* Ethnic-
    ity; Identity; Postethnicity School

Call and Response, 389, 406. *See also* African
    American(s); Oral Traditions
Cameroon, 55 n 36
Canada, 47 n 7, 162, 190, 210, 215 n 16,
    293, 335 n 31, 375–76, 384–85 n 5, 434 n
    15
Caribbean, the, 300–18, 338–48, 375–76.
    See also Barbados; Carriacou; Cuba; Gre-
    nada; Jamaica; Puerto Rico; Trinidad
Carriacou, 305, 309, 312. *See also* Caribbean,
    the
Catholicism, 41
Caucasian(s), 321–22, 324, 329. *See also* Race;
    Whiteness Studies
Cherokee, 155–58
Chicana/o(s), 12, 103–21, 133, 388–410,
    413; culture, 105–06, 405; literary tradi-

tion, 392, 405; Movement, 110, 112–14;
    nationalism, 109–12, 398, 406; women,
    406–08; women writers, 338–410. *See also*
    Latina/o(s)
China, 37, 127, 136–37, 138, 226
Chinese Americans, 126, 133, 136–37,
    373–75
Citizenship, 4, 9, 13, 30–31, 36, 39, 40, 160,
    321, 323, 328, 333 n 9, 334 n 27, 371. *See
    also* Immigration; Legislation (U.S.); Natu-
    ralization
Civil Rights Movement (U.S.), 9, 43, 47 n 8,
    100, 324, 402. *See also* African Americans
Civil War (U.S.), 55 n 36, 415
Class, 265–68, 302, 307, 313–14, 316
Classification, 326–27, 329–32, 332 n 1,
    333 n 10, 334 n 21, 334 n 23. *See also* Iden-
    tification; Identity
Colonial discourse, 152–53, 160–61, 292,
    372
Colonialism, 18, 29, 73–74; and historiogra-
    phy, 156, 157, 158; internal, 45 n 3, 73,
    152, 290; and jurisprudence, 156. *See also*
    American Imperialism; Imperialism; Neo-
    colonialism
Commodification, xix–xx, 37, 44, 180–82,
    380
Community, 186, 192, 194 n 13, 288–95,
    303, 305, 307, 310–12, 317, 340–41,
    344, 388, 392, 401, 404, 408; African
    American, 177–79; Chicano/Mexicano,
    105–07; in literature, 388–411; Native
    American, 279–96; Pueblo Laguna,
    294–96; and self, 389–96; women's role
    in, 394–99, 408. *See also* Ethnicity; Iden-
    tity; Immigration
Complicity, 17, 19, 22–29
Confucianism, 48 n 10
"Consent and Descent" (Sollors), 48 n 11,
    371
Creole/Creolization, 17, 28, 301, 314. *See also*
    Half-Breed Figure; Hybridity; Identity
Cuba, 189–91, 202, 212, 224, 231, 235,
    237, 345
Cultural/Culture, 8, 23, 87–89, 281, 289,
    291, 376, 381, 388, 392, 397–99, 401,
    404–06; agency, 33, 55 n 27, 105–06;
    anxiety in classic U.S. literature, 197–202,
    208–13; difference, 287, 397–98; hegem-

ony, 16, 103, 113, 178; hybridity, 209, 375, 391; transgression of, 388–411; Wars, 9–15. *See also* Community; Ethnicity; Identity; Individualism

Cultural Studies, 3–56, 95–102, 132–33, 263, 434n 10

Decolonization, 355–56, 361, 365

Deconstruction, 25–27, 315

Democracy, 9–10, 44, 222–23, 226–29

"Denied Knowledges" (Bhabha), 182

"Denationalization" (Wong), 122–44, 373

Diaspora, vii–ix, xix, 4, 11–15, 21–31, 38–41, 45n 3, 50n 16, 53n 29, 56n 39, 122–44, 280; African, 392, 400, 409; and Aztlán, 106–09; and ethnic authenticity, 375–78; and homosexuality, 375–76; and Latinos, 107, 392, 395; and postcolonialism, 32–35, 370–83. *See also* Immigration; Migrant/Migration; Transnationalism

"Double Consciousness" (Du Bois)/"Double Vision," 3–4, 13–14, 20–21, 24, 29, 45n 1, 259–62, 267–68, 371, 393, 403–04, 409n 3. *See also* Complicity; Creole/Creolization; Hybridity; Identity; Mestizaje/Mestizo; Mimicry

Dred Scott Case, 177

Dublin, 21

Egypt, 55n 36, 331, 333n 13

Empire, ix, 5, 53–54n 30, 226–29. *See also* American Imperialism; Colonialism; Imperialism

Essentialism, 14, 27, 54n 32, 269–72

Ethnic Studies, 9–15, 49–50n 15, 53n 29, 370, 383. *See also* Cultural/Culture; Ethnicity; Identity; Postethnicity School

Ethnicity, 3, 7–8, 10, 21, 48n 11, 53–54n 30, 262, 280, 286, 298n 12, 320, 370–81, 414; ethnocriticism, 91–92n 17; fetishization of, 33, 113, 281, 383; postcolonial-diasporic, 29, 374; postethnicity, 4–8, 10–12, 38–45, 48n 10, 332. *See also* Border(s)/Borderlands; Borders School; Identity; Race

Euroamerica(ns), 79, 89, 90, 199–202, 285, 287

Eurocentrism, 10, 16–20, 27, 54n 31, 190, 205–10

Exile, 143n 24, 371, 374–75

Exotic, the, 200–01, 291, 328–32

Feminism, xi, 4, 32–35, 50n 16, 54n 33, 101, 232–34, 300, 314, 376–77, 388–411; and Caribbean Literature, 300–19; Chicana, 388, 406–08; and imperialist discourse, 232–34; and postcolonialism, 32–35; and science fiction, 306, 309; and women of color, 388–91, 406–09, 435n 29. *See also* Androgyny; Gender; Lesbianism; Women

Fetishism/Fetishization, 33, 113, 273n 10, 281, 383

Filipino-American(s), 129, 133–34, 137, 143n 16, 143n 25, 349–66; "born again Filipinos," 357, 360, 366; cultural identity, 352–60; "flip" generation, 349, 353–54; folklore, 359–62; identity formation, 351–52, 362; indigenization, 351–60; language, 351–57; literature, 137, 138, 352, 355, 362–64, 366–67, 375; transculturation, 360, 363–64; and U.S. imperialism, 355–57. *See also* Asian American(s)

Fisk University Jubilee Singers, 264–65. *See also* "Sorrow Songs"

Folk culture, 291, 301–05, 309, 314, 359–62. *See also* Oral Traditions

France, 20

Francophone Caribbean Literature, 421–37

Frontier, the (Turner), 4–6, 9–13, 30, 46–47n 6, 48n 10, 49n 13, 222, 226–29

Fugitive Slave Law, 177. *See also* Legislation (U.S.)

Gender, 306–09, 376, 383. *See also* Androgyny; Feminism; Women

General Allotment Act, 280

Georgia, 158–59

Ghana, 19

Gikuyu, 22

Global Capitalism/Globalism/Globalization, vii, xi, 4–5, 7, 19, 29, 38–41, 50n 16, 56n 37, 56n 39, 73–74, 122–44, 270–72, 297n 4, 370–85, 431–32

Greater Syria, 321, 323

Grenada, 202, 313

Half-Breed Figure, 78–83, 289–96. *See also* Creole/Creolization; Identity; Tragic Mulatta/o
Harlem Renaissance, 21–22, 51 n 21, 393
Hawaii, 7, 29
Hegemony, 16, 103, 113, 178
Hindi, 55 n 34
Hindu, 375
Historical novel/romance, xx; and empire, 221, 226–29; formulaic plot of, 221, 225–26; and gender, 229–36; and masculinity, 221, 229–36; and nostalgia, 221, 224–25; popularity of, in 1890s, 225–26. *See also* Romance (genre)
Historiography, 11–15, 25, 26
Holy Land, 323, 328–29
Home/Homeland, 20, 28, 34, 133, 371–72, 374, 376, 378–80, 388, 394; Aztlán as, 105–06, 114; mythic, 103, 107; spiritual, 106; utopian, 104. *See also* Ethnicity; Identity; Nationalism; Nativism
Hopewell Treaty of 1802, 159
Hopi, 287
Hybridity, viii, 4, 17, 19, 22–29, 39, 41–45, 47 n 6, 116–17, 182, 209, 246–47, 250–51, 259, 261–63, 269, 271–72, 291, 344, 412–37. *See also* Border(s)/Borderlands; Complicity; Identity; Immigration; Mimicry

Ibo, 308–09
Identity, 10, 13, 20, 23–24, 27–29, 32, 34, 37, 43, 103–04, 106, 117, 179, 280, 282, 290, 296, 300, 309, 316, 320, 327, 340, 346, 371–72, 375; "American," viii, 7, 12–13, 322–23, 325, 329, 331, 335 n 27; Biracial, 82, 244–49, 255, 290–96, 304; Christian, 323, 328–29; Collective, 193 n 2, 294, 297 n 4; and gender, 33–34, 388–409; postcolonial, 28–35, 269–72; psychological, 164, 167 n 4, 300, 312–13, 317. *See also* African American(s); Arab American(s); Asian American(s); Chicana/o(s); Filipino-American(s); Latina/o(s); Puerto Rico(ans)
Identification, 122–44, 279–96, 327, 331–32, 334 n 21, 334 n 25, 370. *See also* Identity
Immigration, vii–ix, 4, 6, 7, 10, 13, 15, 37,

38, 41, 43, 46 n 4, 51 n 22, 104, 106, 110, 199, 320–28, 333 n 12, 334 n 25, 357, 370–79, 380–82, 384 n 1, 384 n 3; and diaspora, 28–35; and women, 32–35. *See also* Postcoloniality; Transnationalism
Imperialism, 16, 18, 19, 29, 226–29, 269–70, 314, 357. *See also* American Imperialism; Colonialism; Empire
Indigenous cultures/Indigenization, 300, 351–52, 356–57, 358–63, 365. *See also* Nativism; Settlers
India, vii, ix, 18, 35, 36, 55 n 36, 208, 212, 421–32. *See also* South Asian American(s)
Indian Nations (U.S.), 151–75. *See also* Native Americans
Indian Reorganization Act of 1934, 282. *See also* Legislation (U.S.)
Indian-Americans (Asian Indians), 133, 274 n 21, 370–85. *See also* Asian Americans; South Asian Americans
Individualism, 390, 393, 400; and community, 389–96
Internal colony, 20, 45 n 3, 90, 98. *See also* American Imperialism; Colonialism; Empire
International Monetary Fund (IMF), 10
Islam, 22, 41, 322–24, 327–29, 331, 333 n 10, 377

Jamaica, 314–16. *See also* Caribbean, the
Japan, 142 n 2, 370
Japanese-Americans, 134, 370
Jazz, 305, 315. *See also* Blues; "Sorrow Songs"; Spirituals
Jim Crow Laws, 35, 247, 252–53, 256. *See also* "One-drop Rule"; Segregation
Johnson v. M'Intosh (1823), 154

Kansas-Nebraska Act, 177. *See also* Legislation (U.S.)
Kashmir, 378–79. *See also* India; South Asian Americans
King Philip's War, 153, 156–58, 160, 161
Kinship, 111, 289, 290, 310–12
Korea, 370
Korean-Americans, 370

Language, 14, 74–75, 84–85, 208–09, 300–01, 340, 344–45, 348 n 2, 351, 353–54, 357. *See also* Translation

Latina/o(s), 6–7, 12–14, 31, 38, 41–42, 103–21, 198, 338–48, 388–41. *See also* Chicana/o(s); Mexican-Americans; Puerto Rico(ans)

Lesbianism, 306, 309, 316, 375–76. *See also* Androgyny; Feminism

Lebanon, 326

Left Bank, 342

Legislation (U.S.): Anti-terrorism Bill, 326; Fugitive Slave Law, 177; General Allotment Act, 280; Indian Arts and Crafts Act, 282; Indian Reorganization Act, 282; Kansas-Nebraska Act, 177; Naturalization Act, 321

Lion City, Calif., 142 n 11

Louisiana, 36

Lower East Side, 347

Madness, 301, 312, 317. *See also* Psychoanalysis

Marginality/Marginalization, 53 n 28, 300–01, 305, 312, 373

Marxism, 19–27, 50 n 19, 51 n 19, 110, 269–70

Masculinity, U.S., 220–41

Mashpee Indians of Cape Cod, 160, 164–65

Memory, 8, 91–92 n 17, 87, 338, 340, 342–44, 398, 404. *See also* Nostalgia

Mestizaje/Mestizo, 42, 105–06, 115, 293, 406–07, 415. *See also* Border(s)/Borderlands; "Double Consciousness" (Du Bois)/ "Double Vision"; Half-Breed Figure; Hybridity; Identity; Tragic Mulatta/o

Mexican-Americans, 42, 392, 396–97. *See also* Chicana/o(s)

Mexico, 42, 110, 293

Middle Passage, 35, 312. *See also* Slavery

Migration, vii–viii, 23, 34, 39, 42, 43, 48 n 11, 104–06, 115, 263–65, 375. *See also* Diaspora; Immigration

Mimicry, 16, 22–29, 37. *See also* Complicity; Hybridity; Identity

Mississippi, 7

Mohawks, 161

Motherhood, 301, 310–11, 376–77. *See also* Feminism; Gender

Mount Lebanon, 321

Mulatta/o. *See* Tragic Mulatta/o

Multiculturalism, 23, 320–21, 334 n 17, 383. *See also* Community; Ethnicity

Multinational Corporations, 4, 10, 19, 39, 43. *See also* Global Capitalism/Globalism/ Globalization

Muslims. *See* Islam

Myth, 241 n 12, 308, 318, 389. *See also* Folklore; Spiritual Practices

NAFTA, 240

National Art, 199–202, 209–10, 263–65

National Museum of American Indians, 282; oral traditions, 151–52; and postcolonialism, 73–94, 152–53, 167–68 n 9; sovereignty, 152, 167, 168 n 9. *See also* Indian Nations (U.S.)

Nationalism, 79, 103–21, 280, 373; African American, 110, 190, 274 n 20; cultural, 22, 106, 109, 127–29; and U.S. literature, 153, 209–10. *See also* Identity; Immigration; Nativism; Transnationalism

Nation-state, 10, 11, 21, 54 n 30, 109–21, 280, 373

Native American(s), 29, 42, 151–71, 210, 279–98; Half-Breed Figure, 292, 298 n 10; inferiority theories about, 152–53, 155, 159; literature and writing, 73–94, 151–75, 279–98

Native American Studies, 73–94, 133, 151–75, 279–98

Native Informants, 27

Nativism, 14, 22–29, 51 n 22, 52 n 27, 82, 89, 110. *See also* Hybridity; Indigenous Cultures/Indigenization; Settlers

Naturalization, 36, 321–24. *See also* Citizenship; Immigration

Naturalization Act of 1790, 321. *See also* Legislation (U.S.)

Negritude, 20, 21, 22, 52 n 24, 210, 270, 306

Neocolonialism, vii, 5, 7, 19–20, 27, 45 n 3, 47 n 8, 177, 192–93, 375, 379. *See also* American Imperialism; Colonialism; Imperialism

New Ireland, 21

Niger Valley, 189

Nigeria, 210

Nostalgia, xix, 221, 224–25, 235, 237–38, 378–80, 383. *See also* Memory

Nyorican Literature, 341–42

Obeah, 316–17

Oklahoma City Bombing of 1995, 326–27

"One-drop Rule," 244, 247. *See also* Identity; Jim Crow Laws; Segregation

Oral Traditions, 78–79, 286, 290, 294, 301–05, 308. *See also* Folk culture

Orientalism (Said), 16–17, 324–25, 328–29

"Other"/"Othering," 4, 23, 371, 381, 383

Pakistani-Americans, 376–77. *See also* Asian American(s); South Asian American(s)

Palestine, 334 n 18, 342

Pan-Africanism, 19, 189, 267, 270, 274 n 20

Panama, 202

Pan-Americanism, 90

Pan-Asian Ethnicity, 350, 360–61, 363–65

Pan-Indianism (U.S.), 89–90

"Passing," 8, 34, 246, 255

Patriarchy, 3–6, 309, 375–77, 406. *See also* Feminism; Gender

Pequot, 167 n 4

Philippines, 29, 220, 231, 234, 349–66. *See also* Asian American(s); Filipino-American(s)

Plessy v Ferguson (1896), 244, 253–56

Pocahantas Myth, 230–31, 241 n 12

Postcolonial *v.* Post-colonial, 18, 50 n 17

Postcolonialism/Postcoloniality, 258, 265–68, 300–01, 305, 375–80, 384 n 5, 433 n 1; and alienation, 300–01, 305, 379; and class, 265–68; and essentialism, 269–72; and ethnicity, 122–47; and the Harlem Renaissance, 21–22; and Native Americans, 73–94, 152–53, 167–68 n 9; and South Asian Americans, 370–85; and women, 32–35, 54 n 33. *See also* Complicity; Creole/Creolization; "Double Consciousness" (Du Bois)/ "Double Vision"; Hybridity; Mestizaje/Mestizo; Mimicry; Nativism; "Third space"

Postcolonial Studies, xi, 3, 39, 203–13, 272, 413; and the academy, 17–18; antecedents of, 20–22, 258–74; and Borders School, 29–43; critique of, 28–29, 40, 50 n 18, 50–51 n 19, 53 n 29; and feminism, 25, 32–35, 54 n 33; and issues of representation, 15–16; and Marxism, 25, 50–51 n 19, 52 n 25, 53 n 29, 268–69; review of,

15–29; and Subaltern Studies, 25–27; and whiteness studies, 35–38

Postethnicity School, viii, 4–8, 10–12, 38–45, 48 n 10, 332. *See also* Border(s)/Borderlands; Borders School; Ethnicity; Identity

Postmodernism, 21–22, 44, 291, 301

Post-nativism, 82, 89

Post-structuralism, 8, 25–27, 50 n 19, 51 n 19, 400–01, 403–04

"Productive Complicity" (Spivak), 27

Progressivism (U.S.), 6, 46 n 5. *See also* Borders School

Psychoanalysis, 20, 273 n 10, 300, 310, 311–13, 317. *See also* Fetishism/Fetishization; Madness

Pueblos, 290, 294, 297 n 8

Puerto Rico(ans), 29, 338–48

Purdah, 32

Puritans, 9, 163, 199–201

Race/Racial/Racism, 4–8, 55 n 35, 55 n 36, 244–45, 251–53, 256, 301, 314, 320–37, 371, 381–83, 433 n 8, 434 n 15; and gender, 183, 391, 393; and Native Americans, 279–96. *See also* African American(s); Borders School; Ethnicity; Identity; Postethnicity School

Racialization, 301, 314, 333 n 10

Reconstruction (U.S.), 244–45, 247–49

Resistance, 5, 10, 12, 28, 31, 41, 43, 104, 106, 108, 118, 293, 297 n 8

Rhode Island, 284

Roanoke, 292

Romance (genre), xx, 184, 305. *See also* Historical novel/romance

Sati, 32

Segregation/Desegregation, 4–8, 244–45, 253, 256, 325, 374, 433 n 5. *See also* Identity; Jim Crow Laws; "One-drop Rule"; Race

Settlers, literature of, 196–99, 213; violence and duplicity of, 157, 159, 161, 162. *See also* Indigenous Cultures/Indigenization; Nativism

Sistern (Caribbean Theater Collective), 314–15, 318 n 18

Slave Narratives, 177–82, 405

Slavery, 179–80, 188, 316, 399. *See also* Middle Passage

"Slippage" (Bhabha), 24

"Sorrow Songs" (Du Bois), 35, 44, 259–64, 305. *See also* African American(s); Blues; Jazz

South Africa, vii, 55 n 36

South Asian American(s), 42–43, 129, 370–87. *See also* Asian American(s); India; Indian-Americans (Asian Indians); Pakistani-American(s)

Spanglish, 344. *See also* Language; Hybridity

Spanish-American War: and Cuba, 237; and historical romance, 225–26; and Philippines, 220, 235–36; and U.S. imperialism, 220

Spiritual Practices: Aztec, 400; female-centered, 399, 402, 403, 406–08; Native American, 297 n 4

Spokane, 284

Subaltern Studies, 25–27, 52 n 26–27, 73, 204. *See also* Postcolonial Theory

Syria/Syrians, 321, 322, 323, 325, 328, 329, 333 n 3, 334 n 26

"Talented Tenth" (Du Bois), 264, 267

Taos, 284

Tarzan, 241 n 10

Territory, 8, 116, 285, 296, 374, 392, 397, 399, 403

Thailand, 55 n 36

Thayer and Eldridge (publisher), 176, 180

"Third space" (Bhabha), xix, 4, 13, 23–24, 343, 375

Tragic mulatta/o, 182–91, 245, 304. *See also* African American(s); Identity

Transgression, 343, 388–401

Translation, xii, 74–79, 87, 167–68 n 9. *See also* "Anti-imperial Translation"; Language

Transnationalism, viii, xi, 3, 4, 30–32, 38–39, 50 n 16, 53–54 n 30, 122–44, 370–85. *See also* Diaspora; Global Capitalism/ Globalism/Globalization; Immigration; Language; Translation

Trinidad, 19, 307, 316, 375–76. *See also* Caribbean, the

United Nations, 283

United States, 5, 43, 284–85, 372–75; Census Bureau, 321, 327; frontier novel, 238–39; masculinity, 32–35, 220–36, 54 n 33; and Mexico, 6, 42, 47 n 7, 103–19; and nineteenth century U.S. literature, vii–viii, 151–276, 412–37; and Philippines, 220–36; and postcoloniality, 177, 196–213, 412, 414; and Puerto Rico, 29, 338–48; and twentieth century U.S. literature, vii–viii, 279–437. *See also* American Imperialism; Legislation (U.S.)

U.S. Studies, 4, 28, 31, 44–45, 56 n 40. *See also* American Studies

Urdu, 55 n 34, 376–77, 380

Utopia, 306, 309–10, 391–94

West Bank, 342

Whiteness Studies, xi, 4, 16, 35–38, 108, 322. *See also* Identity; Race

Women, 4, 32–35, 50 n 16, 54 n 33, 101, 300–01, 314–15, 388–90, 404, 406–09. *See also* Androgyny; Feminism; Gender; Lesbianism

World Columbian Exposition of 1893, 11, 13

World War II, 5, 18, 46 n 5, 110, 325, 334 n 27